BENTHAM TO RUSSELL

A
HISTORY OF PHILOSOPHY

VOLUME VIII
BENTHAM TO RUSSELL

BY
FREDERICK COPLESTON, S.J.

*Professor at the Pontifical Gregorian University, Rome
and at Heythrop College*

SEARCH PRESS • LONDON

PAULIST PRESS • NEW JERSEY

Published in the United States by
Paulist Press
997 Macarthur Boulevard, Mahwah, N.J. 07430

Published in Great Britain by
Search Press Limited
Wellwood, North Farm Road
Tunbridge Wells, Kent TN2 3DR, England

First published 1966

ISBN (USA) 0-8091-0072-X

Printed and bound in the
United States of America

CONTENTS

Part II

THE IDEALIST MOVEMENT IN GREAT BRITAIN

Part III

IDEALISM IN AMERICA

CONTENTS

PREFACE

In the preface to Volume VII of this *History of Philosophy* I said that I hoped to devote a further volume, the eighth, to some aspects of French and British thought in the nineteenth century. This hope has been only partially fulfilled. For the present volume contains no treatment of French philosophy but is devoted exclusively to some aspects of British and American thought. It covers rather familiar ground. But in a general history of Western philosophy this ground obviously ought to be covered.

As I have strayed over well into the twentieth century, some explanation may be needed of the fact that the philosophy of Bertrand Russell, who is happily still with us, has been accorded relatively extensive treatment, whereas the thought of Ludwig Wittgenstein, who died in 1951, has been relegated to the epilogue, apart from a few allusions in the chapter on Russell. After all, it may be pointed out, Russell was himself influenced to a certain extent by Wittgenstein, both in regard to the interpretation of the logical status of the propositions of logic and pure mathematics and in regard to logical atomism.

The explanation is simple enough. Russell's thought fits naturally into the context of the revolt against idealism; and though he has obviously exercised a powerful influence on the rise and development of the analytic movement in twentieth-century British thought, in some important respects he has maintained a traditional view of the function of philosophy. His lack of sympathy with Wittgenstein's later ideas and with certain aspects of recent 'Oxford philosophy' is notorious. Further, though he has emphasized the limitations of empiricism as a theory of knowledge, in some respects he can be regarded as prolonging the empiricist tradition into the twentieth century, even if he has enriched it with new techniques of logical analysis. Wittgenstein, however, frankly proposed a revolutionary concept of the nature, function and scope of philosophy. Certainly, there is a very considerable difference between the ideas of language expounded in the *Tractatus* and those expounded in *Philosophical Investigations*; but in both cases the concept of philosophy is far from being a traditional one. And as limitations of space excluded the possibility of according extensive treatment to the concentration

on language which is associated with the name of Wittgenstein, I
decided to confine my discussion of the subject to some brief
remarks in an epilogue. This fact should not, however, be interpreted as implying a judgment of value in regard to the philosophy
either of Russell or of Wittgenstein. I mean, the fact that I have
devoted three chapters to Russell does not signify that in my
opinion his thought is simply a hangover from the nineteenth
century. Nor does the fact that I have relegated Wittgenstein to
the epilogue, apart from some allusions in the chapters on Russell,
mean that I fail to appreciate his originality and importance.
Rather is it a matter of not being able to give equally extensive
treatment to the ideas of both these philosophers.

A word of explanation may also be appropriate in regard to my
treatment of Cardinal Newman. It will be obvious to any attentive
reader that in distinguishing the currents of thought in the
nineteenth century I have used traditional labels, 'empiricism',
'idealism' and so on, none of which can properly be applied to
Newman. But to omit him altogether, because of the difficulty of
classifying him, would have been absurd, especially when I have
mentioned a considerable number of much less distinguished
thinkers. I decided, therefore, to make a few remarks about some
of his philosophical ideas in an appendix. I am well aware, of
course, that this will not satisfy Newman enthusiasts; but a writer
cannot undertake to satisfy everybody.

Volumes VII and VIII having been devoted respectively to
German and British-American philosophy in the nineteenth
century, the natural procedure would be to devote a further
volume, the ninth, to aspects of French and other European
philosophy during the same period. But I am inclined to postpone
the writing of this volume and to turn my attention instead to the
subject to which I referred in the preface to Volume VII, that is,
to what may be called the philosophy of the history of philosophy
or general reflection on the development of philosophical thought
and on its implications. For I should like to undertake this task
while there is a reasonable possibility of fulfilling it.

ACKNOWLEDGMENTS

THE author has pleasure in expressing his gratitude to the Right Hon. the Earl Russell, O.M., for his generous permission to quote from his writings, and to the following publishers and holders of copyright for permission to quote from the works indicated below.

The Clarendon Press: *Collected Essays, Ethical Studies, Principles of Logic, Appearance and Reality, Essays on Truth and Reality,* by F. H. Bradley; *The Idea of God in the Light of Recent Philosophy* by A. S. Pringle-Pattison; *The Nature of Truth* by H. H. Joachim; *Statement and Inference* by J. Cook Wilson; and *Essays in Ancient and Modern Philosophy* by H. W. B. Joseph.

The Oxford University Press: *The Problems of Philosophy* and *Religion and Science* by Bertrand Russell; and *A Common Faith* by John Dewey.

Macmillan and Co., Ltd. (London): *Logic, Essentials of Logic, The Philosophical Theory of the State, The Principle of Individuality and Value, The Value and Destiny of the Individual* by Bernard Bosanquet; *Humanism, Formal Logic* and *Axioms as Postulates* (contained in *Personal Idealism,* edited by H. Sturt) by F. C. S. Schiller; and *Space, Time and Deity* by S. Alexander.

The Cambridge University Press: *The Nature of Existence* by J. M. E. McTaggart.

W. Blackwood and Sons, Ltd: *Hegelianism and Personality* by A. S. Pringle-Pattison.

A. and C. Black, Ltd.: *Naturalism and Agnosticism* by James Ward.

Miss S. C. Campbell: *The Realm of Ends* by James Ward.

The Belknap Press of the Harvard University Press: *Collected Papers of Charles Sanders Peirce;* Vols. I and II, copyright 1931, 1932, 1959, 1960; Vols. III and IV, copyright 1933, 1961; Vols. V and VI, copyright 1934, 1935, 1962, 1963 by the President and Fellows of Harvard College.

G. Bell and Sons, Ltd.: *The Influence of Darwin on Philosophy* by John Dewey.

Constable and Co., Ltd.: *Experience and Nature* by John Dewey.

Yale University Press: *A Common Faith* by John Dewey; *The*

Meaning of God in Human Experience and *Human Nature and Its Remaking* by W. E. Hocking. Acknowledgment is also due to Professor W. E. Hocking.

The University of Chicago Press: *Theory of Valuation* by John Dewey. (*International Encyclopaedia of Unified Science*, Vol. 2, no. 4, copyright 1939.)

The Philosophical Library Inc. (N.Y.): *Problems of Men* (copyright 1946) by John Dewey and *The Development of American Pragmatism* by John Dewey (contained in *Twentieth Century Philosophy*, edited by Dagobert D. Runes, copyright 1943).

Holt, Rinehart and Winston Inc. (N.Y.) and the John Dewey Foundation: *Human Nature and Conduct, Logic: The Theory of Inquiry* and *The Public and Its Problems* by John Dewey.

Putnam's and Coward-McCann (N.Y.): *Quest For Certainty* (copyright 1929, renewed 1957) by John Dewey.

The Macmillan Co. Inc. (N.Y.): *Democracy and Education* (copyright 1916) by John Dewey; *The New Realism: Cooperative Studies in Philosophy* (copyright 1912) by E. B. Holt and Others; *Process and Reality* (copyright 1929 and 1949) by A. N. Whitehead.

Professor G. Ryle, Editor of *Mind: The Nature of Judgment* (*Mind*, 1899) by G. E. Moore.

Mrs. G. E. Moore: *Principia Ethica* by G. E. Moore.

Routledge and Kegan Paul, Ltd.: *Philosophical Studies* by G. E. Moore; and *What I Believe* by Bertrand Russell.

George Allen and Unwin, Ltd.: *The Metaphysical Theory of the State* by L. T. Hobhouse; *Philosophical Papers and Some Main Problems of Philosophy* by G. E. Moore; *The Principles of Mathematics, Introduction to Mathematical Philosophy, Philosophical Essays, The Analysis of Mind, Our Knowledge of the External World, Principles of Social Reconstruction, Mysticism and Logic, An Outline of Philosophy, The Scientific Outlook, Power, An Inquiry into Meaning and Truth, A History of Western Philosophy, Human Knowledge: Its Scope and Limits, Logic and Knowledge, My Philosophical Development, Unpopular Essays* and *Authority and the Individual* by Bertrand Russell; *Contemporary British Philosophy*, First Series (1924) and Second Series (1925), edited by J. H. Muirhead.

W. W. Norton and Co., Inc. (N.Y.): *The Principles of Mathematics* by Bertrand Russell.

Simon and Schuster Inc. (N.Y.): *A History of Western Philosophy* (c. 1945), *Human Knowledge: Its Scope and Limits* (c. 1948),

Authority and the Individual (*c.* 1949), *Unpopular Essays* (*c.* 1950) and *My Philosophical Development* (*c.* 1959), by Bertrand Russell.

Macdonald and Co., Ltd. (London) and Doubleday and Co. Inc. (N.Y.): *Wisdom of the West* by Bertrand Russell (copyright Rathbone Books Ltd., London 1959).

The Library of Living Philosophers Inc., formerly published by The Tudor Publishing Co., N.Y., and now published by The Open Court Publishing Co., La Salle, Illinois: *The Philosophy of John Dewey* (1939 and 1951) and *The Philosophy of Bertrand Russell* (1946), both edited by Paul Arthur Schilpp.

PART I

BRITISH EMPIRICISM

CHAPTER I

THE UTILITARIAN MOVEMENT (1)

Introductory remarks—The life and writings of Bentham—The principles of Benthamism, followed by some critical comments—The life and writings of James Mill—Altruism and the associationist psychology; Mill's polemic against Mackintosh—James Mill on the mind—Remarks on Benthamite economics.

1. THE philosophy of David Hume, which represented the culmination of classical British empiricism, called forth a lively reaction on the part of Thomas Reid and his successors.[1] Indeed, as far as the Universities were concerned, in the first decades of the nineteenth century the so-called Scottish School was the one living and vigorous movement of thought. Moreover, though in the meantime it had received some serious blows and had lost its first vigour, its place in the Universities was eventually taken by idealism rather than by empiricism.

It would, however, be a great mistake to suppose that empiricism was reduced to a moribund condition by Reid's attack on Hume, and that it remained in this position until it was given a fresh lease of life by J. S. Mill. Philosophy is not confined to the Universities. Hume himself never occupied an academic chair, though, admittedly, this was not due to lack of effort on his part. And empiricism continued its life, despite attack by Reid and his followers, though its leading representatives were not university professors or lecturers.

The first phase of nineteenth-century empiricism, which is known as the utilitarian movement, may be said to have originated with Bentham. But though we naturally tend to think of him as a philosopher of the early part of the nineteenth century, inasmuch as it was then that his influence made itself felt, he was born in 1748, twenty-eight years before the death of Hume. And some of his works were published in the last three decades of the eighteenth

[1] See Vol. V of this *History*, pp. 364–94.

I

century. It is no matter of surprise, therefore, if we find that there is a conspicuous element of continuity between the empiricism of the eighteenth century and that of the nineteenth. For example, the method of reductive analysis, the reduction, that is to say, of the whole to its parts, of the complex to its primitive or simple elements, which had been practised by Hume, was continued by Bentham. This involved, as can be seen in the philosophy of James Mill, a phenomenalistic analysis of the self. And in the reconstruction of mental life out of its supposed simple elements use was made of the associationist psychology which had been developed in the eighteenth century by, for instance, David Hartley,[1] not to speak of Hume's employment of the principles of association of ideas. Again, in the first chapter of his *Fragment on Government* Bentham gave explicit expression to his indebtedness to Hume for the light which had fallen on his mind when he saw in the *Treatise of Human Nature* how Hume had demolished the fiction of a social contract or compact and had shown how all virtue is founded on utility. To be sure, Bentham was also influenced by the thought of the French Enlightenment, particularly by that of Helvétius.[2] But this does not alter the fact that in regard to both method and theory there was a notable element of continuity between the empiricist movements of the eighteenth and nineteenth centuries in Great Britain.

But once the element of continuity has been noted, attention must be drawn to the considerable difference in emphasis. As traditionally represented at any rate, classical British empiricism had been predominantly concerned with the nature, scope and limits of human knowledge, whereas the utilitarian movement was essentially practical in outlook, orientated towards legal, penal and political reform. It is true that emphasis on the role of the theory of knowledge in classical empiricism can be overdone. Hume, for example, was concerned with the development of a science of human nature. And it can be argued, and has indeed been argued, that he was primarily a moral philosopher.[3] But Hume's aim was chiefly to understand the moral life and the moral judgment, whereas Bentham was mainly concerned with providing the criterion for judging commonly received moral ideas and legal and political institutions with a view to their reformation. Perhaps we can apply Marx's famous assertion and

---

[1] See Vol. V of this *History*, pp. 191–3.
[2] See Vol. VI of this *History*, pp. 35–8.
[3] Cf. Vol. V of this *History*, pp. 260–3, 318–19 and 342–3.

say that Hume was primarily concerned with understanding the world, whereas Bentham was primarily concerned with changing it.

Of the two men Hume was, indeed, by far the greater philosopher. But Bentham had the gift of seizing on certain ideas which were not his own inventions, developing them and welding them into a weapon or instrument of social reform. Benthamism in a narrow sense, and utilitarianism in general, expressed the attitude of liberal and radical elements in the middle class to the weight of tradition and to the vested interests of what is now often called the Establishment. The excesses connected with the French Revolution produced in England a strong reaction which found notable expression in the reflections of Edmund Burke (1729–97), with their emphasis on social stability and tradition. But after the Napoleonic Wars at any rate the movement of radical reform was more easily able to make its influence felt. And in this movement utilitarianism possesses an undeniable historical importance. Considered as a moral philosophy, it is over-simplified and skates lightly over awkward and difficult questions. But its over-simplified character, together with an at least *prima facie* clarity, obviously facilitated its use as an instrument in the endeavour to secure practical reforms in the social and political fields.

During the nineteenth century social philosophy in Great Britain passed through several successive phases. First, there was the philosophical radicalism which is associated with the name of Bentham and which had been already expressed by him in the closing decades of the eighteenth century. Secondly, there was Benthamism as modified, added to and developed by J. S. Mill. And thirdly, there was the idealist political philosophy which arose in the last part of the nineteenth century. The term 'utilitarianism' covers the first two phases, but not, of course, the third. Utilitarianism was individualistic in outlook, even though it aimed at the welfare of society, whereas in idealist political theory the idea of the State as an organic totality came to the fore under the influence of both Greek and German thought.

This and the following chapters will be devoted to an account of the development of utilitarianism from Bentham to J. S. Mill inclusively. The latter's theories in the fields of logic, epistemology and ontology will be discussed separately in a subsequent chapter.

2. Jeremy Bentham was born on February 15th, 1748. A

precocious child, he was learning Latin grammar at the age of four. Educated at Westminster School and the University of Oxford, neither of which institutions captivated his heart, he was destined by his father for a career at the Bar. But he preferred the life of reflection to that of a practising lawyer. And in the law, the penal code and the political institutions of his time he found plenty to think about. To put the matter in simple terms, he asked questions on these lines. What is the purpose of this law or of this institution? Is this purpose desirable? If so, does the law or institution really conduce to its fulfilment? In fine, how is the law or institution to be judged from the point of view of utility?

In its application to legislation and to political institutions the measure of utility was for Bentham the degree of conduciveness to the greater happiness of the greatest possible number of human beings or members of society. Bentham himself remarks that the principle of utility, as so interpreted, occurred to him when he was reading the *Essay on Government* (1768) by Joseph Priestley (1733–1804) who stated roundly that the happiness of the majority of the members of any State was the standard by which all the affairs of the State should be judged. But Hutcheson, when treating of ethics, had previously asserted that that action is best which conduces to the greatest happiness of the greatest number.[1] Again, in the preface to his famous treatise on crimes and punishments (*Dei delitti e delle pene*, 1764), Cesare Beccaria (1738–94) had spoken of the greatest happiness divided among the greatest possible number. There were utilitarian elements in the philosophy of Hume, who declared, for example, that 'public utility is the sole origin of justice'.[2] And Helvétius, who, as already noted, strongly influenced Bentham, was a pioneer in utilitarian moral theory and in its application to the reform of society. In other words, Bentham did not invent the principle of utility: what he did was to expound and apply it explicitly and universally as the basic principle of both morals and legislation.

Bentham was at first principally interested in legal and penal reform. Radical changes in the British constitution did not enter into his original schemes. And at no time was he an enthusiast for democracy as such. That is to say, he had no more belief in the sacred right of the people to rule than he had in the theory of

---

[1] See Vol. V of this *History*, p. 182.
[2] *An Enquiry concerning the Principles of Morals*, 3, 1, 145.

natural rights in general, which he considered to be nonsense. But whereas he seems to have thought at first that rulers and legislators were really seeking the common good, however muddled and mistaken they might be about the right means for attaining this end, in the course of time he became convinced that the ruling class was dominated by self-interest. Indifference and opposition to his plans for legal, penal and economic reform doubtless helped him to come to this conclusion. Hence he came to advocate political reform as a prerequisite for other changes. And eventually he proposed the abolition of the monarchy and the House of Lords, the disestablishment of the Church of England, and the introduction of universal suffrage and annual parliaments. His political radicalism was facilitated by the fact that he had no veneration for tradition as such. He was far from sharing Burke's view of the British constitution; and his attitude had much more affinity with that of the French *philosophes*,[1] with their impatience with tradition and their belief that everything would be for the best if only reason could reign. But his appeal throughout was to the principle of utility, not to any belief that democracy possesses some peculiarly sacred character of its own.

Nor was Bentham primarily moved by humanitarian considerations. In the movement of social reform in Great Britain throughout the nineteenth century, humanitarianism, sometimes based on Christian beliefs and sometimes without any explicit reference to Christianity, undoubtedly played a very important role. But though, for example, in his campaign against the outrageously severe penal code of his time and against the disgraceful state of the prisons, Bentham often demanded changes which humanitarian sentiment would in fact suggest, he was primarily roused to indignation by what he considered, doubtless rightly, to be the irrationality of the penal system, its incapacity to achieve its purposes and to serve the common good. To say this is not, of course, to say that he was what would normally be called inhumane. It is to say that he was not primarily moved by compassion for the victims of the penal system, but rather by the 'inutility' of the system. He was a man of the reason or understanding rather than of the heart or of feeling.

In 1776 Bentham published anonymously his *Fragment on Government* in which he attacked the famous lawyer Sir William

---

[1] Allusion to the influence of Helvétius's writings on Bentham's mind has already been made. We may add that he corresponded with d'Alembert.

Blackstone (1723–80) for his use of the fiction of a social compact or contract. The work had no immediate success, but in 1781 it brought Bentham the friendship of Lord Shelburne, afterwards Marquis of Lansdowne, who was Prime Minister from July 1782 to February 1783. And through Shelburne the philosopher met several other important people. He also formed a friendship with Étienne Dumont, tutor to Shelburne's son, who was to prove of invaluable help in publishing a number of his papers. Bentham not infrequently left manuscripts unfinished and went on to some other topic. And many of his writings were published through the agency of friends and disciples. Sometimes they first appeared in French. For example, a chapter of his *Manual of Political Economy*, written in 1793, appeared in the *Bibliothèque britannique* in 1798; and Dumont made use of the work in his *Théorie des peines et des récompenses* (1811). Bentham's work was published in English for the first time in John Bowring's edition of his *Works* (1838–43).

Bentham's *Defence of Usury* appeared in 1787 and his important *Introduction to the Principles of Morals and Legislation* in 1789.[1] The *Introduction* was intended as a preparation and scheme for a number of further treatises. Thus Bentham's *Essay on Political Tactics* corresponded to one section in this scheme. But though a part of this essay was sent to the Abbé Morellet in 1789, the work was first published by Dumont in 1816,[2] together with *Anarchical Fallacies* which had been written in about 1791.

In 1791 Bentham published his scheme for a model prison, the so-called *Panopticon*. And he approached the French National Assembly with a view to the establishment of such an institution under its auspices, offering his gratuitous services as supervisor. But though Bentham was one of the foreigners on whom the Assembly conferred the title of citizen in the following year, his offer was not taken up.[3] Similar efforts to induce the British government to implement the scheme for a model prison promised at first to be successful. But they eventually failed, partly, so Bentham at any rate liked to believe, through the machinations of King George III. However, in 1813 Parliament voted the philosopher a large sum of money in compensation for his expenditure on the Panopticon scheme.

[1] This work had been printed in 1788.
[2] A partial English text appeared in 1791.
[3] Obviously, the prisoners whom Bentham had in mind were not at all of the type of those who later became victims of the Jacobin Terror. He turned to the new French Assembly in the hope that now at last the reign of unclouded reason was beginning, that philosophy was coming into its own.

In 1802 Dumont published a work entitled *Traités de législation de M. Jérémie Bentham*. This consisted partly of papers written by Bentham himself, some of which had been originally composed in French, and partly of a digest by Dumont of the philosopher's ideas. And the work contributed greatly to the rise of Bentham's fame. At first this was more evident abroad than in England. But in the course of time the philosopher's star began to rise even in his own country. From 1808 James Mill became his disciple and a propagator of his doctrines. And Bentham became what might be called the background leader or inspirer of a group of radicals devoted to the principles of Benthamism.

In 1812 James Mill published an *Introductory View of the Rationale of Evidence*, a version of some of Bentham's papers. A French version of the papers was published by Dumont in 1823 under the title *Traité des preuves judiciaires*; and an English translation of this work appeared in 1825. A five-volume edition of Bentham's papers on jurisprudence which was much fuller than James Mill's was published by J. S. Mill in 1827 under the title *Rationale of Judicial Evidence*.

Bentham also gave his attention both to questions of constitutional reform and to the subject of the codification of the law. Characteristically, he was impatient of what he regarded as the chaotic condition of English law. His *Catechism of Parliamentary Reform* appeared in 1817, though it had been written in 1809. The year 1817 also saw the publication of *Papers upon Codification and Public Instruction*. In 1819 Bentham published a paper entitled *Radical Reform Bill, with Explanations*, and in 1823 *Leading Principles of a Constitutional Code*. The first volume of his *Constitutional Code*, together with the first chapter of the second volume, appeared in 1830. The whole work, edited by R. Doane, was published posthumously in 1841.

It is not possible to list all Bentham's publications here. But we can mention two or three further titles. *Chrestomathia*, a series of papers on education, appeared in 1816, while in the following year James Mill published his edition of Bentham's *Table of the Springs of Action*[1] which is concerned with the analysis of pains and pleasures as springs of action. The philosopher's *Deontology or Science of Morality* was published posthumously by Bowring in 1834 in two volumes, the second volume being compiled from notes. Reference has already been made to Bowring's edition of

---

[1] The work had been written at a considerably earlier period.

Bentham's *Works*.[1] A complete and critical edition of the philosopher's writings is yet to come.

Bentham died on June 6th, 1832, leaving directions that his body should be dissected for the benefit of science. It is preserved at University College, London. This College was founded in 1828, largely as a result of pressure from a group of which Bentham himself was a member. It was designed to extend the benefits of higher education to those for whom the two existing universities did not cater. Further, there were to be no religious tests, as there still were at Oxford and Cambridge.

3. Benthamism rested on a basis of psychological hedonism, the theory that every human being seeks by nature to attain pleasure and avoid pain. This was not, of course, a novel doctrine. It had been propounded in the ancient world, notably by Epicurus, while in the eighteenth century it was defended by, for example, Helvétius in France and Hartley and Tucker in England.[2] But though Bentham was not the inventor of the theory, he gave a memorable statement of it. 'Nature has placed mankind under the governance of two sovereign masters, *pain* and *pleasure*. . . . They govern us in all we do, in all we say, in all we think: every effort we can make to throw off our subjection will serve but to demonstrate and confirm it. In words a man may pretend to abjure their empire, but in reality he will remain subject to it all the while.'[3]

Further, Bentham is at pains to make clear what he means by pleasure and pain. He has no intention of restricting the range of meaning of these terms by arbitrary or 'metaphysical' definitions. He means by them what they mean in common estimation, in common language, no more and no less. 'In this matter we want no refinement, no metaphysics. It is not necessary to consult Plato, nor Aristotle. *Pain* and *pleasure* are what everybody feels to be such.'[4] The term 'pleasure' covers, for example, the pleasures of eating and drinking; but it also covers those of

[1] In the *Works* Bowring included a number of fragments, some of which are of philosophical interest. Thus in the fragment entitled *Ontology* Bentham distinguishes between real entities and fictitious entities. The latter, which are not to be compared with fabulous entities, the products of the free play of the imagination, are creations of the exigencies of language. For example, we require to be able to speak of relations, using the noun 'relation'. But though things can be related, there are no separate entities called 'relations'. If such entities are postulated through the influence of language, they are 'fictitious'.

[2] For Tucker see Vol. V of this *History*, pp. 193–4.

[3] *An Introduction to the Principles of Morals and Legislation*, ch. 1, sect. 1. This work will be referred to in future as *Introduction*.

[4] *Theory of Legislation*, translated from the French of Étienne Dumont by R. Hildreth, p. 3 (London, 1896).

reading an interesting book, listening to music or performing a kind action.

But Bentham is not concerned simply with stating what he takes to be a psychological truth, namely that all men are moved to action by the attraction of pleasure and the repulsion of pain. He is concerned with establishing an objective criterion of morality, of the moral character of human actions. Thus after the sentence quoted above, in which Bentham says that Nature has placed mankind under the government of pain and pleasure, he adds that 'it is for them alone to point out what we ought to do, as well as to determine what we shall do. On the one hand the standard of right and wrong, on the other the chain of causes and effects, are fastened to their throne.'[1] If, therefore, we assume that pleasure, happiness and good are synonymous terms and that pain, unhappiness and evil are also synonymous, the question immediately arises whether it makes any sense to say that we ought to pursue what is good and avoid what is evil, if, as a matter of psychological fact, we always do pursue the one and endeavour to avoid the other.

To be able to answer this question affirmatively, we have to make two assumptions. First, when it is said that man seeks pleasure, it is meant that he seeks his greater pleasure or the greatest possible amount of it. Secondly, man does not necessarily perform those actions which will as a matter of fact conduce to this end.[2] If we make these assumptions and pass over the difficulties inherent in any hedonistic ethics, we can then say that right actions are those which tend to increase the sum total of pleasure while wrong actions are those which tend to diminish it, and that we ought to do what is right and not do what is wrong.[3]

We thus arrive at the principle of utility, also called the greatest happiness principle. This 'states the greatest happiness of all those whose interest is in question, as being the right and proper, and only right and proper and universally desirable, end of human

[1] *Introduction*, ch. 1, sect. 1.

[2] For example, under the attraction of an immediate pleasure a man might neglect the fact that the course of action which causes this pleasure leads to a sum total of pain which outweighs the pleasure.

[3] Strictly speaking, an action which tends to add to the sum total of pleasure is for Bentham a 'right' action, in the sense of an action which we ought to perform, or at any rate not an action which we are obliged not to perform, that is, a 'wrong' action. It may not always be the case that an addition to the sum of pleasure cannot exist otherwise than through my action here and now. Hence I may not be obliged to act, though, if I do, the action will certainly not be wrong.

action'.[1] The parties whose interest is in question may, of course, differ. If we are thinking of the individual agent as such, it is his greatest happiness which is referred to. If we are thinking of the community, it is the greater happiness of the greatest possible number of the members of the community which is being referred to. If we are thinking of all sentient beings, then we must also consider the greater pleasure of animals. Bentham is chiefly concerned with the greater happiness of the human community, with the common good or welfare in the sense of the common good of any given human political society. But in all cases the principle is the same, namely that the greatest happiness of the party in question is the only desirable end of human action.

If we mean by proof deduction from some more ultimate principle or principles, the principle of utility cannot be proved. For there is no more ultimate ethical principle. At the same time Bentham tries to show that any other theory of morals involves in the long run an at least tacit appeal to the principle of utility. Whatever may be the reasons for which people act or think that they act, if we once raise the question why we *ought* to perform a certain action, we shall ultimately have to answer in terms of the principle of utility. The alternative moral theories which Bentham has in mind are principally intuitionist theories or theories which appeal to a moral sense. In his opinion such theories, taken by themselves, are incapable of answering the question why we ought to perform this action and not that. If the upholders of such theories once try to answer the question, they will ultimately have to argue that the action which ought to be performed is one which conduces to the greater happiness or pleasure of whatever party it is whose interest is in question. In other words, it is utilitarianism alone which can provide an objective criterion of right and wrong.[2] And to show that this is the case, is to give the only proof of the principle of utility which is required.

In passing we can note that though hedonism represented only one element in Locke's ethical theory,[3] he explicitly stated that

[1] *Introduction*, ch. 1, sect. 1, note 1.

[2] Bentham insists that the rightness or wrongness of actions depends on an objective criterion and not simply on the motive with which they are performed. 'Motive' and 'intention' are often confused, though they ought, Bentham maintains, to be carefully distinguished. If 'motive' is understood as a tendency to action when a pleasure, or the cause of a pleasure, is contemplated as the consequent of one's action, it makes no sense to speak of a bad motive. But in any case the criterion of right and wrong is primarily an objective criterion, not a subjective one.

[3] See Vol. V of this *History*, pp. 123-7.

'things then are good or evil only in reference to pleasure or pain. That we call good which is apt to cause or increase pleasure or diminish pain in us. . . . And on the contrary we name that evil which is apt to increase any pain or diminish any pleasure in us. . . .'[1] The property which is here called 'good' by Locke is described by Bentham as 'utility'. For 'utility is any property in any object, whereby it tends to produce benefit, advantage, pleasure, good or happiness, or . . . to prevent the happening of mischief, pain, evil or unhappiness to the party whose interest is considered.'[2]

Now, if actions are right in so far as they tend to increase the sum total of pleasure or diminish the sum total of pain of the party whose interest is in question, as Bentham puts it, the moral agent, when deciding whether a given action is right or wrong, will have to estimate the amount of pleasure and the amount of pain to which the action seems likely to give rise, and to weigh the one against the other. And Bentham provides a hedonistic or 'felicific' calculus for this purpose.[3] Let us suppose that I wish to estimate the value of a pleasure (or pain) for myself. I have to take into account four factors or dimensions of value: intensity, duration, certainty or uncertainty, propinquity or remoteness. For example, one pleasure might be very intense but of short duration, while another might be less intense but so much more lasting that it would be quantitatively greater than the first. Further, when considering actions which tend to produce pleasure or pain, I have to bear in mind two other factors, fecundity and purity. If of two types of action, each of which tends to produce pleasurable sensations, the one type tends to be followed by further pleasurable sensations while the other type does not or only in a lesser degree, the first is said to be more fecund or fruitful than the second. As for purity, this signifies freedom from being followed by sensations of the opposite kind. For instance, the cultivation of an appreciation of music opens up a range of enduring pleasure which does not yield those diminishing returns that result from the action of taking certain habit-forming drugs.

So far Bentham's calculus follows the same lines as that of Epicurus. But Bentham is chiefly concerned, in the application of his ethical theory, with the common good. And he adds that when a number of persons or community is the party whose interest is in question, we have to take into account a seventh factor in

[1] *Essay*, Bk. 2, ch. 20, sect. 2.   [2] *Introduction*, ch. 1, sect. 3.
[3] *Ibid.*, ch. 4.

addition to the six just mentioned. This seventh factor is extent, that is, the number of persons who are affected by the pleasure or pain in question.

It has sometimes been said that Bentham's calculus is useless but that one could quite well discard it while retaining his general moral theory. But it seems to the present writer that some distinctions are required. If one chose to look on this theory as no more than an analysis of the meaning of certain ethical terms, it would doubtless be possible to maintain that the analysis is correct and at the same time to disregard the hedonistic calculus. But if one looks on Bentham's moral theory as he himself looked on it, that is, not simply as an analysis but also as a guide for action, the case is somewhat different. We could indeed maintain, and rightly, that no exact mathematical calculation of pains and pleasures can be made. It is fairly obvious, for example, that in many cases a man cannot make a precise mathematical calculation of the respective quantities of pleasure which would probably result from alternative courses of action. And if it is the community whose interest is in question, how are we going to calculate the probable sum total of pleasure when it is a notorious fact that in many cases what is pleasurable to one is not pleasurable to another? At the same time, if we admit, as Bentham admitted, only quantitative differences between pleasures, and if we regard hedonistic ethics as providing a practical rule for conduct, some sort of calculation will be required, even if it cannot be precise. And in point of fact people do make such rough calculations on occasion. Thus a man may very well ask himself whether it is really worth while pursuing a certain course of pleasurable action which will probably involve certain painful consequences. And if he does seriously consider this question, he is making use of one of the rules of Bentham's calculus. What relation this sort of reasoning bears to morality is another question. And it is irrelevant in the present context. For the hypothesis is that Bentham's general moral doctrine is accepted.

Now, the sphere of human action is obviously very much wider than legislation and acts of government. And in some cases it is the individual agent as such whose interest is in question. Hence I can have duties to myself. But if the sphere of morality is coterminous with the sphere of human action, legislation and acts of government fall within the moral sphere. Hence the principle of utility must apply to them. But here the party whose interest is in question is the community. Although, therefore, as Bentham says, there are many actions which are as a matter of fact useful to the community but the regulation of which by law would not be in the public interest, legislation ought to serve this interest. It ought to be directed to the common welfare or happiness. Hence an act of legislation or of government is said to conform with or be dictated by the principle of utility when 'the tendency which it has to augment the happiness of the community is greater than any which it has to diminish it'.[1]

The community, however, is 'a fictitious *body*, composed of the individual persons who are considered as constituting as it were its members'.[2] And the interest of the community is 'the sum of the interests of the several members who compose it'.[3] To say, therefore, that legislation and government should be directed to the common good is to say that they should be directed to the greater happiness of the greatest possible number of individuals who are members of the society in question.

Obviously, if we assume that the common interest is simply the sum total of the private interests of the individual members of the community, we might draw the conclusion that the common good is inevitably promoted if every individual seeks and increases his own personal happiness. But there is no guarantee that individuals will seek their own happiness in a rational or enlightened manner, and in such a way that they do not diminish the happiness of other individuals, thus diminishing the sum total of happiness in the community. And in point of fact it is clear that clashes of interest do occur. Hence a harmonization of interests is required with a view to the attainment of the common good. And this is the function of government and legislation.[4]

It is sometimes said that any such harmonization of interests presupposes the possibility of working altruistically for the common good, and that Bentham thus makes an abrupt and unwarranted transition from the egoistic or selfish pleasure-seeker to the public-spirited altruist. But some distinctions are required. In the first place Bentham does not assume that all men are by

---

[1] *Introduction*, ch. 1, sect. 7.
[2] *Ibid*., ch. 1, sect. 4. For Bentham's use of the word 'fictitious' see Note 1 on p. 15.
[3] *Ibid*.
[4] Bentham and his followers were indeed convinced that in the sphere of the economic market the removal of legal restrictions and the introduction of free trade and competition would, in the long run at any rate, inevitably make for the greater happiness of the community. But further reference to Benthamite economics will be made in the last section of this chapter.

nature necessarily egoistic or selfish in the sense in which these terms would generally be understood. For he recognizes social affections as well as their contrary. Thus in his table of pleasures he includes among the so-called simple pleasures those of benevolence, which are described as 'the pleasures resulting from the view of any pleasures supposed to be possessed by the beings who may be the objects of benevolence; to wit the sensitive beings we are acquainted with'.[1] In the second place, though Benthamism doubtless assumes that the man who takes pleasure in witnessing the pleasure of another does so originally because it is pleasurable to himself, it invokes the principles of the associationist psychology to explain how a man can come to seek the good of others without any advertence to his own.[2]

At the same time there is obviously no guarantee that those whose task it is to harmonize private interests will be notably endowed with benevolence, or that they will in fact have learned to seek the common good in a disinterested spirit. Indeed, it did not take Bentham long to come to the conclusion that rulers are very far from constituting exceptions to the general run of men, who, left to themselves, pursue their own interests, even if many of them are perfectly capable of being pleased by the pleasure of others. And it was this conclusion which was largely responsible for his adoption of democratic ideas. A despot or absolute monarch generally seeks his own interest, and so does a ruling aristocracy. The only way, therefore, of securing that the greater happiness of the greatest possible number is taken as the criterion in government and legislation is to place government, so far as this is practicable, in the hands of all. Hence Bentham's proposals for abolishing the monarchy[3] and the House of Lords and for introducing universal suffrage and annual parliaments. As the common interest is simply the sum total of private interests, everyone has a stake, so to speak, in the common good. And education can help the individual to understand that in acting for the common good he is also acting for his own good.

To avoid misunderstanding, it must be added that the harmonization of interests by law which Bentham demanded was primarily a removal of hindrances to the increase of the happiness of the greatest possible number of citizens rather than what would

---

[1] *Introduction*, ch. 5, sect. 10. 'Sensitive beings' includes animals.
[2] This theme will be treated in connection with James Mill.
[3] In Bentham's time the British monarch was able to exercise considerably more effective influence in political life than is possible today.

generally be thought of as positive interference with the freedom of the individual. This is one reason why he gave so much attention to the subject of penology, the infliction of penal sanctions for diminishing the general happiness or good by infringing laws which are or at any rate ought to be passed with a view to preventing actions which are incompatible with the happiness of the members of society in general. In Bentham's opinion the primary purpose of punishment is to deter, not to reform. Reformation of offenders is only a subsidiary purpose.

Bentham's remarks on concrete issues are often sensible enough. His general attitude to penal sanctions is a case in point. As already remarked, the primary purpose of punishment is to deter. But punishment involves the infliction of pain, of a diminution of pleasure in some way or other. And as all pain is evil, it follows that 'all punishment in itself is evil'.[1] And the conclusion to be drawn is that the legislator ought not to attach to the infringement of the law a penal sanction which exceeds what is strictly required to obtain the desired effect. True, it might be argued that if the primary aim of punishment is to deter, the most ferocious penalties will be the most efficacious. But if punishment is in itself an evil, even though in the concrete circumstances of human life in society a necessary evil, the relevant question is, what is the least amount of punishment which will have a deterrent effect? Besides, the legislator has to take into account public opinion, though this is indeed a variable factor. For the more people come to consider a given penal sanction to be grossly excessive or inappropriate, the more they tend to withhold their co-operation in the execution of the law.[2] And in this case the supposedly deterrent effect of the punishment is diminished. Again, it has a bad educative effect and is not for the public good if some heavy penalty, such as the death penalty, is inflicted for a variety of offences which differ very much in gravity, that is, in the amount of harm which they do to others or to the community at large. As for the subsidiary aim of punishment, namely to contribute to the reformation of offenders, how can this aim be fulfilled when the prisons are notoriously hotbeds of vice?

[1] *Introduction*, ch. 13, sect. 2.
[2] It was certainly not unknown at the time for juries to refuse to convict even when they were well aware that the accused was guilty. Further, the death sentence, when passed for what would now be considered comparatively minor offences and even on children, was frequently commuted. In other words, there was a growing discrepancy between the actual state of the law and educated opinion as to what it should be.

It is possible, of course, to hold a different view about the primary purpose of punishment. But it would require a considerable degree of eccentricity for a man of today to disagree with Bentham's conclusion that the penal system of his time stood in need of reform. And even if we do hold a somewhat different view about the function of punishment, we can none the less recognize that his arguments in favour of reform are, generally speaking, intelligible and persuasive.

But when we turn from such discussions about the need for reform to Bentham's general philosophy, the situation is somewhat different. For example, J. S. Mill objected that Bentham's idea of human nature betrayed a narrowness of vision. And inasmuch as Bentham tends to reduce man to a system of attractions and repulsions in response to pleasures and pains, together with an ability to make a quasi-mathematical computation of the pluses of pleasures and the minuses of pains, many would find themselves in full agreement with Mill on this point.

At the same time J. S. Mill awards high marks to Bentham for employing a scientific method in morals and politics. This consists above all in 'the method of detail; of treating wholes by separating them into their parts, abstractions by resolving them into things —classes and generalities by distinguishing them into the individuals of which they are made up; and breaking every question into pieces before attempting to solve it'.[1] In other words, Mill commends Bentham for his thoroughgoing use of reductive analysis and for this reason regards him as a reformer in philosophy.

In regard to the question of fact Mill is, of course, quite right. We have seen, for example, how Bentham applied a kind of quantitative analysis in ethics. And he applied it because he thought that it was the only proper scientific method. It was the only method which would enable us to give clear meanings to terms such as 'right' and 'wrong'. Again, for Bentham terms such as 'community' and 'common interest' were abstractions which stood in need of analysis if they were to be given a cash-value. To imagine that they signified peculiar entities over and above the elements into which they could be analysed was to be misled by language into postulating fictitious entities.

But though there can obviously be no valid *a priori* objection to experimenting with the method of reductive analysis, it is also clear that Bentham skates lightly over difficulties and treats that

[1] *Dissertations and Discussions*, I, pp. 339–40 (2nd edition, 1867).

which is complicated as though it were simple. For example, it is admittedly difficult to give a clear explanation of what the common good is, if it is not reducible to the private goods of the individual members of the community. But it is also difficult to suppose that a true statement about the common good is always reducible to true statements about the private goods of individuals. We cannot legitimately take it for granted that such a reduction or translation is possible. Its possibility ought to be established by providing actual examples. As the Scholastics say, *ab esse ad posse valet illatio*. But Bentham tends to take the possibility for granted and to conclude without more ado that those who think otherwise have fallen victims to what Wittgenstein was later to call the bewitchment of language. In other words, even if Bentham was right in his application of reductive analysis, he did not pay anything like sufficient attention to what can be said on the other side. Indeed, Mill draws attention to 'Bentham's contempt of all other schools of thinkers'.[1]

According to Mill, Bentham 'was not a great philosopher, but he was a great reformer in philosophy'.[2] And if we are devotees of reductive analysis, we shall probably agree with this statement. Otherwise we may be inclined to omit the last two words. Bentham's habit of over-simplifying and of skating over difficulties, together with that peculiar narrowness of moral vision to which Mill aptly alludes, disqualifies him from being called a great philosopher. But his place in the movement of social reform is assured. His premises are often questionable but he is certainly skilled in drawing from them conclusions which are frequently sensible and enlightened. And, as has already been remarked, the over-simplified nature of his moral philosophy facilitated its use as a practical instrument or weapon.

4. James Mill, Bentham's leading disciple, was born on April 6th, 1773, in Forfarshire. His father was a village shoemaker. After schooling at the Montrose Academy Mill entered the University of Edinburgh in 1790, where he attended the lectures of Dugald Stewart.[3] In 1798 he was licensed to preach; but he never received a call from any Presbyterian parish, and in 1802 he went to London with the hope of earning a living by writing and editorship. In 1805 he married. At the end of the following year he began work on his history of British India which appeared in three

[1] *Ibid.*, I, p. 353.   [2] *Ibid.*, I, p. 339.
[3] See Vol. V of this *History*, pp. 375–83.

volumes in 1817. In 1819 this brought him a post in the East India Company, and subsequent advancement, with increases in salary, set him free at last from financial worries.

In 1808 Mill met Bentham and became a fervent disciple. By this time the would-be Presbyterian minister had become an agnostic. For some years he wrote for the *Edinburgh Review*, but he was too much of a radical to win the real confidence of the editors. In 1816–23 he wrote for the *Supplement* to the *Encyclopaedia Britannica* series of political articles which set forth the views of the utilitarian circle.[1] In 1821 he published his *Elements of Political Economy* and in 1829 his *Analysis of the Phenomena of the Human Mind*. Between these two dates he contributed for a time to the *Westminster Review*, which was founded in 1824 as an organ of the radicals.

James Mill died on June 23rd, 1836, a champion of Benthamism to the last. He was not perhaps a particularly attractive figure. A man of vigorous though somewhat narrow intellect, he was extremely reserved and apparently devoid of any poetic sensibility, while for passionate emotions and for sentiment he had little use. His son remarks that though James Mill upheld an Epicurean ethical theory (Bentham's hedonism), he was personally a Stoic and combined Stoic qualities with a Cynic's disregard for pleasure. But he was certainly an extremely hard-working and conscientious man, devoted to propagating the views which he believed to be true.

With James Mill, as with Bentham, we find a combination of *laissez-faire* economics with a reiterated demand for political reform. As every man naturally seeks his own interest, it is not surprising that the executive does so. The executive, therefore, must be controlled by the legislature. But the House of Commons is itself the organ of the interests of a comparatively small number of families. And its interest cannot be made identical with that of the community in general unless the suffrage is extended and elections are frequent.[2] Like other Benthamites, Mill also had a

[1] This circle comprised, among others, the economists David Ricardo and J. R. McCulloch, T. R. Malthus, the famous writer on population, and John Austin, who applied utilitarian principles to jurisprudence in his work *The Province of Jurisprudence Determined* (1832).

[2] Mill was indeed quite right in thinking that the House of Commons of his time was effectively representative of only a small part of the population. He seems, however, to have thought that a legislature which represented the prosperous middle classes would represent the interests of the country as a whole. At the same time he saw no logical stopping-point in the process of extending the suffrage, though he assumed, rather surprisingly, that the lower classes would be governed by the wisdom of the middle class.

somewhat simple faith in the power of education to make man see that their 'real' interests are bound up with the common interest. Hence political reform and extended education should go hand in hand.

5. James Mill undertook to show, with the aid of the associationist psychology, how altruistic conduct on the part of the pleasure-seeking individual is possible. He was indeed convinced that 'we never feel any pains or pleasures but our own. The fact, indeed, is, that our very idea of the pains or pleasures of another man is only the idea of our own pains, or our own pleasures, associated with the idea of another man.'[1] But these remarks contain also the key to understanding the possibility of altruistic conduct. For an inseparable association can be set up, say between the idea of my own pleasure and the idea of that of the other members of the community to which I belong, an association such that its result is analogous to a chemical product which is something more than the mere sum of its elements. And even if I originally sought the good of the community only as a means to my own, I can then seek the former without any advertence to the latter.

Given this point of view, it may seem strange that in his *Fragment on Mackintosh*, which was published in 1835 after having been held up for a time, Mill indulges in a vehement attack on Sir James Mackintosh (1765–1832), who in 1829 had written on ethics for the *Encyclopaedia Britannica*. For Mackintosh not only accepted the principle of utility but also made use of the associationist psychology in explaining the development of the morality which takes the general happiness as its end. But the reason for the attack is clear enough. If Mackintosh had expounded an ethical theory quite different from that of the Benthamites, the Kantian ethics for example, Mill would presumably not have been so indignant. As it was, Mackintosh's crime in Mill's eyes was to have adulterated the pure milk of Benthamism by adding to it the moral sense theory, derived from Hutcheson and to a certain extent from the Scottish School, a theory which Bentham had decisively rejected.

Although Mackintosh accepted utility as the criterion for

[1] *Analysis of the Phenomena of the Human Mind*, II, p. 217 (1869, edited by J. S. Mill). Commenting on his father's statement, J. S. Mill draws attention to its ambiguity. To say that if I take pleasure in another man's pleasure, the pleasure which I feel is my own and not the other man's, is one thing. And it is obviously true. To imply that if I seek another man's pleasure I do so as a means to my own, is something different.

distinguishing between right and wrong actions, he also insisted on the peculiar character of the moral sentiments which are experienced in contemplating such actions and, in particular, the qualities of the agents as manifested in such actions. If we group together these sentiments as forming the moral sense, we can say that it is akin to the sense of beauty. True, a virtuous man's moral qualities are indeed useful in that they contribute to the common good or happiness. But one can perfectly well approve and admire them without any more reference to utility than when we appreciate a beautiful painting.[1]

In discussing Mackintosh's view James Mill urged that if there were a moral sense, it would be a peculiar kind of faculty, and that we ought logically to admit the possibility of its overriding the judgment of utility. True, Mackintosh believed that in point of fact the moral sentiments and the judgment of utility are always in harmony. But in this case the moral sense is a superfluous postulate. If, however, it is a distinct faculty which, in principle at least, is capable of overriding the judgment of utility, it should be described as an immoral rather than a moral sense. For the judgment of utility is the moral judgment.

Many people would probably feel that, apart from the question whether the term 'moral sense' is appropriate or inappropriate, we certainly can experience the kind of sentiments described by Mackintosh. So what is all the fuss about? A general answer is that both Bentham and Mill looked on the theory of the moral sense as a cloudy and in some respects dangerous doctrine which had been superseded by utilitarianism, so that any attempt to reintroduce it constituted a retrograde step. In particular, Mill doubtless believed that Mackintosh's theory implied that there is a superior point of view to that of utilitarianism, a point of view, that is to say, which rises above such a mundane consideration as that of utility. And any such claim was anathema to Mill.

The long and the short of it is that James Mill was determined to maintain a rigid Benthamism.[2] Any attempt, such as that made by Mackintosh, to reconcile utilitarianism with intuitionist ethics simply aroused his indignation. As will be seen later, however, his son had no such devotion to the letter of the Benthamite gospel.

---

[1] Similarly, the sentiments which we feel in contemplating the undesirable qualities of a bad man need not involve any reference to their lack of utility.

[2] This determination also shows itself in Mill's attack on Mackintosh for making the morality of actions depend on motive, when Bentham had shown that it does not.

6. Obviously, the use made by James Mill of the associationist psychology in explaining the possibility of altruistic conduct on the part of the individual who by nature seeks his own pleasure presupposes a general employment of the method of reductive analysis which was characteristic of classical empiricism, especially in the thought of Hume, and which was systematically practised by Bentham. Thus in his *Analysis of the Phenomena of the Human Mind* Mill tries to reduce man's mental life to its basic elements. In general he follows Hume in distinguishing between impressions and ideas, the latter being copies or images of the former. But Mill actually speaks of sensations, not of impressions. Hence we can also say that he follows Condillac[1] in depicting the development of mental phenomena as a process of the transformation of sensations. It must be added, however, that Mill groups together sensations and ideas under the term 'feelings'. 'We have two classes of feelings; one, that which exists when the object of sense is present; another, that which exists after the object of sense has ceased to be present. The one class of feelings I call sensations; the other class of feelings I call *ideas*.'[2]

After reducing the mind to its basic elements Mill is then faced with the task of reconstructing mental phenomena with the aid of the principles of the association of ideas. Hume, he remarks, recognized three principles of association, namely contiguity in time and place, causation and resemblance. But causation, in Mill's view, can be identified with contiguity in time, that is, with the order of regular succession. 'Causation is only a name for the order established between an antecedent and consequent; that is, the established or constant antecedence of the one, and consequence of the other.'[3]

Mill's work covers such topics as naming, classification, abstraction, memory, belief, ratiocination, pleasurable and painful sensations, the will and intentions. And at the end the author remarks that the work, which constitutes the theoretical part of the doctrine of the mind, should be followed by a practical part comprising logic, considered as practical rules for the mind in its search for truth, ethics and the study of education as directed to training the individual to contribute actively to the greatest possible good or happiness for himself and for his fellow men.

We cannot follow Mill in his reconstruction of mental

---

[1] See Vol. VI of this *History*, pp. 28–35.   [2] *Analysis*, I, p. 52.
[3] *Ibid.*, I, p. 110.

phenomena. But it is worth while drawing attention to the way in which he deals with reflection, which was described by Locke as the notice which the mind takes of its own operations. The mind is identified with the stream of consciousness. And consciousness means having sensations and ideas. As, therefore, 'reflection is nothing but consciousness',[1] to reflect on an idea is the same thing as to have it. There is no room for any additional factor.

Commenting on his father's theory J. S. Mill remarks that 'to reflect on any of our feelings or mental acts is more properly identified with *attending* to the feeling than (as stated in the text) with merely having it'.[2] And this seems to be true. But James Mill is so obstinately determined to explain the whole mental life in terms of the association of primitive elements reached by reductive analysis that he has to explain away those factors in consciousness to which it is difficult to apply such treatment. In other words, empiricism can manifest its own form of dogmatism.

7. To turn briefly to Benthamite economics. As far as the economic market was concerned, Bentham believed that in a freely competitive market a harmony of interest is inevitably attained, at least in the long run. Such State action as he demanded consisted in the removal of restrictions, such as the abolition of the tariffs which protected the English market in grain and which Bentham thought of as serving the sectional interest of the land-owners.

Behind this *laissez-faire* theory lay the influence of the French physiocrats, to whom allusion has already been made, though elements were also derived, of course, from English writers, particularly from Adam Smith.[3] But it was obviously not simply a question of deriving ideas from previous writers. For the *laissez-faire* economics can be said to have reflected the needs and aspirations of the expanding industrial and capitalist system of the time. In other words, it reflected the interests, real or supposed, of that middle class which James Mill considered to be the wisest element in the community.

The theory found its classical expression in the writings of David Ricardo (1772–1823), especially in his *Principles of Political Economy*, which was published in 1817. Bentham is reported to have said that James Mill was his spiritual child, and that Ricardo was the spiritual child of James Mill. But though it was largely

---

[1] *Analysis*, II, p. 177.   [2] *Ibid.*, II, p. 179, note 34.
[3] See Vol. V of this *History*, pp. 354–5.

as a result of Mill's encouragement that Ricardo published his *Principles* when he did, in economic theory Mill was more dependent on Ricardo than the other way round. In any case it was Ricardo's work which became the classical statement of Benthamite economics.

In the view of his disciple J. R. McCulloch (1789–1864) Ricardo's great service was to state the fundamental theorem of the science of value. This was to the effect that in a free market the value of commodities is determined by the amount of labour required for their production. In other words, value is crystallized labour.

Now, if this theory were true, it would appear to follow that the money obtained from the sale of commodities belongs rightfully to those whose labour produced the commodities in question. That is to say, the conclusion drawn by Marx[1] from the labour theory of value appears to be amply justified, unless perhaps we wish to argue that the capitalist is to be included among the labourers. But Ricardo and the other economists of the *laissez-faire* School were far from using the labour theory of value as a means of showing that capitalism by its very nature involves exploitation of the workers. For one thing they were conscious that the capitalist contributes to production by the investment of capital in machinery and so on. For another thing they were interested in arguing that in a competitive market, free from all restrictions, prices tend naturally to represent the real values of commodities.

This line of argument seems to involve the at least implicit assumption that a free market is governed by some sort of natural economic law which ultimately ensures a harmonization of interests and operates for the common good, provided that nobody attempts to interfere with its functioning. But this optimistic view represents only one aspect of Benthamite economics. According to T. R. Malthus (1766–1834), population always increases when living becomes easier, unless, of course, its rate of increase is restricted in some way. Thus population tends to outrun the means of subsistence. And it follows that wages tend to remain constant, at a subsistence level that is to say. Hence there is a law of wages which can hardly be said to operate in favour of the greater happiness of the greatest possible number.

If the Benthamites had made in the economic sphere a thoroughgoing application of the principle of utility, they would have had to demand in this sphere a harmonization of interests

[1] See Vol. VII of this *History*, p. 312.

through legislation similar to the harmonization of interests through legislation which they demanded in the political sphere. Indeed, in his essay on government for the *Encyclopaedia Britannica* James Mill declared that the general happiness is promoted by assuring to every man the greatest possible amount of the fruit of his own labour, and that the government should prevent the powerful robbing the weak. But their belief in certain economic laws restricted the Benthamites' view both of the possibility and of the desirability of State action in the economic sphere.

And yet they themselves made breaches in the wall set up round the economic sphere by the belief in natural economic laws. For one thing Malthus argued that while wages tend to remain constant, rents tend to increase with the increasing fertility of the land. And these rents represent profit for the landlords though they contribute nothing to production. In other words, the landlords are parasites on society. And it was the conviction of the Benthamites that their power should be broken. For another thing, while those who were strongly influenced by Malthus's reflections on population may have thought that the only way of increasing profits and wages would be by restricting the growth of population, and that this would be impracticable, the very admission of the possibility in principle of interfering with the distribution of wealth in one way should have encouraged the exploration of other ways of attaining this end. And in point of fact J. S. Mill came to envisage legislative control, in a limited form at least, of the distribution of wealth.

In other words, if the Benthamite economists began by separating the economic sphere, in which a *laissez-faire* policy should reign, from the political sphere, in which a harmonization of interests through legislation was demanded, in J. S. Mill's development of utilitarianism the gap between the economic and political spheres tended to close. As will be seen presently, J. S. Mill introduced into the utilitarian philosophy elements which were incompatible with strict Benthamism. But it seems to the present writer at any rate that in proposing some State interference in the economic sphere with a view to the general happiness, Mill was simply applying the principle of utility in a way in which it might well have been applied from the start, had it not been for the belief in the autonomy of the economic sphere, governed by its own iron laws.

CHAPTER II

THE UTILITARIAN MOVEMENT (2)

Life and writings of J. S. Mill—Mill's development of the utilitarian ethics—Mill on civil liberty and government—Psychological freedom.

1. JOHN STUART MILL was born in London on May 20th, 1806. A fascinating account of the extraordinary education to which he was subjected by his father is to be found in his *Autobiography*. Having apparently started to learn Greek at the age of three, by the time he was about twelve years old he was sufficiently acquainted with Greek and Latin literature, history and mathematics to enter on what he calls more advanced studies, including logic. In 1819 he was taken through a complete course of political economy, during which he read Adam Smith and Ricardo. As for religion, 'I was brought up from the first without any religious belief, in the ordinary acceptation of the term',[1] though his father encouraged him to learn what religious beliefs mankind had in point of fact held.

In 1820 J. S. Mill was invited to stay in the South of France with Sir Samuel Bentham, brother of the philosopher. And during his time abroad he not only studied the French language and literature but also followed courses at Montpellier on chemistry, zoology, logic and higher mathematics, besides making the acquaintance of some economists and liberal thinkers. Returning to England in 1821 Mill started to read Condillac, studied Roman law with John Austin (1790–1859), and gave further attention to the philosophy of Bentham. He also extended his philosophical reading to the writings of thinkers such as Helvétius, Locke, Hume, Reid and Dugald Stewart. Through personal contact with men such as John Austin and his younger brother Charles, Mill was initiated into the utilitarian circle. Indeed, in the winter of 1822–3 he founded a little Utilitarian Circle of his own, which lasted for about three and a half years.

---

[1] *Autobiography*, p. 38 (2nd edition, 1873). Though James Mill was an agnostic rather than a dogmatic atheist, he refused to admit that the world could possibly have been created by a God who combined infinite power with infinite wisdom and goodness. Moreover, he thought that this belief had a detrimental effect upon morality.

In 1823 Mill obtained, through his father's influence, a clerkship in the East India Company. And after successive promotions he became head of the office in 1856 with a substantial salary. Neither father nor son ever held an academic chair.

Mill's first printed writings consisted of some letters published in 1822, in which he defended Ricardo and James Mill against attack. After the foundation of the *Westminster Review* in 1824 he became a frequent contributor. And in 1825 he undertook the editing of Bentham's *Rationale of Evidence* in five volumes, a labour which, so he tells us, occupied about all his leisure time for almost a year.

It is hardly surprising that prolonged overwork, culminating in the editing of Bentham's manuscripts, resulted in 1826 in what is popularly called a nervous breakdown. But this mental crisis had a considerable importance through its effect on Mill's outlook. In his period of dejection the utilitarian philosophy, in which he had been indoctrinated by his father, lost its charms for him. He did not indeed abandon it. But he came to two conclusions. First, happiness is not attained by seeking it directly. One finds it by striving after some goal or ideal other than one's own happiness or pleasure. Secondly, analytic thought needs to be complemented by a cultivation of the feelings, an aspect of human nature which Bentham had mistrusted. This meant in part that Mill began to find some meaning in poetry and art.[1] More important, he found himself able to appreciate Coleridge and his disciples, who were generally regarded as the antithesis to the Benthamites. In the course of time he even came to see some merit in Carlyle, a feat which his father was never able to achieve. True, the effect of Mill's crisis should not be exaggerated. He remained a utilitarian, and, though modifying Benthamism in important ways, he never went over to the opposite camp. As he himself puts it, he did not share in the sharp reaction of the nineteenth century against the eighteenth, a reaction represented in Great Britain by the names of Coleridge and Carlyle. At the same time he became conscious of the narrowness of Bentham's view of human nature, and he formed the conviction that the emphasis laid by the French *philosophes* and by Bentham on the analytic reason needed to be supplemented, though not supplanted, by an understanding of the importance of other aspects of man and his activity.

In 1829–30 Mill became acquainted with the doctrines of the

[1] Mill started to read Wordsworth in 1828.

followers of Saint-Simon.[1] While he disagreed with them on many issues, their criticism of the *laissez-faire* economics appeared to him to express important truths. Further, 'their aim seemed to me desirable and rational, however their means might be inefficacious'.[2] In a real sense Mill always remained an individualist at heart, a staunch upholder of individual liberty. But he was quite prepared to modify individualism in the interest of the common welfare.

In 1830–1 Mill wrote five *Essays on Some Unsettled Questions of Political Economy*, though they were not published until 1844.[3] In 1843 he published his famous *System of Logic*, on which he had been working for some years. For part of the work he found stimulus in W. Whewell's *History of the Inductive Sciences* (1837) and in Sir John Herschel's *Discourse on the Study of Natural Philosophy* (1830), while in the final rewriting of the work he found further help in Whewell's *Philosophy of the Inductive Sciences* (1840) and the earlier volumes of Auguste Comte's *Cours de philosophie positive*.[4] His correspondence with the celebrated French positivist, whom he never actually met, began in 1841. But in the course of time this epistolary friendship waned and then ceased. Mill continued to respect Comte, but he found himself entirely out of sympathy with the positivist's later ideas for the spiritual organization of humanity.

In 1848 Mill published his *Principles of Political Economy*.[5] In 1851 he married Harriet Taylor, with whom he had been on terms of intimate friendship from 1830 and whose first husband died in 1849. In 1859, the year following that of his wife's death, Mill published his essay *On Liberty*, in 1861 his *Considerations on Representative Government*, and in 1863 *Utilitarianism*.[6] *An Examination of Sir William Hamilton's Philosophy* and the small volume on *Auguste Comte and Positivism* appeared in 1865.

From 1865 until 1868 Mill was a Member of Parliament for Westminster. He spoke in favour of the Reform Bill of 1867, and he denounced the policy of the British government in Ireland. Of his pamphlet *England and Ireland* (1868) he remarks that it 'was

---

[1] Comte Claude Henri de Rouvroy de Saint-Simon (1760–1825) was a French socialist, whose ideas gave rise to a group or School.

[2] *Autobiography*, p. 167. Mill is referring to the aim or ideal of organizing labour and capital for the general good of the community.

[3] The fifth essay was partially rewritten in 1833.

[4] Auguste Comte (1798–1857) published the first volume of this work in 1830.

[5] Subsequent editions appeared in 1849 and 1852.

[6] This short work had previously appeared in instalments in *Fraser's Magazine*.

not popular, except in Ireland, as I did not expect it to be.'[1] Mill also advocated proportional representation and the suffrage for women.

Mill died at Avignon on May 8th, 1873. His *Dissertations and Discussions* appeared in four volumes between 1859 and 1875, while his *Essays in Religion* were published in 1874. Further reference to the last-named work, in which Mill discusses sympathetically the hypothesis of a finite God, that is, God limited in power, will be made in the next chapter.

2. In *Utilitarianism* Mill gives an often-quoted definition or description of the basic principle of utilitarian ethics which is quite in accord with Benthamism. 'The creed which accepts as the foundation of morals, Utility, or the Greatest Happiness Principle, holds that actions are right in proportion as they tend to promote happiness, wrong as they tend to produce the reverse of happiness. By happiness is intended pleasure, and the absence of pain; by unhappiness, pain, and the privation of pleasure.'[2]

True, Mill is anxious to show that utilitarianism is not a philosophy either of egoism or of expediency. It is not a philosophy of egoism because happiness, in the moral context, 'is not the agent's own greatest happiness, but the greatest amount of happiness altogether'.[3] As for expediency, the expedient as opposed to the right generally means that which serves the interests of the individual as such, without regard to the common good, 'as when a minister sacrifices the interests of his country to keep himself in place'.[4] Such conduct is clearly incompatible with the greatest happiness principle. At the same time, though Mill is anxious to show that utilitarianism does not deserve the accusations to which Bentham's doctrine seemed to some people to lay it open, he provides plenty of evidence that his thought moves within a Benthamite framework. This can be seen easily enough if one considers his discussion of the sense in which the principle

[1] *Autobiography*, p. 294.
[2] *Utilitarianism*, pp. 9–10 (2nd edition, 1864).
[3] *Ibid.*, p. 16.
[4] *Ibid.*, p. 32. Mill recognizes that the expedient may mean that which is expedient or useful for securing some temporary advantage when the securing of this advantage involves violation of a rule 'whose observance is expedient in a much higher degree' (*ibid.*). And it is clear that not only the individual but also the community, as represented by public authority, might succumb to the temptation to seek its immediate temporary advantage in this way. But Mill argues that the expedient in this sense is not really 'useful' at all. It is harmful. Hence there can be no question of choice of the expedient being justified by the principle of utility.

of utility is susceptible of proof.[1] Mill's first point is that happiness is universally recognized to be a good. 'Each person's happiness is a good to that person, and the general happiness, therefore, a good to the aggregate of all persons.'[2] This remark implies an acceptance of Bentham's analysis of such terms as 'community' and 'common interest'. Mill then goes on to argue that happiness is not merely *a* good but *the* good: it is the one ultimate end which all desire and seek. True, it can be objected that some people seek virtue or money or fame for its own sake, and that such things cannot properly be described as happiness. But the fact that such things can be sought for their own sakes is explicable in terms of the association of ideas. Take virtue, for example. 'There was no original desire of it, or motive to it, save its conduciveness to pleasure; and especially to protection from pain.'[3] But that which is originally sought as a means to pleasure can, by association with the idea of pleasure, come to be sought for its own sake. And it is then sought not as a means to pleasure or happiness but as a constituent part of it. Evidently, this line of argument, with its appeal to the associationist psychology, is in line with Benthamism.

Nobody, of course, disputes the facts that Mill began with the Benthamism in which he had been indoctrinated by his father, and that he never formally rejected it, and that he always retained elements of it. The significant aspect of Mill's brand of utilitarianism, however, is not to be found in the ideas which he took over from Bentham and James Mill. It is to be found in the ideas which Mill himself added, and which strained the original Benthamite framework to such an extent that it ought to have been radically refashioned or even abandoned.

Foremost among the ideas which Mill introduced was that of intrinsic qualitative differences between pleasures. He does indeed admit that 'utilitarian writers in general have placed the superiority of mental over bodily pleasures chiefly in the greater permanency, safety, uncostliness, etc., of the former—that is, in their circumstantial advantages rather than in their intrinsic

---

[1] Mill agrees with Bentham that the principle of utility cannot be proved by deduction from any more ultimate principle or principles. For the point at issue is the ultimate end of human action. And 'questions of ultimate ends do not admit of proof, in the ordinary acceptation of the term' (*Utilitarianism*, p. 52). It can, however, be shown that all men seek happiness, and only happiness, as the end of action. And this is sufficient proof of the statement that happiness is the one ultimate end of action.

[2] *Utilitarianism*, p. 53.   [3] *Ibid.*, pp. 56–7.

nature'.[1] But he goes on to argue that the utilitarians in question might have adopted another point of view 'with entire consistency. It is quite compatible with the principle of utility to recognize the fact, that some *kinds* of pleasure are more desirable and more valuable than others. It would be absurd that while, in estimating all other things, quality is considered as well as quantity, the estimation of pleasures should be supposed to depend on quantity alone.'[2]

Mill may be quite right in claiming that it is absurd that in discriminating between pleasures no account should be taken of qualitative differences. But the suggestion that the recognition of intrinsic qualitative differences is compatible with Benthamism is quite unjustified. And the reason is clear. If we wish to discriminate between different pleasures without introducing any standard or criterion other than pleasure itself, the principle of discrimination can only be quantitative, whatever Mill may say to the contrary. In this sense Bentham adopted the only possible consistent attitude. If, however, we are determined to recognize intrinsic qualitative differences between pleasures, we have to find some standard other than pleasure itself. This may not be immediately evident. But if we reflect, we can see that when we say that one kind of pleasure is qualitatively superior to another, we really mean that one kind of pleasure-producing activity is qualitatively superior to or intrinsically more valuable than another. And if we try to explain what this means, we shall probably find ourselves referring to some ideal of man, to some idea of what the human being ought to be. For example, it makes little sense to say that the pleasure of constructive activity is qualitatively superior to that of destructive activity except with reference to the context of man in society. Or, to put the matter more simply, it makes little sense to say that the pleasure of listening to Beethoven is qualitatively superior to the pleasure of smoking opium, unless we take into account considerations other than that of pleasure itself. If we decline to do this, the only relevant question is, which is the greater pleasure, quantity being measured not simply by intensity but also according to the other criteria of the Benthamite calculus.

In point of fact Mill does introduce a standard other than pleasure itself. On occasion at least he appeals to the nature of man, even if he does not clearly understand the significance of

---

[1] *Utilitarianism*, p. 11.　　　　[2] *Ibid.*, pp. 11–12.

what he is doing. 'It is better to be a human being dissatisfied than a pig satisfied; better to be Socrates dissatisfied than a fool satisfied.'[1] After all, when Mill is engaged in discussing explicitly Bentham's strong and weak points, one of the main features of Bentham's thought to which he draws attention is its inadequate conception of human nature. 'Man is conceived by Bentham as a being susceptible of pleasures and pains, and governed in all his conduct partly by the different modifications of self-interest, and the passions commonly classed as selfish, partly by sympathies, or occasionally antipathies, towards other beings. And here Bentham's conception of human nature stops. . . . Man is never recognized by him as a being capable of pursuing spiritual perfection as an end; of desiring, for its own sake, the conformity of his own character to his standard of excellence, without hope of good or fear of evil from other source than his own inward consciousness.'[2]

It is very far from being the intention of the present writer to find fault with Mill for introducing the idea of human nature as a standard for determining qualitative differences between pleasure-producing activities. The point is rather that he does not appear to understand the extent to which he is subjecting the original Benthamite framework of his thought to acute stresses and strains. There is no need to consult Aristotle, said Bentham. But to come closer to Aristotle is precisely what Mill is doing. In his essay *On Liberty* he remarks that 'I regard utility as the ultimate appeal on all ethical questions; but it must be utility in the largest sense, grounded on the permanent interests of man as a progressive being.'[3] Mill does not hesitate to refer to man's 'higher faculties',[4] to which higher or superior pleasures are correlative. And in the essay *On Liberty* he quotes with approval the statement of Wilhelm von Humboldt that 'the end of man is the highest and most harmonious development of his powers to a complete and consistent whole.'[5] True, Mill does not produce a clear and full account of what he means by human nature. He lays stress, indeed, on the perfecting and improving of human nature, and he emphasizes the idea of individuality. Thus he says, for example, that 'individuality is the same thing with development', and that 'it is only the cultivation of individuality which

[1] *Dissertations and Discussions*, I, pp. 358–9.   [2] *Ibid.*
[3] *On Liberty*, p. 9 (edited by R. B. McCallum, Oxford, 1946).
[4] *Utilitarianism*, pp. 13 and 16.
[5] *On Liberty*, p. 50.

produces, or can produce, well-developed human beings'.[1] But he makes it clear that individual self-development does not mean for him a surrender to any impulses which the individual is inclined to follow, but rather the individual fulfilment of the ideal of harmonious integration of all one's powers. It is not a question of sheer eccentricity, but of unity in diversity. Hence there must be a standard of excellence; and this is not fully worked out. The relevant point in the present context, however, is not Mill's failure to elaborate a theory of human nature. Rather is it the fact that he grafts on to Benthamism a moral theory which has little or nothing to do with the balancing of pleasures and pains according to the hedonistic calculus of Bentham, and that he does not see the necessity of subjecting his original starting-point to a thorough criticism and revision. As we have seen, he does indeed criticize Bentham's narrowness of moral vision. But at other times he tends to slur over the differences between them, especially, of course, when it is a question of uniting against what they would consider reactionary forces.

The reference to Aristotle in the last paragraph is not so far-fetched as may at first sight appear. As Bentham was primarily interested in questions of practical reform, he not unnaturally emphasized the consequences of actions. The moral character of actions is to be estimated according to the consequences which they tend to have. This view is, of course, essential to utilitarianism, in some form or other at least. And Mill often speaks in the same way. But he also sees, as Aristotle saw, that the exercise of human activities cannot properly be described as a means to an end, happiness, when the end is taken to be something purely external to these activities. For the exercise of the activities can itself constitute a part of happiness. The enjoyment of good health, for example, and the appreciative hearing of good music are, or can be, constituent elements in happiness, and not simply means to some abstract external end. 'Happiness is not an abstract idea, but a concrete whole.'[2] This is a thoroughly Aristotelian notion.

Now, in the first two paragraphs of this section we saw that according to Mill actions are right in proportion as they tend to promote happiness, wrong in so far as they tend to produce the reverse of happiness. We also noted Mill's explanation that in this ethical context happiness does not mean the individual agent's

[1] *On Liberty*, p. 56.   [2] *Utilitarianism*, p. 56.

own greater happiness, but the greatest amount of happiness altogether. And if we ask why the general happiness is desirable, Mill answers that 'no reason can be given why the general happiness is desirable, except that each person, so far as he believes it to be attainable, desires his own happiness'.[1] It is therefore incumbent on him to make clear the relation between the agent's own happiness and the general happiness.

One line of argument employed by Mill represents orthodox Benthamism. 'Each person's happiness is a good to that person, and the general happiness, therefore, a good to the aggregate of all persons.'[2] If the general happiness is related to my happiness as a whole to a part, in desiring the general happiness I am desiring my own. And by the force of association of ideas I can come to desire the general happiness without adverting to my own. It can thus be explained not only how altruism is possible but also how egoism is possible. For it is no more necessary that all should attain to an altruistic point of view than it is necessary that all those who desire money as a means to an end should become misers, seeking money for its own sake.

This may sound reasonable. But reflection discloses a difficulty. If the general happiness is, as Bentham maintained, nothing but the sum total resulting from an addition of the happinesses of individuals, there is no reason why I should be unable to seek my own happiness without seeking the general happiness. And if I ask why I ought to seek the latter, it is no use replying that I seek the former. For this reply to have any relevance, it must be assumed that the general happiness is not simply the result of an addition sum, the aggregate which results from a juxtaposition of individual happinesses, but rather an organic whole of such a kind that he who promotes his own happiness necessarily promotes the general happiness. For he actualizes a constituent part of an organic whole. But it can hardly be shown that this is the case unless emphasis is placed on the social nature of man. For one can then argue that the individual does not attain his own real happiness except as a social being, a member of society, and that his happiness is a constituent element in an organic whole.

This seems indeed to be the sort of idea towards which Mill is working. He remarks, for example, that the firm foundation of the utilitarian morality is to be found in 'the social feelings of mankind'.[3] These social feelings can be described as the 'desire to be in

---

[1] Ibid., p. 53.   [2] Ibid.   [3] Ibid., p. 46.

unity with our fellow creatures, which is already a powerful principle in human nature, and happily one of those which tend to become stronger, even without express inculcation, from the influences of advancing civilization. The social state is at once so natural, so necessary, and so habitual to man, that, except in some unusual circumstances, or by an effort of voluntary abstraction, he never conceives himself otherwise than as a member of a body.'[1] True, Mill emphasizes the fact that the social feelings grow through the influence of education and of advancing civilization, and that the more they grow the more does the common good or general happiness appear as desirable, as an object to be sought. At the same time he also emphasizes the fact that social feeling has its root in human nature itself, and that 'to those who have it, it possesses all the characters of a natural feeling. It does not present itself to their minds as a superstition of education, or a law despotically imposed by the power of society, but as an attitude which it would not be well for them to be without. This conviction is the ultimate sanction of the greatest happiness morality.'[2]

Once again, therefore, we receive the impression that Mill is working away from Benthamism to an ethics based on a more adequate view of the human person. At the same time the new theory is not developed in such a way as to make clear its relations to and differences from the framework of thought with which Mill started and which he never actually abandoned.

Though, however, the difficulty of passing from the man who seeks his own personal happiness to the man who seeks the common good is diminished in proportion as emphasis is laid on the nature of man as a social being, there remains an objection which can be brought against the utilitarian theory of obligation, whether utilitarianism is understood in its original Benthamite form or as developed by Mill.[3] For anyone at least who accepts Hume's famous assertion that an 'ought' cannot be derived from an 'is', an ought-statement from a purely factual or empirical statement, is likely to object that this is precisely what the utilitarians try to do. That is to say, they first assert that as a matter of empirical fact man seeks happiness, and they then

---

[1] *Utilitarianism*, p. 46.   [2] *Ibid.*, p. 50.

[3] This line of objection is not confined, of course, to utilitarianism. It can be brought against any form of teleological ethics which interprets the moral imperative as what Kant would call an assertoric hypothetical imperative. (See Vol. VI of this *History*, pp. 321-3.)

conclude that he ought to perform those actions which are required to increase happiness and that he ought not to perform those actions which diminish happiness or increase pain or unhappiness.

One possible way of dealing with this objection is, of course, to challenge its validity. But if it is once admitted that an ought-statement cannot be derived from a purely factual statement, then, to defend utilitarianism, we have to deny the applicability of the objection in this case. Obviously, we cannot deny that the utilitarians start with a factual statement, namely that all men seek happiness. But it might be argued that this factual statement is not the only statement which functions as a premiss. For example, it might be maintained that a judgment of value about the end, namely happiness, is tacitly understood. That is to say, the utilitarians are not simply stating that as a matter of empirical fact all men pursue happiness as the ultimate end of action. They are also stating implicitly that happiness is the only end worthy of being an ultimate end. Or it might be maintained that together with the factual statement that all men seek for happiness as the ultimate end of action, the utilitarians tacitly include the premisses that to act in the way which effectively increases happiness is the only rational way of acting (given the fact that all seek this end), and that to act in a rational manner is worthy of commendation. Indeed, it is fairly clear that Bentham does assume that, as all seek pleasure, to act in the way which will effectively increase pleasure is to act rationally, and that to act rationally is commendable. And it is also clear that Mill assumes that to act in such a way as to develop a harmonious integration of the powers of human nature or of the human person is commendable.

It is not the purpose of these remarks to suggest that in the opinion of the present writer utilitarianism either in its original Benthamite form or in the somewhat incoherent shape that it assumes with J. S. Mill, is the correct moral philosophy. The point is that though in word the utilitarians derive ought-statements from a purely factual, empirical statement, it is perfectly reasonable to argue that they tacitly presuppose other premisses which are not purely factual statements. Hence, even if it is admitted that an ought-statement cannot be derived from a purely factual statement, the admission is not by itself necessarily fatal to utilitarian moral theory.

As for the general merits and demerits of utilitarian moral theory, this is too broad a question for discussion here. But we can make two points. First, when we are asked why we think that one action is right and another action wrong, we frequently refer to consequences. And this suggests that a teleological ethics finds support in the way in which we ordinarily think and speak about moral questions. Secondly, the fact that a man of the calibre of J. S. Mill found himself driven to transcend the narrow hedonism of Bentham and to interpret happiness in the light of the idea of the development of the human personality suggests that we cannot understand man's moral life except in terms of a philosophical anthropology. Hedonism certainly tends to recur in the history of ethical theory. But reflection on it prompts the mind to seek for a more adequate theory of human nature than that which is immediately suggested by the statement that all men pursue pleasure. This fact is well illustrated by Mill's development of Benthamism.

3. Mill's idea of the self-development of the individual plays a central role in his reflections on civil or social liberty. As he follows Hume and Bentham in rejecting the theory of 'abstract right, as a thing independent of utility',[1] he cannot indeed appeal to a natural right on the part of the individual to develop himself freely. But he insists that the principle of utility demands that every man should be free to develop his powers according to his own will and judgment, provided that he does not do so in a way which interferes with the exercise of a similar freedom by others. It is not in the common interest that all should be moulded or expected to conform to the same pattern. On the contrary, society is enriched in proportion as individuals develop themselves freely. 'The free development of individuality is one of the principal ingredients of human happiness, and quite the chief ingredient of individual and social progress.'[2] Hence the need for liberty.

When he is thinking of the value of free self-development on the part of the individual, Mill not unnaturally pushes the idea of liberty to the fullest extent which is consistent with the existence and maintenance of social harmony. 'The liberty of the individual must be thus far limited; he must not make himself a nuisance to other people.'[3] Provided that he refrains from interfering with other people's liberty and from actively inciting others to crime, the individual's freedom should be unrestricted. 'The only part of

---

[1] *On Liberty*, p. 9. All page references to this essay and to that *On Representative Government* are to the edition of the two essays in one volume by R. B. McCallum (Oxford, 1946).
[2] *Ibid.*, p. 50.   [3] *Ibid.*, p. 49.

the conduct of anyone, for which he is amenable to society, is that which concerns others. In the part which merely concerns himself, his independence is, of right, absolute. Over himself, over his own body and mind, the individual is sovereign.'[1]

In the passage just cited the phrase 'of right' suggests, at first sight at least, that Mill has forgotten for the moment that the theory of natural rights does not form part of his intellectual baggage. It would not indeed be matter for astonishment if after inheriting the rejection of this theory from Bentham and his father Mill then tended to reintroduce the theory. But presumably he would comment that what he rejects is the theory of 'abstract' rights which are not based on the principle of utility and which are supposed to be valid irrespective of the historical and social context. 'Liberty, as a principle, has no application to any state of things anterior to the time when mankind have become capable of being improved by free and equal discussion.'[2] In a society of barbarians despotism would be legitimate, 'provided that the end be their improvement, and the means justified by actually effecting that end'.[3] But when civilization has developed up to a certain point, the principle of utility demands that the individual should enjoy full liberty, except the liberty to do harm to others. And if we presuppose a society of this sort, we can reasonably talk about a 'right' to liberty, a right grounded on the principle of utility.

Mill's general thesis is, therefore, that in a civilized community the only legitimate ground for the exercise of coercion in regard to the individual is 'to prevent harm to others. His own good, either physical or moral, is not a sufficient warrant.'[4] But where does the boundary lie between what does harm to others and what does not, between purely self-regarding conduct and conduct which concerns others? We have noted that Mill quotes with approval Wilhelm von Humboldt's statement that the end of man is 'the highest and most harmonious development of his powers to a complete and consistent whole'.[5] And Mill is, of course, convinced that the common happiness is increased if individuals do develop themselves in this way. Might it not be argued, therefore, that harm is done to others, to the community, if the individual acts in such a way as to prevent the harmonious integration of his powers and becomes a warped personality?

This difficulty is, of course, seen and discussed by Mill himself.

[1] *Ibid.*, p. 9.   [2] *Ibid.*   [3] *Ibid.*   [4] *Ibid.*, p. 8.   [5] *Ibid.*, p. 50.

And he suggests various ways of dealing with it. In general, however, his answer is on these lines. The common good demands that as much liberty as possible should be conceded to the individual. Hence injury to others should be interpreted as narrowly as possible. The majority is by no means infallible in its judgments about what would be beneficial to an individual. Hence it should not attempt to impose its own ideas about what is good and bad on all. The community should not interfere with private liberty except when 'there is a definite damage, or a definite risk of damage, either to an individual or to the public'.[1]

Obviously, this does not constitute a complete answer to the objection from the purely theoretical point of view. For questions can still be asked about what constitutes 'definite damage' or 'a definite risk of damage'.[2] At the same time Mill's general principle is, by and large, that which tends to be followed in our Western democracies. And most of us would doubtless agree that restrictions on private liberty should be kept to the minimum demanded by respect for the rights of others and for the common interest. But it is idle to suppose that any philosopher can provide us with a formula which will settle all disputes about the limits of this minimum.

Mill's insistence on the value of private liberty and on the principle of individuality or originality, the principle, that is to say, of individual self-development, naturally affects his ideas on government and its functions. It affects his concept of the most desirable form of government, and it also leads him to see how democracy can be threatened by a danger to which Bentham and James Mill had not really paid attention. We can consider these two points successively.

Though Mill is well aware of the absurdity of supposing that the form of constitution which one considers to be, abstractly speaking, the best is necessarily the best in the practical sense of being suited to all people and to all stages of civilization, he none the less insists that 'to inquire into the best form of government in the abstract (as it is called) is not a chimerical, but a highly practical

---

[1] *On Liberty*, p. 73.

[2] Mill makes a distinction between violating specific duties to society and causing perceptible hurt to assignable individuals on the one hand and merely 'constructive injury' on the other (cf. *On Liberty*, p. 73). But though most people would make a clear distinction between, say, driving a car to the danger of the public when the driver is drunk and getting drunk in the privacy of one's own home, there are bound to be many cases in which the application of general categories is a matter for dispute.

employment of scientific intellect'.[1] For political institutions do not simply grow while men sleep. They are what they are through the agency of the human will. And when a political institution has become obsolete and no longer corresponds to the needs and legitimate demands of a society, it is only through the agency of the human will that it can be changed or developed or supplanted by another institution. But this demands thought about what is desirable and practicable, about the ideally best form of government. For, 'the ideally best form of government, it is scarcely necessary to say, does not mean one which is practicable or eligible in all states of civilization, but the one which, in the circumstances in which it is practicable and eligible, is attended with the greatest amount of beneficial consequences, immediate and prospective.'[2]

If we presuppose that a stage of civilization has been reached in which democracy is practicable, the ideally best form of government is, for Mill, that in which sovereignty is vested in the community as a whole, in which each citizen has a voice in the exercise of sovereignty, and in which each citizen is sometimes called on to take an actual part in government, whether local or national, in some capacity or other. For one thing, the individual is more secure from being harmed by others in proportion as he is able to protect himself. And he can do this best in a democracy. For another thing, a democratic constitution encourages an active type of character, gifted with initiative and vigour. And it is more valuable to promote an active than a passive type of character. Obviously, this consideration weighs heavily with Mill. In his opinion a democratic constitution is the most likely to encourage that individual self-development on which he lays so much emphasis. Further, it promotes the growth in the individual of a public spirit, of concern with the common good, whereas under a benevolent despotism individuals are likely to concentrate simply on their private interests, leaving care for the common good to a government in which they have no voice or share.

It is clear that Mill is not primarily concerned with an external harmonization of interests among atomic human individuals, each of which is supposed to be seeking simply his own pleasure. For if this were the chief concern of government, one might conclude that benevolent despotism is the ideal form of government and that democracy is preferable only because despots are, in practice,

---

[1] *On Representative Government*, p. 115.   [2] *Ibid.*, p. 141.

generally as self-seeking as anyone else. It was partly this idea that drove Bentham to adopt a radically democratic point of view. Mill, however, while by no means blind to the need for harmonizing interests, is concerned above all with the superior educative effect of democracy. True, it presupposes a certain level of education. At the same time it encourages, more than any other form of government, private liberty and free self-development on the part of the individual.

Ideally, direct democracy would be the best form of government, at least in the sense of a democracy in which all citizens would have the opportunity of sharing in government in some capacity. 'But since all cannot, in a community exceeding a single small town, participate personally in any but some very minor portions of the public business, it follows that the ideal type of a perfect government must be representative.'[1]

Mill is not, however, so naïve as to suppose that a democratic constitution automatically ensures a due respect for individual liberty. When democracy means in effect the rule, by representation, of a numerical majority, there is no guarantee that the majority will not oppress the minority. For example, legislation might be made to serve the interest of a racial or religious majority or that of a particular economic class[2] rather than the interests of the whole community. In fine, what Bentham called 'sinister interests' can operate in a democracy as elsewhere.

As a safeguard against this danger Mill insists that minorities must be effectively represented. And to secure this he advocates a system of proportional representation, referring to Thomas Hare's *Treatise on the Election of Representatives* (1859) and to Professor Henry Fawcett's pamphlet *Mr. Hare's Reform Bill Simplified and Explained* (1860). But constitutional devices such as universal suffrage and proportional representation will not be sufficient without a process of education which inculcates a genuine respect for individual liberty and for the rights of all citizens, whatever may be their race, religion or position in society.

Given Mill's insistence on the value of individual self-development and initiative, it is not surprising that he disapproves of any tendency on the part of the State to usurp the functions of

---

[1] *On Representative Government*, p. 151.

[2] Mill envisages the possibility of a majority of unskilled workers obtaining legislation to protect what it conceives to be its own interest, to the detriment of the interests of skilled workers and of other classes. Cf. *On Representative Government*, p. 183.

voluntary institutions and to hand them over to the control of a State bureaucracy. 'The disease which afflicts bureaucratic governments, and which they usually die of, is routine. . . . A bureaucracy always tends to become a pedantocracy.'[1] The tendency for all the more able members of the community to be absorbed into the ranks of State functionaries 'is fatal, sooner or later, to the mental activity and progressiveness of the body itself.'[2]

This does not mean, however, that Mill condemns all legislation and State control other than that required to maintain peace and order in the community. It seems true to say that he is drawn in two directions. On the one hand the principle of individual liberty inclines him to disapprove of any legislation or State control of conduct which goes beyond what is required for preventing or deterring the individual from injuring others, whether assignable individuals or the community at large. On the other hand the principle of utility, the greatest happiness principle, might well be used to justify a very considerable amount of legislation and State control with a view to the common good or happiness. But, as we have seen, the principle of individuality is itself grounded on the principle of utility. And the idea of preventing the individual from injuring others can be interpreted in such a way as to justify a good deal of State 'interference' with the individual's conduct.

Education is a case in point. We have seen that according to Mill the community has no right to coerce the individual simply for his own good. But this applies, as Mill explains, only to adults, not to children. For the latter must be protected not only from being harmed by others but also from harming themselves. Hence Mill does not hesitate to say, 'is it not almost a self-evident axiom, that the State should require and compel the education, up to a certain standard, of every human being who is born its citizen?'[3] He is not suggesting that parents should be compelled to send their children to State schools. For 'a general State education is a mere contrivance for moulding people to be exactly like one another':[4] it might easily become an attempt to establish 'a despotism over the mind'.[5] But if parents do not provide in some way for the education of their children, they are failing in their duty and are harming both individuals, namely the children, and

[1]*Ibid.*, p. 179.   [2] *Ibid.*, p. 102.
[3] *On Liberty*, p. 94.   [4] *Ibid.*, p. 95.   [5] *Ibid.*

the community.[1] Hence the State should prevent them from injuring others in this way. And if the parents are genuinely unable to pay for their children's education, the State should come to their aid.

On occasion Mill's interpretation of the principle of preventing the individual from injuring others is astonishingly broad. Thus in the essay *On Liberty* he remarks that in a country in which the population is or threatens to become so great that wages are reduced through superabundant labour, with the consequence that parents are unable to support their children, a law to forbid marriages unless the parties could show that they had the means of supporting a family would not exceed the legitimate power of the State. True, the expediency of such a law is open to dispute. But the law would not constitute a violation of liberty. For its aim would be to prevent the parties concerned from injuring others, namely the prospective offspring. And if anyone objected to the law simply on the ground that it would violate the liberty of parties who wished to marry, he would give evidence of a misplaced notion of liberty.

In point of fact Mill came to modify his view that no man should be compelled to act or to refrain from acting in a certain way simply for his own good. Take the case of proposed legislation to reduce the hours of labour. Mill came to the conclusion that such legislation would be perfectly legitimate, and also desirable, if it were in the real interest of the workmen. To pretend that it violates the worker's freedom to work for as many hours as he likes is absurd. It is indeed obviously true that he would choose to work for an excessive length of time, if the alternative were to starve. But it by no means follows that he would not choose to work for shorter hours, provided that the reduction were universally enforced by law. And in enacting such a law the legislator would be acting for the good of the worker and in accordance with his real desire.

Given his belief in the value of voluntary associations and of initiative uncontrolled by the State, together with his rooted mistrust of bureaucracy, Mill would hardly take kindly to the idea of the so-called Welfare State. At the same time in his later years he came to envisage a degree of State-control of the distribution of wealth which he at any rate was prepared to describe as

---

[1] Mill insists, for example, that some education is a prerequisite for exercise of the suffrage, and so for democracy.

socialist in character. And the development of his thought on social legislation has often been depicted, though not necessarily with disapproval of course, as constituting an implicit desertion of his original principles. But though it is perfectly reasonable to see in his thought a shift of emphasis from the idea of private liberty to that of the demands of the common good, it seems to the present writer that the charge of inconsistency or of making a *volte-face* can easily be overdone. After all, Mill did not mean by liberty merely freedom from external control. He emphasized liberty as freedom to develop oneself as a human being in the full sense, a freedom which is demanded by the common good. Hence it is reasonable to conclude that it is the business of the community, that it makes for the common good or general happiness, to remove obstacles to such self-development on the part of the individual. But the removal of obstacles may very well entail a considerable amount of social legislation.

What is true, of course, is that Mill departs very far from Benthamism. And this departure from Benthamism can also be seen in the sphere of economics. For example, when Mill condemned laws against trade unions and associations formed to raise wage-levels, the condemnation may have been based primarily on his belief that free rein should be given to private enterprises in general and to voluntary economic experiments in particular. But it implied that, within the limits set by other factors, something can be done to raise wages by human effort. In other words, there is no iron law of wages which renders nugatory all attempts to raise them.

To conclude this section. Bentham, with what we may call his quantitative point of view, naturally emphasized the individual unit. Each is to count, so to speak, as one and not as more than one. And this idea naturally led him in the direction of democratic convictions. Mill shared these convictions; but he came to lay the emphasis on quality, on the development of the individual personality, a value which is best assured in a democratically constituted society. And this shift in emphasis, involving a change from the concept of the pleasure-seeking and pain-avoiding unit to the concept of the personality seeking the harmonious and integrated active development of all his powers, is perhaps the most salient characteristic of Mill's development of utilitarianism from the philosophical point of view. From the practical point of view, that of the reformer, the feature of Mill's thought which usually strikes the observer is the way in which he discerns the growing movement towards social legislation and approves it in so far as he feels that he can reconcile it with his profound belief in the value of individual liberty. But the two points of view go together, as has already been remarked. For Mill's qualified approval of social legislation is motivated very largely by his conviction that such legislation is required to create the conditions for, by the removal of hindrances to, the fuller self-development of the individual. To the extent that he envisages the removal by the State of obstacles or hindrances to the leading by all of a full human life, Mill approximates to the point of view expounded by the British idealists in the latter part of the nineteenth century. But veneration for the State as such, the kind of veneration which had been shown by Hegel, is entirely absent from his outlook. In a very real sense he remains an individualist to the last. What exists is the individual, though the individual character and personality cannot be fully developed apart from social relations.

4. The topics of civil liberty and government are obviously connected. Freedom of the will or liberty in a psychological sense is discussed by Mill in his *A System of Logic*, under the general heading of the logic of the mental sciences, and in his *An Examination of Sir William Hamilton's Philosophy*. But as interest in the problem of freedom of the will is generally prompted by its bearing on ethics and on questions, whether moral or legal, about responsibility, it seems permissible to take the problem out of the general logical setting in which Mill actually discusses it and to consider it here.

Mill assumes that according to libertarians, upholders, that is to say, of the doctrine of freedom of the will, 'our volitions are not, properly speaking, the effects of causes, or at least have no causes which they uniformly and implicitly obey'.[1] And as he himself believes that all volitions or acts of the will are caused, he embraces, to this extent at least, what he calls the doctrine of philosophical necessity. By causation he understands 'invariable, certain and unconditional sequence',[2] a uniformity of order or sequence which permits predictability. And it is this empiricist idea of causation which he applies to human volitions and actions.

The causes which are relevant in this context are motives and

[1] *A System of Logic*, II, p. 421 (10th edition, 1879). All further page-references to this work will be to this edition, denoted by the title *Logic*.
[2] *Logic*, II, p. 423.

character. Hence the doctrine of philosophical necessity means that, 'given the motives which are present to an individual's mind, and given likewise the character and disposition of the individual, the manner in which he will act might be unerringly inferred'.[1] It is scarcely necessary to say that Mill is referring to predictability in principle. The less knowledge we have of a man's character and of the motives which present themselves to his mind with varying degrees of force, the less able are we to predict his actions in practice.

One obvious objection to this theory is that it presupposes either that a man's character is fixed from the start or that it is formed only by factors which lie outside his control. In point of fact, however, Mill is quite prepared to admit that 'our character is formed by us as well as for us'.[2] At the same time he adds, and indeed must add if he is to preserve consistency with his premiss about causality, that the will to shape our character is formed for us. For example, experience of painful consequences of the character which he already possesses, or some other strong feeling, such as admiration, which has been aroused in him, may cause a man to desire to change his character.

It is true that when we yield, for example, to a stray temptation, we tend to think of ourselves as capable of having acted differently. But, according to Mill, this does not mean that we are actually aware or conscious that we could have acted in a different manner, all other things being equal. We are not conscious of liberty of indifference in this sense. What we are conscious of is that we could have acted differently if we had preferred to do so, that is, if the desire not to act in the way in which we did act or to act in a different manner had been stronger than the desire which, as a matter of fact, operated in us and caused our choice.

We can say, therefore, if we like, that Mill embraces a theory of character-determinism. But though he speaks, as we have seen, about the doctrine of philosophical necessity, he does not relish the use of such terms as 'necessity' and 'determinism'. He argues instead that the predictability in principle of human actions is perfectly compatible with all that the upholders of freedom of the will can reasonably maintain. Some religious metaphysicians, for instance, have found no difficulty in claiming both that God foresees all human actions and that man acts freely. And if God's foreknowledge is compatible with human liberty, so is any other

---

[1] *Ibid.*, II, p. 422.   [2] *Ibid.*, II, p. 426.

foreknowledge. Hence an admission of predictability in principle does not prevent us from saying that man acts freely. It is rather a question of analysing what is meant by freedom. If it is taken to mean that when I am faced with alternative courses of action, I could make a different choice from the one which I actually make, even though all factors, including character, desires and motives, are assumed to be the same, it cannot be allowed that man is free. For freedom in this sense would be incompatible with predictability in principle: it would follow that human actions are uncaused and random events. But if by saying that man is free we mean simply that he could act differently from the way in which he does act if his character and motives were otherwise than they are, and that he himself has a hand in shaping his character, it is then quite legitimate to say that man is free. Indeed, those who assert human freedom can mean no more than this unless they are prepared to say that human actions are chance, inexplicable events.

Mill is naturally convinced that his analysis of human freedom is not at odds with the utilitarian ethics. For he does not deny that character is malleable or that moral education is possible. All that follows from the causal activity of motives, in conjunction with character, is that moral education must be directed to the cultivation of the right desires and aversions, that is, to the cultivation of those desires and aversions which are demanded by the principle of utility. 'The object of moral education is to educate the will: but the will can only be educated through the desires and aversions.'[1] As for penal sanctions and punishment in general, the statement that all human actions are in principle predictable does not entail the conclusion that all punishment is unjust. Let us assume that punishment has two ends, 'the benefit of the offender himself and the protection of others'.[2] Appropriate punishment can serve to strengthen the offender's aversion to wrong-doing and his desire to obey the law. As for protection of others, punishment, provided that unnecessary suffering is not inflicted, needs no defence other than that provided by common sense. Whatever position we may adopt on the subject of free will, murderers can no more be allowed to commit their crimes with impunity than a mad dog can be allowed to roam the streets.

[1] *An Examination of Sir William Hamilton's Philosophy*, p. 505 (2nd edition, 1865). This work will be referred to in future page-references as *Examination*.
[2] *Ibid.*, p. 511.

In maintaining that all human actions are predictable in principle, Mill can draw, of course, on some empirical evidence. For it is an undoubted fact that the better we know a man the more confident we feel that in a given set of circumstances he would act in one way rather than in another. And if he does not act as we expected, we may conclude either that his character was stronger than we suspected or that there was a hidden flaw in his character, as the case may be. Similarly, if we find that our friends are surprised that we have resisted, say, a temptation to use a given opportunity of making money by some shady means, we may very well comment that they ought to have known us better. But though plenty of examples can be found in ordinary speech which seem to imply that a perfect knowledge of a man's character would enable the possessor of the knowledge to predict the man's actions, examples can also be found which suggest a belief to the contrary. After all, there are occasions on which we resent the suggestion that all our utterances and actions can be predicted, as though we were automata, incapable of any originality. Ultimately, however, Mill asserts the predictability in principle of all human actions more as the alternative to admitting uncaused events than as an empirical generalization.

If we assume that Mill is right in saying that we have to choose between these two alternatives, and if we are not prepared to describe human volitions and actions as chance or random events which happen without being caused, the question then arises whether the admission that all human volitions and actions are predictable in principle is or is not compatible with describing some actions as free. In one sense at any rate it is certainly compatible. For some of our actions are performed deliberately, with a conscious purpose, while others are not, reflex acts for instance. And if we wish to use the word 'free' simply to describe actions of the first kind, as distinct from the second kind, the question of predictability is irrelevant. For even if actions of both types are predictable in principle, the difference between them remains. And the word 'free' is being used simply to mark this difference. If, however, we wish to maintain that to say that an action is performed freely necessarily implies that the agent could act otherwise without being a different sort of person, unerring predictability in virtue of a knowledge of the person's character is ruled out. And if we have already accepted the validity of Mill's thesis that we have to choose between asserting predictability in principle and asserting that free actions are random events, we shall find it difficult to claim at the same time that an agent is morally responsible for his free actions.

If, however, we wish to maintain that Mill is not justified in forcing us to choose between admitting that all human actions are predictable in principle in virtue of the agent's character and admitting that free actions are random or chance events, we have to find an acceptable alternative. And this is not easy to do. It is hardly sufficient to say that the action is indeed caused but that it is caused by the agent's will, and that no other cause is required save a final cause, namely a purpose or motive. For Mill would immediately ask, what is the cause of the volition? Or is it an uncaused event? As for the motive, what causes this motive rather than another to be the stronger, actually prevailing motive? Must it not be the agent's character, the fact that he is the sort of man that he is?

It may be said that Mill himself gets into difficulties. For example, he admits that the individual can play a part in shaping his own character. And it is indeed essential for him to admit this, if any sense is to be given to his idea of civil liberty as required for self-development. But on Mill's own premises every effort that a man makes with a view to self-improvement must be caused. And in the long run what can be meant by the statement that a man plays an active part in shaping his own character except that the causes of his character are not simply external, educational and environmental, but also internal, physiological and psychological? But this hardly squares with what the ordinary person understands by the claim that man is free, and that he is not simply a product of his environment, but can freely play an active part in shaping his character. Hence Mill should either embrace and assert determinism, which he tries to avoid, or make it clear that he is using terms such as 'free' and 'freedom' in some peculiar sense of his own, in what Bentham would call a 'metaphysical' sense.

But the fact that difficulties can be raised in regard to Mill's position does not necessarily get other people out of their difficulties. And it might very well be argued that we cannot escape these difficulties if we once allow ourselves to share Mill's analytic approach, speaking about the agent, his character and his motives as though they were distinct entities which interact on one another. We ought instead to find another way of talking, based on a conception of the human person and his acting which cannot be expressed in Mill's terms. Bergson made an attempt to develop, or at least to indicate, such a language. And others have followed suit. We cannot talk about God in the language of, say, physics. For the concept of God is not a concept of physical science. Nor can we talk about freedom in the language used by Mill. If we try to do so, we shall find freedom being translated into something else.

The aim of the foregoing remarks is not to solve the problem of freedom, but simply to indicate some lines of reflection which arise out of Mill's discussions of the matter. For the matter of that, there is a great deal more that could be said in connection with Mill's approach and line of thought. But it would be inappropriate to devote more space to the subject in a book which is not intended to be a treatise on human liberty, whether in the civil or in the psychological sense of the term.

CHAPTER III

J. S. MILL: LOGIC AND EMPIRICISM

Introductory remarks—Names and propositions, real and verbal—The nature of mathematics—Syllogistic reasoning—Induction and the principle of the uniformity of Nature—The law of causation—Experimental inquiry and deduction—Method in the Moral Sciences—Matter as a permanent possibility of sensations—The analysis of mind and the spectre of solipsism—Mill on religion and natural theology.

1. In the eighteenth century the study of logic had been comparatively neglected. And in the introduction to his *System of Logic* Mill pays a tribute to Richard Whateley (1787–1863), Archbishop of Dublin, as 'a writer who has done more than any other person to restore this study to the rank from which it had fallen in the estimation of the cultivated class in our own country.'[1] But it does not follow, of course, that Mill is in full agreement with Whateley's idea of the nature and scope of logic. Logic was defined by Whateley as the science and art of reasoning.[2] But this definition, Mill contends, is in any case too narrow to cover all logical operations. More important, Whateley regarded syllogistic deduction as the standard and type of all scientific inference, and he refused to admit that the logic of induction could be given a scientific form analogous to the theory of the syllogism. He did not mean, he explained, that no rules for inductive investigation could be laid down. But in his opinion such rules must always remain comparatively vague and could not be synthesized in a properly scientific theory of inductive logic. Mill, however, sets out with the aim of showing that the opposite is true. He is careful to remark that he does not despise the syllogism. And in his *System of Logic* he deals with syllogistic inference. But he lays emphasis on the nature of logic as 'the science which treats of the operations of the human mind in the pursuit of truth'.[3] That is to say, he lays emphasis on the function of logic in generalizing and

[1] *Logic*, I, p. 2 (I, *Introduction*, 2). Whateley's *Elements of Logic* appeared in 1826.
[2] Whateley regarded the description of logic as the art of reasoning as inadequate. Logic is also the science of reasoning. As far as this emendation is concerned, Mill agrees with him.
[3] *Logic*, I, p. 4 (I, *Introduction*, 4).

synthesizing the rules for estimating evidence and advancing from known to unknown truths rather than on its function as providing rules for formal consistency in reasoning. Hence what is primarily required for the development of logic is precisely the fulfilment of the task which according to Whateley could not be fulfilled, or at least not with any degree of scientific exactitude, namely to generalize 'the modes of investigating truth and estimating evidence, by which so many important and recondite laws of nature have, in the various sciences, been aggregated to the stock of human knowledge'.[1]

But Mill is not interested simply in developing a systematic theory of inductive logic as employed in natural science. He is also concerned with working out a logic of what he calls the moral sciences, which include psychology and sociology. True, he actually considered this topic before he found himself able to complete a satisfactory account of inductive logic as given in the third book of the *System of Logic*. But this does not prevent Mill from presenting the sixth book, which deals with the logic of the moral sciences, as an application to them of the experimental method of the physical sciences. He thus makes his own the programme envisaged by David Hume, namely that of employing the experimental method in the development of a science of human nature.[2]

If it is asked whether Mill's point of view is that of an empiricist, the answer obviously depends to a great extent on the meaning which is given to this term. As Mill himself uses the term, he is not, or at any rate does not wish to be, an empiricist. Thus in the *System of Logic* he speaks of 'bad generalization *a posteriori* or empiricism properly so called',[3] as when causation is inferred from casual conjunction. Again, Mill refers to induction by simple enumeration as 'this rude and slovenly mode of generalization',[4] a mode of generalization which was demanded by Francis Bacon and which confuses merely empirical laws with causal laws. A simple example is offered by the way in which many people generalize from the people of their own country to the peoples of other countries, 'as if human beings felt, judged and acted everywhere in the same manner'.[5] Again, in Mill's work on Comte we are told that 'direct induction [is] usually no better than

---

[1] *Ibid.*, I, p. vii (in the Preface to the first edition).
[2] See Vol. V of this *History*, pp. 260–2.   [3] *Logic*, II, p. 368 (II, 5, 5, 5).
[4] *Ibid.*, II, p. 363 (II, 5, 5, 4).
[5] *Ibid.*, II, p. 368 (II, 5, 5, 4).

empiricism',[1] 'empiricism' being obviously employed in a depreciatory sense. And similar remarks occur elsewhere.

But though Mill certainly rejects empiricism in the sense in which he understands the term, in the sense, that is to say, of bad and slovenly generalization, of a procedure which bears little relation to scientific method or methods, he equally certainly takes his stand with Locke in holding that the material of all our knowledge is provided by experience. And if this is what is meant by empiricism, Mill is indubitably an empiricist. True, he admits intuition as a source of knowledge. Indeed, 'the truths known by intuition are the original premises from which all others are inferred'.[2] But by intuition Mill means consciousness, immediate awareness of our sensations and feelings. If by intuition is meant 'the direct knowledge we are supposed to have of things external to our minds',[3] he is not prepared to admit that there is any such thing. Indeed, the *System of Logic* 'supplies what was much wanted, a text-book of the opposite doctrine—that which derives all knowledge from experience, and all moral and intellectual qualities principally from the direction given to the associations'.[4]

Mill's rejection of what he calls the German or *a priori* view of human knowledge, which is to be found in the philosophy of Coleridge and to a certain extent in that of Whewell, is complicated by the fact that he regards it as having undesirable consequences in moral and political theory, or even as being invoked to support undesirable social attitudes and convictions. 'The notion that truths external to the mind may be known by intuition or consciousness, independently of observation and experience, is, I am persuaded, in these times the great intellectual support of false doctrines and bad institutions. . . . There never was such an instrument devised for consecrating all deep-seated prejudices.'[5] Hence when the *System of Logic* endeavours to explain mathematical knowledge, the stronghold of the intuitionists, without recourse to the idea of intuitive or *a priori* knowledge, it is performing a valuable social service as well as attempting to settle a purely theoretical problem.

It may be objected that these remarks are really quite inadequate for settling the question whether or not Mill is to be

---

[1] *Auguste Comte and Positivism*, p. 121 (2nd edition, 1866).
[2] *Logic*, I, p. 5 (I, *Introduction*, 4). [3] *Ibid.*, I, footnote (I, *Introduction*, 4).
[4] *Autobiography*, p. 225.
[5] *Ibid.*, pp. 225–6.

described as an empiricist. On the one hand, if empiricism is equated with bad and slovenly generalization, it is indeed obvious that neither Mill nor any other serious thinker would wish to be called an empiricist. For the term becomes one of abuse or at least of depreciation. On the other hand, a conviction that the material of our knowledge is furnished by experience is not by itself sufficient warrant for calling a philosopher an empiricist. Hence to observe that Mill attacks empiricism in a certain sense of the term while at the same time he maintains that all our knowledge is grounded in experience, does not do more than narrow down the question to a certain extent. It does not answer it. We are not told, for instance, whether Mill admits metaphysical principles which, though we come to know them as a basis of experience and not *a priori*, nevertheless go beyond any actual experience, in the sense that they apply to all possible experience.

This line of objection is perfectly reasonable. But it is difficult to give a simple answer to the question raised. On the one hand Mill certainly takes up an empiricist position when he explicitly asserts that we cannot attain absolute truth and that all generalizations are revisable in principle. On the other hand, when he is differentiating between properly scientific induction and slovenly generalization, he tends to speak in such a way as to imply that hitherto unknown truths can be inferred with certainty from known truths and, consequently, that Nature possesses a stable structure, as it were, which could be expressed in statements which would be true of all possible experience. In view of Mill's general position in the history of British philosophy and in view of the influence exercised by his thought it is perfectly natural that we should emphasize the first aspect of his thought and call him an empiricist. But it is as well to remember that he sometimes adopts positions which imply a different point of view. In any case the different strands in his thought can be seen only by considering what he says on particular topics.

2. Logic, Mill maintains, is concerned with inferences from truths previously known, not, of course, in the sense that the logician increases our knowledge of the world by actually making substantial inferences, but in the sense that he provides the tests or criteria for determining the value of inference or proof, and consequently of belief in so far as it professes to be grounded on proof. But inference is 'an operation which usually takes place by means of words, and in complicated cases can take place in no

other way'.[1] Hence it is proper to begin a systematic study of logic by a consideration of language.

We might perhaps expect that Mill would turn immediately to propositions. For it is propositions which are inferred. But as he regards the proposition as always affirming or denying a predicate of a subject, one name, as he puts it, of another name, he actually begins by discussing names and the process of naming.

It is unnecessary to mention here all the distinctions which Mill draws between different types of names. But the following points can be noted. According to Mill, whenever a name given to objects has in the proper sense a meaning, its meaning consists in what it connotes, not in what it denotes. All concrete general names are of this kind. For example, the word 'man' can denote or refer to an indefinite number of individual things which together are said to form a class; but its meaning resides in what it connotes, namely the attributes which are predicated when the word 'man' is applied to certain beings. It follows, therefore, that proper names, such as John, which can be applied to more than one individual but which have no connotation, possess, strictly speaking, no meaning. It does not follow, however, that the word 'God' has no meaning. For this term is not, according to Mill, a proper name. To be sure, as used by the monotheist the term is applicable to only one being. But this is because, as so used, it connotes a certain union of attributes which in fact limits its range of application. It is thus a connotative term, not a proper name like John or Mary.

Mill does indeed distinguish between words which name things or attributes and words which enter into the naming-process. For instance, in 'the wife of Socrates' the word 'of' is not itself a name.[2] But Mill has been criticized by later logicians for passing over words such as 'or' and 'if', which can certainly not be described as parts of names.

Turning to propositions, we find, as already indicated, that Mill's over-emphasis on names and naming leads him to regard all propositions as affirming or denying one name or another. The words which are commonly, though not necessarily, used to signify affirmative or negative predication are 'is' or 'is not', 'are' or 'are not'. Thus Mill takes the subject-copula-predicate form of proposition as the standard, though not invariable, form. And he

---

[1] *Logic*, I, p. 17 (I, I, I, I).

[2] The phrase 'the wife of Socrates' would be for Mill a name, but not a proper name. For it is a connotative name, whereas proper names, such as John, are not connotative but solely denotative.

warns his readers about the ambiguity of the term 'is'. For example, if we fail to distinguish between the existential use of the verb 'to be' and its use as a copula, we may be led into such absurdities as supposing that unicorns must possess some form of existence because we can say that the unicorn is an animal with one horn, or even because we can say that it is an imaginary beast.

In the course of his discussion of the import or meaning of propositions Mill distinguishes between real and verbal propositions. In a real proposition we affirm or deny of a subject an attribute which is not already connoted by its name, or a fact which is not already comprised in the signification of the name of the subject. In other words, a real proposition conveys new factual information, true or false as the case may be, information which is new in the sense that it cannot be obtained simply by analysis of the meaning of the subject term. As proper names are not connotative terms and, strictly speaking, possess no 'meaning', every proposition, such as 'John is married', which has as its subject a proper name, must necessarily belong to this class. Verbal propositions, however, are concerned simply with the meanings of names: the predicate can be obtained by analysis of the connotation or meaning of the subject term. For example, in 'man is a corporeal being' the predicate already forms part of the connotation or meaning of the term 'man'. For we would not call anything a man unless it were a corporeal being. Hence the proposition says something about the meaning of a name, about its usage: it does not convey factual information in the sense that 'John is married' or 'the mean distance of the moon from the earth is 238,860 miles' conveys factual information.

The most important class of verbal propositions are definitions, a definition being 'a proposition declaratory of the meaning of a word: namely, either the meaning which it bears in common acceptance or that which the speaker or writer, for the particular purposes of his discourse, intends to annex to it'.[1] Mill thus does not exclude the use of words in new ways for specific purposes. But he insists on the need for examining ordinary usage very carefully before we undertake to reform language. For an examination of the different shades of meaning which a word has in common usage, or changes in its use, may bring to light distinctions and

---

[1] *Logic*, I, p. 151 (I, I, 8, I). As proper names do not possess meaning, they cannot be defined.

other relevant factors which it is important that the would-be reformer of language should bear in mind.

Obviously, when Mill says that definitions are verbal propositions, he does not intend to imply that they are by nature purely arbitrary or that inquiries into matters of fact are never relevant to the framing of definitions. It would be absurd, for example, to define man with complete disregard for the attributes which those beings whom we call men possess in common. Mill's point is that though the connotation of the term 'man' is grounded in experience of men, and though inquiries into matters of fact can render this connotation less vague and more distinct, what the definition as such does is simply to make this connotation or meaning explicit, either wholly or in part, that is, by means of selected differentiating attributes. True, we may be inclined to suppose that the definition is not purely verbal. But the inclination can be easily explained if we bear in mind the ambiguity of the copula. A general connotative term such as 'man' denotes an indefinite number of things and connotes certain attributes which they have in common. When, therefore, it is said that 'man is . . .', we may be inclined to suppose that the definition asserts that there are men. In this case, however, we tacitly presuppose the presence of two propositions, corresponding to two possible uses of the verb 'to be'; on the one hand the definition, which simply makes explicit the meaning of the term 'man', and on the other hand an existential proposition which asserts that there are beings which possess the attributes mentioned in the definition. If we omit the existential proposition which we have surreptitiously introduced, we can see that the definition is purely verbal, concerned simply with the meaning of a name.

Let us return for a moment to real propositions and consider a general proposition such as 'All men are mortal.'[1] Looked at from one point of view, as a portion of speculative truth, as Mill puts it, this means that the attributes of man are always accompanied by the attribute of being mortal. And under analysis this means that certain phenomena are regularly associated with other phenomena. But we can also look at the proposition under the aspect of a memorandum for practical use. And it then means that 'the attributes of man are *evidence of*, are a *mark* of, mortality'.[2] In other words, it tells us what to expect. According to Mill these

[1] This is, for Mill, a real proposition, and not an 'essential' or purely verbal proposition.
[2] *Logic*, I, p. 13 (I, I, 6, 5).

different meanings are ultimately equivalent. But in scientific inference it is the practical aspect of meaning, its predictive aspect, which is of special importance.

We have, therefore, a distinction between verbal propositions in which the predicate is either identical with or a part of the meaning of the subject term, and real propositions, in which the predicate is not contained in the connotation of the subject. And Mill remarks that 'this distinction corresponds to that which is drawn by Kant and other metaphysicians between what they term analytic and synthetic judgments; the former being those which can be evolved from the meaning of the terms used'.[1] We may add that Mill's distinction also corresponds more or less to Hume's distinction between propositions which state relations between ideas and propositions which state matters of fact.

If we mean by truth correspondence between a proposition and the extra-linguistic fact to which it refers,[2] it obviously follows that no purely verbal proposition can be properly described as true. A definition can be adequate or inadequate; it can correspond or not correspond with linguistic usage. But by itself it makes no statement about matters of extra-linguistic fact. The question arises, however, whether for Mill there are real propositions which are necessarily true. Does he agree with Hume that no real proposition can be necessarily true? Or, to use Kantian terminology, does he recognize the existence of synthetic *a priori* propositions?

It is a notorious fact that Mill tends to speak in different ways, his way of speaking being influenced by his reaction to the type of theory which he happens to be discussing. Hence it is difficult to say what *the* view of Mill is. However, he is undoubtedly opposed to the view that there is any *a priori* knowledge of reality. And this opposition naturally inclines him to reject synthetic *a priori* propositions. Mill is not indeed prepared to say that when the negation of a given proposition appears to us as unbelievable, the proposition must be merely verbal. For there are doubtless some real propositions which reflect a uniformity or regularity of experience such that the negations of these propositions seem to us unbelievable. And for all practical purposes we are justified in treating them as though they were necessarily true. Indeed, we

[1] *Ibid.*, I, p. 129, footnote (1, 1, 6, 4, footnote). Mill tends to use the term 'metaphysics' in the sense of theory of knowledge.
[2] It is not denied, of course, that there can be true propositions which state matters of linguistic fact, propositions about the English language, for example.

can hardly do otherwise, because *ex hypothesi* we have had no experience which has led us to question their universal applicability. But a real proposition can be necessarily true in the psychological sense that we find its opposite unbelievable, without being necessarily true in the logical sense that it must be true of all possible experience, of all unobserved or unexperienced phenomena.

This seems to be more or less Mill's characteristic position. But to appreciate the complexity of the situation it is advisable to consider what he has to say about mathematical propositions, the great stronghold of intuitionists and upholders of *a priori* knowledge.

3. It is scarcely necessary to say that Mill recognizes that mathematics possesses some peculiar characteristics. He remarks, for example, that 'the propositions of geometry are independent of the succession of events'.[1] Again, the truths of mathematics 'have no connection with laws of causation. . . . That when two straight lines intersect each other the opposite angles are equal, is true of all such lines and angles, by whatever cause produced.'[2] Again, mathematical reasoning 'does not suffer us to let in, at any of the joints in the reasoning, an assumption which we have not faced in the shape of an axiom, postulate or definition. This is a merit which it has in common with formal Logic.'[3]

When, however, we start inquiring into Mill's general theory of mathematics, complications arise. Dugald Stewart maintained that mathematical propositions do not express matters of fact but only connections between suppositions or assumptions and certain consequences. He further maintained that the first principles of geometry are Euclid's definitions, not the postulates and axioms. And as he regarded the definitions as arbitrary, he made it difficult to explain how pure mathematics can be applied. That mathematics can fit reality, so to speak, and be successfully applied in physics becomes for him a matter of pure coincidence. Mill, however, was not satisfied with this position. He wished to say that mathematical propositions are true. Hence he could not admit that Euclid's theorems are deducible from definitions. For Mill held, as we have seen, that definitions are neither true nor false. He had to maintain, therefore, that Euclid's theorems are deduced from postulates, which can be true or false. And he

---

[1] *Logic*, I, p. 373 (I, 3, 5, 1).   [2] *Ibid.*, II, p. 147 (II, 3, 24, 3).
[3] *Examination*, p. 526.

argued that any Euclidean definition is only partly a definition.
For it also involves a postulate. In other words, any Euclidean
definition can be analysed into two propositions, of which one is
a postulate or assumption in regard to a matter of fact while the
other is a genuine definition. Thus the definition of a circle can be
analysed into the following two propositions: 'a figure may exist,
having all the points in the line which bounds it equally distant
from a single point within it', (and) 'any figure possessing this
property is called a circle'.[1] The first proposition is a postulate;
and it is such postulates, not the pure definitions, which form the
premisses for the deduction of Euclid's theorems. The gap which
Stewart created between pure and applied mathematics is thus
closed. For the propositions of geometry, for instance, are not
derived from arbitrary definitions but from postulates or assumptions concerning matters of fact.

We can say, therefore, that in geometry 'our reasonings are
grounded on the matters of fact postulated in definitions, and not
on the definitions themselves'.[2] And 'this conclusion', Mills remarks, 'is one which I have in common with Dr. Whewell'.[3] But
though Mill may find himself in agreement with Whewell when it
is a question of attacking Stewart's idea that the theorems of
Euclidean geometry are deduced from definitions, agreement
immediately ceases when it is a question of our knowledge of the
first principles of mathematics. According to Whewell these first
principles are self-evident, underived from experience and known
intuitively. They constitute examples of *a priori* knowledge. And
this is a position which Mill is unwilling to accept. He maintains
instead that in mathematics 'these original premisses, from which
the remaining truths of the science are deduced, are, notwithstanding all appearances to the contrary, results of observations
and experiences, founded, in short, on the evidence of the senses'.[4]
We have never come across a case which would refute a mathematical axiom; and the operation of the laws of association is
quite sufficient to explain our belief in the necessity of such
axioms.

In the general class of 'original premisses' Mill makes a distinction between axioms and the postulates involved in definitions.
Axioms are exactly true. 'That things which are equal to the same
thing are equal to one another, is as true of the lines and figures in

---

[1] *Logic*, I, p. 165 (I, I, 8, 5).   [2] *Ibid.*, I, p. 171 (I, I, 8, 6).   [3] *Ibid.*
[4] *Ibid.*, II, pp. 148–9 (II, 3, 24, 4).

nature, as it would be of the imaginary ones assumed in the definitions.'[1] But the postulates or assumptions involved in the definitions of Euclidean geometry 'are so far from being necessary, that they are not even true; they purposely depart, more or less widely, from the truth'.[2] For example, it is not true that a line as defined by the geometer can exist. But it does not follow that the geometer intuits some peculiar mathematical entity. When he defines the line as having length but not breadth, he is deciding, for his own purposes, to ignore the element of breadth, to abstract from it, and to consider only length. Hence both axioms and postulates are derived from experience.

Obviously, when Mill describes the first principles of mathematics as generalizations from experience, he is not suggesting that our knowledge of all mathematical propositions is in fact the result of inductive generalization. What he is saying in effect is that the ultimate premisses of mathematical demonstration are empirical hypotheses. He therefore finds himself in agreement with Dugald Stewart as against Whewell. As we have seen, he disagrees with Stewart's derivation of Euclidean geometry from pure definitions; but this disagreement is played down when it is a question of noting their substantial agreement about the nature of mathematics. 'The opinion of Dugald Stewart respecting the foundations of geometry is, I conceive, substantially correct; that it is built on hypotheses.'[3] All that Whewell can show, when arguing against this opinion, is that the hypotheses are not arbitrary. But 'those who say that the premisses of geometry are hypotheses, are not bound to maintain them to be hypotheses which have no relation whatever to fact'.[4]

Having said this, Mill then proceeds to get himself into an impossible position. An hypothesis, he remarks, is usually taken to be a postulate or assumption which is not known to be true but is surmised to be true, because, if it were true, it would account for certain facts. But the hypotheses of which he is speaking are not at all of this kind. For, as we have seen, the postulates involved in the definitions of Euclidean geometry are known *not* to be literally true. Further, as much as is true in the hypotheses under discussion 'is not hypothetical, but certain'.[5] The hypotheses, therefore, appear to fall into two parts, one part being known not to be literally true, the other part being certain. And it is thus

---

[1] *Logic*, I, p. 265 (I, 2, 5, 3).　　　[2] *Ibid.*, I, p. 262 (I, 2, 5, 1).
[3] *Ibid.*, I, p. 261 (I, 2, 5, 1).　　　[4] *Ibid.*, I, p. 263 (I, 2, 5, 2).
[5] *Ibid.*, I, p. 261, note (I, 2, 5, 1, note).

rather difficult to see what justification there is for speaking of 'hypotheses' at all. Nor is the situation improved when Mill says that to call the conclusions of geometry necessary truths is really to say that they follow correctly from suppositions which 'are not even true'.[1] What he means, of course, is that the necessity of the conclusions consists in the fact that they follow necessarily from the premisses. But if we were to take literally the suggestion that necessary truths are necessary because they follow from untrue assumptions, we should have to say that Mill was talking nonsense. However, it would be unfair to understand him in this way.

In his *Autobiography* Mill makes it clear that the interpretation of mathematics which he regards as his own is the explanation of so-called necessary truths in terms of 'experience and association'.[2] Hence it would be going too far if one suggested that after the publication of the *System of Logic* Mill later produced a new interpretation of mathematics. It may even be going too far if one suggests that he consciously entertained second thoughts about the interpretation, or interpretations, given in the *Logic*. But it can hardly be denied that he made remarks which implied a different conception of mathematics. For example, in his *Examination of Sir William Hamilton's Philosophy* Mill informs his readers that the laws of number underlie the laws of extension, that these two sets of laws underlie the laws of force, and that the laws of force 'underlie all the other laws of the material universe'.[3] Similarly, in the Address which he wrote in 1866 for the University of St. Andrews Mill implies that mathematics gives us the key to Nature, and that it is not so much that the first principles of mathematics are formed by inductive generalization from observation of phenomena which might be otherwise than they are as that phenomena are what they are because of certain mathematical laws. Obviously, this would not necessarily affect the thesis that we come to know mathematical truths on a basis of experience and not *a priori*. But it would certainly affect the thesis that the necessity of mathematics is purely hypothetical.

Perhaps the situation can be summed up in this way. According to Mill, for the development of the science of number or arithmetic no more is required than two fundamental axioms, namely 'things which are equal to the same thing are equal to one another' and

---

[1] *Ibid.*, I, p. 262 (I, 2, 5, 1). [2] *Autobiography*, p. 226.
[3] *Examination*, p. 533.

'equals added to equals make equal sums', 'together with the definitions of the various numbers'.[1] These axioms can hardly be described as empirical hypotheses, unless one resolutely confuses the psychological question of the way in which we come to recognize them with the question of their logical status. And though Mill speaks of them as inductive truths, he also speaks of their 'infallible truth'[2] being recognized 'from the dawn of speculation'.[3] It would thus be quite possible to regard such axioms as necessarily true by virtue of the meanings of the verbal symbols used, and to develop a formalist interpretation of mathematics. But Mill was not prepared to admit that the fundamental axioms of mathematics are verbal propositions. Hence, if he was determined, as he was, to undermine the stronghold of the intuitionists, he had to interpret them as inductive generalizations, as empirical hypotheses. And the necessity of mathematical propositions had to be interpreted simply as a necessity of logical connection between premisses and the conclusions derived from them. At the same time Mill was acutely conscious of the success of applied mathematics in increasing our knowledge of the world; and he came to make remarks which remind us of Galileo, not to mention Plato. He thought, no doubt, that talk about laws of number lying at the basis of the phenomenal world was quite consistent with his interpretation of the basic principles of mathematics. But though it was consistent with the psychological statement that our knowledge of mathematical truths actually presupposes experience of things, it was hardly consistent with the logical statement that mathematical axioms are empirical hypotheses. And we have seen how Mill got himself into a difficult position when he tried to explain in what sense they are hypotheses.

In fine, we can say one of two things. Either we can say that Mill held an empiricist view of mathematics, but that he made assertions which were inconsistent with this view. And this is the traditional way of depicting the situation. Or we can say with certain writers[4] that though Mill seems to have thought that he was expounding one unified interpretation of mathematics, in actual fact we can discern several alternative interpretations in his writings, interpretations between which he continued to hesitate, in practice if not in theory.

[1] *Logic*, II, p. 150 (II, 3, 24, 5). [2] *Ibid.*, II, p. 149 (II, 3, 24, 4). [3] *Ibid.*
[4] Notably R. P. Anschutz in *The Philosophy of J. S. Mill*, ch. 9.

4. Most of the propositions which we believe, Mill remarks, are believed not because of any immediate evidence for their truth but because they are derived from other propositions, the truth of which we have already assumed, whether justifiably or not. In short, most of the propositions which we believe are inferred from other propositions. But inference can be of two main kinds. On the one hand we can infer propositions from others which are equally or more general. On the other hand we can infer propositions from others which are less general than the propositions inferred from them. In the first case we have what is commonly called deductive inference or ratiocination, while in the second case we have inductive inference.

Now, according to Mill there is 'real' inference only when a new truth is inferred, that is, a truth which is not already contained in the premisses. And in this case only induction can be accounted real inference, inasmuch as 'the conclusion or induction embraces more than is contained in the premisses'.[1] When the conclusion is precontained in the premisses inference makes no real advance in knowledge. And this is true of syllogistic inference. For 'it is universally allowed that a syllogism is vicious if there be anything more in the conclusion than was assumed in the premisses. But this is, in fact, to say that nothing ever was, or can be, proved by syllogism, which was not known, or assumed to be known, before.'[2]

If this were all that Mill had to say on the matter, it would be natural to conclude that for him there are two distinct types of logic. On the one hand there is deductive inference, in which from more general propositions we infer less general propositions. And as the inference is invalid unless the conclusion is precontained in the premisses, no new truth can be discovered in this way. Syllogistic reasoning can ensure logical consistency in thought. For example, if someone speaks in such a way as to show that he is really asserting both that all X's are Y and that a particular X is not Y, we can employ the forms of syllogistic reasoning to make clear to him the logical inconsistency of his thought. But no new truth is, or can be, discovered in this way. For to say that all X's are Y is to say that every X is Y. On the other hand we have inductive inference, the inference employed in physical science, whereby the mind moves from what is known to a truth which is unknown before the process of inference establishes it. In short,

---

[1] *Logic*, I, p. 187 (I, 2, I, 3). [2] *Ibid.*, I, p. 209 (I, 2, 3, I).

on the one hand we have a logic of consistency, on the other hand a logic of discovery.

In reality, however, the situation is much more complicated than this preliminary account suggests. Consider one of the arguments mentioned by Mill: 'All men are mortal; the Duke of Wellington is a man: therefore the Duke of Wellington is mortal.' It is indeed obvious that to concede the major and minor premisses and deny the conclusion would involve one in logical inconsistency. But Mill sometimes speaks as though to assume the truth of the major premiss is to assume the truth of the conclusion in such a way that to know the truth of the major is already to know the truth of the conclusion. And this seems to be questionable on either of the interpretations of the major premiss which he puts forward.

We have already seen that according to Mill the proposition 'all men are mortal', when it is considered as what he calls a portion of speculative truth, means that 'the attributes of man are always accompanied by the attribute mortality'.[1] Mill here fixes his attention on the connotation of the word 'man'. And if the proposition 'all men are mortal' is interpreted in terms of the connotation of the word 'man', it is natural to say that the proposition concerns universals, not particulars. Further, if we were to interpret 'always' as meaning 'necessarily', there would be no cogent ground for saying that the man who asserts that the attributes which make up the connotation of the word 'man' are always accompanied by the attribute of mortality, must already know that the Duke of Wellington is mortal. True, the assertion in question can be said to imply that if there is a being which can properly be described as the Duke of Wellington and which also possesses the attributes that make up the connotation of the word 'man', this being also possesses the attribute of mortality. But the fact remains that the assertion does not necessarily presuppose any knowledge whatsoever of the Duke of Wellington.

It may be objected that Mill does not interpret 'always' as 'necessarily'. If he did, this would make 'all men are mortal' an essential or verbal proposition. For mortality would then be one of the attributes which make up the connotation of the word 'man'. In point of fact Mill regards 'all men are mortal' as a real proposition. Hence 'always' does not mean 'necessarily' but 'so far as all observation goes'. Moreover, though Mill may some-

[1] *Logic*, i, p. 130 (i, i, 6, 5).

times speak in a way which implies or suggests a realistic theory of universals, it is a notorious fact that in the course of his discussion of the syllogism he supports a nominalist theory. In other words, 'all men' must be understood in terms of denotation. It means 'all particular men'. And if we *know* that *all* particular men are mortal, we know that any particular man is mortal.

The premisses of this argument are correct. That is to say, Mill does regard 'all men are mortal' as a real and not as a verbal proposition, and he does take up a nominalist position in his discussion of the syllogism. But the conclusion of the argument does not follow from the premisses. For according to Mill's nominalist theory 'all men are mortal' is a record of experience of particular facts, that is, of facts such as that Socrates and Julius Caesar both died. And if the Duke of Wellington is a living man, his death is obviously not included among these particular facts. Hence it cannot be reasonably claimed that to know that all men are mortal presupposes or includes knowledge of the mortality of the Duke of Wellington. The conclusion that the Duke of Wellington is mortal is not precontained in the proposition 'all men are mortal'. And it seems to follow that inference from 'all men are mortal' to 'the Duke of Wellington is mortal' is invalid.

In order to make the inference valid we have to say that 'all men are mortal' is not simply a record of past experience of people dying but also an inductive inference which goes beyond the empirical evidence and serves as a prediction, telling us what to expect. Having observed in the past that the attributes which make up the connotation of the term 'man' have in fact been accompanied by mortality, we infer that the same is to be expected in the future. In other words, 'all men are mortal' becomes not so much a premiss from which the mortality of living and future men is deduced as a formula for making future inferences, that is, from the possession of certain other attributes to the attribute of mortality. And this is precisely what Mill says. 'General propositions are merely registers of such inferences already made, and short formulae for making more. The major premiss of a syllogism, consequently, is a formula of this description: and the conclusion is not an inference drawn *from* the formula, but an inference drawn *according* to the formula.'[1] And the rules of syllogistic

[1] *Ibid.*, I, p. 221 (I, 2, 3, 4). The notion of a formula 'according to which' was suggested to Mill by Dugald Stewart's doctrine that the axioms of geometry are principles according to which, not from which, we reason.

inferences are rules for the correct interpretation of the formula. As such, they are useful. And Mill can enter 'a protest, as strong as that of Archbishop Whateley himself, against the doctrine that the syllogistic art is useless for the purposes of reasoning'.[1]

But if the major premiss is not a proposition *from* which the conclusion is derived but a formula *according to which* the conclusion is drawn, it follows that it is particular observed facts which constitute the real logical antecedent. In other words 'all inference is from particulars to particulars'.[2] A multitude of particular factual connections between being a man and being mortal have been observed in the past. As we cannot carry them all in our heads, we record them in a compendious memorandum. But the record is not simply an historical note. It runs beyond the empirical evidence observed in the past and predicts the future, serving as a guide to or formula for making inferences. And though we need not cast our reasoning according to the formula in syllogistic form, we can do so. The rules of syllogistic inference are a set of rules or precautions for ensuring correctness and consistency in our interpretation of the formula, correctness being measured by our purpose in establishing the formula, namely to simplify the making of future inferences in accordance with our past inferences. Syllogistic reasoning then becomes the latter half in the total process, as Mill puts it, of travelling from premisses to conclusions, that is, from particulars to particulars. In other words, the gap between deductive and inductive inference is diminished.

But there is more to come. Mill admits that there are cases in which syllogistic reasoning constitutes the whole process of reasoning from premisses to conclusion. These cases occur, for example, in theology and in law, when the major premiss is derived from the appropriate authority, and not by inductive inference from particular cases. Thus a lawyer may receive his major premiss, in the form of a general law, from the legislator and then argue that it applies or does not apply in some particular case or set of circumstances. But Mill adds that the lawyer's process of reasoning is then 'not a process of inference, but a process of interpretation'.[3]

We have already seen, however, that when syllogistic inference constitutes the second half of a total process of reasoning from

---

[1] *Logic*, I, p. 225 (I, 2, 3, 5).   [2] *Ibid.*, I, p. 221 (I, 2, 3, 4).
[3] *Ibid.*, I, p. 223 (I, 2, 3, 4).

premisses to conclusion, it is in effect a process of interpreting a formula, namely the major premiss. And in this case the sharp distinction between two kinds of logic collapses. Syllogistic reasoning is simply a process of interpretation. It can stand on its own, so to speak, as may happen when a theologian takes his major premiss from the authority of the Scripture or the Church. Or it can form one phase in a total process of inference from particulars to particulars. But in neither case is it, taken in itself, an example of inference. And the rules of the syllogism are rules for the correct interpretation of a general proposition, not rules of inference, in the proper sense of the term at least.

5. In view of the fact that Mill represents syllogistic reasoning as a process of interpreting a general proposition which is itself the result of induction, it is not surprising that he defines inductive inference as 'the operation of discovering and proving general propositions'.[1] At first sight the definition may indeed appear somewhat strange. For, as we have seen, all inference is said to be from particulars to particulars. However, 'generals are but collections of particulars definite in kind but indefinite in number'.[2]

This amounts to saying that to prove a general proposition is to prove that something is true of a whole class of particulars. Hence induction can be defined as 'that operation of the mind by which we infer that what we know to be true in a particular case or cases will be true in all cases which resemble the former in certain assignable respects'.[3] Obviously, Mill is not thinking of so-called perfect induction, in which the general proposition simply records what has already been observed to be true in regard to every single member of a class. For induction in this sense does not represent any advance in knowledge.[4] He is thinking of inference which goes beyond the actual data of experience and argues, for example, from the known truth that some X's are Y to the conclusion that anything at any time which possesses the attributes in virtue of which X's are considered as members of a class will also be found to possess the attribute Y.

The basic presupposition implied by this process of going

[1] *Ibid.*, I, p. 328 (I, 3, I, 2).   [2] *Ibid.*
[3] *Ibid.*, I, p. 333 (I, 3, 2, I). The use of the word 'will' should not be taken to mean that inductive inference is exclusively a process of inferring the future from the past. The general proposition refers also, of course, to unobserved contemporary members of a class, and indeed to unobserved past members.
[4] If, for instance, I first discover that each Apostle is a Jew and then say, 'all the Apostles are Jews', this general proposition does not represent any real advance in knowledge.

beyond the actual empirical data to the enunciation of a general proposition is, according to Mill, the principle of the uniformity of Nature, that all phenomena take place according to general laws. 'The proposition that the course of Nature is uniform, is the fundamental principle, or general axiom, of Induction.'[1] And he goes on to say that if inductive inference from particulars to particulars were to be put in syllogistic form by supplying a major premiss, this same principle would constitute the ultimate major premiss.

Now, if the principle of the uniformity of Nature is described as a fundamental principle or axiom or postulate of induction, this may tend to suggest that the principle is explicitly conceived and postulated before any particular scientific inference is made. But this is not at all Mill's point of view. He means rather that the uniformity of Nature is the necessary condition for the validity of scientific inference, and that in embarking on any particular inference we tacitly presuppose it, even though we are not consciously aware of the fact. When, therefore, he says that if an inductive inference were to be cast into syllogistic form, the principle of the uniformity of Nature would be found to constitute the ultimate major premiss, he means that the principle is the 'suppressed' premiss of induction. And, following his general doctrine of syllogistic reasoning, he means that it is a tacit formula or axiom *in accordance with which* inferences are made, not a proposition *from* which the conclusion of the inference is deduced. True, mention of the syllogism is rather confusing. For, as we have seen, Mill regards syllogistic reasoning as the interpretation of a formula; and this suggests deliberate interpretation of a consciously conceived and enunciated formula. But though the principle of the uniformity of Nature would obviously have to be explicitly enunciated if we were actually to cast inference into syllogistic form by supplying the suppressed major premiss, it by no means follows that all scientific inference involves conscious awareness of the principle or axiom in accordance with which it operates.

Mill has no intention, therefore, of suggesting that the principle of the uniformity of Nature is a self-evident truth which is known antecedently to the discovery of particular regularities or uniformities. On the contrary, 'this great generalization is itself founded on prior generalizations.'[2] And so far from being the first

---

[1] *Logic*, I, p. 355 (I, 3, 3, 1).   [2] *Ibid.*

induction to be made, it is one of the last. This may indeed appear at first sight to be incompatible with Mill's view that the uniformity of Nature is the basic presupposition of scientific inference. But his position seems to be more or less as follows. Scientific inference would not be valid unless there was uniformity in Nature. Hence when we turn to the investigation of Nature and embark on scientific inference, we tacitly presuppose that there is uniformity in Nature, even though we are unaware of the fact. The explicit idea of the uniformity of Nature arises through the discovery of particular uniformities. And the more we discover such uniformities, the more we tend to prove the validity of the idea, and thus of the implicit presupposition of all inference.

Now, if the principle of the uniformity of Nature is taken to mean that the course of Nature is always uniform in the sense that the future will always repeat or resemble the past, the principle, as a universal proposition, is patently untrue. As Mill observes, the weather does not follow a uniform course in this sense, nor does anyone expect it to do so. But what is called the uniformity of Nature 'is itself a complex fact, compounded of all the separate uniformities which exist in respect to single phenomena',[1] these separate uniformities being commonly called laws of Nature. Presumably, therefore, to say that scientific inference presupposes the uniformity of Nature is simply to say that the scientific investigation of Nature tacitly presupposes that there are uniformities in Nature. In other words, the condition of the validity of scientific inference is that there should be uniformities in the context or sphere with which the inference is concerned. And the progressive discovery of particular uniformities constitutes the progressive validation of scientific inference.

It is often said that Mill attempts to 'justify' scientific inference from the unknown to the known. And so he does in a sense. But in what sense? He tells us indeed that 'the real proof that what is true of John, Peter, etc. is true of all mankind, can only be, that a different supposition would be inconsistent with the uniformity which we know to exist in the course of Nature'.[2] But we do not know in advance that the course of Nature is uniform. We may assume it, and if the assumption is partly a rule for making inferences, consistency demands that we should follow it. But consistency alone can hardly constitute a proof of the assumption. If at any rate we concentrate our attention on the empiricist

[1] *Ibid.*, I, p. 364 (I, 3, 4, I).   [2] *Ibid.*, I, p. 357 (I, 3, 3, I).

aspects of Mill's thought, on his denial of *a priori* knowledge and on his view that all inference is from particulars to particulars, generals being but collections of particulars, it seems that the only possible justification of inductive generalization is partial verification coupled with absence of falsification. We cannot observe all possible instances of a law or asserted uniformity. But if the law is verified in those cases where we do test it empirically and if we know of no case in which it is falsified, this appears to be the only sort of justification of the inductive leap from the known to the unknown, from the observed to the unobserved, from 'some' to 'all', which can be provided. And if the uniformity of Nature is simply the complex of particular uniformities, it follows that the uniformity of Nature in a general sense tends to be proved, in the only sense in which it can ever be proved, in proportion as particular inductive generalizations are found, through partial verification and absence of falsification, to be successful predictions of phenomena.

6. In common parlance, as Mill puts it, the various uniformities in Nature are called the laws of Nature. But in stricter scientific language the laws of Nature are the uniformities in Nature when reduced to their simplest expression. They are 'the fewest and simplest assumptions, which being granted, the whole existing order of Nature would result',[1] or 'the fewest general propositions from which all the uniformities which exist in the universe might be deductively inferred'.[2] The task of the scientific study of Nature is to ascertain what these laws are and what subordinate uniformities can be inferred from them, while the task of inductive logic is to determine the principles and rules governing the arguments by which such knowledge is established.

We can note in passing how Mill shifts his position under the influence of the actual nature of science. When speaking as an empiricist, he tells us that all inference is from particulars to particulars, and that general propositions, reached by inductive generalization, are formulas for making inferences but not propositions *from* which conclusions are deduced. Now he tells us that the scientific study of Nature involves deducing less general from more general laws. Obviously, it remains true that particulars as such cannot be deduced from any general proposition. The general proposition tells us what to expect, and we then have to examine empirically whether the prediction is confirmed or

[1] *Logic*, i, p. 366 (i, 3, 4, 1).   [2] *Ibid.*

falsified. At the same time there seems to be a change of emphasis. When discussing the syllogism, Mill gives a nominalist account of the process of inference. When he turns to induction he tends to adopt a more realist position. He tends to assume that Nature possesses a stable structure which can be represented in the edifice of science.

Some laws or uniformities, such as the propositions of geometry, are unrelated to temporal succession. Others, such as the propositions of arithmetic, apply both to synchronous or coexisting and to successive phenomena. Others again are related only to temporal succession. And the most important of these is the law of causation. 'The truth that every fact which has a beginning has a cause, is coextensive with human experience.'[1] Indeed, recognition of the law of causation is 'the main pillar of inductive science'.[2] That is to say, inductive science establishes causal laws, and it presupposes that every event happens in accordance with such a law. Hence in developing a theory of induction it is essential to define the idea of causality as clearly as possible.

Mill disclaims any intention of concerning himself with ultimate causes in a metaphysical sense.[3] Moreover, as he intends to determine the idea of causality only in so far as it can be obtained from experience, he does not propose to introduce the notion of any mysterious necessary bond between cause and effect. Such a notion is not required for a theory of inductive science. There is no need to go beyond 'the familiar truth, that invariability of succession is found by observation to obtain between every fact in nature and some other fact which has preceded it'.[4]

At the same time it is misleading to assert that Mill reduces the causal relation to invariable sequence. For this might be taken to imply that in his view the cause of a given phenomenon can be identified with any other phenomenon which is found by experience always to precede it. Rather does he identify the cause of a given phenomenon with the totality of antecedents, positive and negative, which are required for the occurrence of the phenomenon and which are sufficient for its occurrence. 'Invariable sequence, therefore, is not synonymous with causation, unless the sequence, besides being invariable, is unconditional.'[5] And the cause of a phenomenon is, properly speaking, 'the antecedent, or the

---

[1] *Ibid.*, I, p. 376 (I, 3, 5, 1).   [2] *Ibid.*, I, p. 377 (I, 3, 5, 2).
[3] Adopting a distinction made by Reid, Mill says that he is concerned only with 'physical' causes, and not with 'efficient' causes.
[4] *Logic*, I, p. 377 (I, 3, 5, 2).   [5] *Ibid.*, I, p. 392 (I, 3, 5, 6).

concurrence of antecedents, on which it is invariably and *un-conditionally* consequent'.[1]

Now, Mill says of the law of causation that 'on the universality of this truth depends the possibility of reducing the inductive process to rules'.[2] And he certainly assumes in practice that every phenomenon has a cause in the sense explained above. All the phenomena of Nature are the 'unconditional' consequences of previous collocations of causes.[3] And any mind which knew all the causal agents existing at a given moment, together with their positions and the laws of their operations, 'could predict the whole subsequent history of the universe, at least unless some new volition of a power capable of controlling the universe should supervene'.[4]

But how do we know that the law of causation is a universal truth? Mill is certainly not prepared to say that it is a self-evident *a priori* proposition, nor that it is deducible from any such proposition. Hence he must hold that it is a product of inductive inference. But what sort of inductive inference? In ascertaining particular causal laws the method recommended by Mill is that of elimination, as will be seen in the next section. But the method, or rather methods, of experimental inquiry by the process of elimination presuppose the truth of the law of causation. Hence it can hardly be itself established by this process. And this means that we have to fall back on induction by simple enumeration. That is to say, we find in ordinary experience that every event has a cause. And when we come to the scientific study of Nature, we already believe in and expect to find causal connections.

It can hardly be denied, I think, that Mill is in rather a difficult position. On the one hand he wishes to say that the law of causation is a universal and certain truth which validates scientific inference. And he maintains that induction by simple enumeration becomes more and more certain in proportion as the sphere of observation is widened. Hence 'the most universal class of truths, the law of causation for instance, and the principles of number and of geometry, are duly and satisfactorily proved by that method alone, nor are they susceptible of any other proof'.[5] The law of causation 'stands at the head of all observed uniformities, in point of universality, and therefore (if the preceding observations are

---

[1] *Logic*, I, p. 392 (I, 3, 5, 6).   [2] *Ibid.*, I, p. 378 (I, 3, 5, 2).
[3] Mill recognizes in the universe 'permanent causes', natural agents which precede all human experience and of whose origin we are ignorant.
[4] *Logic*, I, p. 400 (I, 3, 5, 8).   [5] *Ibid.*, II, p. 102 (II, 3, 21, 3).

correct) in point of certainty'.[1] Again, 'the law of cause and effect, being thus certain, is capable of imparting its certainty to all other inductive propositions which can be deduced from it'.[2] On the other hand Mill maintains that induction by simple enumeration is fallible. True, the certainty of the law of causation is 'for all practical purposes complete'.[3] At the same time 'the uniformity in the succession of events, otherwise called the law of causation, must be received not as a law of the universe, but of that portion of it only which is within the range of our means of sure observation, with a reasonable degree of extension to adjust cases. To extend it further is to make a supposition without evidence, and to which, in the absence of any ground of experience for estimating its degree of probability, it would be idle to attempt to assign any.'[4]

The upshot seems to be more or less this. In ordinary experience we find that events have causes. And experience, together with the operation of the laws of the association of ideas, can explain our undoubting assurance in the universal validity of the law of causation. And the law can thus fulfil, in regard to scientific inference, the function which Mill assigns to the major premiss in a syllogism. That is to say, it is at once a record of past experience and a prediction of what we are to expect. It is a rule or formula for scientific induction. Moreover, scientific inference always confirms the law of causation and never falsifies it. If we in fact arrive at a wrong conclusion and assert that A is the cause of C when it is not, we eventually find that something else, say B, is the cause of C, not that C is uncaused. Hence for all practical purposes the law of causation is certain, and we can safely rely on it. But from the purely theoretical point of view we are not entitled to say that it infallibly holds good in regions of the universe which lie outside all human experience.

If it is objected that Mill clearly wishes to attribute to the law of causation an absolute certainty which enables it to constitute the absolutely sure foundation of scientific inference, the objection can be conceded. 'That every fact which begins to exist has a cause . . . may be taken for certain. The whole of the present facts are the infallible result of all past facts, and more immediately of all facts which existed at the moment previous. Here, then, is a great sequence, which we know to be uniform. If the whole prior

[1] *Ibid.*, II, p. 103 (II, 3, 21, 3).
[3] *Ibid.*, II, p. 106 (II, 3, 21, 4).
[2] *Ibid.*, II, p. 104 (II, 3, 21, 3).
[4] *Ibid.*, II, p. 108 (II, 3, 21, 4).

state of the entire universe could again recur, it would again be followed by the present state.'[1] But though Mill may believe in the universality and infallibility of the law of causation, the point is that on his premisses he has no adequate justification for his belief. And, as we have seen, he finds himself compelled to recognize this fact.

7. Mill is very far from thinking that empiricism, in the sense of mere observation, can do much to advance scientific knowledge. Nor does he think that experimentalism, in the sense of the making of controlled experiments, constitutes the whole of scientific method. He is conscious that the function of hypotheses is 'one which must be reckoned absolutely indispensable in science. . . . Without such assumptions, science could never have attained its present state; they are necessary steps in the progress to something more certain; and nearly everything which is now theory was once hypothesis.'[2] Nor, of course, does he pass over the role of deduction. 'To the Deductive Method, thus characterized in its three constituent parts, Induction, Ratiocination and Verification, the human mind is indebted for its most conspicuous triumphs in the investigation of Nature.'[3] As attention is generally concentrated on Mill's methods of experimental inquiry, of which a brief account will shortly be given, it is as well to recognize from the outset that the experimentalism which he contrasts with mere empiricism does not involve a total blindness to the actual nature of scientific method.

A distinction is made by Mill between purely descriptive and explanatory hypotheses. Take the bare assertion that the orbits of the planets are ellipses. This merely describes the movements of the planets without offering any causal explanation. And if the hypothesis is verified, this is the only proof of its truth which is required. 'In all these cases, verification is proof; if the supposition accords with the phenomena there needs no other evidence of it.'[4] But in the case of explanatory hypotheses the situation is different. Let us suppose that from hypothesis X we deduce that if the hypothesis is true, phenomena a, b and c should occur in certain given circumstances. And let us suppose that the prediction is verified. The verification does not prove the truth of X; for the same consequences might also be deducible from hypotheses Y and Z. We are then faced with three possible causes. And in order to

[1] *Logic*, I, p. 437 (I, 3, 7, I).　　　　[2] *Ibid.*, II, pp. 16–17 (II, 3, 14, 5).
[3] *Ibid.*, I, p. 538 (I, 3, 11, 3).　　　[4] *Ibid.*, II, p. 15 (II, 3, 14, 4).

discover the true one we have to eliminate two. When this has been done, what was originally an hypothesis becomes a law of Nature.

The implied view of physical science is clearly realistic. Mill speaks as though we already know that Nature is uniform, in the sense that 'the whole of the present facts are the infallible result of all past facts'.[1] But when we contemplate Nature, we are not immediately presented with particular uniformities. And no amount of mere observation will enable us to resolve general uniformity into particular uniformities. For 'the order of Nature, as perceived at a first glance, presents at every instant a chaos followed by another chaos'.[2] In other words, when we look for the cause of a given event, we are faced with a plurality of *prima facie* causes or of possible causes; and observation alone will not enable us to determine the true cause. Nor for the matter of that will purely mental analysis or reasoning. Reasoning is indeed indispensable. For in science we have to form hypotheses and deduce their consequences. But an hypothesis cannot be turned into a law of Nature unless alternative possibilities are eliminated. And this requires methods of experimental inquiry. Obviously, all this presupposes the existence of an objective uniformity of Nature, and so of real causal laws waiting to be discovered. Given the empiricist aspects of Mill's thought, we cannot indeed prove the general uniformity of Nature except *a posteriori* and progressively, in proportion as we discover factual causal connections. But this does not alter the fact that Mill is clearly convinced that there are such connections to be discovered. And this is doubtless why he tends to speak, as we have seen, as though the general uniformity of Nature can be known in advance of the scientific discovery of particular causal laws.

Mill gives four methods of experimental inquiry. The first two methods are respectively those of agreement and disagreement. The canon or regulating principle of the method of agreement states that 'if two or more instances of the phenomenon under investigation have only one circumstance in common, the circumstance in which alone all the instances agree is the cause (or effect) of the given phenomenon'.[3] The canon of the method of disagreement states that if we consider a case in which the phenomenon under investigation occurs and a case in which it does not occur, and if we find that the two cases have all circumstances in common save one, which is present only in the former case, this one

---

[1] *Ibid.*, I, p. 437 (I, 3, 7, 1).   [2] *Ibid.*   [3] *Ibid.*, I, p. 451 (I, 3, 8, 1).

circumstance is the effect or the cause, or an indispensable part of the cause, of the phenomenon in question. Both methods are obviously methods of elimination, the first resting on the axiom that whatever can be eliminated is not connected by any causal law with the occurrence of the phenomenon under investigation, the second on the axiom that whatever cannot be eliminated is so connected. And Mill combines the two methods in the joint method of agreement and disagreement.[1]

The canon of the third experimental method, the method of residues, is stated as follows. 'Subduct from any phenomenon such part as is known by previous inductions to be the effect of certain antecedents, and the residue of the phenomenon is the effect of the remaining antecedents.'[2] The fourth method, that of concomitant variations, is especially used in cases where artificial experiment is not practicable. Its canon declares that whatever phenomenon varies whenever another phenomenon varies in a given manner is either a cause of this phenomenon or its effect or connected with it through some causal fact. For example, if we find that variations in the moon's position are always followed by corresponding variations in the tides, we are entitled to conclude that the moon is the cause, total or partial, which determines the tides, even though we are obviously not able to remove the moon and see what happens in its absence.

Now, Mill does indeed speak as though his four methods of experimental inquiry, which he regards as 'the only possible modes of experimental inquiry',[3] were methods of discovery. And it has been sometimes objected that they are in reality only ways of checking the validity of scientific hypotheses which have been worked out by other means. But in justice to Mill it must be added that he insists more on the status of the methods as methods of proof than on their function as possible methods of discovery. 'If discoveries are ever made by observation and experiment without Deduction, the four methods are methods of discovery: but even if they were not methods of discovery, it would not be the less true that they are the sole methods of Proof; and in that character even the results of deduction are amenable to them.'[4]

Mill recognizes, of course, that experimentation has a limited field of application. In astronomy we cannot perform the experiments which we can perform in chemistry. And the same is more

---

[1] *Logic*, I, p. 458 (I, 3, 8, 4). [2] *Ibid.*, I, p. 460 (I, 3, 8, 5).
[3] *Ibid.*, I, p. 470 (I, 3, 8, 7). [4] *Ibid.*, I, p. 502 (I, 3, 9, 6).

or less true of psychology and sociology. Hence the method of these sciences, 'in order to accomplish anything worthy of attainment, must be to a great extent, if not principally deductive'.[1] But his general principle is that 'observation without experiment (supposing no aid from deduction) can ascertain sequences and coexistences, but cannot prove causation'.[2] And the four methods mentioned above are the methods of proof, the methods of turning an hypothesis into an assured causal law. Mill is therefore not prepared to accept the view, which he attributes to Whewell, that in the absence of empirical falsification we should be content to let an hypothesis stand until a simpler hypothesis, equally consistent with the empirical facts, presents itself. In his opinion absence of falsification is by no means the only proof of physical laws which is required. And for this reason he insists on the use of the methods of experimental inquiry, whenever this is practicable.

Does Mill succeed in justifying inductive inference from the observed to the unobserved, from the known to the unknown? If we concentrate attention on his explicit assertion that all inference is from particulars to particulars, and if we take it that particulars are all entirely separate entities (that is, if we concentrate attention on the nominalist elements in Mill's thought), a negative answer must be given. Mill might, of course, have tried to work out a theory of probability. But in the absence of such a theory he would perhaps have done best to say that science is justified by its success and requires no further theoretical justification. At the same time we can say that he does provide such a justification. But he provides it only by assuming that throughout Nature there is a structure of real uniformities which are something more than purely factual sequences. In other words, he justifies scientific inference by assuming a realist position and forgetting the implications of nominalism.

8. Hume's programme of extending the reign of science from the study of the non-human material world to man himself, by creating a science of human nature, had found a partial fulfilment in Mill's empiricist predecessors. The associationist psychologists aimed at setting psychology, the study of man's mental life, on a scientific basis. And Bentham thought of himself as developing a science of man's moral life and of man in society. As we have seen, J. S. Mill considered that Bentham's idea of human nature was narrow and short-sighted. And he was well aware that the science

---

[1] *Ibid.*, I, p. 443 (I, 3, 7, 3).   [2] *Ibid.*, I, p. 446 (I, 3, 7, 4).

of human nature had not made an advance comparable to that made by the physical sciences. Hence for the would-be creator of a logic of the 'moral sciences' it could not be simply a question of stating in abstract and explicit form a method or methods of proof which had already been employed to obtain impressive concrete results. His work must be necessarily in large measure tentative, a pointing out of a path to be followed in the future rather than a reflection on a road already traversed. But in any case it was natural that Mill should lay emphasis on the need for developing a logic of the moral sciences. I do not intend to imply that he was influenced exclusively by his British predecessors. For French social philosophy was also a stimulative factor. But, given the general movement of thought, it was natural that a man who wished to work out a logic of inductive inference and who was at the same time deeply interested in social thought and reform, should include man in society in the field of his reflections about scientific method.

The sixth book of the *System of Logic* is entitled 'On the Logic of the Moral Sciences'. By the moral sciences Mill means those branches of study which deal with man, provided that they are neither strictly normative in character nor classifiable as parts of physical science. The first condition excludes practical ethics or 'morality', that is, ethics in so far as it is expressed in the imperative mood. 'The imperative mood is the characteristic of art, as distinguished from science.'[1] The second condition excludes consideration of states of mind in so far as they are considered as caused immediately by bodily states. Study of the laws governing the relations between states of mind belongs to psychology as a moral science; but study of the laws governing sensations regarded as proximately dependent on physical conditions belongs to physiology, which is a natural science. Provided that we bear in mind these qualifications, we can say that the moral sciences include psychology, ethology or the science of the formation of character,[2] sociology and history, though the science of history is really part of general sociology, the science of man in society.

What is needed, in Mill's opinion, is to rescue the moral sciences from 'empiricism'. That is to say, purely empirical descriptive laws must be turned into explanatory or causal laws or deduced from such laws. We may, for example, have observed that in all

---

[1] *Logic*, II, p. 546 (II, 6, 12, 1).
[2] The study of the formation of national character had been suggested, for example, by Montesquieu.

known cases human beings behave in a certain way in certain circumstances. We then state in a generalized form that human beings behave in this way. But mere observation of a certain number of instances does not really provide us with any reliable assurance that the empirical law holds universally. Such assurance can be provided only by ascertaining the cause or causes which determine human behaviour under given conditions. And it is only by ascertaining such causal connections that a genuine science of human nature can be developed. It does not follow, of course, that we can always ascertain exact laws in practice. But this at least is the ideal. Thus once more, in the distinction between empiricism and science we see evidence of Mill's firm belief in the existence of objective causal connections waiting to be discovered.

The subject-matter of psychology as a moral science is 'the uniformities of succession, the laws, whether ultimate or derivative, according to which one mental state succeeds another; is caused by, or at least is caused to follow, another'.[1] These laws are those of the association of ideas, which have been ascertained, and in Mill's opinion could only be ascertained, by the methods of experimental inquiry. Hence psychology is 'altogether, or principally, a science of observation and experiment'.[2]

When, however, in ethology we turn to the formation of character, especially national character, there is little room for experiment. But mere observation is not sufficient to establish ethology as a science. Hence its method must be 'altogether deductive'.[3] That is to say, it must presuppose psychology, and its principles must be deduced from the general laws of psychology, while the already accepted empirical laws relating to the formation of character, individual or national, must be shown to be derivable from, and hence to function as verifications of, these principles. Moreover, once the principles of ethology have been firmly established, the way will lie open for the development of a corresponding art, namely that of practical education, which will be able to make use of the principles with a view to producing desirable effects or preventing undesirable effects.

Social science, the science of man in society, studies 'the actions of collective masses of mankind, and the various phenomena which constitute social life'.[4] It includes, of course, the study of politics. In social science or sociology, as in ethology, the making

---

[1] *Logic*, II, p. 439 (II, 6, 4, 3). [2] *Ibid.*, II, p. 458 (II, 6, 5, 5).
[3] *Ibid.* [4] *Ibid.*, II, p. 464 (II, 6, 6, 1).

of artificial experiments is impracticable, while mere observation is not sufficient to create a science. At the same time the deductive method as practised in geometry does not provide an appropriate model. Bentham, indeed, endeavoured to deduce a social-political theory from one principle, namely that men always seek their own interests. But in point of fact it is not always true that men are always governed in their actions by selfish interests. Nor, for that matter, is it universally true that they are governed by altruistic motives. In general, social phenomena are too complex and are the results of too many diverse factors for it to be possible to deduce them from one principle. If he is seeking a model of method, the sociologist should look not to geometry but to physical science. For the physical scientist allows for a variety of causes contributing to the production of an effect, and so for a variety of laws.

Mill emphasizes the utility in social science of what he calls the inverse deductive or historical method. In employing this method the sociologist does not deduce conclusions *a priori* from laws and then verify them by observation. He first obtains the conclusions, as approximate empirical generalizations, from experience and then connects them 'with the principles of human nature by *a priori* reasonings, which reasonings are thus a real Verification'.[1] This idea was borrowed, as Mill frankly acknowledges, from Auguste Comte. 'This was an idea entirely new to me when I found it in Comte: and but for him I might not soon (if ever) have arrived at it.'[2]

But while he emphasizes the utility of the inverse deductive method Mill is not prepared to allow that it is the only method suitable for employment in sociology. For we can also make use of the direct deductive method, provided that we recognize its limitations. For example, if we know that X is a law of human nature, we can deduce that human beings will tend to act in a certain manner. But we cannot know and positively predict that they will act in this way in concrete fact. For we cannot know in advance, or at any rate only rarely, all the other causal agents at work, which may counteract the operation of the cause which we have in mind or combine with it to produce an effect rather different from that which would be produced if there were no other causal agents. However, the direct deductive method

---

[1] *Logic*, II, p. 490 (II, 6, 9, 1). That is to say, the empirical generalizations are verified by ascertaining whether they follow from known general principles relating to human nature.

[2] *Autobiography*, p. 211.

undoubtedly has its own use in predicting tendencies to action. And this is of value for practical politics. Further, it is especially fitted for use in a science such as political economy which 'considers mankind as occupied solely in acquiring and consuming wealth'.[1] Obviously, this is not all that mankind does. But the point is that the more simplified a view of man we take, the more scope can we attribute to the direct deductive method. Conversely, the more complex the situation considered, the more we have to turn to the inverse deductive method.

In sociology Mill follows Comte in making a distinction between social statics and dynamics. The former is concerned with ascertaining and verifying uniformities of coexistence in society. That is to say, it investigates the mutual actions and reactions of contemporaneous social phenomena, abstracting, as far as possible, from the continuous process of change which is always, if gradually, modifying the whole complex of phenomena. Social dynamics, however, studies society considered as being in a constant state of movement or change, and it tries to explain the historical sequences of social conditions. But though we can ascertain some general laws of historical change or progress, we cannot predict the rate of progress. For one thing, we cannot predict the appearance of those exceptional individuals who exercise a marked influence on the course of history.

In this connection Mill refers to Macaulay's essay on Dryden and criticizes the view, there expressed, of the comparative inoperativeness of great historical individuals. We cannot legitimately assume, for example, that without Socrates, Plato and Aristotle European philosophy would have developed as it did, or even that it would have developed at all. Nor can we justifiably assume that if Newton had not lived his natural philosophy would have been worked out practically just as soon by someone else. It is a complete mistake to suppose that the truth that all human volitions and actions are caused, entails the conclusion that outstandingly gifted individuals cannot exercise an exceptional influence.

Obviously, Mill's conception of social science as involving the explanation of human behaviour in terms of causal laws presupposes the predictability in principle of all human volitions and actions. This subject has already been touched on in connection with Mill's ethical theory. But he insists that this predictability is

[1] *Logic*, ii, p. 496 (ii, 6, 9, 3).

not to be confused with 'fatalism', when fatalism is understood as meaning that the human will is of no account in determining the cause of events. For the human will is itself a cause, and a powerful one.[1] Further, in sociology we have to steer a middle course between thinking that no definite causal laws can be ascertained and imagining that it is possible to predict the course of history. Social laws are hypothetical, and statistically-based generalizations by their very nature admit of exceptions.

Mill does indeed express his belief that with the progress of civilization collective agencies tend to predominate more and more, and that in proportion as this happens prediction becomes easier. But he is thinking, for example, of the difference between a society in which much depends on the caprices of an individual, the absolute monarch, and a society in which the people at large expresses its will through universal suffrage. In other words, empirical generalizations have a greater predictive power when we are dealing with men in the mass than when we are dealing with the individual agent.[2] True, one of the main aims of social science is to connect these empirical generalizations with the laws of human nature. But the situation is too complex for it to be possible to predict infallibly the course of history, even if, in Mill's opinions, changes in human society have made it easier to approximate to a science of history or of social dynamics.

9. Mill's whole conception of the sciences, whether physical or moral, obviously presupposes the existence of the external world. And we can now turn to his discussion of the grounds of our belief in such a world, a discussion which is carried on for the most part within the framework of his criticism of Sir William Hamilton's philosophy.

Hamilton maintained that in perception we have an immediate knowledge of the ego and the non-ego, of the self and of something existing which is external to the self. Mill, however, while readily admitting that we have, as Hume claimed, a natural belief in the existence of an external world, endeavours to show how this belief can be psychologically explained without its being necessary

---

[1] Mill can, of course, evade fatalism, if fatalism is understood as omitting the human will from the chain of operative causes. At the same time if, given the antecedent conditions, a human volition cannot be otherwise than it is, it is difficult to see how he can evade fatalism if this is understood as synonymous with rejection of liberty of indifference.,

[2] For instance, statistically-based generalizations may enable us to predict the approximate number of people in a given county who will post letters incorrectly addressed. But the statistician is not in a position to say which individual citizens will be guilty of this oversight.

to suppose that it expresses an original datum of consciousness. He makes two postulates. The first is that the mind is capable of expectation, while the second is the validity of the associationist psychology. On the basis of these two postulates he argues that there are associations 'which, supposing no intuition of an external world to have existed in consciousness, would inevitably generate the belief in a permanent external world, and would cause it to be regarded as an intuition'.[1]

Let us suppose that I have certain visual and tactual sensations which produce in my mind an association of ideas. For example, when sitting at the table in my study, I have those visual sensations which I call seeing the table and the tactual sensations which I call touching or feeling the table. And an association is set up such that when I have a visual sensation of this kind, a tactual sensation is present as a possibility. Conversely, when I have only a tactual sensation, as when the room is completely dark, a visual sensation is there as a possibility. Further, when I leave the room and later re-enter it, I have similar sensations. Hence an association is formed in my mind of such a kind that when I am out of the room, I am firmly persuaded that, if I were at any moment to re-enter it, I should or could have similar sensations. Further, as these possible sensations form a group, and as moreover the group is found to enter into various causal relations, I inevitably think of the permanent possibilities of sensations as an abiding physical object. Actual sensations are transient and fugitive. But the possibilities of sensation, associated as a group, remain. Hence we come to distinguish between sensations and physical objects. But the ground of our belief in these external objects is the existence of different mutually associated clusters or groups of possible sensations, these groups being permanent in comparison with actual sensations.[2]

A further point. We find that the permanent possibilities of sensation which we think of as physical objects 'belong as much to other human or sentient beings as to ourselves',[3] though they certainly do not experience the same actual sensations as we do. And this puts the final seal to our belief in a common external world.

---

[1] *Examination*, p. 192.
[2] Obviously, in the illustration which has just been given of someone sitting at a table, a belief in the existence of an external world is already present. But it can serve to show the general line of Mill's psychological reconstruction of the belief.
[3] *Examination*, p. 196.

Now, Mill's theory, as so far outlined, might possibly be taken as being simply a psychological account of the genesis of a belief. That is to say, it might be understood as being free from any ontological commitment, as not involving any statement about the ontological nature of physical objects. In point of fact, however, Mill proceeds to define matter as 'a Permanent Possibility of Sensation',[1] bodies being groups of simultaneous possibilities of sensation. To be sure, he remarks that it is a question of defining matter rather than of denying its existence. But he makes it clear that he, like 'all Berkeleians',[2] believes in matter only in the sense of this definition, a definition which, he claims, includes the whole meaning which ordinary people attach to the term, whatever some philosophers and theologians may have done. Hence Mill clearly commits himself to an ontological statement.

The definition of matter as a permanent possibility of sensation is, however, ambiguous. For it easily suggests the idea of a permanent ground of possible sensations, a ground which is itself unknowable. And if this were what Mill intended to imply, a rift would inevitably be introduced between the world of science and the underlying physical reality. Scientific truths would relate to phenomena, not to things-in-themselves. But though he remarks elsewhere that 'all matter apart from the feelings of sentient beings has but an hypothetical and unsubstantial existence: it is a mere assumption to account for our sensations',[3] he makes it clear that he does not intend to assert the validity of this hypothesis.

Of course, if we interpret Mill on the lines on which Berkeley is often interpreted, namely as saying simply that material things are simply what we perceive and can perceive them to be, and that there is no unknowable substratum as postulated by Locke, the nature of science, as depicted by Mill, does not appear to be affected. But though it is doubtless part of what Mill means, as is shown by his conviction that in defining matter as he does he is on the side of the common man, the fact remains that he speaks of material things as 'sensations'. Thus he says, for example, that 'the brain, just as much as the mental functions, is, like matter

---

[1] *Examination*, p. 198.

[2] *Ibid.* Needless to say, Mill does not accept the theological conclusions which Berkeley drew from his theory of material things as 'ideas'. But he regards his own analysis of what it means to say that there are material things which continue to exist even when unperceived, as being substantially the same as that given by the good bishop.

[3] *Three Essays on Religion*, p. 86 (1904 edition).

itself, merely a set of human sensations either actual or inferred as possible—namely, those which the anatomist has when he opens the skull. . . .'[1] And from this it appears to follow that physical science inquires into the relations between sensations, principally, of course, possible sensations, but still sensations. Indeed, Mill himself speaks of causal relations or constant sequences as being found to exist between sets of possible sensations.

It is understandable that later empiricists have endeavoured to avoid this conclusion by forbearing from saying that material things *are* sensations or sense-data. Instead they have contented themselves with claiming that a sentence in which a physical or material object is mentioned can in principle be translated into other sentences in which only sense-data are mentioned, the relation between the original sentence and the translation being such that if the former is true (or false), the latter is true (or false), and conversely. The question whether this claim has been made good need not detain us here.[2] The point is that, as far as Mill himself is concerned, he speaks in such a way that the subject-matter of physical science is human sensations.

This, however, is a very difficult position to maintain. Let us suppose that sensations are to be understood as subjective states. This would make great difficulties in regard to Mill's account of the genesis of our belief in an external world, as outlined above. For instance, Mill says that we 'find' that there are possibilities of sensation which are common to other people as well as to ourselves. But other people will be for me simply permanent possibilities of sensation. And if the word 'sensation' is understood in terms of a subjective state, it seems to follow that other people, and indeed everything else, are reduced to my subjective states. As for science, this would become a study of the relations between my sensations. But is it credible that if an anatomist looks at a human brain, the object of his examination is simply a set of his own subjective states, actual and possible? In short, the logical result of defining physical objects in terms of sensations, when sensation is understood as a subjective state, is solipsism. And nobody really believes that solipsism is true.

It may be objected that Mill never intended to say that science

[1] *Ibid.*, p. 85.
[2] It is widely recognized that the only sufficient proof of the possibility of such a translation would be to perform it, and that no adequate translation has in fact been made.

is simply concerned with subjective states in any ordinary sense of the term. And the objection is obviously valid. It is perfectly clear that Mill had no intention of maintaining that the whole physical world consisted of his, Mill's, sensations in a subjective sense. But then we must either reify sensations, turning them into public physical objects, or we must assume that to say that a physical object is a permanent possibility of sensations is to say that a physical object is that which is capable of causing sensations in a sentient subject. The first alternative would be a very peculiar thesis, while the second would tend to reintroduce the concept of things-in-themselves and the rift between the world of science and physical reality to which allusion has already been made.

The fact of the matter is that after showing, to his own satisfaction at least, how our belief in the external world can be explained genetically in terms of the association of ideas, Mill slides into ontological assertions without really considering their implications in regard to the nature of physical science. And it seems clear to the present writer at any rate that Mill's empiricist analysis of the physical object is not really compatible with the realist conception of science which underlies his doctrine about causal laws.

10. Mill was obviously predisposed by the empiricist tradition to give an analogous analysis of the concept of the mind. 'We have no conception of Mind itself, as distinguished from its conscious manifestations. We neither know nor can imagine it, except as represented by the succession of manifold feelings which metaphysicians call by the name of States or Modifications of Mind.'[1] It is quite true, of course, that we tend to speak of the mind as something permanent in comparison with changing mental states. But if there were no special factor in the situation to be considered, we could perfectly well define the mind as a permanent possibility of mental states.

In point of fact, however, the phenomenalistic analysis of the mind presents special difficulties. For 'if we speak of the Mind as a series of feelings, we are obliged to complete the statement by calling it a series of feelings which is aware of itself as past and

---

[1] *Examination*, p. 205. According to Mill's use of the term, metaphysics is 'that portion of mental philosophy which attempts to determine what part of the furniture of the mind belongs to it originally, and what part is constructed out of materials furnished to it from without'. *Logic*, I, p. 7 (I, *Introduction*, 4). For the use of the term 'feeling' see reference on p. 21 to James Mill's use of the word.

future'.[1] And how can the series be aware of itself as a series? We have no reason to suppose that the material thing enjoys self-consciousness. But the mind certainly does.

But though he draws attention to this difficulty and admits that language suggests the irreducibility of the mind to the series of mental phenomena, Mill is unwilling to sacrifice phenomenalism. Hence he is compelled to hold that the series of feelings, as he puts it, can be aware of itself as a series, even though he is admittedly unable to explain how this is possible. 'I think, by far the wisest thing we can do, is to accept the inexplicable fact, without any theory of how it takes place; and when we are obliged to speak of it in terms which assume a theory, to use them with a reservation as to their meaning.'[2]

In connection with the analysis of the concept of mind Mill raises the question of solipsism. According to Reid, he remarks, I have no evidence at all of the existence of other selves if I am but a series of feelings or a thread of consciousness. My so-called awareness of other selves is simply an awareness of my own private feelings. But this line of argument, Mill contends, is 'one of Reid's most palpable mistakes'.[3] For one thing, even if I believe that my own mind is a series of feelings, there is nothing to prevent my conceiving other minds as similar series of feelings. For another thing, I have inferential evidence of the existence of minds other than my own, as the following line of reflection shows.

Modifications in the permanent possibility of sensations which I call my body evoke in me actual sensations and mental states which form part of the series which I call my mind. But I am aware of the existence of other permanent possibilities of sensations which are not related to my mental life in this way. And at the same time I am aware of actions and other external signs in these permanent possibilities of sensation or bodies, which I am warranted in interpreting as signs or expressions of inner mental states analogous to my own.

The view that we know the existence of other minds by inference from overt bodily behaviour is common enough. The trouble is, however, that Mill has already analysed bodies in terms of sensations. Obviously, he never intended to say or to imply that another person's body is simply and solely a group of *my* sensations, actual and possible. But he has at any rate to meet the objection that I am aware of another person's body only through

---

[1] *Examination*, p. 212.   [2] *Ibid.*, p. 213.   [3] *Ibid.*, p. 207.

my sensations, and that if the body is defined in terms of sensations, he must admit either that these sensations are mine or that sensations can exist on their own or that a body is a ground of possible sensations. In the first case solipsism is the logical conclusion. In the second case we are presented with a very peculiar thesis. In the third case, as has already been noted, the phenomenalistic analysis of the material thing collapses. And as, on Mill's own explicit admission, there is a special difficulty in the phenomenalistic analysis of mind, this is *a fortiori* subject to doubt.

Solipsism has proved the haunting spectre of phenomenalism. It is not that phenomenalists have actually embraced solipsism. For they have done nothing of the kind. The difficulty has been rather that of stating phenomenalism in such a way that it leads neither to a solipsistic conclusion on the one hand nor to an implicit abandonment of phenomenalism on the other. Perhaps the most successful attempt to state the phenomenalist position has been the modern linguistic version, to which reference was made in the previous section. But this can easily appear as an evasion of critical problems. At the same time, if we once start looking for hidden substrates, we shall find ourselves in other difficulties. And one can sympathize with the down-to-earth common-sense approach of some recent devotees of the cult of ordinary language. The trouble is, however, that once we have brought things back to ordinary language, the familiar philosophical problems tend to start up all over again.

11. Mill, as was mentioned in the sketch of his life, was brought up by his father without any religious beliefs. But he did not share James Mill's marked hostility to religion as inherently detrimental to morality. Hence he was more open to considering evidence for the existence of God. Of the ontological argument in its Cartesian form he remarks that it 'is not likely to satisfy anyone in the present day'.[1] And as he regarded the causal relation as being essentially a relation between phenomena, it is not surprising that he argues with Hume and Kant that 'the First Cause argument is in itself of no value for the establishment of Theism'.[2] But he is prepared to give serious consideration to the argument from design in Nature, as this is 'an argument of a really scientific character, which does not shrink from scientific tests, but claims

[1] *Three Essays on Religion*, p. 70. This work will be referred to as *Three Essays*.
[2] *Ibid.*, p. 67.

to be judged by the established canons of Induction. The design argument is wholly grounded on experience.'[1] Whether any argument to a metaphenomenal reality can properly be called a 'scientific' argument is open to question. But Mill's main point is that even if the argument from design in Nature concludes with affirming the existence of a divine being which in itself transcends the reach of scientific inquiry, it bases itself on empirical facts in a manner which is easily understood and makes an inference, the validity of which is open to reasonable discussion.

Paley's form of the argument will not do. It is true that if we found a watch on a desert island, we should indeed infer that it had been left there by a human being. But we should do so simply because we already know by experience that watches are made and carried by human beings. We do not, however, have previous experience of natural objects being made by God. We argue by analogy. That is to say, we argue from resemblances between phenomena which we already know to be products of human design and other phenomena which we then attribute to the productive work of a supramundane intelligence.

It must be added, however, that the argument from design in Nature rests on a special resemblance, namely the working together of various factors to one common end. For instance, the argument infers the operation of a supramundane intelligence from the arrangement and structure of the various parts of the visual apparatus which together produce sight. We cannot indeed exclude all other explanations of such phenomena. Hence the argument cannot lead to a conclusion which possesses more than some degree of probability. But the argument is none the less a reasonable inductive inference.[2] 'I think it must be allowed that, in the present state of our knowledge, the adaptations in Nature afford a large balance of probability in favour of creation by intelligence.'[3]

In Mill's opinion, however, we cannot accept the existence of God as a probable truth and at the same time affirm the divine omnipotence. For design implies the adaptation of means to an end, and the need to employ means reveals a limitation of power. 'Every indication of Design in the Kosmos is so much evidence against the omnipotence of the designer.'[4]

---

[1] *Ibid.*, p. 72.
[2] Mill does not think that an account of the matter simply in terms of the survival of the fittest is at all conclusive.
[3] *Three Essays*, p. 75.　　　　[4] *Ibid.*

This does not seem to me a very telling argument. For though the argument from design, taken by itself, concludes simply with assertion of the existence of a designer, not a creator, this does not show that the designer is not the creator. And it is difficult to see how the mere fact of using means to an end is any argument against omnipotence. But Mill's chief interest lies elsewhere, namely in arguing that there is an evident incompatibility between asserting at the same time that God is omnipotent and infinitely good. And this is a much more impressive line of argument.

Mill's point is that if God is omnipotent, he can prevent evil, and that if he does not do so, he cannot be infinitely good. It is no use saying with Dean Mansel that the term 'good' is predicated of God analogically and not in the same sense in which it is used of human beings. For this is really equivalent to saying that God is not good in any sense which we can give to the term. In fine, if we wish to maintain that God is good, we must also say that his power is limited or finite.

Mill is prepared to admit the reasonableness of believing that God desires the happiness of man. For this is suggested by the fact that pleasure seems to result from the normal functioning of the human organism and pain from some interference with this functioning. At the same time we can hardly suppose that God created the universe for the sole purpose of making men happy. Appearances suggest that if there is an intelligent creator, he has other motives besides the happiness of mankind, or of sentient beings in general, and that these other motives, whatever they may be, are of greater importance to him.

In other words, natural theology does not carry us very far. It is not indeed unreasonable, at least in the present state of the evidence, to believe in an intelligent divine being of limited power. But the proper attitude to adopt is what Mill calls a rational scepticism, which is more than sheer agnosticism but less than firm assent.

This might be all very well if those who are really interested in the question of the existence of God were concerned simply and solely with finding an explanatory hypothesis. But it is quite evident that they are not. For a religious person belief in the existence of God is not quite like belief that the architect of St. Paul's Cathedral was Sir Christopher Wren. And Mill sees this to the limited extent of raising the question of the pragmatic value or utility of religion. While recognizing that much evil has been done in the name of religion and that some religious beliefs can be detrimental to human conduct, he is not prepared to subscribe to his father's view that religion is 'the greatest enemy of morality'.[1] For religion, like poetry, can supply man with ideals beyond those which we actually find realized in human life. 'The value, therefore, of religion to the individual, both in the past and present, as a source of personal satisfaction and of elevated feelings, is not to be disputed.'[2] And in Christianity we find a conception of ideal goodness embodied in the figure of Christ.

To be sure, some people look on any suggestion that the pragmatic value of religion provides a reason for believing in God as an immoral suggestion, a betrayal of our duty to pay attention simply to the weight of the empirical evidence. But though this point of view is understandable, Mill does at any rate see that the function of religion in human history is something more than the solving of an intellectual puzzle in terms of an inductive hypothesis.

At the same time Mill raises the question whether the moral uplift of the higher religions cannot be preserved without belief in a supernatural Being. And as far as the provision of an ideal object of emotion and desire is concerned, he suggests that the 'need is fulfilled by the Religion of Humanity in as eminent a degree, and in as high a sense, as by the supernatural religions even in their best manifestations, and far more so than in any of the others'.[3] True, some religions have the advantage of holding out the prospect of immortality. But as the conditions of this life improve and men grow happier and more capable of deriving happiness from unselfish action, human beings, Mill thinks, 'will care less and less for this flattering expectation'.[4] However, if we include in the religion of humanity that belief in the existence of a God of limited power which natural theology justifies as a probable truth, it superadds to other inducements for working for the welfare of our fellow men the conviction that 'we may be co-operating with the unseen Being to whom we owe all that is enjoyable in life'.[5] Hence even if the religion of humanity is destined to be the religion of the future, this does not necessarily exclude belief in God.

Mill is thus in agreement with Auguste Comte that the so-called

---

[1] *Autobiography*, p. 40.   [2] *Three Essays*, p. 48.   [3] *Ibid.*, p. 50.
[4] *Ibid.*, p. 54. Mill maintains that while science does not provide any cogent evidence against immortality, there is no positive evidence in favour of it.
[5] *Ibid.*, p. 108.

religion of humanity is the religion of the future, though he has no sympathy with Comte's fantastic proposals for the organization of this religion. At the same time he does not rule out belief in a finite God with whom man can co-operate. And though his idea of religion is clearly not such as to satisfy Kierkegaard or indeed anyone who understands religion as involving absolute self-commitment to the personal Absolute, he does not think, like some empiricists before him, that religion can be disposed of either by a psychological account of the way in which religious belief could have arisen or by drawing attention to the evils which have been done in the name of religion. Though his empiricist premisses actually determine his evaluation of the force of the arguments for God's existence, he endeavours to keep an open mind. And though he regarded the evidence as amounting 'only to one of the lower degrees of probability',[1] when the *Three Essays on Religion* were published posthumously in 1874 some surprise was felt in positivist circles at the extent to which Mill made concessions to theism. He had travelled at any rate a modest distance beyond the point at which his father had stopped.

[1] *Three Essays*, p. 102.

CHAPTER IV

EMPIRICISTS, AGNOSTICS, POSITIVISTS

Alexander Bain and the associationist psychology—Bain on utilitarianism—Henry Sidgwick's combination of utilitarianism and intuitionism—Charles Darwin and the philosophy of evolution—T. H. Huxley; evolution, ethics and agnosticism— Scientific materialism and agnosticism; John Tyndall and Leslie Stephen—G. J. Romanes and religion—Positivism; the Comtist groups, G. H. Lewes, W. K. Clifford, K. Pearson— B. Kidd; concluding remarks.

1. THE associationist psychology was further developed by Alexander Bain (1818–1903), who occupied the chair of logic in the University of Aberdeen from 1860 until 1880. He was of some help to J. S. Mill in the preparation of his *System of Logic*,[1] and prepared some of the psychological notes for Mill's edition of his father's *Analysis of the Phenomena of the Human Mind*. But though he is sometimes described as a disciple of Mill, Mill himself remarks that the younger man did not really stand in need of any predecessor except the common precursors of them both.

Bain was primarily interested in developing empirical psychology as a separate science, rather than in employing the principle of the association of ideas to solve specifically philosophical problems. Further, he was particularly concerned with correlating psychical processes with their physiological bases, and in this respect he continued the interests of Hartley rather than of the two Mills.[2] While, however, his thought remained within the general framework of the associationist psychology,[3] the titles of his chief works, *The Senses and the Intellect* (1855) and *The Emotions and the Will* (1859), show that he extended his field of study from sensation and intellectual activity to the emotive and volitional aspects of human nature.[4] And this shift of emphasis

---

[1] See J. S. Mill's *Autobiography*, p. 245, note.

[2] Though certainly not blind to the relevance of physiological investigations, J. S. Mill, like his father, was chiefly interested in the psychology of consciousness and in its philosophical relevance.

[3] Bain introduced, however, a good many modifications into the associationist psychology as received from his predecessors.

[4] Mind is thus described from the start. 'It has Feeling, in which term I include what is commonly called Sensation and Emotion. It can Act according to Feeling. It can Think.' *The Senses and the Intellect*, p. 1 (1st edition).

enabled him to surmount, to some extent at least, the tendency of associationist psychologists to depict man's mental life as the result of a purely mechanical process.

Bain's emphasis on human activity shows itself, for example, in his account of the genesis of our belief in an external, material world. If we were simply subjects of purely passive sensations, of sensations or impressions, that is to say, considered apart from any activity or putting forth of energy on our part, our waking state of consciousness would resemble the dream-state. In point of fact, however, 'in us sensation is never wholly passive, and in general is much the reverse. Moreover, the tendency to movement exists before the stimulus of sensation; and movement gives a new character to our whole percipient existence'.[1] Impressions received from without arouse movement, activity, the display of energy or force; and 'it is in this exercise of force that we must look for the peculiar feeling of externality of objects'.[2] For instance, in the case of touch, the sense which is the first to make us clearly aware of an external world, 'it is hard contact that suggests externality; and the reason is that in this contact we put forth force of our own'.[3] Reacting to a sensation of touch by muscular exertion, we have a sense of resistance, 'a feeling which is the principal foundation of our notion of externality'.[4] In fine, 'the sense of the external is the consciousness of particular energies and activities of our own';[5] and our external world, the external world as it is presented to our minds, can be described as 'the sum total of all the occasions for putting forth active energy, or for conceiving this as possible to be put forth'.[6] Bain thus defines the external world, as it exists for our consciousness,[7] in terms of possible active responses to sensations rather than, as Mill defined it, of possible sensations.

It is not surprising, therefore, that Bain emphasizes the intimate connection between belief in general and action. 'Belief has no meaning, except in reference to our actions.'[8] Whenever a man, or an animal for the matter of that, performs an action as a means to an end, the action is sustained by a primitive belief or credulity which can be described 'as expectation of some contingent future about to follow on an action'.[9] It is this primitive credulity which leads a sentient being to repeat its successful experiment,

---

[1] *The Senses and the Intellect*, p. 371.   [2] *Ibid.*   [3] *Ibid.*, p. 372.
[4] *Ibid.*   [5] *Ibid.*, p. 371.   [6] *Ibid.*, p. 372.
[7] According to Bain, we cannot even discuss the existence of a material world entirely apart from consciousness.
[8] *The Emotions and the Will*, p. 524 (2nd edition).   [9] *Ibid.*, p. 525.

say of running to a brook to quench its thirst. It does not follow, however, that the force of belief rises gradually from zero to a state of full development in proportion to the length and uniformity of experience. For there is a primitive impulse or tendency to belief, which is derived from the natural activity of the organic system, and the strength of which is proportionate to the strength of the 'will'. 'The creature that wills strongly believes strongly at the origin of its career.'[1] What experience does is to determine the particular forms taken by a primitive impulse which it does not itself generate. And the factor which is of most importance in establishing sound belief is absence of contradiction or factual invariability of sequence, between, that is, expectation and its fulfilment.

If we assume, therefore, our instinctive responses in action to pleasure and pain, we can say that experience, with the inferences which follow on it, is the cardinal factor in stabilizing beliefs. But it is certainly not the only factor which is influential in shaping particular beliefs. For though feeling and emotion do not alter the objective facts, they may, and often do, affect our way of seeing and interpreting the facts. Evidence and feeling: 'the nature of the subject, and the character of the individual mind, determine which is to predominate; but in this life of ours, neither is the exclusive master'.[2]

If one wished to draw general conclusions about Bain's philosophical position, one could draw different conclusions from different groups of statements. On the one hand the emphasis which he lays on the physiological correlates of psychical processes might suggest a materialistic position. On the other hand a position of subjective idealism is suggested when he speaks, for example, of 'the supposed perception of an external and independent material world'[3] and adds that 'what is here said to be perceived is a convenient fiction, which by the very nature of the case transcends all possible experience'.[4] In point of fact, however, Bain tries to steer clear of metaphysics and to devote himself to empirical and genetic psychology, even if some of his statements have philosophical implications.

Bain's psychological investigations were continued by James Sully (1842–1923), who occupied the chair of philosophy at University College, London, from 1892 until 1903. In his *Outlines of Psychology* (1884) and in his two-volume work *The Human*

---

[1] *Ibid.*, p. 538.   [2] *Ibid.*, p. 548.
[3] *Ibid.*, p. 585.   [4] *Ibid.*

Mind (1892) he followed Bain in emphasizing the physiological correlates of psychical processes and in employing the principle of the association of ideas. Further, he extended his reflections into the field of the theory of education and applied himself to child-psychology in his *Studies of Childhood* (1895).

Already in Bain's lifetime, however, the associationist psychology was subjected to attack by James Ward and others. It is doubtless true that the emphasis laid by Bain on the emotive and volitional aspects of man gave to his thought a rather more modern tone than one finds in his predecessors. But it can also be argued that his introduction of fresh ideas into the old psychology helped to prepare the way for the lines of thought which supplanted it. Obviously, association continued to be recognized as a factor in mental life. But it could no longer be taken as a key to unlock all doors to the understanding of psychical processes, and the old atomistic associationist psychology had had its day.

2. In the ethical field Bain introduced into utilitarianism important modifications or supplementary considerations. These modifications doubtless impaired the simple unity of the utilitarian ethics. But Bain considered them necessary if an adequate account was to be given of the moral consciousness as it actually exists, that is, as Bain saw it in himself and in the members of the society or culture to which he belonged.

Utilitarianism, Bain remarks, has this great advantage over the moral sense theory, that it provides an external standard of morality, substituting 'a regard to consequences for a mere unreasoning sentiment, or feeling'.[1] It is also opposed to the theory that all human actions are the result of selfish impulses, a theory which is committed to misinterpreting affection and sympathy, 'the main foundations of disinterestedness'.[2] To be sure, these impulses belong to the self. But it does not follow that they can properly be described as 'selfish' impulses. In point of fact selfishness has never been the sole foundation of men's ideas of what is right. And it certainly is not the present sole foundation of men's moral convictions. This is recognized by the utilitarians, who connect the notion of utility with that of the common good.

At the same time utilitarianism cannot constitute the whole truth about morality. For one thing, we must find room for a distinction between 'utility made compulsory and what is left

---

[1] *The Emotions and the Will*, p. 272.
[2] *Ibid.*, p. 258. Bain also notes that we can have disinterested antipathies and aversions.

free'.[1] After all, there are many actions which are useful to the community but which are not regarded as obligatory. For another thing, it is clear that the moral rules which prevail in most communities are grounded partly on sentiment, and not only on the idea of utility. Hence, even though the principle of utility is an essential feature of ethics, we must add sentiment and also tradition, 'which is the continuing influence of some former Utility or Sentiment'.[2] That is to say, we must add them if we wish to give a comprehensive account of existing moral practices.

Bain is not concerned, therefore, with working out an *a priori* theory of ethics. He is concerned with exhibiting the empirical foundations of morality as it exists. He approaches morality very much from the point of view of a psychologist. And if we bear this approach in mind, we can understand his genetic treatment of conscience and the feeling of obligation. In contrast to the view of Dugald Stewart that conscience is 'a primitive and independent faculty of the mind, which would be developed in us although we never had any experience of external authority',[3] Bain holds that 'conscience is an imitation within us of the government without us'.[4] In other words, conscience is an interior reflection of the voices of parents, educators and external authority in general. And the sense of obligation and duty arises out of the association established in the infant mind between the performance of actions forbidden by external authority and the sanctions imposed by this authority.

Now, if we interpret J. S. Mill as offering utilitarianism as an adequate description of the existing moral consciousness, Bain is doubtless right in saying that for an adequate description other factors have to be taken into account besides the principle of utility. But if we interpret Mill as recommending a particular system of ethics and as preferring this system to the moral sense theory on the ground that the principle of utility provides a criterion of moral conduct which is lacking in any pure moral sense theory, it is arguable that Bain is really more of a positivist than Mill. For though, as we have seen, he recognizes the advantage which utilitarianism possesses in having an external standard, he tends to emphasize the relativity of moral convictions. If someone asks, what is the moral standard? the proper answer would be that it is 'the enactments of the existing society, as

<hr>

[1] *Ibid.*, p. 274.   [2] *Ibid.*, p. 277.
[3] *Ibid.*, p. 283.   [4] *Ibid.*

derived from some one clothed in his day with a moral legislative authority'.[1] Instead of treating morality as if it were one indivisible whole, we ought to consider particular codes and moral rules separately. And then we shall see that behind the phenomena of conscience and obligation there lies authority. Bain allows for the influence of outstanding individuals; but the assent of the community at large, whatever it may be, is required to complete the legislative process. And once it is completed, the external authority is present which shapes conscience and the sense of duty in the individual.

Bain would have done well to reflect on his own admission that outstanding individuals are capable of moulding afresh the moral outlook of a society. That is to say, he might well have asked himself whether this admission was really consistent with an ethics of social pressure. Some have concluded that there is a field of objective values into which different degrees of insight are possible, while Bergson thought it necessary to make a distinction between what he called 'closed' and 'open' morality. But the problem does not seem to have troubled Bain, even though the data for the raising of the problem were present in his account of morality.

3. A much more radical change in the utilitarian ethics was made by Henry Sidgwick (1838–1900), Fellow of Trinity College, Cambridge, who was elected to the chair of moral philosophy in that university in 1883. His reputation rests principally on *The Methods of Ethics* (1874). Other writings include his *Outlines of the History of Ethics for English Readers* (1886) and his posthumously published *Lectures on the Ethics of Green, Spencer and Martineau* (1902).

In Sidgwick's account of the development of his ethical views, which was printed in the sixth edition (1901) of *The Methods of Ethics*, he remarked that 'my first adhesion to a definite Ethical system was to the Utilitarianism of Mill'.[2] But he soon came to see a discrepancy between psychological hedonism, the thesis that every man seeks his own pleasure, and ethical hedonism, the thesis that every man ought to seek the general happiness. If psychological hedonism is taken to mean that as a matter of fact every man seeks exclusively his own pleasure, the thesis is questionable, or, rather, false. But in any case a purely psychological thesis

---

[1] *The Emotions and the Will*, p. 281.
[2] *The Methods of Ethics*, p. XV (6th edition.)

cannot establish an ethical thesis. As Hume maintained, we cannot deduce an 'ought' from an 'is', an ought-statement from a purely factual descriptive statement. James Mill may have tried to show how it is psychologically possible for a person who by nature pursues his own pleasure or happiness to act altruistically. But even if his account of the matter were valid from a psychological point of view, this would not show that we *ought* to act altruistically. If, therefore, ethical or universalistic hedonism is to have a philosophical basis, we must look elsewhere for it than in psychology.

Sidgwick came to the conclusion that this philosophical basis could be found only in the intuition of some fundamental moral principle or principles. He was thus drawn away from the utilitarianism of Bentham and J. S. Mill to intuitionism. But further reflection convinced him that the principles which were implicit in the morality of common sense, as distinct from philosophical theories about morality, were either utilitarian in character or at any rate compatible with utilitarianism. 'I was then a Utilitarian again, but on an Intuitional basis.'[1]

In Sidgwick's view, therefore, there are certain moral principles which are self-evidently true. Thus it is evident that one should prefer a future greater good to a present lesser one.[2] This is the principle of prudence. It is also self-evident that as rational beings we ought to treat others in the way in which we think that we ought to be treated, unless there is some difference 'which can be stated as a reasonable ground for difference of treatment'.[3] This is the principle of justice. It is also self-evident both that from the point of view of the Universe the good of any one individual is of no more importance than the good of any other individual, and that as a rational being I ought to aim at the general good, so far as it is attainable by my efforts. From these two propositions we can deduce the principle of benevolence, namely that 'each one is morally bound to regard the good of any other individual as much as his own, except in so far as he judges it to be less, when impartially viewed, or less certainly knowable or attainable by him'.[4]

[1] *Ibid.*, p. XX.

[2] This does not mean that we ought to prefer a future uncertain good to a lesser but certain present one. As self-evident, the principle simply states that priority in time, considered simply by itself, is not a reasonable ground for preferring one good to another. Cf. *The Methods of Ethics*, p. 381.

[3] *The Methods of Ethics*, p. 380. The difference might be one of circumstances or between the persons considered. We would not necessarily think it right to treat a child in the way that we consider we ought to be treated.

[4] *Ibid.*, p. 382.

The principle of prudence or of 'rational egoism', as mentioned above, implies that a man ought to seek his own good. And Sidgwick is in fact convinced, with Butler, that this is a manifest obligation. The principle of rational benevolence, however, states that we ought to seek for the good of others, under certain conditions at any rate. If therefore we combine them, we have the command to seek the good of all, including one's own, or to seek one's own good as a constituent part of the general good. For the general good is made up of individual goods. Now, the general good can be equated with universal happiness, provided that we do not understand by happiness simply the pleasures of sense, and provided that we do not intend to imply that happiness is always best attained by aiming at it directly. Hence 'I am finally led to the conclusion that the Intuitional method rigorously applied yields as its final result the doctrine of pure Universalistic Hedonism—which it is convenient to denote by the single word, Utilitarianism'.[1]

If we look at Sidgwick's moral philosophy in the light of the utilitarian tradition, we naturally tend to focus our attention on his rejection of the claims of genetic psychology to provide an adequate basis for our moral convictions, especially of the consciousness of obligation, and on his use of the idea of intuitively perceived moral axioms, a use which was encouraged by his reading of Samuel Clarke and other writers.[2] He can be described as an intuitionist utilitarian or as an utilitarian intuitionist, if such descriptions do not involve a contradiction in terms. Sidgwick, indeed, maintained that there is no real incompatibility between utilitarianism and intuitionism. At the same time he was too honest a thinker to assert that he had given a definitive solution to the problem of reconciling the claims of interest and duty, of prudence or rational egoism and of benevolence, a benevolence capable of expressing itself not only in altruistic conduct but also in complete self-sacrifice in the service of others or in the pursuit of some ideal end.

If, however, we look at Sidgwick's moral philosophy in relation to what was to come later instead of in relation to what went before, we shall probably lay more stress on his method. He laid emphasis on the need for examining what he called the morality of common sense; and he attempted to discover the principles

---

[1] *The Methods of Ethics*, pp. 406–7.
[2] For Samuel Clarke see Vol. V of this *History*, pp. 160–1.

which are implicit in the ordinary moral consciousness, to state them precisely and to determine their mutual relations. His method was analytic. He selected a problem, considered it from various angles, proposed a solution and raised objections and counter-objections. He may have tended to lose himself in details and to suspend final judgment because he was unable to see his way clearly through all difficulties. To say this, however, is in a sense to commend his thoroughness and careful honesty. And though his appeal to self-evident truths may not appear very convincing, his devotion to the analysis and clarification of the ordinary moral consciousness puts one in mind of the later analytic movement in British philosophy.

4. The associationist psychology, the phenomenalism of J. S. Mill and the utilitarian ethics, all had their roots in the eighteenth century. Soon after the middle of the nineteenth century, however, a new idea began to colour the empiricist current of thought. This was the idea of evolution. We cannot indeed fix on a certain date and say that after this date empiricism became a philosophy of evolution. Herbert Spencer, the great philosopher of evolution in nineteenth-century England, had started publishing his *System of Philosophy* before J. S. Mill published his work on Hamilton, and Bain, who died in the same year as Spencer, continued the tradition represented by the two Mills. Moreover, it is less a question of the empiricist movement as a whole coming under the domination of the idea of evolution than of the idea becoming prominent in certain representatives of the movement. We can, however, say that in the second half of the century the theory of evolution invaded and occupied not only the relevant parts of the scientific field but also a considerable part of the field of empiricist philosophy.

The idea of biological evolution was not, of course, an invention of the middle of the nineteenth century. As a purely speculative idea it had appeared even in ancient Greece. In the eighteenth century the way had been prepared for it by Georges-Louis de Buffon (1707–88), while Jean-Baptiste Pierre Lamarck (1744–1829) had proposed his theories that in response to new needs brought about by changes in the environment changes take place in the organic structure of animals, some organs falling into disuse and others being evolved and developed, and that acquired habits are transmitted by heredity. Moreover, when the idea of evolution was first publicized in Britain, the publicist was a philosopher,

Spencer, rather than a scientist. At the same time this does not affect the importance of Darwin's writings in setting the theory of evolution on its feet and in giving an enormously powerful impetus to its propagation.

Charles Robert Darwin (1809–82) was a naturalist, not a philosopher. During his famous voyage on the 'Beagle' (1831–6), observation of variations between differently situated animals of the same species and reflection on the differences between living and fossilized animals led him to question the theory of the fixity of species. In 1838 study of Malthus's *Essay on the Principle of Population* helped to lead him to the conclusions that in the struggle for existence favourable variations tend to be preserved and unfavourable variations to be destroyed, and that the result of this process is the formation of new species, acquired characteristics being transmitted by heredity.

Similar conclusions were reached independently by another naturalist, Alfred Russel Wallace (1823–1913), who, like Darwin, was influenced by a reading of Malthus in arriving at the idea of the survival of the fittest in the struggle for existence. And on July 1st, 1858, a joint communication by Wallace and Darwin was presented at a meeting of the Linnean Society in London. Wallace's contribution was a paper *On the Tendency of Varieties to Depart Indefinitely from the Original Type*, while Darwin contributed an abridgment of his own ideas.

Darwin's famous work on the *Origin of Species by Means of Natural Selection, or The Preservation of Favoured Races in the Struggle for Life* was published in November 1859, all copies being sold out on the day of publication. This was followed in 1868 by *The Variation of Animals and Plants under Domestication*. And the year 1871 saw the publication of *The Descent of Man, and Selection in Relation to Sex*. Darwin published a number of further works, but he is chiefly known for *The Origin of Species* and *The Descent of Man*.

Being a naturalist, Darwin was sparing of philosophical speculation and devoted himself primarily to working out a theory of evolution based on the available empirical evidence. He did indeed interpret morality as evolving out of the purposiveness of animal instinct and as developing through changes in social standards which confer survival value on societies. And he was obviously well aware of the flutter in theological dovecotes which was caused by his theory of evolution, particularly in its application to man. In 1870 he wrote that while he could not look on the universe as the product of blind chance, he could see no evidence of design, still less of beneficent design, when he came to consider the details of natural history. And though he was originally a Christian, he arrived in the course of time at an agnostic suspension of judgment. He tended, however, to avoid personal involvement in theological controversy.

Unless perhaps we happen to live in one of the few surviving pockets of fundamentalism, it is difficult for us now to appreciate the ferment which was caused in the last century by the hypothesis of organic evolution, particularly in its application to man. For one thing, the idea of evolution is now common coin and is taken for granted by very many people who would be quite unable either to mention or to weigh the evidence adduced in its favour. For another thing, the hypothesis is no longer an occasion for bitter theological controversy. Even those who question the sufficiency of the evidence to prove the evolution of the human body from some other species commonly recognize that the first chapters of *Genesis* were not intended to solve scientific problems, and that the matter is one which has to be settled according to the available empirical evidence. Again, if we except the Marxists, who are in any case committed to materialism, reflective unbelievers do not generally maintain that the hypothesis of organic evolution, taken by itself, disproves Christian theism or is incompatible with religious belief. After all, the presence of evil and suffering in the world, which constitutes one of the main objections to Christian theism, remains an indubitable fact whether the hypothesis is accepted or rejected. Further, we have seen philosophers such as Bergson developing a spiritualistic philosophy within the framework of the general idea of creative evolution, and, more recently, a scientist such as Teilhard de Chardin making an enthusiastic use of the same idea in the service of a religious world-view. Hence the controversies of the last century naturally seem to many people to have accumulated a great deal of dust and cobwebs in the interval.

We have to remember, however, that in the middle of the last century the idea of the evolution of species, especially as applied to man himself, was for the general educated public a complete novelty. Moreover, the impression was commonly given, not only by exponents of the idea but also by some of its critics, that the Darwinian theory rendered superfluous or, rather, positively excluded any teleological interpretation of the cosmic process. For example, T. H. Huxley wrote as follows. 'That which struck the present writer most forcibly on his first perusal of the *Origin of Species* was the conviction that Teleology, as commonly understood, had received its deathblow at Mr. Darwin's hands.'[1] Those species survive which are the best fitted for the struggle for existence; but the variations which make them the best fitted are fortuitous.

Our concern here is with the impact of the theory of evolution on philosophy rather than with the theological controversies to which it gave rise. Herbert Spencer, the foremost philosopher of evolution in the nineteenth century, merits a chapter to himself. Meanwhile we can consider briefly two or three writers who contributed to publicizing the idea of evolution and to developing some philosophical theories based on or connected with this idea. It is to be noted, however, that they were scientists who made excursions into philosophy, rather than professional philosophers. Generally speaking, the academic or university philosophers held aloof from the topic and maintained a reserved attitude. As for Spencer, he never occupied an academic post.

5. The name which immediately suggests itself in this context is that of Thomas Henry Huxley (1825–95). As a naval surgeon aboard the 'Rattlesnake' Huxley had opportunity for studying the marine life of the tropical seas, and as a result of his researches he was elected a Fellow of the Royal Society in 1851. In 1854 he was appointed lecturer in natural history at the School of Mines. In the course of time he became more and more involved in public life, serving on some ten royal commissions and taking an active part in educational organization. From 1883 to 1885 he was president of the Royal Society.

In Huxley's opinion Darwin had placed the theory of evolution on a sound footing by following a method in accordance with the rules of procedure laid down by J. S. Mill. 'He has endeavoured to determine great facts inductively, by observation and experiment; he has then reasoned from the data thus furnished; and lastly, he has tested the validity of his ratiocination by comparing his deductions with the observed facts of Nature.'[2] It is true that the

---

[1] *Lectures and Essays* (The People's Library edition), pp. 178–9. Huxley was commenting on an essay by a certain Professor Kölliker of Würzburg who had interpreted Darwin as a teleologist and had criticized him on this score.

[2] *Lay Sermons, Addresses and Reviews*, p. 294 (6th edition). The quotation is taken from an 1860 article on *The Origin of Species*.

origin of species by natural selection has not been proved with certainty. The theory remains an hypothesis which enjoys only a high degree of probability. But it is 'the only extant hypothesis which is worth anything in a scientific point of view'.[1] And it is a marked improvement on Lamarck's theory.[2]

But though Huxley accepted the view that organic evolution proceeds by natural selection or the survival of the fittest in the struggle for existence, he made a sharp distinction between the evolutionary process and man's moral life. Those who expound an ethics of evolution, according to which man's moral life is a continuation of the evolutionary process, are probably right in maintaining that what we call the moral sentiments have evolved like other natural phenomena. But they forget that the immoral sentiments are also the result of evolution. 'The thief and the murderer follow nature just as much as the philanthropist.'[3]

In fine, morality involves going against the evolutionary process. In the struggle for existence the strongest and most self-assertive tend to trample down the weaker, whereas 'social progress means a checking of the cosmic process at every step and the substitution for it of another, which may be called the ethical process'.[4] Originally, human society was probably just as much a product of organic necessity as the societies of bees and ants. But in the case of man social progress involves strengthening the bonds of mutual sympathy, consideration and benevolence, and self-imposed restrictions on anti-social tendencies. True, in so far as this process renders a society more fitted for survival in relation to Nature or to other societies, it is in harmony with the cosmic progress. But in so far as law and moral rules restrict the struggle for existence between members of a given society, the ethical process is plainly at variance with the cosmic process. For it aims at producing quite different qualities. Hence we can say that 'the ethical progress of society depends, not on imitating the cosmic process, still less in running away from it, but in combating it'.[5]

[1] *Ibid.*, p. 295.
[2] In regard to Lamarck's theory that environmental changes produce new needs in animals, that new needs produce new desires, and that new desires result in organic modifications which are transmitted by heredity, Huxley remarks that it does not seem to have occurred to Lamarck to inquire 'whether there is any reason to believe that there are any limits to the amount of modifications producible, or to ask how long an animal is likely to endeavour to gratify an impossible desire;' *Lectures and Essays*, p. 124. The quotation is taken from an 1850 essay on 'The Darwinian Hypothesis'.
[3] *Evolution and Ethics and Other Essays*, p. 80. The discourse on *Evolution and Ethics* was originally given at Oxford as the second Romanes lecture.
[4] *Ibid.*, p. 81.   [5] *Ibid.*, p. 83.

There is thus a marked difference between the views of T. H. Huxley and his grandson, Sir Julian Huxley, on the relation between evolution and ethics. I do not mean to imply, of course, that Sir Julian Huxley rejects the moral qualities and ideals which his grandfather considered desirable. The point is that whereas Sir Julian Huxley emphasizes the element of continuity between the general movement of evolution and moral progress, T. H. Huxley emphasized the element of discontinuity, maintaining that 'the cosmic process has no sort of relation to moral ends'.[1] T. H. Huxley might, of course, have called for a new type of ethics, involving a Nietzschean exaltation of Nature's strong men, which could have been interpreted as a continuation of what he called the cosmic process. But he did not aim at any such transvaluation of values. Rather did he accept the values of sympathy, benevolence, consideration for others, and so on; and in the cosmic process he found no respect for such values.

Though, however, man's moral life formed for Huxley a world of its own within the world of Nature, it does not follow that he looked on man as possessing a spiritual soul which cannot be accounted for in terms of evolution. He maintained that 'consciousness is a function of the brain'.[2] That is to say, consciousness is an epiphenomenon which arises when matter has developed a special form of organization. And this theory, together with his defence of determinism, led to his being described as a materialist.

Huxley, however, stoutly denied the applicability to himself of this description. One reason which he gave for this denial is perhaps not very impressive, because it involved a very narrow interpretation of materialism. Materialism, according to Huxley, maintains that there is nothing in the universe but matter and force, whereas the theory of the epiphenomenal nature of consciousness neither denies the reality of consciousness nor identifies it with the physical processes on which it depends.[3] But Huxley went on to remark, with a rather charming unexpectedness, that 'the arguments used by Descartes and Berkeley to show that our certain knowledge does not extend beyond our states of consciousness, appear to me to be as impregnable now as they did when I first became acquainted with them some half-century ago. . . . Our one certainty is the existence of the mental world, and that of

[1] *Evolution and Ethics, and Other Essays*, p. 83.   [2] *Ibid.*, p. 135.
[3] The Marxist, for example, does not deny the reality of mind. Nor does he identify psychical with physical processes. But he looks on himself none the less as a materialist. And so he is in a metaphysical sense.

Kraft und Stoff falls into the rank of, at best, a highly probable hypothesis.'[1] Further, if material things are resolved into centres of force, one might just as well speak of immaterialism as of materialism.

It is not perhaps very easy to understand how the doctrine that we can never really know anything with certainty but our states of consciousness can be harmonized with the doctrine that consciousness is a function of the brain. But the first doctrine enables Huxley to say that 'if I were forced to choose between Materialism and Idealism, I should elect for the latter'.[2]

It must be added, however, that Huxley has no intention of letting himself be forced to choose between materialism and idealism. And the same applies to the issue between atheism and theism. Huxley proclaims himself an agnostic, and in his work on David Hume he expresses agreement with the Scottish philosopher's suspension of judgment about metaphysical problems. We have our scientific knowledge, and 'the man of science has learned to believe in justification, not by faith, but by verification'.[3] In regard to that which lies beyond the scope of verification we must remain agnostic, suspending judgment.

As one might expect in the case of a naturalist who makes excursions into philosophy, Huxley's philosophical theories are not well worked out. Nor is their mutual consistency clearly exhibited, to put it mildly. At the same time they manifest the not uncommon English attitude which shows itself in a dislike of extremes and a reluctance to submit to the imposition of restrictive labels. Huxley was quite prepared to defend evolution against attack, as he did in his famous encounter with Bishop Samuel Wilberforce in 1860. And he was prepared to criticize orthodox theology. But though he clearly did not believe in the Christian doctrine of God, he refused to commit himself either to atheism or to materialism. Behind the veil of phenomena lies the unknowable. And in regard to the unknowable agnosticism is, by definition, the appropriate attitude.

6. (i) The label 'materialist', repudiated by Huxley, was accepted by John Tyndall (1820–93), who in 1853 was appointed professor of natural philosophy in the Royal Institution, where he

---

[1] *Evolution and Ethics, and Other Essays*, p. 130. *Kraft und Stoff* is the title of a well-known book by the German materialist, Ludwig Büchner. See Vol. VII of this *History*, pp. 352–3.
[2] *Ibid.*, p. 133.
[3] *Lay Sermons, Addresses and Reviews*, p. 18.

was a colleague of Faraday.[1] Tyndall was chiefly concerned with inorganic physics, particularly with the subject of radiant heat; and he was much less inclined than Huxley to make prolonged excursions into the field of philosophy. But he did not hesitate to profess openly what he called 'scientific materialism'.

The scientific materialism accepted by Tyndall was not, however, the same thing as the materialism which was rejected by Huxley. For it meant in large part the hypothesis that every state of consciousness is correlated with a physical process in the brain. Thus in his address to the British Association in 1868 on the *Scope and Limit of Scientific Materialism* Tyndall explained that 'in affirming that the growth of the body is mechanical, and that thought, as exercised by us, has its correlative in the physics of the brain, I think that the position of the "Materialist" is stated, as far as that position is a tenable one'.[2] In other words, the materialist asserts that two sets of phenomena, mental processes and physical processes in the brain, are associated, though he is 'in absolute ignorance'[3] of the real bond of union between them. Indeed, in his so-called Belfast Address, delivered before the British Association in 1874, Tyndall asserted roundly that 'man the *object* is separated by an impassible gulf from man the *subject*. There is no motor energy in the human intellect to carry it, without logical rupture, from the one to the other.'[4]

Tyndall did indeed understand scientific materialism as involving 'a provisional assent'[5] to the hypothesis that the mind and all its phenomena 'were once latent in a fiery cloud'[6] and that they are 'a result of the play between organism and environment through cosmic ranges of time'.[7] But the conclusion which he drew from the theory of evolution was that matter could not properly be looked on as mere 'brute' matter. It had to be regarded as potentially containing within itself life and mental phenomena. In other words, scientific materialism demanded a revision of the concept of matter as something essentially dead and opposed to biological and mental life.

Beyond the phenomena of matter and force, which form the object of scientific inquiry, 'the real mystery of the universe lies

---

[1] On Faraday's death in 1867 Tyndall succeeded him as Superintendent of the Institution.
[2] *Fragments of Science for Unscientific People*, pp. 121–2 (2nd edition).
[3] *Ibid.*, p. 122.
[4] *Lectures and Essays*, p. 40 (Rationalist Press Association edition, 1903).
[5] *Fragments of Science*, p. 166.
[6] *Ibid.*, p. 163.   [7] *Lectures and Essays*, p. 40.

unsolved, and, as far as we are concerned, is incapable of solution'.[1] But this acknowledgment of mystery in the universe was not intended by Tyndall as a support for belief in God as conceived by Christians. In his *Apology for the Belfast Address* (1874), he spoke of the idea of creative activity by 'a Being standing outside the nebula'[2] not only as based on no empirical evidence but also as 'opposed to the very spirit of science'.[3] Further, when answering a Catholic critic he remarked, in the same *Apology*, that he would not disavow the charge of atheism, as far as any concept of the Supreme Being was concerned which his critics would be likely to accept.

Tyndall's scientific materialism was not confined, therefore, to a methodological point of view presupposed by scientific inquiry. He was not simply saying, for example, that the scientific psychologist should pursue his inquiries into the relation between mind and body on the assumption that we shall find a correlation between any given mental phenomenon and a physical process. He was saying that as far as knowledge is concerned, science is omnicompetent. Problems which cannot be answered by science are unanswerable in principle. Religion, for example, is immune from disproof as long as it is regarded simply as a subjective experience.[4] But if it is regarded as claiming to extend our knowledge, its claim is bogus. In a general sense of the term, therefore, Tyndall was a positivist. By admitting a sphere for agnosticism, mysteries or enigmas, that is to say, which cannot be solved, he stopped short of the position to be adopted later by the neo-positivists or logical positivists. But this does not alter the fact that scientific materialism involved for him a positivist view of the omnicompetence of science in the field of knowledge.

(ii) The view that agnosticism is the only attitude which is really in harmony with the genuinely scientific spirit was also maintained by Sir Leslie Stephen (1832–1904), author of a two-volume *History of English Thought in the Eighteenth Century* (1876) and of a three-volume work on *The English Utilitarians* (1900). At first a clergyman, he came successively under the influence of J. S. Mill, Darwin and Spencer, and in 1875 he finally abandoned his clerical status.

In a discussion of the nature of materialism Stephen maintains

[1] *Fragments of Science*, p. 93.   [2] *Lectures and Essays*, p. 47.   [3] *Ibid*.
[4] 'No atheistic reasoning can, I hold, dislodge religion from the human heart. Logic cannot deprive us of life, and religion is life to the religious. As an experience of consciousness it is beyond the assaults of logic', *ibid*., p. 45.

that it 'represents the point of view of the physical inquirer. A man is a materialist for the time being so long as he has only to do with that which may be touched, handled, seen or otherwise perceived through the senses'.[1] In other words, scientific inquiry demands a methodical materialism. It does not demand acceptance of the doctrine that matter is the ultimate reality.

It by no means follows, however, that we are entitled to assert spiritualism, the doctrine that mind is the ultimate reality. The truth of the matter is that 'we cannot get behind the curtain, which is reality'.[2] If we try to do so, we are at once plunged into 'the transcendental region of antinomies and cobwebs of the brain'.[3] The unknowable which lies beyond 'reality' is 'a mere blank':[4] it is not itself converted into a reality by being spelt with a capital letter. 'The ancient secret is a secret still; man knows nothing of the Infinite and Absolute.'[5]

One would have thought that if the phenomenal world is once equated with 'reality', there is no good reason for supposing that there is any unknowable beyond it. What is the reason for supposing that there *is* a secret which always remains a secret? Conversely, if there is good reason for supposing that there is an unknowable Absolute, there is no good reason for equating the phenomenal world with reality. But Stephen's agnosticism represents less a carefully thought out position than a general attitude. Science alone provides us with definite knowledge. Science knows nothing of any meta-empirical Absolute. But we feel that even if all scientific problems were answered, the universe would still be mysterious, enigmatic. The enigma, however, is insoluble.

Needless to say, scientific materialism and agnosticism were by no means regarded as entailing the rejection of moral values. Tyndall insisted that moral values are independent of religious creeds, and that scientific materialism must not be understood as involving or implying a belittlement of man's highest ideals. As for Sir Leslie Stephen, in his work *The Science of Ethics* (1882) he tried to continue and develop Spencer's attempt to ground morals on evolution. Abstractly considered, the function of morality is to further the health and vitality of the social organism. Historically considered, moral principles undergo a process of natural selection, and those which are most effective in furthering the good

---

[1] *An Agnostic's Apology and Other Essays*, p. 52 (Rationalist Press Association edition, 1904). The quotation is taken from an 1886 essay. *What is Materialism?*
[2] *Ibid.*, p. 66.   [3] *Ibid.*, p. 57.   [4] *Ibid.*   [5] *Ibid.*, p. 20.

of the social organism prevail over the less effective. That is to say, they are approved by the society in question. Thus even morality is brought under the law of the survival of the fittest. Obviously, Stephen's point of view was different from that of T. H. Huxley.

7. Agnosticism was not, of course, the only attitude adopted by those who embraced the theory of evolution. Henry Drummond (1851–97), for example, a writer whose books once enjoyed great popularity, tried to bring together science and religion, Darwinism and Christianity, in terms of the operation of one law of continuing evolution. More interesting, however, is the case of George John Romanes (1848–94), biologist and author of a number of works on evolution, who passed from early religious belief to agnosticism and from agnosticism by way of pantheism back in the direction of Christian theism.

The agnostic phase in Romanes's thought found expression in *A Candid Examination of Theism*, which he published in 1878 under the pseudonym of *Physicus*. There is, he maintained, no real evidence for the existence of God, though it may possibly be true, for all we know, that there would be no universe unless there were a God. Some years later, however, in a lecture entitled *Mind, Motion and Monism* (1885), Romanes proposed a form of pantheism, while his adoption of a more sympathetic attitude towards Christian theism was represented by *Thoughts on Religion* (1895), edited by Charles Gore, later Bishop of Oxford. This work comprises some articles which Romanes wrote for the *Nineteenth Century* but did not publish, together with notes for a second *Candid Examination of Theism* which was to have been signed *Metaphysicus*.

In the articles on the influence of science on religion, which form part of *Thoughts on Religion*, Romanes argues that this influence has been destructive in the sense that it has progressively revealed the invalidity of appeals to direct intervention in Nature or to alleged evidence of special cases of design. At the same time science necessarily presupposes the idea of Nature as a system, as exemplifying universal order; and theism provides a reasonable explanation of this universal order. If, however, we wish to speak of the postulated creator of universal order as a divine Mind, we must remember that none of the qualities which characterize the minds with which we are acquainted can be properly attributed to God. Hence 'the word

Mind, as applied to the supposed agency, stands for a blank'.[1] In this sense, therefore, the argument for theism leads to agnosticism.

In his notes for the proposed second version of his *Candid Examination of Theism* Romanes adopts a somewhat different point of view by arguing that the advance of science, 'far from having weakened religion, has immeasurably strengthened it. For it has proved the uniformity of natural causation'.[2] But the question whether one is to look on the universal causal order as a continuing expression of the divine will or simply as a natural fact, is not one which can be settled by the human understanding alone. Science provides an empirical basis, as it were, for a religious vision of the world, but the transition to this vision requires an act of faith. True, 'no one is entitled to deny the possibility of what may be termed an organ of spiritual discernment',[3] manifested in the religious consciousness; and 'reason itself tells me it is not unreasonable to expect that the heart and will should be required to join with reason in seeking God'.[4] The way to become a Christian is to act as one, 'and if Christianity be true, the verification will come, not indeed immediately through any course of speculative reason, but immediately by spiritual intuition'.[5] At the same time faith, definite self-commitment to a religious view of the world, demands 'a severe effort of the will',[6] an effort which Romanes himself is not prepared to make.

It is thus a mistake to say that Romanes came to commit himself definitely to a theistic position. In a sense he not only begins but also ends with agnosticism. At the same time there is a considerable difference between the initial and the terminal agnosticism. For whereas in one period of his life Romanes was evidently convinced that his scientific conscience demanded of him an agnostic position, in later years he came to insist that the religious view of the world may be justified, though it would be justified by something of the nature of spiritual intuition. The agnostic has no right to rule out this possibility or to say that the venture of faith is a fool's venture. For the experiment of faith may well have its own peculiar mode of verification, about which science cannot pronounce judgment. In other words, Romanes was neither satisfied with agnosticism nor fully prepared to reject it. He developed a sympathy with religious belief which Tyndall did not share. But he did not feel able to commit himself to it by

---

[1] *Thoughts on Religion*, p. 87.   [2] *Ibid.*, p. 124.   [3] *Ibid.*, p. 140.
[4] *Ibid.*, p. 132.   [5] *Ibid.*, p. 168.   [6] *Ibid.*, p. 131.

that effort of the will which he considered necessary before the internal validation of the religious consciousness could manifest itself.

8. (i) As we have seen, J. S. Mill admired Auguste Comte and was prepared to talk in a general way about the religion of humanity. But he had no use for Comte's proposals for organizing a cult for the new religion or for his dreams of a spiritual and intellectual domination to be exercised by the positivist philosophers. Again, Spencer, who also derived stimulus from Comte, adopted a critical attitude towards some of the Frenchman's theories,[1] while T. H. Huxley described the philosophy of Comte as Catholicism minus Christianity. For real disciples of Comte we have to turn to Richard Congreve (1818–99), Fellow of Wadham College, Oxford, who translated Comte's positivist catechism into English and to his circle. This included John Henry Bridges (1832–1906), Frederic Harrison (1831–1923) and Edward Spencer Beesley (1831–1915).

The London Positivist Society was founded in 1867, and in 1870 it opened a positivist temple in Chapel Street. But after some years a split occurred in the ranks of the Comtists, and those who accepted the leadership of Pierre Laffitte (1823–1903), friend and successor of Comte as high priest of positivism, formed the London Positivist Committee which opened a centre of its own in 1881. Bridges was the first president of the new Committee (1878–80), and he was succeeded by Harrison. The original group was led by Congreve. In 1916 the two groups were reunited.[2]

(ii) The independent thinkers are obviously of more interest than those who were primarily engaged in spreading the pure word of Comtism. One of these independent thinkers was George Henry Lewes (1817–78), author of the once popular but long superseded two-volume *Biographical History of Philosophy* (1845–6). In his earlier years Lewes was an enthusiastic follower of Comte, and in 1853 he published *Comte's Philosophy of the Positive Sciences*. But though he remained a positivist in the sense of holding that philosophy consists in the widest generalizations from the results of the particular sciences and should abstain from any treatment of the meta-empirical, he moved away from Comte and came more under the influence of Spencer. In 1874–9 he published five volumes of *Problems of Life and Mind*.

---

[1] In 1864 Spencer wrote his *Reasons for Dissenting from the Philosophy of Comte*.

[2] In 1893 the London Positivist Committee founded *The Positivist Review*. But the periodical ceased publication in 1925, after having been called *Humanity* during the last two years of its life.

Lewes made a distinction between the phenomenon which is understandable simply in terms of its constituent factors and the phenomenon which emerges from its constituent factors as something new, a novelty. The former he called a 'resultant', the latter an 'emergent'. The idea of this distinction was not Lewes's invention, but he appears to have coined the term 'emergent', which was later to play a conspicuous role in the philosophy of evolution.

(iii) A more interesting figure was William Kingdon Clifford (1845–79), who from 1871 was professor of applied mathematics in University College, London. An eminent mathematician, he was also extremely interested in philosophical topics. And he was a fervent preacher of the religion of humanity.

Clifford's best known philosophical idea is probably that of 'mind-stuff', which he proposed as a means of solving the problem of the relation between the psychical and the physical and of avoiding the necessity of postulating the emergence of mind from a completely heterogeneous matter. Like other defenders of the ancient theory of panpsychism, Clifford did not mean to imply that all matter enjoys consciousness. His thesis was that the relation between the psychical and the physical is comparable to that between a read sentence and the same sentence as written or printed. There is a complete correspondence, and every atom, for example, has a psychical aspect. Emergence is not indeed excluded. For consciousness arises when a certain organization of mind-stuff has developed. But any leap from the physical to the psychical, which might seem to imply the causal activity of a creative agent, is avoided.[1]

In the field of ethics Clifford emphasized the idea of the tribal self. The individual has indeed his egoistic impulses and desires. But the concept of the human atom, the completely solitary and self-contained individual, is an abstraction. In actual fact every individual is by nature, in virtue of the tribal self, a member of the social organism, the tribe. And moral progress consists in subordinating the egoistic impulses to the interests or good of the tribe, to that which, in Darwinian language, makes the tribe most fit for survival. Conscience is the voice of the tribal self; and the

---

[1] As Clifford presupposed something like the phenomenalism of Hume, he had to maintain that impressions or sensations, composed of mind-stuff, can exist antecedently to consciousness. When consciousness arises, they become, or can become, its objects; but to be objects of consciousness is not essential for their existence.

ethical ideal is to become a public-spirited and efficient citizen. In other words, morality as described by Clifford corresponds pretty well to what Bergson was later to call 'closed morality'.

On the subject of religion Clifford was something of a fanatic. Not only did he speak of the clergy as enemies of humanity, and of Christianity as a plague, but he also attacked all belief in God. He was thus more akin to some of the writers of the French Enlightenment than to the nineteenth-century English agnostics, who were generally polite in what they said about religion and its official representatives. And he has been compared not inaptly with Nietzsche. At the same time he proclaimed a substitute religion, that of humanity, though he looked to the progress of science to establish the kingdom of man rather than to any organization on the lines proposed by Comte. Clifford did indeed speak of the 'cosmic emotion' which man can feel for the universe; but it was not his intention to replace theism by pantheism. He was concerned rather with substituting man for God, as he thought that belief in God was inimical to human progress and morality.

(iv) Clifford's successor in his chair of applied mathematics was Karl Pearson (1857–1936), who was later (1911–33) Galton professor of eugenics in the University of London.[1] In Pearson's writings we find a clear exposition of the positivist spirit. He was not indeed the man to look with a kindly eye on Comte's ideas about religious cult, but he was a firm believer in the omnicompetence of science. And his attitude towards metaphysics and theology was very similar to that advanced later by the neopositivists.

According to Pearson, the function of science is 'the classification of facts, the recognition of their sequence and relative significance',[2] while the scientific frame of mind is the habit of forming impersonal judgments upon the facts, judgments, that is to say, which are unbiased by personal feeling and by the idiosyncrasies of the individual temperament. This is not, however, a frame of mind which is characteristic of the metaphysician. Metaphysics, in fact, is poetry which masquerades as something else. 'The poet is a valued member of the community, for he is known to be a poet. . . . The metaphysician is a poet, often a very great one, but unfortunately he is not known to be a poet, because he strives to

---

[1] Sir Francis Galton (1822–1911), a cousin of Darwin, was the founder of the science of eugenics and envisaged the deliberate application in human society of the principle of selection which works automatically in Nature.

[2] *The Grammar of Science*, p. 6 (2nd edition, revised and enlarged, 1900).

clothe his poetry in the language of reason, and hence it follows that he is liable to be a dangerous member of the community.'[1] Rudolf Carnap was to expound exactly the same point of view.

What, then, are the facts which form the basis for scientific judgment? Ultimately they are simply sense-impressions or sensations. These are stored up in the brain, which acts as a kind of telephone exchange; and we project groups of impressions outside ourselves and speak of these as external objects. 'As such we call it [a group thus projected] a *phenomenon*, and in practical life term it *real*.'[2] What lies behind sense-impressions, we do not and cannot know. The claims of philosophers to have penetrated to things-in-themselves are completely bogus. Indeed, we cannot with propriety even raise the question what causes sense-impressions. For the causal relation is simply a relation of regular sequence between phenomena. Pearson therefore prefers the term 'sensations' to 'sense-impressions', as the latter term naturally suggests the causal activity of an unknown agent.

Obviously, Pearson does not intend to say that science consists simply of noting sensations or sense-impressions. Concepts are derived from sensations; and deductive inference is an essential feature of scientific method. But science is grounded in sensations and it also terminates in them, in the sense that we test the conclusions of an inference by the process of verification. As a body of propositions science is a mental construction, but it rests at either end, so to speak, on sense-impressions.

The statement that science is a mental construction is to be taken literally. On the level of pre-scientific thought the permanent physical object is, as we have seen, a mental construct. And on the level of scientific thought both laws and scientific entities are both mental constructs. The descriptive laws of science[3] are general formulas constructed for economy of thought, and 'the logic man finds in the universe is but the reflection of his own reasoning faculty'.[4] As for postulated entities such as atoms, the term 'atom' denotes neither an observed object nor a thing-in-itself. 'No physicist ever saw or felt an individual atom. Atom and molecule are intellectual conceptions by aid of which physicists

---

[1] *The Grammar of Science*, p. 17.
[2] *Ibid.*, p. 64.
[3] Science, Pearson insists, is purely descriptive, and not explanatory. Scientific laws 'simply *describe*, they never explain the routine of our perceptions, the sense-impressions we project into an "outside world" ', *ibid.*, p. 99.
[4] *Ibid.*, p. 91. No argument from 'design' to the existence of God, therefore, could ever be valid.

classify phenomena, and formulate the relationships between their sequences.'[1] In other words, it is not sufficient to write off metaphysics as a possible source of knowledge about things-in-themselves. Science itself needs to be purified of its superstitions and of the tendency to think that its useful concepts refer to hidden entities or forces.

The beneficent social effects of science are strongly emphasized by Pearson. In addition to the technical application of scientific knowledge and its use in special departments such as that of eugenics, there is the general educative effect of scientific method. 'Modern science, as training the mind to an exact and impartial analysis of facts, is an education specially fitted to promote sound citizenship.'[2] Indeed, Pearson goes so far as to quote with approval a remark by Clifford to the effect that scientific thought is human progress itself, and not simply an accompaniment to or condition of such progress.

On the basis, therefore, of a phenomenalism which stood in the tradition of Hume and J. S. Mill Pearson developed a theory of science akin to that of Ernst Mach.[3] In fact, Mach dedicated to Pearson his *Beiträge zur Analyse der Empfindungen*. Common to both men is the idea of science as enabling us to predict and as practising, for this purpose, a policy of economy of thought by linking phenomena in terms of the fewest and simplest concepts possible. And both men interpret unobserved scientific entities as mental constructions. Further, as both Pearson and Mach resolve phenomena ultimately into sensations, we seem to arrive at the odd conclusion that though science is purely descriptive, there is really no world to be described, apart from the contents of consciousness. Thus empiricism, which began by stressing the experimental foundations of all knowledge, ends, through its phenomenalistic analysis of experience, in having no world left, outside the sphere of sensations. To put the matter in another way, empiricism started with the demand for respect for facts and then went on to resolve facts into sensations.

9. Generally speaking, the thinkers mentioned in this chapter can be said to have given expression to a vivid recognition of the part played by scientific method in the enormous increase in man's knowledge of the world. And it is understandable that this recognition was accompanied by the conviction that scientific

---

[1] *Ibid.*, p. 95.   [2] *Ibid.*, p. 9.
[3] See Vol. VII of this *History*, p. 359.

method was the only means of acquiring anything that could properly be called knowledge. Science, they thought, continually extends the frontiers of human knowledge; and if there is anything which lies beyond the reach of science, it is unknowable. Metaphysics and theology claim to make true statements about the metaphenomenal; but their claims are bogus.

In other words, the growth of a genuinely scientific outlook is necessarily accompanied by a growth of agnosticism. Religious belief belongs to the childhood of the human race, not to a truly adult mentality. We cannot indeed prove that there is no reality beyond the phenomena, the relations between which are studied by the scientist. Science is concerned with description, not with ultimate explanations. And there may be, for all we know, such an explanation. Indeed, the more phenomena are reduced to sensations or sense-impressions, the more difficult it is to avoid the concept of a metaphenomenal reality. But in any case a reality of this kind could not be known. And the adult mind simply accepts this fact and embraces agnosticism.

With Romanes, it is true, agnosticism came to mean something much more than a mere formal acknowledgment of the impossibility of proving the non-existence of God. But with the more positivist-minded thinkers religion, as far as the adult man was concerned, was deprived of intellectual content. That is to say, it would not comprise belief in the truth of propositions about God. In so far as religion could be retained by the adult mind, it would be reduced to an emotive element. But the emotive attitude would be directed either to the cosmos, as the object of cosmic emotion or feeling, or to humanity, as in the so-called religion of humanity. In fine, the emotive element in religion would be detached from the concept of God and re-directed elsewhere, traditional religion being something that should be left behind in the onward march of scientific knowledge.

We can say, therefore, that a large number of thinkers considered in this chapter were forerunners of the so-called scientific humanists of today, who look on religious belief as lacking any rational support and tend to emphasize the alleged detrimental effect of religion on human progress and morality. Obviously, if one is convinced that man is essentially related to God as his last end, one will question the propriety of the use of the term 'humanism' for any atheistic philosophy of man. But if one regards the movement of evolution in human society as simply an advance in the scientific knowledge and control by man both of his environment and of himself, one can hardly keep any room for religion in so far as it directs man's attention to the transcendent. Scientism is necessarily opposed to traditional religion.

A rather different point of view was advanced by Benjamin Kidd (1858–1916), author of the once popular works *Social Evolution* (1894), *The Principles of Western Civilization* (1902), and *The Science of Power* (1918). In his opinion natural selection in human society tends to favour the growth of man's emotional and affective rather than of his intellectual qualities. And as religion is grounded on the emotive aspects of human nature, it is not surprising if we find that religious peoples tend to prevail over communities in the struggle for existence. For religion encourages, in a way that science can never do, altruism and devotion to the interests of the community. In its ethical aspects especially religion is the most potent of social forces. And the highest expression of the religious consciousness is Christianity, on which Western civilization is built.

In other words, Kidd belittled the reason as a constructive force in social evolution and laid the emphasis on feeling. And as he deprived religion of its intellectual content and interpreted it as the most powerful expression of the emotive aspect of man's nature, he depicted it as an essential factor in human progress. Hostile criticism of religion by the destructive reason was thus for him an attack on progress.

Kidd's recognition of the influence of religion in human history was obviously quite justified. But the emphasis which he placed on the emotive aspects of religion laid him open to the retort that religious beliefs belong to the class of emotively-sustained myths which have as a matter of fact exercised a great influence but the need of which should be outgrown by the adult mentality. Kidd would answer, of course, that such a retort presupposes that progress is secured by the exercise of the critical reason, whereas in his view progress is secured by the development of the emotional and affective aspects of man, not by the development of a reason which is destructive rather than constructive. It seems, however, to be obvious that though the emotive aspects of man are essential to his nature, reason should retain control. And if religion has no rational warrant at all, it is necessarily suspect. Further, though the influence exercised by religions on human societies is an undoubted fact, it by no means necessarily follows that this influence has been invariably beneficial. We need rational principles of discrimination.

There is, however, one main belief which is common to both Kidd and those whom he attacked, namely the belief that in the struggle for existence the principle of natural selection works automatically for progress.[1] And it is precisely this dogma of progress which has been called in question in the course of the twentieth century. In view of the cataclysmic events of this century we can hardly retain a serene confidence in the beneficent effects of collective emotion. But, equally, we find it difficult to suppose that the advance of science, taken by itself, is synonymous with social progress. There is the all-important question of the purposes to be realized by scientific knowledge. And consideration of this question takes us outside the sphere of descriptive science. Obviously, we should all agree that science should be used in the service of man. But the question arises, how are we to interpret man? And our answer to this question will involve metaphysics, either explicit or implicit. The attempt to by-pass or exclude metaphysics will often be found to involve a concealed metaphysical assumption, an unavowed theory of being. In other words, the idea that scientific advance pushes metaphysics out of the picture is mistaken. Metaphysics simply reappears in the form of concealed assumptions.

[1] As we have seen, T. H. Huxley was an exception, inasmuch as he believed that moral progress runs counter to the process of evolution in Nature.

CHAPTER V

THE PHILOSOPHY OF HERBERT SPENCER

Life and writings—The nature of philosophy and its basic concepts and principles—The general law of evolution: the alternation of evolution and dissolution—Sociology and politics —Relative and absolute ethics—The Unknowable in religion and science—Final comments.

1. IN 1858, the year preceding that of the publication of Darwin's *The Origin of Species*, Herbert Spencer mapped out a plan for a system which was to be based on the law of evolution or, as he expressed it, the law of progress. He is one of the few British thinkers who have deliberately attempted the construction of a comprehensive philosophical system. He is also one of the few British philosophers who have acquired a world-wide reputation during their lifetime. Seizing on an idea which was already in the air and to which Darwin gave an empirical basis in a restricted field, Spencer turned it into the key-idea of a synoptic vision of the world and of human life and conduct, an optimistic vision which appeared to justify nineteenth-century belief in human progress and which made of Spencer one of the major prophets of an era.

Though, however, Spencer remains one of the great figures of the Victorian age, he now gives the impression of being one of the most dated of philosophers. Unlike Mill, whose writings well repay study, whether one agrees or not with the views expressed. Spencer is little read nowadays. It is not merely that the idea of evolution has become common coin and no longer arouses much excitement. It is rather that after the brutal challenges of the twentieth century we find it difficult to see how the scientific hypothesis of evolution, taken by itself, can provide any adequate basis for that optimistic faith in human progress which was, generally speaking, a characteristic feature of Spencer's thought. On the one hand positivism has changed its character and fights shy of explicit and comprehensive world-visions. On the other hand those philosophers who believe that the trend of evolution is in some real sense beneficent to man generally appeal to metaphysical theories which were foreign to the mind of Spencer. Moreover, while Mill not only dealt with many problems which are still examined by British philosophers but also treated them in a way which is still considered relevant, Spencer is notable for his large-scale exploration of one leading idea rather than for any detailed analyses. However, though Spencer's thought is so closely wedded to the Victorian era that it can scarcely be described as a living influence today, the fact remains that he was one of the leading representative members of the nineteenth century. Hence he cannot be passed over in silence.

Herbert Spencer was born at Derby on April 27th, 1820. Whereas Mill began Greek at the age of three, Spencer admits that at the age of thirteen he knew nothing worth mentioning of either Latin or Greek. By the age of sixteen, however, he had at any rate acquired some knowledge of mathematics; and after a few months as a schoolmaster at Derby he became a civil engineer employed by the Birmingham and Gloucester Railway. When the line was completed in 1841, Spencer was discharged. 'Got the sack—very glad', as he noted in his diary. But though in 1843 he moved to London to take up a literary career, he returned for a short while to the service of the railways and also tried his hand at inventions.

In 1848 Spencer became sub-editor of the *Economist*, and he entered into relations of friendship with G. H. Lewes, Huxley, Tyndall and George Eliot. With Lewes in particular he discussed the theory of evolution; and among the articles which he wrote anonymously for Lewes's *Leader* there was one on 'The Development Hypothesis', in which the idea of evolution was expounded on Lamarckian lines. In 1851 he published *Social Statics* and in 1855, at his own expense, *The Principles of Psychology*. At this time the state of his health was causing him serious concern, and he made several excursions to France, where he met Auguste Comte. He was able, however, to publish a collection of his essays in 1857.

At the beginning of 1858 Spencer drew up a scheme for *A System of Synthetic Philosophy*; and the prospectus, distributed in 1860, envisaged ten volumes. *First Principles* appeared in one volume in 1862, and *The Principles of Biology* in two volumes in 1864–7. *The Principles of Psychology*, originally published in one volume in 1855, appeared in two volumes in 1870–2, while the three volumes of *The Principles of Sociology* were published in 1876–96. *The Data of Ethics* (1879) was subsequently included with two other parts to form the first volume of *The Principles of Ethics* (1892), while the second volume of this work (1893) utilized

Justice (1891). Spencer also published new editions of several volumes of the *System*. For example, the sixth edition of *First Principles* appeared in 1900, while a revised and enlarged edition of *The Principles of Biology* was published in 1898–9.

Spencer's *System of Synthetic Philosophy* constituted a remarkable achievement, carried through in spite of bad health and, at first at any rate, of serious financial difficulties. Intellectually, he was a self-made man; and the composition of his great work involved writing on a number of subjects which he had never really studied. He had to collect his data from various sources, and he then interpreted them in the light of the idea of evolution. As for the history of philosophy, he knew little about it, except from secondary sources. He did indeed make more than one attempt to read Kant's first *Critique*; but when he came to the doctrine of the subjectivity of space and time, he laid the book aside. He had little appreciation or understanding of points of view other than his own. However, if he had not practised what we might call a rigid economy of thought, it is unlikely he would ever have completed his self-imposed task.

Of Spencer's other publications we can mention *Education* (1861), a small but very successful book, *The Man Versus the State* (1884), a vigorous polemic against what the author regarded as the threatening slavery, and the posthumous *Autobiography* (1904). In 1885 Spencer published in America *The Nature and Reality of Religion*, comprising a controversy between himself and the positivist Frederic Harrison. But the work was suppressed, as Harrison protested against the re-publication of his articles without permission, especially as an introduction in support of Spencer's position by a Professor Yeomans had been included in the volume.

With the exception of membership of the Athenaeum Club (1868) Spencer consistently refused all honours. When invited to stand for the chair of mental philosophy and logic at University College, London, he refused; and he also declined membership of the Royal Society. He seems to have felt that when he had really had need of such offers they had not been made, and that when they were made, he no longer had need of them, his reputation being already established. As for honours offered by the government, his opposition to social distinctions of this kind militated against acceptance, quite apart from his annoyance at the lateness of the offers.

Spencer died on December 8th, 1903. At the time of his death he was extremely unpopular in his own country, mainly because of his opposition to the Boer War (1899–1902), which he regarded as an expression of the militaristic spirit that he so much hated.[1] Abroad, however, there was considerable criticism of English indifference to the passing of one of the country's outstanding figures. And in Italy the Chamber adjourned on receiving the news of Spencer's death.

2. Spencer's general account of the relation between philosophy and science bears a marked resemblance to that given by the classical positivists such as Auguste Comte. Both science and philosophy treat of phenomena, of, that is to say, the finite, conditioned and classifiable. True, in Spencer's opinion phenomena are manifestations to consciousness of infinite, unconditioned Being. But as knowledge involves relating and classification, whereas infinite, unconditional Being is by its very nature unique and unclassifiable, to say that such Being transcends the sphere of phenomena is to say that it transcends the sphere of the knowable.[2] Hence it cannot be investigated by the philosopher any more than by the scientist. Metaphenomenal or 'ultimate' causes lie outside the reach of both philosophy and science.

If, therefore, we are to distinguish between philosophy and science, we cannot do so simply in terms of the objects of which they treat. For both are concerned with phenomena. We have to introduce the idea of degrees of generalization. 'Science' is the name of the family of particular sciences. And though every science, as distinct from the unco-ordinated knowledge of particular facts, involves generalization, even the widest of such generalizations are partial in comparison with those universal truths of philosophy which serve to unify the sciences. 'The truths of Philosophy thus bear the same relation to the highest scientific truths, that each of these bears to lower scientific truths. . . . Knowledge of the lowest kind is un-unified knowledge; Science is *partially-unified* knowledge; Philosophy is *completely-unified* knowledge.'[3]

The universal truths or widest generalizations of philosophy can be considered in themselves, as 'products of exploration'.[4] And we are then concerned with general philosophy. Or the universal truths can be considered according to their active role as 'instruments of exploration'.[5] That is to say, they can be considered as

---

[1] Spencer's attitude to the Boer War prompted an attack on him by *The Times*.
[2] We shall return later to Spencer's doctrine of the 'unknowable'.
[3] *First Principles*, p. 119 (6th edition).   [4] *Ibid.*, p. 120.   [5] *Ibid.*

truths in the light of which we investigate different specific areas of phenomena, such as the data of ethics and sociology. And we are then concerned with special philosophy. Spencer's *First Principles* is devoted to general philosophy, while subsequent volumes of the *System* deal with the parts of special philosophy.

Taken by itself, Spencer's account of the relation between science and philosophy in terms of degrees of unification tends to suggest that in his view the basic concepts of philosophy are derived by generalization from the particular sciences. But this is not the case. For he insists that there are fundamental concepts and assumptions which are involved in all thinking. Let us suppose that a philosopher decides to take one particular datum as the point of departure for his reflections, and that he imagines that by acting in this way he is making no assumptions. In actual fact the choice of one particular datum implies that there are other data which the philosopher might have chosen. And this involves the concept of existence other than the existence actually asserted. Again, no particular thing can be known except as like some other things, as classifiable in virtue of a common attribute, and as different from or unlike other things. In fine, the choice of one particular datum involves a number of 'unacknowledged postulates',[1] which together provide the outlines of a general philosophical theory. 'The developed intelligence is framed upon certain organized and consolidated conceptions of which it cannot divest itself; and which it can no more stir without using than the body can stir without help of its limbs.'[2]

It can hardly be claimed that Spencer makes his position crystal clear. For he speaks of 'tacit assumptions',[3] 'unavowed data',[4] 'unacknowledged postulates',[5] 'certain organized and consolidated conceptions',[6] and 'fundamental intuitions',[7] as though the meanings of these phrases stood in no need of further elucidation and as though they all meant the same thing. It is indeed clear that he does not intend to assert a Kantian theory of the *a priori*. The fundamental concepts and assumptions have an experimental basis. And sometimes Spencer speaks as though it were a question of the individual experience or consciousness. He says, for example, that 'we cannot avoid accepting as true the verdict of consciousness that some manifestations are like one another and some are unlike one another'.[8] The situation is

---

[1] *Ibid.*, p. 123.   [2] *Ibid.*   [3] *Ibid.*, p. 122.   [4] *Ibid.*, p. 123.
[5] *Ibid.*   [6] *Ibid.*   [7] *Ibid.*   [8] *Ibid.*, p. 125.

complicated, however, by the fact that Spencer accepts the idea of a relative *a priori*, that is, of concepts and assumptions which are, from the genetic point of view, the product of the accumulated experience of the race[1] but which are *a priori* in relation to a given individual mind, in the sense that they came to it with the force of 'intuitions'.

The basic assumptions of the process of thought have to be taken provisionally as unquestionable. They can be justified or validated only by their results, that is, by showing the agreement or congruity between the experience which the assumptions logically lead us to expect and the experiences which we actually have. Indeed, 'the complete establishment of the congruity becomes the same thing as the complete unification of knowledge in which Philosophy reaches its goal'.[2] Thus general philosophy makes explicit the basic concepts and assumptions, while special philosophy shows their agreement with the actual phenomena in distinct fields or areas of experience.

Now, according to Spencer 'knowing is classifying, or grasping the like and separating the unlike'.[3] And as likeness and unlikeness are relations, we can say that all thinking is relational, that '*relation* is the universal form of thought'.[4] We can distinguish, however, between two kinds of relations, those of sequence and those of co-existence.[5] And each gives rise to an abstract idea. 'The abstract of all sequences is Time. The abstract of all co-existences is Space.'[6] Time and Space are not indeed original forms of consciousness in an absolute sense. But as the generation of these ideas takes place through an organization of experiences which proceeds throughout the entire evolution of mind or intelligence, they can have a relatively *a priori* character, as far as a given individual mind is concerned.

Our concept of Space is fundamentally that of co-existent positions which offer no resistance. And it is derived by abstraction from the concept of Matter, which in its simplest form is that of co-existent positions which offer resistance. In turn, the concept of Matter is derived from an experience of force. For 'forces, standing in certain co-relations, form the whole content of our

---

[1] Some of these may have their remoter origin in animal experience.
[2] *First Principles*, p. 125.   [3] *Ibid.*, p. 127.   [4] *Ibid.*, p. 145.
[5] In Spencer's opinion the idea of co-existence is derived from that of sequence, inasmuch as we find that the terms of certain relations of sequence can be presented with equal facility in reverse order. Co-existence cannot be an original datum of a consciousness which consists in serial states.
[6] *First Principles*, p. 146.

idea of Matter'.[1] Similarly, though the developed concepts of
Motion involves the ideas of Space, Time and Matter, the rudimentary consciousness of Motion is simply that of 'serial
impressions of force'.[2]

Spencer argues, therefore, that psychological analysis of the
concepts of Time, Space, Matter and Motion shows that they are
all based on experiences of Force. And the conclusion is that 'we
come down, then, finally to Force, as the ultimate of ultimates'.[3]
The principle of the indestructibility of matter is really that of the
indestructibility of force. Similarly, all proofs of the principle of
the continuity of motion 'involve the postulate that the quantity
of Energy is constant',[4] energy being the force possessed by matter
in motion. And in the end we arrive at the principle of the persistence of Force, 'which, as being the basis of science, cannot be
established by science',[5] but transcends demonstration, a principle which has as its corollary that of the uniformity of law, the
persistence of relations between forces.

It may be objected that such principles as that of the indestructibility of matter belong to science rather than to philosophy. But Spencer answers that they are 'truths which unify
concrete phenomena belonging to all divisions of Nature, and so
must be components of that all-embracing conception of things
which Philosophy seeks'.[6] Further, though the word 'force'
ordinarily signifies 'the consciousness of muscular tension',[7] the
feeling of effort which we have when we set something in motion
or resist a pressure is a symbol of Absolute Force. And when we
speak of the persistence of Force, 'we really mean the persistence
of some Cause which transcends our knowledge and conception'.[8]
How we can intelligibly predicate persistence of an unknowable
reality is not perhaps immediately evident. But if the assertion of
the persistence of Force really means what Spencer says that it
means, it clearly becomes a philosophical principle, even apart
from the fact that its character as a universal truth would in any
case qualify it for inclusion among the truths of philosophy
according to Spencer's account of the relation between philosophy
and science.

3. Though, however, such general principles as the indestructibility of matter, the continuity of motion and the persistence of
force are components of the synthesis which philosophy seeks to

[1] *Ibid.*, p. 149.   [2] *Ibid.*, p. 151.   [3] *Ibid.*
[4] *Ibid.*, p. 167.   [5] *Ibid.*, p. 175.   [6] *Ibid.*, p. 249.
[7] *Ibid.*, p. 175.   [8] *Ibid.*, p. 176.

achieve, they do not, even when taken together, constitute this synthesis. For we require a formula or law which specifies the course of the transformations undergone by matter and motion, and which thus serves to unify all the processes of change which are examined in the several particular sciences. That is to say, if we assume that there is no such thing as absolute rest or permanence but that every object is constantly undergoing change, whether by receiving or losing motion or by changes in the relations between its parts, we need to ascertain the general law of the continuous redistribution of matter and motion.

Spencer finds what he is looking for in what he calls indiscriminately a 'formula', 'law' or 'definition' of evolution. 'Evolution is an integration of matter and concomitant dissipation of motion; during which the matter passes from a relatively indefinite, incoherent homogeneity to a relatively definite, coherent heterogeneity; and during which the retained motion undergoes a parallel transformation.'[1] This law can be established deductively, by deduction from the persistence of force. It can also be established or confirmed inductively. For whether we contemplate the development of solar systems out of the nebular mass, or that of more highly organized and complex living bodies out of more primitive organisms, or that of man's psychological life, or the growth of language, or the evolution of social organization, we find everywhere a movement from relative indefiniteness to relative definiteness, from incoherence to coherence, together with a movement of progressive differentiation, the movement from relative homogeneity to relative heterogeneity. For example in the evolution of the living body we see a progressive structural and functional differentiation.

But this is only one side of the picture. For the integration of matter is accompanied by a dissipation of motion. And the process of evolution tends towards a state of equilibrium, of a balance of forces, which is succeeded by dissolution or disintegration. For example, the human body dissipates and loses its energies, dies and disintegrates; any given society loses its vigour and decays; and the heat of the sun is gradually dissipated.

Spencer is careful to avoid claiming that we can legitimately extrapolate what is true of a relatively closed system to the totality of things, the universe as a whole. We cannot, for example,

---

[1] *First Principles*, p. 367. In a note Spencer remarks that the word 'relatively', omitted in the original text, needs to be inserted in two places as above.

argue with certainty from the running-down, so to speak, of our solar system to the running-down of the universe. And it is possible, for all we know, that when life has been extinguished on our planet through the dissipation of the sun's heat, it will be in process of development in some other part of the universe. In fine, we are not entitled to argue that what happens to a part *must* happen to the whole.

At the same time, if there is an alternation of evolution and dissolution in the totality of things, we must 'entertain the conception of Evolutions that have filled an immeasurable past and Evolutions that will fill an immeasurable future'.[1] And if this represents Spencer's personal opinion, we can say that he gives an up-to-date version of certain early Greek cosmologies, with their ideas of a cyclic process. In any case there is a rhythm of evolution and dissolution in the parts, even if we are not in a position to make dogmatic assertions about the whole. And though at first Spencer spoke about the law of evolution as the law of progress, his belief in alternations of evolution and dissolution evidently set limits to his optimism.

4. Spencer's ideal of a complete philosophical synthesis demands the inclusion of a systematic treatment of the inorganic world in the light of the idea of evolution. And he remarks that if this topic had been treated in the *System of Philosophy*, it 'would have occupied two volumes, one dealing with Astrogeny and the other with Geogeny'.[2] In point of fact, however, Spencer confines himself, in special philosophy, to biology, psychology, sociology and ethics. He alludes, of course, to astronomical, physical and chemical topics, but the *System* contains no systematic treatment of evolution in the inorganic sphere.

As limitations of space exclude a recapitulation of all the parts of Spencer's system, I propose to pass over biology and psychology and to make some remarks in this section about his sociological and political ideas, devoting the following section to the subject of ethics.

The sociologist is concerned with the growth, structures, functions and products of human societies.[3] The possibility of a science of sociology follows from the fact that we can find regular sequences among social phenomena, which permit prediction; and

---

[1] *Ibid.*, p. 506.　　　　[2] *The Principles of Sociology*, I, p. 3.
[3] The study of what Spencer calls super-organic evolution, which presupposes organic or biological evolution, would include, if understood in the widest sense, the study of, for example, the societies of bees and ants.

it is not excluded by the fact that social laws are statistical and predictions in this field approximate. 'Only a moiety of science is exact science.'[1] It is the possibility of generalization which is required, not quantitative exactitude. As for the utility of sociology, Spencer claims in a somewhat vague way that if we can discern an order in the structural and functional changes through which societies pass, 'knowledge of that order can scarcely fail to affect our judgments as to what is progressive and what retrograde—what is desirable, what is practicable, what is Utopian'.[2]

When we consider the struggle for existence in the general process of evolution, we find obvious analogies between the inorganic, organic and super-organic (social) spheres. The behaviour of an inanimate object depends on the relations between its own forces and the external forces to which it is exposed. Similarly, the behaviour of an organic body is the product of the combined influences of its intrinsic nature and of its environment, both inorganic and organic. Again, every human society 'displays phenomena that are ascribable to the character of its units and to the conditions under which they exist'.[3]

It is indeed true that the two sets of factors, intrinsic and extrinsic, do not remain static. For example, man's powers, physical, emotional and intellectual, have developed in the course of history, while evolving society has produced remarkable changes in its organic and inorganic environment. Again, the products of evolving society, its institutions and cultural creations, bring fresh influences into being. Further, the more human societies develop, so much the more do they react on one another, so that the super-organic environment occupies a position of even greater importance. But in spite of the growing complexity of the situation an analogous interplay of forces, intrinsic and extrinsic, is discernible in all three spheres.

Though, however, there is continuity between the inorganic, organic and super-organic spheres, there is also discontinuity. If there is similarity, there is also dissimilarity. Consider, for example, the idea of a society as an organism. As in the case of an organic body in the proper sense, the growth of society is accompanied by a progressive differentiation of structures, which results in a progressive differentiation of functions. But this point of similarity between the organic body and human society is also

---

[1] *The Study of Sociology*, p. 44 (26th thousand, 1907).   [2] *Ibid.*, p. 70.
[3] *The Principles of Sociology*, I, pp. 9–10.

a point of dissimilarity between them both and the inorganic body. For according to Spencer the actions of the different parts of an inorganic thing cannot properly be regarded as functions. Further, there is an important difference between the process of differentiation in an organic body and that in the social organism. For in the latter we do not find that kind of differentiation which in the former results in one part alone becoming the organ of intelligence and in some parts becoming sense-organs while others do not. In the organic body 'consciousness is concentrated in a small part of the aggregate', whereas in the social organism 'it is diffused throughout the aggregate: all the units possess the capacity for happiness and misery, if not in equal degrees, still in degrees that approximate'.[1]

An enthusiast for the interpretation of political society as an organism might, of course, try to find detailed analogies between differentiation of functions in the organic body and in society. But this might easily lead him into speaking, for example, as though the government were analogous to the brain and as though the other parts of society should leave all thinking to the government and simply obey its decisions. And this is precisely the sort of conclusion which Spencer wishes to avoid. Hence he insists on the relative independence of the individual members of a political society and denies the contention that society is an organism in the sense that it is more than the sum of its members and possesses an end which is different from the ends of the members. 'As, then, there is no social sensorium, it results that the welfare of the aggregate, considered apart from that of the members, is not an end to be sought. The society exists for the benefit of its members; not its members for the benefit of society.'[2] In other words, we can say that the arms and the legs exist for the good of the whole body. But in the case of society we have to say that the whole exists for the parts. Spencer's conclusion at any rate is clear. And even if his arguments are sometimes obscure and perplexing, it is also clear that in his opinion the analogy of an organism, as applied to a political society, is not only misleading but also dangerous.

The situation is in fact this. Spencer's determination to use the idea of evolution throughout all fields of phenomena leads him to speak of political society, the State, as a super-organism. But as he is a resolute champion of individual liberty against the claims

[1] *Ibid.*, I, p. 479.   [2] *Ibid.*

and encroachment of the State, he tries to deprive this analogy of its sting by pointing out essential differences between the organic body and the body political. And he does this by maintaining that while political development is a process of integration, in the sense that social groups become larger and individual wills are merged together, it is also a movement from homogeneity to heterogeneity, so that differentiation tends to increase. For example, with the advance of civilization towards the modern industrialized State the class-divisions of relatively more primitive societies tend, so Spencer believes, to become less rigid and even to break down. And this is a sign of progress.

Spencer's point depends in part on his thesis that 'the state of homogeneity is an unstable state; and where there is already some heterogeneity, the tendency is towards greater heterogeneity'.[1] Given this idea of the movement of evolution, it obviously follows that a society in which differentiation is relatively greater is more evolved than one in which there is relatively less differentiation. At the same time it is clear that Spencer's point of view also depends on a judgment of value, namely that a society in which individual liberty is highly developed is intrinsically more admirable and praiseworthy than a society in which there is less individual liberty. True, Spencer believes that a society which embodies the principle of individual liberty possesses a greater survival-value than societies which do not embody the principle. And this can be understood as a purely factual judgment. But it seems obvious to me at any rate that Spencer considers the first type of society to be more deserving of survival because of its greater intrinsic value.

If we pass over Spencer's account of primitive societies and their development, we can say that he concentrates most of his attention on the transition from the militaristic or militant type of society to the industrial type. The militant society is basically 'one in which the army is the nation mobilized while the nation is the quiescent army, and which, therefore, acquires a structure common to army and nation'.[2] There can indeed be development within this kind of society. For example, the military leader becomes the civil or political head, as in the case of the Roman emperor; and in the course of time the army becomes a specialized professional branch of the community instead of being co-extensive with the adult male population. But in the militant

---

[1] *The Principles of Sociology*, II, p. 288.   [2] *Ibid.*, I, p. 577.

society in general integration and cohesion are dominant features. The primary aim is the preservation of the society, while the preservation of individual members is a matter for concern only as a means to the attainment of the primary aim. Again, in this kind of society there is constant regulation of conduct, and 'the individuality of each member has to be so subordinated in life, liberty, and property, that he is largely, or completely *owned* by the State'.[1] Further, as the militant type of society aims at self-sufficiency, political autonomy tends to be accompanied by economic autonomy.[2] The Germany of National Socialism would doubtless have represented for Spencer a good example of a revival of the militant type of society in the modern industrial era.

Spencer does not deny that the militant type of society had an essential role to play in the process of evolution considered as a struggle for existence in which the fittest survive. But he maintains that though inter-social conflict was necessary for the formation and growth of societies, the development of civilization renders war increasingly unnecessary. The militant type of society thus becomes an anachronism, and a transition is required to what Spencer calls the industrial type of society. This does not mean that the struggle for existence ceases. But it changes its form, becoming 'the industrial struggle for existence',[3] in which that society is best fitted to survive which produces 'the largest number of the best individuals—individuals best adapted for life in the industrial state'.[4] In this way Spencer tries to avoid the accusation that when he has arrived at the concept of the industrial type of society, he abandons the ideas of the struggle for existence and of the survival of the fittest.

It would be a great mistake to suppose that by the industrial type of society Spencer means simply a society in which the citizens are occupied, exclusively or predominantly, in the economic life of production and distribution. For an industrial society in this narrow sense would be compatible with a thorough-going regulation of labour by the State. And it is precisely this element of compulsion which Spencer is concerned to exclude. On the economic level, he is referring to a society dominated by the principle of *laissez-faire*. Hence in his view socialist and communist

---

[1] *Ibid.*, II, p. 607.
[2] The militant type of society also tends to manifest itself in characteristic forms of law and judicial procedure.
[3] *The Principles of Sociology*, II, p. 610.   [4] *Ibid.*

States would be very far from exemplifying the essence of the industrial type of society. The function of the State is to maintain individual freedom and rights, and to adjudicate, when necessary, between conflicting claims. It is not the business of the State to interfere positively with the lives and conduct of the citizens, except when interference is required for the maintenance of internal peace.

In other words, in the ideal type of industrial society, as Spencer interprets the term, emphasis is shifted from the totality, the society as a whole, to its members considered as individuals. 'Under the industrial *régime* the citizen's individuality, instead of being sacrificed by the society, has to be defended by the society. Defence of his individuality becomes the society's essential duty.'[1] That is to say, the cardinal function of the State becomes that of equitably adjusting conflicting claims between individual citizens and preventing the infringement of one man's liberty by another.

Spencer's belief in the universal applicability of the law of evolution obviously committed him to maintaining that the movement of evolution tends to the development of the industrial type of State, which he regarded, rather over-optimistically, as an essentially peaceful society. But the tendencies to interference and regulation by the State which were showing themselves in the last decades of his life led him to express his fear of what he called 'the coming slavery'[2] and to attack violently any tendency on the part of the State or of one of its organs to regard itself as omnicompetent. 'The great political superstition of the past was the divine right of kings. The great political superstition of the present is the divine right of parliaments.'[3] Again, 'the function of Liberalism in the past was that of putting a limit to the powers of kings. The function of true Liberalism in the future will be that of putting a limit to the powers of Parliaments.'[4]

Obviously, in this resolute attack on 'the coming slavery' Spencer could not appeal simply to the automatic working-out of any law of evolution. His words are clearly inspired by a passionate conviction in the value of individual liberty and initiative, a conviction which reflected the character and temperament of a man who had never at any period of his life been inclined to bow before constituted authority simply because it was authority. And it is a notorious fact that Spencer carried his attack on what

---

[1] *The Principles of Sociology*, ii, p. 607.
[2] This is the title of one of his essays.
[3] *The Man Versus the State*, p. 78 (19th thousand, 1910).   [4] *Ibid.*, p. 107.

he regarded as encroachments by the State on private liberty to the extent of condemning factory legislation, sanitary inspection by government officials, State management of the Post Office, poor relief by the State and State education. Needless to say, he did not condemn reform as such or charitable relief work or the running of hospitals and schools. But his insistence was always on voluntary organization of such projects, as opposed to State action, management and control. In short, his ideal was that of a society in which, as he put it, the individual would be everything and the State nothing, in contrast with the militant type of society in which the State is everything and the individual nothing.

Spencer's equation of the industrial type of society with peace-loving and anti-militaristic society is likely to strike us as odd, unless we make the equation true by definition. And his extreme defence of the policy of *laissez-faire* is likely to appear to us as eccentric, or at least as a hangover from a bygone outlook. He does not seem to have understood, as Mill came to understand, at least in part, and as was understood more fully by an idealist such as T. H. Green, that social legislation and so-called interference by the State may very well be required to safeguard the legitimate claims of every individual citizen to lead a decent human life.

At the same time Spencer's hostility to social legislation which nowadays is taken for granted by the vast majority of citizens in Great Britain should not blind us to the fact that he, like Mill, saw the dangers of bureaucracy and of any exaltation of the power and functions of the State which tends to stifle individual liberty and originality. To the present writer at any rate it seems that concern with the common good leads to an approval of State action to a degree far beyond what Spencer was prepared to endorse. But it should never be forgotten that the common good is not something entirely different from the good of the individual. And Spencer was doubtless quite right in thinking that it is for the good both of individuals and of society in general that citizens should be able to develop themselves freely and show initiative. We may well think that it is the business of the State to create and maintain the conditions in which individuals can develop themselves, and that this demands, for example, that the State should provide for all the means of education according to the individual's capacity for profiting by it. But once we accept the principle that the State should concern itself with positively

creating and maintaining the conditions which will make it possible
for every individual to lead a decent human life in accordance
with his or her capacities, we expose ourselves to the danger of
subsequently forgetting that the common good is not an abstract
entity to which the concrete interests of individuals have to be
ruthlessly sacrificed. And Spencer's attitude, in spite of its
eccentric exaggerations, can serve to remind us that the State
exists for man and not man for the State. Further, the State is
but one form of social organization: it is not the only legitimate
form of society. And Spencer certainly understood this fact.

As has already been indicated, Spencer's political views were
partly the expression of factual judgments, connected with his
interpretation of the general movement of evolution, and partly
an expression of judgments of value. For example, his assertion
that what he calls the industrial type of society possesses a greater
survival value than other types was partly equivalent to a
prediction that it would in fact survive, in virtue of the trend of
evolution. But it was also partly a judgment that the industrial
type of society deserved to survive, because of its intrinsic value.
Indeed, it is clear enough that with Spencer a positive evaluation
of personal liberty was the really determining factor in his view
of modern society. It is also clear that if a man is resolved that, as
far as depends on him, the type of society which respects individual
freedom and initiative *will* survive, this resolution is based
primarily on a judgment of value rather than on any theory about
the automatic working-out of a law of evolution.

5. Spencer regarded his ethical doctrine as the crown of his
system. In the preface to *The Data of Ethics* he remarks that his
first essay, on *The Proper Sphere of Government* (1842), vaguely
indicated certain general principles of right and wrong in political
conduct. And he adds that 'from that time onwards my ultimate
purpose, lying behind all proximate purposes, has been that of
finding for the principles of right and wrong in conduct at large,
a scientific basis'.[1] Belief in supernatural authority as a basis for
ethics has waned. It thus becomes all the more imperative to give
morality a scientific foundation, independent of religious beliefs.
And for Spencer this means establishing ethics on the theory of
evolution.

Conduct in general, including that of animals, consists of acts

---

[1] *The Data of Ethics*, p. V (1907 edition). This preface is reprinted in the first
volume of *The Principles of Ethics*, the reference being to p. VII (1892 edition).

adjusted to ends.[1] And the higher we proceed in the scale of evolution, the clearer evidence do we find of purposeful actions directed to the good either of the individual or of the species. But we also find that teleological activity of this kind forms part of the struggle for existence between different individuals of the same species and between different species. That is to say, one creature tries to preserve itself at the expense of another, and one species maintains itself by preying on another.

This type of purposeful conduct, in which the weaker goes to the wall, is for Spencer imperfectly evolved conduct. In perfectly evolved conduct, ethical conduct in the proper sense, antagonisms between rival groups and between individual members of one group will have been replaced by co-operation and mutual aid. Perfectly evolved conduct, however, can be achieved only in proportion as militant societies give place to permanently peaceful societies. In other words it cannot be achieved in a stable manner except in the perfectly evolved society, in which alone can the clash between egoism and altruism be overcome and transcended.

This distinction between imperfectly and perfectly evolved conduct provides the basis for a distinction between relative and absolute ethics. Absolute ethics is 'an ideal code of conduct formulating the behaviour of the completely adapted man in the completely evolved society',[2] while relative ethics is concerned with the conduct which is the nearest approximation to this ideal in the circumstances in which we find ourselves, that is, in more or less imperfectly evolved societies. According to Spencer, it is simply not true that in any set of circumstances which call for purposeful action on our part we are always faced with a choice between an action which is absolutely right and one which is absolutely wrong. For example, it may happen that circumstances are such that, however I act, I shall cause some pain to another person. And an action which causes pain to another cannot be absolutely right. In such circumstances, therefore, I have to try to estimate which possible course of action is relatively right, that is, which possible course of action will probably cause the greatest amount of good and the least amount of evil. I cannot expect to make an infallible judgment. I can only act as seems to me best, after devoting to the matter the amount of reflection which appears to be demanded by the relative importance of the issue.

[1] Purposeless actions are excluded from 'conduct'.
[2] *The Data of Ethics*, p. 238.

I can indeed bear in mind the ideal code of conduct of absolute ethics; but I cannot legitimately assume that this standard will serve as a premiss from which I can infallibly deduce what action would be relatively best in the circumstances in which I find myself.

Spencer accepts the utilitarian ethics in the sense that he takes happiness to be the ultimate end of life and measures the rightness or wrongness of actions by their relation to this end. In his opinion the 'gradual rise of a utilitarian ethic has, indeed, been inevitable'.[1] True, there was from the start a nascent utilitarianism, in the sense that some actions were always felt to be beneficial and other injurious to man and society. But in past societies ethical codes were associated with authority of some sort or another, or with the idea of divine authority and divinely imposed sanctions, whereas in the course of time ethics has gradually become independent of non-ethical beliefs, and there has been growing up a moral outlook based simply on the ascertainable natural consequences of actions. In other words, the trend of evolution in the moral sphere has been towards the development of utilitarianism. It must be added, however, that utilitarianism must be understood in such a way that room is found for the distinction between relative and absolute ethics. Indeed, the very idea of evolution suggests progress towards an ideal limit. And in this progress advance in virtue cannot be separated from social advance. 'The co-existence of a perfect man and an imperfect society is impossible.'[2]

As Spencer regards utilitarianism as the scientifically-based ethics, it is understandable that he wishes to show that it is not simply one among many mutually exclusive systems, but that it can find room for the truths contained in other systems. Thus he maintains, for example, that utilitarianism, when rightly understood, finds room for the point of view which insists on the concepts of right, wrong and obligation rather than on the attainment of happiness. Bentham may have thought that happiness is to be aimed at directly, by applying the hedonistic calculus. But he was wrong. He would indeed have been right if the attainment of happiness did not depend on the fulfilment of conditions. But in this case any action would be moral if it produced pleasure. And this notion is incompatible with the moral consciousness. In point of fact the attainment of happiness depends on the fulfilment of

[1] *The Principles of Ethics*, I, p. 318.   [2] *The Data of Ethics*, p. 241.

certain conditions, that is, on the observance of certain moral precepts or rules.[1] And it is at the fulfilment of these conditions that we ought to aim directly. Bentham thought that everyone knows what happiness is, and that it is more intelligible than, say, the principles of justice. But this view is the reverse of the truth. The principles of justice are easily intelligible, whereas it is far from easy to say what happiness is. Spencer advocates, therefore, what he calls a 'rational' utilitarianism, one which 'takes for its immediate object of pursuit conformity to certain principles which, in the nature of things, causally determine welfare'.[2]

Again, the theory that moral rules can be inductively established by observing the natural consequences of actions does not entail the conclusion that there is no truth at all in the theory of moral intuitionism. For there are indeed what can be called moral intuitions, though they are not something mysterious and inexplicable but 'the slowly organized results of experiences received by the race'.[3] What was originally an induction from experience can come in later generations to have for the individual the force of an intuition. The individual may see or feel instinctively that a certain course of action is right or wrong, though this instinctive reaction is the result of the accumulated experience of the race.

Similarly, utilitarianism can perfectly well recognize truth in the contention that the perfection of our nature is the object for which we should seek. For the trend of evolution is towards the emergence of the highest form of life. And though happiness is the supreme end, it is 'the concomitant of that highest life which every theory of moral guidance has distinctly or vaguely in view'.[4] As for the theory that virtue is the end of human conduct, this is simply one way of expressing the doctrine that our direct aim should be that of fulfilling the conditions for the attainment of the highest form of life to which the process of evolution tends. If it were attained, happiness would result.

Needless to say, Spencer could not reasonably claim to ground his ethical theory on the theory of evolution without admitting a continuity between evolution in the biological sphere and that in the moral sphere. And he maintains, for example, that 'human justice must be a further development of sub-human justice'.[5]

---

[1] Obviously, the idea of moral precepts must be understood in such a way as to admit the distinction between principles of conduct in an imperfectly evolved society and the ideal principles which would obtain in a perfectly evolved society.
[2] *The Data of Ethics*, p. 140.   [3] *Ibid.*, p. 148.   [4] *Ibid.*
[5] *Justice* (*The Principles of Ethics*, Part IV), p. 17.

At the same time, in a preface, subsequently withdrawn, to the fifth and sixth parts of *The Principles of Ethics* he admits that the doctrine of evolution has not furnished guidance to the hoped-for extent. He seems, however, never to have understood clearly that the process of evolution, considered as an historical fact, could not by itself establish the value-judgments which he brought to bear upon its interpretation. For example, even if we grant that evolution is moving towards the emergence of a certain type of human life in society and that this type is therefore shown to be the most fitted for survival, it does not necessarily follow that it is morally the most admirable type. As T. H. Huxley saw, factual fitness for survival in the struggle for existence and moral excellence are not necessarily the same thing.

Of course, if we assume that evolution is a teleological process directed towards the progressive establishment of a moral order, the situation is somewhat different. But though an assumption of this kind may have been implicit in Spencer's outlook, he did not profess to make any such metaphysical assumptions.

6. The explicit metaphysical element in Spencer's thought is, somewhat paradoxically, his philosophy of the Unknowable. This topic is introduced in the context of a discussion about the alleged conflict between religion and science. 'Of all antagonisms of belief the oldest, the widest, the most profound, and the most important is that between Religion and Science.'[1] Of course, if religion is understood simply as a subjective experience, the question of a conflict between it and science hardly arises. But if we bear in mind religious beliefs, the case is different. In regard to particular events supernatural explanations have been superseded by scientific or natural explanations. And religion has had to confine itself more or less to offering an explanation of the existence of the universe as a totality.[2] But the arguments are unacceptable to anyone who possesses a scientific outlook. In this sense, therefore, there is a conflict between the religious and scientific mentalities. And it can be resolved, according to Spencer, only through a philosophy of the Unknowable.

If we start from the side of religious belief, we can see that both pantheism and theism are untenable. By pantheism Spencer

---

[1] *First Principles*, p. 9.

[2] It may occur to the reader that religion and the offering of explanations are not precisely the same thing. But in ordinary language 'religion' is generally understood as involving an element or elements of belief. And Spencer obviously understands the term in this way.

understands the theory of a universe which develops itself from potential to actual existence. And he contends that this idea is inconceivable. We do not really know what it means. Hence the question of its truth or falsity hardly arises. As for theism, understood as the doctrine that the world was created by an external agent, this too is untenable. Apart from the fact that the creation of space is inconceivable, because its non-existence cannot be conceived, the idea of a self-existent Creator is as inconceivable as that of a self-existent universe. The very idea of self-existence is inconceivable. 'It is not a question of probability, or credibility, but of conceivability.'[1]

It is true, Spencer concedes, that if we inquire into the ultimate cause or causes of the effects produced on our senses, we are led inevitably to the hypothesis of a First Cause. And we shall find ourselves driven to describe it as both infinite and absolute. But Mansel[2] has shown that though the idea of a finite and dependent First Cause involves manifest contradictions, the idea of a First Cause which is infinite and absolute is no more free from contradictions, even if they are not so immediately evident. We are unable, therefore, to say anything intelligible about the nature of the First Cause. And we are left in the end with nothing more than the idea of an inscrutable Power.

If, however, we start from the side of science, we are again brought face to face with the Unknowable. For science cannot solve the mystery of the universe. For one thing, it cannot show that the universe is self-existent, for the idea of self-existence is, as we have seen, inconceivable or unintelligible. For another thing, the ultimate ideas of science itself 'are all representative of realities that cannot be comprehended'.[3] For example, we cannot understand what force is 'in itself'. And in the end 'ultimate religious ideas and ultimate scientific ideas alike turn out to be merely symbols of the actual, not cognitions of it'.[4]

This point of view is supported by an analysis of human thought. All thinking, as we have seen, is relational. And that which is not classifiable by being related to other things through relations of similarity and dissimilarity is not a possible object of knowledge. Hence we cannot know the unconditioned and

---

[1] *First Principles*, p. 29.
[2] Henry L. Mansel (1820–71), who became Dean of St. Paul's, developed Sir William Hamilton's doctrine about the unknowable unconditioned and gave the Bampton lectures on *The Limits of Religious Thought* (1858) from which Spencer quotes (*First Principles*, pp. 33–6) in support of his own agnosticism.
[3] *First Principles*, p. 55. [4] *Ibid.*, p. 57.

absolute. And this applies not only to the Absolute of religion but also to ultimate scientific ideas if considered as representing meta-phenomenal entities or things-in-themselves. At the same time to assert that all knowledge is 'relative' is to assert implicitly that there exists a non-relative reality. 'Unless a real Non-relative or Absolute be postulated, the Relative itself becomes absolute, and so brings the argument to a contradiction.'[1] In fact, we cannot eliminate from our consciousness the idea of an Absolute behind appearances.

Thus whether we approach the matter through a critical examination of religious beliefs or through reflection on our ultimate scientific ideas or through an analysis of the nature of thought and knowledge, we arrive in the end at the concept of an unknowable reality. And a permanent state of peace between religion and science will be achieved 'when science becomes fully convinced that its explanations are proximate and relative, while Religion becomes fully convinced that the mystery it contemplates is ultimate and absolute'.[2]

Now, the doctrine of the Unknowable forms the first part of *First Principles* and thus comes at the beginning of Spencer's system of philosophy as formally arranged. And this fact may incline the unwary reader to attribute to the doctrine a fundamental importance. When, however, he discovers that the inscrutable Absolute or Power of religion is practically equiparated with Force, considered in itself, he may be led to conclude that the doctrine is not much more, if anything, than a sop politely offered to the religious-minded by a man who was not himself a believer in God and who was buried, or rather cremated, without any religious ceremony. It is thus easy to understand how some writers have dismissed the first part of *First Principles* as an unhappy excrescence. Spencer deals with the Unknowable at considerable length. But the total result is not impressive from the metaphysical point of view, as the arguments are not well thought out, while the scientist is likely to demur at the notion that his basic ideas pass all understanding.

The fact remains, however, that Spencer recognizes a certain mystery in the universe. His arguments for the existence of the Unknowable are indeed somewhat confused. Sometimes he gives the impression of accepting a Humian phenomenalism and of arguing that the modifications produced on our senses must be

[1] *First Principles*, pp. 82–3.   [2] *Ibid.*, p. 92.

caused by something which transcends our knowledge. At other times he seems to have at the back of the mind a more or less Kantian line of thought, derived from Hamilton and Mansel. External things are phenomena in the sense that they can be known only in so far as they conform to the nature of human thought. Things-in-themselves or noumena cannot be known; but as the idea of the noumenon is correlative to that of the phenomenon, we cannot avoid postulating it.[1] Spencer also relies, however, on what he calls an all-important fact, namely that besides 'definite' consciousness 'there is also an *indefinite* consciousness which cannot be formulated'.[2] For example, we cannot have a definite consciousness of the finite without a concomitant indefinite consciousness of the infinite. And this line of argument leads to the assertion of the infinite Absolute as a positive reality of which we have a vague or indefinite consciousness. We cannot know *what* the Absolute is. But even though we deny each successive definite interpretation or picture of the Absolute which presents itself, 'there ever remains behind an element which passes into new shapes'.[3]

This line of argument appears to be intended seriously. And though it might be more convenient to turn Spencer into a complete positivist by dismissing the doctrine of the Unknowable as a patronizing concession to religious people, there does not seem to be any adequate justification for this summary dismissal. When Frederic Harrison, the positivist, exhorted Spencer to transform the philosophy of the Unknowable into the Comtist religion of humanity, Spencer turned a deaf ear. It is easy to poke fun at him for using a capital letter for the Unknowable, as though, as it has been said, he expected one to take off one's hat to it. But he seems to have been genuinely convinced that the world of science is the manifestation of a reality which transcends human knowledge. The doctrine of the Unknowable is unlikely to satisfy many religious people. But this is another question. As far as Spencer himself is concerned, he appears to have sincerely believed that the vague consciousness of an Absolute or Unconditioned is an uneliminable feature of human thought, and that it is, as it were, the heart of religion, the permanent element which survives the succession of different creeds and different metaphysical systems.

7. Needless to say, Spencer's philosophy contains a good deal

---

[1] Spencer actually employs the Kantian terms.   [2] *First Principles*, p. 74.
[3] *Ibid.*, p. 80.

of metaphysics. Indeed, it is difficult to think of any philosophy which does not. Is not phenomenalism a form of metaphysics? And when Spencer says, for example, that 'by reality we mean *persistence* in consciousness',[1] it is arguable that this is a metaphysical assertion. We might, of course, try to interpret it as being simply a definition or as a declaration about the ordinary use of words. But when we are told that 'persistence is our ultimate test of the real whether as existing under its unknown form or under the form known to us',[2] it is reasonable to classify this as a metaphysical assertion.

Obviously, Spencer cannot be described as a metaphysician if we mean by this a philosopher who undertakes to disclose the nature of ultimate reality. For in his view it cannot be disclosed. And though he is a metaphysician, to the extent of asserting the existence of the Unknowable, he then devotes himself to constructing a unified overall interpretation of the knowable, that is, of phenomena. But if we like to call this general interpretation 'descriptive metaphysics', we are, of course, free to do so.

In developing this interpretation Spencer adheres to the empiricist tradition. It is true that he is anxious to reconcile conflicting points of view. But when he is concerned with showing that his own philosophy can recognize truth in non-empiricist theories, his method of procedure is to give an empiricist explanation of the data on which the theories are based. As has already been mentioned, he is quite prepared to admit that there are what can be called moral intuitions. For an individual may very well feel a quasi-instinctive approval or disapproval of certain types of action and may 'see', as though intuitively and without any process of reasoning, that such actions are right or wrong. But in Spencer's opinion moral intuitions in this sense are 'the results of accumulated experiences of Utility, gradually organized and inherited'.[3] Whether there are such things as inherited experiences of utility, is open to question. But in any case it is abundantly clear that Spencer's way of showing that there is truth in moral intuitionism is to give an empiricist explanation of the empirical data to which this theory appeals.

Similarly, Spencer is prepared to admit that there is something which can be called an intuition of space, in the sense that as far as the individual is concerned it is practically a form independent

---

[1] *First Principles*, p. 143. [2] *Ibid.*, pp. 143–4.
[3] *The Data of Ethics*, p. 106.

of experience. But it by no means follows that Spencer is trying to incorporate into his own philosophy the Kantian doctrine of the *a priori*. What he does is to argue that this theory is based on a real fact, but that this fact can be explained in terms of the 'organized and consolidated experiences of all antecedent individuals who bequeathed to him [a given subsequent individual] their slowly-developed nervous organizations'.[1]

Though, however, we are not entitled to conclude from Spencer's concern with reconciling conflicting points of view that he throws empiricism overboard, he is, we can say, an empiricist with a difference. For he does not simply tackle individual problems separately, as many empiricists are apt to do. In his autobiography he speaks of his architectonic instinct, his love for system-building. And in point of fact his philosophy was designed as a system: it did not simply become a system in the sense that different lines of investigation and reflection happened to converge towards the formation of an overall picture. Spencer's general principle of interpretation, the so-called law of evolution, was conceived at an early stage and then used as an instrument for the unification of the sciences.

It can hardly be claimed that Spencer's architectonic instinct, his propensity for synthesis, was accompanied by an outstanding gift for careful analysis or for the exact statement of his meaning. But his weak health and the obstacles which he had to face in the fulfilment of his self-imposed mission did not in any case leave him the time or the energy for much more than he was able in fact to achieve. And though most readers probably find his writings extremely dull, his ambitions and pertinacious attempt to unify our knowlege of the world and of man, as well as our moral consciousness and social life, in the light of one all-pervading idea demands the tribute of our admiration. He has relapsed, as it were, into the Victorian era; and, as has already been remarked, in regard to living influence there is no comparison between Spencer and J. S. Mill. But though Spencer's philosophy may be covered with dust it deserves something better than the contemptuous attitude adopted by Nietzsche, who regarded it as a typical expression of the tame and limited mentality of the English middle class.

[1] *Ibid.*

PART II

THE IDEALIST MOVEMENT IN·GREAT BRITAIN

CHAPTER VI
THE BEGINNINGS OF THE MOVEMENT

Introductory historical remarks—Literary pioneers; Coleridge and Carlyle—Ferrier and the subject-object relation—John Grote's attack on phenomenalism and hedonism—The revival of interest in Greek philosophy and the rise of interest in Hegel; B. Jowett and J. H. Stirling.

1. In the second half of the nineteenth century idealism became the dominant philosophical movement in the British universities. It was not, of course, a question of subjective idealism. If this was anywhere to be found, it was a logical consequence of the phenomenalism associated with the names of Hume in the eighteenth century and J. S. Mill in the nineteenth century. For the empiricists who embraced phenomenalism tended to reduce both physical objects and minds to impressions or sensations, and then to reconstruct them with the aid of the principle of the association of ideas. They implied that, basically, we know only phenomena, in the sense of impressions, and that, if there are metaphenomenal realities, we cannot know them. The nineteenth-century idealists, however, were convinced that things-in-themselves, being expressions of the one spiritual reality which manifests itself in and through the human mind, are essentially intelligible, knowable. Subject and object are correlative because they are both rooted in one ultimate spiritual principle. It was thus a question of objective rather than subjective idealism.[1]

Nineteenth-century British idealism thus represented a revival of explicit metaphysics.[2] That which is the manifestation of Spirit can in principle be known by the human spirit. And the whole

---

[1] The foregoing remarks constitute a generalization which is open to criticism on a number of counts. But in such introductory observations one has to prescind from the differences between the various idealist systems.

[2] Empiricism, it is true, had its own implicit metaphysics. And the empiricists not infrequently used the term 'metaphysics' in regard to some of their tenets. But in so far as metaphysics involves an attempt to disclose the nature of ultimate reality, idealism can legitimately be said to represent a revival of metaphysics.

world is the manifestation of Spirit. Science is simply one level of knowledge, one aspect of the complete knowledge to which the mind tends, even if it cannot fully actualize its ideal. Metaphysical philosophy endeavours to complete the synthesis.

The idealist metaphysics was thus a spiritualist metaphysics, in the sense that for it ultimate reality was in some sense spiritual. And it follows that idealism was sharply opposed to materialism. In so far indeed as the phenomenalists tried to go beyond the dispute between materialism and spiritualism by reducing both minds and physical objects to phenomena which cannot properly be described either as spiritual or as material, we cannot legitimately call them materialists. But these phenomena were evidently something very different from the one spiritual reality of the idealists. And in any case we have seen that on the more positivistic side of the empiricist movement there appeared an at least methodological materialism, the so-called scientific materialism, a line of thought for which the idealists had no sympathy.

With its emphasis on the spiritual character of ultimate reality and on the relation between the finite spirit and infinite Spirit idealism stood for a religious outlook as against materialistic positivism and the tendency of empiricism in general to by-pass religious problems or to leave room, at best, for a somewhat vague agnosticism. Indeed, a good deal of the popularity of idealism was due to the conviction that it stood firmly on the side of religion. To be sure, with Bradley, the greatest of the British idealists, the concept of God passed into that of the Absolute, and religion was depicted as a level of consciousness which is surpassed in metaphysical philosophy, while McTaggart, the Cambridge idealist, was an atheist. But with the earlier idealists the religious motive was much in evidence, and idealism seemed to be the natural home of those who were concerned with preserving a religious outlook in face of the threatening incursions of agnostics, positivists and materialists.[1] Further, after Bradley and Bosanquet idealism turned from absolute to personal idealism and was once again favourable to Christian theism, though by that time the impetus of the movement was already spent.

It would, however, be a mistake to conclude that British

[1] In Catholic countries idealism, with its tendency to subordinate theology to speculative philosophy, was commonly regarded as a disintegrating influence, so far as the Christian religion was concerned. In England the situation was somewhat different. A good many of the British idealists were themselves religious men, who found in their philosophy both an expression of and a support for their religious view of the world and of human life.

idealism in the nineteenth century represented simply a retreat from the practical concerns of Bentham and Mill into the metaphysics of the Absolute. For it had a part to play in the development of social philosophy. Generally speaking, the ethical theory of the idealists emphasized the idea of self-realization, of the perfecting of the human personality as an organic whole, an idea which had more in common with Aristotelianism than with Benthamism. And they looked on the function of the State as that of creating the conditions under which individuals could develop their potentialities as persons. As the idealists tended to interpret the creation of such conditions as a removal of hindrances, they could, of course, agree with the utilitarians that the State should interfere as little as possible with the liberty of the individual. They had no wish to replace freedom by servitude. But as they interpreted freedom as freedom to actualize the potentialities of the human personality, and as the removal of hindrances to freedom in this sense involved in their opinion a good deal of social legislation, they were prepared to advocate a measure of State-activity which went beyond anything contemplated by the more enthusiastic adherents of the policy of *laissez faire*. We can say, therefore, that in the latter part of the nineteenth century idealist social and political theory was more in tune with the perceived needs of the time than the position defended by Herbert Spencer. Benthamism or philosophical radicalism doubtless performed a useful task in the first part of the century. But the revised liberalism expounded by the idealists later in the century was by no means 'reactionary'. It looked forward rather than backward.

The foregoing remarks may appear to suggest that nineteenth-century idealism in Great Britain was simply a native reaction to empiricism and positivism and to *laissez faire* economic and political theory. In point of fact, however, German thought, especially that of Kant and Hegel successively, exercised an important influence on the development of British idealism. Some writers, notably J. H. Muirhead,[1] have maintained that the British idealists of the nineteenth century were the inheritors of a Platonic tradition which had manifested itself in the thought of the Cambridge Platonists in the seventeenth century and in the philosophy of Berkeley in the eighteenth century. But though it is useful to draw attention to the fact that British philosophy has not been exclusively empiricist in character, it would be difficult

[1] In *The Platonic Tradition in Anglo-Saxon Philosophy* (1931).

to show that nineteenth-century idealism can legitimately be considered as an organic development of a native Platonic tradition. The influence of German thought, particularly of Kant and Hegel,[1] cannot be dismissed as a purely accidental factor. It is indeed true that no British idealist of note can be described as being in the ordinary sense a disciple of either Kant or Hegel. Bradley, for example, was an original thinker. But it by no means follows that the stimulative influence of German thought was a negligible factor in the development of British idealism.

A limited knowledge of Kant was provided for English readers even during the philosopher's lifetime. In 1795 a disciple of Kant, F. A. Nitzsch, gave some lectures on the critical philosophy at London, and in the following year he published a small work on the subject. In 1797 J. Richardson published his translation of *Principles of Critical Philosophy* by J. J. Beck, and in 1798 A. F. M. Willich published *Elements of Critical Philosophy*. Richardson's translation of Kant's *Metaphysic of Morals* appeared in 1799; but the first translation of the *Critique of Pure Reason*, by F. Haywood, did not appear until 1838. And the serious studies of Kant, such as E. Caird's great work, *A Critical Account of the Philosophy of Kant* (1877), did not appear until a considerably later date. Meanwhile the influence of the German philosopher, together with a host of other influences, was felt by the poet Coleridge, whose ideas will be discussed presently, and in a more obvious way by Sir William Hamilton, though the element of Kantianism in Hamilton's thought was most conspicuous in his doctrine about the limits of human knowledge and in his consequent agnosticism in regard to the nature of ultimate reality.

Among the British idealists proper, Kant's influence may be said to have been felt particularly by T. H. Green and E. Caird. But it was mixed with the influence of Hegel. More accurately, Kant was seen as looking forward to Hegel or was read, as it has been put, through Hegelian spectacles. Indeed, in J. H. Stirling's *The Secret of Hegel* (1865) the view was explicitly defended that the philosophy of Kant, if properly understood and evaluated, leads straight to Hegelianism. Hence, though we can say with truth that the influence of Hegel is more obvious in the absolute

---

[1] Fichte and Schelling exercised little influence, though the former had some stimulative effect on Carlyle, and the latter on Coleridge. There is one obvious reason for this. The classical German idealist movement was already over when the British began; and it was regarded as having culminated in Hegel, considered as the true successor of Kant.

idealism of Bradley and Bosanquet than in the philosophy of Green, there is no question of suggesting that we can divide up the British idealists into Kantians and Hegelians. Some pioneers apart, the influence of Hegel was felt from the beginning of the movement. And it is thus not altogether unreasonable to describe British idealism, as is often done, as a Neo-Hegelian movement, provided at least that it is understood that it was a question of receiving stimulus from Hegel rather than of following him in the relation of pupil to master.

In its earlier phases the British idealist movement was characterized by a marked concentration on the subject-object relationship. In this sense idealism can be said to have had an epistemological foundation, inasmuch as the subject-object relationship is basic in knowledge. The metaphysics of the Absolute was not indeed absent. For subject and object were regarded as grounded in and manifesting one ultimate spiritual reality. But the point of departure affected the metaphysics in an important way. For the emphasis placed in the first instance on the finite subject militated against any temptation to interpret the Absolute in such a manner as to entail the conclusion that the finite is no more than its 'unreal' appearance. In other words, the earlier idealists tended to interpret the Absolute in a more or less theistic, or at any rate in a panentheistic, sense, the monistic aspect of metaphysical idealism remaining in the background. And this, of course, made it easier to represent idealism as an intellectual support for traditional religion.

Gradually, however, the idea of the all-comprehensive organic totality came more and more into the foreground. Thus with Bradley the self was depicted as a mere 'appearance' of the Absolute, as something which is not fully real when regarded in its *prima facie* independence. And this explicit metaphysics of the Absolute was understandably accompanied by a greater emphasis on the State in the field of social philosophy. While Herbert Spencer on the one hand was engaged in asserting an opposition between the interests of the free individual and those of the State, the idealists were engaged in representing man as achieving true freedom through his participation in the life of the totality.

In other words, we can see in the idealist movement up to Bradley and Bosanquet the increasing influence of Hegelianism. As has already been indicated, the influence of Kant was never unmixed. For the critical philosophy was seen as looking forward to metaphysical idealism. But if we make allowances for this fact and also for the fact that there were very considerable differences between Bradley's theory of the Absolute and that of Hegel, we can say that the change from emphasis on the subject-object relationship to emphasis on the idea of the organic totality represented a growing predominance of the stimulative influence of Hegelianism over that of the critical philosophy of Kant.

In the final phase of the idealist movement emphasis on the finite self became once again prominent, though it was a question this time of the active self, the human person, rather than of the epistemological subject. And this personal idealism was accompanied by a reapproximation to theism, except in the notable case of McTaggart, who depicted the Absolute as the system of finite selves. But though this phase of personal idealism is of some interest, inasmuch as it represents the finite self's resistance to being swallowed up in some impersonal Absolute, it belongs to a period when idealism in Britain was giving way to a new current of thought, associated with the names of G. E. Moore, Bertrand Russell, and, subsequently, Ludwig Wittgenstein.

2. As far as the general educated public was concerned, the influence of German thought first made itself felt in Great Britain through the writings of poets and literary figures such as Coleridge and Carlyle.

(i) Samuel Taylor Coleridge (1772–1834) seems to have made his first acquaintance with philosophy through the writings of Neo-Platonists, when he was a schoolboy at Christ's Hospital. This early attraction for the mystical philosophy of Plotinus was succeeded, however, by a Voltairean phase, during which he was for a short time a sceptic in regard to religion. Then at Cambridge Coleridge developed a perhaps somewhat surprising enthusiasm for David Hartley and his associationist psychology.[1] Indeed, Coleridge claimed to be more consistent than Hartley had been. For whereas Hartley, while maintaining that psychical processes depend on and are correlated with vibrations in the brain, had not asserted the corporeality of thought, Coleridge wrote to Southey in 1794 that he believed thought to be corporeal, that is, motion. At the same time Coleridge combined his enthusiasm for Hartley with religious faith.[2] And he came to think that the scientific

[1] That is to say, it is from one point of view somewhat surprising to find that the romantic poet was ever an enthusiast for Hartley of all people. But the associationist psychology was then regarded as 'advanced', and this doubtless helped to commend it to the intellectually alive undergraduate.
[2] For the matter of that, Hartley himself had been a religious believer.

understanding is inadequate as a key to reality, and to speak of
the role of intuition and the importance of moral experience. Later
on he was to declare that Hartley's system, in so far as it differs
from that of Aristotle, is untenable.[1]

Coleridge's distinction between the scientific understanding
and the higher reason or, as the Germans would put it, between
Verstand and *Vernunft* was one expression of his revolt against
the spirit of the eighteenth-century Enlightenment. He did not,
of course, mean to imply that the scientific and critical understanding should be rejected in the name of a higher and intuitive
reason. His point was rather that the former is not an omnicompetent instrument in the interpretation of reality, but that it
needs to be supplemented and balanced by the latter, namely the
intuitive reason. It can hardly be claimed that Coleridge made his
distinction between understanding and reason crystal clear. But
the general line of his thought is sufficiently plain. In *Aids to
Reflection* (1825) he describes the understanding as the faculty
which judges according to sense. Its appropriate sphere is the
sensible world, and it reflects and generalizes on the basis of
sense-experience. Reason, however, is the vehicle of ideas which
are presupposed by all experience, and in this sense it predeter-
mines and governs experience. It also perceives truths which are
incapable of verification in sense-experience, and it intuitively
apprehends spiritual realities. Further, Coleridge identifies it with
the practical reason, which comprises the will and the moral aspect
of the human personality. J. S. Mill is thus perfectly justified in
saying in his famous essay on Coleridge that the poet dissents
from the 'Lockian' view that all knowledge consists of generalizations from experience, and that he claims for the reason, as
distinct from the understanding, the power to perceive by direct
intuition realities and truths which transcend the reach of the
senses.[2]

In his development of this distinction Coleridge received
stimulus from the writings of Kant, which he began to study
shortly after his visit to Germany in 1798–9.[3] But he tends to
speak as though Kant not only limited the scope of the understanding to knowledge of phenomenal reality but also envisaged

[1] See Coleridge's *Biographia Literaria*, ch. 6.
[2] See Mill's *Dissertations and Discussions*, I, p. 405.
[3] 'The writings of the illustrious sage of Koenigsberg, the founder of the
Critical Philosophy, more than any other works, at once invigorated and dis-
ciplined my understanding', *Biographia Literaria*, p. 76 (Everyman's Library
edition).

an intuitive apprehension of spiritual realities by means of the reason, whereas in point of fact in attributing this power to the reason, identified moreover with the practical reason, Coleridge obviously parts company with the German philosopher. He is on firmer ground when he claims an affinity with Jacobi[1] in maintaining that the relation between reason and spiritual realities is analogous to that between the eye and material objects.

Nobody, however, would wish to maintain that Coleridge was a Kantian. It was a question of stimulus, not of discipleship. And though he recognized his debt to German thinkers, especially to Kant, it is clear that he regarded his own philosophy as being fundamentally Platonic in inspiration. In *Aids to Reflection* he asserted that every man is born either a Platonist or an Aristotelian. Aristotle, the great master of understanding, was unduly earthbound. He 'began with the sensual, and never received that which was above the senses, but by necessity, but as the only remaining hypothesis. . . .'[2] That is to say, Aristotle postulated spiritual reality only as a last resort, when forced to do so by the need of explaining physical phenomena. Plato, however, sought the supersensible reality which is revealed to us through reason and our moral will. As for Kant, Coleridge sometimes describes him as belonging spiritually to the ranks of the Aristotelians, while at other times he emphasizes the metaphysical aspects of Kant's thought and finds in him an approach to Platonism. In other words, Coleridge welcomes Kant's restriction of the reach of understanding to phenomenal reality and then tends to interpret his doctrine of reason in the light of Platonism, which is itself interpreted in the light of the philosophy of Plotinus.

These remarks should not be understood as implying any contempt for Nature on Coleridge's part. On the contrary, he disliked Fichte's 'boastful and hyperstoic hostility to Nature, as lifeless, godless, and altogether unholy'.[3] And he expressed a warm sympathy with Schelling's philosophy of Nature, as also with his system of transcendental idealism, in which 'I first found a genial coincidence with much that I had toiled out for myself, and a powerful assistance in what I had yet to do'.[4] Coleridge is indeed at pains to reject the charge of plagiarism, and he maintains that both he and Schelling have drunk at the same springs, the writings of Kant, the philosophy of Giordano Bruno and the

[1] See Vol. VI of this *History*, pp. 146–8.
[2] *Philosophical Lectures*, edited by K. Coburn, p. 186.
[3] *Biographia Literaria*, p. 78.   [4] *Ibid.*, p. 79.

speculations of Jakob Boehme. However, the influence of Schelling seems to be sufficiently evident in the line of thought which we can now briefly outline.

'All knowledge rests on the coincidence of an object with a subject.'[1] But though subject and object are united in the act of knowledge, we can ask which has the priority. Are we to start with the object and try to add to it the subject? Or are we to start with the subject and try to find a passage to the object? In other words, are we to take Nature as prior and try to add to it thought or mind, or are we to take thought as prior and try to deduce Nature? Coleridge answers that we can do neither the one nor the other. The ultimate principle is to be sought in the identity of subject and object.

Where is this identity to be found? 'Only in the self-consciousness of a spirit is there the required identity of object and of representation.'[2] But if the spirit is originally the identity of subject and object, it must in some sense dissolve this identity in order to become conscious of itself as object. Self-consciousness, therefore, cannot arise except through an act of will, and 'freedom must be assumed as a *ground* of philosophy, and can never be deduced from it'.[3] The spirit becomes a subject knowing itself as object only through 'the act of constructing itself objectively to itself'.[4]

This sounds as though Coleridge begins by asking the sort of question which Schelling asks, then supplies Schelling's answer, namely that we must postulate an original identity of subject and object, and finally switches to Fichte's idea of the ego as constituting itself as subject and object by an original act. But Coleridge has no intention of stopping short with the ego as his ultimate principle, especially if we mean by this the finite ego. Indeed, he ridicules the 'egoism' of Fichte.[5] Instead, he insists that to arrive at the absolute identity of subject and object, of the ideal and the real, as the ultimate principle not only of human knowledge but also of all existence we must 'elevate our conception to the absolute self, the great eternal *I am*'.[6] Coleridge criticizes Descartes's *Cogito, ergo sum* and refers to Kant's distinction between the empirical and the transcendental ego. But he then tends to speak as though the transcendental ego were the absolute

---

[1] *Biographia Literaria*, p. 136.   [2] *Ibid.*, p. 145.   [3] *Ibid.*
[4] *Ibid.*, p. 144.
[5] Fichte did not, of course, make the finite ego or self his ultimate principle. And Coleridge tends to caricature his thought.   [6] *Biographia Literaria*, p. 144.

I am that I am of *Exodus*[1] and the God in whom the finite self is called to lose and find itself at the same time.

All this is obviously cloudy and imprecise. But it is at any rate clear that Coleridge opposes a spiritualistic interpretation of the human self to materialism and phenomenalism. And it is clearly this interpretation of the self which in his view provides the basis for the claim that reason can apprehend supersensible reality. Indeed, in his essay on faith Coleridge describes faith as fidelity to our own being in so far as our being is not and cannot become an object of sense-experience. Our moral vocation demands the subordination of appetite and will to reason; and it is reason which apprehends God as the identity of will and reason, as the ground of our existence, and as the infinite expression of the ideal which we are seeking as moral beings. In other words, Coleridge's outlook was essentially religious, and he tried to bring together philosophy and religion. He may have tended, as Mill notes, to turn Christian mysteries into philosophical truths. But an important element in the mission of idealism, as conceived by its more religious adherents, was precisely that of giving a metaphysical basis to a Christian tradition which seemed to be signally lacking in any philosophical backbone.

In the field of social and political theory Coleridge was conservative in the sense that he was opposed to the iconoclasm of the radicals and desired the preservation and actualization of the values inherent in traditional institutions. At one time he was indeed attracted, like Wordsworth and Southey, by the ideas which inspired the French Revolution. But he came to abandon the radicalism of his youth, though his subsequent conservatism arose not from any hatred of change as such but from a belief that the institutions created by the national spirit in the course of its history embodied real values which men should endeavour to realize. As Mill put it, Bentham demanded 'the extinction of the institutions and creeds which had hitherto existed', whereas Coleridge demanded 'that they be made a reality'.[2]

(ii) Thomas Carlyle (1795–1881) belonged to a later generation than that of Coleridge; but he was considerably less systematic in the presentation of his philosophical ideas, and there are doubtless very many people today who find the turbulent prose of *Sartor Resartus* quite unreadable. However, he was one of the channels

---

[1] *Exodus*, 3, 14.
[2] *Dissertations and Discussions*, I, p. 436.

through which German thought and literature were brought to the attention of the British public.

Carlyle's first reaction to German philosophy was not exactly favourable, and he made fun both of Kant's obscurity and of the pretensions of Coleridge. But in his hatred of materialism, hedonism and utilitarianism he came to see in Kant the brilliant foe of the Enlightenment and of its derivative movements. Thus in his essay on the *State of German Literature* (1827) he praised Kant for starting from within and proceeding outwards instead of pursuing the Lockian path of starting with sense-experience and trying to build a philosophy on this basis. The Kantian, according to Carlyle, sees that fundamental truths are apprehended by intuition in man's inmost nature. In other words, Carlyle ranges himself with Coleridge in using Kant's restriction of the power and scope of the understanding as a foundation for asserting the power of reason to apprehend intuitively basic truths and spiritual realities.

Characteristic of Carlyle was his vivid sense of the mystery of the world and of its nature as an appearance of, or veil before, supersensible reality. In the *State of German Literature* he asserted that the ultimate aim of philosophy is to interpret phenomena or appearances, to proceed from the symbol to the reality symbolized. And this point of view found expression in *Sartor Resartus*,[1] under the label of the philosophy of clothes. It can be applied to man, the microcosm. 'To the eye of vulgar Logic what is man? An omnivorous Biped that wears Breeches. To the eye of Pure Reason what is he? A Soul, a Spirit, and divine Apparition. . . . Deep-hidden is he under that strange Garment.'[2] And the analogy is applicable also to the macrocosm, the world in general. For the world is, as Goethe divined, *'the living visible Garment of God'*.[3]

In the *State of German Literature* Carlyle explicitly connects his philosophy of symbolism with Fichte, who is regarded as having interpreted the visible universe as the symbol and sensible manifestation of an all-pervading divine Idea, the apprehension of which is the condition of all genuine virtue and freedom. And there is indeed no great difficulty in understanding Carlyle's predilection for Fichte. For seeing, as he does, human life and

---

[1] As no publisher would accept this work, it first appeared in instalments in *Fraser's Magazine*, 1833–4. An American edition of the book appeared in 1836, and an English edition in 1838.

[2] *Sartor Resartus*, I, 10, p. 57 (Scott Library edition). The 'Garment' is, of course, the body.

[3] *Ibid.*, I, 8, p. 48.

history as a constant struggle between light and darkness, God and the devil, a struggle in which every man is called to play a part and to make an all-important choice, he naturally feels an attraction for Fichte's moral earnestness and for his view of Nature as being simply the field in which man works out his moral vocation, the field of obstacles, so to speak, which man has to overcome in the process of attaining his ideal end.

This outlook helps to explain Carlyle's concern with the hero, as manifested in his 1840 lectures *On Heroes, Hero-Worship and the Heroic in History*. Over against materialism and what he calls profit-and-loss philosophy he sets the ideas of heroism, moral vocation and personal loyalty. Indeed, he is prepared to assert that 'the life-breath of all society [is] but an effluence of Hero-worship, submissive admiration for the truly great. Society is founded on Hero-worship.'[1] Again, 'Universal History, the history of what man has accomplished in the world, is at bottom the History of the Great Men who have worked here'.[2]

In his insistence on the role of history's 'great men' Carlyle resembles Hegel[3] and anticipates Nietzsche in some aspects, though hero-worship in the political field is an idea which we are likely to regard with mixed feelings nowadays. However, it is clear that what especially attracted Carlyle in his heroes was their earnestness and self-devotion and their freedom from a morality based on the hedonistic calculus. For example, while aware of Rousseau's shortcomings and faults of character, which made him 'a sadly *contracted* Hero',[4] Carlyle insists that this unlikely candidate for the title possessed 'the first and chief characteristic of a Hero: he is heartily *in earnest*. In earnest, if ever man was; as none of these French Philosophes were.'[5]

3. In spite of the fact that both men delivered lectures it would be idle to look either to Coleridge or Carlyle for a systematic development of idealism. For a pioneer in this field we have to turn rather to James Frederick Ferrier (1808–64), who occupied the chair of moral philosophy in the University of St. Andrews from 1845 until the year of his death, and who made a great point of systematic procedure in philosophy.

In 1838–9 Ferrier contributed a series of articles to *Blackwood's*

[1] *On Heroes*, lecture I, p. 193 (London, Chapman and Hall).
[2] *Ibid.*, p. 185.
[3] Hegel, however, regarded his 'word-historical individuals' as instruments of the World-Spirit.
[4] *On Heroes*, lecture V, p. 323.   [5] *Ibid.*

Magazine, which was published with the title *Introduction to the Philosophy of Consciousness*. In 1854 he published his main work, *The Institutes of Metaphysics*, which is remarkable for the way in which the author develops his doctrine in a series of propositions, each of which, with the exception of the first fundamental proposition, is supposed to follow with logical rigour from its predecessor. In 1856 he published *Scottish Philosophy*, while his *Lectures on Greek Philosophy and Other Philosophical Remains* appeared posthumously in 1866.

Ferrier claimed that his philosophy was Scottish to the core. But this does not mean that he regarded himself as an adherent of the Scottish philosophy of common sense. On the contrary, he vigorously attacked Reid and his followers. In the first place a philosopher should not appeal to a multitude of undemonstrated principles, but should employ the deductive method which is essential to metaphysics and not an optional expository device. In the second place the Scottish philosophers of common sense tended to confuse metaphysics with psychology, trying to solve philosophical problems by psychological reflections, instead of by rigorous logical reasoning.[1] As for Sir William Hamilton, his agnosticism about the Absolute was quite misplaced.

When Ferrier said that his philosophy was Scottish to the core, he meant that he had not borrowed it from the Germans. Though his system was not uncommonly regarded as Hegelian, he claimed that he had never been able to understand Hegel.[2] Indeed, he expressed a doubt whether the German philosopher had been able to understand himself. In any case Hegel starts with Being, whereas his own system took knowledge as its point of departure.[3]

Ferrier's first move is to look for the absolute starting-point of metaphysics in a proposition which states the one invariable and essential feature in all knowledge, and which cannot be denied without contradiction. This is that 'along with whatever any intelligence knows, it must, as the ground or condition of its knowledge, have some cognizance of itself'.[4] The object of know-

---

[1] According to Ferrier, if we wish to find the solution to a metaphysical problem, we might well inquire what the psychologists have said about the matter and then assert the exact opposite.

[2] This did not prevent Ferrier from writing articles on Schelling and Hegel for the *Imperial Dictionary of Universal Biography*.

[3] We can hardly exclude all influence of German thought on Ferrier's mind. But he was doubtless right in claiming that his system was his own creation, and not the result of borrowing.

[4] *Institutes of Metaphysics*, I, prop. 1, p. 79 (Works, I, 3rd edition). This work will henceforth be referred to simply as *Institutes*.

ledge is a variable factor. But I cannot know anything without knowing that I know. To deny this is to talk nonsense. To assert it is to admit that there is no knowledge without self-consciousness, without some awareness of the self.

It follows from this, Ferrier argues, that nothing can be known except in relation to a subject, a self. In other words, the object of knowledge is essentially object-for-a-subject. And Ferrier draws the conclusion that nothing is thinkable except in relation to a subject. From this it follows that the material universe is unthinkable as existing without any relation to subject.

The critic might be inclined to comment that Ferrier is really saying no more than that I cannot think of the universe without thinking of it, or know it without knowing it. If anything more is being said, if, in particular, a transition is being made from an epistemological point to the assertion of an ontological relation, a solipsistic conclusion seems to follow, namely that the existence of the material world is unthinkable except as dependent on myself as subject.

Ferrier, however, wishes to maintain two propositions. First, we cannot think of the universe as 'dissociated from *every* me. You cannot perform the abstraction.'[1] Secondly, each of us can dissociate the universe from himself in particular. And from these two propositions it follows that though 'each of us can unyoke the universe (so to speak) from himself, he can do this only by yoking it on, in thought, to some other self'.[2] This is an essential move for Ferrier to make, because he wishes to argue that the universe is unthinkable except as existing in synthesis with the divine mind.

The first section of the *Institutes of Metaphysics* thus purports to show that the absolute element in knowledge is the synthesis of subject and object. But Ferrier does not proceed at once to his final conclusion. Instead, he devotes the second section to 'agnoiology', the theory of 'ignorance'. We can be said to be in a state of nescience in regard to the contradictions of necessarily true propositions. But this is obviously no sign of imperfection in our minds. As for ignorance, we cannot properly be said to be ignorant except of what is in principle knowable. Hence we cannot be ignorant of, for example, matter 'in itself' (without relation to a subject). For this is unthinkable and unknowable. Further, if we

---

[1] *Ibid.*, I, prop. 13, observation 3, p. 312.
[2] *Ibid.*, observation 2, p. 311.

assume that we are ignorant of the Absolute, it follows that the Absolute is knowable. Hence Hamilton's agnosticism is untenable.

But what is the Absolute or, as Ferrier expresses it, Absolute Existence? It cannot be either matter *per se* or mind *per se*. For neither is thinkable. It must be, therefore, the synthesis of subject and object. There is, however, only one such synthesis which is necessary. For though the existence of a universe is not conceivable except as object-for-a-subject, we have already seen that the universe can be unyoked or dissociated from any given finite subject. Hence 'there is one, but only one, Absolute Existence which is strictly *necessary*; and that existence is a supreme, and infinite, and everlasting Mind in synthesis with all things'.[1]

By way of comment it is not inappropriate to draw attention to the rather obvious fact, that the statement 'there can be no subject without an object and no object without a subject' is analytically true, if the terms 'subject' and 'object' are understood in their epistemological senses. It is also true that no material thing can be conceived except as object-for-a-subject, if we mean by this that no material thing can be conceived except by constituting it ('intentionally', as the phenomenologists would say) as an object. But this does not seem to amount to much more than saying that a thing cannot be thought of unless it is thought of. And from this it does not follow that a thing cannot exist unless it is thought of. Ferrier could retort, of course, that we cannot intelligibly speak of a thing as existing independently of being conceived. For by the mere fact that we speak of it, we conceive it. If I try to think of material thing X as existing outside the subject-object relationship, my effort is defeated by the very fact that I am thinking of X. In this case, however, the thing seems to be irrevocably yoked, as Ferrier puts it, to me as subject. And how can I possibly unyoke it? If I try to unyoke it from myself and yoke it to some other subject, whether finite or infinite, does not this other subject, on Ferrier's premises, become object-for-a-subject, the subject in question being myself?

It is not my intention to suggest that in point of fact the material universe could exist independently of God. The point is rather that the conclusion that it cannot so exist does not really follow from Ferrier's epistemological premises. The conclusion which does seem to follow is solipsism. And Ferrier escapes from

---

[1] *Institutes*, III, prop. 11, p. 522. It will be noted that for Ferrier the Absolute is not God alone but the synthesis of God and the world, of the infinite subject and its object in relation to one another.

this conclusion only by an appeal to common sense and to our knowledge of historical facts. That is to say, as I cannot seriously suppose that the material universe is simply object for me as subject, I must postulate an eternal, infinite subject, God. But on Ferrier's premises it appears to follow that God Himself, as thought by me, must be object-for-a-subject, the subject being myself.

4. Among Ferrier's contemporaries John Grote (1813–66), brother of the historian, deserves mention. Professor of moral philosophy at Cambridge from 1855 until 1866, he published the first part of *Exploratio philosophica* in 1865. The second part appeared posthumously in 1900. His *Examination of Utilitarian Philosophy* (1870) and *A Treatise on the Moral Ideals* (1876) were also published after his death. It is true that nowadays Grote is even less known than Ferrier; but his criticism of phenomenalism and of hedonistic utilitarianism is not without value.

Grote's critique of phenomenalism can be illustrated in this way. One of the main features of positivistic phenomenalism is that it first reduces the object of knowledge to a series of phenomena and then proceeds to apply a similar reductive analysis to the subject, the ego or self. In effect, therefore, the subject is reduced to its own object. Or, if preferred, subject and object are both reduced to phenomena which are assumed to be the basic reality, the ultimate entities out of which selves and physical objects can be reconstructed by thought. But this reduction of the self or subject can be shown to be untenable. In the first place talk about phenomena is not intelligible except in relation to consciousness. For that which appears, appears to a subject, within the ambit, so to speak, of consciousness. We cannot go behind consciousness; and analysis of it shows that it essentially involves the subject-object relationship. In primitive consciousness subject and object are virtually or confusedly present; and they are progressively distinguished in the development of consciousness until there arises an explicit awareness of a world of objects on the one hand and of a self or subject on the other, this awareness of the self being developed especially by the experience of effort. As, therefore, the subject is present from the start as one of the essential poles even in primitive consciousness, it cannot be legitimately reduced to the object, to phenomena. At the same time reflection on the essential structure of consciousness shows that we are not presented with a self-enclosed ego from which we have to find a bridge, as in the philosophy of Descartes, to the non-ego.

In the second place it is important to notice the way in which the phenomenalists overlook the active role of the subject in the construction of an articulated universe. The subject or self is characterized by teleological activity; it has ends. And in pursuit of its ends it constructs unities among phenomena, not in the sense that it imposes *a priori* forms on a mass of unrelated, chaotic data,[1] but rather in the sense that it builds up its world in an experimental way by a process of auto-correction. On this count too, therefore, namely the active role of the self in the construction of the world of objects, it is clear that it cannot be reduced to a series of phenomena, its own immediate objects.[2]

In the sphere of moral philosophy Grote was strongly opposed to both egoistic hedonism and utilitarianism. He did not object to them for taking into account man's sensibility and his search for happiness. On the contrary, Grote himself admitted the science of happiness, 'eudaemonics' as he called it, as a part of ethics. What he objected to was an exclusive concentration on the search for pleasure and a consequent neglect of other aspects of the human personality, especially man's capacity for conceiving and pursuing ideals which transcend the search for pleasure and may demand self-sacrifice. Hence to 'eudaemonics' he added 'aretaics', the science of virtue. And he insisted that the moral task is to achieve the union of the lower and higher elements of man's nature in the service of moral ideals. For our actions become moral when they pass from the sphere of the merely spontaneous, as in following the impulse to pleasure, into the sphere of the deliberate and voluntary, impulse supplying the dynamic element and intellectually-conceived principles and ideals the regulative element.

Obviously, Grote's attack on utilitarianism as neglecting the higher aspects of man through an exclusive concentration on the search for pleasure was more applicable to Benthamite hedonism than to J. S. Mill's revised version of utilitarianism. But in any case it was a question not so much of suggesting that a utilitarian philosopher could not have moral ideals as of maintaining that the utilitarian ethics could not provide an adequate theoretical frame-

---

[1] According to Grote, in its construction of an articulated world the self discovers or recognizes categories in Nature, which are the expression of the divine mind.
[2] In Grote's view, things-in-themselves are known intuitively, even if not distinctly, through knowledge by acquaintance, as contrasted with knowledge about.

work for such ideals. Grote's main point was that this could be provided only by a radical revision of the concept of man which Bentham inherited from writers such as Helvétius. Hedonism, in Grote's opinion, could not account for the consciousness of obligation. For this arises when man, conceiving moral ideals, feels the need of subordinating his lower to his higher nature.

5. We can reasonably see a connection between the idealists' perception of the inadequacy of the Benthamite view of human nature and the revival of interest in Greek philosophy which occurred in the universities, especially at Oxford, in the course of the nineteenth century. We have already seen that Coleridge regarded his philosophy as being fundamentally Platonic in inspiration and character. But the renewal of Platonic studies at Oxford can be associated in particular with the name of Benjamin Jowett (1817–93), who became a Fellow of Balliol College in 1838 and occupied the chair of Greek from 1855 to 1893. The defects in his famous translation of Plato's *Dialogues* are irrelevant here. The point is that in the course of his long teaching career he contributed powerfully to a revival of interest in Greek thought. And it is not without significance that T. H. Green and E. Caird, both prominent in the idealist movement, were at one time his pupils. Interest in Plato and Aristotle naturally tended to turn their minds away from hedonism and utilitarianism towards an ethics of self-perfection, based on a theory of human nature within a metaphysical framework.

The revival of interest in Greek thought was accompanied by a growing appreciation of German idealist philosophy. Jowett himself was interested in the latter, particularly in the thought of Hegel;[1] and he helped to stimulate the study of German idealism at Oxford. The first large-scale attempt, however, to elucidate what Ferrier had considered to be the scarcely intelligible profundities of Hegel was made by the Scotsman, James Hutchison Stirling (1820–1909), in his two-volume work *The Secret of Hegel*, which appeared in 1865.[2]

Stirling developed an enthusiasm for Hegel during a visit to Germany, especially during a stay at Heidelberg in 1856; and the result was *The Secret of Hegel*. In spite of the comment that if the

---

[1] While he explicitly acknowledged the stimulus which he had received from Hegel, Jowett gradually moved further away from rather than nearer to Hegelianism.

[2] A one-volume edition appeared in 1898. Stirling never held an academic post; but he gave the Gifford Lectures at Edinburgh in 1899–90. These were published in 1890 with the title *Philosophy and Theology*.

author knew the secret of Hegel, he kept it successfully to himself, the book marked the beginning of the serious study of Hegelianism in Great Britain. In Stirling's view Hume's philosophy was the culmination of the Enlightenment, while Kant,[1] who took over what was valuable in Hume's thought and used it in the development of a new line of reflection, fulfilled and at the same time overcame and transcended the Enlightenment. While, however, Kant laid the foundations of idealism, it was Hegel who built and completed the edifice. And to understand the secret of Hegel is to understand how he made explicit the doctrine of the concrete universal, which was implicit in the critical philosophy of Kant.

It is noteworthy that Stirling regarded Hegel not only as standing to modern philosophy in the relation in which Aristotle stood to preceding Greek thought but also as the great intellectual champion of the Christian religion. He doubtless attributed to Hegel too high a degree of theological orthodoxy; but his attitude serves to illustrate the religious interest which characterized the idealist movement before Bradley. According to Stirling, Hegel was concerned with proving, among other things, the immortality of the soul. And though there is little evidence that Hegel felt much interest in this matter, Stirling's interpretation can be seen as representing the emphasis placed by the earlier idealists on the finite spiritual self, an emphasis which harmonized with their tendency to retain a more or less theistic outlook.

[1] Stirling published a *Text-Book to Kant* in 1881.

CHAPTER VII

THE DEVELOPMENT OF IDEALISM

T. H. Green's attitude to British empiricism and to German thought—Green's doctrine of the eternal subject, with some critical comments—The ethical and political theory of Green— E. Caird and the unity underlying the distinction between subject and object—J. Caird and the philosophy of religion— W. Wallace and D. G. Ritchie.

1. PHILOSOPHERS are not infrequently more convincing when they are engaged in criticizing the views of other philosophers than when they are expounding their own doctrines. And this perhaps somewhat cynical remark seems to be applicable to Thomas Hill Green (1836–82), Fellow of Balliol College, Oxford, and Whyte professor of moral philosophy in that university from 1878 to the year of his death. In his *Introductions to Hume's Treatise of Human Nature*,[1] which he published in 1874 for the Green and Grose edition of Hume, he made an impressive broadside attack on British empiricism. But his own idealist system is no less open to criticism than the views against which he raised objections.

From Locke onwards, according to Green, empiricists have assumed that it is the philosopher's business to reduce our knowledge to its primitive elements, to the original data, and then to reconstruct the world of ordinary experience out of these atomic data. Apart, however, from the fact that no satisfactory explanation has ever been offered of the way in which the mind can go behind the subject-object relationship and discover the primitive data out of which both minds and physical objects are supposed to be constructed, the empiricist programme lands us in an impasse. On the one hand, to construct the world of minds and physical objects the mind has to relate the primitive atomic data, discrete phenomena. In other words, it has to exercise activity. On the other hand, the mind's activity is inexplicable on empiricist principles. For it is itself reduced to a series of phenomena. And how can it construct itself? Further, though empiricism professes to account for human knowledge, it does not in fact do anything of the kind. For the world of ordinary experience is interpreted

---

[1] This work will be referred to as *Introductions*.

as a mental construction out of discrete impressions; and we have no way of knowing that the construction represents objective reality at all. In other words, a consistent empiricism leads inevitably to scepticism.

Hume himself, as Green sees him, was an outstanding thinker who discarded compromise and carried the principles of empiricism to their logical conclusion. 'Adopting the premisses and method of Locke, he cleared them of all illogical adaptations to popular belief, and experimented with them on the basis of professed knowledge. . . . As the result of the experiment, the method, which began with professing to explain knowledge, showed knowledge to be impossible.'[1] 'Hume himself was perfectly cognizant of this result, but his successors in England and Scotland would seem so far to have been unable to look it in the face.'[2]

Some philosophers after Hume, and here Green is evidently referring to the Scottish philosophers of common sense, have thrust their heads back into the thicket of uncriticized belief. Others have gone on developing Hume's theory of the association of ideas, apparently oblivious of the fact that Hume himself had shown the insufficiency of the principle of association to account for anything more than natural or quasi-instinctive belief.[3] In other words, Hume represented both the culmination and the bankruptcy of empiricism. And the torch of inquiry 'was transferred to a more vigorous line in Germany'.[4]

Kant, that is to say, was the spiritual successor of Hume. 'Thus the *Treatise of Human Nature* and the *Critique of Pure Reason*, taken together, form the real bridge between the old world of philosophy and the new. They are the essential "Propaedeutik" without which no one is a qualified student of modern philosophy.'[5] It does not follow, however, that we can remain in the philosophy of Kant. For Kant looks forward to Hegel or at any rate to something resembling Hegelianism. Green agrees with Stirling that Hegel developed the philosophy of Kant in the right direction; but he is not prepared to say that Hegel's system as it stands is satisfactory. It is all very well for the Sundays of speculation, as Green puts it; but it is more difficult to accept on the weekdays of ordinary thought. There is need for reconciling the judgments of

[1] *Introductions*, I, 2–3. Green and Grose edition of Hume's *Treatises*, I, p. 2.
[2] *Ibid.*, 3.
[3] Green is clearly thinking of philosophers such as the two Mill's.
[4] *Introductions*, I, 3. Green and Grose, I, pp. 2–3.
[5] *Ibid.* Green and Grose, I, p. 3.

speculative philosophy with our ordinary judgments about matters of fact and with the sciences. Hegelianism, however, if taken as it stands, cannot perform this task of synthesizing different tendencies and points of view in contemporary thought. The work has to be done over again.

In point of fact the name of Hegel does not loom large in the writings of Green. The name of Kant is far more prominent. But Green maintained that by reading Hume in the light of Leibniz and Leibniz in the light of Hume, Kant was able to free himself from their respective presuppositions. And we can justifiably say that though Green derived a great deal of stimulus from Kant, he read him in the light of his conviction that the critical philosophy needed some such development, though not precisely the same, as that which it actually received at the hands of the German metaphysical idealists, and of Hegel in particular.

2. In the introduction to his *Prolegomena to Ethics*, which was published posthumously in 1883, Green refers to the temptation to treat ethics as though it were a branch of natural science. This temptation is indeed understandable. For growth in historical knowledge and the development of theories of evolution suggest the possibility of giving a purely naturalistic and genetic explanation of the phenomena of the moral life. But what becomes then of ethics considered as a normative science? The answer is that the philosopher who 'has the courage of his principles, having reduced the speculative part of them [our ethical systems] to a natural science, must abolish the practical or preceptive part altogether'.[1] The fact, however, that the reduction of ethics to a branch of natural science involves the abolition of ethics as a normative science should make us reconsider the presuppositions or conditions of moral knowledge and activity. Is man merely a child of Nature? Or is there in him a spiritual principle which makes knowledge possible, whether it be knowledge of Nature or moral knowledge?

Green thus finds it necessary to start his inquiry into morals with a metaphysics of knowledge. And he argues in the first place that even if we were to decide in favour of the materialists all those questions about particular facts which have formed the subject of debate between them and the spiritualists, the possibility of our explaining the facts at all still remain to be accounted for. 'We shall still be logically bound to admit that in a man who

---

[1] *Prolegomena to Ethics*, p. 9 (first edition). This work will be referred to henceforth as *Prolegomena*.

can know a Nature—for whom there is a "cosmos of experience"
—there is a principle which is not natural and which cannot
without a ὕστερον πρότερον be explained as we explain the facts
of nature.'[1]

According to Green, to say that a thing is real is to say that it
is a member in a system of relations, the order of Nature. But
awareness or knowledge of a series of related events cannot itself
be a series of events. Nor can it be a natural development out of
such a series. In other words, the mind as an active synthesizing
principle is irreducible to the factors which it synthesizes. True,
the empirical ego belongs to the order of Nature. But my awareness
of myself as an empirical ego manifests the activity of a principle
which transcends that order. In fine, 'an understanding—for that
term seems as fit as any other to denote the principle of consciousness in question—irreducible to anything else, "makes nature"
for us, in the sense of enabling us to conceive that there is such a
thing'.[2]

We have just seen that for Green a thing is real in virtue of its
membership in a system of related phenomena. At the same time
he holds that 'related appearances are impossible apart from the
action of an intelligence'.[3] Nature is thus made by the synthesizing
activity of a mind. It is obvious, however, that we cannot seriously
suppose that Nature, as the system of related phenomena, is
simply the product of the synthesizing activity of any given
finite mind. Though, therefore, it can be said that each finite mind
constitutes Nature in so far as it conceives the system of relations,
we must also assume that there is a single spiritual principle, an
eternal consciousness, which ultimately constitutes or produces
Nature.

From this it follows that we must conceive the finite mind as
participating in the life of an eternal consciousness or intelligence
which 'partially and gradually reproduces itself in us, com-
municating piece-meal, but in inseparable correlation, understanding and the facts understood, experience and the experienced
world'.[4] This amounts to saying that God gradually reproduces
his own knowledge in the finite mind. And, if this is the case, what
are we to say about the empirical facts relating to the origin and

---

[1] *Prolegomena*, p. 14. The phrase 'cosmos of experience' is taken from G. H.
Lewes, one of Green's targets of attack.
[2] *Ibid.*, p. 22. Clearly, Kant's transcendental ego is given an ontological status.
[3] *Ibid.*, p. 28.
[4] *Ibid.*, p. 38.

growth of knowledge? For these hardly suggest that our knowledge is imposed by God. Green's answer is that God reproduces his own knowledge in the finite mind by making use, so to speak, of the sentient life of the human organism and of its response to stimuli. There are thus two aspects to human consciousness. There is the empirical aspect, under which our consciousness appears to consist 'in successive modifications of the animal organism'.[1] And there is the metaphysical aspect, under which this organism is seen as gradually becoming 'the vehicle of an eternally complete consciousness'.[2]

Green thus shares with the earlier idealists the tendency to choose an epistemological point of departure, the subject-object relationship. Under the influence of Kant, however, he depicts the subject as actively synthesizing the manifold of phenomena, as constituting the order of Nature by relating appearances or phenomena. This process of synthesis is a gradual process which develops through the history of the human race towards an ideal term. And we can thus conceive the total process as an activity of one spiritual principle which lives and acts in and through finite minds. In other words, Kant's idea of the synthesizing activity of the mind leads us to the Hegelian concept of infinite Spirit.

At the same time Green's religious interests militate against any reduction of infinite Spirit to the lives of finite spirits considered simply collectively. It is true that he wishes to avoid what he regards as one of the main defects of traditional theism, namely the representation of God as a Being over against the world and the finite spirit. Hence he depicts the spiritual life of man as a participation in the divine life. But he also wishes to avoid using the word 'God' simply as a label either for the spiritual life of man considered universally, as something which develops in the course of the evolution of human culture, or for the ideal of complete knowledge, an ideal which does not yet exist but towards which human knowledge progressively approximates. He does indeed speak of the human spirit as 'identical' with God; but he adds, 'in the sense that He *is* all which the human spirit is capable of becoming'.[3] God is the infinite eternal subject; and His complete knowledge is reproduced progressively in the finite subject in dependence, from the empirical point of view, on the modifications of the human organism.

[1] *Ibid.*, pp. 72–3.   [2] *Ibid.*, p. 72.   [3] *Ibid.*, p. 198.

If we ask why God acts in this way, Green implies that no answer can be given. 'The old question, why God made the world, has never been answered, nor will be. We know not why the world should be; we only know that there it is. In like manner we know not why the eternal subject of that world should reproduce itself, through certain processes of the world, as the spirit of mankind, or as the particular self of this or that man in whom the spirit of mankind operates. We can only say that, upon the best analysis we can make of our experience, it seems that so it does.'[1]

In Green's retention of the idea of an eternal subject which 'reproduces itself' in finite subjects and therefore cannot be simply identified with them it is not unreasonable to see the operation of a religious interest, a concern with the idea of a God in whom we live and move and have our being. But this is certainly not the explicit or formal reason for postulating an eternal subject. For it is explicitly postulated as the ultimate synthesizing agent in constituting the system of Nature. And in making this postulate Green seems to lay himself open to the same sort of objection that we brought against Ferrier. For if it is once assumed, at least for the sake of argument, that the order of Nature is constituted by the synthesizing or relating activity of intelligence, it is obvious that I cannot attribute this order to an eternal intelligence or subject unless I have myself first conceived, and so constituted, it. And it then becomes difficult to see how, in Ferrier's terminology, I can unyoke the conceived system of relations from the synthesizing activity of my own mind and yoke it on to any other subject, eternal or otherwise.

It may be objected that this line of criticism, though possibly valid in the case of Ferrier, is irrelevant in that of Green. For Green sees the individual finite subject as participating in a general spiritual life, the spiritual life of humanity, which progressively synthesizes phenomena in its advance towards the ideal goal of complete knowledge, a knowledge which would be itself the constituted order of Nature. Hence there is no question of unyoking my synthesis from myself and yoking it to any other spirit. My synthesizing activity is simply a moment in that of the human race as a whole or of the one spiritual principle which lives in and through the multiplicity of finite subjects.

In this case, however, what becomes of Green's eternal subject? If we wish to represent, say, the advancing scientific knowledge

[1] *Prolegomena*, pp. 103–4.

of mankind as a life in which all scientists participate and which moves towards an ideal goal, there is, of course, no question of 'unyoking' and 'yoking'. But a concept of this sort does not by itself call for the introduction of any eternal subject which reproduces its complete knowledge in a piecemeal manner in finite minds.

Further, how precisely, in Green's philosophy, are we to conceive the relation of Nature to the eternal subject or intelligence? Let us assume that the constitutive activity of intelligence consists in relating or synthesizing. Now if God can properly be said to create Nature, it seems to follow that Nature is reducible to a system of relations without terms. And this is a somewhat perplexing notion. If, however, the eternal subject only introduces relations, so to speak, between phenomena, we seem to be presented with a picture similar to that painted by Plato in the *Timaeus*, in the sense, that is to say, that the eternal subject or intelligence would bring order out of disorder rather than create the whole of Nature out of nothing. In any case, though it may be possible to conceive a divine intelligence as creating the world by thinking it, terms such as 'eternal subject' and 'eternal consciousness' necessarily suggest a correlative eternal object. And this would mean an absolutization of the subject-object relationship, similar to that of Ferrier.

Objections of this sort may appear to be niggling and to indicate an inability to appreciate Green's general vision of an eternal consciousness in the life of which we all participate. But the objections serve at any rate the useful purpose of drawing attention to the fact that Green's often acute criticism of other philosophers is combined with that rather vague and woolly speculation which has done so much to bring metaphysical idealism into disrepute.[1]

3. In his moral theory Green stands in the tradition of Plato and Aristotle, in the sense that for him the concept of good is primary, not that of obligation. In particular, his idea of the good for man as consisting in the full actualization of the potentialities of the human person in an harmonious and unified state of being recalls the ethics of Aristotle. Green does indeed speak of 'self-satisfaction' as the end of moral conduct, but he makes it clear

---

[1] Obviously, metaphysical idealists are by no means the only philosophers whose criticism of their opponents has been more telling than their own positive contributions to philosophy. Indeed, the frequency with which this situation occurs raises general problems about philosophy. But they cannot be discussed here.

that self-satisfaction signifies for him self-realization rather than pleasure. We must distinguish between 'the quest for self-satisfaction which all moral activity is rightly held to be, and the quest for pleasure which morally *good* activity is not'.[1] This does not mean that pleasure is excluded from the good for man. But the harmonious and integrated actualization of the human person's potentialities cannot be identified with the search for pleasure. For the moral agent is a spiritual subject, not simply a sensitive organism. And in any case pleasure is a concomitant of the actualization of one's powers rather than this actualization itself.

Now it is certain that it is only through action that a man can realize himself, in the sense of actualizing his potentialities and developing his personality towards the ideal state of harmonious integration of his powers. And it is also obvious that every human act, in the proper sense of the term, is motivated. It is performed in view of some immediate end or goal. But it is arguable that a man's motives are determined by his existing character, in conjunction with other circumstances, and that character is itself the result of empirical causes. In this case are not a man's actions determined in such a way that what he will be depends on what he is, what he is depending in turn on circumstances other than his free choice? True, circumstances vary; but the ways in which men react to varying circumstances seem to be determined. And if all a man's acts are determined, is there any room for an ethical theory which sets up a certain ideal of human personality as that which we ought to strive to realize through our actions?

Green is quite prepared to concede to the determinists a good deal of the ground on which they base their case. But at the same time he tries to take the sting out of these concessions. 'The propositions, current among "determinists", that a man's action is the joint result of his character and circumstances, is true enough in a certain sense, and, in that sense, is quite compatible with an assertion of human freedom.'[2] In Green's view, it is not a necessary condition for the proper use of the word 'freedom' that a man should be able to do or to become anything whatsoever. To justify our describing a man's actions as free, it is sufficient that they should be his own, in the sense that he is truly the author of them. And if a man's action follows from his character, if, that is to say, he responds to a situation which calls for action in a

[1] *Prolegomena*, p. 169.   [2] *Ibid.*, p. 109.

certain way because he is a certain sort of man, the action is his own; he, and nobody else, is the responsible author of it.

In defending this interpretation of freedom Green lays emphasis on self-consciousness. In the history of any man there is a succession of natural empirical factors of one kind or another, natural impulses for example, which the determinist regards as exercising a decisive influence on the man's conduct. Green argues, however, that such factors become morally relevant only when they are assumed, as it were, by the self-conscious subject, that is, when they are taken up into the unity of self-consciousness and turned into motives. They then become internal principles of action; and, as such, they are principles of free action.

This theory, which is in some respects reminiscent of Schelling's theory of freedom, is perhaps hardly crystal clear. But it is clear at least that Green wishes to admit all the empirical data to which the determinist can reasonably appeal,[1] and at the same time to maintain that this admission is compatible with an assertion of human freedom. Perhaps we can say that the question which he asks is this. Given all the empirical facts about human conduct, have we still a use for words such as 'freedom' and 'free' in the sphere of morals? Green's answer is affirmative. The acts of a self-conscious subject, considered precisely as such, can properly be said to be free acts. Actions which are the result of physical compulsion, for example, do not proceed from the self-conscious subject as such. They are not really his own actions; he cannot be considered the true author of them. And we need to be able to distinguish between actions of this type and those which are the expression of the man himself, considered not merely as a physical agent but also as a self-conscious subject or, as some would say, a rational agent.

Mention of the fact that for Green self-realization is the end of moral conduct may suggest that his ethical theory is individualistic. But though he does indeed lay emphasis on the individual's realization of himself, he is at one with Plato and Aristotle in regarding the human person as essentially social in character. In other words, the self which has to be realized is not an atomic self, the potentialities of which can be fully actualized and harmonized without any reference to social relations. On the contrary, it is only in society that we can fully actualize our

---

[1] Obviously, if Green had lived at a later date, he would have had to cope with theories of the infra-conscious springs of human action.

potentialities and really live as human persons. And this means in effect that the particular moral vocation of each individual has to be interpreted within a social context. Hence Green can use a phrase which Bradley was afterwards to render famous, by remarking that 'each has primarily to fulfil the duties of his station'.[1]

Given this outlook, it is understandable that Green lays emphasis, again with Plato and Aristotle but also, of course, with Hegel, on the status and function of political society, the State, which is 'for its members the society of societies'.[2] It will be noted that this somewhat grandiloquent phrase itself indicates a recognition of the fact that there are other societies, such as the family, which are presupposed by the State. But Hegel himself recognized this fact, of course. And it is clear that among societies Green attributes a pre-eminent importance to the State.

Precisely for this reason, however, it is important to understand that Green is not recanting, either explicitly or implicitly, his ethical theory of self-realization. He continues to maintain his view that 'our ultimate standard of worth is an ideal of *personal* worth. All other values are relative to value for, of, or in a person.'[3] This ideal, however, can be fully realized only in and through a society of persons. Society is thus a moral necessity. And this applies to that larger form of social organization which we call political society or the State as well as to the family. But it by no means follows that the State is an end itself. On the contrary, its function is to create and maintain the conditions for the good life, that is, the conditions in which human beings can best develop themselves and live as persons, each recognizing the others as ends, not merely as means. In this sense the State is an instrument rather than an end in itself. It is indeed an error to say that a nation or a political society is *merely* an aggregate of individuals. For use of the word 'merely' shows that the speaker overlooks the fact that the individual's moral capacities are actualized only in concrete social relations. It implies that individuals could possess their moral and spiritual qualities and fulfil their moral vocation quite apart from membership of society. At the same time the premiss that the nation or the State is not 'merely' a collection of individuals does not entail the conclusion that it is a kind of self-subsistent entity over and above the individuals who compose it.

[1] *Prolegomena*, p. 192.
[2] *Lectures on the Principles of Political Obligation*, p. 146 (1901 edition). This work will be referred to as *Political Obligation*.
[3] *Prolegomena*, p. 193.

'The life of the nation has no real existence except as the life of the individuals composing the nation.'[1]

Green is therefore quite prepared to admit that in a certain sense there are natural rights which are presupposed by the State. For if we consider what powers must be secured for the individual with a view to the attainment of his moral end, we find that the individual has certain claims which should be recognized by society. It is true that rights in the full sense of the term do not exist until they have been accorded social recognition. Indeed, the term 'right', in its full sense, has little or no meaning apart from society.[2] At the same time, if by saying that there are natural rights which are antecedent to political society we mean that a man, simply because he is a man, has certain claims which ought to be recognized by the State as rights, it is then perfectly true to say that 'the State presupposes rights, and rights of individuals. It is a form which society takes in order to maintain them.'[3]

It is sufficiently obvious from what has been said that in Green's view we cannot obtain a philosophical understanding of the function of the State simply by conducting an historical investigation into the ways in which actual political societies have in fact arisen. We have to consider the nature of man and his moral vocation. Similarly, to have a criterion for judging laws we have to understand the moral end of man, to which all rights are relative. 'A law is not good because it enforces "natural rights", but because it contributes to the realization of a certain end. We only discover what rights are natural by considering what powers must be secured to a man in order to the attainment of this end. These powers a perfect law will secure to their full extent.'[4]

From this close association of political society with the attainment of man's moral end it follows that 'morality and political subjection have a common source, "*political* subjection" being distinguished from that of a slave, as a subjection which secures

---

[1] *Ibid.*, p. 193. Hegel could, of course, say the same. For the universal, in his view, exists only in and through particulars. At the same time, in speaking of the State, Green does not employ the exalted epithets used by the German philosopher.

[2] Society in this context does not necessarily mean the State. The members of a family, for example, enjoy rights. The point is that 'right' is, so to speak, a social term.

[3] *Political Obligation*, p. 144. The State, of course, presupposes the family, a form of society in which the claims of individuals are already recognized. The State maintains these rights.

[4] *Ibid.*, p. 41.

rights to a subject. That common source is the rational recognition by certain human beings—it may be merely by children of the same parent—of a common well-being which is their well-being, and which they conceive as their well-being, whether at any moment any one of them is inclined to it or no, . . .'[1] Obviously, any given individual may be disinclined to pursue what promotes this common well-being or good. Hence there is need for moral rules or precepts and, in the political sphere, for laws. Moral obligation and political obligation are thus closely linked by Green. The real basis of an obligation to obey the law of the State is neither fear nor mere expediency but man's moral obligation to avoid those actions which are incompatible with the attainment of his moral end and to perform those actions which are required for its attainment.

It follows that there can be no right to disobey or rebel against the State as such. That is to say, 'so far as the laws anywhere or at any time in force fulfil the idea of a State, there can be no right to disobey them'.[2] But, as Hegel admitted, the actual State by no means always measures up to the idea or ideal of the State; and a given law may be incompatible with the real interest or good of society as a whole. Hence civil disobedience in the name of the common good or well-being can be justifiable. Obviously, men have to take into account the fact that it is in the public interest that laws should be obeyed. And the claim of this public interest will usually favour working for the repeal of the objectionable law rather than downright disobedience to it. Further, men ought to consider whether disobedience to an objectionable law might result in some worse evil, such as anarchy. But the moral foundation of political obligation does not entail the conclusion that civil disobedience is never justified. Green sets rather narrow limits to the scope of civil disobedience by saying that to justify our practising it we ought to be able 'to point to some public interest, generally recognized as such'.[3] But from what he subsequently says it does not seem that the proviso 'generally recognized as such' is intended to exclude entirely the possibility of a right to civil disobedience in the name of an ideal higher than that shared by the community in general. The reference is rather to an appeal to a generally recognized public interest against a law which is promulgated not for the public good but in the private interest of a special group or class.

[1] *Political Obligation*, p. 125.   [2] *Ibid.*, p. 147.   [3] *Ibid.*, p. 149.

Given Green's view that the State exists to promote the common good by creating and maintaining the conditions in which all its citizens can develop their potentialities as persons, it is understandable that he has no sympathy with attacks on social legislation as violating individual liberty, when liberty signifies the power to do as one likes without regard to others. Some people, he remarks, say that their rights are being violated if they are forbidden, for example, to build houses without any regard to sanitary requirements or to send their children out to work without having received any education. In point of fact, however, no rights are being violated. For a man's rights depend on social recognition in view of the welfare of society as a whole. And when society comes to see, as it has not seen before, that the common good requires a new law, such as a law enforcing elementary education, it withdraws recognition of what may formerly have been accounted a right.

Clearly, in certain circumstances the appeal from a less to a more adequate conception of the common good and its requirements might take the form of insisting on a greater measure of individual liberty. For human beings cannot develop themselves as persons unless they have scope for the exercise of such liberty. But Green is actually concerned with opposing *laissez-faire* dogmas. He does not advocate curtailment of individual liberty by the State for the sake of such curtailment. Indeed, he looks on the social legislation of which he approves as a removal of obstacles to liberty, that is, the liberty of all citizens to develop their potentialities as human beings. For example, a law determining the minimum age at which children can be sent to work removes an obstacle to their receiving education. It is true that the law curtails the liberty of parents and prospective employers to do what they like without regard to the common good. But Green will not allow any appeal from the common good to liberty in this sense. Private, sectional and class interests, however hard they may mask themselves under an appeal to private liberty, cannot be allowed to stand in the way of the creation by the State of conditions in which all its citizens have the opportunity to develop themselves as human beings and to live truly human lives.

With Green, therefore, we have a conspicuous example of the revision of liberalism in accordance with the felt need for an increase in social legislation. He tries to interpret, we can say, the operative ideal of a movement which was developing during the closing decades of the nineteenth century. His formulation of a theory may be open to some criticism. But it was certainly preferable not only to *laissez-faire* dogmatism but also to attempts to retain this dogmatism in principle while making concessions which were incompatible with it.

In conclusion it is worth remarking that Green is not blind to the fact that fulfilment of our moral vocation by performing the duties of our 'station' in society may seem to be a rather narrow and inadequate ideal. For 'there may be reason to hold that there are capacities of the human spirit not realizable in persons under the conditions of any society that we know, or can positively conceive, or that may be capable of existing on the earth'.[1] Hence, unless we judge that the problem presented by unfulfilled capacities is insoluble, we may believe that the personal life which is lived on earth in conditions which thwart its full development is continued in a society in which man can attain his full perfection. 'Or we may content ourselves with saying that the personal self-conscious being, which comes from God, is for ever continued in God.'[2] Green speaks in a rather non-committal fashion. But his personal attitude seems to be much more akin to that of Kant, who postulated continued life after death as an unceasing progress in perfection, than to that of Hegel, who does not appear to have been interested in the question of personal immortality, whether he believed in it or not.

4. The idea of a unity underlying the distinction between subject and object becomes prominent in the thought of Edward Caird (1835–1908), Fellow of Merton College, Oxford (1864–6), professor of moral philosophy in the University of Glasgow (1866–93) and Master of Balliol College, Oxford (1893–1907). His celebrated work, *A Critical Account of the Philosophy of Kant*, appeared in 1877, a revised edition in two volumes being published in 1889 under the title *The Critical Philosophy of Kant*. In 1883 Caird published a small work on Hegel,[3] which is still considered one of the best introductions to the study of this philosopher. Of Caird's other writings we may mention *The Social Philosophy and Religion of Comte* (1885), *Essays on Literature and Philosophy* (two volumes, 1892), *The Evolution of Religion* (two volumes, 1893) and *The Evolution of Theology in the Greek Philosophers* (two volumes,

---

[1] *Prolegomena*, p. 195.   [2] *Ibid.*
[3] *Hegel*, published in Blackwood's Philosophical Classics series.

1904). The two last named works are the published versions of sets of Gifford Lectures.

Though Caird wrote on both Kant and Hegel, and though he used metaphysical idealism as an instrument in interpreting human experience and as a weapon for attacking materialism and agnosticism, he was not, and did not pretend to be, a disciple of Hegel or of any other German philosopher. Indeed, he considered that any attempt to import a philosophical system into a foreign country was misplaced.[1] It is idle to suppose that what satisfied a past generation in Germany will satisfy a later generation in Great Britain. For intellectual needs change with changing circumstances.

In the modern world, Caird maintains, we have seen the reflective mind questioning man's spontaneous certainties and breaking asunder factors which were formerly combined. For example, there is the divergence between the Cartesian point of departure, the self-conscious ego, and that of the empiricists, the object as given in experience. And the gulf between the two traditions has grown so wide that we are told that we must either reduce the physical to the psychical or the psychical to the physical. In other words, we are told that we must choose between idealism and materialism, as their conflicting claims cannot be reconciled. Again, there is the gulf which has developed between the religious consciousness and faith on the one hand and the scientific outlook on the other, a gulf which implies that we must choose between religion and science, as the two cannot be combined.

When oppositions and conflicts of this kind have once arisen in man's cultural life, we cannot simply return to the undivided but naïve consciousness of an earlier period. Nor is it sufficient to appeal with the Scottish School to the principles of common sense. For it is precisely these principles which have been called in question, as by Humian scepticism. Hence the reflective mind is forced to look for a synthesis in which opposed points of view can be reconciled at a higher level than that of the naïve consciousness.

Kant made an important contribution to the fulfilment of this task. But its significance has, in Caird's opinion, been misunderstood, the misunderstanding being due primarily to Kant himself.

[1] On this subject see Caird's Preface to *Essays in Philosophical Criticism*, edited by A. Seth and R. B. Haldane (1883).

For instead of interpreting the distinction between appearance and reality as referring simply to different stages in the growth of knowledge, the German philosopher represented it as a distinction between phenomena and unknowable things-in-themselves. And it is precisely this notion of the unknowable thing-in-itself which has to be expelled from philosophy, as indeed Kant's successors have done. When we have got rid of this notion, we can see that the real significance of the critical philosophy lies in its insight into the fact that objectivity exists only for a self-conscious subject. In other words, Kant's real service was to show that the fundamental relationship is that between subject and object, which together form a unity-in-difference. Once we grasp this truth, we are freed from the temptation to reduce subject to object or object to subject. For this temptation has its origin in an unsatisfactory dualism which is overcome by the theory of an original synthesis. The distinction between subject and object emerges within the unity of consciousness, a unity which is fundamental.

According to Caird, science itself bears witness in its own way to this unity-in-difference. True, it concentrates on the object. At the same time it aims at the discovery of universal laws and at correlating these laws; and it thus tacitly presupposes the existence of an intelligible system which cannot be simply heterogeneous or alien to the thought which understands it. In other words, science bears witness to the correlativity of thought and its object.

Though, however, one of the tasks allotted to the philosopher by Caird is that of showing how science points to the basic principle of the synthesis of subject and object as a unity-in-difference, he himself gives his attention chiefly to the religious consciousness. And in this sphere he finds himself driven to go behind subject and object to an underlying unity and ground. Subject and object are distinct. Indeed, 'all our life moves between these two terms which are essentially distinct from, and even opposed to, each other'.[1] Yet they are at the same time related to each other in such a way that neither can be conceived without the other.[2] And 'we are forced to seek the secret of their being in a higher principle, of whose unity they in their action and reaction are the manifestations, which they presuppose as their beginning and to which they point as their end'.[3]

[1] *The Evolution of Religion*, I, p. 65.
[2] This is obviously true in regard to the *terms* 'subject' and 'object'.
[3] *The Evolution of Religion*, I, p. 67.

This enveloping unity, which is described in Platonic phrases as being 'at once the source of being to all things that are, and of knowing to all beings that know',[1] is the presupposition of all consciousness. And it is what we call God. It does not follow, Caird insists, that all men possess an explicit awareness of God as the ultimate unity of being and knowing, of objectivity and subjectivity. An explicit awareness is in the nature of the case the product of a long process of development. And we can see in the history of religion the main stages of this development.[2]

The first stage, that of 'objective religion', is dominated by awareness of the object, not indeed as the object in the abstract technical sense of the term, but in the form of the external things by which man finds himself surrounded. At this stage man cannot form an idea of anything 'which he cannot body forth as an existence in space and time'.[3] We can assume that he has some dim awareness of a unity comprehending both himself and other things; but he cannot form an idea of the divine except by objectifying it in the gods.

The second stage in the development of religion is that of 'subjective religion'. Here man returns from absorption in Nature to consciousness of himself. And God is conceived as a spiritual being standing apart from both Nature and man, and as revealing Himself above all in the inner voice of conscience.

In the third stage, that of 'absolute religion', the self-conscious subject and its object, Nature, are seen as distinct yet essentially related, and at the same time as grounded in an ultimate unity. And God is conceived 'as the Being who is at once the source, the sustaining power, and the end of our spiritual lives'.[4] This does not mean, however, that the idea of God is completely indeterminate, so that we are forced to embrace the agnosticism of Herbert Spencer. For God manifests Himself in both subject and object; and the more we understand the spiritual life of humanity on the one hand and the world of Nature on the other, so much the more do we learn about God who is 'the ultimate unity of our life and of the life of the world'.[5]

Insofar as Caird goes behind the distinction between subject and object to an ultimate unity, we can say that he does not

---

[1] *Ibid.*, I, p. 68.
[2] Caird's three stages correspond more or less to Hegel's stages; natural religion, the religion of spiritual individuality and absolute religion.
[3] *The Evolution of Religion*, I, p. 189.
[4] *Ibid.*, I, p. 195.   [5] *Ibid.*, I, p. 140.

absolutize the subject-object relationship in the way that Ferrier does. At the same time his epistemological approach, namely by way of their relationship, seems to create a difficulty. For he explicitly recognizes that 'strictly speaking, there is but one object and one subject for each of us'.[1] That is to say, for me the subject-object relationship is, strictly, that between myself as subject and my world as object. And the object must include other people. Even if, therefore, it is granted that I have from the beginning a dim awareness of an underlying unity, it seems to follow that this unity is the unity of myself as subject and of my object, other persons being part of 'my object'. And it is difficult to see how it can then be shown that there are other subjects, and that there is one and only one common underlying unity. Common sense may suggest that these conclusions are correct. But it is a question not of common sense but rather of seeing how the conclusions can be established, once we have adopted Caird's approach. Taken by itself, the idea of an underlying unity may well be of value.[2] But arrival at the conclusion at which Caird wishes to arrive is not facilitated by his point of departure. And it is certainly arguable that Hegel showed wisdom in starting with the concept of Being rather than with that of the subject-object relationship.

5. It has been said of John Caird (1820–98), brother of Edward, that he preached Hegelianism from the pulpit. A Presbyterian theologian and preacher, he was appointed professor of divinity in the University of Glasgow in 1862, becoming Principal of the University in 1873. In 1880 he published *An Introduction to the Philosophy of Religion*, and in 1888 a volume on Spinoza in Blackwood's Philosophical Classics. Some other writings, including his Gifford Lectures on *The Fundamental Ideas of Christianity* (1899), appeared posthumously.

In arguing against materialism John Caird maintains not only that it is unable to explain the life of the organism and of consciousness,[3] but also that the materialists, though undertaking to reduce the mind to a function of matter, tacitly and inevitably

---

[1] *Evolution of Religion*, I, p. 65.

[2] This idea appears, for example, though in a rather different setting, in the philosophy of Karl Jaspers, under the form of The Comprehensive.

[3] In the organism, John Caird argues, we find immanent teleology which shows itself in the way that an internal spontaneity or energy differentiates members and functions and at the same time reintegrates them into a common unity, realizing the immanent end of the whole organism. As for the life of reflective consciousness, the idea of mechanical causality loses all relevance in this sphere.

presuppose from the outset that the mind is something different from matter. After all, it is the mind itself which has to perform the reduction. In an analogous manner he argues that the agnostic who says that God is unknowable betrays by his very statement the fact that he has an implicit awareness of God. 'Even in maintaining that the human mind is incapable of absolute knowledge the sceptic presupposes in his own mind an ideal of absolute knowledge in comparison with which human knowledge is pronounced defective. The very denial of an absolute intelligence in us could have no meaning but for a tacit appeal to its presence. An implicit knowledge of God in this sense is proved by the very attempt to deny it.'[1]

As expressed in this particular quotation, Caird's theory is obscure. But it can be elucidated in this way. Caird is applying to knowledge in particular Hegel's thesis that we cannot be aware of finitude without being implicitly aware of infinity. Experience teaches us that our minds are finite and imperfect. But we could not be aware of this except in the light of an implicit idea of complete or absolute knowledge, a knowledge which would be in effect the unity of thought and being. It is this implicit or virtual idea of absolute knowledge which constitutes a vaguely-conceived standard in comparison with which our limitations become clear to us. Further, this idea draws the mind as an ideal goal. It thus operates in us as a reality. And it is in fact an absolute intelligence, in the light of which we participate.

Obviously, it is essential for Caird to maintain the view expressed in the last two sentences. For if he said simply that we strive after complete or absolute knowledge as an ideal goal, we should probably conclude that absolute knowledge does not yet exist, whereas Caird wishes to arrive at the conclusion that in affirming the limitations of our knowledge we are implicitly affirming a living reality. Hence he has to argue that in asserting the limitations of my intelligence I am implicitly asserting the existence of an absolute intelligence which operates in me and in whose life I participate. He thus utilizes the Hegelian principle that the finite cannot be understood except as a moment in the life of the infinite. Whether the employment of these Hegelian principles can really serve the purpose for which Caird employed them, namely to support Christian theism, is open to dispute. But he at any rate is convinced that they can.

[1] *An Introduction to the Philosophy of Religion*, p. 112.

John Caird also argues, in the same way as his brother, that the interrelation of subject and object reveals an ultimate unity underlying the distinction. As for the traditional proofs of God's existence, they are exposed to the customary objections, if they are taken as claiming to be strictly logical arguments. If, however, they are interpreted more as phenomenological analyses of ways 'by which the human spirit rises to the knowledge of God, and finds therein the fulfilment of its own highest nature, these proofs possess great value'.[1] It is not quite clear perhaps where this great value is supposed to lie. Caird can hardly mean that logically invalid arguments possess great value if they exhibit ways in which the human mind has as a matter of fact reached a conclusion by faulty reasoning. So presumably he means that the traditional arguments possess value as illustrating ways in which the human mind can become explicitly conscious of an awareness which they already possess in an implicit and obscure manner. This point of view would allow him to say both that the arguments beg the question by presupposing the conclusion from the start and that this does not really matter, inasmuch as they are really ways of making the implicit explicit.[2]

Like Hegel, John Caird insists on the need for advancing from the level of ordinary religious thought to a speculative idea of religion, in which 'contradictions' are overcome. For example, the opposed and equally one-sided positions of pantheism and deism are both overcome in a truly philosophical conception of the relation between the finite and the infinite, a conception which is characteristic of Christianity when rightly understood. As for specifically Christian doctrines, such as that of the Incarnation, Caird's treatment of them is more orthodox than Hegel's. He is, however, too convinced of the value of the Hegelian philosophy as an ally in the fight against materialism and agnosticism to consider seriously whether, as McTaggart was later to put it, the ally may not turn out in the long run to be an enemy in disguise, inasmuch as the use of Hegelianism in the interpretation of Christianity tends, by the very nature of the Hegelian system, to involve the subordination of the content of the Christian faith

---

[1] *An Introduction to the Philosophy of Religion*, p. 125.

[2] In more recent times, it has sometimes been said that the traditional proofs of God's existence, while logically invalid, possess value as 'pointers' to God. But unless we know what is meant by saying this, it is difficult to discuss the thesis. We need to be told something more than that the traditional proofs are 'pointers to God' or, as by Caird, that they possess great value as phenomenological analyses. This is the point that I have been trying to make.

to speculative philosophy and, indeed, a tie-up with a particular system.

In point of fact, however, John Caird does not adopt the Hegelian system lock, stock and barrel. What he does is rather to adopt from it those general lines of thought which seem to him to possess intrinsic validity and to be of service in supporting a religious outlook in the face of contemporary materialist and positivist tendencies. He thus provides a good example of the religious interest which characterized a large part of the idealist movement in Great Britain.

6. Among those who contributed to spreading a knowledge of Hegelianism in Great Britain William Wallace (1844–97), Green's successor as Whyte professor of moral philosophy at Oxford, deserves a mention. In 1874 he published a translation, furnished with prolegomena or introductory material, of Hegel's *Logic* as contained in the *Encyclopaedia of the Philosophical Sciences*.[1] He later published a revised and enlarged edition in two volumes, the translation appearing in 1892 and the greatly augmented *Prolegomena*[2] in 1894. Wallace also published in 1894 a translation, with five introductory chapters, of Hegel's *Philosophy of Mind*, again from the *Encyclopaedia*. In addition he wrote the volume on Kant (1882) for Blackwood's Philosophical Classics series and a *Life of Schopenhauer* (1890). His *Lectures and Essays on Natural Theology and Ethics*, which appeared posthumously in 1898, show clearly the affinity between his thought and John Caird's speculative interpretation of religion in general and of Christianity in particular.

Though we must refrain from multiplying brief references to philosophers who stood within the ambit of the idealist movement, there is a special reason for mentioning David George Ritchie (1853–1903), who was converted to idealism by Green at Oxford and who in 1894 became professor of logic and metaphysics in the University of St. Andrews. For while the idealists in general were unsympathetic to systems of philosophy based on Darwinism, Ritchie undertook to show that the Hegelian philosophy was perfectly capable of assimilating the Darwinian theory of evolution.[3] After all, he argued, does not Darwin's theory of the survival of the fittest harmonize very well with Hegel's doctrine that the real is the rational and the rational the real, and that the

[1] This is, of course, the so-called shorter or lesser *Logic*, of Hegel.
[2] *Prolegomena to the Study of Hegel, and especially of his Logic.*
[3] Cf. for example, *Darwin and Hegel, with Other Philosophical Studies* (1893).

rational, representing a value, triumphs over the irrational? And does not the disappearance of the weaker and less fitted for survival correspond with the overcoming of the negative factor in the Hegelian dialectic?

It is true, Ritchie admitted, that the Darwinians were so concerned with the origin of species that they failed to understand the significance of the movement of evolution as a whole. We must recognize the facts that in human society the struggle for existence takes forms which cannot be properly described in biological categories, and that social progress depends on co-operation. But it is precisely at this point that Hegelianism can shed a light which is shed neither by the biological theory of evolution taken purely by itself nor by the empiricist and positivist systems of philosophy which are professedly based on this theory.

Though, however, Ritchie made a valiant attempt to reconcile Darwinism and Hegelianism, the construction of 'idealist' philosophies of evolution, in the sense of philosophies which endeavoured to show that the total movement of evolution is towards an ideal term or goal, was actually to take place outside rather than inside the Neo-Hegelian current of thought.

CHAPTER VIII

ABSOLUTE IDEALISM: BRADLEY

Introductory remarks—The Presuppositions of Critical History
—*Morality and its self-transcending in religion*—*The relevance
of logic to metaphysics*—*The basic presupposition of meta-
physics*—*Appearance: the thing and its qualities, relations and
their terms, space and time, the self*—*Reality: the nature of the
Absolute*—*Degrees of truth and reality*—*Error and evil*—*The
Absolute, God and religion*—*Some critical discussion of
Bradley's metaphysics.*

1. IT was in the philosophy of Francis Herbert Bradley (1846–
1924) that emphasis on the subject-object relationship was
decisively supplanted by the idea of the supra-relational One, the
all-embracing Absolute. Of Bradley's life there is little which
needs to be said. In 1870 he was elected a Fellow of Merton
College, Oxford, and he retained this post until his death. He did
not lecture. And the quantity of his literary output, though
substantial, was not exceptional. But as a thinker he is of considerable interest, especially perhaps for the way in which he
combines a radical criticism of the categories of human thought,
when considered as instruments for apprehending ultimate reality,
with a firm faith in the existence of an Absolute in which all contradictions and antinomies are overcome.

In 1874 Bradley published an essay on *The Presuppositions of
Critical History*, to which reference will be made in the next
section. *Ethical Studies* appeared in 1876, *The Principles of Logic*
in 1883,[1] *Appearance and Reality* in 1893,[2] and *Essays on Truth
and Reality* in 1914. Other essays and articles were collected
and published posthumously in two volumes in 1935 under the
title *Collected Essays*.[3] A small book of *Aphorisms* appeared in
1930.

Bradley's enemies were those of the idealists in general, namely
empiricists, positivists and materialists, though in his case we have
to add the pragmatists. As a polemical writer he did not always
represent his opponents' views in a manner which they considered

---

[1] The second edition appeared in two volumes in 1922.
[2] A second edition, with an added Appendix, appeared in 1897.
[3] *The Presuppositions of Critical History* is reprinted in the first volume.

fair; but he could be devastating, and on occasion none too polite. His own philosophy has often been described as Neo-Hegelian. But though he was undoubtedly influenced by Hegelianism, the description is not altogether appropriate. It is true that both Hegel and Bradley were concerned with the totality, the Absolute. But the two men held markedly different views about the capacity of the human reason to grasp the Absolute. Hegel was a rationalist, in the sense, that is to say, that he regarded reason (*Vernunft*), as distinct from understanding (*Verstand*), as capable of penetrating the inner life of the Absolute. He endeavoured to lay bare the essential structure of the self-developing universe, the totality of Being; and he showed an overwhelming confidence in the power of dialectical thought to reveal the nature of the Absolute both in itself and in its concrete manifestations in Nature and Spirit. Bradley's dialectic, however, largely took the form of a systematic self-criticism by discursive thought, a criticism which, in his opinion at least, made clear the incapacity of human thought to attain any adequate grasp of ultimate reality, of what is really real. The world of discursive thought was for him the world of appearance; and metaphysical reflection showed that it was precisely this, by revealing the antinomies and contradictions engendered by such thought. Bradley was indeed convinced that the reality which is distorted by discursive thought is in itself free from all contradictions, a seamless whole, an all-comprehensive and perfectly harmonious act of experience. The point is, however, that he did not pretend to be able to show dialectically precisely how antinomies are overcome and contradictions solved in the Absolute. To be sure, he did in fact say a good deal about the Absolute. And in view of his thesis that ultimate reality transcends human thought, it is arguable that in doing so he showed a certain inconsistency. But the point which is relevant here is that Bradley gave expression not so much to Hegelian rationalism as to a peculiar combination of scepticism and fideism; of scepticism through his depreciation of human thought as an instrument of grasping reality as it really is, and of fideism by his explicit assertion that belief in a One which satisfies all the demands of ideal intelligibility rests on an initial act of faith that is pre-supposed by all genuinely metaphysical philosophy.

In reaching this characteristic position Bradley was influenced to a certain extent by Herbart's view that contradictions do not belong to reality itself but emerge only through our inadequate ways of conceiving reality.[1] This is not to suggest that Bradley was an Herbartian. He was a monist, whereas the German philosopher was a pluralist. But the late Professor A. E. Taylor relates that when he was at Merton College, he was recommended by Bradley to study Herbart as a wholesome correction to undue absorption in Hegelian ways of thinking.[2] And an understanding of Herbart's influence on Bradley helps to correct any overemphasis on Hegelian elements in the latter's philosophy.

Bradley's philosophy, however, cannot be adequately described in terms of influence exercised by other thinkers. It was in fact an original creation, in spite of the stimulus derived from such different German philosophers as Hegel and Herbart. In some respects, for instance in the way in which the concept of 'God' is represented as transcended in that of the suprapersonal Absolute, Bradley's thought shows clear signs of the influence of German absolute idealism. And the way in which the tendency of earlier British idealists to absolutize the subject-object relationship gives way before the idea of the totality, the One, can be said to represent the triumph of the absolute idealism which is associated above all with the name of Hegel. But British absolute idealism, especially in the case of Bradley, was a native version of the movement. It may not be as impressive as the Hegelian system; but this is no good reason for depicting it as no more than a minor replica of Hegelianism.

2. In his essay on *The Presuppositions of Critical History* Bradley writes that the critical mind must provisionally suspect the reality of everything before it. At the same time 'critical history must have a presupposition, and this presupposition is the uniformity of law'.[3] That is to say, 'critical history assumes that its world is one',[4] this unity being that of the universality of law and of 'what loosely may be termed causal connection'.[5] History does not start by proving this unity; it presupposes it as the condition of its own possibility, though developed history confirms the truth of the presupposition.

There is no mention here of the Absolute. Indeed, the world of causal connections is relegated by Bradley in his metaphysics to the sphere of appearance. But in the light of the later development of his thought we can see in the idea of the unity of the world of

---

[1] See Vol. VII of this *History*, p. 251.
[2] See *Contemporary British Philosophy, Second Series*, p. 271, edited by J. H. Muirhead (1925).
[3] *Collected Essays*, I, p. 24.   [4] *Ibid.*, I, p. 20.   [5] *Ibid.*, I, p. 21.

history as a presupposition of historiography a hint of the idea of a total organic unity as the presupposition of metaphysics. And this suggestion seems to be supported by Bradley's assertion in a note that 'the universe seems to be one system; it is an organism (it would appear) and more. It bears the character of the self, the personality to which it is relative, and without which it is as good as nothing. Hence any portion of the universe by itself cannot be a consistent system; for it refers to the whole, and has the whole present in it. Potentially the whole (since embodying that which is actually the whole), in trying to fix itself on itself, it succeeds only in laying stress on its character of relativity; it is carried beyond and contradicts itself'.[1] To be sure, this is not precisely a statement of the doctrine of the Absolute as we find it in *Appearance and Reality*, where the Absolute is certainly not depicted as a self. At the same time the passage serves to show how Bradley's mind was dominated by the idea of the universe as an organic whole.

3. Bradley's *Ethical Studies* is not a metaphysical work. Indeed, on reading the first essay one may receive the impression that the writer's line of thought has more affinity with the modern analytic movement than with what would naturally be expected from a metaphysical idealist. For Bradley concerns himself with examining what the ordinary man understands by responsibility and imputability, and he then shows how two theories of human action are incompatible with the conditions of moral responsibility which are implicitly presupposed by 'the vulgar'.

On the one hand, the ordinary man implicitly assumes that he cannot legitimately be held morally responsible for an action unless he is the same man who performed the action. And if this assumption is taken to be correct, it excludes that form of determination which is based on the associationist psychology and to all intents and purposes does away with any permanent self-identity. 'Without personal identity responsibility is sheer nonsense; and to the psychology of our Determinists personal identity (with identity in general) is a word without a vestige of meaning.'[2] On the other hand, the ordinary man assumes that he cannot legitimately be held morally responsible for an action unless he is truly the author of it, unless it proceeds from him as effect from

---

[1] *Collected Essays*, I, pp. 69–70.

[2] *Ethical Studies*, p. 36 (2nd edition). It is in this context that Bradley makes his famous comment: 'Mr Bain collects that the mind is a collection. Has he ever thought who collects Mr Bain?' (p. 39, note 1).

cause. And this assumption rules out any theory of indeterminism which implies that human free actions are uncaused and does away with the relation between a man's action and his self or character. For the agent as described by this sort of theory is 'a person who is *not* responsible, who (if he is anything) is idiotic'.[1]

Bradley is, of course, the last man to suggest that we should take the beliefs of the ordinary man as a final court of appeal. But for the moment he is concerned not with expounding a metaphysical theory of the self but with arguing that both determinism and indeterminism, when understood in the senses mentioned above, are incompatible with the presuppositions of the moral consciousness. And the positive conclusion to be drawn is that the moral consciousness of the ordinary man implies a close relation between actions for which one can legitimately be held responsible and one's self in the sense of character.

Though, however, *Ethical Studies* is not a metaphysical work, either in the sense that Bradley sets out to derive ethical conclusions from metaphysical premises or in the sense that he explicitly introduces his metaphysical system,[2] it certainly has a metaphysical bearing or significance. For the upshot of the work is that morality gives rise to contradictions which cannot be resolved on the purely ethical level, and that it points beyond itself. True, in this work morality is depicted as leading on to religion. But elsewhere religion is depicted as leading on to the philosophy of the Absolute.

For Bradley the end of morality, of moral action, is self-realization. And it follows that the good for man cannot be identified with 'the feeling of self-realizedness',[3] or indeed with any feeling. Hedonism therefore, which looks on the feeling of pleasure as the good for man, is ruled out. In Bradley's view, as in that of Plato, the hedonist should logically assert that any action is moral which produces greater pleasure in the agent. For consistent hedonism admits only of a quantitative standard of discrimination. Once we introduce, with J. S. Mill, a qualitative distinction between pleasures, we require a standard other than the feeling of pleasure and have thus in effect abandoned hedonism. The truth of the matter is that Mill's utilitarianism expresses a groping after the ethical idea of self-realization, and that it is hindered

---

[1] *Ibid.*, p. 12.
[2] The book includes indeed some metaphysical excursions; but Bradley does not explicitly introduce his metaphysics of the Absolute.
[3] *Ethical Studies*, p. 125.

from arriving fully at this idea by its illogical attempt to retain
hedonism at the same time. 'May we suggest, in conclusion, that
of all our utilitarians there is perhaps not one who has not still a
great deal to learn from Aristotle's *Ethics?*'[1]

In making pleasure the sole good hedonism is a hopelessly one-
sided theory. Another one-sided theory is the Kantian ethics of
duty for duty's sake. But here the trouble is the formalism of the
theory. We are told to realize the good will, 'but as to that which
the good will is, it [the ethics of duty for duty's sake] tells us
nothing, and leaves us with an idle abstraction'.[2] Bradley safe-
guards himself from the charge of caricaturing the Kantian ethics
by saying that he does not intend to give an exegesis of Kant's
moral theory. At the same time he states his belief that the
Kantian ethical system 'has been annihilated by Hegel's
criticism'.[3] And Hegel's main criticism was precisely that the
Kantian ethics was involved in an empty formalism.

Bradley does not disagree, any more than Hegel did, with the
view that the end of morality is the realization of a good will.
His point is that content must be given to this idea. And to do this
we must understand that the good will is the universal will, the
will of a social organism. For this means that one's duties are
specified by one's membership of the social organism, and that 'to
be moral, I must will my station and its duties'.[4]

At first sight this Hegelian point of view, with its reminiscences
of Rousseau, may seem to be at variance with Bradley's doctrine
that the end of morality is self-realization. But all depends, of
course, on how the term 'self' is understood. For Bradley, as for
Hegel, the universal will, which is a concrete universal existing in
and through its particulars, represents the individual's 'true' self.
Apart from his social relations, his membership of a social
organism, the individual man is an abstraction. 'And individual
man is what he is because of and by virtue of community.'[5] Hence
to identify one's private will with the universal will is to realize
one's true self.

What does this mean in less abstract terms? The universal will
is obviously the will of a society. And as the family, the basic
society, is at the same time preserved and taken up in political
society, the State, the emphasis is placed by Bradley, as by
Hegel, on the latter. To realize oneself morally, therefore, is to

---

[1] *Ethical Studies*, pp. 125–6.   [2] *Ibid.*, p. 159.   [3] *Ibid.*, p. 148, note 1.
[4] *Ibid.*, p. 180.   [5] *Ibid.*, p. 166.

act in accordance with social morality, that is, with 'the morality already existing ready to hand in laws, institutions, social usages, moral opinions and feelings'.[1]

This view obviously gives content to the moral law, to the command of reason to realize the good will. But, equally obviously, morality becomes relative to this or that human society. Bradley does indeed try to maintain a distinction between lower and higher moral codes. It is true that the essence of man is realized, however imperfectly, at any and every stage of moral evolution. But 'from the point of view of a higher stage, we can see that lower stages failed to realize the truth completely enough, and also, mixed and one with their realization, did present features contrary to the true nature of man as we now see it'.[2] At the same time Bradley's view that one's duties are specified by one's station, by one's place and function in the social organism, leads him to assert that morality not only is but ought to be relative. That is to say, it is not simply a question of noting the empirical fact that moral convictions have differed in certain respects in different societies. Bradley maintains in addition that moral codes would be of no use unless they were relative to given societies. In fine, 'the morality of every stage is justified for that stage; and the demand for a code of right in itself, apart from any stage, is seen to be the asking for an impossibility'.[3]

It scarcely needs saying that the very idea of a moral code involves the idea of a relation to possible conduct, and that a code which has no relation at all to a man's historical and social situation would be useless to him. But it does not necessarily follow that I must identify morality with the existing moral standards and outlook of the society to which I happen to belong. Indeed if, as Bradley admits, a member of an existing society can see the defects in the moral code of a past society, there does not seem to be any adequate reason why an enlightened member of the past society should not have seen these defects for himself and have rejected social conformism in the name of higher moral standards and ideals. This is, after all, precisely what has happened in history.

In point of fact, however, Bradley does not reduce morality simply to social morality. For in his view it is a duty to realize the ideal self; and the content of this ideal self is not exclusively social. For example, 'it is a moral duty for the artist or the

[1] *Ibid.*, pp. 199–200.   [2] *Ibid.*, p. 192.   [3] *Ibid.*

inquirer to lead the life of one, and a moral offence when he fails to do so'.[1] True, the activities of an artist or of a scientist can, and generally do, benefit society. But 'their social bearing is indirect, and does not lie in their very essence'.[2] This idea is doubtless in tune with Hegel's attribution of art to the sphere of absolute spirit, rather than that of objective spirit, where morality belongs. But the point is that Bradley's assertion that 'man is not man at all unless social, but man is not much above the beasts unless more than social'[3] might well have led him to revise such statements as that 'there is nothing better than my station and its duties, nor anything higher or more truly beautiful'.[4] If morality is self-realization, and if the self cannot be adequately described in purely social categories, morality can hardly be identified with conformity to the standards of the society to which one belongs.

Yet in a sense all this is simply grist to Bradley's mill. For, as has already been mentioned, he wishes to show that morality gives rise to antinomies or contradictions which cannot be overcome on the purely ethical level. For example, and this is the principal contradiction, the moral law demands the perfect identification of the individual will with the ideally good and universal will, though at the same time morality cannot exist except in the form of an overcoming of the lower self, a striving which presupposes that the individual will is not identified with the ideally good will. In other words, morality is essentially an endless process; but by its very nature it demands that the process should no longer exist but should be supplanted by moral perfection.

Obviously, if we deny either that overcoming of the lower or bad self is an essential feature of the moral life or that the moral law demands the cessation of this overcoming, the antinomy disappears. If, however, we admit both theses, the conclusion to be drawn is that morality seeks its own extinction. That is to say, it seeks to transcend itself. 'Morality is an endless process and therefore a self-contradiction; and, being such, it does not remain standing in itself, but feels the impulse to transcend its existing reality.'[5] If the moral law demands the attainment of an ideal which cannot be attained as long as there is a bad self to be overcome, and if the existence in some degree of a bad self is a necessary presupposition of morality, the moral law, we must conclude,

---

[1] *Ethical Studies*, p. 223.   [2] *Ibid.*   [3] *Ibid.*
[4] *Ibid.*, p. 201.   [5] *Ibid.*, p. 313.

demands the attainment of an ideal or end which can be attained only in a supra-ethical sphere.

As far as *Ethical Studies* is concerned, this sphere is that of religion. The moral ideal is 'not realized in the objective world of the State';[1] but it can be realized for the religious consciousness. It is true that 'for religion the world is alienated from God, and the self is sunk in sin'.[2] At the same time for the religious consciousness the two poles, God and the self, the infinite and the finite, are united in faith. For religious faith the sinner is reconciled with God and justified, and he is united with other selves in the community of the faithful. Thus in the sphere of religion man reaches the term of his striving and he fulfils the demand of morality that he should realize himself as 'an infinite whole',[3] a demand which can be only imperfectly fulfilled on the ethical level through membership in political society.

Morality, therefore, consists in the realization of the true self. The true self, however, is 'infinite'. This means that morality demands the realization of the self as a member of an infinite whole. But the demand cannot be fully met on the level of the ethics of my station and its duties. Ultimately, indeed, it can be met only by the transformation of the self in the Absolute. And in this sense Bradley's account of morality is pregnant with metaphysics, the metaphysics of the Absolute. But in *Ethical Studies* he is content to take the matter as far as the self-transcending of morality in religion. The self-transcending of religion is left to the explicit metaphysics of *Appearance and Reality*.

4. Turning to Bradley's logical studies, we must note in the first place his concern with separating logic from psychology. Needless to say, he does not question the legitimacy of inquiries into the origin of ideas and into the association between ideas, inquiries which had occupied so prominent a place in empiricist philosophy from Locke to J. S. Mill. But he insists that they belong to the province of psychology, and that if we confuse logical and psychological inquiries, we shall find ourselves giving psychological answers to logical questions, as the empiricists were inclined to do. 'In England at all events we have lived too long in the psychological attitude.'[4]

Bradley starts his logical studies with an examination of the judgment, considered not as a combination of ideas, which have

---

[1] *Ibid.*, p. 316.   [2] *Ibid.*, p. 322.   [3] *Ibid.*, p. 74.
[4] *The Principles of Logic*, I, p. 2 (2nd edition).

to be previously treated, but as an act of judging that something is or is not the case. It is true, of course, that we can distinguish various elements within the judgment. But the logician is concerned not with the psychological origin of ideas or concepts nor with the influence of mental associations but with the symbolic function, the reference, which concepts acquire in the judgment. 'For logical purposes ideas are symbols, and they are nothing but symbols.'[1] Terms acquire a definite meaning or reference in the proposition; and the proposition says something which is either true or false. The logician should concern himself with these aspects of the matter, leaving psychological questions to the psychologist.

Bradley's anti-psychologizing attitude in logic has won him a good mark from modern logicians including those whose general philosophical outlook is more or less empiricist. But the connection between his logic and his metaphysics is generally regarded much less benevolently. On this point, however, we have to be careful. On the one hand Bradley does not identify logic with metaphysics. And he regards his inquiries into the forms, quantity and modality of judgments and into the characteristics and types of inference as pertaining to logic, not to metaphysics. On the other hand in the preface to the first edition of *The Principles of Logic* he implicitly admits that 'I am not sure where logic begins or ends'.[2] And some of his logical theories have an obvious connection with his metaphysics, a connection which I wish to illustrate briefly by one or two examples.

As every judgment is either true or false, we are naturally inclined to assume that it asserts or denies a fact, its truth or falsity depending on its correspondence or lack of correspondence with some factual state of affairs. But while a singular judgment such as 'I have a toothache' or 'This leaf is green' seems at first sight to mirror a particular fact, reflection shows that the universal judgment is the result of inference and that it is hypothetical in character. For example, if I say that all mammals are warm-blooded, I infer from a limited number of instances a universal conclusion; and what I am actually asserting is that if at any time there is something which possesses the other attributes of being a mammal, it also possesses that of warm-bloodedness.[3] The judgment is thus hypothetical; and a gap is introduced between ideal

[1] *The Principles of Logic*, I, pp. 2–3.   [2] *Ibid.*, I, p. ix.
[3] It is presupposed that the judgment is not what Bradley calls a 'collective' judgment, a mere summation of observed cases, but a genuine abstract universal judgment.

content and actual fact. For the judgment is asserted as being true even if at any given time there are no actually existing mammals.

According to Bradley, however, it is a mistake to assume that though the universal judgment is hypothetical, the singular affirmative judgment enjoys the privilege of being tied to a particular fact or experience, which it mirrors. If I say that I have a toothache, I am referring, of course, to a particular pain of my own; but the judgment which I enunciate could perfectly well be enunciated by someone else, who would obviously be referring to a different toothache, his own and not mine. True, we can try to pin down the reference of singular judgments by the use of words, such as 'this', 'that', 'here' and 'now'. But though this device serves very well for practical purposes, it is not possible to eliminate every element of generality from the meaning of these particularizing expressions.[1] If someone holds an apple in his hand and says 'This apple is unripe', I am obviously perfectly well aware what apple is being referred to. But the judgment 'This apple is unripe' is not tied to this particular apple: it could be uttered by someone else, or indeed by the same man, with reference to some other apple. The singular affirmative judgment, therefore, does not enjoy any special privilege of being a mirror of existent fact.

The conclusion which Bradley wishes to draw is that if the judgment is regarded as a synthesis or union of ideas, every judgment is general, and that a gap is thus introduced between ideal content and reality. 'Ideas are universal, and, no matter what it is that we try to say and dimly mean, what we really express and succeed in asserting is nothing individual.'[2] If, therefore, an abstract universal judgment is hypothetical and so divorced to some extent from actual reality, it is no use thinking that in the singular judgment we can find an unequivocal reference to a particular fact. All judgments are tarred with the same brush.

In point of fact, however, 'judgment is not the synthesis of ideas, but the reference of ideal content to reality'.[3] And it is Bradley's contention that the latent and ultimate subject of any judgment is reality as a whole, reality, we may say, with a capital letter. 'Not only (this is our doctrine) does all judgment affirm of Reality, but in every judgment we have the assertion that

[1] Hegel had already drawn attention to this point. See Vol. VII of this *History*, p. 182.
[2] *The Principles of Logic*, I, p. 49.   [3] *Ibid.*, I, p. 56.

"Reality is such that *S* is *P*".[1] If, for example, I assert that this leaf is green, I am asserting that reality as a whole, the universe, is such that this leaf is green. There is no such thing as an isolated particular fact. So-called particular facts are what they are only because reality as a whole is what it is.

This point of view has an evident bearing on the relative adequacy of different types of judgment. For if reality as a whole is the latent ultimate subject of every judgment, it follows that the more particular a judgment is, the less adequate is it as a description of its ultimate subject. Further, an analytic judgment, in the sense of one which analyses a particular given sense-experience, distorts reality by arbitrarily selecting elements from a complex whole and treating them as though they constituted a self-sufficient particular fact, whereas there are no such facts. The only self-sufficient fact is reality as a whole.

Bradley thus turns his back on the empiricist belief that the more we analyse, the closer we approach to truth.[2] It has been assumed that 'analysis is no alteration, and that, whenever we distinguish, we have to do with divisible existence'.[3] This assumption, however, is a 'cardinal principle of error and delusion'.[4] In reality truth, as Hegel saw, is the whole.

This may suggest that we shall come nearer to an apprehension of reality if we turn away from the immediate judgments of sense to the general hypotheses of the sciences. But though in this sphere there is less fragmentation, there is also a much higher degree of abstraction and of mental construction. If reality consists of what is presented to the senses, the abstractions of the sciences seem to be further removed from reality than the immediate judgments of sense. And if reality does not consist of the wealth of sensuous phenomena, can we really suppose that it consists of logical constructions and scientific abstractions? 'It may come from a failure in my metaphysics, or from a weakness of the flesh which continues to blind me, but the notion that existence could be the same as understanding strikes as cold and ghost-like as the dreariest materialism. That the glory of this world in the end is appearance leaves the world more glorious, if we feel it is a show of some fuller splendour; but the sensuous

[1] *The Principles of Logic*, II, p. 623 (terminal essays, 2).
[2] As Bradley turned his back on Hume, so have modern logical atomists turned their back on Bradley. Thus for Bertrand Russell analysis is the path to truth, to a knowledge of reality, rather than a distortion or mutilation of reality. In actual fact, however, we need both analysis and synthesis.
[3] *The Principles of Logic*, I, p. 95.　　　　[4] *Ibid.*

curtain is a deception and a cheat, if it hides some colourless movement of atoms, some spectral woof of impalpable abstractions, or unearthly ballet of bloodless categories.'[1]

This oft-quoted passage is directed not only against the reduction of reality to scientific generalizations which form a web through whose meshes there slips the whole wealth of sensible particulars, but also against the Hegelian idea that logical categories reveal to us the essence of reality and that the movement of dialectical logic represents the movement of reality.[2] And Bradley's general point of view is that the process of judgment and inference, or, better, the process of discursive thought, is unable to grasp and represent reality. To be sure, for the purposes of practical life and of the sciences discursive thought is a perfectly adequate instrument. This is shown by its success. But it does not necessarily follow that it is a fit instrument for grasping ultimate reality as it is in itself.

When Bradley was writing *The Principles of Logic*, he tried to avoid metaphysics as much as he felt possible. In the second edition, published twenty-nine years after the publication of *Appearance and Reality*, there is naturally more reference to metaphysics, together with modifications or corrections of some of the logical views advanced in the first edition. In other words, Bradley's explicit metaphysics reacted on his logic. In any case, however, it is quite clear that his logical theories have from the start a metaphysical relevance, even if the main conclusion is perhaps a negative one, namely that discursive thought cannot comprehend reality. At the same time, as Bradley remarks in his additional notes, if reality is the whole, the totality, it must somehow include thought within itself.

5. In his introduction to *Appearance and Reality* Bradley remarks that 'we may agree, perhaps, to understand by metaphysics an attempt to know reality as against mere appearance, or the study of first principles or ultimate truths, or again the effort to comprehend the universe, not simply piecemeal or by fragments, but somehow as a whole'.[3] Most of us would probably accept his contention that a dogmatic and *a priori* assertion of the impossibility of metaphysics should be ruled out of court. And it is obviously reasonable to say that if we are going to make the

---

[1] *Ibid.*, II, p. 591.

[2] In Bradley's developed metaphysics movement, becoming, belongs to the sphere of appearance.

[3] *Appearance and Reality*, p. 1 (2nd edition, 1897).

attempt to understand reality as a whole, it should be made 'as thoroughly as our nature permits'.[1] But in view of what has been said in the last section about the shortcomings of discursive thought it may seem odd that Bradley is prepared to make the attempt at all. He insists, however, that it is natural for the reflective mind to desire to comprehend reality, and that even if comprehension in the full sense turns out to be unattainable, a limited knowledge of the Absolute is none the less possible.

Now, if we describe metaphysics from the start as an attempt to know reality as contrasted with appearance, we presuppose that this distinction is meaningful and valid. And if we say that metaphysics is an attempt to understand reality as a whole, we assume, at least by way of hypothesis, that reality is a whole, that there is in the same sense a One. But Bradley is perfectly prepared to admit that metaphysics rests on an initial presupposition. 'Philosophy demands, and in the end it rests on, what may fairly be termed faith. It has, we may say, to presuppose its conclusion in order to prove it.'[2]

What precisely is the content of this assumption or presupposition or initial act of faith? In the appendix which he added to the second edition of *Appearance and Reality* Bradley tells us that 'the actual starting-point and basis of this work is an assumption about truth and reality. I have assumed that the object of metaphysics is to find a general view which will satisfy the intellect, and I have assumed that whatever succeeds in doing this is real and true, and that whatever fails is neither. This is a doctrine which, so far as I can see, can neither be proved nor questioned.'[3]

The natural way of interpreting this passage, if it is taken simply by itself, seems to be this. The scientist assumes that there are uniformities to be discovered within his field of investigation. Otherwise he would never look for them. And he has to assume that the generalizations which satisfy his intellect are true. Further investigations may lead him to modify or change his conclusions. But he cannot proceed at all without making some presupposition. Similarly, we are free to pursue metaphysics or to leave it alone; but if we pursue it at all, we inevitably assume that a 'general view' of reality is possible, and therefore that reality as a whole is intelligible in principle. We further inevitably assume that we can recognize the truth when we find it. We assume, that

---

[1] *Appearance and Reality*, p. 4.   [2] *Essays on Truth and Reality*, p. 15.
[3] *Appearance and Reality*, pp. 553–4.

is to say, that the general view which satisfies the intellect is true and valid. For our only way of discriminating between rival general views is by choosing the one which most adequately satisfies the demands of the intellect.

Considered in itself this point of view is reasonable enough. But difficulties arise when we bear in mind Bradley's doctrine about the shortcomings of discursive thought. And it is perhaps not surprising to find expression being given to a somewhat different view. Thus in a supplementary note to the sixth chapter of his *Essays on Truth and Reality* Bradley maintains that the One which is sought in metaphysics is not reached simply by a process of inference but is given in a basic feeling-experience. 'The subject, the object, and their relation, are experienced as elements or aspects in a One which is there from the start.'[1] That is to say, on the pre-reflective level there is an experience 'in which there is no distinction between my awareness and that of which it is aware. There is an immediate feeling, a knowing and being in one, with which knowledge begins.'[2] Indeed, 'at no stage of mental development is the mere correlation of subject and object actually given'.[3] Even when distinctions and relations emerge in consciousness, there is always the background of 'a felt totality'.[4]

This point of view is possibly compatible with that previously mentioned, though one would not normally describe a basic immediate experience as an 'assumption'. In any case Bradley's thesis that there is such an experience enables him to give some content to the idea of the Absolute, in spite of the shortcomings of discursive thought. Metaphysics is really an attempt to think the One which is given in the alleged primitive feeling-experience. In a sense this attempt is foredoomed to failure. For thought is inevitably relational. But inasmuch as thought can recognize the 'contradictions' which emerge when reality is conceived as a Many, as a multiplicity of related things, it can see that the world of common sense and of science is appearance. And if we ask, 'Appearance of what?', reference to the basic experience of a felt totality enables us to have some inkling at any rate of what the Absolute, ultimate reality, must be. We cannot attain a clear vision of it. To do so, we should have to be the comprehensive unified experience which constitutes the Absolute. We should have to get outside our own skins, so to speak. But we can have a

---

[1] *Essays on Truth and Reality*, p. 200.   [2] *Ibid.*, p. 159.
[3] *Ibid.*, p. 200.   [4] *Ibid.*

limited knowledge of the Absolute by conceiving it on an analogy with the basic sentient experience which underlies the emergence of distinctions between subject and object and between different objects. In this sense the experience in question can be regarded as an obscure, virtual knowledge of reality which is the 'presupposition' of metaphysics and which the metaphysician tries to recapture at a higher level.

In other words, Bradley admits the truth of the objection that metaphysics presupposes its own conclusion, but he regards it not as an objection but rather as a clarification of the nature of metaphysics. In view, however, of the importance of the theme it is regrettable that he does not develop his thesis more at length. As it is, he speaks in a variety of ways, employing terms such as presupposition, assumption, faith and immediate experience. And though these different ways of speaking may be compatible, we are left in some doubt about his precise meaning. However, we are probably justified in laying emphasis on Bradley's thesis that there is an immediate experience of 'a many felt in one',[1] and that this experience gives us an inkling of the nature of the Absolute.

6. By the nature of the case there is not much that can be said by way of positive description either about the alleged prereflective experience of a felt totality or about the infinite act of experience which constitutes the Absolute. And it is hardly surprising if Bradley concentrates his attention on showing that our ordinary ways of conceiving reality give rise to contradictions and cannot yield a 'general view' capable of satisfying the intellect. But it is not possible to enter here into all the details of his dialectic. We must confine ourselves to indicating some of the phases of his line of thought.

(i) We are accustomed to group the world's contents into things and their qualities, in Scholastic language into substances and accidents, or, as Bradley puts it, into the substantive and adjectival. But though this way of regarding reality is embedded in language and undoubtedly has a practical utility, it gives rise, Bradley maintains, to insoluble puzzles.

Consider, for example, a lump of sugar which is said to have the qualities of whiteness, hardness and sweetness. If we say that the sugar is white, we obviously do not mean that it is identical with the quality of whiteness. For if this were what we meant, we could

---

[1] *Essays on Truth and Reality*, p. 174. Bradley argued against James Ward that there is in fact such an experience.

not then say that the lump of sugar is hard, unless indeed we were prepared to identify whiteness and hardness. It is natural, therefore, to conceive the sugar as a centre of unity, a substance which possesses different qualities.

If, however, we try to explain what this centre of unity is in itself, we are entirely at a loss. And in our perplexity we are driven to say that the sugar is not an entity which possesses qualities, a substance in which accidents inhere, but simply the qualities themselves as related to one another. Yet what does it mean to say, for example, that the quality of whiteness is related to the quality of sweetness? If, on the one hand, being related to sweetness is identical with being white, to say that whiteness is related to sweetness is to say no more than that whiteness is whiteness. If, on the other hand, being related to sweetness is something different from being white, to say that whiteness is related to sweetness is to predicate of it something different from itself, that is, something which it is not.

Obviously, Bradley is not suggesting that we should cease to speak about things and their qualities. His contention is that once we try to explain the theory implied by this admittedly useful language, we find the thing dissolving into its qualities, while at the same time we are unable to give any satisfactory explanation of the way in which the qualities form the thing. In brief, no coherent account can be given either of the substance-accident theory or of phenomenalism.

(ii) Now let us rule out the substance-accident theory and confine our attention to qualities and relations. In the first place we can say that qualities without relations are unintelligible. For one thing, we cannot think of a quality without conceiving it as possessing a distinct character and so as different from other qualities. And this difference is itself a relation.

In the second place, however, qualities taken together with their relations are equally unintelligible. On the one hand qualities cannot be wholly reduced to their relations. For relations require terms. The qualities must support their relations; and in this sense qualities can be said to make their relations. On the other hand a relation makes a difference to what is related. Hence we can also say that qualities are made by their relations. A quality must be 'at once condition and result'.[1] But no satisfactory account of this paradoxical situation can be given.

[1] *Appearance and Reality*, p. 31.

Approaching the matter from the side of relations we can say at once that without qualities they are unintelligible. For relations must relate terms. But we are also driven to say that relations are unintelligible even when they are taken together with their terms, namely qualities. For a relation must be either nothing or something. If it is nothing, it cannot do any relating. But if it is something, it must be related to each of its terms by another relation. And we are then involved in an endless series of relations.

A Scholastic reader of this ingenious piece of dialectic would probably be inclined to remark that a relation is not an 'entity' of the same logical category as its terms, and that it makes no sense to say that it requires to be related to its terms by other relations. But Bradley does not, of course, intend to say that it is sensible to talk about relations being related to their terms. His point is that they must either be so related or be nothing at all, and that both theses are unacceptable.[1] And his conclusion is that 'a relational way of thought—any one that moves by the machinery of terms and relations—must give appearance, and not truth. It is a makeshift, a device, a mere practical compromise, most necessary, but in the end most indefensible.'[2]

To say roundly that thinking which employs the categories of terms and relations does not give us truth, seems to be an exaggeration even on Bradley's premises. For, as will be seen later, he expounds a theory of degrees of truth, a theory which does not admit any simple distinction between truth and error. It is clear, however, that what he means is that relational thinking cannot give us Truth with a capital letter. That is to say, it cannot disclose the nature of reality as contrasted with appearance. For if the concept of relations and their terms gives rise to insoluble puzzles, it cannot be an instrument for attaining the 'general view' which will satisfy the intellect.

Bradley's position can be clarified in this way. It has sometimes been said that he denied external relations and accepted only internal relations. But this statement can be misleading. It is true that in Bradley's view all relations make a difference to their terms. In this sense they are internal. At the same time they cannot be simply identified with the terms which they relate. And in this sense there not only can but also must be external relations,

---

[1] Obviously, if we wish to avoid Bradley's conclusion, we must refuse to be compelled to choose between these bald theses. For example, we can distinguish two possible meanings of the statement 'a relation is nothing'.

[2] *Appearance and Reality*, p. 33.

though there cannot indeed be a relation which exists entirely on its own, and to which it is purely accidental whether it happens to connect terms or not. Hence Bradley can say: 'External relations, if they are to be absolute, I in short cannot understand except as the supposed necessary alternative when internal relations are denied. But the whole "Either-Or", between external and internal relations, to me seems unsound.'[1]

At the same time it is precisely the rejection of 'Either-Or' and the assertion of 'Both-And' which gives rise to Bradley's critique of relational thought. Relations cannot be external in an absolute sense. But neither can they be wholly internal, completely merged with their terms. And it is the difficulty in combining these two points of view which leads Bradley to conclude that relational thought is concerned with the sphere of appearance, and that ultimate reality, the Absolute, must be supra-relational.

(iii) Bradley remarks that anyone who has understood the chapter in *Appearance and Reality* on relation and quality 'will have seen that our experience, where relational, is not true; and he will have condemned, almost without a hearing, the great mass of phenomena'.[2] We need not, therefore, say much about his critique of space, time, motion and causality. It is sufficient to illustrate his line of thought by reference to his critique of space and time.

On the one hand space cannot be simply a relation. For any space must consist of parts which are themselves spaces. And if space were merely a relation, we should thus be compelled to make the absurd statement that space is nothing but the relation which connects spaces. On the other hand, however, space inevitably dissolves into relations and cannot be anything else. For space is infinitely differentiated internally, consisting of parts which themselves consist of parts, and so on indefinitely. And these differentiations are clearly relations. Yet when we look for the terms, we cannot find them. Hence the concept of space, as giving rise to a contradiction, must be relegated to the sphere of appearance.

A similar critique is applied to the concept of time. On the one hand time must be a relation, namely that between 'before' and 'after'. On the other hand it cannot be a relation. If it is a relation between units which have no duration, 'then the whole time has no duration, and is not time at all'.[3] If, however, time is a relation

---

[1] *Essays on Truth and Reality*, p. 238.
[2] *Appearance and Reality*, p. 34.　　　[3] *Ibid.*, p. 37.

between units which themselves possess duration, the alleged units cannot be really units but dissolve into relations. And there are no terms. It may be said that time consists of 'now's'. But as the concept of time involves the ideas of before and after, diversity is inevitably introduced into the 'now'; and the game starts once more.

(iv) Some people, Bradley remarks, are quite prepared to see the external spatio-temporal world relegated to the sphere of appearance, but will assure us that the self at least is real. For his own part, however, he is convinced that the idea of the self, no less than the ideas of space and time, gives rise to insoluble puzzles. Obviously, the self exists in some sense. But once we start to ask questions about the nature of the self, we soon see how little value is to be attached to people's spontaneous conviction that they know perfectly well what the term means.

On the one hand a phenomenalistic analysis of the self cannot be adequate. If we try to equate a man's self with the present contents of his experience, our thesis is quite incompatible with our ordinary use of the word 'self'. For we obviously think and speak of the self as having a past and a future, and so as enduring beyond the present moment. If, however, we try to find a relatively enduring self by distinguishing between the relatively constant average mass of a man's psychical states and those states which are clearly transitory, we shall find that it is impossible to say where the essential self ends and the accidental self begins. We are faced with 'a riddle without an answer'.[1]

On the other hand, if we abandon phenomenalism and locate the self in a permanent unit or monad, we are again faced with insoluble difficulties. If all the changing states of consciousness are to be attributed to this unit, in what sense can it be called a unit? And how is personal identity to be defined? If, however, the unit or monad is depicted as underlying all these changing states, 'it is a mere mockery to call it the self of a man'.[2] It would be absurd to identify a man's self with a kind of metaphysical point.

Bradley's conclusion is that 'the self is no doubt the highest form of experience which we have, but, for all that, is not a true form'.[3] The earlier idealists may have thought that the subject-object relationship was a firm rock on which to build a philosophy of reality, but in Bradley's opinion the subject, no less than the object, must be relegated to the sphere of appearance.

---

[1] *Appearance and Reality*, p. 80.   [2] *Ibid.*, p. 87.   [3] *Ibid.*, p. 119.

7. Reality for Bradley is one. The splintering of reality into finite things connected by relations belongs to the sphere of appearance. But to say of something that it is appearance is not to deny that it exists. 'What appears, for that sole reason, most indubitably *is*; and there is no possibility of conjuring its being away from it.'[1] Further, inasmuch as they exist, appearances must be comprised within reality; they are real appearances. Indeed, 'reality, set on one side and apart from all appearance, would assuredly be nothing'.[2] In other words, the Absolute is the totality of its appearances: it is not an additional entity lying behind them.

At the same time appearances cannot exist in the Absolute precisely as appearances. That is to say, they cannot exist in the Absolute in such a way as to give rise to contradictions or antinomies. For the whole which we seek in metaphysics must be one which completely satisfies the intellect. In the Absolute, therefore, appearances must be transformed and harmonized in such a way that no contradictions remain.

What must the Absolute, or reality, be, for such a trans-formation of appearances to be possible? Bradley answers that it must be an infinite act of experience, and moreover, sentient experience. 'Being and reality are, in brief, one thing with sentience; they can neither be opposed to, nor even in the end distinguished from it.'[3] Again, 'the Absolute is one system, and its contents are nothing but sentient experience. It will hence be a single and all-inclusive experience, which embraces every partial diversity in concord.'[4]

Use of the term 'sentient experience' should not, of course, be taken to imply that according to Bradley the Absolute can be identified with the visible universe as animated by some kind of world-soul. The Absolute is spirit. 'We may fairly close this work then by insisting that Reality is spiritual. . . . Outside of spirit there is not, and there cannot be, any reality, and, the more that anything is spiritual, so much the more is it veritably real.'[5]

We may very well ask, however, what Bradley means by saying that reality is spiritual, and how this statement is compatible with describing reality as sentient experience. And to answer these questions we must recall his theory of an immediate basic feeling-experience or sentient experience in which the distinction between

[1] *Ibid.*, p. 132.   [2] *Ibid.*   [3] *Ibid.*, p. 146.
[4] *Ibid.*, pp. 146–7.   [5] *Ibid.*, p. 552.

subject and object, with the consequent sundering of ideal content from that of which it is predicated, has not yet emerged. On the level of human reflection and thought this basic unity, a felt totality, breaks up and externality is introduced. The world of the manifold appears as external to the subject. But we can conceive as a possibility an experience in which the immediacy of feeling, of primitive sentient experience, is recovered, as it were, at a higher level, a level at which the externality of related terms such as subject and object ceases utterly. The Absolute is such an experience in the highest degree. In other words, the Absolute is not sentient experience in the sense of being below thought and infra-relational: it is above thought and supra-relational, including thought as transformed in such a way that the externality of thought to being is overcome.

When, therefore, the Absolute is described as sentient experience, this term is really being used analogically. 'Feeling, as we have seen, supplies us with a positive idea of non-relational unity. The idea is imperfect, but is sufficient to serve as a positive basis',[1] as a positive basis, that is to say, for conceiving ultimate reality. And reality or the Absolute can properly be described as spiritual inasmuch as spirit is definable as 'a unity of the manifold in which the externality of the manifold has utterly ceased'.[2] In the human mind we find a unification of the manifold; but the externality of the manifold has by no means utterly ceased. The human mind is thus only imperfectly spiritual. 'Pure spirit is not realized except in the Absolute.'[3]

It is important to understand that when Bradley describes the Absolute as spiritual, he does not mean to imply that it is a spirit, a self. Inasmuch as the Absolute *is* its appearances, as transformed, it must include within itself all the elements, so to speak, of selfhood. 'Every element of the universe, sensation, feeling, thought and will, must be included within one comprehensive sentience.'[4] But it would be extremely misleading to apply to the infinite universe a term such as 'self', which connotes finitude, limitation. The Absolute is supra-personal, not infra-personal; but it is not a person, and it should not be described as a personal being.

In other words, the Absolute is not a sentient life below consciousness. But consciousness involves externality; and though it

---

[1] *Appearance and Reality*, p. 530.   [2] *Ibid.*, p. 498.
[3] *Ibid.*, p. 499   [4] *Ibid.*, p. 159.

must be comprised within the Absolute, it must be comprised within it as transformed in such a way that it is no longer what it appears to us to be. Hence we cannot properly speak of the Absolute as conscious. All that we can say is that it includes and at the same time transcends consciousness.

As for personal immortality, Bradley admits that it is just possible. But he considers that a future life 'must be taken as decidedly improbable'.[1] And he evidently does not believe in it, though his main concern is with arguing that a belief in personal immortality is required neither for morality nor for religion. True, the finite self, as an appearance of the Absolute, must be included within it. But it is included only as somehow transformed. And it is clear that the transformation required is for Bradley of such a kind that an assertion of the personal immortality of the finite self would be quite inappropriate.

8. The Absolute, therefore, is all its appearances, every one of them; but 'it is not all equally, but one appearance is more real than another'.[2] That is to say, some appearances or phenomena are less far removed than others from all-inclusiveness and self-consistency. Hence the former require less alteration than the latter in order to fit into the harmonious, all-inclusive and self-consistent system which constitutes reality. 'And this is what we mean by degrees of truth and reality.'[3]

The criteria of truth are coherence and comprehensiveness. 'Truth is an ideal expression of the Universe, at once coherent and comprehensive. It must not conflict with itself, and there must be no suggestion which fails to fall inside it. Perfect truth in short must realize the idea of a systematic whole.'[4] Thought sunders, as Bradley puts it, the *what* from the *that*. We try to reconstitute the unity of ideal content and being by proceeding beyond singular judgments of perception to ever more comprehensive descriptions of the universe. Our goal is thus a complete apprehension of the universe in which every partial truth would be seen as internally, systematically and harmoniously related to every other partial truth in a self-coherent whole.

This goal is, however, unattainable. We cannot combine comprehensiveness with an understanding of all particular facts. For the wider and more comprehensive our relational scheme becomes, the more abstract it becomes: the meshes of the net become wider,

---

[1] *Ibid.*, p. 506.   [2] *Ibid.*, p. 487.   [3] *Ibid.*, p. 365.
[4] *Essays on Truth and Reality*, p. 223.

and particular facts fall through. Further, our relational thinking, as we have already seen, is not in any case fitted to grasp reality as it is, as one fully coherent and comprehensive whole. 'There is no possible relational scheme which in my view in the end will be truth. . . . I had long ago made it clear (so I thought) that for me no truth in the end was quite true. . . .'[1]

Now, if we take it that for Bradley the standard in reference to which we have to measure degrees of truth is the ideal truth which perpetually eludes our grasp, we seem to be left without any standard or criterion which can be of practical use. But Bradley's line of thought seems to be this. 'The criterion of truth, I should say, as of everything else, is in the end the satisfaction of a want of our nature.'[2] We do not know in advance what satisfies the intellect. But by using our intellect in the attempt to understand the world we discover that what satisfies us is coherence and comprehensiveness, as far as we are able to find them. This, then, is what we are aiming at, the ideal goal of perfect coherence and comprehensiveness. But to be able to distinguish between different degrees of truth it is not necessary to have attained this goal. For reflection on the degrees of satisfaction and dissatisfaction which we experience in our actual attempt to understand the world will enable us to make corresponding distinctions between degrees of truth.

9. If the Absolute is its appearances, it must in some sense be or contain error and evil. And though Bradley disclaims the ability to explain precisely how they are transformed in the Absolute, he at any rate feels that it is incumbent on him to show that they are not positively incompatible with his theory of ultimate reality.

The line which Bradley takes in regard to error follows from his theory of degrees of truth. If undiluted truth, so to speak, is identified with the complete truth, every partial truth must be infected with some degree of error. In other words, any sharp distinction between truth and error disappears. An erroneous judgment does not constitute a peculiar kind of judgment. All human judgments are appearance; and all are transformed in the Absolute, though some need a more radical transformation than others. The transformation of what we call erroneous judgments, therefore, does not demand special treatment. It is all a question of degree.

<hr>

[1] *Essays on Truth and Reality*, p. 239.   [2] *Ibid.*, p. 219.

As for evil in the sense of pain and suffering, Bradley suggests that it does not exist, as such, in the infinite act of experience which constitutes the Absolute. The possibility of this can be verified to some extent within the field of our own experience, by the way in which a small pain can be swallowed up, as it were, or neutralized by an intense pleasure. This suggestion is hardly a source of much consolation to the finite sufferer; but Bradley is understandably unwilling to envisage the Absolute as undergoing pain.

In treating of moral evil Bradley makes use of the interpretation to which reference has already been made. Moral evil is in a sense a condition of morality, inasmuch as the moral life consists in an overcoming of the lower self. But morality tends, as we have seen, to transcend itself. And in the Absolute it no longer exists as morality. Absolute experience transcends the moral order, and moral evil has no meaning in this context.

10. Can Bradley's Absolute be properly described as God? Bradley's answer is plain enough: 'for me the Absolute is not God'.[1] Obviously, if we meant by God simply ultimate reality, without any further specification, the Absolute would be God. But Bradley is thinking of the concept of God as a personal being; and he will not allow that personality can be predicated of the Absolute. True, to speak of the Absolute as impersonal would be misleading. For this would suggest that the Absolute is infra-personal. In point of fact personality must be contained within reality, so that the Absolute cannot be less than personal. But, as so contained, personality is transformed to such an extent that we cannot speak of the Absolute as personal 'if the term "personal" is to bear anything like its ordinary sense'.[2] Reality 'is not personal, because it is personal and more. It is, in a word, suprapersonal.'[3]

Some theistic philosophers would obviously comment that they predicate personality of God in an analogical sense and not, as Bradley seems to suppose, in a univocal sense. As predicated of God, the term 'personal' does not imply finitude or limitation. This, however, is precisely the line of argument to which Bradley objects. In his view theistic philosophers begin by wishing to satisfy the demands of the religious consciousness.[4] That is to say, they desire to reach the conclusion that God is personal, a being

---

[1] *Ibid.*, p. 335.
[2] *Appearance and Reality*, p. 531.   [3] *Ibid.*
[4] When speaking of the religious consciousness, it is primarily Christianity which Bradley has in mind. It can hardly be claimed that in all forms of religion the divine, or ultimate reality, is conceived as personal.

to whom man can pray and who can hear man's prayers. But they then pursue a line of argument which progressively eliminates from the concept of personality all that gives it concrete content or meaning for us. And the proper conclusion of this line of argument is that God is not personal but super-personal, above personality. The conclusion, however, which these philosophers actually assert is the one which they wish to arrive at, not the one which follows from the line of argument which they actually employ. It is not that they are deliberately dishonest. It is rather that they take a word which has a definite range of meaning when applied to human beings, evacuate it of its content and then imagine that it can be meaningfully applied to God. In point of fact, if we once admit that terms such as 'personal' cannot be applied to God in the sense which they ordinarily bear in our language, we create a chasm between personality and God. 'Nor will you bridge the chasm by the sliding extension of a word. You will only make a fog, where you can cry out that you are on both sides at once. And towards increasing this fog I decline to contribute.'[1]

The question, however, is not simply whether God should be called personal or super-personal. It must be remembered that Bradley's Absolute *is* its appearances. It is the universe as transformed. If therefore we understand by God a being who transcends the world in such a way that he cannot be identified with it, it is obvious that God and the Absolute cannot be equated. We *could* call the Absolute 'God'. But Bradley's contention is that the term already has in ordinary speech a meaning which is different from that of the term 'Absolute'. Hence confusion results if the two are identified. And in the interest of clarity, and of intellectual honesty, it is preferable to say that the Absolute is not 'God'.

This point of view affects what Bradley has to say of religion. If we assume that for the religious consciousness God is a being distinct from the external world and the finite self, we can only conclude that this consciousness is involved in a self-contradiction. On the one hand it looks on God as the one true reality. And in this case God must be infinite. On the other hand it conceives God as distinct from the multiplicity of creatures and so as one being, even if the greatest, among many. And in this case God must be limited, finite. If, therefore, when we speak of religion, we are thinking of its concept of ultimate reality, we are compelled to

---

[1] *Appearance and Reality*, p. 533.

conclude that it belongs to the sphere of appearance, and that, just as morality passes into religion, so does religion pass into the metaphysics of the Absolute. 'If you identify the Absolute with God, that is not the God of religion. . . . Short of the Absolute God cannot rest, and having reached that goal, he is lost and religion with him.'[1]

There is, however, another point of view to which Bradley gives expression. The essence of religion he maintains is not knowledge. Nor is it feeling. 'Religion is rather the attempt to express the complete reality of goodness through every aspect of our being. And, so far as this goes, it is at once something more, and something higher, than philosophy.'[2] The precise meaning of this definition of religion may not be immediately evident; but it is at any rate clear that there is no question of religion, as so defined, passing into metaphysics. Religion may still be appearance; but so is philosophy. And 'the completion of each is not to be found except in the Absolute'.[3] It is obvious from what has been said that Bradley by no means has the desire of some of the earlier British idealists to use metaphysics to support the Christian religion. But it is equally obvious that he does not share Hegel's sublime confidence in the power of speculative philosophy.

In conclusion we can mention Bradley's passing suggestion of the need for a new religion and religious creed. He obviously does not think that metaphysics can justify Christianity, as Hegel thought that it could. Indeed, Bradley would doubtless think it misleading to apply the name of Christianity to 'absolute religion' as interpreted by Hegel. At the same time it might be possible to have 'a religious belief founded otherwise than on metaphysics, and a metaphysics able in some sense to justify that creed. . . . Though this fulfilment is a thing which I cannot myself expect to see, and though the obstacles in the way are certainly great, on the other hand I cannot regard it as impossible.'[4]

11. In the preface to *Appearance and Reality* Bradley quotes from his note-book the celebrated aphorism, 'metaphysics is the finding of bad reasons for what we believe upon instinct, but to find these reasons is no less an instinct'.[5] This remark is clearly not intended as a flat denial of the view expressed in the same preface that 'the metaphysician cannot perhaps be too much in earnest

[1] *Ibid.*, p. 447.   [2] *Ibid.*, p. 453.   [3] *Ibid.*, p. 454.
[4] *Essays on Truth and Reality*, pp. 446–7.
[5] *Appearance and Reality*, p. XIV.

with metaphysics',[1] provided at any rate that he recognizes the limitations of metaphysics and does not exaggerate its importance. Bradley himself takes seriously his own contention that 'the chief need of English philosophy is, I think, a sceptical study of first principles . . . an attempt to become aware of and to doubt all preconceptions'.[2] This element of scepticism, 'the result of labour and education',[3] is represented by the dialectic of appearance, the critique of our ordinary ways of thought. At the same time the element of belief 'upon instinct' is represented by Bradley's explicit statement, to which reference has already been made, that metaphysics rests on a basic presupposition or assumption or initial act of faith,[4] and by the whole doctrine of the Absolute as a completely self-coherent and comprehensive totality.

This element of belief 'upon instinct' occupies a prominent position in the development of Bradley's metaphysics. Consider, for example, the theory of the transformation of appearances in the Absolute. The theory is not, of course, eschatological in character. That is to say, Bradley is not suggesting that at some future apocalyptic date the phenomena which give rise to contradictions or antinomies will undergo a transformation. He maintains that they exist here and now in the Absolute otherwise than they appear to us to exist. The completely harmonious and all-inclusive experience which constitutes the Absolute is a present reality, not simply something which will come into being in the future. But Bradley does not profess to be able to tell us precisely in what this transformation consists. What he does is to argue from possibility to actuality. We can show, for instance, that the transformation of error is not impossible. And if it is not impossible, it is possible. And if it is possible, it is an actual reality. 'For what is *possible*, and what a general principle compels us to say *must be*, that certainly *is*.'[5]

The same holds good of the transformation of pain. 'That which is both possible and necessary we are bound to think real.'[6] Similarly, of the transformation of moral evil Bradley remarks that 'if possible, then, as before, it is indubitably real'.[7] Again, 'the "this" and "mine" are now absorbed as elements within our Absolute. For their resolution must be, and it may be, and so certainly is *is*.'[8] And as a final example we can mention the

---

[1] *Appearance and Reality*, p. XIV.   [2] *Ibid.*, p. XII.   [3] *Ibid.*
[4] As we have seen, this is also described by Bradley as a dim virtual knowledge.
[5] *Appearance and Reality*, p. 196.
[6] *Ibid.*, p. 201.   [7] *Ibid.*, p. 203.   [8] *Ibid.*, p. 240.

transformation of finite centres of consciousness, which 'evidently is real, because on our principle it is necessary, and because again we have no reason to doubt that it is possible'.[1]

An obvious objection to this line of argument is that we can hardly be said to know that the required transformation is possible, unless we are able to show how it can take place. How, for example, can we legitimately claim to know that finite centres of consciousness can exist as elements within one infinite absolute experience without any disharmony or 'contradiction', unless we are able to show how they can so exist? It is really not enough to say that nobody can prove the impossibility of our thesis. After all, there is very considerable difficulty, *prima facie* at least, in seeing how finite centres of consciousness can be said to exist as elements within one unified and harmonious experience. And the burden of proof lies on the shoulders of those who claim that it is possible rather than of those who say that it is not possible.

It may be said in reply that as Bradley believes both that reality is one infinite self-coherent and all-inclusive experience and that appearances are real, and not simply illusory, appearances, he must also believe that the required transformation of appearances is not only possible but also actual. This is quite true. The point is, however, that Bradley is forced to draw this conclusion only because of an initial assumption or presupposition or hypothesis about reality. The assumption is not proved by the dialectic of appearance. True, the elimination of substance, of the substantial, is skilfully used to suggest that all finite things are adjectival to one reality. But Bradley's criticism of substance is itself open to criticism. And in any case the fact, if it is a fact, that our ordinary ways of conceiving reality give rise to contradictions and antinomies does not of itself prove that reality is a self-coherent whole. For reality might be precisely what the dialectic reveals it as being, namely incoherent. If we go on to assert that reality, as contrasted with appearance, is a self-coherent totality, this is because we have already decided that reality *must* be of this nature. References to a primitive sentient experience of a 'felt totality' will not help us much. The idea of such an experience may indeed serve as an analogue for conceiving the Absolute, if we have already decided that there must be an Absolute. But it can hardly be said to prove that it is necessary to postulate the Absolute, as Bradley conceives it.

[1] *Ibid.*, p. 227.

It is true that Bradley's line of thought can be presented in a plausible way. If we are going to try to understand reality at all, we must assume that reality is intelligible. Hence we must take it that the real is that which satisfies the demands of the intellect. An account of reality which is riddled with self-contradictions does not satisfy the intellect. We must therefore conclude that in reality, as contrasted with appearance, all contradictions are overcome. And in the end this means that we must accept the doctrine of a completely harmonious and all-inclusive totality, the Absolute.

Though, however, it is reasonable to claim that no account of reality which is riddled with contradictions can be accepted as true, it obviously does not follow that we have to accept Bradley's contention that all our ordinary and scientific ways of conceiving reality are in fact riddled with contradictions. True, concepts such as those of space, time and the self have for centuries provided philosophers with problems or puzzles. But we would probably not be inclined to acquiesce in the conclusion that the problems are insoluble on the ground that the concepts are inherently self-contradictory, unless we already believed that reality is different from what it appears to be.

Further, when Bradley makes statements about the Absolute, they are apt to cause no less difficulty than, say, the concept of an enduring self. For example, we are told that 'the Absolute has no history of its own, though it contains histories without number. . . . The Absolute has no seasons, but all at once it bears its leaves, fruit and blossoms.'[1] Now if Bradley's Absolute were transcendent, we could understand the statement that it has no history of its own. But, in his view, the appearances of the Absolute are internal to it: it is nothing apart from them. Hence history, change, development are internal to it. Yet at the same time it 'has no seasons'. The thesis is, of course, that change is 'transformed' in the Absolute. But if it is so transformed that it is no longer what we call change, it is difficult to see how the Absolute can be said to contain histories without number. And if change is not so transformed as to be no longer change, it is difficult to see how the Absolute can be said to have no history. For, to repeat, it *is* its appearances.

The obvious answer to this line of criticism is that it is illegitimate to expect perfect self-coherence from metaphysics. For,

---

[1] *Appearance and Reality*, pp. 499–500.

given Bradley's interpretation of the shortcomings of human thought, it follows necessarily that any concept of the Absolute which we are capable of forming belongs itself to the sphere of appearance. Indeed, the whole of metaphysics is appearance. Nor does Bradley hesitate to admit this. As we have seen, he declares that philosophy, no less than religion, reaches its completion in the Absolute. That is to say, philosophy is an appearance which, as transformed, is included in the infinite experience which constitutes the Absolute but which transcends our grasp. It is no matter for surprise, therefore, if metaphysical statements themselves fail to attain an ideal standard of self-coherence.

This is true enough. But it simply adds point to the contention that in the long run Bradley's assertion of the Absolute rests on an initial act of faith. In the long run it is the '*must* be' which is decisive. For Bradley's sceptical mind all constructions of human thought, including the metaphysics of the Absolute, must be relegated to the sphere of appearance. He allows indeed for degrees of truth. And he is convinced that the metaphysics of the Absolute in truer than, say, a concept of reality as consisting of many separate things linked by relations. But this does not alter the fact that speculative philosophy is appearance, and not identical with absolute experience. As has been already noted, Bradley does not share Hegel's confident 'rationalism'. Hence we can say that his scepticism extends even to metaphysics, as is indeed suggested by the aphorism quoted at the beginning of this section. This scepticism is combined, however, with a firm belief that reality in itself, transcending our powers of comprehension, is a comprehensive, completely harmonious totality, an all-embracing perfectly self-coherent eternal experience.

It is not altogether surprising if contemporary British philosophers, when writing on Bradley, have tended to concentrate on the puzzles which he raises in regard to our ordinary ways of thought and to pass over his doctrine of the Absolute in a rather cursory manner. One reason for this is that the logical puzzles raised by Bradley can often be treated on their own, without reference to any act of faith in the One, and that they are in principle capable of being definitely solved. For example, in order to decide whether it is true to say that space cannot be and at the same time must be a relation or set of relations, it is not necessary to discuss the transformation of space in the Absolute. What we need in the first place is to clarify the meaning or meanings of 'space'. Again, if we take Bradley's thesis that the concept of relation is self-contradictory, as on the one hand all relations make a difference to their terms and so must be internal to them, while on the other hand they must in some sense fall between and connect their terms and so be external to them, we have a problem which we can hope to solve, provided that we are prepared for the requisite clarificatory analysis. We can understand what is meant by Bradley's thesis and what questions have to be answered in order to decide whether or not it is true.

At the same time we obviously miss what one might call the essential Bradley, if we use *Appearance and Reality* simply as a quarry for detached logical puzzles. For the philosopher is clearly a man who is possessed by the idea of the Absolute, of a completely self-consistent and all-inclusive whole. And it is easy to understand how his philosophy has been able to arouse the interest of Indian thinkers who have not abandoned the native traditions of Hindu speculation, and of some Western philosophers who have an initial sympathy with this line of speculation. For there is at any rate some affinity between Bradley's theory of speculation and the Indian doctrine of Maya, the phenomenal world which veils the one true reality. Obviously, both Bradley and the Indian philosophers in question are faced with the same difficulty, namely that every concept which we can form of ultimate reality must itself belong to the sphere of appearance. But their initial 'visions' are similar, and it is a vision which can exercise a powerful attraction on some minds. Perhaps what we need is a serious inquiry into the bases of this vision or initial inspiration, an inquiry which is not dominated by the *a priori* assumption that what Bradley speaks of as a presupposition or act of faith must be devoid of objective value. It is an inquiry which possesses considerable importance in regard to the foundations of speculative metaphysics.

CHAPTER IX

ABSOLUTE IDEALISM: BOSANQUET

Life and writings—Logic; judgment and reality—The meta-physics of individuality—Bosanquet's philosophy of the State—Hobhouse's criticism of Bosanquet—R. B. Haldane; Hegelianism and relativity—H. H. Joachim and the coherence theory of truth.

1. BRADLEY was a recluse. The other leading absolute idealist in Great Britain, Bernard Bosanquet (1848–1923), was not. After studying at Balliol College, Oxford, where he came under the influence of T. H. Green and R. L. Nettleship, he was elected a Fellow of University College, Oxford, in 1871. But in 1881 he took up residence in London with a view to devoting himself not only to writing but also to lecturing for the adult education movement, which was just beginning, and to social work. From 1903 until 1908 he occupied the chair of moral philosophy in the University of St. Andrews.

Bosanquet was a prolific writer. In 1883 his essay on *Logic as the Science of Knowledge* appeared in *Essays in Philosophical Criticism*, edited by A. Seth and R. B. Haldane. *Knowledge and Reality* was published in 1885 and the two-volume *Logic or the Morphology of Knowledge* in 1888.[1] There followed in quick succession *Essays and Addresses* (1889), *A History of Aesthetic* (1892, 2nd edition 1904), *The Civilization of Christendom and Other Studies* (1893), *Companion to Plato's Republic* (1895), *Essentials of Logic* (1895), and *The Psychology of the Moral Self* (1897). In 1899 Bosanquet published what is probably his best known work, *The Philosophical Theory of the State*.[2] Two sets of Gifford lectures, *The Principle of Individuality and Value* and *The Value and Destiny of the Individual*, appeared respectively in 1912 and 1913. Among other publications we may mention *The Distinction between Mind and Its Objects* (1913), *Three Lectures on Aesthetic* (1915), *Social and International Ideals* (1917), *Some Suggestions in Ethics* (1918), *Implication and Linear Inference* (1920), *What Religion Is* (1920), *The Meeting of Extremes in Contemporary Philosophy* (1921) and *Three chapters on the Nature of Mind* (1923).

[1] A second edition appeared in 1911.
[2] A fourth edition appeared in 1923, the year of Bosanquet's death.

In spite of this extensive literary activity Bosanquet has tended to pass into oblivion and, in comparison with Bradley, is rarely mentioned nowadays, except perhaps in connection with a certain brand of political theory.[1] One reason is probably that Bosanquet is a duller and less paradoxical thinker than Bradley. A more important factor, however, seems to be the belief that, political and aesthetic theory apart, he has little to offer that is not to be found in the writings of his more famous contemporary. Indeed, in 1920 Bosanquet himself wrote to an Italian philosopher that from the publication of *Ethical Studies* in 1876 he had recognized Bradley as his master. But this modest remark hardly does justice to the facts. For example, Bosanquet strongly criticized Bradley's work *The Principles of Logic* on the ground that it created a gulf between thought and reality. And Bradley recognized his indebtedness to Bosanquet's ideas in connection with the material added to the second edition of *The Principles of Logic*. As for *Appearance and Reality*, Bosanquet was deeply influenced by it; but, though he was, like Bradley, a monist, he developed his own metaphysics which in some respects stood closer to Hegelianism. He was convinced of the truth of Hegel's principle that the rational is the real and the real the rational, and he did not share Bradley's marked sceptical tendencies.

2. In a certain sense, Bosanquet maintains, it is true to say that the world is for every individual *his* world, the course of his consciousness, built up out of his perceptions. 'The real world for every individual is emphatically *his* world; an extension and determination of his present perception, which perception is to him not indeed reality as such, but his point of contact with reality as such.'[2] That is to say, we must distinguish between the course of consciousness considered as a series of psychical phenomena and consciousness considered as 'intentional', as presenting a system of interrelated objects.[3] 'Consciousness is consciousness of a world only in so far as it *presents* a system, a whole of objects, acting on one another, and therefore independent of the presence or absence of the consciousness which presents them.'[4] We must also allow for a distinction between my objective world and the creations of

---

[1] Bosanquet's history of aesthetic theory remains, however, a valuable contribution to the subject.

[2] *Logic*, I, p. 3.

[3] Bosanquet is concerned with phenomenology rather than with psychology. The individual's world is not built up out of his perceptions considered as psychological entities, but rather out of his perceptions considered as presenting objects.

[4] *Essentials of Logic*, p. 15.

my imagination. Hence we can say that 'the whole world, for each of us, *is* our course of consciousness, in so far as this is regarded as a system of objects which we are obliged to think'.[1]

Reflection on this factor of constraint shows us that the worlds of different individuals are constructed by definite processes common to intelligence as such. In a sense each of us begins with his or her private world. But the more the constructive process of building up a systematic world of objects is developed, so much the more do these several worlds correspond with one another and tend to merge into a common world.

This process of constructing a world is the same as knowledge, in the sense of coming to know. Thus knowledge is the mental construction of reality, the medium in which the world exists for us as a system of interrelated objects. And logic is the analysis of this constructive process. 'The work of intellectually constituting that totality which we call the real world is the work of knowledge. The work of analyzing the process of this constitution or determination is the work of logic, which might be described as the self-consciousness of knowledge, or the reflection of knowledge upon itself.'[2]

Now, knowledge exists in the judgment. And it follows, therefore, if logic is the self-consciousness of knowledge, that the study of the judgment is fundamental in logic. True, we can say that the proposition, the expression of the judgment, has 'parts'. And the enunciation of a proposition is a temporal process. But the judgment in itself is an identity-in-difference: it is 'not a relation between ideas, nor a transition from one idea to another, nor does it contain a third idea which indicates a particular kind of connection between two other ideal contents'.[3]

The ultimate subject of the judgment is reality as a whole, and 'the essence of Judgment is the reference of an ideal content to Reality'.[4] Hence every judgment could be introduced by some such phrase as 'Reality is such that . . .' or 'The real world is characterized by. . . .'[5]

As for inference, we can indeed make a *prima facie* distinction between judgment and inference by saying that the former is the immediate and the latter the mediate reference of an ideal content to reality. But on closer examination the distinction tends to

---

[1] *Ibid.*, pp. 14–15.　　　　　　　　　　[2] *Logic*, I, p. 3.
[3] *Ibid.*, I, pp. 83–4. By 'a third idea' Bosanquet means the copula considered as a distinct element in the judgment.
[4] *Ibid.*, II, p. 1.　　　　　　　　　　[5] *Ibid.*, I, p. 78.

break down. For, properly speaking, no judgment can be said to express knowledge unless it possesses the characteristics of necessity and 'precision', precision depending on the mediating conditions being made explicit. And in this case no absolute distinction between judgment and inference is possible. Instead we have the ideal of one ultimate judgment which would predicate the whole of reality, as an ideal content, of itself. This ultimate judgment would not, of course, be simple. For it would include within itself all partial truths as organically interrelated, as coherent. It would be the all-inclusive identity-in-difference in the form of knowledge. 'The whole is the truth.'[1] And particular truths are true in so far as they cohere with other truths in this whole.

Obviously, Bosanquet is in agreement with Bradley on many points: on the fundamental importance of the judgment in logic, on reality as the ultimate subject of every judgment, and on truth in the full sense as being the complete system of truth. But in spite of the many points of agreement there are important differences of attitude. Thus for Bosanquet reality or the universe is 'not only of such a nature that it can be known by intelligence, but further of such a nature that it can be known and handled by *our* intelligence'.[2] True, Bosanquet carefully refrains from claiming that the finite mind can fully comprehend reality. At the same time he is anxious to avoid what he regards as Bradley's marked tendency to drive a wedge between human thought on the one hand and reality on the other. Every finite mind approaches reality from a particular point of view and builds up its own conception of reality. But though there are degrees of truth, and so of error, no judgment is entirely out of touch with reality; and intelligence as such forces us to conceive the universe in certain ways, so that, despite private points of view, a common objective world is presented in consciousness. Further, human thought as a whole approximates more and more to a comprehension of reality, even though the ideal ultimate judgment is a goal which transcends the capacity of any given finite mind.[3]

3. With Bosanquet, as with Bradley, there is evidently a close connection between logic and metaphysics. For both hold that the

---

[1] *The Principle of Individuality and Value*, p. 43.
[2] *Essentials of Logic*, p. 166.
[3] To a certain extent Bradley would be prepared to speak in much the same way. But it is true that he so emphasizes the deficiencies of human thought that Bosanquet is justified in seeing in Bradley's philosophy the creation of a gap between thought and reality.

ultimate subject of every judgment is reality as a whole. But it would be a mistake to think that because Bosanquet describes logic as the self-consciousness of knowledge, he intends to imply that logic can provide us with factual knowledge about the world. He does not maintain this any more than Bradley does. Logic is the morphology of knowledge: it does not provide us with the content of knowledge.

Indeed, it is a mistake to look to philosophy at all for a knowledge of hitherto unknown facts. 'Philosophy can tell you no new facts, and can make no discoveries. All that it can tell you is the significant connection of what you already know. And if you know little or nothing, philosophy has little or nothing to tell you.'[1] In other words, we acquire factual knowledge by ordinary experience and by the study of physics, chemistry, and so on. Philosophy neither deduces nor adds to this knowledge. What it does is to exhibit a pattern of connections between already known facts.

Obviously, the sciences do not present us with unrelated atomic facts; they exhibit relations, connections, bringing facts under what we call laws. Hence, if philosophy has any such function to perform, to exhibit the 'significant connection' of what we already know must mean showing how the facts which are known otherwise than through philosophy are members of an overall system in which each member contributes to the total unity in virtue of the very characteristics which distinguish it from other members. In other words, the philosopher is not primarily concerned with class-concepts formed by abstraction from differentiating characteristics but rather with the concrete universal, which is an identity-in-difference, the universal existing in and through its particulars.

The concrete universal is called by Bosanquet, following Hegel, the 'individual'. And it is clear that in the fullest sense of the term there can be only one individual, namely the Absolute. For this universal of universals is the all-embracing system which alone can fully satisfy the criteria proposed by Bosanquet, that is, non-contradiction and wholeness. These criteria are said to be really one. For it is only in the complete whole or totality that there is complete absence of contradiction.

Though, however, individuality belongs in a pre-eminent sense to the Absolute, it is also attributed to human beings, even if in a secondary sense. And when examining this use of the term

[1] *Essentials of Logic*, p. 166.

Bosanquet insists that individuality should not be understood in a predominantly negative fashion, as though it consisted chiefly in not being someone else. After all, in the case of the supreme individual, the Absolute, there is no other individual from which it can be distinguished. Rather should individuality be conceived positively, as consisting 'in the richness and completeness of a self'.[1] And it is in social morality, art, religion and philosophy that 'the finite mind begins to experience something of what individuality must ultimately mean'.[2] In social morality, for example, the human person transcends what Bosanquet calls the repellent self-consciousness, for the private will is united with other wills without being annulled in the process. Again, in religion the human being transcends the level of the narrow and poverty-stricken self and feels that he attains a higher level of richness and completeness in union with the divine. At the same time morality is subsumed within religion.

Reflection on the development of the individual self can thus give us some idea of how various levels of experience can be comprehended and transformed in the one unified and all-inclusive experience which constitutes the Absolute. And here Bosanquet has recourse to the analogy of Dante's mind as expressed in the *Divine Comedy*. The external world and the world of selves are both present in the poet's mind and find expression in the poem. The human selves are indeed presented as thinking and acting beings, as real selves existing in an external sphere. At the same time all these selves live only through their participation in the thoughts, emotions and acts which make up the poet's mind as expressed in the poem.

This analogy should not be interpreted as meaning that for Bosanquet the Absolute is a mind behind the universe, a mind which composes a divine poem. The Absolute is the totality. Hence it cannot be a mind. For mind is a perfection which depends on physical preconditions and constitutes a certain level of reality. Nor can the Absolute be simply equated with the God of the religious consciousness, who is a being distinct from the world and who does not contain evil. 'The whole, considered as a perfection in which the antagonism of good and evil is unnoted, is not what religion means by God, and must rather be taken as the Absolute.'[3] Here Bosanquet is at one with Bradley.

---

[1] *The Principle of Individuality and Value*, p. 69.   [2] *Ibid.*, p. 80.
[3] *The Value and Destiny of the Individual*, p. 251.

Though, however, the Absolute cannot be a mind or a self, reflection on self-consciousness, the chief characteristic of mind, can furnish us with clues for deciphering the nature of reality. For example, the self attains satisfaction and richness of experience only by passing out of itself: it must die, as it were, to live. And this suggests that a perfect experience embodies the character of the self to this extent at least, that it passes out of itself to regain itself. In other words, Bosanquet, unlike Bradley, is attempting to offer some explanation of the existence of finite experience. 'Not of course that the infinite being can lose and regain its perfection, but that the burden of the finite is inherently a part or rather an instrument of the self-completion of the infinite. The view is familiar. I can only plead that it loses all point if it is not taken in bitter earnest.'[1] One objection against this Hegelian idea of a self-developing Absolute is that it seems to introduce temporal succession into the infinite being. But unless we are prepared to say that the concept of the Absolute is for us a vacuous concept, we cannot help ascribing to the Absolute a content which, from our point of view, is developed in time.

It may be objected that Bosanquet has done nothing to show that there is an Absolute. He simply assumes its existence and tells us what it must be. His reply, however, is that at all levels of experience and thought there is a movement from the contradictory and partial to the non-contradictory and complete, and that the movement can find no end save in the concept of the Absolute. 'I am aware of no point at which an arrest in the process can be justified.'[2] The idea of the Absolute, the totality, is in fact the motive-force, the final end, of all thought and reflection.

Now, individuality is the criterion of value, a concept on which much more emphasis is laid by Bosanquet than by Bradley. And as individuality is to be found in its complete form only in the Absolute, the Absolute must be the ultimate standard of value, as well as of truth and reality. It follows from this that we cannot attribute an ultimate or absolute value to the finite self. And as Bosanquet conceives self-perfection as involving an overcoming of self-enclosedness and a conscious entry into membership of a greater whole, we would hardly expect him to regard personal immortality as the destiny of the finite self. He claims indeed that the best in the finite self is preserved, in a transformed state, in the Absolute. But he also admits that that which persists of myself

---

[1] *The Principle of Individuality and Value*, pp. 243–4.   [2] *Ibid.*, pp. 267–8.

would not appear to my present consciousness to be a continuation of 'myself'. This, however, is not for Bosanquet any cause for
regret. The self, as we know it, is a mixture, as it were, of the finite
and the infinite; and it is only in shedding the restricting vesture
of finite limited selfhood that it achieves its destiny.

As has already been noted, Bosanquet is much less concerned
than Bradley with illustrating the defectiveness of human thought
as an instrument for grasping reality, and much more concerned
with understanding the universe as a whole and with determining
degrees of perfection or value. Yet in the long run both maintain
that the universe is something very different from what it appears
to be. Bosanquet rather plays down this aspect of the matter.
And for this reason his thought may appear less exciting than that
of Bradley. But both men represent the universe as an infinite
experience, as something, that is to say, which it certainly does
not appear to be at first sight. Though, however, there is a fundamental affinity, Bosanquet is notable as making explicit the value-
judgment which is basic in idealist monism, namely that the
supreme value and the ultimate criterion of all value is the
totality, the all-inclusive concrete universal in which all 'contradictions' are overcome.

4. Given Bosanquet's absolute idealism, one would not expect
him to favour the type of political theory which regards the State
as a device for enabling individuals (in the ordinary sense of the
term) to pursue their private ends in peace and security. All such
theories are condemned as superficial, as theories 'of the first
look'. 'It is the first look of the man in the street or of the traveller,
struggling at a railway station, to whom the compact self-
containedness and self-direction of the swarming human beings
before him seems an obvious fact, while the social logic and
spiritual history which lie behind the scene fail to impress themselves on his perceptive imagination.'[1]

These theories assume that every man is a self-enclosed unit
which undergoes the impact of other such units. And government
tends to appear as the impact of others when systematized,
regularized and reduced to a minimum. In other words, it appears
as something alien to the individual, bearing upon him from without, and so as an evil, though admittedly a necessary evil.

A quite different point of view is represented by Rousseau's
theory of the General Will. Here we have the idea of an 'identity

[1] *The Philosophical Theory of the State*, p. 80 (1st edition).

between my particular will and the will of all my associates in the body politic which makes it possible to say that in all social co-operation, and in submitting even to forcible restraint, when imposed by society in the true common interest, I am obeying only myself, and am actually attaining my freedom'.[1] Yet in the process of expressing his enthusiasm for direct democracy and his hostility to representative government Rousseau really enthrones the Will of All in the place of the General Will, which becomes a nonentity.

We must therefore go beyond Rousseau and give a real content to the idea of the General Will, without reducing it in effect to the Will of All. And this means identifying it with the State when considered not merely as a governmental structure but rather as 'a working conception of life . . . the conception by the guidance of which every living member of the commonwealth is enabled to perform his function, as Plato has taught us'.[2] If the State or political society is understood in this way, we can see that the relation of the individual mind and will to the mind of society and the General Will is comparable to the relation between the individual physical object and Nature as a whole. In both cases the self-enclosed individual is an abstraction. The individual man's real will, therefore, by which he wills his own nature as a rational being, is identical with the General Will. And in this identification 'we find the only true account of political obligation'.[3] In obeying the State the individual obeys his real will. And when he is constrained by the State to act in a certain manner, he is constrained to act in accordance with his real will, and so to act freely.

In other words, the alleged antithesis between the individual and the State is for Bosanquet a false antithesis. And it follows that the alleged problem of justifying interference by the State with private liberty is not a genuine problem. But this is not to say that no genuine problem can arise in regard to some particular concrete issue. For the ultimate end of the State, as of its members, is a moral end, the attainment of the best life, the life which most develops man's potentialities or capacities as a human being. Hence we can always ask, in regard to a proposed law for example, 'how far and in what way the use of force and the like by the State is a hindrance to the end for which the States exists',[4] and which is at the same time the end of each of its members. An appeal simply to private liberty against so-called State interference

[1] *Ibid.*, p. 107.   [2] *Ibid.*, p. 151.
[3] *Ibid.*, p. 154.   [4] *Ibid.*, p. 183.

in general betrays a misunderstanding of the nature of the State and of its relations to its members. But it by no means follows that any and every use of compulsion contributes to the end for which the State exists.

Bosanquet's point of view can be clarified in this way. As the end of the State is a moral end, it cannot be attained unless the citizens act morally, which includes intention as well as external action. Morality in this full sense, however, cannot be enforced by law. Individuals can be compelled, for instance, to refrain from certain actions; but they cannot be compelled to refrain from them for high moral motives. It is indeed clearly conducive to the common good that people should refrain from murder, even if their motive is simply the avoidance of punishment. It remains true, however, that the employment of force, so far as it is the determining cause of an action, reduces the resultant actions to a lower level than they would occupy if they were the result of reason and free choice. Hence the employment of force and compulsion should be restricted as far as possible, not because it is thought to represent an interference by society with self-enclosed individuals (for this is a false antithesis), but because it interferes with the attainment of the end for which the State exists.

In other words, Bosanquet shares the view of T. H. Green that the primary function of legislation is to remove hindrances to the development of the good life. How far, for example, social legislation should extend is not a question which can be answered *a priori*. As far as general principles go, we can only say that to justify compulsion we ought to be able to show that 'a definite tendency to growth, or a definite reserve of capacity, . . . is frustrated by a known impediment, the removal of which is a small matter compared to the capacities to be set free'.[1] On this principle we can justify, for instance, compulsory education as the removal of a hindrance to the fuller and wider development of human capacities. Obviously, the legislation itself is positive. But the object of the law is primarily that of removing hindrances to the attainment of the end for which political society exists, an end which is 'really' willed by every member as a rational being.

If we assume that the moral end is the fullest possible development of man's capacities, and that it is attained or at any rate approached only in the context of society, it seems only natural to look beyond the national State to the ideal of a universal society,

[1] *The Philosophical Theory of the State*, p. 192.

humanity in general. And Bosanquet does at least admit that the idea of humanity must have a place 'in any tolerably complete philosophical thinking'.[1] At the same time he claims that the ethical idea of humanity does not form an adequate basis for an effective community. For we cannot presuppose in mankind at large a sufficient unity of experience, such as exists in a national State, for the exercise of a General Will. Further, Bosanquet condemns proposals for a World-State with plans for substituting a universal language for national languages, a substitution which, in his opinion, would destroy literature and poetry and reduce intellectual life to a level of mediocrity. Like Hegel, therefore, Bosanquet is unable to transcend the idea of the national State, animated by a common spirit which expresses itself in objective institutions and submits these institutions to a critical evaluation in the light of experience and present needs.

Again, like Hegel, Bosanquet is prepared to admit that no actual State is immune from criticism. It is possible in principle for the State to act 'in contravention of its main duty to sustain the conditions of as much good life as possible'.[2] But though this admission would appear to most people to be obviously justified, it creates a special difficulty for anyone who holds with Bosanquet that the State is in some sense identical with the General Will. For by definition the General Will wills only what is right. Hence Bosanquet tends to make a distinction between the State as such and its agents. The latter may act immorally, but the former, the State as such, cannot be saddled with responsibility for the misdeeds of its agents 'except under circumstances which are barely conceivable'.[3]

It can hardly be claimed that this is a logically satisfactory position. If the State as such means the General Will, and if the General Will always wills what is right, it seems to follow that there are no conceivable circumstances in which the State as such could be said to act immorally. And in the long run we are left with a tautology, namely that a will which always wills what is right, always wills what is right. Indeed, Bosanquet himself seems to feel this, for he suggests that on a strict definition of State action we ought to say that the State does not really will an immoral action which we would ordinarily attribute to 'the State'. At the same time he understandably feels bound to admit that there may be circumstances in which we can legitimately speak of

[1] *Ibid.*, p. 328.   [2] *Ibid.*, p. 327.   [3] *Ibid.*, p. 322.

the State acting immorally. But by speaking of 'barely conceivable' circumstances he inevitably gives the impression that for practical purposes the State is immune from criticism. For those who maintain that statements about action by the State are always reducible in principle to statements about individuals, there is obviously no difficulty in speaking about the State as acting immorally. But if we assume that we can make meaningful statements about 'the State as such' which are not reducible in principle to a set of statements about assignable individuals, the question certainly arises whether we can legitimately apply the criteria of personal morality when judging the actions of this somewhat mysterious entity.

5. It is understandable that when some British writers undertook to show that ultimate responsibility for the First World War rested fairly and squarely on the shoulders of German philosophers such as Hegel, Bosanquet's political philosophy came in for its share of criticism. For example, in *The Metaphysical Theory of the State* (1918) by L. T. Hobhouse,[1] the author, though principally concerned with Hegel, devoted a good deal of criticism to Bosanquet, in whom he rightly saw the British political philosopher who stood nearest to Hegel.

Hobhouse sums up what he calls the metaphysical theory of the State in the three following propositions. 'The individual attains his true self and freedom in conformity to his real will'; 'this real will is the general will'; and 'the general will is embodied in the State'.[2] The State is thus identified to all intents and purposes with the entire social fabric, with society in general; and it is regarded as the guardian and expression of morality, as the highest moral entity. But if the State is identified with society, the result is the absorption of the individual by the State. And why should the national State be regarded as the highest product of social development? If we assume for the sake of argument that there is such a thing as the General Will and that it is the real or true will of man,[3] it should find a much more adequate expression in a universal world-society than in the national State. True, a world-society is not yet in existence. But the creation of such a

[1] Leonard Trelawny Hobhouse (1864–1929), professor of sociology in the University of London from 1907 until the year of his death, was a philosopher of wide interests and the author of a number of books on philosophical and sociological topics. The work mentioned in the text represents a course of lectures given at the London School of Economics in 1917.

[2] *The Metaphysical Theory of the State*, pp. 117–18.

[3] As a matter of fact, Hobhouse denies all three propositions mentioned above.

society should be held up as an ideal towards which we ought to strive effectively, whereas in point of fact Bosanquet, following Hegel, shows an unwarranted prejudice in favour of the national State. In this sense idealist political theory is unduly conservative. Further, if the State is regarded as the guardian and expression of morality and as the highest moral entity, the logical consequence is a disastrous moral conformism. In any case, if the State is really, as Bosanquet supposes it to be, a moral entity of a higher order than the individual moral agent, it is very odd that these sublime moral entities, namely different States, have not succeeded in regularizing their mutual relations according to moral standards.[1] In brief, 'to confuse the State with society and political with moral obligation is the central fallacy of the metaphysical theory of the State'.[2]

Having summed up the metaphysical theory of the State in a number of theses, Hobhouse then finds himself driven to admit that Bosanquet sometimes speaks in ways which do not easily fit into this abstract scheme. But his way of coping with this difficulty is to argue that Bosanquet is guilty of inconsistency. He notes, for example, that in the introduction to the second edition of *The Philosophical Theory of the State* Bosanquet refers to a social co-operation which does not belong strictly either to the State or to private individuals simply as such. And he finds this inconsistent with the thesis that every man's true self finds its adequate embodiment in the State. Again, Hobhouse notes that in *Social and International Ideals* Bosanquet speaks of the State as an organ of the community, which has the function of maintaining the external conditions required for the development of the best life. And he finds this way of speaking inconsistent with the thesis that the State is identical with the whole social fabric. Hobhouse's conclusion, therefore, is that if such passages represent what Bosanquet really thinks about the State, he ought to undertake 'the reconstruction of his entire theory'.[3]

By and large, of course, Hobhouse is quite justified in finding in Bosanquet the so-called metaphysical theory of the State.[4] True,

[1] According to Bosanquet, 'moral relations presuppose an organized life; but such a life is only within the State, not in relations between the States and other communities'. *The Philosophical Theory of the State*, p. 325.
[2] *The Metaphysical Theory of the State*, p. 77.   [3] *Ibid.*, p. 121, note 1.
[4] If one sums up a trend of thought common to several philosophers in a number of theses, it is not surprising if the resultant scheme is not fully applicable to all of them, or perhaps to any of them. And one can then find examples of 'inconsistency'. Still, the inconsistency may be with the main operative ideas of a given philosopher's thought.

it is an exaggeration to say that according to Bosanquet a man's true self finds its adequate embodiment in the State, if we mean by this that man's potentialities are completely actualized in what would normally be regarded as his life as a citizen. Like Hegel, Bosanquet considers art, for instance, separately from the State, even if it presupposes society. At the same time it is undoubtedly true that he maintains an organic theory of the State, according to which statements about the State 'as such' are irreducible in principle to statements about assignable individuals. It is also true that Bosanquet ascribes to the national State a pre-eminent role as the embodiment of the General Will, and that he is comparatively insensitive to the ideal of a wider human society. As for the confusion of political with moral obligation, which Hobhouse mentions as a cardinal feature of the metaphysical theory of the State and to which he strongly objects, it seems to the present writer that a distinction must be made.

If we hold a teleological interpretation of morality, in which obligation is regarded as falling on us in regard to those actions which are required for the attainment of a certain end (for example, the actualization and harmonious integration of one's potentialities as a human being), and if at the same time we regard life in organized society as one of the normally requisite means for attaining this end, we can hardly avoid looking on political obligation as one of the expressions of moral obligation. But it by no means follows that we are committed to confusing moral with political obligation, if by this is meant reducing the former to the latter. This confusion can arise only if the State is regarded as being itself the basis and interpreter of the moral law. If we do look on the State in this way, a disastrous conformism is, as Hobhouse notes, the result. But though Bosanquet's theory of the General Will as finding its adequate embodiment in the State undoubtedly favours this exalted view of the latter's moral function, we have seen that he allows, even if with reluctance, for moral criticism of any actual State. Hobhouse's comment, however, is that Bosanquet is here guilty of inconsistency, and that if he really wishes to allow for moral criticism of the State, he should revise his theory of the General Will. The comment seems to the present writer to be just.

6. We have noted that Bosanquet stood closer than Bradley to Hegel. But if we are looking for a British philosopher who openly shared Stirling's enthusiastic veneration for Hegel as the

great master of speculative thought, we must turn rather to Richard Burdon Haldane (1856–1928), the distinguished statesman who in 1911 was created Viscount Haldane of Cloan. In his two-volume work *The Pathway to Reality* (1903–4) Haldane declared that Hegel was the greatest master of speculative method since Aristotle, and that he himself was not only prepared but also desirous to be called an Hegelian.[1] Indeed, his undisguised admiration for German thought and culture led to a rather shameful attack on him at the beginning of the First World War.[2]

Haldane made an attempt to show that the theory of relativity is not only compatible with Hegelianism but also demanded by it. In *The Pathway to Reality* he proposed a philosophical theory of relativity; and when Einstein published his papers on the subject, Haldane regarded them as providing confirmation of his own theory, which he developed in *The Reign of Relativity* (1921). In brief, reality as a whole is one, but knowledge of this unity is approached from various points of view, such as those of the physicist, the biologist and the philosopher. And each point of view, together with the categories which it employs, represents a partial and relative view of the truth and should not be absolutized. This idea not only fits in with but is also demanded by a philosophical outlook for which reality is ultimately Spirit and for which truth is the whole system of truth, reality's complete self-reflection or self-knowledge, a goal which is approached through dialectical stages.

It can hardly be claimed that this general philosophical theory of relativity was, in itself, a novelty. And in any case it was rather late in the day for an attempt to infuse fresh life into Hegelianism by emphasizing the relativistic aspects of the system and by invoking the name of Einstein as a patron. However, it is worth mentioning Haldane as one of those prominent figures in British public life who have had a lasting interest in philosophical problems.

7. We have already had occasion to mention the coherence theory of truth, namely that any particular truth is true in virtue

[1] In the biographical note which prefaces his contribution to the first volume of *Contemporary British Philosophy*, edited by J. H. Muirhead, Haldane remarks that he was influenced more by Hegel's method than by his detailed theory of the Absolute. But he adds that in his opinion Hegel came nearer to the ultimately true view than anyone since the ancient Greeks.

[2] Though he had become Lord Chancellor in 1912, after having done excellent work as Secretary of State for War, Haldane was omitted from the reconstituted ministry of 1915, not indeed because his colleagues had any doubt of his patriotism but rather as a measure of expediency in view of popular prejudice.

of its place in a total system of truth. This theory was discussed and defended in *The Nature of Truth* (1906) by Harold Henry Joachim (1868–1938), who occupied the Wykeham chair of logic at Oxford from 1919 until 1935. And it is not altogether superfluous to say something about the book, because the author showed his awareness of the difficulties to which the theory gives rise and did not attempt to slur them over.

Joachim approaches the coherence theory of truth by way of a critical examination of other theories. Consider, for example, the correspondence theory, according to which a factual statement is true if it corresponds with extra-linguistic reality. If somebody asks us to tell him what the reality is with which, say, a true scientific statement corresponds, our reply will necessarily be expressed in a judgment or set of judgments. When therefore we say that the scientific statement is true because it corresponds with reality, what we are really saying is that a certain judgment is true because it coheres systematically with other judgments. Hence the correspondence of truth is seen to pass into the coherence theory.

Or take the doctrine that truth is a quality of certain entities called 'propositions', a quality which is simply perceived immediately or intuitively. According to Joachim the claim of an immediate experience to be an experience of truth can be recognized only in so far as the intuition is shown to be the outcome of rational mediation, that is, in so far as the truth in question is seen to cohere with other truths. A proposition considered as an independent entity which possesses the quality of truth or of falsity, is a mere abstraction. Hence once more we are driven on to the interpretation of truth as coherence.

Joachim is thus convinced that the coherence theory of truth is superior to all rival theories. 'That the truth itself is one, and whole, and complete, and that all thinking and all experience moves within its recognition and subject to its manifest authority; this I have never doubted.'[1] Similarly, Joachim does not doubt that different judgments and partial systems of judgments are 'more or less true, i.e. as approximating more or less closely to the one standard'.[2] But once we begin to make the coherence theory explicit, really to think out its meaning and implications, difficulties arise which cannot be ignored.

In the first place coherence does not mean simply formal

---

[1] *The Nature of Truth*, p. 178.   [2] *Ibid.*, pp. 178–9.

consistency. It refers in the long run to one all-inclusive significant whole in which form and matter, knowledge and its object, are inseparably united. In other words, truth as coherence means absolute experience. And an adequate theory of truth as coherence would have to provide an intelligible account of absolute experience, the all-inclusive totality, and to show how the various levels of incomplete experience form constitutive moments in it. But it is impossible in principle that these demands should be met by any philosophical theory. For every such theory is the result of finite and partial experience and can be at best only a partial manifestation of the truth.

In the second place truth, as it is attained in human knowledge, involves two factors, thought and its object. And it is precisely this fact which gives rise to the correspondence theory of truth. An adequate theory of truth as coherence must therefore be able to explain how we are to conceive that self-diremption of the totality, absolute experience, which brings about the relative independence of subject and object, of ideal content and external reality, within human knowledge. But no such explanation, Joachim admits, has ever been given.

In the third place, as all human knowledge involves thought about an Other (that is, an other than itself), every theory of the nature of truth, including the coherence theory, must be a theory about truth as its Other, as something about which we think and pronounce judgment. And this is equivalent to saying that 'the coherence theory of truth *on its own admission* can never rise above the level of knowledge which at the best attains to the "truth" of correspondence'.[1]

With admirable candour Joachim is quite ready to speak of the 'shipwreck' of his endeavours to state an adequate theory of truth. In other words, he cannot meet the difficulties to which the coherence theory gives rise. At the same time he is still convinced that this theory carries us further than rival theories into the problem of truth, and that it can maintain itself against objections which are fatal to them, even if it itself gives rise to questions which cannot be answered. It is, however, clear enough that the ultimate reason why Joachim sticks to the coherence theory, in spite of the difficulties to which it admittedly gives rise, is a metaphysical reason, a belief about the nature of reality. Indeed, he explicitly says that he does not believe that 'the Metaphysician is

[1] *Ibid.*, p. 175.

entitled to acquiesce in logical theories, when their success demands that he should accept within the sphere of Logic assumptions which his own metaphysical theory condemns'.[1] In other words, absolute idealism in metaphysics demands the coherence theory of truth in logic. And in spite of the difficulties to which this theory gives rise we are justified in accepting it, if other theories of truth inevitably pass into the coherence theory when we try to state them precisely.

In judging whether other theories of truth do in fact pass into the coherence theory we have to bear in mind Joachim's own observation that coherence in this context does not mean simply formal consistency. An admission that two mutually incompatible propositions cannot both be true at the same time is not equivalent to embracing the coherence theory of truth. As Joachim presents the theory, when he is discussing the difficulties to which it gives rise, it is clearly a metaphysical theory, part and parcel of absolute idealism. Hence it is a question of whether all other theories of truth can be seen ultimately either to suffer complete collapse under critical examination or to imply the validity of absolute idealism. And nobody who is not already an absolute idealist is likely to admit that this is the case. It is not indeed the intention of the present writer to suggest that coherence has nothing to do with truth. In point of fact we often use coherence as a test, coherence with already established truths. And it is arguable that this implies a metaphysical belief about the nature of reality. But it does not necessarily follow that this is an implicit belief in absolute idealism. In any case, as Joachim himself frankly recognizes, if a true proposition is true only in so far as it is included as a moment in an absolute experience which transcends our grasp, it is very difficult to see how we can ever know that any proposition is true. And yet we are sure that we can have some knowledge. Perhaps an essential preliminary to any attempt to formulate 'the' theory of truth is a careful examination of the ways in which terms such as 'true' and 'truth' are used in ordinary discourse.

[1] *The Nature of Truth*, p. 179.

CHAPTER X

THE TURN TOWARDS PERSONAL IDEALISM

Pringle-Pattison and the value of the human person—The pluralistic idealism of McTaggart—The pluralistic spiritualism of J. Ward—General comments.

1. THE attitude adopted by Bradley and Bosanquet to finite personality not unnaturally led to a reaction even within the idealist movement. One of the chief representatives of this reaction was Andrew Seth Pringle-Pattison (1856–1931).[1] In his first work, *The Development from Kant to Hegel* (1882), he described the transition from the critical philosophy of Kant to the metaphysical idealism of Hegel as an inevitable movement. And he always maintained that the mind cannot rest in a system which involves the doctrine of unknowable things-in-themselves. But in 1887 he published *Hegelianism and Personality* in which, somewhat to the surprise of his readers, he submitted absolute idealism to outspoken criticism.

At first sight, Pringle-Pattison admits, Hegelianism appears to magnify man. For, obscure though Hegel's utterances may be, his philosophy certainly suggests that God or the Absolute is identical with the whole historical process, considered as developing dialectically towards self-knowledge in and through the human mind. 'The philosopher's knowledge of God is God's knowledge of himself.'[2] The ground is thus prepared for the Left-wing Hegelian transformation of theology into anthropology.

Reflection, however, shows that in Hegelianism the individual person is of little account. For human beings become 'the foci in which the impersonal life of thought momentarily concentrates itself, in order to take stock of its own contents. These foci appear only to disappear in the perpetual process of this realization.'[3] The human person, in other words, is simply a means whereby impersonal Thought comes to a knowledge of itself. And from the

[1] Originally called Andrew Seth, he adopted the name Pringle-Pattison in 1898 in fulfilment of a condition for succeeding to an estate. He successively occupied chairs of philosophy at Cardiff (1883–7), St. Andrews (1887–91) and Edinburgh (1891–1919).
[2] *Hegelianism and Personality*, p. 196 (2nd edition).
[3] *Ibid.*, p. 199.

point of view of anyone who attaches a real value to personality it is clear that 'Hegel's determination to have one process and one subject was the original fountain of error'.[1] The radical mistake both of Hegelianism itself and of its British derivatives is 'the identification of the human and the divine self-consciousness or, to put it more broadly, the unification of consciousness in a single self'.[2] This unification is ultimately destructive of the reality of both God and man.

Pringle-Pattison insists, therefore, on two points. First, we should recognize a real self-consciousness in God, even though we have to avoid ascribing to it the features of finite self-consciousness considered precisely as finite. Secondly, we must assert the value and relative independence of the human person. For each person has a centre of its own, a will, which is 'impervious' to any other person, 'a centre which I maintain even in my dealings with God Himself'.[3] 'The two positions—the divine personality and human dignity and immortality—are two complementary sides of the same view of existence.'[4]

This sounds like an abandonment of absolute idealism in favour of theism. But in his later writings Pringle-Pattison reaffirms absolute idealism or, more accurately, attempts to revise it in such a way that it permits more value being attached to finite personality than in the philosophies of Bradley and Bosanquet. The result is an unsatisfactory amalgam of absolute idealism and theism.

In the first place we cannot prove, by the sort of arguments employed by the earlier British idealists, that the world of Nature can exist only as object for a subject. Ferrier's line of argument, for example, is quite unsound. It is indeed obviously true that we cannot conceive material things without conceiving them; but 'this method of approach cannot possibly prove that they do not exist out of that relation'.[5] As for Green's argument that relations cannot exist except through the synthesizing activity of a universal consciousness, this presupposes a defunct psychology, according to which experience begins with unrelated sensations. In point of

---

[1] *Hegelianism and Personality*, p. 203.
[2] *Ibid.*, p. 226. Strictly speaking, neither Bradley nor Bosanquet regarded the Absolute as a 'self'. But they did, of course, merge all finite experiences in the unity of a single absolute experience.
[3] *Ibid.*, p. 217.
[4] *Ibid.*, p. 238.
[5] *The Idea of God in the Light of Recent Philosophy* (1917), p. 192. This work will be referred to as *The Idea of God*.

fact relations are just as much given realities as the things related.

It does not follow, however, that, as the 'lower naturalism' maintains, Nature exists apart from a total system which embodies value. On the contrary, we can see in Nature a continuity of process combined with the emergence of qualitatively distinct levels. Man appears as 'the organ through which the universe beholds and enjoys itself'.[1] And among the emergent qualities which characterize the universe we must recognize not only the so-called secondary qualities but also 'the aspects of beauty and sublimity which we recognize in nature and those finer insights which we owe to the poet and the artist'.[2] Moral values too must be taken as qualifying the universe. And the whole process of Nature, with the emergence of qualitatively different levels, is to be looked on as a progressive manifestation of the Absolute or God.

According to Pringle-Pattison, the idea of God as existing 'before' the world and as creating it out of nothing is philosophically untenable. 'The idea of creation tends to pass into that of manifestation';[3] and the infinite and the finite stand to one another in a relation of mutual implication. As for man, 'he exists as an organ of the universe or of the Absolute, the one Being',[4] which should be conceived in terms of its highest manifestation and so as one spiritual life or absolute experience.

Whatever *Hegelianism and Personality* may have seemed to imply, there is thus no radical rejection of absolute idealism in Pringle-Pattison's later work. On the contrary, there is a large measure of agreement with Bosanquet. At the same time Pringle-Pattison is not prepared to accept Bosanquet's view of the destiny of the human individual. In his view differentiation constitutes the very essence of absolute life, and 'every individual is a unique nature . . . an expression or focalization of the universe which is nowhere else repeated'.[5] The higher we ascend in the scale of life, the clearer becomes the uniqueness of the individual. And if value increases in proportion to unique individuality, we cannot suppose that distinct selves achieve their destiny by being merged without distinction in the One. Each must be preserved in its uniqueness.

Pringle-Pattison is thus not prepared to say with Bradley that

---

[1] *Ibid.*, p. 211.   [2] *Ibid.*, p. 212.   [3] *Ibid.*, p. 308.
[4] *Ibid.*, p. 259.   [5] *Ibid.*, p. 267.

the temporal world is appearance. And as he retains the doctrine of the Absolute, he seems to be committed to saying that the Absolute is subject to temporal succession. But he also wishes to maintain that there is a real sense in which the Absolute or God transcends time. Hence he has recourse to the analogies of the drama and the symphony. Where, for example, a symphony is played, the notes succeed one another; yet in a real sense the whole is there from the beginning, giving meaning to and unifying the successive units. 'Somewhat in this fashion we may perhaps conceive that the time-process is retained in the Absolute and yet transcended.'[1]

If such analogies were pressed, the natural conclusion would be that the Absolute is simply the Idea, or perhaps more properly the Value, of the entire cosmic and historical process. But Pringle-Pattison clearly wishes to maintain that God is an absolute personal experience, which could hardly be described as simply the meaning and value of the world. In other words, he tries to combine absolute idealism with elements of theism. And the ambiguous result suggests that he would have done better either to retain the Absolute and identify it with the historical process considered as moving towards the emergence of new values or to make a clear break with absolute idealism and embrace theism. However, it is at any rate clear that within the general framework of absolute idealism he tried to preserve and assert the value of the finite personality.

2. We can now turn to a Cambridge philosopher, John McTaggart Ellis McTaggart (1866–1925), for whom the problem of the relation between finite selves and the Absolute did not and could not arise, inasmuch for him there was no Absolute apart from the society or system of selves. In his philosophy the Absolute as understood by Bradley and Bosanquet simply disappeared from the scene.

McTaggart was elected a Fellow of Trinity College, Cambridge, in 1891. In his view Hegel had penetrated further than any other philosopher into the nature of reality. And he devoted himself to a prolonged study of Hegelianism, which bore fruit in *Studies in the Hegelian Dialectic* (1896; second edition, 1922), *Studies in the Hegelian Cosmology* (1901; second edition, 1918), and *A Commentary on Hegel's Logic* (1910). But McTaggart was by no means only a student of and commentator on Hegel: he was an

---

[1] *The Idea of God*, p. 363.

original thinker. This fact shows itself indeed in the commentaries but much more in the two volumes of *The Nature of Existence*,[1] which together contain his system of philosophy.

In the first part of his sytem McTaggart is concerned with determining the characteristics which belong to all that exists or, as he puts it, to existence as a whole.[2] More accurately, he is concerned with determining the characteristics which the existent *must* have. Hence the method to be employed will be that of *a priori* deduction. McTaggart is thus very far from being what is often described as an inductive metaphysician.

Even in the first part of the system, however, McTaggart admits two empirical premisses, namely that something exists and that what exists is differentiation. The truth of the first premiss is known by immediate experience. For everyone is aware that he at any rate exists. And he cannot deny this without implicitly affirming it. As for the second premiss, 'it would indeed be possible to reach this result *a priori*. For I shall argue later that it is certain *a priori* that no substance can be simple.'[3] But an appeal to perception 'seems more likely to command assent'.[4] What McTaggart really wishes to show is that existence as a whole is differentiated, that there is a plurality of substances. And this is shown by the very fact of perception. If, for example, perception is interpreted as a relation, there must be more than one term.

We can take it, therefore, that something exists. This cannot be existence itself.[5] For if we say that what exists is existence, we are left with an absolute blank. That which exists must possess some quality besides existence. And the compound quality, composed of all the qualities of a thing, can be called its nature. But we cannot resolve a thing without residue into its qualities. 'At the head of the series there will be something existent which has qualities without being itself a quality. The ordinary name for

---

[1] The first volume appeared in 1921. The second, edited by Professor C. D. Broad, was published posthumously in 1927. A summary of the system is presented by McTaggart himself in his contribution to the first volume of *Contemporary British Philosophy*, edited by J. H. Muirhead.

[2] Existence is said to be an indefinable quality which is such that everything which exists is real, though not everything which is real is necessarily existent. In other words, reality or being is for McTaggart a wider concept than that of existence.

[3] *The Nature of Existence*, 45. The work is divided into sections numbered successively from the beginning of the first to the end of the second volume. And references are given here according to these numbered sections.

[4] *Ibid.*

[5] Obviously, McTaggart, interpreting existence as an indefinable quality, could not accept the Thomist thesis that ultimate reality is precisely *ipsum esse subsistens*.

this, and I think the best name, is substance.'[1] It may be objected
that substance apart from its qualities is an inconceivable nothing;
but it does not follow that substance is 'not anything in conjunction with its qualities'.[2]

If therefore there is anything existing, and we know from
experience that there is, there must be at least one substance. But
we have already accepted the empirical premiss of pluralism, of the
differentiation of existence as a whole. It follows therefore that there
must be relations.[3] For if there is a plurality of substances, they
must be similar and dissimilar, similar in being substances, dissimilar
in being distinct.[4] And similarity and dissimilarity are relations.

Now, according to McTaggart every relation generates a
derivative quality in each of its terms, namely the quality of
being a term in this relationship. Further, a derivative relationship is generated between every relation and each of its terms. We
therefore get infinite series. But 'these infinite series are not
vicious, because it is not necessary to complete them to determine
the meaning of the earlier terms'.[5] Hence Bradley's argument to
show that qualities and relations cannot be truly real loses its force.

Substances, we have seen, must be dissimilar in some way. But
there are similarities which permit their arrangement in collections
and collections of collections. A collection is called a 'group', and
the substances which compose it are its 'members'.[6] Taken by
itself, this is a straightforward idea. But there are several points
to notice. First, a group is for McTaggart a substance. Thus the
group of all French citizens is a substance which possesses qualities
of its own, such as being a nation. Secondly, as no substance is
ever absolutely simple, a compound substance cannot have simple
substances as its members. Thirdly, we cannot assume without
more ado that two groups are necessarily two substances. If the
contents are the same, the groups are one substance. For example,
the counties of England and the parishes of England form two
groups but only one substance.

[1] The Nature of Existence, 65.   [2] Ibid., 68.
[3] The term 'relation' is for McTaggart indefinable, though we can clarify the
difference in meaning between words such as 'relation' and 'quality'. For instance,
qualities are not said to exist 'between' terms, whereas relations are.
[4] According to McTaggart, following Leibniz, if two substances had precisely
the same nature, they would be indistinguishable, and therefore one and the same
substance.
[5] The Nature of Existence, 88.
[6] We must distinguish between members and parts. 'If we take the group of
all the counties in Great Britain, neither England nor Whitechapel are members
of the group, but they are parts, of which the group is the whole.' Ibid., 123.

Now, there must be one compound substance which contains all existent content and of which every other substance is a part. 'This substance is to be called the Universe.'[1] It is an organic unity in which 'all that exists, both substances and characteristics, are bound together in one system of extrinsic determination'.[2] At the same time there seems to be a major objection against admitting this idea of an all-inclusive substance. On the one hand McTaggart takes it that a sufficient description of any substance must be possible in principle. On the other hand no sufficient description of the universe seems to be possible. For a sufficient description would have, it appears, to indicate the parts and also their relations to one another and to the whole. But how can this be possible if no substance is simple and is consequently infinitely divisible?[3]

The details of McTaggart's solution of this difficulty are too complicated for discussion here. His general principle, as stated in his summary of his system, is that to avoid a contradiction between the thesis that a sufficient description of any substance is possible and the thesis that no substance is simple 'there must be some description of any substance, A, which implies sufficient descriptions of the members of all its sets of parts which are sequent to some given sets of parts'.[4] Taken by itself, this statement does not indeed convey very much. But McTaggart's line of thought is this. A sufficient description of a substance is possible in principle, if certain conditions are fulfilled. Consider the all-inclusive substance, the universe. This consists of one or more primary wholes, which in turn consist of primary parts. These parts can be differentiated by, for example, distinct qualities. And a sufficient description of the universe is possible in principle, provided that descriptions of the primary parts *imply* sufficient descriptions of the secondary parts, the series of which is indefinitely prolonged. For this implication to be a reality, however, the secondary parts must be related to one another by what McTaggart calls the relation of determining correspondence. For example, let us suppose that A and B are primary parts of a given

---

[1] *Ibid.*, 135.

[2] *Ibid.*, 137. If, for instance, a substance X possesses qualities a, b and c, an alteration in one quality produces an alteration in the nature (composed of the qualities) and so in the substance which is manifested in the nature. The qualities are then said to stand to one another in a relation of extrinsic determination.

[3] As no substance is absolutely simple, the difficulty occurs in regard to every substance.

[4] *Contemporary British Philosophy*, First Series, p. 256.

substance, and that A and B are sufficiently described in terms of the qualities of x and y respectively. The relation of determining correspondence demands that a secondary part of A should be sufficiently describable in terms of y and that a secondary part of B should be sufficiently describable in terms of x. Given such interlocking determining correspondences throughout the whole hierarchy of consequent sets of parts, sufficient descriptions of the primary parts will imply sufficient descriptions of the secondary parts. And a sufficient description of the substance is thus possible in principle, notwithstanding the fact that it is indefinitely divisible.

As McTaggart maintains that a sufficient description of every substance must be possible, it follows that the relation of determining correspondence must hold between the parts of a substance. And if we look on determining correspondence as a label for types of causal relations, we can then say that McTaggart attempts to prove *a priori* the necessity of a certain pattern of causal relations within the universe. That is to say, if, as he assumes, the universe is an intelligible organic unity, there must exist in the hierarchy of its parts a certain pattern of determining correspondence.

Now, we have referred, for instance, to the counties of England, and we have been speaking of the universe. But though in the first part of the system some empirical illustrations are given to facilitate understanding, the conclusions reached are intended to be purely abstract. For example, though it is argued *a priori* that, if anything exists, there must be an all-inclusive substance which we can call the universe, it is a mistake to suppose that this term necessarily refers to the whole complex of entities which we are ordinarily accustomed to think of as the universe. The first part of the system established simply that there must be a universe. It does not tell us which, if any, empirical entities are members of the all-inclusive group which is called the universe. It is only in the second part of the system that McTaggart applies the conclusions of the first part, asking, for instance, whether the characteristics of substance which have been determined *a priori* can belong to those kinds of things which at first sight appear to be substances, or, rather, whether the characteristics which are encountered in or suggested by experience really belong to the existent.

In this field of inquiry, however, McTaggart insists, we cannot obtain absolute certainty. We may indeed be able to show that certain characteristics presented in or suggested by experience cannot belong to the existent, and that they must therefore be assigned to the sphere of appearance. But we cannot show with absolute certainty that characteristics suggested by experience *must* belong to the existent. For there might be characteristics never experienced or imagined by us which would equally well or better satisfy the *a priori* requirements of the first part of the system. However, if it can be shown that characteristics suggested by experience do in fact satisfy these *a priori* demands, and that no others which we know of or can imagine will do so, we have reasonable, though not absolute, certainty. In other words, McTaggart ascribes absolute certainty only to the results of *a priori* demonstration.

'The universe appears, *prima facie*, to contain substances of two very different kinds—Matter and Spirit.'[1] But McTaggart refuses to admit the reality of matter, mainly on the ground that nothing which has the quality of being material can have between its parts that relation of determining correspondence which must exist between the secondary parts of a substance. Let us suppose, for the sake of argument, that a given material thing has two primary parts, one of which can be sufficiently described as blue, while the other can be sufficiently described as red. According to the requirements of the principle of determining correspondence there would have to be a secondary part of the primary part described as blue which would correspond with the primary part described as red. That is to say, this secondary part would be red. But this is not logically possible. For a primary part could not be sufficiently described as blue, if one of its secondary parts were red. And analogous conclusions can be drawn if we consider qualities such as size and shape. Hence matter cannot belong to the existent: it cannot qualify the universe.[2]

We are left therefore with spirit. There is indeed no demonstrative proof that nothing exists save spirit. For there might possibly be a form of substance, which we had never experienced or imagined, which would satisfy the requirements for being a substance and yet not be spiritual. But we have no positive ground for claiming that there is such a substance. Hence it is reasonable to conclude that all substance is spiritual.

[1] *The Nature of Existence*, 352.
[2] According to McTaggart, it is no good saying that the existence of matter can be proved inferentially from sense-data. For what we call sense-data might be caused by spiritual causes. And if we claim that sense-data are themselves material substances, we shall have to meet the arguments which show, in general, that substance cannot be material.

As for the nature of spirit, 'I propose to define the quality of spirituality by saying that it is the quality of having content, all of which is the content of one or more selves'.[1] Thus selves are spiritual, and so are parts of selves and groups of selves, though in deference to common usage the term 'a spirit' can be reserved for a self.[2]

If spirit, therefore, is the only form of substance, the universe or Absolute will be the all-inclusive society or system of selves, selves being its primary parts. The secondary parts, of all grades, are perceptions, which form the contents of selves. In this case there must be relations of determining correspondence between these parts. True, this demands the fulfilment of certain conditions; that 'a self can perceive another self, and a part of another self',[3] that a perception is part of a percipient self, and that a perception of a part of a whole can be part of a perception of this whole. But the fulfilment of these conditions cannot be shown to be impossible; and there are reasons for thinking that they are in fact fulfilled. So we can take it that the Absolute is the system or society of selves.

Are selves immortal? The answer to this question depends on the point of view which we adopt. On the one hand McTaggart denies the reality of time, on the ground that an assertion of the reality of the temporal series of past, present and future compels us to attribute to any given event mutually incompatible determinations.[4] Hence if we adopt this point of view, we should describe selves as timeless or eternal rather than as immortal, a term which implies unending temporal duration. On the other hand time certainly belongs to the sphere of appearance. And the self will appear to persist through all future time. 'In consequence of this, I think we may properly say that the self is immortal',[5] though immortality must then be understood as including pre-existence, before, that is, its union with the body.

Professor C. D. Broad has remarked[6] that he does not suppose that McTaggart made a single disciple, though he exercised a considerable influence on his pupils by his logical subtlety, his intellectual honesty and his striving after clarity. It is not indeed

---

[1] *The Nature of Existence*, 381.
[2] For McTaggart the self is indefinable and is known by acquaintance.
[3] *The Nature of Existence*, 408.
[4] Cf. *The Nature of Existence*, 332, and McTaggart's article on *The Unreality of Time* in *Mind*, 1908.
[5] *The Nature of Existence*, 503.
[6] In *British Philosophy in the Mid-Century*, edited by C. A. Mace, p. 45.

surprising if McTaggart failed to make disciples. For, apart from the fact that he does not explain, any more than Bradley did, how the sphere of appearance arises in the first place, his system provides a much clearer example than the philosophies of either Bradley or Bosanquet of the account of metaphysics which has sometimes been given by anti-metaphysicians, namely as an alleged science which professes to deduce the nature of reality in a purely *a priori* manner. For having worked out in the first part of his system what characteristics the existent must possess, McTaggart blithely proceeds in the second part to reject the reality of matter and time on the ground that they do not fulfil the requirements established in the first part. And though his conclusions certainly make his philosophy more interesting and exciting, their strangeness is apt to make most readers conclude without more ado that there must be something wrong with his arguments. Most people at any rate find it difficult to believe that reality consists of a system of selves, the contents of which are perceptions. 'Ingenious but unconvincing', is likely to be their verdict about McTaggart's arguments.

It may be objected that this is a very philistinian point of view. If McTaggart's arguments are good ones, the strangeness of his conclusions does not alter the fact. And this is true enough. But it is also a fact that few philosophers have been convinced by the arguments adduced to show that reality must be what McTaggart says it is.

3. McTaggart combined the doctrine that existing reality consists of spiritual selves with atheism.[1] But the personal idealists generally adopted some form of theism. We can take as an example James Ward (1843–1925), naturalist, psychologist and philosopher, who studied for a while in Germany, where he came under the influence of Lotze, and eventually occupied the chair of logic and mental philosophy at Cambridge (1897–1925).

In 1886 Ward contributed to the *Encyclopaedia Britannica* a famous article on psychology, which later provided the basis for his *Psychological Principles* (1918), a work which clearly shows the influence of German philosophers such as Lotze, Wundt and Brentano. Ward was strongly opposed to the associationist psychology. In his view the content of consciousness consists of

[1] McTaggart admitted the bare possibility of there being within the society of selves a self which from the standpoint of experience might appear to exercise some controlling, though not creative, function. But he added that we have no reason to suppose that there is in fact such a self. And even if there were, it would not be equivalent to God as customarily represented in theistic thought.

'presentations'; but these form a continuum. They are not discrete isolated events or impressions, into which the presentational continuum can be broken up. Obviously, a new presentation introduces fresh material; but it does not constitute simply an additional item in a series, for it modifies or partially changes the pre-existing field of consciousness. Further, every presentation is a presentation for a subject, being an experience of the subject. The idea of the 'soul' is not for Ward a concept of psychology; but we cannot dispense with the idea of the subject. For consciousness involves selective attention to this or that feature or aspect of the presentational continuum; and this is an activity of the subject under the influence of feelings of pleasure and pain. It is, however, a mistake to regard the subject of consciousness as merely a spectator, a purely cognitive subject. For the conative aspect of experience is fundamental, and the selective activity in question is teleological in character, the active subject selecting and attending to presentational data in view of an end or purpose.[1]

In the first series of his Gifford Lectures, published in 1899 as *Naturalism and Agnosticism*, Ward attacked what he called the naturalistic view of the world. We must distinguish between natural science on the one hand and philosophical naturalism on the other. For example, mechanics which deals simply 'with the quantitative aspects of physical phenomena'[2] should not be confused with the mechanical theory of Nature, 'which aspires to resolve the actual world into an actual mechanism'.[3] The philosopher who accepts this theory believes that the formulas and laws of mechanics are not simply abstract and selective devices for dealing with an environment under certain aspects, devices which possess a limited validity, but that they reveal to us the nature of concrete reality in an adequate manner. And in this belief he is mistaken. Spencer, for instance, attempts to deduce the movement of evolution from mechanical principles and is blind to the fact that in the process of evolution different levels emerge which require their own appropriate categories and concepts.[4]

Dualism, however, as a possible alternative to naturalism, is untenable. It is true that the fundamental structure of experience is the subject-object relationship. But this distinction is not

---

[1] In the opinion of the present writer this approach to psychology was much superior to that of the associationists.
[2] *Naturalism and Agnosticism*, I, p. viii.　　　　[3] *Ibid.*
[4] Ward is not always careful to observe his own distinction between natural science and philosophical naturalism. And he tends to speak as though the science of mechanics does not treat of 'the actual'.

equivalent to a dualism between mind and matter. For even when the object is what we call a material thing, the fact that it is comprised together with the subject within the unity of the subject-object relationship shows that it cannot be entirely heterogeneous to the subject. No ultimate dualism between mind and matter can stand up to criticism.

Having rejected, therefore, materialism, in the form of the mechanical theory of Nature, and dualism, Ward has recourse to what he calls spiritualistic monism. This term does not, however, express a belief that there is only one substance or being. Ward's view is that all entities are in some sense spiritual. That is to say, they all possess a psychical aspect. His theory is thus pluralistic; and in his second set of Gifford Lectures, which appeared in 1911 under the title *The Realm of Ends or Pluralism and Theism* he speaks of pluralistic spiritualism rather than of spiritualistic monism, though, if the latter term is properly understood, both names have the same meaning.

To some readers it may appear extraordinary that a Cambridge professor of comparatively recent date should embrace a theory of panpsychism. But Ward does not intend to imply, any more than Leibniz did,[1] that every entity or monad enjoys what we call consciousness. The idea is rather that there is no such thing as 'brute' matter, but that every centre of activity possesses some degree, often a very low degree, of 'mentality'. Moreover, Ward claims that pluralistic spiritualism is not a doctrine which has been deduced *a priori* but is based on experience.[2] 'The world is taken simply as we find it, as a plurality of active individuals unified only in and through their mutual interactions. These interactions again are interpreted throughout on the analogy of social transactions, as a mutuum commercium; that is to say, as based on cognition and conation.'[3]

---

[1] Ward's pluralism resembles the monadology of Leibniz, except that Ward's monads are not 'windowless' but act on one another.

[2] According to Ward, the only *a priori* statements which are beyond challenge are 'purely formal statements' (*The Realm of Ends*, p. 227), those of logic and mathematics. These do not give factual information about the world. If, however, a philosopher professes to deduce the nature of reality from a table of categories and these are found to apply to the world, it will also be found that they were taken from experience in the first place.

[3] *The Realm of Ends*, p. 225. Obviously, the less fantastic panpsychism is made to appear, the more does it lie open to the comment that no new information is being given, but that it consists simply in interpreting the empirically observable behaviour of things according to certain selected analogies. The question whether it is true or not then appears as a question whether a certain description is appropriate, not whether certain behaviour takes place or not.

Now, Ward admits that it is possible to stop at this idea of a plurality of finite active centres of experience. For Kant has exposed the fallacies in the alleged demonstrative proofs of God's existence. At the same time theism supplies a unity which is missing in pluralism without God. Further, the concepts of creation and conservation throw light on the existence of the Many, though creation should be understood in terms of ground and consequent rather than of cause and effect. 'God is the ground of the world's being, its *ratio essendi*.'[1] In addition, Ward argues in a pragmatist-like way that acceptance of the idea of God has the benefit of increasing the pluralist's confidence in the significance of finite existence and in the eventual realization of the ideal of the kingdom of ends. Without God as both transcendent and immanently active in the universe, 'the world may well for ever remain that *rerum concordia discors*, which at present we find it'.[2]

4. We can safely venture the generalization that one of the basic factors in personal idealism is a judgment of value, namely that personality represents the highest value within the field of our experience. This statement may indeed appear inapplicable to the philosophy of McTaggart, who professes to demonstrate by *a priori* reasoning what characteristics must belong to the existent and then inquires which of the kinds of things that are *prima facie* substances actually possess these characteristics. But it does not necessarily follow, of course, that a judgment of value does not constitute an effective implicit factor even in his philosophy. In any case it is clear that Pringle-Pattison's revision of absolute idealism was prompted by a conviction of the ultimate value of personality, and that James Ward's pluralistic spiritualism was connected with a similar conviction.

Obviously, personal idealism does not consist simply of this judgment of value. It involves also the conviction that personality should be taken as the key to the nature of reality, and a sustained attempt to interpret reality in the light of this conviction. This means that personal idealism tends to pluralism rather than to monism. In the philosophies of McTaggart and Ward a pluralistic conception of the universe is clearly dominant. With Pringle-Pattison it is held in check by his retention of the idea of the Absolute as a single all-inclusive experience. At the same time the value which he attaches to finite personality drives him to

[1] *The Realm of Ends*, p. 234.   [2] *Ibid.*, p. 421.

endeavour to interpret the doctrine of the One in such a way as not to involve the submerging or obliteration of the Many in the One.

The natural result in metaphysics of the turning from monism to pluralism in the light of a conviction of the value of personality is the assertion of some form of theism. In the exceptional case of McTaggart the Absolute is indeed interpreted as the society or system of finite spiritual selves. And with Pringle-Pattison the change to unequivocal theism is checked by the influence which the tradition of absolute idealism still exercises on his mind. But the inner dynamic, so to speak, of personal idealism is towards the interpretation of ultimate reality as being itself personal in character and of such a kind as to allow for the dependent reality of finite persons. According to the absolute idealists, as we have seen, the concept of God must be transformed into the concept of the Absolute. In personal idealism the concept of the Absolute tends to be re-transformed into the concept of God. True, McTaggart looks on his idea of the society or system of spiritual selves as the proper interpretation of the Hegelian Absolute. But with James Ward we find a clear transition to theism. And it is no matter for surprise that he explicitly asserts his affinity with Kant rather than with Hegel.

How far we extend the application of the term 'personal idealism' is, within limits, a matter of choice. Consider, for example, William Ritchie Sorley (1855–1935), who occupied the chair of moral philosophy at Cambridge from 1900 until 1932. He was mainly concerned with problems connected with the nature of values and the judgment of value, and it may be preferable to label him a philosopher of value. But he also inquired into the sort of general philosophical theory which we must embrace when we take values seriously into account as factors in reality. Thus he insisted that persons are 'the bearers of value',[1] and that metaphysics culminates in the idea of God, conceived not only as creator but also as 'the essence and source of all values, and as willing that these values should be shared by the free minds who owe their being to him'.[2] And the total result of his reflections is such that he can reasonably be labelled as a personal idealist.

We cannot, however, be expected to outline the ideas of all those British philosophers who can reasonably be described as personal idealists. Instead we can draw attention to the differences in

---

[1] *Contemporary British Philosophy*, Second Series, p. 254.   [2] *Ibid.*, p. 265.

attitude towards the sciences between the absolute idealists and the personal idealists. Bradley does not, of course, deny the validity of science at its own level. But inasmuch as he relegates all discursive thought to the sphere of appearance, he is involved in holding that the sciences are incapable of revealing to us the nature of reality as distinct from appearance. True we find much the same attitude in McTaggart, for whom the spatio-temporal world is appearance. And even James Ward, in his polemic against naturalism and the mechanical theory of the world, plays down the ability of science to disclose to us the nature of reality and emphasizes the man-made character of abstract scientific concepts, which have to be judged by their utility rather than by any claim to absolute truth. At the same time he is convinced that the concrete sciences, such as biology and psychology, suggest and confirm his pluralistic philosophy. And, in general, the personal idealists are concerned not so much with sitting in judgment on science and relegating it to the sphere of appearance as with challenging the claim of materialist and mechanist philosophies to be the logical outcome of the sciences. The general tendency at any rate of personal idealism is to appeal to the fact that different sciences require different categories to cope with different levels of experience or aspects of reality, and to regard metaphysics as a legitimate and indeed necessary enlargement of the field of interpretation rather than as the unique path to a knowledge of reality from which the empirical sciences, confined to the sphere of appearance, are necessarily debarred. This observation may not apply to McTaggart. But he is really *sui generis*. The general attitude of the personal idealists is to argue that experience and an empirical approach to philosophy support pluralism rather than the type of monism characteristic of absolute idealism, and that if we bear in mind the different types of science,[1] we can see that metaphysical philosophy is not a counterblast to science but a natural crown to that interpretation of reality in which the sciences have their own parts to play.

A final point. If we except the system of McTaggart, personal idealism was calculated by its very nature to appeal to religiously minded philosophers, to the sort of philosophers who would be considered suitable persons to receive invitations to give series of Gifford Lectures. And what the personal idealists wrote was

[1] When Ward writes as though science does not provide us with knowledge of the concretely real, he is thinking primarily of mechanics which he regards as a branch of mathematics. As already noted, he was himself a psychologist.

generally religiously edifying. Their style of philosophy was obviously much less destructive of Christian faith than the absolute idealism of Bradley.[1] But though the various philosophies which can reasonably be regarded as representative of personal idealism are edifying enough from the moral and religious points of view, they tend to give the impression, at least in their more metaphysical aspects, of being a series of personal statements of belief which owe less to rigorous argument than to a selective emphasis on certain aspects of reality.[2] And it is understandable that during the lifetime of Ward and Sorley other Cambridge philosophers were suggesting that instead of rushing to produce large-scale interpretations of reality we should do better to make our questions as clear and precise as possible and treat them one by one. However, though this sounds a very reasonable and practical suggestion, the trouble is that philosophical problems are apt to interlock. And the idea of breaking up philosophy into clearly defined questions which can be answered separately has not in practice proved to be as fruitful as some people hoped. Still, it is undeniable that the idealist systems appear, in the present climate of British philosophy, to belong to a past phase of thought. This makes them indeed apt material for the historian. But it also means that the historian cannot help wondering whether there is really much justification for devoting space to minor systems which do not strike the imagination in the way that the system of Hegel makes an impression. There is, however, this to be said, that personal idealism represents the recurrent protest of the finite personality to absorption in a One, however it is conceived. It is easy to say that personality is 'appearance'; but no monistic system has ever explained how the sphere of appearance arises in the first place.

[1] I do not mean to imply that Bradley can properly be described as an irreligious thinker. At the same time the concept of 'God' belongs for him to the sphere of appearance, and it would be absurd to claim him as a Christian thinker. He was not.

[2] McTaggart certainly professed to reach his conclusion by rigorous argument. But then his conclusions were not particularly edifying from the religious point of view, unless one is prepared to maintain that the existence or non-existence of God is a matter of indifference to religion.

PART III

IDEALISM IN AMERICA

CHAPTER XI
INTRODUCTORY

The beginnings of philosophy in America; S. Johnson and J. Edwards—The Enlightenment in America; B. Franklin and T. Jefferson—The influence of the Scottish philosophy—R. W. Emerson and Transcendentalism—W. T. Harris and his programme for speculative philosophy.

1. THE remote origins of philosophical reflection in America can be traced back to the Puritans of New England. Obviously, the primary aim of the Puritans was to organize their lives according to the religious and moral principles in which they believed. They were idealistic in the non-philosophical sense of the term. They were also Calvinists who allowed no dissent from what they regarded as the principles of orthodoxy. At the same time we can find among them an element of philosophical reflection, stimulated mainly by the thought of Petrus Ramus or Pierre de la Ramée (1515–72) and by the *Encyclopaedia* of Johann Heinrich Alsted (1588–1638). Petrus Ramus, the celebrated French humanist and logician, became a Calvinist in 1561, expounded a congregationalist theory of the Church, and eventually perished in the massacre of St. Bartholomew's Eve. He thus had special qualifications for being regarded as an intellectual patron by the Congregationalists of New England. Alsted, a follower of Melanchthon and also a disciple of Petrus Ramus, published an encyclopaedia of the arts and sciences in 1630. This work, which had a Platonic colouring, contained a section devoted to what Alsted called *archeologia*, the system of the principles of knowledge and being. And it became a popular textbook in New England.

The religious affiliations of the first phase of American philosophical thought are shown by the fact that the earliest philosophers were clerics. Samuel Johnson (1696–1772) is an example. At first a Congregationalist minister, he entered the Anglican Church in 1772 and subsequently received Anglican orders. In

254

1754 he was appointed first president of King's College, New York, which is now Columbia University.

In his autobiography Johnson remarks that when he was studying at Yale the standard of education was low. Indeed, it showed a decline in comparison with the standards of the original settlers who had been brought up in England. True, the names of Descartes, Boyle, Locke and Newton were not unknown, and the introduction of the writings of Locke and Newton were gradually opening up fresh lines of thought. But there was a strong tendency to equate secular learning with some of the works of Ramus and Alsted and to regard the new philosophical currents as a danger to the purity of religious faith. In other words, a 'scholasticism' which had served a useful purpose in the past was being used to check the spread of new ideas.

Johnson himself came under the influence of Berkeley. He made the acquaintance of the philosopher during the latter's sojourn on Rhode Island (1729–31) and it was to Berkeley that he dedicated his *Elementa Philosophica*, which appeared in 1752.[1]

But though deeply impressed by Berkeley's immaterialism, Johnson was not prepared to accept his view that space and time are particular relations between particular ideas, and that infinite space and time are simply abstract ideas. He wished to retain the Newton-Clarke theory of absolute and infinite space and time, on the ground that they are entailed by admission of the existence of a plurality of finite spirits. For example, unless there were absolute space, all finite spirits would coincide with one another. Further, Johnson tried to fit Berkeley's theory of ideas into a Platonic mould, by maintaining that all ideas are ectypes of archetypes existing in the divine mind. In other words, while welcoming Berkeley's immaterialism Johnson endeavoured to adapt it to the Platonic tradition already present in American thought.

A better-known representative of eighteenth-century American thought is Jonathan Edwards (1703–58), a noted Congregationalist theologian. Educated at Yale, in 1717 he made the acquaintance of Locke's *Essay* and in 1730 of Hutcheson's *Inquiry into the Original of Our Ideas of Beauty and Virtue*. Though primarily a Calvinist theologian who for most of his life occupied pastoral posts, he attempted to achieve a synthesis between the Calvinist theology and the new philosophy. Or, to put the matter in another

[1] Johnson's philosophical correspondence with Berkeley can be found in the second volume of the critical edition of the bishop's *Works* edited by Professor T. E. Jessop.

way, he used ideas taken from contemporary philosophy in interpreting the Calvinist theology. In 1757 he became president of the college at Princeton, New Jersey, which is now Princeton University; but he died of smallpox in the following year.

Edwards sees the universe as existing only within the divine mind or spirit. Space, necessary, infinite and eternal, is in fact an attribute of God. Further, it is only spirits which are, properly speaking, substances. There are no quasi-independent material substances which exercise real causal activity. To be sure, Nature exists as appearance; and from the point of view of the scientist, who is concerned with phenomena or appearances, there is uniformity in Nature, a constant order. The scientist as such can speak quite legitimately of natural laws. But from a profounder and philosophical point of view we can admit only one real causal activity, that of God. Not only is the divine conservation of finite things a constantly repeated creation, but it is also true that the uniformity of Nature is, from the philosophical standpoint, an arbitrary constitution, as Edwards puts it, of the divine will. There is really no such thing in Nature as a necessary relation or as efficient causality; all connections depend ultimately as the arbitrary *fiat* of God.

The fact that Edwards rejects, with Berkeley, the existence of material substance but admits the existence of spiritual substances must not, however, be taken to mean that in his view human volition constitutes an exception to the general truth that God is the only real cause. From one point of view, of course, we can say that he gives an empiricist analysis of relations, in particular of the causal relation. But this analysis is combined with the Calvinist idea of the divine omnipotence or causality to produce metaphysical idealism in which God appears as the sole genuine cause. In his work on the *Freedom of the Will* Edwards explicitly rejects the idea of the self-determining human will. In his view it is absurd, and also an expression of Arminianism, to maintain that the human will can choose against the prevailing motive or inclination.[1] Choice is always determined by the prevailing motive, and this in turn is determined by what appears to be the greatest good. Theologically speaking, a man's choice is predetermined by his Creator. But it is a mistake to suppose that this relieves man

---

[1] Obviously if by prevailing inclination or strongest motive we mean the motive which actually 'prevails', it *would* be absurd to claim that we can resist it. But then the statement that we always follow it becomes tautological.

of all moral responsibility. For a moral judgment about an action depends simply on the nature of the action, not on its cause. A bad action remains a bad action, whatever its cause.

An interesting feature of Edwards' thought is his theory of a sense of God or direct awareness of the divine excellence. In general, he was in sympathy with the revivalist 'Great Awakening' of 1740-1. And he considered that the religious affections, on which he wrote a treatise, manifest an apprehension of the divine excellence which is to be attributed to the heart rather than to the head. At the same time he tried to distinguish between the sense of God and the highly emotive states which are characteristic of revivalist meetings. In doing this he developed a theory of the sense of God in which it is reasonable to see the influence of Hutcheson's aesthetic and moral ideas.

According to Edwards, just as a sense of the sweetness of honey precedes and lies at the basis of our theoretical judgment that honey is sweet, so does a sentiment or sense of, say, the divine holiness lie at the basis of the judgment that God is holy. In general, just as a sense of the beauty of an object or of the moral excellence of a person is presupposed by judgments which give expression to this sense or feeling, so is a sense of the divine excellence presupposed by our 'cerebral' judgments about God. Perhaps the term 'just as' is open to criticism. For the sense of God is for Edwards a consent of our being to the divine being and is of supernatural origin. But the point is that man can be aware of God through a form of experience analogous to sense-experience and to the pleasure which we feel in beholding a beautiful object or an expression of moral excellence.

Perhaps we can see in this theory the influence of Lockian empiricism. I do not mean to imply, of course, that Locke himself based belief in God on feeling and intuition. In regard to this matter his approach was rationalistic; and his mistrust of 'enthusiasm' is notorious. But his general insistence on the primacy of sense-experience may well have been one of the foctors which influenced Edwards' mind, though the influence of Hutcheson's idea of the sense of moral beauty or excellence is certainly more obvious.

Edwards did not live long enough to carry out his project of writing a complete theology, developed systematically according to a new method. But he was extremely influential as a theologian; and his attempt to bring together Calvinist theology, idealism,

Lockian empiricism and the world-view of Newton constituted the first major expression of American thought.

2. In Europe the eighteenth century was the age of the Enlightenment. And America too had what is customarily called its Enlightenment. In the field of philosophy it does not indeed bear comparison with its counterparts in England and France. But it is none the less of importance in the history of American life.

The first characteristic which we can notice is the attempt to separate the Puritan moral virtues from their theological setting, an attempt which is well exemplified by the reflections of Benjamin Franklin (1706–90). An admirer of William Wollaston, the English deist, he was certainly not the man to walk in the footsteps of Samuel Johnson or Jonathan Edwards. Revelation, as he declared, had for him no weight. And he was convinced that morals should be given a utilitarian in place of a theological basis. Some types of action are beneficial to man and society, while other types of action are detrimental. The former can be regarded as commanded, the latter as forbidden. Virtues such as temperance and diligence are justified by their utility. Their opposites are blameworthy because they are prejudicial to the interests of society and of personal success.

Famous as he is, Franklin can hardly be described as a profound philosopher, in spite of the fact that he was one of the founders of the American Philosophical Society. And it is a simple matter to caricature his ethical outlook. To be sure, Franklin exalted truthfulness, sincerity and integrity, virtues highly esteemed by the Puritans, as essential for human well-being. But once these virtues are extolled because, on balance, people who are truthful and sincere are more likely to be successful in life than the untruthful and insincere, a certain banal pragmatism takes the place of the religious idealism of the Puritan mind at its best. It is no longer a case of man becoming the image of God, as it was with the more Platonic-minded Puritan theologians. Rather is it a case of 'early to bed and early to rise makes a man healthy and wealthy and wise'. A sensible maxim perhaps, but not particularly uplifting.

However, even if Franklin's reflections tended to assume a somewhat banal character, they represented the same movement to set ethics on its own feet and to separate it from theology which we find in more sophisticated forms in eighteenth-century

European philosophy. And the retention of Puritan virtues in a secularized dress was of considerable historical importance in the development of the American outlook.

Another important feature of the Enlightenment in America was the secularization of the idea of society. Calvinism was opposed from the start to control of the Church by the State. And though the general tendency of the Calvinists was to secure, when possible, widespread control over society, in principle at any rate they recognized a distinction between the body of true believers and political society. Moreover, Calvinism in New England took the form of Congregationalism. And though in practice the clergy, once appointed, exercised great power, the congregations were in theory simply voluntary unions of likeminded believers. When stripped, therefore, of its theological and religious associations, this idea of society lent itself to exploitation in the interest of democratic republicanism. And Locke's theory of the social contract or compact was at hand to serve as an instrument.

The process of secularizing the theory of religious society associated with the Congregationalists of New England was, however, only one factor in a complex situation. Another factor was the growth in the New World of pioneer societies which were not primarily associated, if at all, with particular religious bodies and movements. The new frontier societies[1] had to adapt the ideas of law and social organization which they carried with them to the situations in which they found themselves. And their main desire was clearly that of securing, as far as possible, such conditions of order as would prevent anarchy and enable individuals to pursue their several ends in comparative peace. Needless to say, the members of the pioneer societies were not much concerned with political philosophy, or with philosophy of any sort. At the same time they represented a growing society which tacitly implied a Lockian theory of a free union of human beings organizing themselves and submitting themselves to law with a view to preserving a social fabric and order which would permit the peaceful, though competitive, exercise of individual initiative. Further, the growth of these societies, with emphasis on temporal success, favoured the spread of the idea of toleration, which was scarcely a strong point of the Calvinist theologians and ministers.

The idea of political society as a voluntary union of human

---

[1] Benjamin Franklin, it may be noted, emphasized the virtues and values which proved to be of advantage in the frontier societies.

beings for the purpose of establishing social order as a framework for the peaceful exercise of private initiative was understandably associated with the idea of natural rights which are presupposed by organized society and should be protected by it. The theory of natural rights, sponsored by Locke and by other English and French writers, found expression in *The Rights of Man*[1] by Thomas Paine (1737–1809), a deist who insisted on the sovereignty of reason and on the equal rights of all men. It also found a powerful exponent in Thomas Jefferson (1743–1826) who, as is well known, drafted the Declaration of Independence of 1776. This famous document asserts that it is self-evidently true that all men are created equal, that they are endowed by their Creator with certain inalienable rights, and that among these are the right to life, liberty and the pursuit of happiness. The Declaration further asserts that governments are instituted to secure these rights, and that they derive their powers from the consent of the governed.

It is scarcely necessary to remark that the Declaration of Independence was a national act, not an exercise in political philosophy. And, quite apart from the fact that a good deal of it consists of animadversions on the British monarch and government, the philosophy behind its opening sentences was not fully developed in eighteenth-century America. Thus Jefferson himself simply assumed that the statement that all men are endowed by their Creator with certain inalienable rights is a matter of common sense. That is to say, common reason sees that it must be true, without any need of proof, though, once its truth has been recognized, moral and social conclusions can be drawn from it. At the same time the philosophical portion of the Declaration admirably illustrates the spirit and fruit of the American Enlightenment. And there is, of course, no doubt about its historical importance.

3. Men such as Franklin and Jefferson were obviously not professional philosophers. But in the course of the nineteenth century academic philosophy underwent a very considerable development in the United States. And among the influences contributing to this development was the thought of Thomas Reid and his successors in the Scottish School. In religious quarters the Scottish philosophical tradition was regarded with favour as being at the same time realist in character and a much needed antidote

---

[1] Part I, 1791; Part II, 1792. Paine was also the author of the *Age of Reason*, the two parts of which appeared respectively in 1794 and 1796.

to materialism and positivism. It thus became popular with those Protestant divines who were conscious of the lack of an adequate rational basis for the Christian faith.

One of the principal representatives of this tradition was James McCosh (1811–94), himself a Scottish Presbyterian, who occupied for sixteen years the chair of logic and metaphysics at Queen's College, Belfast, and then in 1868 accepted the presidency of Princeton and made the university a stronghold of the Scottish philosophy. Besides writing a number of other philosophical works, such as *An Examination of John Stuart Mill's Philosophy* (1866) and *Realistic Philosophy* (1887), he published a well-known study, *The Scottish Philosophy*, in 1875.

Among the effects of the popularization in America of the Scottish tradition was the widespread habit of dividing philosophy into mental and moral, the former, namely the science of the human mind or psychology, being looked on as providing the basis for the latter, namely ethics. This division is reflected in the titles of the much-used textbooks published by Noah Porter (1811–92), who in 1847 was nominated to the chair of moral philosophy and metaphysics at Yale, where he was also president for some years. For instance, in 1868 he published *The Human Intellect*, in 1871 *The Elements of Intellectual Science*, an abridgement of the first-named book, and in 1885 *The Elements of Moral Science*. Porter was not, however, simply an adherent of the Scottish School. He had made a serious study not only of British empiricists such as J. S. Mill and Bain but also of Kantian and post-Kantian German thought. And he attempted to effect a synthesis of the Scottish philosophy and German idealism. Thus he maintained that the world is to be regarded as a thought rather than as a thing, and that the existence of the Absolute is a necessary condition of the possibility of human thought and knowledge.

An attempt at combining themes from empiricism, the Scottish philosophy of common sense and German idealism had been made by the French philosopher, Victor Cousin (1792–1867). As rector of the *École normale*, rector of the University of Paris and finally minister of public instruction, Cousin had been in a position to impose his ideas as a kind of philosophical orthodoxy in the centre of French academic life. But an eclectic philosophy, formed from such heterogeneous elements, was obviously open to serious criticism on the ground of incoherence. However, the relevant point here is that his thought exercised a certain influence in America, especially in encouraging a combination of ideas inspired by the Scottish tradition with a transcendentalism inspired by German idealism.

As an example we can mention Caleb Sprague Henry (1804–84), a professor at the University of New York. To all intents and purposes Cousin had based metaphysics on psychology. Psychological observation, properly employed, reveals in man the presence of a spontaneous reason which acts as a bridge between consciousness and being and enables us to pass beyond the limits of subjective idealism, by apprehending, for example, finite substances as objectively existent. Philosophy, as the work of reflective reason, makes explicit and develops the objective truths apprehended immediately by spontaneous reason. This distinction between spontaneous and reflective reason was accepted by Henry who, as a devout Anglican, proceeded to use it in a theological setting and drew the conclusions that religious or spiritual experience precedes and grounds religious knowledge.[1] By religious or spiritual experience, however, he meant primarily the moral consciousness of good and obligation, a consciousness which manifests the power of God to raise man to a new life. Further, with Henry material civilization becomes the fruit of the 'understanding', whereas Christianity, considered historically as the redemptive work of God, aiming at the creation of an ideal society, is the response to the demands of 'reason' or spirit.

4. At the same time that the Scottish philosophy was penetrating into university circles, the famous American writer Ralph Waldo Emerson (1803–82) was preaching his gospel of transcendentalism. In 1829 he became a Unitarian minister. But the man who found inspiration in Coleridge and Carlyle, who laid emphasis on moral self-development and tended to divest religion of its historical associations, who was more concerned with giving expression to his personal vision of the world than with transmitting a traditional message, was not really suited for the ministry. And in 1832 he abandoned it and gave himself to the task of developing and expounding a new idealist philosophy which, he was confident, was capable of renewing the world in a

---

[1] In using the distinction in this way Henry was not simply following Cousin. For Cousin insisted that the existence of God is known by inductive reasoning from the existence of finite substances, though he tried to combine this thesis with an idea of God inspired by German metaphysical idealism, an idea which led to accusations of pantheism by clerical critics. Henry was interested chiefly in the redemptive power of Christianity in history, and while accepting Cousin's idea of reason, he transposed it into the setting of Christian theology.

way in which not only materialism but also traditional religion was incapable of renewing it.

In 1836 Emerson published anonymously a little work entitled *Nature*, which contained the essence of his message. His celebrated *Address*, delivered in 1838 in the divinity school of Harvard, aroused considerable opposition among those who considered it unorthodox. In 1841 and 1844 he published two series of *Essays*, while his *Poems* appeared in 1846. In 1849 he published *Representative Men*, a series of lectures which he had given in 1845–6 on selected famous men from Plato to Napoleon and Goethe. In later years he became a national institution, the Sage of Concord, a fate which sometimes overtakes those who are at first regarded as purveyors of dangerous new ideas.

In a lecture delivered in 1842 in the Masonic Temple at Boston Emerson declares that what are called the 'new views' are really very old thoughts cast into a mould suited to the contemporary world. 'What is popularly called Transcendentalism among us is Idealism; Idealism as it appears in 1842.'[1] The materialist takes his stand on sense-experience and on what he calls facts, whereas 'the idealist takes his departure from his consciousness, and reckons the world an appearance'.[2] Materialism and idealism thus appear to be sharply opposed. Yet once we begin to ask the materialist what the basic facts really are, his solid world tends to break up. And with phenomenalism all is ultimately reduced to the data of consciousness. Hence under criticism materialism tends to pass into idealism, for which 'mind is the only reality . . . [and] Nature, literature, history are only subjective phenomena'.[3]

It does not follow, however, that the external world is simply the creation of the individual mind. Rather is it the product of the one universal spirit or consciousness, 'that Unity, that Over-Soul, within which every man's particular being is contained and made one with all other'.[4] This Over-Soul or eternal One or God is the sole ultimate reality, and Nature is its projection. 'The world proceeds from the same spirit as the body of man. It is a remoter and inferior projection of God, a projection of God in the unconscious. But it differs from a body in one important respect. It is not, like that, now subjected to the human will. Its serene order is inviolable by us. It is, therefore, to us, the present expositor of the divine mind.'[5]

---

[1] *Complete Works*, II, p. 279 (London, 1866). References are given according to volume and page of this edition. [2] *Ibid.*, II, p. 280.
[3] *Ibid.*, II, pp. 280–1. [4] *Ibid.*, I, p. 112. [5] *Ibid.*, II, p. 167.

If we ask how Emerson knows all this, it is no good expecting any systematically developed proofs. He does indeed insist that the human reason presupposes and seeks an ultimate unity. But he also insists that 'we know truth when we see it, let sceptic and scoffer say what they choose'.[1] When foolish people hear what they do not wish to hear, they ask how one knows that what one says is true. But 'we know truth when we see it, from opinion, as we know when we are awake that we are awake'.[2] The announcements of the soul, as Emerson puts it, are 'an influx of the divine mind into our mind':[3] they are a revelation, accompanied by the emotion of the sublime.

We might expect that from this doctrine of the unity of the human soul with the Over-Soul or divine spirit Emerson would draw the conclusion that the individual as such is of little importance, and that moral or spiritual progress consists in submerging one's personality in the One. But this is not at all his point of view. The Over-Soul incarnates itself, as Emerson expresses it, in a particular way in each individual. Hence 'each man has his own vocation. The talent is the call.'[4] And the conclusion is drawn: 'Insist on yourself, never imitate'.[5] Conformism is a vice: self-reliance is a cardinal virtue. 'Whoso would be a man must be a nonconformist.'[6] Emerson provides indeed a theoretical reason for this exaltation of self-reliance. The divine spirit is self-existent, and its embodiments are good in proportion as they share in this attribute. At the same time it is not unreasonable to see in Emerson's moral doctrine the expression of the spirit of a young, vigorous, developing and competitive society.

In Emerson's opinion this self-reliance, if universally practised, would bring about a regeneration of society. The State exists to educate the wise man, the man of character; and 'with the appearance of the wise man, the State expires. The appearance of character makes the State unnecessary.'[7] What is meant is doubtless that if individual character were fully developed, the State as an organ of force would be unnecessary, and that in its place there would be a society based on moral right and love.

It scarcely needs saying that Emerson, like Carlyle, was a seer rather than a systematic philosopher. Indeed, he went so far as to say that 'a foolish consistency is the hobgoblin of little minds, adored by little statesmen and philosophers and divines. With

---

[1] *Works*, I, p. 117.   [2] *Ibid.*   [3] *Ibid.*   [4] *Ibid.*, I, p. 59.
[5] *Ibid.*, I, p. 35.   [6] *Ibid.*, I, p. 20.   [7] *Ibid.*, I, p. 244.

consistency a great soul has simply nothing to do.'[1] True his principal point is that a man should preserve his intellectual integrity and not be afraid to say what he really thinks today simply because it contradicts what he said yesterday. But he remarks, for example, that if in metaphysics we deny personality to God, this should not prevent us from thinking and speaking in a different way 'when the devout motions of the soul come'.[2] And though we can understand what Emerson means, a systematic philosopher who held this point of view would be more likely to follow Hegel in drawing an explicit distinction between the language of speculative philosophy and that of religious consciousness than to content himself with dismissing consistency as a hobgoblin of little minds. In other words, Emerson's philosophy was impressionistic and what is sometimes called 'intuitive'. It conveyed a personal vision of reality, but it was not presented in the customary dress of impersonal argument and precise statement. Some, of course, may consider this to be a point in its favour, but the fact remains that if we are looking for a systematic development of idealism in American thought, we have to look elsewhere.

Emerson was the chief figure in the Transcendentalist Club which was founded at Boston in 1836. Another member, highly esteemed by Emerson, was Amos Bronson Alcott (1799–1888), a deeply spiritual man who, in addition to his attempts to introduce new methods into education, founded a utopian community in Massachusetts, though it did not last long. Given to vague and oracular utterances, he was later pushed by the St. Louis Hegelians into trying to clarify and define his idealism. Among others associated in some way with New England Transcendentalism we may mention Henry David Thoreau (1817–62) and Orestes Augustus Brownson (1803–76). Thoreau, a famous literary figure, was attracted to Emerson when the latter delivered his Phi Beta Kappa Society address on 'The American Scholar' at Harvard in 1857. As for Brownson, his spiritual pilgrimage led him by various stages from Presbyterianism to Catholicism.

5. In 1867 there appeared at St. Louis, Missouri, the first number of *The Journal of Speculative Philosophy*, edited by William Torrey Harris (1835–1909). Harris and his associates contributed powerfully to spreading in America a knowledge of German idealism, and the group are known as the St. Louis

---

[1] *Ibid.*, I, p. 24.   [2] *Ibid.*

Hegelians. Harris was also one of the founders of the Kant-Club (1874). The group had some relations with the Transcendentalists of New England; and Harris helped to start the Concord Summer School of Philosophy in 1880, with which Alcott collaborated. In 1889 he was appointed United States Commissioner of Education by President Harrison.

In the first number of *The Journal of Speculative Philosophy* Harris spoke of the need for a speculative philosophy which would fulfil three main tasks. In the first place it should provide a philosophy of religion suitable for a time when traditional dogmas and ecclesiastical authority were losing their hold on men's minds. In the second place it should develop a social philosophy in accordance with the new demands of the national consciousness, which was turning away from sheer individualism. In the third place it should work out the deeper implications of the new ideas in the sciences, in which field, Harris maintained, the day of simple empiricism was definitely over. As speculative philosophy meant for Harris the tradition which started with Plato and attained its fullest expression in the system of Hegel, he was calling in effect for a development of idealism under the inspiration of post-Kantian German philosophy but in accordance with American needs.

There were various attempts to fulfil this sort of programme, ranging from the personal idealism of Howison and Bowne to the absolute idealism of Josiah Royce. And as both Howison and Bowne were born before Royce, they should perhaps be treated first. I propose, however, to devote the next chapter to Royce and in the following chapter to discuss briefly the personal idealists and some other philosophers who belonged to the idealist tradition, mentioning the names of some thinkers who were junior to Royce.

It may be as well, however, to point out at once that it is difficult to make any very sharp division between personal and absolute idealism in American thought. In a real sense Royce too was a personalist idealist. In other words, the form which absolute idealism took with Bradley, involving the relegation of personality to the sphere of appearances as contrasted with that of reality, was not congenial to the American mind. And, in general, it was felt that the proper fulfilment of Harris's programme required that human personality should not be sacrificed on the altar of the One, though there were, of course, differences in emphasis, some thinkers placing the emphasis on the Many, others more on the

One. Hence a distinction between personal and absolute idealism is legitimate, provided that we allow for the qualification which has just been made.

We may also remark that the term 'personal idealism' is somewhat ambiguous in the context of American thought. It was used, for example, by William James of his own philosophy. But though the use of the term was doubtless justified, James is best discussed under the heading of pragmatism.

CHAPTER XII

THE PHILOSOPHY OF ROYCE

Remarks on Royce's writings previous to his Gifford Lectures
—The meaning of Being and the meaning of ideas—Three
inadequate theories of Being—The fourth conception of Being—
The finite self and the Absolute; moral freedom—The social
aspect of morality—Immortality—Infinite series and the idea
of a self-representative system—Some critical comments.

1. JOSIAH ROYCE (1855–1916) entered the University of California at the age of sixteen and received his baccalaureate in 1875. A paper which he wrote on the theology of the *Prometheus Bound* of Aeschylus won him a grant of money that enabled him to spend two years in Germany, where he read German philosophers such as Schelling and Schopenhauer, and studied under Lotze at Göttingen. After taking his doctorate in 1878 at Johns Hopkins University he taught for a few years in the University of California and then went to Harvard as a lecturer in philosophy. In 1885 he was nominated as assistant professor, and in 1892 professor. In 1914 he accepted the Alford chair of philosophy at Harvard.

In 1885 Royce published *The Religious Aspect of Philosophy*. In it he argues that the impossibility of proving the universal and absolute validity of the moral ideal embraced by any given individual tends to produce moral scepticism and pessimism. Reflection, however, shows that the very search for a universal and absolute ideal reveals in the seeker a moral will which wills the harmonization of all particular ideals and values. And there then arises in the mind of the individual the consciousness that he ought so to live that his life and the lives of other men may form a unity, converging towards a common ideal goal or end. With this idea Royce associates an exaltation of the social order, in particular of the State.[1]

Turning to the problem of God, Royce rejects the traditional proofs of God's existence and develops an argument for the Absolute from the recognition of error. We are accustomed to

---

[1] The exaltation of the State, which is even described as 'divine', reappears in Royce's essay, *California: A Study of American Character* (1886).

think that error arises when our thought fails to conform with its intended object. But we obviously cannot place ourselves in the position of an external spectator, outside the subject-object relationship, capable of seeing whether thought conforms with its object or not. And reflection on this fact may lead to scepticism. Yet it is clear that we are capable of recognizing error. We can not only make erroneous judgments but also know that we have made them. And further reflection shows that truth and falsity have meaning only in relation to a complete system of truth, which must be present to absolute thought. In other words, Royce accepts a coherence theory of truth and passes from it to the assertion of absolute thought. As he was later to express it, an individual's opinions are true or false in relation to a wider insight. And his argument is that we cannot stop until we arrive at the idea of an all-inclusive divine insight which embraces in a comprehensive unity our thinking and its objects and is the ultimate measure of truth and falsity.

In *The Religious Aspect of Philosophy*, therefore, the Absolute is described as thought. 'All reality must be present to the unity of the Infinite Thought.'[1] But Royce does not understand this term in a sense which would exclude descriptions of the Absolute in terms of will or of experience. And in *The Conception of God* (1897) he argues that there is an absolute experience which is related to ours as an organic whole is related to its constituent elements. Though, therefore, Royce frequently uses the term 'God', it is obvious that the divine being is for him the One, the totality.[2] At the same time God or the Absolute is conceived as self-conscious. And the natural conclusion to draw is that finite selves are thoughts of God in his own act of self-knowledge. It is thus perfectly understandable that Royce drew upon himself the criticism of the personal idealists.[3] In point of fact, however, he had no wish to submerge the Many in the One in such a way as to reduce finite self-consciousness to an inexplicable illusion. Hence he had to develop a theory of the relation between the One and the Many which would neither reduce the Many to illusory appearance nor make the term 'One' altogether inappropriate. And this was

---

[1] *The Religious Aspect of Philosophy*, p. 433.
[2] In *The Spirit of Modern Philosophy* (1892), Royce speaks of the one infinite Self of which all finite selves are moments or organic parts.
[3] The sub-title of *The Conception of God* is *A Philosophical Discussion Concerning the Nature of the Divine Idea as a Demonstrable Reality*. Howison, the personal idealist, was one of the participants in the original discussion of 1895.

one of the main themes of Royce's Gifford Lectures, to which we shall turn in the next section.

Royce's idea of God as the absolute and all-inclusive experience naturally compels him, like Bradley, to devote attention to the problem of evil. In *Studies in Good and Evil* (1898) he rejects any attempt to evade the issue by saying that suffering and moral evil are illusions. On the contrary, they are real. We cannot avoid the conclusion, therefore, that God suffers when we suffer. And we must suppose that suffering is necessary for the perfecting of the divine life. As for moral evil, this too is required for the perfection of the universe. For the good will presupposes the evil as something to be overcome. True, from the point of view of the Absolute the world, the object of infinite thought, is a perfect unity in which evil is already overcome and subordinated to the good. But it is none the less a constituent element in the whole.

If God is a name for the universe, and if suffering and evil are real, we must obviously locate them in God. If, however, there is an absolute point of view from which evil is eternally overcome and subordinated to the good, God can hardly be simply a name for the universe. In other words, the problem of the relation between God and the world becomes acute. But Royce's ideas on this subject are best discussed in connection with his main presentation of his philosophy.

2. The two volumes of *The World and the Individual*, representing series of Gifford Lectures, appeared respectively in 1900 and 1901. In them Royce sets out to determine the nature of Being. If it is asserted that God is, or that the world is, or that the finite self is, we can always ask for the meaning of 'is'. This term, which Royce calls 'the existential predicate',[1] is often assumed to be simple and indefinable. But in philosophy the simple and ultimate is as much a subject for reflection as the complex and derived. Royce is not, however, concerned with the verb 'to be' simply in the sense of exist. He is also concerned with determining 'the special sorts of Reality that we attribute to God, to the World, and to the Human Individual'.[2] In traditional language he is concerned with essence as well as with existence, in his own language with the *what* as well as with the *that*. For if we assert

---

[1] *The World and the Individual*, I, p. 12 (1920 edition). This work will be referred to simply as *The World*.

[2] *Ibid.*, I, p. 12.

that X is or exists, we assert that there is an X, something possessing a certain nature.

In point of fact the problem of determining the meaning of what Royce calls the existential or ontological predicate immediately becomes for him the problem of determining the nature of reality. And the question arises, how are we to tackle this problem? It might perhaps appear that the best way to approach it would be to look at reality as presented in experience and try to understand it. But, Royce insists, we can understand reality only by means of ideas. And it thus becomes all-important to understand what an idea is and how it stands to reality. 'I am one of those who hold that when you ask the question: What is an Idea? and: How can Ideas stand in any true relation to Reality? you attack the world-knot in the way that promises most for the untying of its meshes.'[1]

After his initial announcement that he is going to deal with the problem of Being, Royce's shift of attention to the nature of ideas and their relation to reality is likely to appear both disappointing and exasperating to his readers. But his method of procedure is easily explicable. We have seen that in *The Religious Aspect of Philosophy* Royce described God as absolute thought. And his approach to the problem of Being by way of a theory of ideas is suggested by the metaphysical position which he has already adopted, namely the primacy of thought. Thus when he asserts 'the primacy of the World as Idea over the World as Fact',[2] he is speaking in terms of the idealist tradition as he sees it, the tradition according to which the world is the self-realization of the absolute Idea.

In the first place Royce draws a distinction between the external and internal meanings of an idea. Let us suppose that I have an idea of Mount Everest. It is natural to think of this idea as referring to and representing an external reality, namely the actual mountain. And this representative function is what Royce understands by the external meaning of an idea. But now let us suppose that I am an artist, and that I have in my mind an idea of the picture which I wish to paint. This idea can be described as 'the partial fulfilment of a purpose'.[3] And this aspect of an idea is what Royce calls its internal meaning.

Common sense would doubtless be prepared to admit that the idea in the mind of an artist can reasonably be described as the

<hr />

[1] *Ibid.*, I, pp. 16–17.   [2] *Ibid.*, I, p. 19.   [3] *Ibid.*, I, p. 25.

partial fulfilment of a purpose.[1] And to this extent it recognizes the existence of internal meaning. But, left to itself, common sense would probably regard the representative function of the idea as primary, even though it is a question of representing what does not yet exist, namely the projected work of art. And if we consider an idea such as that of the number of the inhabitants of London, common sense would certainly emphasize its representative character and ask whether or not it corresponds with external reality.

Royce, however, maintains that it is the internal meaning of an idea which is primary, and that in the long run external meaning turns out to be only 'an aspect of the completely developed internal meaning'.[2] Suppose, for example, that I wish to ascertain the number of people, or of families, resident in a certain area. Obviously, I have a purpose in wishing to ascertain these facts. Perhaps I am in charge of a housing scheme and wish to ascertain the number of individuals and of families in order to be able to estimate the number of houses or flats required for the already resident population in a district which is to be reconstructed. It is clearly important that my idea of the population should be accurate. External meaning is thus of importance. At the same time I try to obtain an accurate idea with a view to the fulfilment of a purpose. And the idea can be regarded as a partial or incomplete fulfilment of this purpose. In this sense the internal meaning of the idea is primary. According to Royce, its external meaning, taken simply by itself, is an abstraction, an abstraction, that is to say, from its context, namely the fulfilment of a purpose. When it is replaced in its context, the internal meaning is seen to take precedence.

What, it may be asked, is the connection between this theory of the meaning of ideas and the solution of the problem of reality? The answer is obviously that Royce intends to represent the world as the embodiment of an absolute system of ideas which are, in themselves, the incomplete fulfilment of a purpose. 'We propose to answer the question: What is to be? by the assertion that: To

[1] It is certainly not the intention of the present writer to suggest that the artist or poet necessarily first forms a clear idea of the work to be done and then gives concrete embodiment to this idea. If, for example, the poet had a clear idea of the poem, the poem would already have been composed. And all that remained would be to write down a poem already existing in the poet's mind. At the same time the poet would not start working without some sort of conceived purpose, some sort of 'idea' which could reasonably be regarded as the beginning of a total action.

[2] The World, I, p. 36.

be means simply to express, to embody the complete internal meaning of a certain absolute system of ideas—a system, moreover, which is genuinely implied in the true internal meaning or purpose of every finite idea, however fragmentary.'[1] Royce admits that this theory is not novel. For example, it is essentially the same as the line of thought which 'led Hegel to call the world the embodied Idea'.[2] But though the theory is not novel, 'I believe it to be of fundamental and of inexhaustible importance'.[3]

In other words, Royce first interprets the function of human ideas in the light of an already existing idealist conviction about the primacy of thought. And he then uses this interpretation as the basis for an explicit metaphysics. At the same time he works dialectically towards the establishment of his own view of the meaning of 'to be' by examining in turn different types of philosophy with a view to exhibiting their inadequacy. And though we cannot enter into the details of this discussion, it is appropriate to indicate its general lines.

3. The first type of philosophy discussed by Royce is what he calls realism. By this he understands the doctrine that 'the mere knowledge of any Being by any one who is not himself the Being known, "makes no difference whatever" to that known Being'.[4] In other words, if all knowledge were to disappear from the world, the only difference that this would make to the world would be that the particular fact of knowledge would no longer exist. Truth and falsity consist in the correspondence or non-correspondence of ideas with things; and nothing exists simply in virtue of the fact that it is known. Hence we cannot tell by inspecting the relations between ideas whether the objects referred to exist or not. Hence the *what* is sundered from the *that*. And this, Royce remarks, is why the realist has to deny the validity of the ontological argument for God's existence.

Royce's criticism of 'realism' is not always very clear. But his general line of thought is as follows. By realism in this context he evidently means an extreme nominalistic empiricism, according to which the world consists of a plurality of entities that are mutually independent. The disappearance of one would not affect the existence of the rest. Any relations which are superadded to these entities must, therefore, be themselves independent entities. And in this case, Royce argues, the terms of the relations cannot really

[1] *Ibid.*, I, p. 36. [2] *Ibid.*, I, p. 32.
[3] *Ibid.* [4] *Ibid.*, I, p. 93.

be related. If we start with entities which are sundered from one another, they remain sundered. Royce then argues that ideas must themselves be entities, and that on realist premisses an unbridgeable gulf yawns between them and the objects to which they are thought to refer. In other words, if ideas are entities which are completely independent of other entities, we can never know whether they correspond with objects external to themselves, nor indeed whether there are such objects at all. Hence we can never know whether realism, as an idea or set of ideas, is true or false. And in this sense realism, as a theory of reality, is self-defeating: it undermines its own foundations.[1]

From realism Royce proceeds to a consideration of what he calls 'mysticism'. As the core of realism consists in defining as 'real' any being which is essentially independent of any idea which refers to it from without, the realist, Royce claims, is committed to dualism. For he must postulate the existence of at least one idea and one object which is external to it. Mysticism, however, rejects dualism and asserts the existence of a One in which the distinctions between subject and object, idea and the reality to which it refers, vanish.

Mysticism, as understood in this sense, is as self-defeating as realism. For if there is only one simple and indivisible Being, the finite subject and its ideas must be accounted illusory. And in this case the Absolute cannot be known. For it could be known only by ideas. In fact any assertion that there is a One must be illusory. It is true that our fragmentary ideas need completion in a unified system, and that the whole is the truth. But if a philosopher stresses unity to such an extent that ideas have to be accounted illusion, he cannot at the same time consistently maintain that there is a One or Absolute. For it is plain that the Absolute has meaning for us only in so far as it is conceived by means of ideas.

If therefore we wish to maintain that knowledge of reality is possible at all, we cannot take the path of mysticism. We must allow for plurality. At the same time we cannot return to realism as described above. Hence realism must be modified in such a way that it is no longer self-defeating. And one way of attempting such a modification is to take the path of what Royce calls 'critical rationalism'.

The critical rationalist undertakes to 'define Being in terms of

---

[1] The argument might perhaps be summed up in this way. If things are completely independent of ideas, ideas are completely independent of things. And in this case truth, considered as a relation between idea and things, is unattainable.

validity, to conceive that whoever says, of any object, *It is*, means only that a certain idea . . . *is valid*, has truth, defines an experience that, at least as a mathematical ideal, and perhaps as an empirical event, is determinately *possible*'.[1] Suppose that I assert that there are human beings on the planet Mars. According to the critical rationalist, I am asserting that in the progress of possible experience a certain idea would be validated or verified. Royce gives as examples of critical rationalism Kant's theory of possible experience and J. S. Mill's definition of matter as a permanent possibility of sensations. We might add logical positivism, provided that we substitute for 'idea' 'empirical proposition'.

In Royce's view critical rationalism has this advantage over realism that by defining Being in terms of possible experience, the validation of an idea (better, the verification of a proposition), it avoids the objections which arise from realism's complete sundering of ideas from the reality to which they are assumed to refer. At the same time critical rationalism has this great drawback that it is incapable of answering the question, '*what is a valid or a determinately possible experience at the moment when it is supposed to be only possible?* What is a valid truth at the moment when nobody verifies its validity?'[2] If I assert that there are men on Mars, this statement doubtless implies, in a definable sense of this term, that the presence of men on Mars is an object of possible experience. But if the statement happens to be true, their existence is not simply possible existence. Hence we can hardly define Being simply in terms of the possible validation or verification of an idea. And though critical rationalism does not make knowledge of reality impossible, as is done by both realism and mysticism, it is unable to provide an adequate account of reality. Hence we must turn to another and more adequate philosophical theory, which will subsume in itself the truths contained in the three theories already mentioned but which will at the same time be immune from the objections which can be brought against them.

4. It has already been indicated that by 'realism' Royce understands nominalism rather than realism as this term is used in the context of the controversy about universals. And if we bear this fact in mind, we shall not be so startled by his assertion that for the realist the only ultimate form of being is the individual. For the nominalist slogan was that only individuals exist. At the same time we must also bear in mind the fact that Hegel, who was no

---

[1] *The World*, I, pp. 226–7. [2] *Ibid.*, I, p. 260.

nominalist, used the term 'individual' to mean the concrete universal, and that in the Hegelian philosophy the ultimate form of being is the individual in this sense of the term, the Absolute being the supreme individual, the all-inclusive concrete universal. Hence when Royce asserts that the truth contained in realism is that the only ultimate form of being is the individual, it would be misleading to say simply that he is accepting the nominalist slogan. For he re-interprets the term 'individual' under the inspiration of the idealist tradition. According to his use of the term 'an individual being is a Life of Experience fulfilling Ideas, in an absolutely final form. . . . The essence of the Real is to be Individual, or permit no other of its own kind, and this character it possesses only as the unique fulfilment of purpose.'[1]

Now we have seen that an idea is the incomplete or partial fulfilment of a purpose, the expression of will. And the complete embodiment of the will is the world in its entirety. Hence any idea ultimately 'means'[2] the totality. And it follows that in the totality, the world as a whole, I can recognize myself. To this extent therefore we can find truth in 'mysticism' and agree with the oriental mystic who 'says of the self and the World: *That art Thou*'.[3]

It is evident, however, that as embodied in any particular phase of consciousness the will expresses itself in attention only to a part of the world or to certain facts in the world. The rest relapses into a vague background at the margin of consciousness. It becomes in fact the object of possible experience. In other words, it is necessary to introduce a concept from critical rationalism.

So far we have been thinking of the point of view of the individual finite subject. But though there is an obvious sense in which the world is 'my world' and nobody else's, it is also obvious that if I regard the world as being simply and solely the embodiment of my will, I am committed to solipsism. It is also clear that if I postulate the existence of other lives of experience besides my own but regard each life as completely self-enclosed, I fall back into the thesis of realism, namely that reality consists of completely separate and mutually independent entities. Hence to avoid solipsism without returning to the realist thesis which we

---

[1] *The World*, I, p. 348. For example, 'my world' is the embodiment of my will, the fulfilment of my purpose, the expression of my interests. And it is thus unique. But, as is explained in the following paragraphs, we cannot remain simply with the concept of 'my world'.

[2] We must remember that for Royce 'internal meaning' is primary.

[3] *The World*, I, p. 355.

have already rejected we must introduce a new dimension or plane, that of intersubjectivity.

It is commonly said, Royce remarks, that we come to know the existence of other persons by analogical reasoning. That is to say, observing certain patterns of external behaviour we attribute to them wills like our own. But if this means that we first have a clear knowledge of ourselves and then infer the existence of other persons, 'it is nearer the truth to say that we first learn about ourselves from and through our fellows, than that we learn about our fellows by using the analogy of ourselves'.[1] We have indeed ever-present evidence of the existence of others. For they are the source of new ideas. They answer our questions; they tell us things; they express opinions other than our own; and so on. Yet it is precisely through social intercourse or at least in the consciousness of the presence of others, that we form our own ideas and become aware of what we really will and aim at. As Royce puts it, our fellows 'help us to find out what our true meaning is'.[2]

If, however, Royce rejects the view that we first possess a clear consciousness of ourselves and then infer the existence of other persons, still less does he intend to imply that we first have a clear and definite idea of other persons and then infer that we too are persons. He says, indeed, that 'a vague belief in the existence of our fellows seems to antedate, to a considerable extent, the definite formation of any consciousness of ourselves'.[3] But his thesis is that the clear awareness of ourselves and of other persons arises out of a kind of primitive social consciousness, so that it is a question of differentiation rather than of inference. Empirical self-consciousness depends constantly upon a series of contrast-effects. 'The Ego is always known as in contrast to the Alter.'[4] Both emerge from the original social consciousness.

As experience develops, the individual comes more and more to regard the inner lives of others as something private, removed from his direct observation. At the same time he becomes progressively conscious of external objects as instruments of purposes which are common to himself and others as well as of his and their particular purposes or interests. There thus arises the consciousness of a triad, 'my fellow and Myself, with Nature between us'.[5]

[1] Ibid., II, pp. 170–1.   [2] Ibid., II, p. 172.   [3] Ibid., II, p. 170.
[4] Ibid., II, p. 264. Royce expresses his general agreement with the theory of the origins of self-consciousness given in the second volume of Mental Development in the Child and the Race (1896), by James Mark Baldwin (1861–1934), of Princeton University.
[5] The World, II, p. 177.

The world of Nature is known by us only in part, a great deal remaining for us the realm of possible experience. But we have already noted the difficulty encountered by critical rationalism in explaining the ontological status of objects of possible experience; and in any case science makes it impossible for us to believe that Nature is simply and solely the embodiment of human will and purpose. The hypothesis of evolution, for example, leads us to conceive finite minds as products. In this case, however, the question arises, how can we save the idealist definition of Being in terms of the internal meaning of ideas considered as the partial fulfilment of a purpose?

Royce's answer to this question is easy to foresee. The world is ultimately the expression of an absolute system of ideas which is itself the partial fulfilment of the divine will. God, expressing himself in the world, is the ultimate Individual. Or, to put the matter in another way, the ultimate Individual is the life of absolute experience. Each finite self is a unique expression of the divine purpose; and each embodies or expresses itself in its world. But 'my world' and 'your world' are unique facets of 'the world', the embodiment of the infinite divine will and purpose. And what is for us simply the object of possible experience is for God the object of actual creative experience. 'The whole world of truth and being must exist only as present, in all its variety, its wealth, its relationships, its entire constitution, to the unity of a single consciousness, which includes both our own and all finite conscious meanings in one final eternally present insight.'[1] Royce is thus able to preserve his theory of Being, namely that 'whatever is, is consciously known as the fulfilment of some idea, and is so known either by ourselves at this moment, or by a consciousness inclusive of our own'.[2]

5. We have seen that for Royce the individual is a *life* of experience. And if we are looking for the nature of the self in a meta-empirical sense,[3] we have to conceive it in ethical terms, not in terms of a soul-substance. For it is through the possession of a unique ideal, a unique vocation, a unique life-task which is what my past has 'meant' and which my future is to fulfil that '*I am defined and created a Self*'.[4] Perhaps, therefore, we can say,

---

[1] *The World*, I, p. 397.   [2] *Ibid.*, I, p. 396.
[3] That is to say, if we are looking for a metaphysical concept of the self rather than for an empirical account of, say, the origins and development of self-consciousness.
[4] *The World*, II, p. 276.

speaking in a manner that puts us in mind of existentialism, that for Royce the finite individual continually creates himself as this unique self by realizing a unique ideal, by fulfilling a certain unique vocation.[1]

It is in terms of this idea of the self that Royce attempts to meet the objection that absolute idealism deprives the finite self of reality, value and freedom. He has, of course, no intention of denying any of the empirical data relating to the dependence of the psychical on the physical or to the influence on the self of social environment, education and such like factors. But he insists that each finite self has its own unique way of acknowledging and responding by its deeds to this dependence,[2] while from the metaphysical point of view the life of each finite self is a unique contribution to the fulfilment of the general purpose of God. Royce has indeed to admit that when I will, God wills in me, and that my act is part of the divine life. But this admission, he maintains, is quite compatible with the statement that the finite self can act freely. For by the very fact that I am a *unique* expression of the divine will, the will from which my acts proceed is *my* will. 'Your individuality in your act *is* your freedom.'[3] That is to say, my way of expressing the divine will is myself; and if my acts proceed from myself, they are free acts. There is indeed a sense in which it is true to say that the divine Spirit compels us, but 'in the sense that it compels you to be an individual, and to be free'.[4]

Now, Royce maintains that every finite will seeks the Absolute, so much so that 'to seek anything but the Absolute itself is, indeed, even for the most perverse Self, simply impossible'.[5] In other words, every finite self tends by its very nature, whether it is aware of the fact or not, to unite its will ever more closely with the divine will. Obligation bears on us in relation to conduct which would bring us nearer to this end. And a moral rule is a rule which, if followed, would bring us nearer to the end than if we acted in a manner contrary to the rule. It is thus clear enough that in Royce's ethics the concept of the good is paramount, and that obligation bears on us in relation to the means necessary to attain this good, namely the conscious union of our will with the divine will. But it is not so clear how any room can be left for rebellion against the divine will or against a known dictate of the moral

---

[1] Needless to say, for the atheist existentialist, such as Sartre, the idea of a God-given vocation is devoid of validity.
[2] Here again one is put in mind of modern existentialism.
[3] *The World*, I, p. 469.   [4] *Ibid.*, II, p. 293.   [5] *Ibid.*, II, p. 347.

law. For if we all inevitably seek the Absolute, it appears to follow that if a person acts in a manner which will not as a matter of fact bring him nearer to the final end which he is always seeking, he does so simply out of ignorance, out of defective knowledge. Hence the question arises, 'can a finite self, knowing the Ought, in any sense freely choose to rebel or to obey?'[1]

Royce answers in the first place that though a man who has clear knowledge of what he ought to do will act in accordance with this knowledge, he can voluntarily concentrate his attention elsewhere, so that here and now he no longer has clear knowledge of what he ought to do. 'To sin is *consciously to forget*, through a narrowing of the field of attention, an Ought that one already recognizes.'[2]

Given Royce's premisses, this answer is hardly adequate. We can, of course, easily give a cash-value to his idea of a shift of attention. Suppose, for example, that I am sincerely convinced that it would be wrong for me to act in a certain way which I regard as productive of sensual pleasure. The more I concentrate my attention on the pleasurable aspects of this way of acting, so much the more does my conviction of its wrongness tend to retreat to the margin of consciousness and become ineffective. We all know that this sort of situation occurs frequently enough. And the ordinary comment would be that the agent should be careful not to concentrate his attention on the pleasurable aspects of a way of acting which he sincerely believes to be wrong. If he concentrates his attention in this manner, he is ultimately responsible for what happens. But though this point of view is clearly reasonable, the question immediately arises, how can the agent be properly held responsible for choosing to concentrate his attention in a certain direction if he is in his entirety an expression of the divine will? Have we simply not pushed the difficulty a stage further back?

Royce rather tends to evade the issue by turning to the subject of the overcoming of evil in the totality. But his general line of answer seems to be that as a man's direction of his attention proceeds from his will, the man is himself responsible for it and thus for the outcome. The fact that the man's will is itself the expression of the divine will does not alter the situation. In the circumstances it does not appear that Royce can very well say anything else. For though he certainly wishes to maintain human

[1] *The World*, II, p. 351.   [2] *Ibid.*, II, p. 359.

freedom and responsibility in a real sense, his determination to maintain at the same time the doctrine of the all-comprehensive Absolute inevitably influences his account of freedom. Moral freedom becomes 'simply this freedom to hold by attention, or to forget by inattention, an Ought already present to one's finite consciousness'.[1] If it is asked whether the holding or forgetting is not itself determined by the Absolute, Royce can only answer that it proceeds from a man's own will, and that to act in accordance with one's will *is* to act freely, even if one's finite will is a particular embodiment of the divine will.

6. As Royce lays great emphasis, in a manner which reminds us of Fichte, on the uniqueness of the task which each finite self is called to perform, he can hardly be expected to devote much time to developing a theory of universal moral rules.[2] And it is perhaps not an exaggeration to say that the fundamental precept is for him, as for Emerson, 'Be an individual! That is, find and fulfil your unique task.' At the same time it would be quite wrong to depict him as belittling the idea of the community. On the contrary, his ethical theory can be regarded as a contribution to the demand made by Harris in his programme for speculative philosophy, that a social theory should be developed which would fulfil the needs of a national consciousness that was moving away from sheer individualism. For Royce all finite selves are mutually related precisely because they are unique expressions of one infinite will. And all individual vocations or life-tasks are elements in a common task, the fulfilment of the divine purpose. Hence Royce preaches loyalty to the ideal community, the Great Community as he calls it.[3]

In *The Problem of Christianity* (1913) Royce defines loyalty as 'the willing and thoroughgoing devotion of a self to a cause, when the cause is something which unites many selves in one, and which is therefore the interest of a community'.[4] And he sees in the Church, the community of the faithful, especially as represented in the Pauline Epistles, the embodiment of the spirit of loyalty, of

---

[1] *Ibid.*, II, p. 360.

[2] 'By the Ought you mean, at any temporal instant, a rule that, if followed, would guide you so to express, at that instant, your will, that you should be thereby made nearer to union with the divine, nearer to a consciousness of the oneness of your will and the Absolute Will, than you would if you acted counter to this Ought', *The World*, II, pp. 347–8. Here the emphasis is placed on 'the instant', not on the universal.

[3] In 1908 Royce published *The Philosophy of Loyalty* and in 1916 *The Hope of the Great Community*.

[4] *The Problem of Christianity*, I, p. 68.

devotion to a common ideal and of loyalty to the ideal community which should be loved as a person. It does not follow, however, that Royce intended to identify what he calls the Great Community with an historic Church, any more than with an historic State. The Great Community is more like Kant's kingdom of ends; it is the ideal human community. Yet though it is an ideal to be sought after rather than an actual historic society existing here and now, it none the less lies at the basis of the moral order, precisely because it is the goal or *telos* of moral action. It is true that the individual alone can work out his moral vocation; it cannot be done for him. But because of the very nature of the self genuine individuality can be realized only through loyalty to the Great Community, to an ideal cause which unites all men together.

Largely under the influence of C. S. Peirce, Royce came to emphasize the role of interpretation in human knowledge and life; and he applied this idea in his ethical theory. For example, the individual cannot realize himself and attain true selfhood or personality without a life-goal or life-plan, in relation to which concepts such as right and wrong, higher self and lower self, become concretely meaningful. But a man comes to apprehend his life-plan or ideal goal only through a process of interpreting himself to himself. Further, this self-interpretation is achieved only in a social context, through interaction with other people. Others inevitably help me to interpret myself to myself; and I help others to interpret themselves to themselves. In a sense this process tends to division rather than to union, inasmuch as each individual becomes thereby more aware of himself as possessing a unique life-task. But if we bear in mind the social structure of the self, we are led to form the idea of an unlimited community of interpretation, of humanity, that is to say, as engaged throughout time in the common task of interpreting both the physical world and its own purposes, ideals and values. All growth in scientific knowledge and moral insight involves a process of interpretation.

The supreme object of loyalty as a moral category is, Royce came to think, this ideal community of interpretation. But towards the close of his life he stressed the importance of limited communities both for moral development and for the achievement of social reform. If we consider, for instance, two individuals who are disputing about, say, the possession of some property, we can see that this potentially dangerous situation is transformed by the intervention of a third party, the judge. A tryadic relation is substituted for the potentially dangerous dyadic relation; and a small-scale community of interpretation is set up. Thus Royce tries to exhibit the mediating or interpretative and morally educative functions of such institutions as the judicial system, always in the light of the idea of interpretation. He applies this idea even to the institution of insurance and develops, as a safeguard against war, a scheme of insurance on an international scale.[1] Some of his commentators may have seen in such ideas a peculiarly American fusion of idealism with a rather down-to-earth practicality. But it does not follow, of course, that such a fusion is a bad thing. In any case Royce evidently felt that if substantive proposals were to be put forward in ethical theory, something more was required than exhorting men to be loyal to the ideal community of interpretation.

7. From what has been said hitherto it is clear that Royce attaches to the unique personality a value which could not be attributed to it in the philosophy of Bradley. It is not surprising, therefore, that he is far more interested than Bradley in the question of immortality, and that he maintains that the self is preserved in the Absolute.

In discussing this subject Royce dwells, among other aspects of the matter, on the Kantian theme that the moral task of the individual can have no temporal end. 'A consciously last moral task is a contradiction in terms. . . . The service of the eternal is an essentially endless service. There can be no last moral deed.'[2] Obviously, this line of argument could not by itself prove immortality. It is true that if we recognize a moral law at all, we have to regard it as bearing upon us as long as we live. But it does not follow from this premiss alone that the self survives bodily death and is able to continue fulfilling a moral vocation. But for Royce as a metaphysician the universe is of such a kind that the finite self, as a unique expression of the Absolute and as representing an irreplaceable value, must be supposed to continue in existence. The ethical self is always something in the making; and as the divine purpose must be fulfilled, we are justified in believing that after the death of the body the self attains genuine individuality in a higher form. But 'I know not in the least, I pretend not to guess, by what processes the individuality of our human life is further expressed. I wait until this mortal shall put

---

[1] Cf. *War and Insurance* (1914), and *The Hope of the Great Community* (1916).
[2] *The World*, I, pp. 444–5.

on—Individuality.'[1] Evidently, in Royce's assertion of immortality what really counts is his general metaphysical vision of
reality, coupled with his evaluation of personality.

8. At the end of the first volume of Royce's Gifford Lectures
there is a Supplementary Essay in which he takes issue with
Bradley on the subject of an infinite multitude. Bradley, it will be
remembered, maintains that relational thought involves us in
infinite series. If, for example, qualities A and B are related by
relation R, we must choose between saying that R is reducible
without residue to A and B or that it is not so reducible. In the
first case we shall be compelled to conclude that A and B are not
related at all. In the second case we shall have to postulate further
relations to relate both A and B with R, and so on without end.
We are then committed to postulating an actually infinite multitude. But this concept is self-contradictory. Hence we must conclude that relational thought is quite incapable of giving a
coherent account of how the Many proceed from and are unified
in the One, and that the world as presented in such thought
belongs to the sphere of appearance as contrasted with that of
reality. Royce, however, undertakes to show that the One can
express itself in infinite series which are 'well-ordered' and involve
no contradiction, and that thought is thus capable of giving a
coherent account of the relation between the One and the Many.
It is perhaps disputable whether Bradley's difficulties are really
met by first ascribing to him the thesis that an actually infinite
multitude is 'a self-contradictory conception'[2] and then arguing
that an endless series in mathematics does not involve a contradiction. But though Royce develops his own conception of the
relation between the One and the Many in the context of a controversy with Bradley, what he is really interested in is, of course,
the explanation of his own ideas.

Royce's attention was directed by C. S. Peirce to the logic of
mathematics;[3] and the Supplementary Essay shows the fruit of
Royce's reflections on this subject. In an endless mathematical
series, such as that of the whole numbers, the endlessness of the
series is due to a recurrent operation of thought, a recurrent
operation of thought being describable as 'one that, *if once finally
expressed*, would involve, in the region where it had received

---

[1] *The Conception of Immortality*, p. 80.
[2] *The World*, I, p. 475.
[3] Royce's interest in mathematical logic found expression in *The Relation of the
Principles of Logic to the Foundation of Geometry* (1905).

expression, an infinite variety of serially arranged facts, corresponding to the purpose in question'.[1] In general, if we assume a purpose of such a kind that if we try to express it by means of a succession of acts, the ideal data which begin to express it demand as part of their own 'meaning' additional data which are themselves further expressions of the original meaning and at the same time demand still further expressions, we have an endless series produced by a recurrent operation of thought.

A series of this kind can properly be regarded as a totality. To be sure, it is not a totality in the sense that we can count to the end and complete the series. For it is *ex hypothesi* infinite or endless. But if we take, for example, the series of whole numbers, 'the mathematician can view them all as *given* by means of their universal definition, and their consequent clear distinction from all other objects of thought'.[2] In other words, there is no intrinsic repugnance between the idea of a totality and that of an infinite series. And we can conceive the One as expressing itself in an infinite series or, rather, a plurality of co-ordinate infinite series, the plurality of lives of experience. This gives us, of course, a dynamic rather than a static concept of the One. And this is essential to Royce's metaphysics, with its emphasis on divine will and purpose and on the 'internal meaning' of ideas.

An infinite series of this kind is described by Royce as a self-representative system. And he finds examples in 'all continuous and discrete mathematical systems of any infinite type'.[3] But a simple illustration given by Royce himself will serve better to clarify what he means by a self-representative system. Suppose that we decide that on some portion of England a map is to be constructed which will represent the country down to the smallest detail, including every contour and marking, whether natural or artificial. As the map itself will be an artificial feature of England, another map will have to be constructed within the first map and representing it too, if, that is to say, our original purpose is to be carried out. And so on without end. True, this endless representation of England would not be physically possible. But we can conceive an endless series of maps within maps, a series which, though it cannot be completed in time, can be regarded as already given in our original purpose or 'meaning'. The observer who understood the situation and looked at the series of maps, would not see any last map. But he would know why there could be no

[1] *The World*, I, p. 507.   [2] *Ibid.*, I, p. 515.   [3] *Ibid.*, I, p. 513.

last map. Hence he would see no contradiction or irrationality in the endlessness of the series. And the series would constitute a self-representative system.

If we apply this idea in metaphysics, the universe appears as an infinite series, an endless whole, which expresses a single purpose or plan. There are, of course, subordinate and co-ordinate series, in particular the series which constitute the lives of finite selves. But they are all comprised within one unified infinite series which has no last member but which is 'given' as a totality in the internal meaning of the divine idea or absolute system of ideas. The One, according to Royce, must express itself in the endless series which constitutes its life of creative experience. In other words, it must express itself in the Many. And as the endless series is the progressive expression or fulfilment of a single purpose, the whole of reality is one self-representative system.

9. It is clear that Royce, with his emphasis on personality, has no intention of abandoning theism altogether and of using the term 'the Absolute' simply as a name for the world considered as an open totality, a series which has no assignable last member. The world is for him the embodiment of the internal meaning of a system of ideas which are themselves the partial fulfilment of a purpose. And the Absolute is a self; it is personal rather than impersonal; it is an eternal and infinite consciousness. Hence it can reasonably be described as God. And Royce depicts the infinite series which constitutes the temporal universe as present all at once, *tota simul*, to the divine consciousness. Indeed, he is quite prepared to commend St. Thomas Aquinas for his account of the divine knowledge; and he himself uses the analogy of our awareness of a symphony as a whole, an awareness which is obviously quite compatible with the knowledge that this part precedes that. So, according to Royce, God is aware of temporal succession, though the whole temporal series is none the less present to the eternal consciousness.

At the same time Royce rejects the dualistic sundering of the world from God which he regards as characteristic of theism, and he blames Aquinas for conceiving 'the temporal existence of the created world as sundered from the eternal life which belongs to God'.[1] The Many exist within the unity of the divine life. 'Simple unity is a mere impossibility. God cannot be One except by being Many. Nor can we various Selves be Many, unless in Him we are One.'[2]

[1] *The World*, II, p. 143.   [2] *Ibid.*, II, p. 331.

In other words, Royce tries to re-interpret theism in the light of absolute idealism. He tries to preserve the idea of a personal God while combining it with the idea of the all-comprehensive Absolute represented as the Universal of universals.[1] And this is not an easy position to maintain. In fact its ambiguity is well illustrated by Royce's use of the term 'individual'. If we speak of God as the supreme or ultimate Individual, we naturally tend to think of him as a personal being and of the world as the 'external' expression of his creative will. But for Royce the term 'individual' means, as we have seen, a life of experience. And according to this meaning of the term God becomes the life of absolute and infinite experience, in which all finite things are immanent. Whereas the interpretation of the existence of finite things as the expression of purposeful will suggests creation in a theistic sense, the description of God as absolute experience suggests a rather different relation. No doubt Royce tries to bring the two concepts together through the conception of creative experience; but there seems to be in his philosophy a somewhat unstable marriage between theism and absolute idealism.

It is, of course, notoriously difficult to express the relation between the finite and the infinite without tending either to a monism in which the Many are relegated to the sphere of appearance or are submerged in the One or to a dualism which renders the use of the term 'infinite' quite inappropriate. And it is certainly not possible to avoid both positions without a clear theory of the analogy of being. But Royce's statements on the subject of being are somewhat perplexing.

On the one hand we are told that being is the expression or embodiment of the internal meaning of an idea, and so of purpose or will. But though the subordination of being to thought may be characteristic of metaphysical idealism, the question obviously arises whether thought itself is not a form of being. And the same question can be asked in regard to will. On the other hand we are told that the ultimately real, and so presumably the ultimate form of being, is the individual. And as God is the Individual of individuals, it appears to follow that he must be the supreme and absolute being. Yet we are also told to regard 'individuality, and consequently Being, as above all an expression of Will'.[2] To regard individuality as an expression of will is not so difficult, if,

[1] The term 'universal' is used here, needless to say, in the sense of the concrete universal.

[2] *The World*, I, p. 588.

that is to say, we interpret individuality as a life of expression. But to regard being as an expression of will is not so easy. For the question again arises, is will not being? Of course, it would be possible to restrict the use of the term 'being' to material being. But then we could hardly regard individuality, in Royce's sense of the term, as being.

In spite, however, of the ambiguity and lack of precision in his writing, Royce's philosophy impresses by its sincerity. It is evidently the expression of a deeply held faith, a faith in the reality of God, in the value of the human personality and in the unity of mankind in and through God, a unity which can be adequately realized only through individual contributions to a common moral task. Royce was indeed something of a preacher. But the philosophy which he preached certainly meant for him a great deal more than an intellectual exercise or game.

It should be added that in the opinion of some commentators[1] Royce came to abandon his theory of the Absolute Will and to substitute for it the idea of an unlimited community of interpretation, an unlimited community, that is to say, of finite individuals. And from the purely ethical point of view such a change would be understandable. For it would dispose of the objection, of which Royce himself was aware, that it is difficult, if indeed possible at all, to reconcile the theory of the Absolute Will with the view of human beings as genuine moral agents. At the same time the substitution of a community of finite individuals for the Absolute would be a pretty radical change. And it is by no means easy to see how such a community could take over, as it were, the cosmological function of the Absolute. Even if, therefore, the idea of the Absolute retreats into the background in Royce's latest writings, one hesitates to accept the view that he positively rejected the idea, unless, of course, one is driven to do so by strong empirical evidence. There is indeed some evidence. In his last years Royce himself referred to a change in his idealism. Hence we cannot say that the claim that he substituted the unlimited community of interpretation for his earlier concept of the Absolute is unfounded. Royce does not seem, however, to have been explicit as one could wish about the precise nature and extent of the change to which he refers.

[1] Cf., the Appendix to *The Moral Philosophy of Josiah Royce* by Peter Fuss (Cambridge, Mass., 1965).

CHAPTER XIII

PERSONAL IDEALISM AND OTHER TENDENCIES

Howison's criticism of Royce in favour of his own ethical pluralism—The evolutionary idealism of Le Conte—The personal idealism of Bowne—The objective idealism of Creighton—Sylvester Morris and dynamic idealism—Notes on the prolongation of idealism into the twentieth century—An attempt at transcending the opposition between idealism and realism.

1. GEORGE HOLMES HOWISON (1834–1916), a member of the Philosophical Society of St. Louis and of W. T. Harris's Kant-Club, was at first a professor of mathematics. But in 1872 he accepted the chair of logic and philosophy in the Massachusetts Institute of Technology at Boston, a post which he occupied until 1878 when he went to Germany for two years. In Germany he came under the influence of the right-wing Hegelian Ludwig Michelet (1801–93), and, like Michelet himself, he interpreted Hegel's absolute Idea or cosmic Reason as a personal being, God. In 1884 Howison became a professor in the University of California. His work *The Limits of Evolution and Other Essays*, appeared in 1901.

It has already been mentioned that Howison participated in the discussion which formed the basis for *The Conception of God* (1897), a work to which reference was made in the chapter on Royce. In his introduction to the book Howison draws attention to the existence of a certain measure of basic agreement among the participants in the discussion, particularly in regard to the personality of God and about the close relation between the concepts of God, freedom and immortality. But though he recognizes certain family likenesses between different types of idealism, this does not prevent him from developing a sharp criticism of Royce's philosophy.

In the first place, if being is defined in terms of its relation to the internal meaning of an idea, how, Howison asks, are we to decide whether the idea in question is my idea or that of an infinite all-inclusive self? The factor which leads Royce and those who share his general outlook to reject solipsism in favour of absolute idealism is an instinctive response to the demands of common sense rather than any logical and compelling argument. In the second place, though Royce certainly intends to preserve individual freedom and responsibility, he can do so only at the cost of consistency. For absolute idealism logically involves the merging of finite selves in the Absolute.

Howison's own philosophy has been described as ethical pluralism. Existence takes the form of spirits and of the contents and order of their experience, the spatio-temporal world owing its being to the co-existence of spirits. Each spirit is a free and active efficient cause, having the origin of its activity within itself. At the same time each spirit is a member of a community of spirits, the City of God, the members being united in terms of final causality, that is, by their attraction to a common ideal, the full realization of the City of God. The human consciousness is not simply self-enclosed, but, when developed, it sees itself as a member of what Howison describes as Conscience or Complete Reason. And the movement towards a common ideal or end is what is called evolution.

This may sound remarkably like Royce's view, except perhaps for Howison's insistence that the spring of the activity of each spirit is to be sought within itself. But Howison tries to avoid what he regards as the logical and disastrous consequences of Royce's philosophy by emphasizing final causality. God is represented as the personified ideal of every spirit. By this Howison does not mean that God has no existence except as a human ideal. He means that the mode of divine action on the human spirit is that of final causality, rather than that of efficient causality. God draws the finite self as an ideal; but the self's response to God is its own activity rather than the action of God or the Absolute. In other words, God acts by illuminating the reason and attracting the will to the ideal of the unity of free spirits in himself rather than by determining the human will through efficient causality or the exercise of power.

2. Another participant in the discussion referred to above was Joseph Le Conte (1823–1901), professor in the University of California. Trained as a geologist, Le Conte interested himself in the philosophical aspects of the theory of evolution and expounded what can be described as evolutionary idealism.[1] As the ultimate source of evolution he saw a divine Energy which expresses itself

---

[1] Le Conte's writings include *Religion and Science* (1874), and *Evolution: Its Nature, Its Evidence and Its Relation to Religious Thought* (1888).

immediately in the physical and chemical forces of Nature. But the efflux of this divine Energy becomes progressively individuated concomitantly with the advancing organization of matter. Le Conte's philosophy is thus pluralistic. For he maintains that in the process of evolution we find the emergence of successively higher forms of self-active individuals, until we reach the highest form of individual being yet attained, namely the human being. In man the efflux or spark of the divine life is able to recognize and to enter into conscious communion with its ultimate source. In fact we can look forward to a progressive elevation of man to the level of 'regenerated' man, enjoying a higher degree of spiritual and moral development.

Howison's approach to philosophy tended to be through the critical philosophy of Kant, when rethought in the light of metaphysical idealism. Le Conte's approach was rather by way of an attempt to show how the theory of evolution liberates science from all materialistic implications and points the way to a religious and ethical idealism. He exercised some influence on the mind of Royce.

3. Besides Howison, whose philosophy has been labelled as ethical idealism, one of the most influential representatives of personal idealism in America was Borden Parker Bowne (1847–1910). As a student at New York Bowne wrote a criticism of Spencer. During subsequent studies in Germany he came under the influence of Lotze, especially in regard to the latter's theory of the self.[1] In 1876 Bowne became Professor of Philosophy in the University of Boston. His writings include *Studies in Theism* (1879), *Metaphysics* (1882), *Philosophy of Theism* (1887), *Principles of Ethics* (1892), *The Theory of Thought and Knowledge* (1897), *The Immanence of God* (1905), and *Personalism* (1908). These titles show clearly enough the religious orientation of his thought.

Bowne at first described his philosophy as transcendental empiricism, in view of the conspicuous role played in his thought by a doctrine of categories inspired by Kant. These are not simply empirically derived, fortuitous results of adaptation to environment in the process of evolution. At the same time they are the expression of the nature of the self and of its self-experience. And this shows that the self is an active unity and not a mere logical

[1] See Vol. VII of this *History*, p. 378. For Lotze, to recognize the fact of the unity of consciousness is *eo ipso* to recognize the existence of the soul. He thus tries to avoid phenomenalism on the one hand and postulating an occult soul-substance on the other. For Bowne, the self is an immediate datum of consciousness, not a hidden entity which has to be inferred from the existence of faculties and their acts.

postulate, as Kant thought. Indeed, the self or person, characterized by intelligence and will, is the only real efficient cause. For
efficient causality is essentially volitional. In Nature we find
indeed uniformities, but no causality in the proper sense.

This idea of Nature forms the basis for a philosophy of God.
Science describes how things happen. And it can be said to explain
events, if we mean by this that it exhibits them as examples or
cases of empirically discovered generalizations which are called
'laws'. 'But in the causal sense science explains nothing. Here the
alternative is supernatural explanation or none.'[1] True, in science
itself the idea of God is no more required than in shoemaking. For
science is simply classificatory and descriptive. But once we turn
to metaphysics, we see the order of Nature as the effect of the
constant activity of a supreme rational will. In other words, as
far as its causation is concerned, any event in Nature is as supernatural as a miracle would be. 'For in both alike God would be
equally implicated.'[2]

We can now take a broad view of reality. If, as Bowne believes,
to be real is to act, and if activity in the full sense can be attributed
only to persons, it follows that it is only persons who are, so to
speak, fully real. We thus have the picture of a system of persons
standing to one another in various active relations through the
instrumentality of the external world. And this system of persons
must, according to Bowne, be the creation of a supreme Person,
God. On the one hand a being which was less than personal could
not be the sufficient cause of finite persons. On the other hand, if
we can apply the category of causality to a world in which the
infra-personal exercises no real efficient causality, this can only be
because the world is the creation of a personal being who is
immanently active in it. Ultimate reality thus appears as personal
in character, as a system of persons with a supreme Person at
their head.

Personalism, as Bowne came to call his philosophy, is 'the only
metaphysics that does not dissolve away into self-cancelling
abstractions'.[3] Auguste Comte, according to Bowne, was justified
not only in confining science to the study of uniformities of co-
existence and sequence among phenomena and in excluding from
it all properly causal inquiry but also in rejecting metaphysics in
so far as this is a study of abstract ideas and categories which are
supposed to provide causal explanations. But personalism is

---

[1] *The Immanence of God*, p. 19.   [2] *Ibid.*, p. 18.   [3] *Ibid.*, p. 32.

immune from the objections which can be raised against meta-physics as Comte understood the term. For it does not seek the causal explanations which, on Comte's own showing, science cannot provide, in abstract categories. It sees in these categories simply the abstract forms of self-conscious life, and the ultimate causal explanation is found in a supreme rational will. True, personalist metaphysics may seem to involve a return to what Comte regarded as the first stage of human thought, namely the theological stage, in which explanations were sought in divine wills or in a divine will. But in personalism this stage is raised to a higher level, inasmuch as capricious wills are replaced by an infinite rational will.[1]

4. Objective idealism, as it is commonly called, had as its principal representative James Edwin Creighton (1861–1924), who in 1892 succeeded J. G. Schurman[2] as head of the Sage School at Cornell University. In 1920 he became the first president of the American Philosophical Association. His principal articles were collected and published posthumously in 1925 with the title *Studies in Speculative Philosophy*.[3]

Creighton distinguishes two types of idealism. The first, which he calls mentalism, is simply the antithesis of materialism. While the materialist interprets the psychical as a function of the physical, the mentalist reduces material things to psychical phenomena, to states of consciousness or to ideas. And as the material world cannot without absurdity be reduced to any given finite individual's states of consciousness, the mentalist is in-evitably driven to postulate an absolute mind. The clearest example of this type of idealism is the philosophy of Berkeley. But there are variants, such as panpsychism.

The other main type of idealism is objective or speculative idealism, which does not attempt to reduce the physical to the psychical but regards Nature, the self and other selves as three distinct but co-ordinate and complementary moments or factors

---

[1] Obviously, what really needs to be shown is that metaphysical explanation is required at all. That empirical science cannot provide it is clear enough.

[2] Jack Gould Schurman (1854–1942), who became President of Cornell University in 1892, the same year in which he founded *The Philosophical Review*, believed that American culture was destined to prove the great mediator between East and West, and that idealism was peculiarly suited both to America and to the fulfilment of this task. Just as Kant mediated between rationalism and empiricism, so can speculative idealism mediate between the sciences and the arts. It has a synthesizing function in cultural life.

[3] Though not a prolific writer, Creighton's influence as a teacher was considerable. And he and his colleagues at Cornell were responsible for the philosophical education of a good many future American professors.

within experience. In other words, experience presents us with the ego, other selves and Nature as distinct and irreducible factors which are at the same time comprised within the unity of experience. And objective idealism attempts to work out the implications of this basic structure of experience.

For example, though Nature is irreducible to mind, the two are mutually related. Nature, therefore, cannot be simply heterogeneous to mind; it must be intelligible. And this means that though philosophy cannot do the work of the empirical sciences it is not committed merely to accepting the scientific account of Nature, without adding anything. Science puts Nature in the centre of the picture: philosophy exhibits it as a co-ordinate of experience, in its relation to spirit. This does not mean that the philosopher is competent to contradict, or even to call in question scientific discoveries. It means that it is his business to show the significance of the world as represented by the sciences in reference to the totality of experience. In other words, there is room for a philosophy of Nature.

Again, objective idealism is careful to avoid placing the ego in the centre of the picture by taking it as an ultimate point of departure and then trying to prove, for example, the existence of other selves. The objective idealist, while recognizing the distinction between individuals, recognizes also that there are no isolated individual selves apart from society. And he will study, for instance, the significance of morality, political institutions and religion as activities or products, as the case may be, of a society of selves within the human environment, namely Nature.

In conformity with these ideas, which have an obvious affinity with Hegelianism, the Cornell School of idealism emphasized the social aspect of thought. Instead of being divided up into as many systems as there are philosophers, philosophy should be, like science, a work of co-operation. For it is the reflection of spirit, existing in and through a society of selves, rather than of the individual thinker considered precisely as such.

5. Objective idealism, represented chiefly by Creighton, was associated with Cornell University. Another form of idealism, so-called dynamic idealism, was associated with the University of Michigan, where it was expounded by George Sylvester Morris (1840–89).[1] After having studied at Dartmouth College and the

---

[1] Another representative of this form of idealism at Michigan was the author of *Dynamic Idealism* (1898), Alfred Henry Lloyd.

Union Theological Seminary at New York, Morris passed some years in Germany, where he came under the influence of Trendelenburg[1] at Berlin. In 1870 he began to teach modern languages and literature at Michigan, and from 1878 he also lectured on ethics and the history of philosophy at Johns Hopkins University. Subsequently he became dean of the philosophical faculty at Michigan. His writings include *British Thought and Thinkers* (1880), *Philosophy and Christianity* (1883), and *Hegel's Philosophy of the State and of History: An Exposition* (1887). He also translated into English Ueberweg's *History of Philosophy* (1871–3), in the second volume of which he inserted an article on Trendelenburg.

Under the influence of Trendelenburg Morris placed in the forefront of his philosophy the Aristotelian idea of movement, that is, of the actualization of a potentiality, of the active expression of an entelechy. Life is obviously movement, energy; but thought too is a spontaneous activity, akin to other forms of natural energy. And it follows from this that the history of thought is not properly described as a dialectical development of abstract ideas or categories. Rather is it the expression of the activity of the spirit or mind. And philosophy is the science[2] of the mind as an active entelechy. That is to say, it is the science of experience in act or of lived experience.

To say that philosophy is the science of the activity of the spirit or mind, of experience in act, is not, however, to say that it has no connection with being. For the analysis of experience shows that subject and object, knowledge and being, are correlative terms. That which exists or has being is that which is known or knowable. It is that which falls within the potential field of active experience. And this is why we have to reject the Kantian Theory of the unknowable thing-in-itself, together with the phenomenalism which produces this theory.[3]

In his later years Morris moved closer to Hegel, whom he regarded as an 'objective empiricist', concerned with the integration of human experience by the reason. His most famous pupil was John Dewey, though Dewey came to abandon idealism for the instrumentalism associated with his name.

6. Idealism in America obviously owed much to the influence of

---

[1] See Vol. VII of this *History*, pp. 386–7.
[2] For Morris philosophy is as much a science as other sciences.
[3] That is to say, if we regard the object of knowledge as phenomena, in the sense of appearances of what does not itself appear, we are led inevitably to postulate unknowable things-in-themselves.

European thought. But equally obviously, it proved congenial to many minds and received a native stamp, which is shown above all perhaps in the emphasis so often placed on personality. It is not surprising, therefore, that American idealism was by no means simply a nineteenth-century phenomenon, due to the discovery of German thought and to influence from British idealism. It has shown a vigorous life in the present century.

Among the representatives of personal idealism in the first half of the twentieth century we can mention the names of Ralph Tyler Flewelling (1871–), for many years a Professor of Philosophy in the University of South California and founder of *The Personalist* in 1920,[1] Albert Cornelius Knudson (1873–1953)[2] and Edgar Sheffield Brightman (1884–1953), Bowne Professor of Philosophy in the University of Boston.[3] The titles of their publications provide abundant evidence of the continuation of that religious orientation of personalism which we have already had occasion to notice. But apart from the fact that it is so often religiously minded people who are attracted in the first instance to personal idealism, there is, as has been mentioned above, an intrinsic reason for the religious orientation of this line of thought. The basic tenet of personalism has been stated as the principle that reality has no meaning except in relation to persons; that the real is only in, of or for persons. In other words, reality consists of persons and their creations. It follows, therefore, that unless the personal idealist equates ultimate reality with the system of finite selves, as McTaggart did, he must be a theist. There is room, of course, for somewhat different conceptions of God. Brightman, for example, maintained that God is finite.[4] But a concern not only with philosophical theism but also with religion as a form of experience is a universal feature of American personal idealism.

This is not to say, however, that the personal idealists have been

---

[1] Among Flewelling's publications are *Personalism and The Problems of Philosophy* (1915), *The Reason in Faith* (1924), *Creative Personality* (1925) and *Personalism in Theology* (1943).

[2] Knudson is the author of *The Philosophy of Personalism* (1927), *The Doctrine of God* (1930), and *The Validity of Religious Experience* (1937).

[3] Brightman published among other writings, *Religious Values* (1925), *A Philosophy of Ideals* (1928), *The Problem of God* (1930), *Is God a Person?* (1932), *Moral Laws* (1933), *Personality and Religion* (1934), *A Philosophy of Religion* (1940), and *The Spiritual Life* (1942).

[4] Brightman argues, for instance, that the 'waste' involved in the process of evolution suggests the idea of a finite God who meets with opposition. Again, the divine reason sets limits to the divine will and power. Further, there is in God a 'given' element which he progressively masters. But where this 'given' element comes from is left obscure.

concerned only with the defence of a religious outlook. For they have also devoted their attention to the subject of values, connecting them closely with the idea of the self-realization or development of personality. And this in turn has reacted on the theory of education, emphasis being laid on moral development and the cultivation of personal values. Finally, in political theory this type of idealism, with its insistence on freedom and on respect for the person as such, has been sharply opposed to totalitarianism and a strong advocate of democracy.

Evolutionary idealism has been represented in the first half of the present century by John Elof Boodin (1869–1950).[1] The main idea of this type of idealism is familiar enough, namely that in the evolutionary process we can see the emergence of successively higher levels of development through the creative activity of an immanent principle, the nature of which should be interpreted in the light of its higher rather than of its lower products.[2] In other words, evolutionary idealism substitutes for a purely mechanistic conception of evolution, based on laws relating to the redistribution of energy, a teleological conception according to which mechanical processes take place within a general creative movement tending towards an ideal goal.[3] Thus Boodin distinguishes between different interacting levels or fields in the evolutionary process or processes, in each of which there are interacting individual systems of energy. These levels or fields range from the primary physico-chemical level up to the ethical-social level. And the all-inclusive field is the divine creative spirit, 'the spiritual field in which everything lives and moves and has its being'.[4]

Evolutionary idealism does not indeed deny the value of human personality. For Boodin the human spirit participates in the divine creativity by the realization of values. At the same time, inasmuch as the evolutionary idealist fixes his attention chiefly on

[1] Author of *Time and Reality* (1904), *Truth and Reality* (1911), *A Realistic Universe* (1916), *Cosmic Evolution* (1925), *God and Creation* (2 volumes, 1934), and *Religion of Tomorrow* (1943).

[2] In distinguishing between 'lower' and 'higher' judgments of value obviously play an important part.

[3] It would, however, be a mistake to suppose that all philosophers who believe in creative evolution have postulated a fixed, preconceived goal or *telos* of the evolutionary process. Indeed, unless the creative agent is conceived in a recognizably theistic manner, such a postulate is inappropriate.

[4] *God and Creation*, II, p. 34. According to Boodin, God, as conceived according to his intrinsic essence, is eternal; but from another point of view, namely when he is considered as the creative activity comprising the whole history of the cosmos, he is temporal.

the total cosmic process rather than on the finite self,[1] he is more inclined than the personal idealist to a pantheistic conception of God. And this tendency is verified in the case of Boodin.

Absolute idealism has been continued in the present century by the well-known philosopher William Ernest Hocking (b. 1873), a pupil of Royce and William James at Harvard and later Alford Professor of Philosophy in that University.[2] At the level of common sense, Hocking argues, physical objects and other minds appear as entities which are purely external to myself. And it is at this level that the question arises how we come to know that there are other minds or other selves. But reflection shows us that there is an underlying social consciousness which is as real as self-consciousness. In fact they are interdependent. After all, the very attempt to prove that there are other minds presupposes an awareness of them. And further reflection, Hocking maintains, together with intuitive insight, reveals to us the presence of the enveloping divine reality which renders human consciousness possible. That is to say, our participation in social consciousness involves an implicit awareness of God and is in some sense an experience of the divine, of absolute mind. Hence the ontological argument can be stated in this way: 'I have an idea of God, therefore I have an experience of God'.[3]

We have noted that Hocking was a pupil of Royce. And like his former professor he insists that God is personal, a self. For 'there is nothing higher than selfhood and nothing more profound'.[4] At the same time he insists that we cannot abandon the concept of the Absolute. And this means that we must conceive God as in some sense including within himself the world of finite selves and the world of Nature. Indeed, just as the human self, taken apart from its life of experience, is empty, so is the concept of God an empty concept if he is considered apart from his life of absolute experience. 'The domain of religion in fact is a divine self, a Spirit which is as Subject to all finite things, persons and arts as Object,

---

[1] The personal idealist is not, of course, committed to denying the hypothesis of evolution. But he takes the idea of personality as his point of departure and as the fixed point, as one might put it, in his reflections, whereas the evolutionary idealist emphasizes the aspect of the person as a product of a general creative activity immanent in the whole cosmos.

[2] Hocking's writings include *The Meaning of God in Human Experience* (1912), *Human Nature and Its Remaking* (1918), *Man and the State* (1926), *The Self, Its Body and Freedom* (1928), *Lasting Elements of Individualism* (1937), *Thoughts on Life and Death* (1937), *Living Religions and a World Faith* (1940), *Science and the Idea of God* (1944) and *Experiment in Education* (1954).

[3] *The Meaning of God in Human Experience*, p. 314.

[4] *Types of Philosophy*, p. 441.

and presumably to much else that these categories do not include.'[1] The world is thus necessary to God, though at the same time we can conceive it as created. For Nature is in fact an expression of the divine mind, as well as the means by which finite selves communicate with one another and pursue common ideals. In addition to the scientific view of Nature, which treats Nature as a self-contained whole, we need the concept of it as a divine communication to the finite self. As for the divine essence in itself, it transcends the grasp of discursive thought, though mystical experience yields a valid insight.

With Hocking, therefore, as with Royce, we find a form of personalistic absolute idealism. He tries to find a middle position between a theism which would reduce God to the level of being a self among selves, a person among persons, and an absolute idealism which would leave no room for the concept of God as personal. And this desire to find a middle position is shown in Hocking's treatment of religion. On the one hand he dislikes the tendency, shown by some philosophers, to offer as the alleged essence of religion a concept which abstracts from all historical religion. On the other hand he rejects the notion of one particular historical faith becoming the world-faith by displacing all others. And though he attributes to Christianity a unique contribution to the recognition of the ultimate personal structure of reality, he looks to a process of dialogue between the great historical religions to produce, by a convergent movement, the world-faith of the future.

We have already had occasion more than once to note the concern of American idealists with religious problems. It is hardly an exaggeration to say that with some of the personal idealists, such as Bowne, philosophy was practically used as an apologetic in defence of the Christian religion. In the case of personalistic absolute idealism,[2] however, as with Hocking, it is more a question of developing a religious view of the world and of suggesting a religious vision for the future than of defending a particular historical religion. And this is clearly more in line with W. T. Harris's programme for speculative philosophy. For Harris assumed that traditional doctrines and ecclesiastical organization were in process of losing their grip on men's minds, that a new

---

[1] *Human Nature and Its Remaking*, p. 329.
[2] The line of thought of Royce and Hocking is sometimes described as absolutistic personalism in distinction from the pluralistic personalism of Bowne and other 'personal idealists'.

religious outlook was needed, and that it was part of the business of speculative philosophy or metaphysical idealism to meet this need.

At the same time idealism does not necessarily involve either the defence of an already existing religion or positive preparation for a new one. It is, of course, natural to expect of the metaphysical idealist some interest in religion or at least an explicit recognition of its importance in human life. For he aims, in general, at a synthesis of human experience, and in particular, at doing justice to those forms of experience which the materialist and positivist tend either to belittle or to exclude from the scope of philosophy. But it would be a mistake to think that idealism is necessarily so connected either with Christian faith or with the mystical outlook of a philosopher such as Hocking that it is inseparable from profoundly held religious convictions. A preoccupation with religious problems was not a characteristic of the objective idealism of Creighton; nor is it a characteristic of the thought of Brand Blanshard (b. 1892), Sterling Professor of Philosophy at Yale, the twentieth-century American idealist who is best known in Great Britain.[1]

In his notable two-volume work, *The Nature of Thought* (1939–40), Blanshard devotes himself to critical analyses of interpretations of thought and knowledge which he considers false or inadequate and to a defence of reason conceived primarily as the discovery of necessary connections. He rejects the restriction of necessity to purely formal propositions and its reduction to convention, and he represents the movement of thought as being towards the logical ideal of an all-inclusive system of interdependent truths. In other words, he maintains a version of the coherence theory of truth. Similarly, in *Reason and Analysis* (1962) Blanshard devotes himself on the negative side to a sustained criticism of the analytic philosophy of the last forty years, including logical positivism, logical atomism and the so-called linguistic movement, and on the positive side to an exposition and defence of the function of reason as he conceives it. True, he has given two series of Gifford Lectures. But in *Reason and Goodness* (1961), which represents the first series, the emphasis is laid on vindicating the function of reason in ethics, as against, for example, the emotive theory of ethics, certainly not on edification, either moral or religious.[2]

[1] Blanshard studied at Oxford, and he is regarded as carrying on the tradition of Oxford idealism.

[2] The second volume has not appeared at the time of writing.

These remarks are not intended either as commendation or as criticism of Blanshard's freedom from the preoccupation with religious problems and from the tone of uplift which have been conspicuous features of many of the publications of American idealists. The point is rather that the example of Blanshard shows that idealism is able to make out a good case for itself and to deal shrewd blows at its enemies without exhibiting the features which in the eyes of some of its critics rule it out of court from the start, as though by its very nature it served extra-philosophical interests. After all, Hegel himself deprecated any confusion between philosophy and uplift and rejected appeals to mystical insights.

7. In Marxist terminology idealism is commonly opposed to materialism, as involving respectively the assertion of the ultimate priority of mind or spirit to matter and the assertion of the ultimate priority of matter to mind or spirit. And if idealism is understood in this way, no synthesis of the opposites is possible. For the essential dispute is not about the reality of either mind or matter. It is about the question of ultimate priority. And both cannot be ultimately prior at the same time.

Generally, however, idealism is contrasted with realism. It is by no means always clear how these terms are being understood. And in any case their meanings can vary with different contexts. But an attempt has been made by an American philosopher, Wilbur Marshall Urban (b. 1873),[1] to show that idealism and realism are ultimately based on certain judgments of value about the conditions of genuine knowledge, and that these judgments can be dialectically harmonized. He does not mean, of course, that opposed philosophical systems can be conflated. He means that the basic judgments on which idealist and realist philosophies ultimately rest can be so interpreted that it is possible to transcend the opposition between idealism and realism.

The realist, Urban maintains, believes that there cannot be genuine knowledge unless things are in some sense independent of mind. In other words, he asserts the priority of being to knowledge. The idealist, however, believes that there can be no genuine knowledge unless things are in some sense dependent on mind. For their intelligibility is bound up with this dependence. At first sight, therefore, realism and idealism are incompatible, the first

---

[1] Urban is the author of, among other writings, *Valuation: Its Nature and Laws* (1909), *The Intelligible World: Metaphysics and Value* (1929), *Language and Reality* (1939) and *Beyond Realism and Idealism* (1949). In the present context the relevant work is the last-named one.

asserting the priority of being to thought and knowledge, the second asserting the priority of thought to being. But if we consider the basic judgments of value, we can see the possibility of overcoming the opposition between them. For example, the realist claim that knowledge cannot be described as genuine knowledge of reality unless things are in some sense independent of mind can be satisfied provided that we are willing to admit that things are not dependent simply on the human mind, while the idealist claim that knowledge cannot be described as genuine knowledge of reality unless things are in some sense mind-dependent can be satisfied if it is assumed that the reality on which on all finite things ultimately depend is spirit or mind.

It seems to the present writer that there is a great deal of truth in this point of view. Absolute idealism, by rejecting the claim of subjective idealism that the human mind can know only its own states of consciousness, goes a long way towards meeting the realist's claim that genuine knowledge of reality is not possible unless the object of knowledge is in some real sense independent of the subject. And a realism that is prepared to describe ultimate reality as spirit or mind goes a long way towards meeting the idealist claim that nothing is intelligible unless it is either spirit or the self-expression of spirit. At the same time the dialectical harmonization of opposed views, which Urban has in mind, seems to demand certain stipulations. We have to stipulate, for example, that the idealist should cease talking like Royce, who uses the word 'being' for the expression of will and purpose, for the embodiment of the internal meaning of an idea, and should recognize that will is itself a form of being. In fact, to reach agreement with the realist he must, it appears, recognize the priority of existence; *prius est esse quam esse tale*. If, however, he admits this, he has to all intents and purposes been converted to realism. We also have to stipulate, of course, that realism should not be understood as equivalent to materialism. But then many realists would insist that realism in no way entails materialism.

The ideal of transcending the traditional oppositions in philosophy is understandable, and doubtless laudable. But there is this point to consider. If we interpret realism in terms of basic judgments of value about the conditions of genuine knowledge, we have implicitly adopted a certain approach to philosophy. We are approaching philosophy by way of the theme of knowledge, by way of the subject-object relationship. And many philosophers who are customarily labelled realists doubtless do this. We speak, for example, of realist theories of knowledge. But some realists would claim that they take as their point of departure being, particularly in the sense of existence, and that their approach is recognizably different from that of the idealist, and that it is the different approaches to philosophy which determine the different views of knowledge.

PART IV

THE PRAGMATIST MOVEMENT

CHAPTER XIV
THE PHILOSOPHY OF C. S. PEIRCE

The life of Peirce—The objectivity of truth—Rejection of the method of universal doubt—Logic, ideas and the pragmatist analysis of meaning—Pragmatism and realism—The pragmatist analysis of meaning and positivism—Ethics, pure and practical—Peirce's metaphysics and world-view—Some comments on Peirce's thought.

1. ALTHOUGH it is possible to find pragmatist ideas in the writings of some other thinkers,[1] the originator of the pragmatist movement in America was to all intents and purposes Charles Sanders Peirce (1839–1914). To be sure, the term 'pragmatism' is associated chiefly with the name of William James. For James's style as lecturer and writer and his obvious concern with general problems of interest to reflective minds quickly brought him before the public eye and kept him there, whereas during his lifetime Peirce was little known or appreciated as a philosopher. But both James and Dewey recognized their indebtedness to Peirce. And after his death Peirce's reputation has steadily increased, even if, by the nature of his thought, he remains very much a philosopher's philosopher.

Peirce was the son of a Harvard mathematician and astronomer, Benjamin Peirce (1809–80), and his own formal education culminated in the chemistry degree which he received at Harvard in 1863. From 1861 until 1891 he was on the staff of the United States Coast and Geodetic Survey, though from 1869 he was also associated for some years with the Harvard Observatory. And the one book which he published, *Photometric Researches* (1878), embodied the results of a series of astronomical observations which he had made.

In the academic years of 1864–5 and 1869–70 Peirce lectured at

---

[1] See, for example, *Chauncey Wright and the Foundations of Pragmatism* by E. H. Madden (Seattle, 1963).

Harvard on the early history of modern science, and in 1870–1 on logic.[1] From 1879 until 1884 he was a lecturer on logic at Johns Hopkins University; but for various reasons his appointment was not renewed.[2] And he never again held any regular academic post, in spite of William James's efforts on his behalf.

In 1887 Peirce settled with his second wife in Pennsylvania and tried to make ends meet by writing reviews and articles for dictionaries. He wrote indeed a great deal, but apart from a few articles his work remained unpublished until the posthumous publication of his *Collected Papers*, six volumes appearing in 1931–5 and two further volumes in 1958.

Peirce did not approve of the way in which William James was developing the theory of pragmatism, and in 1905 he changed the name of his own theory from pragmatism to pragmaticism, remarking that the term was ugly enough to render it secure from kidnappers. At the same time he appreciated the friendship of James, who did what he could to put remunerative work in the way of the neglected and poverty-stricken philosopher. Peirce died of cancer in 1914.

2. It is probably correct to say that in the minds of most people for whom the word 'pragmatism' has any definite meaning, it is associated primarily with a certain view of the nature of truth, namely with the doctrine that a theory is to be accounted true in so far as it 'works', in so far, for example, as it is socially useful or fruitful. It is therefore just as well to understand from the outset that the essence of Peirce's pragmatism or pragmaticism lies in a theory of meaning rather than in a theory of truth. This theory of meaning will be examined presently. Meanwhile we can consider briefly what Peirce has to say about truth. And it will be seen that whether or not the identification of truth with 'what works' represents the real view of William James, it certainly does not represent that of Peirce.

Peirce distinguishes different kinds of truth. There is, for example, what he calls transcendental truth, which belongs to

---

[1] In 1868 Peirce published some articles in *The Journal of Speculative Philosophy* on certain alleged faculties of the human mind, such as that of recognizing intuitively, without the need of any previous knowledge, the premises which constitute the absolute points of departure for reasoning.

[2] The fact that in 1883 Peirce divorced his first wife and subsequently remarried probably contributed to the termination of his appointment at Johns Hopkins. But there appear to have been other factors too, such as the offence which he sometimes gave by intemperate expressions of moral indignation and his lack of conformity on some points with the requirements of academic life.

things as things.[1] And if we say that science is looking for truth in this sense, we mean that it is inquiring into the real characters of things, the characters which they have whether we know that they have them or not. But here we are concerned with what Peirce calls complex truth, which is the truth of propositions. This again can be subdivided. There is, for example, ethical truth or veracity, which lies in the conformity of a proposition with the speaker's or writer's belief. And there is logical truth, the conformity of a proposition with reality in a sense which must now be defined.

'When we speak of truth and falsity, we refer to the possibility of the proposition being refuted.'[2] That is to say, if we could legitimately deduce from a proposition a conclusion which would conflict with an immediate perceptual judgment, the proposition would be false. In other words, a proposition would be false if experience would refute it. If experience would not refute a proposition, the proposition is true.

This may suggest that for Peirce truth and verification are the same thing. But reflection will show that he is perfectly justified in rejecting this identification. For he is saying, not that a proposition is true if it is empirically verified, but that it is true if it would not be empirically falsified, supposing that such a testing were possible. In point of fact it may not be possible. But we can still say that a proposition is false if, to put it crudely, it *would* conflict with reality as revealed in experience if a confrontation were possible, and that otherwise it is true. Peirce can therefore say without inconsistency that 'every proposition is either *true* or *false*'.[3]

Now, there are some propositions which could not conceivably be refuted. Such, for example, are the propositions of pure mathematics. Hence on the interpretation of truth mentioned above the truth of a proposition in pure mathematics lies in 'the impossibility of ever finding a case in which it fails'.[4] Peirce sometimes writes in a rather disconcerting way about mathematics. He says, for instance, that the pure mathematician deals exclusively with hypotheses which are the products of his own imagination, and that no proposition becomes a statement of pure mathematics 'until it is devoid of all definite meaning'.[5] But

---

[1] Peirce refers in this context to the Scholastic maxim that every being is one, true and good.

[2] 5.569. References are given in the customary way to volume and numbered paragraph of the *Collected Papers of Charles Sanders Peirce*.

[3] 2.327.   [4] 5.567.   [5] *Ibid.*

'meaning' has to be understood here in the sense of reference. A proposition of pure mathematics does not say anything about actual things:[1] the pure mathematician, as Peirce puts it, does not care whether or not there are real things corresponding to his signs. And this absence of 'meaning' is, of course, the reason why the propositions of pure mathematics cannot possibly be refuted and so are necessarily true.

There are other propositions, however, of which we do not know with absolute certainty whether they are true or false. These are what Leibniz calls truths of fact, in distinctions from truths of reason. And they include, for example, scientific hypotheses and metaphysical theories about reality. In the case of a proposition which cannot possibly be refuted we know that it is true.[2] But a scientific hypothesis can *be* true without our knowing that it is. And in point of fact we cannot know with certainty that it is true. For while empirical refutation shows that an hypothesis is false, what we call verification does not prove that an hypothesis is true, though it certainly provides a ground for accepting it provisionally. If from hypothesis x it is legitimately deduced that in certain circumstances event y should occur, and if in these circumstances y does not occur, we can conclude that x is false. But the occurrence of y does not prove with certainty that x is true. For it may be the case, for example, that the conclusion that in the same set of circumstances event y should occur, can be deduced from hypothesis z, which on other grounds is preferable to x. Scientific hypotheses can enjoy varying degrees of probability, but they are all subject to possible revision. In fact all formulations of what passes for human knowledge are uncertain, fallible.[3]

It should not be necessary to add that Peirce's principle of fallibilism does not entail a denial of objective truth. Scientific inquiry is inspired by a disinterested search for objective truth. Nobody would ask a theoretical question unless he believed that there was such a thing as truth. And 'truth consists in a conformity of something *independent of his thinking it to be so*, or of

[1] The question whether it concerns a realm of possibility, as contrasted with actuality, is a question for the metaphysician.

[2] Peirce remarks that an entirely meaningless proposition is to be classed with true propositions, because it cannot be refuted. But he adds the saving provision, 'if it be called a proposition at all' (2.327).

[3] When asked whether his principle of fallibilism, as it is called, the assertion that all assertions are uncertain, is itself fallible or infallible, uncertain or certain, Peirce answers that he does not intend to claim that his assertion is absolutely certain. This may be logical, but it involves a certain weakening of his position.

any man's opinion on that subject'.[1] But if we combine the idea of the disinterested search for objective truth, known as such, with the principle of fallibilism, according to which dogmatism is the enemy of the pursuit of truth, we must conceive absolute and final truth as the ideal goal of inquiry. This ideal stands eternally above our struggles to attain it, and we can only approximate to it.

Truth, therefore, can be defined from different points of view. From one point of view truth can be taken to mean 'the Universe of all Truth'.[2] 'All propositions refer to one and the same determinately singular subject . . . namely, to The Truth, which is the universe of all universes, and is assumed on all hands to be real.'[3] From an epistemological point of view, however, truth can be defined as 'that concordance of an abstract statement with the ideal limit towards which endless investigation would tend to bring scientific belief'.[4]

If such passages recall to our minds the idealist notion of truth as the whole, the total system of truth, rather than anything which would normally be associated with the term 'pragmatism', there is nothing to be surprised at in this. For Peirce openly acknowledged points of similarity between his own philosophy and that of Hegel.

3. In regard to the pursuit of truth Peirce rejects the Cartesian thesis that we should begin by doubting everything until we can find an indubitable and presuppositionless point of departure. In the first place we cannot doubt simply at will. Real or genuine doubt arises when some experience, external or internal, clashes or appears to clash with one of our beliefs. And when this occurs, we undertake further inquiry with a view to overcoming the state of doubt, either by re-establishing our former belief on a firmer basis or by substituting for it a better-grounded belief. Doubt is thus a stimulus to inquiry, and in this sense it has a positive value. But to doubt the truth of a proposition, we must have a reason for doubting the truth of *this* proposition or of a proposition on which it depends. Any attempt to apply the method of universal doubt simply leads to pretended or fictitious doubt. And this is not genuine doubt at all.

Peirce is obviously thinking in the first place of scientific inquiry. But he applies his ideas in a quite general way. We all start with certain beliefs, with what Hume called natural beliefs.

[1] 5.211.   [2] 5.153.   [3] 5.506.   [4] 5.565.

And the philosopher will indeed try to make explicit our un-criticized natural beliefs and subject them to critical scrutiny. But even he cannot doubt them at will: he requires a reason for doubting the truth of this or that particular belief. And if he has or thinks that he has such a reason, he will also find that his very doubt presupposes some other belief or beliefs. In other words, we cannot have, nor do we need, an absolutely presuppositionless point of departure. Cartesian universal doubt is not genuine doubt at all. 'For genuine doubt does not talk of beginning with doubt-ing.'[1] The follower of Descartes would presumably reply that he is primarily concerned with 'methodic' rather than with 'real' or 'genuine' doubt. But Peirce's point is that methodic doubt, in so far as it is distinguishable from genuine doubt, is not really doubt at all. Either we have a reason for doubting or we do not. In the first case the doubt is genuine. In the second case we have only pretended or fictitious doubt.

If we bear in mind this point of view, we can understand Peirce's claim that 'the scientific spirit requires a man to be at all times ready to dump his whole cartload of beliefs, the moment experience is against them'.[2] He is obviously speaking of theoretical beliefs, which are characterized above all by expecta-tion. If a man holds belief x, he believes, for example, that in certain circumstances event y should occur. And if it does not occur, he will, of course, doubt the truth of the belief. Ante-cedently to a clash between experience and belief, anyone who possesses the scientific spirit will be prepared to abandon any belief about the world if such a clash should occur. For, as we have already seen, he regards all such beliefs as subject to possible revision. But it by no means follows from this that he will begin or should begin with universal doubt.

4. Pragmatism, as Peirce conceives it, is 'not a *Weltanschauung* but is a method of reflection having for its purpose to render ideas clear'.[3] It belongs, therefore, to methodology, to what Peirce calls 'methodeutic'. And as he emphasizes the logical foundations and connections of pragmatism, it is appropriate to say something first about his account of logic.

Peirce divides logic into three main parts, the first of which is speculative grammar. This is concerned with the formal conditions of the meaningfulness of signs. A sign, called by Peirce a 'repre-sentamen', stands for an object to someone in whom it arouses a

[1] 6.498.   [2] 1.55.   [3] 5.13, note.

more developed sign, the 'interpretant'. A sign stands, of course, for an object in respect of certain 'characters', and this respect is called the 'ground'. But we can say that the relation of significance or the semiotic function of signs is for Peirce a triadic relation between representamen, object and interpretant.[1]

The second main division of logic, critical logic, is concerned with the formal conditions of the truth of symbols. Under this heading Peirce treats of the syllogism or argument, which can be divided into deductive, inductive and 'abductive' argument. Inductive argument, which is statistical in character, assumes that what is true of a number of members of a class is true of all members of the class. And it is in connection with induction that Peirce considers the theory of probability. Abductive argument is predictive in character. That is to say, it formulates an hypothesis from observed facts and deduces what should be the case if the hypothesis is true. And we can then test the prediction. When looked at from one point of view, Royce tells us, pragmatism can be described as the logic of abduction. The force of this remark will become clear presently.

The third main division of logic, speculative rhetoric, deals with what Peirce calls the formal conditions of the force of symbols or 'the general conditions of the reference of Symbols and other Signs to the Interpretants which they aim to determine'.[2] In communication a sign arouses another sign, the interpretant, in an interpreter. Peirce insists that the interpreter is not necessarily a human being. And as he wishes to avoid psychology as much as possible, he lays emphasis on the interpretant rather than on the interpreter. In any case it simplifies matters if we think of a sign arousing a sign in a person. We can then see that speculative rhetoric will be concerned in large measure with the theory of meaning. For meaning is 'the intended interpretant of a symbol'.[3] Whether we are speaking of a term, a proposition or an argument, its meaning is the entire intended interpretant. And as pragmatism is for Peirce a method or rule for determining meaning, it obviously belongs to or is closely connected with speculative rhetoric, which is also called 'methodeutic'.

More precisely, pragmatism is a method or rule for making ideas clear, for determining the meaning of ideas. But there are

---

[1] Under the general heading of speculative grammar Peirce also considers terms, propositions and the fundamental principles of logic, those of identity, non-contradiction and excluded middle.
[2] 2.93. [3] 5.175.

different types of ideas.[1] First, there is the idea of a percept or
sense-datum considered in itself, without relation to anything
else. Such would be the idea of blueness or of redness. In Peirce's
terminology this is the idea of a 'firstness'. Secondly, there is the
idea of acting which involves two objects, namely the agent and
the patient or that which is acted upon. This is the idea of a
'secondness'.[2] Thirdly, there is the idea of a sign relation, of a sign
signifying to an interpreter that a certain property belongs to a
certain object or, rather, to a certain kind of object. This is an
idea of a 'thirdness'. And such ideas, which can be thought of as
universal ideas, are called by Peirce intellectual concepts or
conceptions.[3] In practice pragmatism is a method or rule for
determining their meaning.

Peirce formulates the principle of pragmatism in several ways.
One of the best known is as follows. *'In order to ascertain the
meaning of an intellectual conception one should consider what
practical consequences might conceivably result by necessity from the
truth of that conception; and the sum of these consequences will
constitute the entire meaning of the conception.'*[4] For example,
suppose that someone tells me that a certain kind of object is
hard, and suppose that I do not know what the word 'hard'
means. It can be explained to me that to say that an object is
hard means, among other things, that if one exerts moderate
pressure on it, it does not give in the way that butter does; that
if someone sits on it, he does not sink through; and so on. And the
sum total of 'practical consequences' which necessarily follow if
it is true to say that an object is hard, gives the entire meaning of
the concept. If I do not believe this, I have only to exclude all such
'practical consequences' from the meaning of the term. I shall then
see that it becomes impossible to distinguish between the meanings of 'hard' and 'soft'.

Now, if we understand Peirce as saying that the meaning of an
intellectual concept is reducible to the ideas of certain sense-data,

[1] Strictly speaking, the theory of ideas belongs to epistemology. But Peirce
insists that it is grounded on the logic of relations. And he emphasizes the relevance
of the theory to pragmatism.

[2] As in human experience acting involves an act of the will, Peirce tends to
speak of this type of idea as the idea of a volition. In any case he insists that an
idea of a 'secondness' cannot be simply reduced to ideas of 'firstness'. If, for
example, we try to reduce the idea of the wind moving the blind to simpler ideas
of sense-data, taken separately, the whole idea of acting disappears.

[3] In theory at least Peirce distinguishes between 'idea' and concept', a universal
idea being subjectively apprehended in an intellectual concept.

[4] 5.9.

we shall have to conclude that he is contradicting his assertion that intellectual concepts are not reducible to ideas of 'firstness'. And if we understand him as saying that the meaning of an intellectual concept is reducible to the ideas of certain actions, we shall have to conclude that he is contradicting his assertion that such concepts are not reducible to ideas of 'secondness'. But he is saying neither the one nor the other. His view is that the meaning of an intellectual concept can be explicated in terms of the ideas of necessary relations between ideas of secondness and ideas of firstness, between, that is to say, ideas of volition or action and ideas of perception. As he explains, when he talks about 'consequences', he is referring to the relation (*consequentia*) between a consequent and an antecedent, not simply about the consequent (*consequens*).

From this analysis it obviously follows that the meaning of an intellectual concept has a relation to conduct. For the conditional propositions in which the meaning is explicated are concerned with conduct. But, equally obviously, Peirce is not suggesting that in order to understand or to explain the meaning of an intellectual concept we have actually to do something, to perform certain actions mentioned in the explication of the meaning. I can explain to an interpreter the meaning of 'hard' by causing to arise in his mind the idea that if he were to perform a certain action in regard to the object which is described as hard, he *would* have a certain experience. It is not required that he should actually perform the action before he can understand what 'hard' means. It is not even necessary that the action should be practicable, provided that it is conceivable. In other words, the meaning of an intellectual concept is explicable in terms of conditional propositions; but, for the meaning to be understood, it is not necessary that the conditions should be actually fulfilled. It is only necessary that they should be conceived.

It is to be noted that this theory of meaning does not contradict Peirce's view, which has been mentioned above, that we must distinguish between truth and verification. If, for example, I say that a given object has weight, and if I explain that this means that in the absence of an opposing force it will fall, the fulfilment of the conditional proposition is said to verify my statement. But to verify means to show that a proposition is true, that is, that it is true antecedently to any verification, true independently of any action performed by me or by anyone else.

5. Although it involves touching on ontology, it is convenient at this point to draw attention to Peirce's conviction that the pragmatist theory of meaning demands the rejection of nominalism and the acceptance of realism. An intellectual concept is a universal concept; and its meaning is explicated in conditional propositions. These conditional propositions are in principle verifiable. And the possibility of verification shows that some at least of the propositions which explicate the meaning of intellectual concepts express something in reality which is so independently of its being expressed in a judgment. For example, a statement such as 'iron is hard' is a prediction: if x, then y. And regularly successful or verified prediction shows that there must be something real now, of a general nature, which accounts for a future actuality. This something real now is for Peirce a real possibility. He compares it to the essence or common nature in the philosophy of Duns Scotus;[1] but for him it has a relational structure, expressed in the conditional proposition which explicates the meaning of a universal concept. Hence he calls it a 'law'. Universal concepts, therefore, have an objective foundation or counterpart in reality, namely 'laws'.

We have been speaking of ideas of thirdness. But Peirce's realism can also be seen in his account of ideas of firstness. The idea of white, for example, has its objective counterpart in reality, namely, not simply white things but whiteness, an essence. Whiteness as such does not indeed exist as an actuality. Only white things exist in this way. But for Peirce whiteness is a real possibility. From the epistemological point of view it is the real possibility of an idea, an idea of a firstness.[2]

In general, human knowledge and science demand as a necessary condition the existence of a realm of real possibilities, 'essences', of a general nature. Hence we cannot accept the nominalist thesis that generality belongs only to words in their function as standing for a plurality of individual entities.[3]

6. When we read the formulation of the pragmatist principle

---

[1] Peirce's realism was not derived from Scotus, but it was to a great extent developed through reflection on and a transformation of the doctrine of the mediaeval Franciscan, or of what Peirce believed to be his doctrine. Indeed, on occasion Peirce even called himself a 'Scotistic realist'. On this subject see *Charles Peirce and Scholastic Realism: A Study of Peirce's Relation to John Duns Scotus*, by John F. Boler (Seattle, 1963).

[2] The 'essence' of whiteness is embodied in an idea through the power of attention, which is said to 'abstract' it.

[3] What Peirce calls 'realism' is not what everyone would understand by the term. But we are concerned here with his use of the word.

which is quoted in the fourth section of this chapter,[1] we are naturally put in mind of the neopositivist criterion of meaning. But in order to be able to discuss the relation between Peirce's theory of meaning and positivism, we have first to make some distinctions with a view to clarifying the issue.

In the first place, when Peirce himself talks about positivism, he is speaking, needless to say, of classical positivism as represented, for example, by Auguste Comte and Karl Pearson. And while he allows that positivism in this sense has been of service to science, he also explicitly attacks some features which he finds in it or at any rate attributes to it. For instance, he attributes to Comte the view that a genuine hypothesis must be practically verifiable by direct observation; and he proceeds to reject this view, on the ground that for an hypothesis to be meaningful it is required only that we should be able to *conceive* its practical consequences, not that it should be practically verifiable. Again, Peirce refuses to allow that nothing except what is directly observable should be postulated in an hypothesis. For in an hypothesis we infer the future, a 'will be' or 'would be', and a 'would be' is certainly not directly observable.[2] Further, it is a mistake to regard hypotheses as being simply fictional devices for stimulating observation. An hypothesis can have, for example, an initial probability, as being the result of legitimate inference. In general, therefore, Peirce regards the positivists as too preoccupied with the process of practical verification and as being far too quick to say that this or that is inconceivable.

We cannot, however, infer without more ado from Peirce's criticism of Comte and Pearson that his theory of meaning has nothing in common with neopositivism (or logical positivism as it is generally called in England). For though the neopositivists were originally given to identifying the meaning of an empirical hypothesis with its mode of verification, they did not intend to imply that its meaning can be identified with the actual process of verification. They identified the meaning with the *idea* of the mode of verification, considered, in Peirce's terminology, as the practical consequences of the hypothesis. Further, they did not insist that an hypothesis should be directly verifiable, in order to

---

[1] P. 311.

[2] Obviously, when a prediction is fulfilled, the result may be directly observable. But Peirce's point is that a scientific hypothesis states what *would* be the case *if* a condition were fulfilled, and that a 'would be' is not, *as such*, directly observable.

be meaningful. It is not the intention of the present writer to express agreement with the neopositivist criterion of meaning. In point of fact he does not agree with it. But this is irrelevant. The relevant point is that the theory of meaning expounded by the neopositivists escapes at any rate some of the criticisms which Peirce levelled, whether fairly or unfairly, against positivism as he knew it.

It must also be emphasized that the question is not whether Peirce was or was not a positivist. For it is perfectly clear that he was not. As will be seen presently, he sketched a metaphysics which under some aspects at least bore a resemblance to Hegelian absolute idealism. The question is rather whether the neopositivists are justified in looking on Peirce as a predecessor, not only in the sense that his 'pragmaticist' analysis of meaning has a clear affinity to their own but also in the sense that genuine consistency with his theory of meaning would have ruled out the sort of metaphysics which he in fact developed. In other words, once given his theory of meaning, ought Peirce to have been a positivist? That is to say, ought he to have anticipated neopositivism to a much great extent than was in fact the case?

In his well-known paper on *How to make our ideas clear* Peirce asserts that 'the essence of belief is the establishment of a habit; and different beliefs are distinguished by the different modes of action to which they give rise'.[1] If there is no difference at all between the lines of conduct or action to which two *prima facie* different beliefs give rise, they are not two beliefs but one.

It is easy to think of a simple example. If one man says that he believes that there are other persons besides himself while another man says that he believes the opposite, and if we find them acting in precisely the same way by talking with others, questioning them, listening to them, writing them letters and so on, we naturally conclude that, whatever he may say, the second man really has exactly the same belief as the first man, namely that there are other persons besides himself.

Peirce applies this idea to the alleged difference in belief between Catholics and Protestants in regard to the Eucharist,[2] maintaining that as there is no difference in action or conduct

[1] 5.398.
[2] The term 'Protestant' in this context is ambiguous. For there is no one belief about the Eucharist which can be called *the* Protestant belief. But Peirce obviously has in mind those who deny the real presence of Christ in the Sacrament, and, more particularly, those who deny a change which justifies the statement that the consecrated bread and wine *are* the Body and Blood of Christ.

between the two parties, there cannot be any real difference in belief. At first sight at any rate this thesis appears to be in flat contradiction with the facts. For example, practising Catholics genuflect before the Blessed Sacrament, pray before the Tabernacle in which the Blessed Sacrament is reserved, and so on, while the Protestants whom Peirce has in mind do not, for the very good reason that they do not believe in the 'real presence'. But closer inspection of what Peirce says on the subject shows that he is really arguing that Catholics and Protestants have the same expectations in regard to the sensible effects of the Sacrament. For, irrespective of their theological beliefs, both parties expect, for example, that consumption of the consecrated bread will have the same physical effects as consumption of unconsecrated bread. And this is, of course, quite true. The Catholic who believes in transubstantiation does not deny that after the consecration the 'species' of bread will have the same sensible effects as unconsecrated bread.

The relevance of Peirce's argument to the subject of his relation to positivism may not be immediately apparent. But in point of fact his line of argument is extremely relevant. For he explicitly says that he wishes to point out 'how impossible it is that we should have an idea in our minds which relates to anything but conceived sensible effects of things. Our idea of anything *is* our idea of its sensible effects; and if we fancy that we have any other we deceive ourselves, and mistake a mere sensation accompanying the thought for a part of the thought itself.'[1] In the immediate context this means that to agree that an object has all the sensible effects of bread and to claim at the same time that it is really the Body of Christ is to indulge in 'senseless jargon'.[2] In a wider context it seems to follow clearly from Peirce's thesis that all metaphysical talk about spiritual realities which cannot be construed as talk about 'sensible effects' is nonsense, or that it has no more than emotive significance.

Needless to say, we are not concerned here with theological controversy between Catholics and Protestants. The point of referring to the passage in which Peirce mentions the matter is simply that in it he explicitly states that our idea of anything *is* the idea of its sensible effects. If such a statement does not give good ground for the contention that certain aspects of Peirce's thought constitute an anticipation of neopositivism, it is difficult

[1] 5.401.   [2] *Ibid.*

to think of statements which would do so. But this does not alter the fact that there are other aspects of his thought which differentiate it sharply enough from positivism. Nor, as far as I know, has anyone attempted to deny the fact.

7. Turning to ethics, we can note that it is described by Peirce in various ways, as, for example, the science of right and wrong, the science of ideals, the philosophy of aims. But he also tells us that 'we are too apt to define ethics to ourselves as the science of right and wrong'.[1] To be sure, ethics is concerned with right and wrong; but the fundamental question is, 'What am I to aim at, what am I after?'[2] In other words, the fundamental problem of ethics is that of determining the end of ethical conduct, conduct meaning here deliberate or self-controlled action. The concept of the good is thus basic in Peirce's ethics.

For Peirce, therefore, ethics consists of two main divisions. Pure ethics inquires into the nature of the ideal, the *summum bonum* or ultimate aim of conduct. 'Life can have but one end. It is Ethics which defines that end.'[3] Practical ethics is concerned with the conformity of action to the ideal, to the end. The former, pure ethics, can be called a pre-normative science, while practical ethics is strictly normative in character. Both are required. On the one hand a system of practical ethics gives us a programme for future deliberate or controlled conduct. But all deliberate conduct has an aim; it is for the sake of an end. And as the ultimate end or aim is determined in pure ethics, this is presupposed by practical ethics. On the other hand pragmatism requires that the concept of the end should be explicated in terms of conceived practical consequences, in conditional propositions relating to deliberate or controlled conduct. It does not follow, however, that in ethics a pragmatist will be an advocate of action for the sake of action. For, as we have seen, deliberate or rational action, and it is with this that ethics is concerned, is directed to the realization of an end, an ideal.

'Pure ethics,' Peirce tells us, 'has been, and always must be, a theatre of discussion, for the reason that its study consists in the gradual development of a distinct recognition of a satisfactory aim.'[4] This satisfactory aim or end of conduct must be an infinite end, that is, one which can be pursued indefinitely. And this is to be found in what we may call the rationalization of the universe. For the rational or reasonable is the only end which is fully

[1] 2.198.   [2] *Ibid.*   [3] *Ibid.*   [4] 4.243.

satisfactory in itself. And this means in effect that the *summum bonum* or supreme good is really the evolutionary process itself considered as the progressive rationalization of reality, as the process whereby that which exists comes more and more to embody rationality. The ultimate end is thus a cosmic end. But 'in its higher stages evolution takes place more and more largely through self-control'.[1] And this is where specifically human action comes in. It is self-control which makes possible 'an ought-to-be of conduct'.[2]

Peirce thus has the vision of the cosmic process as moving towards the realization of reason or rationality, and of man as co-operating in the process. Further, as the ultimate end is a general end, a cosmic aim, so to speak, it follows that it must be a social end, common to all men. Conscience, created and modified by experience, is in a sense pre-ethical: it belongs to what Peirce calls a community-consciousness, existing at a level of the soul at which there are hardly distinct individuals. And in point of fact a great part of one's moral vocation is settled by one's place and function in the community to which one belongs. But our vision should rise above the limited social organism to 'a conceived identification of one's interests with those of an unlimited community'.[3] And universal love is the all-important moral ideal.

Inasmuch as Peirce's pragmatism is primarily a theory of meaning and a method of making our concepts clear, it is primarily a matter of logic. But it has, of course, an application in ethics. For ethical concepts are to be interpreted in terms of conceived modes of conduct, though, as we have seen, reflection or deliberate or controlled conduct leads inevitably to reflection on the end of conduct. If we interpret ethical concepts and propositions in terms of good and bad consequences, we cannot avoid asking the question, what is the good? In other words, pragmatism is not a doctrine simply of practice, of action for action's sake. Theory and practice, Peirce insists, go together. For the matter of that, pragmatism in its application to science is not a doctrine of action for action's sake. We have already noted how Peirce rejected what he regarded as the positivist worship of actual verification. True, the pragmatist analysis of scientific hypotheses can be said to look forward to conduct or action; but in itself the analysis is a theoretical inquiry. Similarly, ethics looks forward to moral conduct; it is a normative science. But it is none the less a science, a

[1] 5.433.   [2] 4.540.   [3] 2.654.

theoretical inquiry, though it would, of course, be barren if no conduct resulted.

Sometimes Peirce speaks as though ethics were fundamental and logic an application of it. For thinking or reasoning is itself a form of conduct, and it is 'impossible to be thoroughly and rationally logical except upon an ethical basis'.[1] Indeed, logic, as concerned with what we ought to think, 'must be an application of the doctrine of what we deliberately choose to do, which is ethics'.[2] At the same time Peirce does not really mean that logic can be derived from ethics, any more than ethics can be derived from logic. They are for him distinct normative sciences. But inasmuch as pragmatism teaches that 'what we think is to be interpreted in terms of what we are prepared to do',[3] there must be connections between logic and ethics.

One connection worth noting is this. We have seen that according to Peirce absolute certainty concerning the truth of an hypothesis cannot be attained at any given moment by any given individual. At the same time there can be an 'infinite' or unending approximation to it through the unlimited or continuing community of observers, by means of repeated verification which raises probability towards the ideal limit of certainty. So in the moral sphere the experiment of conduct, so to speak, tends to increase, through the unlimited community of mankind, clear recognition of the nature of the supreme end of life and of its 'meaning', its implications in regard to concrete action. And we can envisage, at any rate as an ideal limit, universal agreement.

Indeed, Peirce does not hesitate to say that 'in regard to morals we can see ground for hope that debate will ultimately cause one party or other to modify their sentiments up to complete accord'.[4] This obviously presupposes that the basis of morality is objective, that the supreme good or ultimate end is something to be discovered and about which agreement is possible in principle. And this point of view obviously differentiates Peirce's ethics from the emotive theory, especially in its older and cruder form, which is associated with the early phase of modern neopositivism. So does his idea of analyzing moral propositions on lines analogous to his analysis of scientific propositions,[5] not to speak of his general

[1] 2.198.   [2] 5.35.   [3] Ibid.   [4] 2.151.
[5] The upholder of the emotive theory of ethics would claim that this analysis fails to do justice to the peculiar character of moral utterances. But to say this is, of course, to recognize the difference between Peirce's theory of ethics and the emotive theory.

vision of evolution as moving towards the embodiment of reason in the unlimited community, a vision which has much more affinity with absolute idealism than with positivism.

8. Sometimes Peirce speaks of metaphysics in a thoroughly positivist manner. For example, in a paper on pragmatism he states that pragmatism will serve to show that 'almost every proposition of ontological metaphysics is either meaningless gibberish—one word being defined by other words, and they by still others, without any real conception ever being reached—or else is downright absurd'.[1] When this rubbish has been swept away, philosophy will be reduced to problems capable of investigation by the observational methods of the genuine sciences. Pragmatism is thus 'a species of prope-positivism'.[2]

At the same time Peirce goes on to say that pragmatism does not simply jeer at metaphysics but 'extracts from it a precious essence, which will serve to give life and light to cosmology and physics'.[3] In any case he has no intention of rejecting metaphysics, provided that he himself is practising it. And while it is only right to mention the fact that Peirce sometimes derides metaphysics, this does not alter the fact that he has his own brand of it.

Peirce gives a number of different definitions or descriptions of metaphysics, when, that is to say, the term 'metaphysics' is not being used as a term of abuse. We are told, for example, that 'metaphysics consists in the results of the absolute acceptance of logical principles not merely as regulatively valid, but as truths of being'.[4] It is in accordance with this view that Peirce connects the fundamental ontological categories with the logical categories of firstness, secondness and thirdness. And he asserts that as metaphysics results from the acceptance of logical principles as principles of being, the universe must be regarded as having a unifying explanation. At other times Peirce emphasizes the observational basis of metaphysics. 'Metaphysics, even bad metaphysics, really rests on observations, whether consciously or not.'[5] And it is in accordance with this view that Peirce derives the fundamental ontological categories from phenomenology or 'phaneroscopy', by inquiring into the irreducible formal elements in any and every

---

[1] 5.423. [2] *Ibid.*
[3] *Ibid.* Elsewhere (6.3) Peirce says that the chief cause of the backwardness of metaphysics is that it has been so often in the hands of theologians, who have an axe to grind.
[4] 1.487. [5] 6.2

experience. We are also told that 'metaphysics is the science of Reality',[1] reality including for Peirce not only the actually existent but also the sphere of real possibility.

To a certain extent at least these various ways of describing metaphysics can be harmonized. For example, to say that metaphysics is the science of reality is not incompatible with saying that it is based on experience or observation. It may even be possible to harmonize the view that metaphysics rests on observations with the view that it results from the acceptance of logical principles, providing at any rate that we do not interpret this second view as meaning that metaphysics can be deduced from logic without any recourse to experience. At the same time it does not seem to be possible to construct from Peirce's various utterances an absolutely consistent and unambiguous account of metaphysics. For one thing, he does not appear to have made up his mind definitely about the precise relation between ontology and logic. For present purposes, therefore, we had better confine ourselves to indicating briefly some of Peirce's metaphysical ideas. We cannot undertake here to create that consistent system which the philosopher himself did not achieve.

We can start with Peirce's three fundamental categories. The first, that of 'firstness', is 'the idea of that which is such as it is regardless of anything else'.[2] And Peirce calls it the category of quality, in the sense of 'suchness'. From the phenomenological point of view we can conceive a feeling, as of sadness, or a sensed quality, as of blueness, without reference to subject or object but simply as a unique something, 'a purely monadic state of feeling'.[3] To convert the psychological concept into a metaphysical one, Peirce tells us, we have to think of a monad as 'a pure nature, or quality, in itself without parts or features, and without embodiment'.[4] But the term 'monad', with its Leibnizian associations, can be misleading. For Peirce goes on to say that the meanings of the names of the so-called secondary qualities are as good examples of monads as can be given. It is understandable therefore that he speaks of the category of firstness as that of quality. In any case firstness is a pervasive feature of the universe, representing the element of uniqueness, freshness and originality which is everywhere present, in every phenomenon, every fact, every event. To obtain some idea of what is meant, Peirce suggests that we should imagine to ourselves the universe as it appeared to Adam when

[1] 5.21.   [2] 5.66.   [3] 1.303.   [4] Ibid.

he looked on it for the first time, and before he had drawn distinctions and become reflectively aware of his own experience.

The second fundamental category, that of 'secondness', is dyadic, corresponding to the idea of secondness in logic. That is to say, secondness is 'the conception of being relative to, the conception of reaction with, something else'.[1] From one point of view secondness can be called 'fact', while from another point of view it is existence or actuality. For 'existence is that mode of being which lies in opposition to another'.[2] And this category too pervades the universe. Facts are facts, as we say; and this is why we sometimes speak of 'brute' facts. Actuality or existence involves everywhere effort and resistance. It is in this sense dyadic.

The third fundamental category, that of 'thirdness', is said to be the category of mediation, its logical prototype being the mediating function of a sign between object and interpretant. Ontologically, thirdness mediates between firstness, in the sense of quality, and secondness, in the sense of fact or of action and reaction. It thus introduces continuity and regularity, and it takes the form of laws of various types or grades. For instance, there can be laws of quality, determining 'systems of qualities, of which Sir Isaac Newton's law of colour-mixture, with Dr. Thomas Young's supplement thereto, is the most perfect known example'.[3] There can also be laws of fact. Thus if a spark falls into a barrel of gunpowder (treated as a first), it causes an explosion (treated as a second); and it does so according to an intelligible law, which thus has a mediating function.[4] Then again there are laws of regularity which enable us to predict that future facts of secondness will always take on a certain determinate character or quality. In its various forms, however, the category of thirdness, like those of firstness and secondness, pervades the universe; and we can say that everything stands in some relation to every other thing.[5]

Now, quality can be said, in Mill's language, to be a permanent possibility of sensation. It is, however, a real possibility, independent of subjective experience. And we can thus say that the first quality gives us the first mode of being, namely real possibility, though the concept of possibility is admittedly wider than that of quality. Similarly, the second category, being from one point of

---

[1] 6.32.   [2] 4.457.   [3] 1.482.
[4] According to Peirce laws of fact can be divided into logically necessary and logically contingent laws, while logically contingent laws can be subdivided into metaphysically necessary and metaphysically contingent laws (1.483).
[5] Cf. 4.319.

view that of actuality or existence, gives us the second mode of being, namely actuality as distinct from possibility. Again, by involving the concept of law the third category gives us the third mode of being, which Peirce calls 'destiny', as governing future facts. But it must be understood that in Peirce's use of the term the concept of 'destiny' is wider than the concept of law, if we mean by law the idea of it which is associated with determinism. For to be free from determining law is as much 'destiny' as to be subject to it.

We have, therefore, three fundamental ontological categories and three corresponding metaphysical modes of being. Peirce also distinguishes three modes or categories of existence or actuality. The first is what he calls 'chance', a term used 'to express with accuracy the characteristics of freedom or spontaneity'.[1] The second mode of existence is law, laws being of various types but all being the result of evolution. The third mode of existence is habit, or, rather, the tendency to habit-making. The word 'habit', however, must be understood in a wide sense. For, according to Peirce, all things possess a tendency to take habits,[2] whether they are human beings, animals, plants or chemical substances. And the laws which state uniformities or regularities are the results of long periods of such habit-taking.

We can now briefly consider the actual world or universe in the light of these modes or categories of actuality or existence.[3] 'Three elements are active in the world: first, chance; second, law; and third, habit-taking.'[4] We are invited to think of the universe as being originally in a state of pure indetermination, a state in which there were no distinct things, no habits, no laws, a state in which absolute chance reigned. From one point of view this absolute indetermination was 'nullity',[5] the negation of all determination, while from another point of view, considered, that is to say, as the real possibility of all determination, it was 'being'.[6] At the same time chance is spontaneity, freedom, creativity. It thus annuls itself as unlimited possibility or potentiality by taking the form of possibilities of this or that sort, that is to say, of some definite qualities or suchnesses, falling under the ontological category of firstness. And as the universe evolves and

---

[1] 6.201.   [2] Cf. 1.409.
[3] The actual world, it will be remembered, is for Peirce part of the wider sphere of real possibility. It consists of actualized possibilities and of possibilities in the process of actualization.
[4] 1.409.   [5] 1.447.   [6] Ibid.

'monads' act and react in 'secondnesses', habits are formed and there are produced those regularities or laws which fall into the category of thirdness. The ideal limit of the process is the complete reign of law, the opposite of the reign of absolute chance.

The first stage is evidently, in a real sense, an abstraction. For if chance is spontaneity and creativity, we can hardly speak, as Peirce explicitly recognizes, of an assignable time or period during which there was absolutely no determination. Similarly, the complete reign of law, in which all chance or spontaneity is absent, is also in a sense an abstraction, an ideal limit. For according to Peirce's principle of 'tychism',[1] chance is always present in the universe. Hence we can say that the universe is a process of creative and continuous determination, moving from the ideal limit of absolute indetermination to the ideal limit of absolute determination, or, better, from the ideal limit of bare possibility to the ideal limit of the complete actualization of possibility. Another way of putting the matter is to say that evolution is a process of advance from absolute chance considered as 'a chaos of unpersonalized feeling'[2] to the reign of pure reason embodied in a perfectly rational system. We have already seen, in connection with his ethical doctrine, how Peirce regards the universe as moving towards an ever fuller embodiment of rationality.

It does not follow from Peirce's doctrine of absolute chance as the primitive state of the universe that chance is the sole explanation of evolution. On the contrary, 'evolution is nothing more nor less than the working out of a definite end',[3] a final cause. And this idea enables Peirce to adopt and adapt the old idea of the cosmic significance of love, an idea which goes back at any rate to the Greek philosopher Empedocles. A final end works by attraction, and the response is love. To the idea of 'tychism', therefore, we have to add that of 'agapism' as a cosmological category. And to these two we must add a third, namely 'synechism', which is 'the doctrine that all that exists is continuous'.[4]

Synechism, we may note, rules out any ultimate dualism between matter and mind. Indeed, 'what we call matter is not completely dead, but is merely mind hidebound with habits'[5] which make it act with a specially high degree of mechanical regularity. And Peirce remarks that 'tychism' must give rise to a 'Schelling-fashioned idealism which holds matter to be mere

---

[1] 'Tychism' or 'chance-ism', coined by Peirce from the Greek word *tyche*.
[2] 6.33.   [3] 1.204.   [4] 1.172.   [5] 6.158.

specialized and partially deadened mind'.[1] So convinced is he of
this, that he does not hesitate to say that 'the one intelligible
theory of the universe is that of objective idealism, that matter is
effete mind, inveterate habits becoming physical laws'.[2]

Now, if it is asked whether Peirce believed in God, the answer
is affirmative. But if it is asked what part is played in his philosophy by the concept of God, the answer is more complex. His
general principle is that philosophy and religion should not be
mixed up. Not that this prevents him from writing about God.
But when he talks about 'musement' as an activity of the mind
which leads directly to God, he is not thinking of what would
normally be called a systematic metaphysical argument. If, for
example, I contemplate the starry heavens, as Kant did, and
allow instinct and the heart to speak, I cannot help believing in
God. Appeal to one's own 'instinct' is more effective than any
argument.[3] Peirce does indeed make it clear that in his opinion
contemplation of the 'three universes' of tychism, agapism and
synechism 'gives birth to the hypothesis and ultimately to the
belief that they, or at any rate two of the three, have a Creator
independent of them'.[4] But he calls this the 'neglected argument',
also the 'humble argument', and he brings it under the heading of
'musement'. The direction of Peirce's thought is, however,
perfectly plain. A theory of evolution which enthroned mechanical
law above the principle of creative growth or development would
be hostile to religion; but 'a genuine evolutionary philosophy . . .
is so far from being antagonistic to the idea of a personal creator
that it is really inseparable from that idea'.[5] While, therefore, in
his systematic metaphysics Peirce concentrates on the doctrine of
categories, his general world-view is certainly theistic.

9. From the point of view of the history of pragmatism Peirce's
chief contribution is, of course, his analysis of meaning, his rule
for making concepts clear. And if this is considered in a general
way, it has an obvious value. For it can serve as a useful goad or
stimulus, making us give concrete content to our concepts, instead
of letting words do duty for clear ideas. In other words, it stimulates

---

[1] 6.102. Tychism is mentioned because Peirce connects mind with firstness, and
so, rather surprisingly, with chance, while matter is connected with secondness,
and with agapism, and evolution with thirdness, synechism (6.32).
[2] 6.25.
[3] Peirce believed that God's existence is from one point of view evident enough.
'Where would such an idea, say as that of God, come from if not from direct
experience?' (6.493).
[4] 6.483.   [5] 6.157.

to conceptual analysis. It seems to me pretty obvious, for example, that if there were no assignable difference between what Peirce calls the 'practical consequences' or 'practical effects' of the words 'hard' and 'soft', there would in fact be no difference in meaning. True, as a general criterion of meaning Peirce's principle of pragmaticism lies open to the same sort of objections which have been brought against the neopositivist criterion of meaning. There is great difficulty in interpreting all factual statements as predictions or sets of predictions. But this does not alter the fact that the principle of pragmaticism brings out aspects of the semantic situation which have to be taken into account in developing a theory of meaning. In other words, Peirce made a valuable contribution to logic. And if he allowed what he saw clearly to obscure other aspects of the situation, there is nothing exceptional in this.

We have seen, however, that when applying the principle of pragmaticism in a particular context Peirce states roundly that our idea of anything *is* our idea of its sensible effects. If this statement is taken seriously in its universal form, it appears to undermine Peirce's own metaphysical world-view. He does indeed make an attempt to apply his principle to the concept of God without dissolving the concept.[1] And he suggests[2] that if the pragmaticist is asked what he means by 'God', he can reply that just as long acquaintance with the works of Aristotle makes us familiar with the philosopher's mind, so does study of the physico-psychical universe give us an acquaintance with what may be called in some analogous sense the divine 'mind'. But if his statement elsewhere about 'sensible effects' is taken seriously, it seems to follow either that we have no clear concept of God or that the idea of God is simply the idea of his sensible effects. And in point of fact Peirce himself suggests in one place[3] that the question whether there really is such a being as God is the question whether physical science is something objective or simply a fictional construction of the scientists' minds.

It may be objected that the last sentence involves taking a remark out of its general context, and that in any case too much emphasis has been placed on the statement that our idea of anything is the idea of its sensible effects. After all, when he made the statement Peirce was talking about the sensible effects of bread. Further, he gives various formulations of the principle of pragmatism, and in view of the way in which he often uses the principle

[1] 6.489–490. [2] 6.502. [3] 6.503.

we ought not to over-emphasize a statement made in a particular context.

This is doubtless true. But Peirce made the statement in question. And the point which we are trying to make here is that he did not construct a system in which all the elements of his thought were harmonized and rendered consistent. Peirce approached philosophy through mathematics and science, and his theory of meaning was doubtless largely suggested by reflection on scientific statements considered as fallible hypotheses, as verifiable or falsifiable predictions. But his interests were wide and his mind was original and fertile; and he developed a metaphysical world-view in which pragmatism was not forgotten but which demanded reconsideration of the nature and scope of the pragmatist principle. To claim that it is impossible to synthesize Peirce's logic and his metaphysics would be to claim too much, at least if synthesis is understood as permitting revision and modification of the elements to be synthesized. But two things at any rate are clear; first that Peirce did not himself work out such a synthesis, and, secondly, that no synthesis is possible if the pragmatic principle is understood in such a way that it leads straight to neopositivism.

To say, however, that Peirce did not achieve a fully coherent synthesis of the various elements in his thought is not to deny that he was in a real sense a systematic thinker. Indeed, from one point of view it is hardly an exaggeration to claim that he was possessed by a passion for system. We have only to think, for example, of the way in which he used the ideas of firstness, secondness and thirdness, employing them to link together logic, epistemology, ontology and cosmology. It is undeniable that out of his various papers there arise the general outlines of an imposing system.

We have said that Peirce approached philosophy by way of mathematics and science. And we would naturally expect his metaphysics to be a prolongation or extension of his reflections on the scientific view of the world. So it is to some extent. At the same time the general results have a marked affinity with metaphysical idealism. But Peirce was well aware of this; and he considered that if one constructs a world-view based on the scientific conception of the world, one is inevitably pushed in the direction of metaphysical idealism, an idealism which is able to accommodate the 'Scholastic realism' on which Peirce always insisted. In other words, he did not start with idealist premises.

He started with realism and was determined to maintain it. But he recognized that though his approach was different from that of the idealists, his conclusions had a recognizable resemblance to theirs. We find much the same situation in the case of Whitehead in the present century.

We have already noted Peirce's commendation of Schelling's view of matter, and his explicit statement that objective idealism is the one intelligible theory of the universe. Here we can note his partial affinity with Hegel. Sometimes indeed Peirce speaks against Hegel, maintaining, for example, that he was too inclined to forget that there is a world of action and reaction, and that Hegel deprived 'firstness' and 'secondness' of all actuality. But when speaking of his own doctrine of categories, logical and metaphysical, Peirce notes the 'Hegelian sound'[1] of what he has to say and remarks that his statements are indeed akin to those of Hegel. 'I sometimes agree with the great idealist and sometimes diverge from his footsteps.'[2] While prepared to say on occasion that he entirely rejects the system of Hegel, Peirce is also prepared to say on occasion that he has resuscitated Hegelianism in a new form, and even to claim that, so far as a philosophical concept can be identified with the idea of God, God is the absolute Idea of Hegel, the Idea which manifests itself in the world and tends towards its complete self-revelation in the ideal limit or term of the evolutionary process.[3] It is not altogether surprising, therefore, if Peirce speaks of Hegel as 'in some respects the greatest philosopher that ever lived',[4] even if he also criticizes Hegel for a lamentable deficiency in 'critical severity and sense of fact'.[5]

We have mentioned the name of Whitehead. There does not seem to be any evidence that Whitehead was influenced by Peirce, or even that he had studied Peirce's writings. But this renders the resemblance between their thought all the more notable. It is, of course, a limited resemblance, but it is none the less real. For example, Whitehead's doctrine of eternal objects and actual entities was anticipated to some extent by Peirce's distinction between 'generals' and facts. Again, Whitehead's doctrine of novelty in the universe, in the cosmic process, recalls Peirce's doctrine of spontaneity and originality. Further, it is perhaps not

---

[1] 1.453.   [2] *Ibid.*
[3] One can compare Peirce's different ways of alluding to Hegelianism with the different ways in which he speaks of metaphysics. Needless to say, the different statements must in both cases he interpreted in the light of their immediate contexts.
[4] 1.524.   [5] *Ibid.*

altogether fanciful to see in Peirce's thought an anticipation of Whitehead's famous distinction between the primordial and consequent natures of God. For Peirce tells us that God as Creator is the 'Absolute First',[1] while as terminus of the universe, as God completely revealed, he is the 'Absolute Second'.[2] Perhaps one is put in mind more of Hegel than of Whitehead; but then the philosophy of Whitehead himself, anti-idealist though it was by original intention, bears some resemblance in its final form to absolute idealism.

To return finally to Peirce in himself. He was an original philosopher and powerful thinker. Indeed, the claim that he is the greatest of all purely American philosophers is by no means unreasonable. He had a strong tendency to careful analysis and was far from being one of those philosophers whose chief concern appears to be that of providing uplift and edification. At the same time he had a speculative mind which sought for a general or overall interpretation of reality. And this combination is, we may well think, precisely what is required. At the same time the example of Peirce is a living illustration of the difficulty of effecting such a combination. For we find in his thought unresolved ambiguities. For instance, Peirce is a resolute realist. Reality is independent of human experience and thought. Indeed, the real is to be defined precisely in terms of this independence. And it is this account of the real which permits Peirce to attribute independent reality to the world of possibles and to depict God as the only absolute reality. At the same time his pragmatism or pragmaticism seems to demand what Royce called the 'critical rationalist' interpretation of reality, namely in terms of conceivable human experience. That which gives rise to actual experience is actually real. That which is conceived as giving rise to possible experience is potentially actual, a real possibility. On this interpretation of reality we could not claim that God is an actually existing being without claiming that he is the object of actual experience. Alternatively, we would have to analyze the concept of God in such a way as to reduce it to the idea of those effects which we do experience. So we are back once more with the latent tension in Peirce's philosophy as a whole between his metaphysics and a logical analysis of the meaning of concepts which appears to point in quite a different direction from that of his speculative metaphysics.

[1] 1.362.
[2] *Ibid*. The 'third' would be every state of the universe at an assignable point of time, mediating between God as First and God as Second.

CHAPTER XV

THE PRAGMATISM OF JAMES AND SCHILLER

The life and writings of William James—James's conception of radical empiricism and pure experience—Pragmatism as theory of meaning and as theory of truth—The relations between radical empiricism, pragmatism and humanism in the philosophy of James—Pragmatism and belief in God—Pragmatism in America and England—The humanism of C. F. S. Schiller.

1. WILLIAM JAMES (1842–1910) was born at New York and received his school education partly in America and partly abroad, acquiring in the process a fluency in the French and German languages. In 1864 he entered the Harvard Medical School, receiving the degree of doctor of medicine in 1869. After a period of bad health and mental depression he became an instructor in anatomy and physiology at Harvard. But he was also interested in psychology, and in 1875 he began giving courses in the subject. In 1890 he published his *Principles of Psychology* in two volumes.

Apart from an early attempt to become a painter, James's higher education was thus mainly scientific and medical. But like his father, Henry James, senior,[1] he was a man of deep religious feeling, and he found himself involved in a mental conflict between the scientific view of the world, interpreted as a mechanistic view which excluded human freedom, and a religious view which would include belief not only in God but also in the freedom of man. As far as the legitimacy of belief in freedom was concerned, James found help in the writing of the French philosopher Charles Renouvier (1815–1903). And it was largely the desire to overcome the opposition between the outlook to which science seemed to him to point and the outlook suggested by his religious and humanistic inclinations which drove James to philosophy. In 1879 he started to lecture on the subject at Harvard, and in the following year he became an assistant professor of philosophy. In 1885 he was nominated professor of philosophy.

In 1897 James published *The Will to Believe and Other Essays in Popular Philosophy.*[2] His famous *Varieties of Religious*

---

[1] Henry James, junior, the novelist, was a younger brother of William.
[2] The copyright date is 1896, but the volume appeared in 1897.

Experience,[1] appeared in 1902. This was followed by *Pragmatism* in 1907, *A Pluralistic Universe*[2] in 1909 and, in the same year, *The Meaning of Truth*. James's posthumously published writings include *Some Problems of Philosophy* (1911), *Memories and Studies* (1911), *Essays in Radical Empiricism* (1912), and *Collected Essays and Reviews* (1920). His *Letters*, edited by his son, Henry James, appeared in 1926.

2. In the preface to *The Will to Believe* James describes his philosophical attitude as that of radical empiricism. He explains that by empiricism he understands a position which is 'contented to regard its most assured conclusions concerning matters of fact as hypotheses liable to modification in the course of future experience'.[3] As for the word 'radical', this indicates that the doctrine of monism itself is treated as an hypothesis. At first hearing this sounds very odd. But in this context James understands by monism the view that the multiplicity of things forms an intelligible unity. He does not mean by monism the theory that the world is one single entity or one single fact. On the contrary, he excludes this theory in favour of pluralism. What he is saying is that radical empiricism postulates a unity which is not immediately given, but that this postulate, which stimulates us to discover unifying connections, is treated as itself an hypothesis which has to be verified, and not as an unquestionable dogma.[4]

In *Some Problems of Philosophy*, in the context of a discussion of types of metaphysics, empiricism is contrasted with rationalism. 'Rationalists are the men of principles, empiricists the men of facts.'[5] The rationalist philosopher, as James sees him, moves from the whole to its parts, from the universal to the particular, and he endeavours to deduce facts from principles. Further, he tends to claim final truth on behalf of his system of deduced conclusions. The empiricist, however, starts with particular facts; he moves from parts to wholes; and he prefers, if he can, to explain principles as inductions from facts. Further, the claim to final truth is foreign to his mind.

Obviously, there is nothing new here. Familiar lines of contrast between rationalism and empiricism are presented by James in a more or less popular manner. But in the preface to *The Meaning*

---

[1] This work represents Gifford Lectures given at Edinburgh in 1901–2.
[2] This work represents the Hibbert Lectures given at Oxford in 1908–9.
[3] *The Will to Believe*, p. vii (1903 edition).
[4] We shall mention presently another sense of the word 'monism'.
[5] *Some Problems of Philosophy*, p. 35.

of Truth we can find a more clearly defined account of radical empiricism. It is there said to consist 'first of a postulate, next of a statement of fact, and finally of a generalized conclusion'.[1] The postulate is that only those matters which are definable in terms drawn from experience should be considered debatable by philosophers. Hence if there is any being which transcends all possible experience, it also transcends philosophical discussion. The statement of fact is that relations, conjunctive and disjunctive, are as much objects of experience as the things related. And the generalized conclusion from this statement of fact is that the knowable universe possesses a continuous structure, in the sense that it does not consist simply of entities which can be related only through categories imposed from without.

James is insistent on the reality of relations. 'Radical empiricism takes conjunctive relations at their face value, holding them to be as real as the terms united by them.'[2] And among conjunctive relations is the causal relation. Hence what James calls radical empiricism differs from the empiricism of Hume, according to whom 'the mind never perceives any real connection among distinctive existences'.[3] It is also opposed to Bradley's theory of relations. 'Mr. Bradley's understanding shows the most extraordinary power of perceiving separations and the most extraordinary impotence in comprehending conjunctions.'[4]

The meaning of the word 'experience' is notoriously imprecise. But according to James ordinary experience, in which we are aware of distinct things of various kinds and of relations of different types, grows out of pure experience, described as 'the immediate flux of life which furnishes the material to our later reflection with its conceptual categories'.[5] True, only new-born infants and people in a state of semi-coma can be said to enjoy in its purity a state of pure experience, which is 'but another name for feeling or sensation'.[6] But pure experience, the immediacy of feeling or sensation, is the embryo out of which articulated experience develops; and elements or portions of it remain even in our ordinary experience.

From this doctrine of pure experience we can draw two conclusions. First, in this basic flux of experience the distinctions of reflective thought, such as those between consciousness and

---

[1] *The Meaning of Truth*, p. xii.   [2] *Essays in Radical Empiricism*, p. 107.
[3] *Treatise of Human Nature*, Appendix, p. 636 (Selby-Bigge edition).
[4] *Essays in Radical Empiricism*, p. 117.
[5] *Ibid.*, p. 93.   [6] *Ibid.*, p. 94.

content, subject and object, mind and matter, have not yet emerged in the forms in which we make them. In this sense pure experience is 'monistic'. And James can speak of it as the 'one primal stuff or material in the world, a stuff of which everything is composed'.[1] This is the doctrine of 'neutral monism', which James associates with radical empiricism. Pure experience cannot be called, for example, either physical or psychical: it logically precedes the distinction and is thus 'neutral'.

Secondly, however, the fact that radical empiricism is pluralistic rather than monistic in the ontological sense and asserts the reality of many things and of the relations between them, means that pure experience must be regarded as containing in itself potentially the distinctions of developed experience. It is shot through, as James expresses the matter, not only with nouns and adjectives but also with prepositions and conjunctions. The causal relation, for example, is present in the flux of sensation, inasmuch as all sensation is teleological in character.

Now, if pure monism is understood in a purely psychological sense, as simply stating, that is to say, that the primitive and basic form of experience is a state of 'feeling' in which distinctions, such as that between subject and object, are not as yet present, it is doubtless compatible with a realistic pluralism. But if it is understood in an ontological sense, as meaning that the flux of undifferentiated experience is the ontological 'stuff' out of which all emerges, it is difficult to see how it does not lead straight to some form of monistic idealism. However, James assumes that the doctrine of pure experience, which is obviously psychological in origin, is compatible with the pluralistic view of the universe that he associates with radical empiricism.

In so far as radical empiricism involves pluralism and belief in the reality of relations, it can be said to be a world-view. But if it is understood simply in terms of the three elements mentioned above, namely a postulate, a statement of fact, and a generalized conclusion, it is an embryonic rather than a full-grown world-view. The problem of God, for example, is left untouched. James does indeed maintain that there are specifically religious experiences which suggest the existence of a superhuman consciousness that is limited and not all-inclusive in a sense which would conflict with pluralism. And he remarks that if empiricism were to become 'associated with religion, as hitherto, through some strange

[1] *Ibid.*

misunderstanding, it has been associated with irreligion, I believe that a new era of religion as well as of philosophy will be ready to begin'.[1] But James's theism will be more conveniently treated after we have outlined the basic tenets of pragmatism and the relation between pragmatism and radical empiricism.

3. In origin and primarily pragmatism is, James tells us, 'a method only'.[2] For it is in the first place 'a method of settling metaphysical disputes that might otherwise be interminable'.[3] That is to say, if A proposes theory x while B proposes theory y, the pragmatist will examine the practical consequences of each theory. And if he can find no difference between the respective practical consequences of the two theories, he will conclude that they are to all intents and purposes one and the same theory, the difference being purely verbal. In this case further dispute between A and B will be seen to be pointless.

What we have here is obviously a method for determining the meanings of concepts and theories. In an address delivered in 1881 James remarked that if two apparently different definitions of something turn out to have identical consequences, they are really one and the same definition.[4] And this is the theory of meaning which finds expression in *Pragmatism*. 'To attain perfect clearness in our thoughts of an object, we need only consider what conceivable effects of a practical kind the object may involve—what sensations we are to expect from it, and what reactions we must prepare. Our conception of these effects, whether immediate or remote, is then for us the whole of our conception of the object, so far as that conception has positive significance at all.'[5]

As so described, the pragmatism of James evidently follows the main lines of the pragmatist method as conceived by Peirce. James was, indeed, influenced by some other thinkers as well, such as the scientists Louis Agassiz and Wilhelm Ostwald; but he made no secret of his indebtedness to Peirce. He refers to him in a footnote relating to the address of 1881.[6] He again admits his debt to Peirce in a public lecture given in 1898.[7] And after the passage quoted in the last paragraph he adds that 'this is the principle of Peirce, the principle of pragmatism',[8] and remarks that Peirce's doctrine remained unnoticed until he, James, brought it forward in the lecture of 1898 and applied it to religion.

[1] *A Pluralistic Universe*, p. 314. [2] *Pragmatism*, p. 51.
[3] *Ibid.*, p. 45. [4] *The Will to Believe*, p. 124.
[5] *Pragmatism*, p. 47. [6] *The Will to Believe*, p. 124, note 1.
[7] *Collected Essays and Reviews*, p. 410. [8] *Pragmatism*, p. 47.

There are, it is true, certain differences between the positions of Peirce and James. For example, when Peirce spoke about the practical consequences of a concept he emphasized the general idea of a habit of action, the idea of the general manner in which the concept could conceivably modify purposive action. James, however, tends to emphasize particular practical effects. As we have seen in the passage which is quoted above from *Pragmatism*, he there emphasizes particular sensations and reactions. Hence Peirce accused him of having been led away from the universal to the particular under the influence of an ultra-sensationalistic psychology, of being, as Dewey put it, more of a nominalist. In Peirce's terminology, James is concerned with antecedents and consequents more than with consequences, a consequence being the conceived relation between an antecedent and a consequent.

At the same time, if James's pragmatism were simply a method for making concepts clear, for determining their meanings, we could say that he adopts Peirce's principle, even if he gives it, as Dewey expresses it, a 'nominalistic' twist. In point of fact, however, pragmatism is not for James simply a method of determining the meanings of concepts. It is also a theory of truth. Indeed, James explicitly states that 'the pivotal part of my book named *Pragmatism* is its account of the relation called "truth" which may obtain between our idea (opinion, belief, statement, or what not) and its object'.[1] And it was largely James's development of pragmatism into a theory of truth which led Peirce to re-name his own theory 'pragmaticism'.

It is important to understand that James's theory of truth does not presuppose a denial of the correspondence theory. Truth is for him a property of certain of our beliefs, not of things. 'Realities are not *true*, they *are*; and beliefs are true *of* them.'[2] In modern language, logical truth and falsity are predicated of propositions, not of things or of facts. Strictly speaking at any rate, it is the proposition enunciating a fact which is true, not the fact itself. Julius Caesar's existence at a certain period of history cannot properly be called true; but the statement that he existed is true, while the statement that he did not exist is false. At the same time the statement that Julius Caesar existed is not true in virtue of the meanings of the symbols or words employed in the statement. Hence we can say that it is true in virtue of a relation of correspondence with reality or fact.

[1] *The Meaning of Truth*, p. v.   [2] *Ibid.*, p. 196.

In James's opinion, however, to say that a true belief (he also speaks of true ideas) is one which corresponds or agrees with reality raises rather than solves a problem. For what precisely is meant by correspondence in this context? Copying? An image of a sensible object might be called a copy of the object. But it is not so easy to see how a true idea of, say, justice can reasonably be described as a copy.

James's analysis of 'correspondence' is on these lines. Truth is a relation between one part of experience and another. The *terminus a quo* of the relation is an idea, which belongs to the subjective aspect of experience, while the *terminus ad quem* is an objective reality. What, then, is the relation between the terms? Here we have to employ the pragmatist interpretation of an idea as a plan or rule of action. If our following out this plan leads us to the *terminus ad quem*, the idea is true. More accurately, 'such mediating events *make* the idea true'.[1] In other words, the truth of an idea is the process of its verification or validation. If, for example, I am lost in a wood and then come upon a path which I think of as possibly or probably leading to an inhabited house where I can obtain directions or help, my idea is a plan of action. And if my following out this plan verifies or validates the idea, this process of verification constitutes the truth of the idea: it is the 'correspondence' to which the correspondence theory of truth really refers.

Now, it is noticeable that on the same page on which James tells us that an idea '*becomes* true, is *made* true by events',[2] he also tells us that 'true ideas are those that we can assimilate, validate, corroborate and verify'. In other words, he cannot help admitting that there are truths which can or could be verified, but which have not yet been verified. Indeed, he is prepared to state that unverified truths 'form the overwhelmingly large number of the truths we live by',[3] and that truth lives 'for the most part on a credit system'.[4]

If, however, truths are *made* true by verification or validation, it follows that unverified truths are potentially true, truths *in posse*. And this enables James to deal a blow at the philosophical rationalists or intellectualists who exalt static, timeless truths which are true prior to any verification. 'Intellectualist truth is only pragmatist truth *in posse*.'[5] And the total fabric of truth

---

[1] *The Meaning of Truth*, p. 202.   [2] *Pragmatism*, p. 201.
[3] *Ibid.*, p. 206.   [4] *Ibid.*, p. 207.   [5] *The Meaning of Truth*, p. 205.

would collapse if it did not rest on some actually verified truths, that is, on some actual truths, just as a financial system would collapse if it possessed no solid basis in cash.

In discussing James's theory of truth it is obviously important not to caricature it. James was inclined to write in a popular style and to use some rather down-to-earth phrases which gave rise to misunderstanding. For example, his expression of the view that an idea or belief is true if it 'works' was apt to suggest the conclusion that even a falsehood could be called 'true' if it were useful or expedient to believe it. But when James speaks about a theory 'working', he means that it 'must mediate between all previous truths and certain new experiences. It must derange common sense and previous belief as little as possible, and it must lead to some sensible terminus or other that can be verified exactly. To "work" means both these things.'[1]

Misunderstanding was also caused by the way in which James spoke of satisfaction as a basic element in truth. For his way of speaking suggested that in his view a belief could be accounted true if it caused a subjective feeling of satisfaction, and that he was thus opening the door to every kind of wishful thinking. But this was not at any rate his intention. 'Truth in science is what gives us the maximum possible sum of satisfaction, taste included, but consistency both with previous truth and with novel fact is always the most imperious claimant.'[2] The successful 'working' of an hypothesis, in the sense explained above, involves the satisfaction of an interest. But the hypothesis is not accepted simply because one wishes it to be true. If, however, there is no evidence which compels us to choose one rather than the other of two hypotheses which purport to explain the same set of phenomena, it is a matter of scientific 'taste' to choose the more economical or the more elegant hypothesis.

It is indeed true that in his famous essay on *The Will to Believe* James explicitly declares that 'our passional nature not only lawfully may, but must, decide our option between propositions, whenever it is a genuine option that cannot by its nature be decided on intellectual grounds'.[3] But he makes it clear that by a genuine option he means one 'of the forced, living, and momentous kind'.[4] That is to say, when it is a question of a living and important issue, one which influences conduct, when we cannot avoid

---

[1] *Pragmatism*, pp. 216–17. [2] *Ibid.*, p. 217.
[3] *The Will to Believe*, p. 11. [4] *Ibid.*, p. 3.

choosing one of two beliefs, and when the issue cannot be decided on intellectual grounds, we are entitled to choose on 'passional' grounds, to exercise the will to believe, provided that we recognize our option for what it is. It is then a question of the right to believe in certain circumstances. And whether one agrees with James's thesis or not, one should not represent him as claiming that we are entitled to believe any proposition which affords us consolation or satisfaction, even if the balance of evidence goes to show that the proposition is false.[1] It is true, for instance, that according to James we are entitled, other things being equal, to embrace a view of reality which satisfies the moral side of our nature better than another view. And it is by no means everyone who would agree with him. But this is no reason for disregarding the qualification 'other things being equal', where 'other things' include, of course, already known truths and the conclusions deducible from them.

Though, however, we should be careful not to caricature the pragmatist theory of truth, it by no means follows that it is immune from serious criticism. One obvious line of criticism, attributed by James to the 'rationalists', is that in so far as it identifies truth with verification the pragmatist theory confuses the truth of a proposition with the process of showing that it is true. This was one of Peirce's objections to turning pragmatism from a method of determining meaning into a theory of truth.

James's reply is to challenge his critic, the rationalist as he calls him, to explain 'what the *word* true *means*, as applied to a statement, without invoking the *concept of the statement's workings*'.[2] In James's opinion the rationalist cannot explain what he means by correspondence with reality without referring to the practical consequences of the proposition in question, to what would verify or validate it, if it were true. The rationalist thus implicitly commits himself to the pragmatist theory of truth, though he proposes to attack it in the name of a different theory.

In a discussion of this topic confusion is only too apt to arise. Suppose that I say that the statement that Julius Caesar crossed the Rubicon is true in virtue of its correspondence with reality, with historical fact. And suppose that I am asked to explain what

---

[1] One might, however, object against James's thesis that if a question is in principle unanswerable on intellectual grounds, it cannot, on the pragmatist analysis of meaning, be a meaningful question, and that in this case the issue of belief or unbelief does not arise.

[2] *The Meaning of Truth*, p. 221.

I mean by this relation of correspondence with reality. I can hardly do so without mentioning the state of affairs or, rather, the action or series of actions which are referred to in the statement. And it is perfectly true that the occurrence of this series of actions at an assignable date in history is ultimately what validates or 'verifies' the statement. In this sense I cannot explain what I mean by correspondence without referring to what would validate or verify the statement. At the same time the term 'verification' would normally be understood to refer to the measures which we might conceivably take to show that a statement is true, when we already know what the statement means. That is to say, verification would normally be understood as referring to conceivable means of showing that the state of affairs which must obtain or must have obtained if the statement is true actually does or did obtain. And if verification is understood in this sense, it seems perfectly correct to say with the 'rationalist' that it is a case of *showing* a statement to be true rather than of *making* it true.

We might, however, first define 'true' in such a way that it would follow logically that only an actually verified statement is true. A statement which could be verified but has not yet been verified would then be potentially true, a truth *in posse*. But it is evident that James does not regard the pragmatist theory of truth as being simply and solely the result of arbitrary definition. Hence it is not unreasonable to claim that the theory is acceptable or unacceptable according as it is reduced or not reduced to a thesis which, once understood, appears obvious. That is to say, if it is reduced to the thesis that an empirical statement is true or false according as the state of affairs asserted or denied is (was or will be) the case or not, the theory is acceptable, though what is stated is 'trivial'. If, however, the theory identifies the truth of a statement with the process which would show that the state of affairs asserted or denied is the case or not, it is very difficult to see how it does not stand wide open to the objections of the 'rationalists'.

It is not suggested that these remarks constitute an adequate answer to James's question about the nature of correspondence. From the point of view of a professional logician to say, for example, that a proposition is a copy or picture of reality simply will not do. Even apart from the fact that it will not fit the propositions of pure mathematics and formal logic,[1] it is far too

---

[1] For James such propositions are truths *in posse*, which are made (actually) true by successful application, by their 'working'. But this implies that they are empirical hypotheses, a view which is not favoured by most modern logicians.

imprecise a description of the relation between a true empirical proposition and the state of affairs asserted or denied. And it is to James's credit that he saw this. But it is worth noting that he also seems to have felt that his theory of truth ran the risk of being reduced to a triviality. For he says that one can expect the theory to be first attacked, then to be admitted as true but obvious and insignificant, and finally to be regarded as 'so important that its adversaries claim that they themselves discovered it'.[1] If, however, the theory contains something more than what is 'obvious', it is this something more which we may well be inclined to consider the questionable element in James's pragmatism.

4. How does pragmatism stand to radical empiricism? According to James, there is no logical connection between them. Radical empiricism 'stands on its own feet. One may entirely reject it and still be a pragmatist.'[2] And yet he also tells us that 'the establishment of the pragmatist theory of truth is a step of first rate importance in making radical empiricism prevail'.[3]

Up to a certain point James is doubtless justified in saying that radical empiricism and pragmatism are independent of one another. For instance, it is perfectly possible to hold that relations are as real as their terms and that the world has a continuous structure without accepting the pragmatist conceptions of meaning and truth. At the same time the postulate of radical empiricism is, as we have seen, that only those matters should be considered as subjects of philosophical debate which are definable in terms derived from experience. And the pragmatist is said to hold of the truth-relation that 'everything in it is experienceable. ... The "workableness" which ideas must have, in order to be true, means particular workings, physical or intellectual, actual or possible, which they may set up from next to next inside of concrete experience.'[4] In other words, pragmatism will regard as possessing a claim to truth only those ideas which can be interpreted in terms of experienceable 'workings'. And acceptance of this view would obviously tend to make radical empiricism prevail, if by radical empiricism we mean the above-mentioned postulate.

We can put the matter in this way. Pragmatism, James remarks, has 'no doctrines save its method'.[5] Radical empiricism, however, which James develops into a metaphysics or world-view, has its

[1] *Pragmatism*, p. 198.   [2] *Ibid.*, p. ix.
[3] *The Meaning of Truth*, p. xii.   [4] *Ibid.*, p. xiv.
[5] *Pragmatism*, p. 54.

doctrines. These doctrines, considered in themselves, can be held on other grounds than those provided by radical empiricism. This is true, for example, of belief in God. But in James's view the use of the pragmatist theory of truth or method of determining truth and falsity would contribute greatly to making the doctrines of radical empiricism prevail. He may have been over-optimistic in thinking this; but it is what he thought.

Now, James also makes use of the word 'humanism' to describe his philosophy. In a narrower sense of the term he uses it to refer to the pragmatist theory of truth when considered as emphasizing the 'human' element in belief and knowledge. For example, 'humanism says that satisfactoriness is what distinguishes the true from the false'.[1] It sees that truth is reached 'by ever substituting more satisfactory for less satisfactory opinions'.[2] We have already noted that James tries to avoid pure subjectivism by insisting that a belief cannot be accounted satisfactory and so true, if it is incompatible with previously verified beliefs or if the available evidence tells against it. But in his view no belief can be final, in the sense of being incapable of revision. And this is precisely what the 'humanist' sees. He sees, for example, that our categories of thought have been developed in the course of experience, and that even if we cannot help employing them, they might conceivably change in the future course of evolution.

To borrow a Nietzschean phrase, the humanist understands that our beliefs are human, all-too-human. And it is in this sense that we should understand James's definition of humanism as the doctrine that *'though one part of our experience may lean upon another part to make it what it is in any one of several aspects in which it may be considered, experience as a whole is self-containing and leans on nothing'*.[3] What he means is that while there are standards which grow up *within* experience, there is no absolute standard of truth *outside* all experience, to which all our truths must conform. The humanist regards truth as relative to changing experience, and so as relative to man; and he regards absolute truth as 'that ideal vanishing-point towards which we imagine that all our temporary truths will some day converge'.[4] And, to do him justice, James is prepared to apply this outlook to humanism itself.[5]

---

[1] *Essays in Radical Empiricism*, p. 253.   [2] *Ibid.*, p. 255.
[3] *The Meaning of Truth*, p. 124.   [4] *Ibid.*, p. 85.
[5] See, for example, *The Meaning of Truth*, p. 90.

The term 'humanism', however, is also used by James in a wider sense. Thus he tells us that the issue between pragmatism and rationalism, and so between humanism and rationalism, is not simply a logical or epistemological issue: *'it concerns the structure of the universe itself'*.[1] The pragmatist sees the universe as unfinished, changing, growing and plastic. The rationalist, however, maintains that there is one 'really real' universe, which is complete and changeless. James is thinking partly of 'Vivekanda's mystical One'.[2] But he is also thinking, of course, of Bradley's monism, according to which change is not fully real and degrees of truth are measured in relation to a unique absolute experience which transcends our apprehension.[3]

Now, James himself remarks that the definition of humanism which is quoted above in the last paragraph but one seems at first sight to exclude theism and pantheism. But he insists that this is not really the case. 'I myself read humanism theistically and pluralistically.'[4] Humanism thus becomes a pluralistic and theistic metaphysics or world-view, coinciding with developed radical empiricism. But James's theism can be considered separately in the next section.

5. When discussing the application of pragmatism as a method to substantial philosophical problems, James remarks that Berkeley's criticism of the idea of material substance was thoroughly pragmatist in character. For Berkeley gives the 'cash-value',[5] as James puts it, of the term 'material substance' in ideas or sensations. Similarly, when examining the concept of the soul Hume and his successors 'redescend into the stream of experience with it, and cash it into so much small-change value in the way of "ideas" and their peculiar connections with each other'.[6]

James himself applies the pragmatist method to a problem of intimate personal concern, namely to the issue between theism and materialism. In the first place we can consider theism and materialism retrospectively, as James puts it. That is to say, we can suppose that the theist and the materialist see the world itself and its history in the same way, and that the theist then adds the hypothesis of a God who set the world going, while the materialist

---

[1] *Pragmatism*, p. 259.   [2] *Ibid.*, p. 262.
[3] James relates rival theories of the universe to different types of temperament.
[4] *The Meaning of Truth*, p. 125.
[5] James's talk about cash-value is apt to create an unfortunate impression. But he is referring, of course, to analyzing ideas on beliefs in terms of their 'practical consequences'.
[6] *Pragmatism*, p. 92.

excludes this hypothesis as unnecessary and invokes 'matter' instead. How are we to choose between these two positions? On pragmatist principles at any rate we cannot choose. For 'if no future detail of experience or conduct is to be deduced from our hypothesis, the debate between materialism and theism becomes quite idle and insignificant'.[1]

When, however, theism and materialism are considered 'prospectively', in relation to what they promise, to the expectations which they respectively lead us to entertain, the situation is quite different. For materialism leads us to expect a state of the universe in which human ideals, human achievements, consciousness and the products of thought will be as if they had never been,[2] whereas theism 'guarantees an ideal order that shall be permanently preserved'.[3] Somehow or other God will not allow the moral order to suffer shipwreck and destruction.

Looked at from this point of view, therefore, theism and materialism are very different. And on pragmatist principles we are entitled, other things being equal, to embrace that belief which corresponds best with the demands of our moral nature. But James does not mean to imply that there is no evidence at all in favour of theism, other than a desire that it should be true. 'I myself believe that the evidence for God lies primarily in inner personal experiences.'[4] In *A Pluralistic Universe* he resumes what he has already maintained in *The Varieties of Religious Experience* by arguing that 'the believer is continuous, to his own consciousness at any rate, with a wider self from which saving experiences flow in'.[5] Again, 'the drift of all the evidence we have seems to me to sweep us very strongly towards the belief in some form of superhuman life with which we may, unknown to ourselves, be co-conscious'.[6] At the same time the evil and suffering in the world suggest the conclusion that this superhuman consciousness is finite, in the sense that God is limited 'either in power, or in knowledge, or in both at once'.[7]

This idea of a finite God is used by James in his substitution of 'meliorism' for optimism on the one hand and pessimism on the other. According to the meliorist the world is not necessarily becoming better, nor is it necessarily becoming worse: it *can*

---

[1] *Ibid.*, p. 99.
[2] James quotes a well-known passage from A. J. Balfour's *The Foundations of Belief* (p. 30).
[3] *Pragmatism*, p. 106.
[4] *Ibid.*, p. 109.
[5] *A Pluralistic Universe*, p. 307.
[6] *Ibid.*
[7] *Ibid.*, p. 311.

become better, if, that is to say, man freely co-operates with the finite God in making it better.[1] In other words, the future is not inevitably determined, either for better or for worse, not even by God. There is room in the universe for novelty, and human effort has a positive contribution to make in the establishment of a moral order.

James thus used pragmatism to support a religious world-view. But we have seen that when stating the pragmatist theory of meaning he declared that our whole conception of an object is reducible to our ideas of the 'conceivable effects of a practical kind the object may involve',[2] explicitly mentioning the sensations we may expect and the reactions we should prepare. And we may well doubt whether this is a promising foundation for a theistic world-view. But as was noted in the section on his life, the reconciliation of a scientific with a religious outlook constituted for him a personal problem. And taking a theory of truth which was built on to a theory of meaning that originated in an analysis of empirical hypotheses, he used it to support the only world-view which really satisfied him. In the process, of course, he extended the concept of experience far beyond sense-experience. Thus he maintained that religious empiricism is much more truly 'empirical' than irreligious empiricism, inasmuch as the former takes seriously the varieties of religious experience whereas the latter does not. In a sense his problem was the same as that of Kant, to reconcile the scientific outlook with man's moral and religious consciousness. His instrument of unification or harmonization was pragmatism. The result was presented as the development of radical empiricism. And the attitude adopted was described as humanism.

6. The pragmatist movement was above all an American phenomenon. True, one can find manifestations of the pragmatist attitude even in German philosophy. In the seventh volume of this *History* mention was made of the emphasis laid by F. A. Lange[3] on the value for life of metaphysical theories and religious doctrines at the expense of their cognitive value, and the way in which Hans Vaihinger[4] developed what we may call a pragmatist view of truth which had obvious affinities with Nietzsche's fiction-theory.[5] Attention was also drawn to the influence exercised on

---

[1] James applied the pragmatist method to the issue between the theories of free will and determinism, as also to that between pluralism and monism.
[2] *Pragmatism*, p. 47.
[3] Vol. VII, p. 366.
[4] *Ibid.*, pp. 366–7.
[5] *Ibid.*, pp. 408–10.

William James by G. T. Fechner,[1] especially through his distinction between the 'day' and 'night' views of the universe and his claim that, other things being equal, we are entitled to give preference to the view which most contributes to human happiness and cultural development. As for French thought, mention was made in the first section of this chapter of the help derived by James from the writings of Charles Renouvier. And Renouvier, it may be noted, maintained that belief and even certitude are not exclusively intellectual affairs, but that affirmation involves also feeling and will. Though, however, we can certainly find affinities with pragmatism not only in German but also in French thought,[2] the pragmatist movement remains primarily associated with the names of three American philosophers, Peirce, James and Dewey.

This does not mean that England was without its pragmatist movement. But English pragmatism was neither so influential nor so impressive as its American counterpart. It would not be possible to give a reasonable account of American philosophy without including pragmatism. Peirce was an outstanding thinker on any count and nobody would question the influence exercised by James and Dewey on intellectual life in the United States. They brought philosophy to the fore, so to speak, to public notice; and Dewey especially applied it in the educational and social fields. But no great sin of omission would be committed if in an account of the development of modern British philosophy no mention were made of pragmatism, even though it caused a temporary flutter in the philosophical dovecotes. However, in an account of nineteenth-century British thought in which allusion has been made to a considerable number of minor philosophers some mention of pragmatism seems to be desirable.

In 1898 the Oxford Philosophical Society was founded, and an outcome of its discussions was the publication in 1902 of *Personal Idealism*, edited by Henry Sturt. In his preface to this collection of essays by eight members of the Society Sturt explained that the contributors were concerned with developing the theme of personality and with defending personality against naturalism on the one hand and absolute idealism on the other. The naturalist

---

[1] Vol. VII, pp. 375–6. James refers frequently to Fechner in his writings.
[2] It is worth mentioning that Maurice Blondel once used the term *pragmatism* for his philosophy of action. But when he became acquainted with American pragmatism, he dropped the term, as he did not agree with the interpretation given to it by William James.

maintains that the human person is a transitory product of physical processes, while the absolute idealist holds that personality is an unreal appearance of the Absolute.[1] In fine, 'Naturalism and Absolutism, antagonistic as they seem to be, combine in assuring us that personality is an illusion'.[2] Oxford idealism, Sturt went on to say, had always been opposed to naturalism; and to this extent absolute and personal idealism maintained a common front. But for this very reason the personal idealists felt that absolute idealism was a more insidious adversary than naturalism. The absolute idealists adopted the impracticable course of trying to criticize human experience from the point of view of absolute experience. And it failed to give any adequate recognition to the volitional aspect of human nature. Absolute idealism, in brief, was insufficiently empirical. And Sturt suggested 'empirical idealism' as an appropriate name for personal idealism. For personal life is what is closest to us and best known by us.

Needless to say, personal idealism and pragmatism are not interchangeable terms. Of the eight contributors to *Personal Idealism* some became well known outside the sphere of philosophy. R. R. Marett, the anthropologist, is an example. Others, such as G. F. Stout, were philosophers but not pragmatists. The volume contained, however, an essay by F. C. S. Schiller, who was the principal champion of pragmatism in England. And the point which we have been trying to make is that British pragmatism had a background of what we may call 'humanism'. It was to a considerable extent a protest on behalf of the human person not only against naturalism but also against the absolute idealism which was then the dominant factor in Oxford philosophy. It thus had more affinity with the pragmatism of William James than with the pragmatism of Peirce, which was essentially a method or rule for determining the meaning of concepts.

Ferdinand Canning Scott Schiller (1864–1937), came of German ancestry, though he was educated in England. In 1893 he became an instructor at Cornell University in America. In 1897 he was elected to a Tutorial Fellowship at Corpus Christi College, Oxford; and he remained a Fellow of the College until his death, though in 1929 he accepted a chair of philosophy in the University of Southern California at Los Angeles. In 1891 he published anony-

---

[1] Strictly speaking, Bradley did not hold that personality is an 'unreal appearance' of the Absolute. It is a real appearance; but, being appearance, it cannot be fully real.

[2] *Personal Idealism*, p. vi.

mously *Riddles of the Sphinx*,[1] and this was followed in 1902 by his essay, *Axioms as Postulates*, in *Personal Idealism*, the volume referred to above. *Humanism: Philosophical Essays* appeared in 1903, *Studies in Humanism* in 1907, *Plato or Protagoras?* in 1908, *Formal Logic* in 1912, *Problems of Belief* and *Tantalus, or The Future of Man* in 1924, *Eugenics and Politics* in 1926, *Logic for Use* in 1929 and *Must Philosophers Disagree? and Other Essays in Popular Philosophy* in 1934. Schiller also contributed a paper entitled *Why Humanism?* to the first series of *Contemporary British Philosophy* (1924), edited by J. H. Muirhead, and wrote the article on pragmatism for the fourteenth edition of the *Encyclopaedia Britannica* (1929).

7. As the titles of his writings suggest, Schiller's thought centres round man. In his essay *Plato or Protagoras?* he explicitly places himself on the side of Protagoras and makes his own the famous dictum that man is the measure of all things. *In Riddles of the Sphinx*, where he had attacked the absolute idealist theory of the One in the name of pluralistic personalism, he had declared that all our thinking must be anthropomorphic. But he did not at first use the term 'pragmatism' to describe his humanistic outlook. And in the preface to the first edition of *Humanism*, written after he had come under the influence of American pragmatism, especially that of William James, Schiller remarks that 'I was surprised to find that I had all along been a pragmatist myself without knowing it, and that little but the name was lacking to my own advocacy of an essentially cognate position in 1892'.[2] But though Schiller makes frequent use of the term 'pragmatism', once he has taken it over from William James, he insists that humanism is the basic concept. Humanism, which holds that man, and not the Absolute, is the measure of all experience and the maker of the sciences, is the fundamental and permanent attitude of thought of James and himself. Pragmatism 'is in reality only the application of Humanism to the theory of knowledge'.[3] The general need is to re-humanize the universe.

Re-humanization of the universe, humanism in other words, demands in the first place a humanization of logic. This demand is in part a protest against the arid subtleties and mental gymnastics

---

[1] A second edition, with the author's name, appeared in 1894 and a new edition in 1910.

[2] *Humanism*, p. xiii (2nd edition, 1912). Schiller's reference is to an essay, *Reality and Idealism*, which he published in 1892. It is reprinted in *Humanism*, pp. 110–27.

[3] *Ibid.*, p. xxv.

of formal logicians who treat logic as a game to be played for its own sake, a protest which, Schiller notes, was expressed by Albert Sidgwick, himself a logician, whose first work bore the title *Fallacies: A View of Logic from the Practical Side* (1883). But Schiller's demand for a humanization of logic is much more than a protest against the aridities and hair-splitting of some logicians. For it rests on the conviction that logic does not represent a realm of absolute and timeless truth which is unaffected by human interest and purposes. In Schiller's view the idea of absolute truth is an *'ignis fatuus'*,[1] in formal logic as well as in empirical science. The fundamental principles or axioms of logic are not *a priori* necessary truths; they are postulates, demands on experience,[2] which have shown themselves to possess a wider and more lasting value for the fulfilment of human purposes than is possessed by other postulates. And to bring out this aspect of the principles or axioms of logic is one of the tasks involved in the humanization of this science.

But we can go considerably further than this. The pragmatist believes that the validity of any logical procedure is shown by its successful working. But it works only in concrete contexts. And it is therefore idle to suppose that complete abstraction from all subject-matter introduces us into a realm of changeless, absolute truth. Indeed, Schiller goes so far as to say that formal logic *'is in the strictest and completest sense meaningless'*.[3] If someone says, 'it is too light' and we do not know the context, his statement is for us meaningless. For we do not know whether he is referring to the weight of an object, to the colour of something or to the quality of a lecture or a book. Similarly, we cannot abstract completely from the use of logic, from its application, *'without incurring thereby a total loss, not only of truth but also of meaning'*.[4]

If, therefore, logical principles are postulates made in the light of human desires and purposes, and if their validity depends on their success in fulfilling these desires and purposes, it follows that we cannot divorce logic from psychology. 'Logical value must be found in psychological fact *or nowhere*. . . . Logical possibilities (or even "necessities") are nothing until they have somehow become psychologically actual and active.'[5] So much for all attempts to de-psychologize logic and to set it on its own feet.

---

[1] *Contemporary British Philosophy*, First Series, p. 401.
[2] See *Axioms as Postulates* in *Personal Idealism*, p. 64.
[3] *Formal Logic*, p. 382.   [4] *Ibid.*, p. ix.
[5] *Axioms as Postulates* in *Personal Idealism*, p. 124.

What has been said of logical truth, namely that it is relative to human desires and aims, can be said of truth in general. Truths are in fact valuations. That is to say, to assert that a proposition is true is to say that it possesses practical value by fulfilling a certain purpose. 'Truth is the useful, efficient, workable, to which our practical experience tends to restrict our truth-valuations.'[1] Conversely, the false is the useless, what does not work. This is *'the great Pragmatist principle of selection'*.[2]

Schiller sees, of course, that ' "working" is clearly a vague generic term, and it is legitimate to ask what precisely is covered by it'.[3] But he finds this a difficult question to answer. It is comparatively easy to explain what is meant by the working of a scientific hypothesis. But it is not at all so easy to explain, for example, what forms of 'working' are to be accounted relevant to assessing the truth of an ethical theory. We have to admit that 'men take up different attitudes towards different workings because they themselves are temperamentally different'.[4] In other words, no clear and precise general answer can be given to the question.

As one would expect, Schiller is anxious to show that a distinction can be made on pragmatist principles between 'all truths are useful' and 'everything useful is true'. One of his arguments is that 'useful' means useful for a particular purpose, which is determined by the general context of a statement. For example, if I were threatened with torture if I did not say that the earth is flat, it would certainly be useful for me to say this. But the utility of my statement would not make it true. For statements about the shape of the earth pertain to empirical science; and it is certainly not useful for the advancement of science to assert that the earth is flat.

Another way of dealing with the matter is to insist on social recognition. But Schiller is alive to the fact that to recognize a truth is to recognize it as true. And on his principles to recognize it as true is to recognize it as useful. Hence social recognition cannot make a proposition useful, and so true. It is accorded to propositions which have already shown their utility. 'The use-criterion selects the individual truth-valuations, and constitutes thereby the objective truth which obtains social recognition.'[5]

Schiller tends to fall back on a biological interpretation of truth

---

[1] *Humanism*, p. 59.   [2] *Ibid.*, p. 58.
[3] *Contemporary British Philosophy*, First Series, p. 405.
[4] *Ibid.*, p. 406.   [5] *Humanism*, p. 59.

and to stress the idea of survival-value.[1] There is a process of natural selection among truths. Truths of inferior value are eliminated, while truths of superior value survive. And the belief which proves to have most survival-value shows itself to be the most useful, and so the most true. But what is survival-value? It can be described as 'a sort of working, which, while wholly devoid of any rational appeal, yet exercises a far-reaching influence on our beliefs, and is capable of determining this adoption and the elimination of their contraries'.[2] So we are back once more with the admittedly imprecise and vague idea of 'working'.

As we have seen, Schiller maintains that from 'all truths are useful' it does not follow that 'any proposition which is useful is true'. This is perfectly correct, of course. But then one might quite well hold that all truths are 'useful' in some sense or other without holding that their utility constitutes their truth. If one *does* hold that truth is constituted by utility, one can hardly deny at the same time that every useful proposition is true in so far as it is useful. And if the doctrine of non-convertibility is to be maintained successfully one has to show that true propositions possess some property or properties which useful falsehoods do not. Human beings are organisms, but not all organisms are human beings. And this is so because human beings possess properties which are not possessed by all organisms. What are the properties which are peculiar to true propositions over and above a utility which can also be possessed by a proposition which is false? This is a question to which Schiller never really faces up. Mention has been made of Sturt's opinion that absolute idealism did not give sufficient recognition to the volitional side of human nature. One of the troubles with Schiller is that he accords it too much recognition.

Schiller was much less inclined than James to indulge in metaphysical speculation. He did indeed maintain that humanism, an anthropocentric outlook, demands that we should look on the world as 'wholly plastic',[3] as indefinitely modifiable, as what we can make of it. But though he allows that humanists or pragmatists will regard the efforts of metaphysicians with tolerance and will concede aesthetic value to their systems, at the same time 'metaphysics seem doomed to remain *personal guesses* at ultimate reality, and to remain inferior in objective value to the

---

[1] See especially *Logic in Use*, also *Problems of Belief*, chapters XI–XII.
[2] *Contemporary British Philosophy*, First Series, p. 406.
[3] *Axioms as Postulates* in *Personal Idealism*, p. 61.

sciences, which are essentially "common" *methods* for dealing with phenomena'.[1] Here again we see the difficulty encountered by Schiller in explaining precisely what 'working' can mean outside the sphere of scientific hypotheses. So he attributes aesthetic value rather than truth-value to metaphysical theories. This is obviously because he regards scientific hypotheses as empirically verifiable whereas metaphysical systems are not. And we are back again with the question whether verification, a species of 'working', does not show an hypothesis to be true (or tend to show it) rather than constitute its truth.

Schiller's main contribution to pragmatism lay in his treatment of logic, which was more professional and detailed than that of William James. But his overall interpretation of logic cannot be said to have demonstrated its 'survival-value'.

[1] *Contemporary British Philosophy*, First Series, p. 409.

CHAPTER XVI

THE EXPERIMENTALISM OF JOHN DEWEY

Life and writings—Naturalistic empiricism: thought, experience and knowledge—The function of philosophy—Instrumentalism: logic and truth—Moral theory—Some implications in social and educational theory—Religion in a naturalistic philosophy —Some critical comments on Dewey's philosophy.

1. JOHN DEWEY (1859–1952) was born at Burlington, Vermont. After studying at the University of Vermont he became a high school teacher. But his interest in philosophy led him to submit to W. T. Harris an essay on the metaphysical assumptions of materialism with a view to publication in *The Journal of Speculative Philosophy*,[1] and the encouragement which he received resulted in his entering Johns Hopkins University in 1882. At the university Dewey attended courses on logic by C. S. Peirce, but the chief influence on his mind was exercised by G. S. Morris, the idealist, with whom Dewey entered into relations of personal friendship.

From 1884 until 1888 Dewey lectured at the University of Michigan, first as an instructor in philosophy and later as an assistant professor, after which he spent a year as professor at the University of Minnesota. In 1889 he returned to Michigan as head of the department of philosophy, and he occupied this post until 1894 when he went to Chicago. During this period Dewey occupied himself with logical, psychological and ethical questions, and his mind moved away from the idealism which he had learned from Morris.[2] In 1887 he published *Psychology*, in 1891 *Outlines of a Critical Theory of Ethics*, and in 1894 *The Study of Ethics: A Syllabus*.

From 1894 until 1904 Dewey was head of the department of philosophy in the University of Chicago, where he founded his Laboratory School[3] in 1896. The publications of this period include *My Pedagogic Creed* (1897), *The School and Society* (1900), *Studies in Logical Theory* (1903) and *Logical Conditions of a Scientific Treatment of Morality* (1903).

---

[1] The article was published in the issue of April, 1882.
[2] In this connection Dewey notes the influence exercised on his mind by William James's *Principles of Psychology*.
[3] An experimental school, commonly known as The Dewey School.

In 1904 Dewey went as professor of philosophy to Columbia University, becoming professor emeritus in 1929.[1] In 1908 he published *Ethics*,[2] in 1910 *How We Think* and *The Influence of Darwin and Other Essays in Contemporary Thought*, in 1915 *Schools of Tomorrow*, in 1916 *Democracy and Education* and *Essays in Experimental Logic*, in 1920 *Reconstruction in Philosophy*, in 1922 *Human Nature and Conduct*, in 1925 *Experience and Nature*, and in 1929 *The Quest for Certainty*. As for later publications *Art as Experience* and *A Common Faith* appeared in 1934, *Experience and Education* and *Logic: The Theory of Inquiry* in 1938, *Theory of Valuation* in 1939, *Education Today* in 1940, *Problems of Men* in 1946 and *Knowing and The Known* in 1949.

Outside the United States at least Dewey is probably best known for his instrumentalism, his version of pragmatism. But he was certainly not the man to concern himself simply with general theories about thought and truth. As the foregoing partial list of his publications indicates, he was deeply interested in problems of value and of human conduct, of society and of education. In the last-named field especially he exercised a great influence in America. Obviously, his ideas did not win universal acceptance. But they could not be ignored. And, in general, we can say that William James and John Dewey were the two thinkers who did most to bring philosophy to the attention of the educated public in the United States.

2. Dewey often describes his philosophy as empirical naturalism or naturalistic empiricism. And the meaning of these descriptions can perhaps best be illustrated by saying something about his account of the nature and function of thought. We can begin by considering the bearing in this context of the term 'naturalism'.

In the first place thought is not for Dewey an ultimate, an absolute, a process which creates objective reality in a metaphysical sense. Nor is it something in man which represents a non-natural element, in the sense that it sets man above or over against Nature. It is in the long run a highly developed form of the active relation between a living organism and its environment. To be sure, in spite of a tendency to use behaviourist language Dewey is well aware that the intellectual life of man has its own peculiar characteristics. The point is, however, that he refuses to start, for instance, from the distinction between subject and object as from

---

[1] During this period Dewey made several journeys abroad, to Europe, the Far East, Mexico and, in 1928, to Russia.
[2] Written in collaboration with J. H. Tufts.

an absolute and ultimate point of departure, but sees man's intellectual life as presupposing and developing out of antecedent relations, and thus as falling wholly within the sphere of Nature. Thought is one among other natural processes or activities.

All things react in some way to their environment. But they obviously do not all react in the same way. In a given set of circumstances an inanimate thing, for example, can be said simply to react or not to react. A situation does not pose any problem which the thing can recognize as a problem and to which it can react in a selective manner. When, however, we turn to the sphere of life, we find selective responses. As living organisms become more complex, their environment becomes more ambivalent. That is to say, it becomes more uncertain what responses or actions are called for in the interests of living, what actions will best fit into a series which will sustain the continuity of life. And 'in the degree that responses take place to the doubtful *as* the doubtful, they acquire *mental* quality'.[1] Further, when such responses possess a directed tendency to change the precarious into the secure and the problematic into the resolved, 'they are *intellectual* as well as mental'.[2]

We can say therefore that for Dewey thought is a highly developed form of the relation between stimulus and response on the purely biological level. True, in its interaction with its environment the human organism, like any other organism, acts primarily according to established habits. But situations arise which reflection recognizes as problematic situations, and thus as calling for inquiry or thought, the immediate response being thus in a sense interrupted. But in another sense the response is not interrupted. For the aim of thought, stimulated by a problematic situation, is to transform or reconstruct the set of antecedent conditions which gave rise to the problem or difficulty. In other words, it aims at a change in the environment. 'There is no inquiry that does not involve the making of *some* change in environing conditions.'[3] That is to say, the conclusion at which the process of inquiry arrives is a projected action or set of actions, a plan of possible action which will transform the problematic situation. Thought is thus instrumental and has a practical function. It is not, however, quite accurate to say that it subserves activity. For it is itself a form of activity. And it can be seen as part of a total process of activity whereby man seeks to resolve problematic

---

[1] *The Quest for Certainty*, p. 225.   [2] *Ibid.*   [3] *Logic*, I, p. 42.

situations by effecting changes in his environment, by changing an 'indeterminate' situation, one in which the elements clash or do not harmonize and so give rise to a problem for reflection, into a 'determinate' situation, a unified whole. In this sense, therefore, thought does not interrupt the process of response; for it is itself part of the total response. But the process of inquiry presupposes recognition of a problematic situation *as* problematic. It can thus be said to interrupt the response, if we mean by response one that is instinctive or follows simply in accordance with some established habit.

A man can, of course, react to a problematic situation in an unintelligent manner. To take a simple example, he may lose his temper and smash a tool or instrument which is not functioning properly. But this sort of reaction is clearly unhelpful. To solve his problem the man has to inquire into what is wrong with the instrument and consider how to put things right. And the conclusion at which he arrives is a plan of possible action calculated to transform the problematic situation.

This is an example taken from the level of common sense. But Dewey will not allow that there is any impassable gulf or rigid distinction between the level of common sense and that of, say, science. Scientific inquiry may involve prolonged operations which are not overt actions in the ordinary sense but operations with symbols. Yet the total process of hypothesis, deduction and controlled experiment simply reproduces in a much more sophisticated and complex form the process of inquiry which is stimulated by some practical problem in everyday life. Even the complicated operations with symbols aim at transforming the problematic situation which gave rise to the hypothesis. Thus thought is always practical in some way, whether it takes place at the level of common sense or at the level of scientific theory. In both cases it is a way of dealing with a problematic situation.

It is to be noted that when Dewey speaks of effecting a change in the environment, the last-mentioned term should not be understood as referring exclusively to man's physical environment, the world of physical Nature. 'The environment in which human beings live, act and inquire, is not simply physical. It is cultural as well.'[1] And a clash of values, for example, in a given society gives rise to a problematic situation, the resolution of which would effect a change in the cultural environment.

[1] *Ibid.*, p. 42.

This account of thought and its basic function corresponds with the fact that 'man who lives in a world of hazards is compelled to seek for security'.[1] And it is, of course, obvious that when man is faced with threatening and perilous situations, recognized as such, it is action which is called for, not simply thought. At the same time Dewey is, needless to say, well aware that inquiry and thought do not necessarily lead to action in the ordinary sense. For example, a scientist's inquiry may terminate in an idea or set of ideas, that is, in a scientific theory or hypothesis. Dewey's account of thought does indeed entail the view that 'ideas are anticipatory plans and designs which take effect in concrete reconstruction of antecedent conditions of existence'.[2] A scientific hypothesis is predictive, and it thus looks forward, so to speak, to verification. But the scientist may not be in a position to verify it here or now. Or he may not choose to do so. His inquiry then terminates in a set of ideas; and he does not possess warranted knowledge. But this does not alter the fact that the ideas are predictive, that they are plans for possible action.

Analogously, if a man is stimulated to inquiry or reflection by a morally problematic situation, the moral judgment which he finally makes is a plan or directive for possible action. When a man commits himself to a moral principle, he expresses his preparedness to act in certain ways in certain circumstances. But though his thought is thus directed to action, action does not necessarily follow. The judgment which he makes is a direction for possible action.

Now, there is a real sense in which each problematic situation is unique and unrepeatable. And when Dewey is thinking of this aspect of the matter, he tends to depreciate general theories. But it is obvious that the scientist works with general concepts and theories; and Dewey's recognition of the fact is shown in his insistence that a theory's connection with action is 'with *possible* ways of operation rather than with those found to be *actually* and immediately required'.[3] At the same time the tension between a tendency to depreciate general concepts and theories, in view of the fact that inquiry is stimulated by particular problematic situations and aims at transforming them, and a recognition of the fact that scientific thought operates with general ideas and constructs general theories, general solutions, shows itself in what

---

[1] *The Quest for Certainty*, p. 3.   [2] *Ibid.*, p. 166.
[3] *Logic*, p. 49.

Dewey has to say about the nature of philosophy. But this matter can be left to the next section.

We have seen that Dewey's account of thought is 'naturalistic' in the sense that it depicts thought as developing out of the relation between an organism and its environment. 'Intellectual operations are foreshadowed in behaviour of the biological kind, and the latter prepares the way for the former.'[1] Naturalism does not deny differences, of course, but it is committed to accounting for these differences without invoking any non-natural source or agent. In other words, thought must be represented as a product of evolution.

Further, Dewey's account of thought can be described as 'empiricist' in the sense that thought is depicted as starting from experiences and as leading back to experiences. The process of inquiry is set in motion when the subject encounters a problematic situation in its environment, and it terminates, whether actually or ideally, in some change in the environment, or indeed in man himself. At the same time Dewey asserts that the object of knowledge is made or constructed by thought. And as this statement seems at first sight to represent an idealist rather than an empiricist position, it stands in need of some explanation.

Experience in general is said to be a transaction, a process of doing and undergoing, an active relation between an organism and its environment. And according to Dewey primary or immediate experience is non-cognitive in character. It contains 'no division between act and material, subject and object, but contains them both in an unanalyzed totality'.[2] What is experienced is not objectified by a subject as a sign possessing significance or meaning. Distinctions such as that between subject and object arise only for reflection. And a thing assumes, or, rather, is clothed with significance only as the result of a process of inquiry or thought. A fountain pen, for example, takes on significance for me in terms of its function or functions. And it does so as the result of a process of inquiry or thought. Inasmuch, therefore, as Dewey reserves the term 'object of knowledge' for the term of this process, he can say that thought makes or constructs the object of knowledge.

On the one hand Dewey is at pains to point out that his account of the activity of knowing does not entail the conclusion that

[1] *Ibid.*, p. 43.
[2] *Experience and Nature*, p. 8 (Dover Publications edition 1958).

things do not exist antecedently to being experienced or to being thought about.[1] On the other hand by identifying the object of knowledge with the term of inquiry he is committed to saying that it is in some sense the product of thought. For the term of inquiry is the determinate situation which replaces an indeterminate or problematic situation. Dewey argues, however, that 'knowledge is not a distortion or perversion which confers upon *its* subject-matter traits which *do* not belong to it, but is an act which confers upon non-cognitive material traits which *did* not belong to it'.[2] The resolution of a problematic situation or the process of clothing with determinate significance is no more a distortion or perversion than is the act of the architect who confers upon stone and wood qualities and relations which they did not formerly possess.

If it is asked why Dewey adopts this odd theory of knowledge, which identifies the object of knowledge with the term of the process of inquiry, one reason is that he wishes to get rid of what he calls 'the spectator theory of knowledge'.[3] According to this theory we have on the one hand the knower and on the other the object of knowledge, which is entirely unaffected by the process of knowing. We are then faced with the problem of finding a bridge between the process of knowing which takes place wholly within the spectator-subject and the object which is indifferent to being known. If, however, we understand that the object of knowledge as such comes into being through the process of knowing, this difficulty does not arise.

The statement that the object of knowledge comes into being through the process of knowing might, considered by itself, be a tautology. For it is tautological to say that nothing is constituted an object of knowledge except by being known. But Dewey obviously does not intend the statement to be a tautology: he intends to say something more. And what he intends is to depict the process of knowing as a highly developed form of the active relation between an organism and its environment, a relation whereby a change is effected in the environment. In other words, he is concerned with giving a naturalistic account of knowledge and with excluding any concept of it as a mysterious phenomenon which is entirely *sui generis*. He is also concerned with uniting theory and practice. Hence knowledge is represented as being

---

[1] Dewey remarks, for example, that 'I should think it fairly obvious that we experience most things *as* temporally prior to our experiencing of them', *The Influence of Darwin*, p. 240.

[2] *Experience and Nature*, p. 381.   [3] *The Quest for Certainty*, p. 23.

itself a doing or making rather than, as in the so-called spectator theory, a 'seeing'.

3. Dewey's account of thought and knowledge is obviously relevant to his concept of philosophy and to his judgments about other philosophers. For example, he is sharply opposed to the idea of philosophy as being concerned with a sphere of unchanging, timeless being and truth. We can indeed explain the genesis of this idea. 'The *world* is precarious and perilous.'[1] That is to say, the hazards to which men are exposed are objective situations. And when they are recognized as hazards, they become problematic situations which man seeks to resolve. But his means for doing so are limited. Further, in his search for security, and so for certainty, man becomes aware that the empirical world, which is a changing world, cannot provide him with absolute security and certainty. And we find Greek philosophers such as Plato making a sharp distinction between the changing, empirical world and the sphere of immutable being and truth. Theory thus becomes divorced from practice.[2] True, philosophy remains an activity. For thought is always an activity. But with Aristotle, for example, purely theoretical activity, the life of contemplation, is exalted above the practical life, the life of action in a changing world. And it becomes necessary to recall thought to its true function of being directed to resolving indeterminate or problematic situations by effecting changes in the environment and in man himself. Thought and practice have to be once more joined together.

This union of thought and practice is seen most strikingly in the rise of modern science. In the early stages of history man either tried to control the mysterious and threatening forces of Nature by magic or personified them and sought to appease them, though he also practised simple acts such as that of agriculture. Later, as we have seen, there arose that divorce between theory and practice which was effected by philosophy, the idea of man as spectator being substituted for that of man as actor. But with the rise of modern science a new attitude to change shows itself. For the scientist sees that it is only by correlating phenomena that we can understand the process of change and, within limits, control it, bringing about the changes which we desire and preventing

---

[1] *Experience and Nature*, p. 42.
[2] Dewey is, of course, aware of the practical aspects of the thought of Plato and Aristotle. But he is opposed to the whole idea of a sphere of immutable Being and Truth, and the dichotomy between the sphere of Being and the sphere of Becoming is the aspect of Plato's philosophy which he emphasizes.

those which we regard as undesirable. Thought is thus no longer directed to a celestial sphere of unchanging being and truth; it is redirected to the experienced environment, though on a surer basis than it was in the early stages of humanity. And with the constant growth and progress of the sciences the whole attitude of man towards thought and knowledge has been altered. And this new attitude or vision of the function of thought and knowledge needs to be reflected in our concept of philosophy.

Now, the particular sciences are not themselves philosophy. But science has been commonly conceived as presenting us with the picture of a world which is indifferent to moral values, as eliminating from Nature all qualities and values. And 'thus is created the standing problem of modern philosophy: the relation of science to the things we prize and love and which have authority in the direction of conduct'.[1] This problem, which occupied the mind of, for example, Immanuel Kant, became 'the philosophic version of the popular conflict of science and religion'.[2] And philosophers of the spiritualistic and idealistic traditions, from the time of Kant, or rather from that of Descartes, onwards have tried to solve the problem by saying that the world of science can safely be presented as the sphere of matter and mechanism, stripped of qualities and values, because 'matter and mechanism have their foundation in immaterial mind'.[3] In other words, philosophers have tried to reconcile the scientific view of the world, as they conceived it, with an assertion of the reality of values by developing their several versions of the same sort of dichotomy or dualism which was characteristic of Platonism.

Obviously, Dewey will have nothing to do with this way of solving the problem. For in his view it amounts simply to a resuscitation of an outmoded metaphysics. But though he rejects the notion that there are immutable values, transcending the changing world, he has not the slightest intention of belittling, much less of denying, values. Hence he is committed by his naturalism to maintaining that they are in some sense comprised within Nature, and that advance in scientific knowledge constitutes no threat whatever to the reality of value. 'Why should we not proceed to employ our gains in science to improve our judgments about values, and to regulate our actions so as to make values more secure and more widely shared in existence?'[4] It is not

---

[1] *The Quest for Certainty*, p. 103.   [2] *Ibid.*, p. 41.
[3] *Ibid.*, p. 42.   [4] *Ibid.*

the business of the philosopher to prove in general that there are values. For beliefs about values and value-judgments are inevitable characteristics of man; and any genuine philosophy of experience is aware of this fact. 'What is inevitable needs no proof for its existence.'[1] But man's affections, desires, purposes and devices need direction; and this is possible only through knowledge. Here philosophy can give guidance. The philosopher can examine the accepted values and ideals of a given society in the light of their consequences, and he can at the same time attempt to resolve the conflicts between values and ideals which arise within a society by pointing the way to new possibilities, thus transforming indeterminate or problematic situations in the cultural environment into determinate situations.

The function of philosophy is thus both critical and constructive or, rather, reconstructive. And it is critical with a view to reconstruction. Hence we can say that philosophy is essentially practical. And inasmuch as there is no question of the philosopher competing with the scientist on his own ground, Dewey naturally lays emphasis on moral and social philosophy and on the philosophy of education. True, the philosopher is by no means confined to these topics. As Dewey maintains in *Studies in Logical Theory*, a philosophy of experience includes within its area of inquiry all modes of human experience, including the scientific as well as the moral, religious and aesthetic, and also the social-cultural world in its organized form. And it should investigate the interrelations between these different fields. But if we are thinking of the resolution of specific problematic situations, the philosopher is obviously not in a better position than the scientist to solve scientific problems. From this point of view, therefore, it is natural that Dewey should have come to say that 'the task of future philosophy is to clarify men's ideas as to the social and moral strifes of their own day. Its aim is to become so far as is humanly possible an organ for dealing with these conflicts.'[2]

Now, if the philosopher is conceived as being called upon to throw light on specific problematic situations, it is understandable that general notions and theories should be depreciated. We can understand, for example, Dewey's assertion that whereas philosophical discussion in the past has been carried on 'in terms of *the* state, *the* individual',[3] what is really required is light upon 'this

[1] *Ibid.*, p. 299. [2] *Reconstruction in Philosophy*, p. 26.
[3] *Ibid.*, p. 188.

or that group of individuals, this or that concrete human being, this or that special institution or social arrangement'.[1] In other words, when he is concerned with emphasizing the practical function of philosophy, Dewey tends to depreciate general concepts and theories as divorced from concrete life and experience and as associated with a view of philosophy as a purely contemplative activity. His attitude is an expression of his protest against the divorce of theory from practice.

The reader will doubtless object that it is no more the business of the philosopher as such to solve, for instance, specific political problems than it is to solve specific scientific problems. But Dewey does not really intend to say that it is the philosopher's business to do this. What he claims is that 'the true impact of philosophical reconstruction'[2] is to be found in the development of *methods* for reconstructing specific problematic situations. In other words, Dewey is concerned with the 'transfer of experimental method from the technical field of physical experience to the wider field of human life'.[3] And this transfer obviously requires a general theory of experimental method, while the use of the method 'implies direction by ideas and knowledge'.[4] True, Dewey has not the slightest intention of encouraging the development of a method which is supposed to possess an *a priori*, absolute and universal validity. He insists that what is needed is an intelligent examination of the actual consequences of inherited and traditional customs and institutions with a view to intelligent examination of the ways in which their customs and institutions should be modified in order to produce the consequences which we consider desirable. But this does not alter the fact that a great part of his reflection is devoted to developing a general logic of experience and a general theory of experimental method.

It would thus be a gross caricature of Dewey's actual practice if one were to represent him as despising all general concepts and all general theories, still more if we were to represent him as actually doing without such concepts and theories. Without them one could not be a philosopher at all. It is true that in his contribution to a volume of essays entitled *Creative Intelligence* (1917) Dewey roundly asserts that because 'reality' is a denotative term, designating indifferently everything that happens, no general theory of reality 'is possible or needed',[5] a conclusion which does

[1] *Reconstruction in Philosophy*, p. 188. [2] *Ibid.*, p. 193.
[3] *The Quest for Certainty*, p. 273. [4] *Ibid.*
[5] *Creative Intelligence*, p. 55.

not appear to follow from the premisses. But in *Experience and Nature* (1925) he can fairly be said to have himself developed such a theory, though admittedly not a theory of any reality transcending Nature. Similarly, though in *Reconstruction in Philosophy* he rules out talk about 'the State', this does not prevent him from developing a theory of the State. Again, when he asserts that any philosophy which is not isolated from modern life must grapple with 'the problem of restoring integration and co-operation between man's beliefs about the world in which he lives and his beliefs about the values and purposes that should direct his conduct',[1] he is indicating a problem which cannot possibly be discussed without general ideas. It is not indeed a question of maintaining that Dewey is perpetually contradicting himself. For example, one might rule out talk about 'the State', meaning by this an eternal essence, and yet make generalizations based on reflection about actual States. Rather is it a question of maintaining that Dewey's insistence on practice, as the termination of inquiry in the reconstruction of a specific problematic situation, leads him at times to speak in a way which does not square with his actual practice.

4. We have noted the stress which Dewey lays on inquiry, inquiry being defined as 'the controlled or directed transformation of an indeterminate situation into one that is so determinate in its constituent distinctions and relations as to convert the elements of the original situation into a unified whole'.[2] He calls, therefore, for a new logic of inquiry. If the Aristotelian logic is considered purely historically, in relation to Greek culture, 'it deserves the admiration it has received'.[3] For it is an admirable analysis of 'discourse in isolation from the operations in which discourse takes effect'.[4] At the same time the attempt to preserve the Aristotelian logic when the advance of science has undermined the ontological background of essences and species on which it rested is 'the main source of existing confusion in logical theory'.[5] Moreover, if this logic is retained when its ontological presuppositions have been repudiated, it inevitably becomes purely formal and quite inadequate as a logic of inquiry. True, Aristotle's logic remains a model in the sense that it combined in a unified scheme both the

[1] *The Quest for Certainty*, p. 255.
[2] *Logic*, pp. 104–5. Bertrand Russell objects that this definition would apply to the activity of a drill sergeant in transforming a collection of new recruits into a regiment, though this activity could hardly be described as a process of inquiry. Cf. *The Philosophy of John Dewey*, edited by P. A. Schilpp, p. 143.
[3] *Ibid.*, p. 94.   [4] *Ibid.*   [5] *Ibid.*

common sense and the science of his day. But his day is not our day. And what we need is a unified theory of inquiry which will make available for use in other fields 'the authentic pattern of experimental and operational inquiry in science'.[1] This is not to demand that all other fields of inquiry should be reduced to physical science. It is rather that the logic of inquiry has hitherto found its chief exemplification in physical science, and that it needs to be abstracted, so to speak, and turned into a general logic of inquiry which can be employed in all 'inquiries concerned with deliberate reconstruction of experience'.[2] We are thus reminded of Hume's demand that the experimental method of inquiry which had proved so fruitful in physical science or natural philosophy should be applied in the fields of aesthetics, ethics and politics. But Dewey, unlike Hume, develops an elaborate account of this logic of inquiry.

It would be impracticable to summarize this account here. But certain features can be mentioned. In general, logic is regarded, of course, as instrumental, that is, as a means of rendering intelligent, instead of blind, the action involved in reconstructing a problematic or indeterminate situation. Intelligent action presupposes a process of thought or inquiry, and this requires symbolization and propositional formulation. Propositions in general are the necessary logical instruments for reaching a final judgment which has existential import; and the final judgment is reached through a series of intermediate judgments. Hence judgment can be described as 'a continuous process of resolving an indeterminate, unsettled situation into a determinately unified one, through operations which transform subject-matter originally given'.[3] The whole process of judgment and ratiocination can thus be considered as a phase of intelligent actions, and at the same time as instrumental to actual reconstruction of a situation. Universal propositions, for instance, are formulations of possible ways of acting or operating.[4] They are all of the *'if/then'* type.

If logical thought is instrumental, its validity is shown by its success. Hence the standard of validity is 'precisely the degree in which the thinking actually disposes of the difficulty [the problematic situation] and allows us to proceed with more direct modes of experiencing that are forthwith possessed of more assured and deepened value'.[5] In accordance with this view Dewey rejects the

[1] *Logic*, p. 98.   [2] *Reconstruction in Philosophy*, p. 138.
[3] *Logic*, p. 283.   [4] *Ibid.*, p. 264.
[5] *Studies in Logical Theory*, p. 3. Dewey often depicts the term of inquiry as an enrichment and deepening of experience.

idea of the basic principles of logic as being *a priori* truths which are fixed antecedently to all inquiry and represents them as generated in the process of inquiry itself. They represent conditions which have been found, during the continued process of inquiry, to be involved in or demanded by its success. Just as causal laws are functional in character, so are the so-called first principles of logic. Their validity is measured by their success. Instrumentalism in logic thus has a connection with Dewey's naturalism. The basic logical principles are not eternal truths, transcending the changing empirical world and to be apprehended instinctively; they are generated in the actual process of man's active relation with his environment.

In an essay on the development of American pragmatism Dewey defines instrumentalism as 'an attempt to constitute a precise logical theory of concepts, of judgments and inferences in their various forms, by considering primarily how thought functions in the experimental determinations of future consequences'.[1] But there is also an instrumentalist theory of truth. And some brief remarks must be made about this topic.

In a footnote in his *Logic* Dewey remarks that 'the best definition of *truth* from the logical standpoint which is known to me is that of Peirce',[2] namely that the true is that opinion which is fated to be ultimately accepted by all investigators. He also quotes with approval Peirce's statement that truth is the concordance of an abstract statement with the ideal limit towards which endless inquiry would tend to bring scientific belief. Elsewhere, however, Dewey insists that if it is asked what truth is here and now, so to speak, without reference to an ideal limit of all inquiry, the answer is that a statement or an hypothesis is true or false in so far as it leads us to or away from the end which we have in view. In other words, 'the hypothesis that works is the *true* one'.[3] In Dewey's opinion this view of truth follows as a matter of course from the pragmatist concept of meaning.

Dewey is careful to point out that if it is said that truth is utility or the useful, this statement is not intended to identify truth with 'some purely personal end, some profit upon which a particular individual has set his heart'.[4] The idea of utility in this context must be interpreted in relation to the process of

---

[1] *Twentieth Century Philosophy*, edited by D. D. Runes, pp. 463–4 (New York, 1943).
[2] *Logic*, p. 345, note 6.
[3] *Reconstruction in Philosophy*, p. 156.   [4] *Ibid.*, p. 157.

transforming a problematic situation. And a problematic situation is something public and objective. A scientific problem, for example, is not a private neurotic worry but an objective difficulty which is resolved by appropriate objective methods. For this reason Dewey avoids speaking with James of truth as the satisfactory or that which satisfies. For this way of speaking suggests a private emotive satisfaction. And if the term 'the satisfactory' is employed, we must understand that the satisfaction in question is that of the demands of a public problematic situation, not the satisfaction of the emotive needs of any individual. For the matter of that, the solution of a scientific problem might occasion great unhappiness to the human race. Yet in so far as it worked or manifested its utility by transforming an objective problematic situation, it would be true and 'satisfactory'.

Though, however, he insists that instrumentalism does not deny the objectivity of truth by making it relative to the individual's whims, wishes and emotive needs, Dewey is, of course, well aware that his theory is opposed to that of eternal, unchanging truths. Indeed, he obviously intends this opposition. He regards the theory of eternal, unchanging truths as implying a certain metaphysics or view of reality, namely the distinction between the phenomenal sphere of becoming and the sphere of perfect and unchanging being, which is apprehended in the form of eternal truths. This metaphysics is, of course, at variance with Dewey's naturalism. Hence the so-called timeless truths have to be represented by him as being simply instruments for application in knowing the one world of becoming, instruments which constantly show their value in use. In other words, their significance is functional rather than ontological. No truth is absolutely sacrosanct, but some truths possess in practice a constant functional value.

This theory that there are no sacrosanct eternal truths, but that all statements which we believe to be true are revisible in principle or from the purely logical point of view, obviously has important implications in the fields of morals and politics. 'To generalize the recognition that the true means the verified and nothing else places upon men the responsibility for surrendering political and moral dogmas, and subjecting to the test of consequences their most cherished prejudices.'[1] In Dewey's opinion this is one of the main reasons why the instrumentalist theory of truth raises fear and hostility in many minds.

[1] *Reconstruction in Philosophy*, p. 160.

5. Passing over for the present any criticism of the instrumentalist theory of truth, we can turn to ethics which Dewey regards as concerned with intelligent conduct in view of an end, with consciously directed conduct. A moral agent is one who proposes to himself an end to be achieved by action.[1] But Dewey insists that activity, consciously directed to an end which is thought worth while by the agent, presupposes habits as acquired dispositions to respond in certain ways to certain classes of stimuli. 'The act must come before the thought, and a habit before an ability to evoke the thought at will.'[2] As Dewey puts it, it is only the man who already has certain habits of posture and who is capable of standing erect that can form for himself the idea of an erect stance as an end to be consciously pursued. Our ideas, like our sensations, depend on experience. 'And the experience upon which they both depend is the operation of habits—originally of instincts.'[3] Our purposes and aims in action come to us through the medium of habits.

Dewey's insistence on the relevance to ethics of the psychology of habit is partly due to his conviction that habits, as demands for certain kinds of action, 'constitute the self',[4] and that 'character is the interpenetration of habits'.[5] For if such interpenetration, in the sense of an harmonious and unified integration, is something to be achieved rather than an original datum, it obviously follows that moral theory must take habits into account, in so far as it is concerned with the development of human nature.

But Dewey's emphasis on the psychology of habit is also due to his determination to include ethics in his general naturalistic interpretation of experience. Naturalism cannot accommodate such ideas as those of eternal norms, subsistent absolute values or a supernatural moral legislator. The whole moral life, while admittedly involving the appearance of fresh elements, must be represented as a development of the interaction of the human organism with its environment. Hence a study of biological and social psychology is indispensable for the moral philosopher who is concerned with the moral life as it actually exists.

It has already been noted that for Dewey environment does not mean simply the physical, non-human environment. Indeed, from the moral point of view man's relations with his social environment are of primary importance. For it is a mistake to think that

---

[1] Cf., for example, *Outlines of a Critical Theory of Ethics*, p. 3.
[2] *Human Nature and Conduct*, p. 30.　　　[3] *Ibid.*, p. 32.
[4] *Ibid.*, p. 25.　　　[5] *Ibid.*, p. 38.

morality *ought* to be social: 'morals *are* social'.[1] This is simply an empirical fact. It is true that to a considerable extent customs, which are widespread uniformities of habit, exist because individuals are faced by similar situations to which they react in similar ways. 'But to a larger extent customs persist because individuals form their personal habits under conditions set by prior customs. An individual usually acquires the morality as he inherits the speech of his social group.'[2] This may indeed be more obvious in the case of earlier forms of society. For in modern society, at least of the Western democratic type, the individual is offered a wide range of custom-patterns. But in any case, customs, as demands for certain ways of acting and as forming certain outlooks, constitute moral standards. And we can say that 'for practical purposes morals mean customs, folk-ways, established collective habits'.[3]

At the same time customs, as widespread uniformities of habit, tend to perpetuate themselves even when they no longer answer the needs of man in his relations with his environment. They tend to become matter of mechanical routine, a drag on human growth and development. And to say this is to imply that there is in man another factor, besides habit, which is relevant to morals. This factor is impulse. Indeed, habits, as acquired dispositions to act in certain ways, are secondary to unacquired or unlearned impulses.

This distinction, however, gives rise to a difficulty. On the one hand impulse represents the sphere of spontaneity and thus the possibility of reorganizing habits in accordance with the demands of new situations. On the other hand man's impulses are for the most part not definitely organized and adapted in the way in which animal instincts are organized and adapted. Hence they acquire the significance and definiteness which are required for human conduct only through being canalized into habits. Thus 'the direction of native activity depends upon acquired habits, and yet acquired habits can be modified only by redirection of impulses'.[4] How, then, can man be capable of changing his habits and customs to meet fresh situations and the new demands of a changing environment? How can he change himself?

This question can be answered only by introducing the idea of intelligence. When changing conditions in the environment render a habit useless or detrimental or when a conflict of habits occurs,

---

[1] *Human Nature and Conduct*, p. 319.　　[2] *Ibid.*, p. 58.
[3] *Ibid.*, p. 75.　　[4] *Ibid.*, p. 126.

impulse is liberated from the control of habit and seeks redirection. Left to itself, so to speak, it simply bursts the chains of habit asunder in a wild upsurge. In social life this means that if a society's customs have become outmoded or harmful, and if the situation is left to itself, revolution inevitably occurs, unless perhaps the society simply becomes lifeless and fossilized. The alternative is obviously the intelligent redirection of impulse into new customs and the intelligent creation of fresh institutions. In fine, a 'breach in the crust of the cake of custom releases impulses; but it is the work of intelligence to find the ways of using them'.[1]

In some sense, therefore, intelligence, when seeking to transform or reconstruct a problematic moral situation, has to deliberate about ends and means. But for Dewey there are no fixed ends which the mind can apprehend as something given from the start and perennially valid. Nor will he allow that an end is a value which lies beyond the activity which seeks to attain it. 'Ends are foreseen consequences which arise in the cause of activity and which are employed to give activity added meaning and to direct its further course.'[2] When we are dissatisfied with existing conditions, we can, of course, picture to ourselves a set of conditions which, if actualized, would afford satisfaction. But Dewey insists that an imaginary picture of this kind becomes a genuine aim or end-in-view only when it is worked out in terms of the concrete, possible process of actualizing it, that is, in terms of 'means'. We have to study the ways in which results similar to those which we desire are actually brought about by causal activity. And when we survey the proposed line of action, the distinction between means and ends arises within the series of contemplated acts.

It is obviously possible for intelligence to operate with existing moral standards. But we are considering problematic situations which demand something more than manipulating the current moral ideas and standards of a society. And in such situations it is the task of intelligence to grasp and actualize possibilities of growth, of the reconstruction of experience. Indeed, 'growth itself is the only moral "end" '.[3] Again, 'growing, or the continuous reconstruction of experience, is the only end'.[4]

A natural question to ask is, growth in what direction? Reconstruction for what purpose? But if such questions concern a final end other than growth itself, reconstruction itself, they can have

[1] *Ibid.*, p. 170.   [2] *Ibid.*, p. 225.
[3] *Reconstruction in Philosophy*, p. 177.   [4] *Ibid.*, p. 184.

no meaning in terms of Dewey's philosophy. He does indeed admit that happiness or the satisfaction of the forces of human nature is the moral end. But as happiness turns out to be living, while 'life means growth',[1] we seem to be back at the same point. The growth which is the moral end is one which makes possible further growth. In other words, growth itself is the end.

We must remember, however, that for Dewey no genuine end is separable from the means, from the process of its actualization. And he tells us that 'good consists in the meaning that is experienced to belong to an activity when conflict and entanglement of various incompatible impulses and habits terminate in a unified orderly release in action'.[2] So we can say perhaps that for Dewey the moral end is growth in the sense of the dynamic development of harmoniously integrated human nature, provided that we do not envisage a fixed and determinate state of perfection as the final end. There is for Dewey no final end save growth itself. The attainment of a definite and limited end-in-view opens up new vistas, new tasks, fresh possibilities of action. And it is in grasping and realizing these opportunities and possibilities that moral growth consists.

Dewey tries, therefore, to get rid of the concept of a realm of values distinct from the world of fact. Values are not something given; they are constituted by the act of evaluating, by the value-judgment. This is not a judgment that something is 'satisfying'. For to say this is simply to make a statement of fact, like the statement that something is sweet or white. To make a value-judgment is to say that something is 'satisfactory' in the sense that it fulfils specifiable conditions.[3] For example, does a certain activity create conditions for further growth or does it prevent them? If I say that it does, I declare the activity to be valuable or a value.

It may be objected that to say that something fulfils certain specifiable conditions is no less a statement of fact than to say that an object is satisfying, in the sense that I myself or many people or all men find it satisfying. But Dewey is aware that to ask whether something is a value is to ask whether it is 'something to be prized and cherished, *to be* enjoyed',[4] and that to say that it is a value is to say that it is something *to be* desired and enjoyed.[5]

---

[1] *Democracy and Education*, p. 61.   [2] *Human Nature and Conduct*, p. 210.
[3] Cf. *The Quest for Certainty*, p. 260.   [4] *Ibid.*, p. 260.
[5] 'A judgment about what is *to be* desired and enjoyed is therefore a claim on future action; it possesses *de jure* and not merely *de facto* quality', *Ibid.*, p. 263.

Hence the following definition. 'Judgments about values are judgments about the conditions and the results of experienced objects; judgments about that which should regulate the formation of our desires, affections and enjoyments.'[1]

The emphasis, however, is placed by Dewey on the judgment of value as the term of a process of inquiry, stimulated by a problematic situation. For this enables him to say that his theory of values does not do away with their objectivity. Something is a value if it is adapted 'to the needs and demands imposed by the situation',[2] that is to say, if it meets the demands of an objective problematic situation, in regard to its transformation or reconstruction. A judgment of value, like a scientific hypothesis, is predictive, and it is thus empirically or experimentally verifiable. 'Appraisals of courses of action as better and worse, more or less serviceable, are as experimentally justified as are non-valuative propositions about impersonal subject matter.'[3] The transfer of the experimental method from physics to ethics would mean, of course, that all judgments and beliefs about values would have to be regarded as hypotheses. But to interpret them in this way is to transfer them from the realm of the subjective into that of the objective, of the verifiable. And as much care should be devoted to their framing as is devoted to the framing of scientific hypotheses.

6. Dewey's insistence on growth obviously implies that personality is something to be achieved, something in the making. But the human person is not, of course, an isolated atom. It is not simply a question of the individual being under an obligation to consider his social environment: he *is* a social being, whether he likes it or not. And all his actions 'bear the stamp of his community as assuredly as does the language he speaks'.[4] This is true even of those courses of activity of which society in general disapproves. It is a man's relations with his fellow-men which provide him both with the opportunities for action and with the instruments for taking advantage of such opportunities. And this is verified in the case of the burglar or the dealer in the white slave traffic no less than in that of the philanthropist.

At the same time the social environment, with its institutions, has to be organized and modified in the manner best suited for promoting the fullest possible development in desirable ways of

---

[1] *Ibid.*, p. 265.
[2] *Theory of Valuation*, p. 17.
[3] *Ibid.*, p. 22.
[4] *Human Nature and Conduct*, p. 317.

the capacities of individuals. And at first sight we are faced with a vicious circle. On the one hand the individual is conditioned by the existing social environment in regard to his habits of action and his aims. On the other hand, if the social environment is to be changed or modified, this can be accomplished only by individuals, even though by individuals working together and sharing common aims. How, then, is it possible for the individual, who is inevitably conditioned by his social environment, to devote himself to changing that environment in a deliberate and active manner?

Dewey's answer is what one would expect, namely that when a problematic situation arises, such as a clash between man's developing needs on the one hand and existing social institutions on the other, impulse stimulates thought and inquiry directed to transforming or reconstructing the social environment. As in morals, the task-in-hand is always in the forefront of Dewey's mind. The function of political philosophy is to criticize existing institutions in the light of man's development and changing needs and to discern and point out practical possibilities for the future to meet the needs of the present. In other words, Dewey looks on political philosophy as an instrument for concrete action. This means that it is not the business of the political philosopher to construct Utopias. Nor should he allow himself to succumb to the temptation of delineating 'the State', the essential concept of a state, which is supposed to be perennially valid. For to do this is in effect to canonize, even though unconsciously, an existing state of affairs, probably one that has already been challenged and subjected to criticism. In any case inquiry is hindered rather than helped by solutions which purport to cover all situations. If, for example, we are concerned with determining the value of the institution of private property in a given society at a certain period, it is no help to be told either that private property is a sacred, inviolable and perennial right or that it is always theft.

Obviously, the process of criticizing existing social institutions and of pointing the way to fresh concrete possibilities requires some standard to which men can refer. And for Dewey the test for all such institutions, whether political, juridical or industrial, is 'the contributions they make to the all-around growth of every member of society'.[1] It is for this reason that he favours democracy, namely as founded on 'faith in the capacities of human nature, faith in human intelligence and in the power of pooled and

[1] *Reconstruction in Philosophy*, p. 186.

co-operative experience'.[1] Yet 'the prime condition of a democratically organized public is a kind of knowledge and insight which does not yet exist',[2] though we can indicate some of the conditions which have to be fulfilled if it is to exist. Democracy as we know it is thus the settling for the free use of the experimental method in social inquiry and thought, which is required for the solution of concrete social, political and industrial problems.

We have seen that for Dewey the moral end is growth, and that the degree to which they facilitate growth provides a test for assessing the value of social and political institutions. The idea of growth is also the key to his educational theory. Indeed, 'the educative process is all one with the moral process'.[3] And education is 'getting from the present the degree and kind of growth there is in it'.[4] It follows that as the potentiality for growth or development does not cease with the close of adolescence, education should not be regarded as a preparation for life. It is itself a process of living.[5] In fact, 'the educational process has no end beyond itself; it is its own end'.[6] True, formal schooling comes to an end; but the educative influence of society, social relations and social institutions affects adults as well as the young. And if we take, as we should, a broad view of education, we can see the importance of effecting those social and political reforms which are judged most likely to foster the capacity for growth and to evoke those responses which facilitate further development. Morals, education and politics are closely interconnected.

Given this general view of education, Dewey naturally stresses the need of making the school as far as possible a real community, to reproduce social life in a simplified form and thus to promote the development of the child's capacity to participate in the life of society in general. Further, he emphasizes, as one would expect, the need for training children in intelligent inquiry. Struck by the contrast between the lack of interest shown by many children in their school instruction and their lively interest in those activities outside the school in which they are able to share personally and actively, he concludes that scholastic methods should be so changed as to allow the children to participate actively as much

[1] *Problems of Men*, p. 59.
[2] *The Public and Its Problems*, p. 166. It is in this work that Dewey's most detailed discussion of the State is to be found.
[3] *Reconstruction in Philosophy*, p. 183.
[4] *Ibid.*, pp. 184–5.
[5] This point of view is expanded in, for example, *My Pedagogic Creed*.
[6] *Democracy and Education*, p. 59.

as possible in concrete processes of inquiry leading from problematic situations to the overt behaviour or actions needed to transform the situation. But we cannot enter into further details of Dewey's ideas about education in the ordinary sense. His main conviction is that education should not be simply instruction in various subjects but rather a coherent unified effort to foster the development of citizens capable of promoting the further growth of society by employing intelligence fruitfully in a social context.

7. For many years Dewey was comparatively reticent about religion. In *Human Nature and Conduct* (1922), he spoke of religion as 'a sense of the whole',[1] and remarked that 'the religious experience is a reality in so far as in the midst of effort to foresee and regulate future objects we are sustained and expanded in feebleness and failure by the sense of an enveloping whole'.[2] And in *The Quest for Certainty* (1929) we find him maintaining that Nature, including humanity, when it is considered as the source of ideals and possibilities of achievement and as the abode of all attained goods, is capable of evoking a religious attitude which can be described as a sense of the possibilities of existence and as devotion to the cause of their actualization.[3] But these were more or less incidental remarks, and it was not until 1934 that Dewey really tackled the subject of religion in *A Common Faith*, which was the published version of a series of Terry Foundation Lectures delivered at Yale University.

Although, however, Dewey had previously written little about religion, he made it clear that he himself rejected all definite creeds and religious practices. And it was indeed obvious that his empirical naturalism had no room for belief in or worship of a supernatural divine being. At the same time Dewey had also made it clear that he attached some value to what he called a religious attitude. And in *A Common Faith* we find him distinguishing between the noun 'religion' and the adjective 'religious'. The noun he rejects, in the sense of rejecting definite religious creeds, institutions and practices. The adjective he accepts, in the sense that he affirms the value of religion as a quality of experience.

It must be understood, however, that Dewey is not speaking of any specifically religious and mystical experience, such as might be used to support belief in a supernatural Deity. The quality which he has in mind is one which can belong to an experience

---

[1] *Human Nature and Conduct*, p. 331.　　[2] *Ibid.*, p. 264.
[3] Cf. *The Quest for Certainty*, pp. 288–91.

that would not ordinarily be described as religious. For example, the experience or feeling of being at one with the universe, with Nature as a whole, possesses this quality. And in *A Common Faith* Dewey associates the quality of being 'religious' with faith in 'the unification of the self through allegiance to inclusive ideal ends, which imagination presents to us and to which the human will responds as worthy of controlling our desires and choices'.[1]

As for the word 'God', Dewey is prepared to retain it, provided that it is used to signify not an existent supernatural being but rather the unity of the ideal possibilities which man can actualize through intelligence and action. 'We are in the presence neither of ideals completely embodied in existence nor yet of ideals that are mere rootless ideals, fantasies, utopias. For there are forces in nature and society that generate and support the ideals. They are further unified by the action that gives them coherence and solidity. It is this *active* relation between ideal and actual to which I would give the name "God".'[2]

A naturalistic philosophy, in other words, can find no room for God as conceived in the Jewish, Christian and Mohammedan religions. But a philosophy of experience must find room for religion in some sense of the term. Hence the quality of being 'religious' must be detached, as it were, from specifically religious experiences, in the sense of experience which purports to have for its object a supernatural being, and reattached to other forms of experience. As Dewey notes in *A Common Faith* the adjective 'religious' can apply to attitudes which can be adopted towards any object or any ideal. It can apply to aesthetic, scientific or moral experience or to experience of friendship and love. In this sense religion can pervade the whole of life. But Dewey himself emphasizes the religious character of the experience of the unification of the self. As 'the self is always directed toward something beyond itself',[3] its ideal unification depends upon a harmonizing of the self with the universe, with Nature as a totality. And here Dewey stresses, as we have seen, the movement towards the realization of ideal possibilities. One might perhaps expect him to recognize an active divine principle operating in and through Nature for the realization and conservation of values. But even if much of what he says points in the direction of some such idea, his naturalism effectively prevents him from taking such a step.

[1] *A Common Faith*, p. 33.   [2] *Ibid.*, pp. 50–1.   [3] *Ibid.*, p. 19.

8. Obviously, Dewey's philosophy is not a metaphysics if by this term we mean a study or doctrine of meta-empirical reality. But though, as has already been noted, he denies, in one place at least, that any general theory of reality is needed or even possible, it is clear enough that he develops a world-view. And world-views are generally classed under the heading of metaphysics. It would be ingenuous to say that Dewey simply takes the world as he finds it. For the plain fact is that he interprets it. For the matter of that, in spite of all that he has to say against general theories, he does not really prohibit all attempts to determine the generic traits, as he puts it, of existence of all kinds. What he does is to insist that 'the generic insight into existence which alone can define metaphysics in any empirically intelligible sense is itself an added fact of interaction, and is therefore subject to the same requirement of intelligence as any other natural occurrence: namely, inquiry into the bearings, leadings and consequences of what it discovers. The universe is no infinite self-representative series, if only because the addition within it of a representation makes it a different universe.'[1] So far as metaphysics in the sense of ontology is admitted,[2] its findings become working hypotheses, as much subject to revision as are the hypotheses of physical science. Presumably Dewey's own world-view is such a working hypothesis.

It is arguable that this world-view shows traces of its author's Hegelian past, in the sense at any rate that Nature is substituted for Hegel's Spirit and that Dewey tends to interpret the philosophical systems of the past in relation to the cultures which gave birth to them. This second point helps to explain the fact that when Dewey is treating of past systems, he bothers very little, if at all, about the arguments advanced on their behalf by their authors and dwells instead on the inability of these systems to deal with the problematic situations arising out of contemporary culture. This attitude is, of course, in accordance with his instrumentalist view of truth. But the result is that the attentive and critical reader of his books receives the impression that the naturalistic view of the world is assumed, not proved. And in the opinion of the present writer this impression is justified. Dewey simply assumes, for example, that the day of theological and metaphysical explanations is past, and that such explanations

---

[1] *Experience and Nature*, pp. 414–15. The reference to an infinite self-representative series is to the doctrine of Royce.

[2] Dewey himself deals, for example, with the category of causality.

were bogus. And the observation that such explanations do not serve as instruments to solve, say, contemporary social problems is insufficient to show the validity of the assumption.

The reply may be made that if Dewey's philosophy of experience, his general world-view, succeeds in giving a coherent and unified account of experiences as a whole, no further justification is required for excluding superfluous hypotheses which go beyond the limits of naturalism. But it is open to question whether Dewey's philosophy as a whole is really coherent. Consider, for example, his denial of absolute values and fixed ends. He asserts, as we have seen, the objectivity of values; but he regards them as relative to the problematic situations which give rise to the processes of inquiry that terminate in value-judgments. Yet it certainly appears that Dewey himself speaks of 'growth' as though it were an absolute value and an end in itself, an end fixed by the nature of man and ultimately by the nature of reality. Again, Dewey is careful to explain that he has no intention of denying the existence of a world antecedently to human experience; and he asserts that we experience many things *as* antecedently prior to our experiencing them. At the same time there is a strong tendency to interpret 'experience' in terms of the reconstruction of situations, a reconstruction which makes the world different from what it would have been without human operational thinking. And this points to a theory of creative experience which tends to turn the antecedently given into a kind of mysterious thing-in-itself.

Obviously, the presence of inconsistencies in Dewey's thought does not disprove naturalism. But it does at any rate render an assumption of a naturalistic point of view more open to criticism than it would have been if Dewey had succeeded in giving a perfectly unified and coherent world-view or interpretation of experience. It is clearly not sufficient to answer that on Dewey's own premises his world-view is a working hypothesis which must be judged by its 'consequences' and not by the comparative absence of antecedent arguments in its favour. For the 'working' of a world-view is shown precisely in its ability to give us a coherent and unified conceptual mastery over the data.

If we turn to Dewey's logical theory, we again encounter difficulties of some moment. For instance, though he recognizes, of course, that there are basic logical principles which have constantly shown themselves to be objectively useful instruments in coping with problematic situations, he insists that from a purely logical point of view no principle is sacrosanct; all are revisible in principle. At the same time Dewey evidently assumes that intelligence cannot rest satisfied with a problematic situation, with an unresolved conflict or 'contradiction'. As in the philosophy of Hegel, the mind is forced on towards an overcoming of such contradictions.[1] And this seems to imply an absolute demand of the intellect, a demand which it is difficult to reconcile with the view that no logical principles are absolute.

Again, there seems to be some ambiguity in the use of the word 'consequences'. A scientific hypothesis is interpreted as predictive, and it is verified if the predicted consequences, which constitute the meaning of the hypothesis, are realized. Whether verification brings subjective satisfaction to people or not, is irrelevant. In this context Dewey is careful to avoid the objection, to which James exposes himself, that the 'satisfying' character of a proposition is the test of its truth. But when we come to the social and political spheres, we can see a tendency to slide into the interpretation of 'consequences' as desirable consequences. Dewey would probably reply that what he is talking about is 'intended' consequences. The solution to a social or political problematic situation 'intends', has as its meaning, certain consequences. And, as in the case of scientific hypotheses, verification validates the proposed solution. Whether people like the solution or not is beside the point. In both cases, in that of the social or political solution or plan as in that of the scientific hypothesis, the test of truth or validity is objective. Yet it seems fairly obvious that in practice Dewey discriminates between political plans and solutions and theories in terms of their contribution to 'growth', their promotion of an end which he considers desirable. One might, of course, apply the same criterion in an analogous sense to scientific hypotheses. For example, an hypothesis which tends to arrest further scientific inquiry and advance cannot be accepted as true. But then the test of truth is no longer simply the verification of the consequences which are said to form the meaning of the hypothesis, though it may indeed tend to coincide with Peirce's conception of truth as the ideal limit to which all inquiry converges.

The strength of Dewey's philosophy doubtless lies in the fact

---

[1] There is, of course, a big difference between the attitudes of Hegel and Dewey. For Dewey is concerned with the active transformation of a situation, and not simply with the dialectical overcoming of a contradiction. But both men assume that contradiction *is* something to be overcome.

that its author always has his eye on empirical reality, or concrete situations and on the power of human intelligence and will to deal with these situations and to create possibilities of further development. Dewey brings philosophy down to earth and tries to show its relevance to concrete problems, moral, social and educational. And this helps to explain his great influence. He is a rather dull writer. And he is not a conspicuously precise and clear writer. His success in bringing his ideas to the attention of so many of his fellow-countrymen is not due to his literary gifts: it must be attributed in great part to the practical relevance of his ideas. Besides, his general world-view is undoubtedly capable of appealing to those who look on theological and metaphysical tenets as outmoded, and perhaps also as attempts to preserve vested interests, and who at the same time seek a forward-looking philosophy which does not appeal in any way to supernatural realities but in some sense justifies a faith in indefinite human progress.

For these reasons the activity of finding inconsistencies and ambiguities in Dewey's thought may appear to some minds a poor sort of game to play, a futile sniping at a philosophy which, by and large, is firmly rooted in the soil of experience. To others, however, it may well appear that practical relevance is bought, so to speak, at the expense of a thorough explicitation, examination and justification of the foundations of the philosophy. It may also appear that in the long run Dewey's philosophy rests on a judgment of value, the value of action. One can, of course, base a philosophy on a judgment or on judgments of value. But it is desirable that in this case the judgments should be brought into the open. Otherwise one may think, for example, that the instrumentalist theory of truth is simply the result of a dispassionate analysis.

PART V

THE REVOLT AGAINST IDEALISM

CHAPTER XVII

REALISM IN BRITAIN AND AMERICA

An introductory remark—Some Oxford realists—Brief notes on an ethical discussion at Oxford—American neo-realism—Critical realism in America—The world-view of Samuel Alexander—A reference to A. N. Whitehead.

1. WHEN we think of the revolt against idealism in Great Britain, the names which immediately come to mind are those of two Cambridge men, G. E. Moore and Bertrand Russell. Moore, however, is universally acknowledged to be one of the chief inspirers of the analytic movement, as it is commonly called, which has enjoyed a spectacular success in the first half of the twentieth century. And Russell, besides being another of the principal pioneers of this movement, is by far the most widely known British philosopher of this century. The present writer, therefore, has decided to postpone the brief treatment of them which is all that the scope of this volume allows and to treat first of a number of comparatively minor figures, even if this means neglecting the demands of chronological order.

2. Mention has already been made of the way in which idealism came to occupy a dominating position in the British universities, especially at Oxford, during the second half of the nineteenth century. But even at Oxford the triumph of idealism was not complete. For example, Thomas Case (1844–1925), who occupied the chair of metaphysics from 1899 until 1910 and was President of Corpus Christi College from 1904 until 1924, published *Realism in Morals* in 1877 and *Physical Realism* in 1888. It is indeed true that in itself Case's realism was opposed to subjective idealism and to phenomenalism rather than to objective or to absolute idealism. For it consisted basically in the thesis that there is a real and knowable world of things existing independently of sense-data.[1]

[1] It must be noted, however, that though for Case independent physical things are knowable, their existence and nature is known mediately, being inferred from sense-data, which are caused modifications of the nervous system.

At the same time, while in the war against materialism Case was on the side of the idealists, he regarded himself as continuing or restoring the realism of Francis Bacon and of scientists such as Newton and as an opponent of the then fashionable idealist movement.[1]

A more notable opponent of idealism was John Cook Wilson (1849–1915), who occupied the chair of logic at Oxford from 1889 until the year of his death. He published very little, his main influence being exercised as a teacher. But a two-volume collection of lectures on logic, essays and letters, together with a memoir by the editor, A. S. L. Farquharson, appeared posthumously in 1926 with the title *Statement and Inference*.

As an undergraduate Cook Wilson had been influenced by T. H. Green, and later he went to Göttingen to hear Lotze. But he gradually became a sharp critic of idealism. He did not, however, oppose to it a rival world-view. His strength lay partly in attack and partly in the way in which he selected particular problems and tried to follow them through with meticulous care and thoroughness. In this sense his thought was analytic. Further, he had an Aristotelian respect for the distinctions expressed in or implied by ordinary language. And he was convinced that logicians would do well to pay both attention and defence to the natural logic of common linguistic usage.

One of Cook Wilson's grievances against the logic of Bradley and Bosanquet is their doctrine of judgment. In his view they assume that there is one mental act, namely judging, which finds expression in every statement. And to make this assumption is to confuse mental activities, such as knowing, opining and believing, which ought to be distinguished. Further, it is a serious mistake to suppose that there is an activity called judging which is distinct from inference. 'There is no such thing.'[2] If logicians paid more attention to the ways in which we ordinarily use such terms as 'judge', they would see that to judge that something is the case is to infer it. In logic we can get along quite well with statement and inference, without introducing a fictitious separate activity, namely judging.

A statement, therefore, can express various activities. But of these knowing is fundamental. For we cannot understand what is

---

[1] It is significant that Case was the author of the article on Aristotle in the eleventh edition of the *Encyclopædia Britannica*.
[2] *Statement and Inference*, I, p. 87.

meant by, for example, having an opinion or wondering whether something is true except by way of a contrast with knowledge. It by no means follows, however, that knowledge can be analyzed and defined. We can indeed ask how we come to know or what we know, but the question, What is knowledge itself? is absurd. For to demand an answer is to presuppose that we can estimate its truth, and it is thus presupposed that we are already aware what knowledge is. Knowledge can be exemplified but not explained or defined. Nor does it stand in need of any further justification than pointing to examples of it.

We can indeed exclude false accounts of knowledge. These take two main forms. On the one hand there is the attempt to reduce the object to the act of apprehension by interpreting knowledge as a making, a construction of the object. On the other hand there is the tendency to describe the act of apprehension in terms of the object, by maintaining that what we know is a 'copy' or representation of the object. This thesis makes knowledge impossible. For if what we know immediately is always a copy or idea, we can never compare it with the original, to see whether it tallies or not.

Refutations of false accounts of knowledge presuppose, however, that we are already well aware of what knowledge is. And we are aware of it by actually knowing something. Hence to ask, what is knowledge? as though we were ignorant, is just as much an improper question as Bradley's query, how is a relation related to its term? A relation is simply not the sort of thing which can be intelligibly said to be related. And knowledge is an indefinable and *sui generis* relation between a subject and an object. We can say what it is not, that it neither makes the object nor terminates in a copy of the object; but we cannot define what it is.

Cook Wilson's realism obviously assumes that we perceive physical objects which exist independently of the act of perception. In other words, he denies the thesis that *esse est percipi*, to be is to be perceived.[1] At the same time he finds it necessary to qualify his realism. Thus when dealing with the so-called secondary qualities he takes the example of heat and maintains that what we perceive is our own sensation of heat, while that which exists in the physical object is simply a power to cause or produce this sensation in a subject. This power 'is not perceived but inferred

---

[1] According to G. E. Moore, *esse est percipi* is the basic tenet of idealism. But he understands the thesis in a wide sense.

by a scientific theory'.[1] When, however, he is dealing with the so-called primary qualities, Cook Wilson maintains that we feel, for example, the extension of an actual body and not simply our tactual and muscular sensations. In other words, in his discussion of the relation of qualities to physical things he occupies a position close to that of Locke.

Indeed, we can say that Cook Wilson's realism involves the contention that the world which we know is simply the world as conceived by the classical Newtonian scientists. Thus he rejects the idea of non-Euclidean space or spaces. In his view mathematicians actually employ only the Euclidean concept of space, 'none other of course being possible for thought, while they imagine themselves to be talking of another kind of space'.[2]

The general outlook of Cook Wilson was shared by H. A. Prichard (1871–1947), who occupied the chair of moral philosophy at Oxford. In the first place 'it is simply *impossible* to think that any reality depends upon our knowledge of it, or upon any knowledge of it. If there is to be knowledge, there must first *be* something to be known.'[3] Obviously, the activities of Sherlock Holmes, as related by Conan Doyle, depend upon the mind in a sense in which stones and stars do not. But I could not claim to 'know' what Sherlock Holmes did unless there was first something to be known. In the second place 'knowledge is *sui generis*, and, as such, cannot be explained'.[4] For any alleged explanation necessarily presupposes that we are aware what knowledge is. In the third place secondary qualities cannot exist independently of a percipient subject, and consequently they 'cannot be qualities of things, since the qualities of a thing must exist independently of the perception of a thing'.[5]

In view of the last-mentioned point it is not surprising to find Prichard maintaining, in his posthumously published collection of essays *Knowledge and Perception* (1950), that we never actually see physical objects but only coloured and spatially related extensions, which we 'mistake' for physical bodies. If we ask how it comes about that we judge these sense-data to be physical

---

[1] *Statement and Inference*, II, p. 777. Cook Wilson prefers the example of heat to that of colour. For people who are innocent of theory are accustomed to speak of themselves as 'feeling hot', whereas nobody speaks of 'feeling coloured'. To see the relation between colour and the subject, a greater degree of reflection is required.

[2] *Ibid.*, II, p. 567.

[3] *Kant's Theory of Knowledge* (1909), p. 118.

[4] *Ibid.*, p. 124.   [5] *Ibid.*, p. 86.

objects, Prichard replies that it is not a case of judging at all.[1] We are naturally under the impression that what we see are physical bodies existing independently of perception. And it is only in the course of subsequent reflection that we come to infer or judge that this is not the case.

If, therefore, we start with the position of common sense or naïve realism, we must say that both Cook Wilson and Prichard modified this position, making concessions to the other side. Further concessions were made by H. W. B. Joseph (1867–1943), Fellow of New College, Oxford, and an influential teacher. Thus in a paper on Berkeley and Kant which he read to the British Academy Joseph remarks that common sense realism is badly shaken by reflection, and he suggests that though the things outside us are certainly not private in the sense in which my pain is private, they may be bound up 'with the being of knowing and perceiving minds'.[2] Joseph also suggests that reflection on the philosophies of Berkeley and Kant points to the conclusion that the conditions of our knowledge of objects may depend 'upon a reality or intelligence which shows itself in nature to itself in minds'.[3]

The last remark is clearly a concession to metaphysical idealism rather than to any form of subjective idealism. But this simply illustrates the difficulty in maintaining that in our knowledge of physical objects knowing is a relation of compresence between a subject and an object which is entirely heterogeneous to mind. As for the discussion of sense-data, a discussion which received a powerful impetus at Oxford from Professor H. H. Price's *Perception*,[4] this illustrates the difficulty in maintaining successfully a position of naïve realism. That is to say, problems arise for reflection which suggest that the position has to be modified. One way of coping with this situation is to dismiss the problems as pseudo-problems. But this was not an expedient adopted by the older Oxford philosophers whom we have been considering.

3. H. A. Prichard, who was mentioned in the last section, is probably best known for his famous essay in *Mind* (1912) on the

---

[1] According to Prichard, we could judge or infer that the direct objects of perception are physical bodies which are entirely independent of the perceiving subject, if we could be said to 'know' the former. But perception, for Prichard, is never knowledge.

[2] *Essays in Ancient and Modern Philosophy*, p. 231.   [3] *Ibid.*

[4] This book, published in 1932, shows the influence of Cambridge thinkers, such as Moore and Russell, whereas Cook Wilson had shown little respect for Cambridge thought.

question, 'Does Moral Philosophy rest on a Mistake?'[1] Moral philosophy is conceived by Prichard as being largely concerned with trying to find arguments to prove that what seem to be our duties really are our duties. And his own thesis is that in point of fact we simply see or intuit our duties, so that the whole attempt to prove that they are duties is mistaken. True, there can be argument in some sense. But what is called argument is simply an attempt to get people to look more closely at actions in order that they may see for themselves the characteristic of being obligatory. There are, of course, situations which give rise to what we are accustomed to call a conflict of duties. But in the case of an apparent conflict of this kind it is a mistake to try to resolve it by arguing, as so many philosophers have done, that one of the alternative actions will produce a greater good of some sort, this good being external to and a consequence of the action. The question at issue is, which action has the greater degree of obligatoriness? And the question cannot be answered in any other way than by looking closely at the actions until we *see* which is the greater obligation. This is, after all, what we are accustomed to do in practice.

This ethical intuitionism obviously implies that the concepts of right and obligation are paramount in ethics and take precedence over the concept of good. In other words, teleological ethical systems, such as the Aristotelian and the Utilitarian, rest on a fundamental mistake. And in the period after the First World War a discussion took place at Oxford on the themes raised by Prichard. It was conducted more or less independently of, though not without some reference to, the views of G. E. Moore. But we can say that it expressed a strong reaction against the type of position represented by the Cambridge philosopher. For though Moore had maintained in *Principia Ethica* (1903) that goodness is an indefinable quality,[2] he made it quite clear that in his opinion a moral obligation is an obligation to perform that action which will produce the greater amount of goodness.

In 1922 Prichard devoted his inaugural lecture as professor of moral philosophy at Oxford to the theme 'Duty and Interest', developing therein his point of view. In 1928 E. F. Carritt published *The Theory of Morals* in which he maintained that the idea of a *summum bonum*, a supreme good, is the *ignis fatuus* of moral

[1] Reprinted in *Moral Obligation: Essays and Lectures* (1949).
[2] This does not mean that we cannot say what things possess this quality or have intrinsic value. Moore was convinced that we can.

philosophy, and that any attempt to prove that certain actions are duties because they are means to the realization of some end considered as good is foredoomed to failure. The famous Aristotelian scholar, Sir W. D. Ross, then Provost of Oriel College, Oxford, contributed to the discussion by his book on *The Right and The Good* (1930). And this was followed in 1931 by Joseph's *Some Problems in Ethics*, in which the author characteristically tried to combine admission of the thesis that obligation is not derived from the goodness of the consequences of an action with the thesis that obligation is none the less not independent of any relation to goodness.

In other words, Joseph attempted to compromise between Prichard's view and the Aristotelian tradition. And in his little work *Rule and End in Morals* (1932), which was intended as a summing-up of the Oxford discussions, Professor J. H. Muirhead of the University of Birmingham drew attention to signs of a return, welcomed by himself, towards an Aristotelian-idealist view of ethics. But in 1936 there appeared *Language, Truth and Logic*, the celebrated logical positivist manifesto by A. J. Ayer, in which a statement such as 'actions of type X are wrong' was interpreted, not as the expression of any intuition, but as an utterance expressing an emotive attitude towards actions of type X and as also calculated to arouse a similar emotive attitude in others. And though the emotive theory of ethics certainly cannot be said to have won the universal assent of British moral philosophers, it stimulated a new phase of discussion in ethical theory, a phase which lies outside the scope of this volume.[1] Hence when Sir David Ross published *The Foundations of Ethics* in 1939, his intuitionism seemed to some at any rate to belong to a past phase of thought. However, on looking back we can see how the discussion by Prichard, Ross, Joseph and others of concepts such as those of the right and the good represented an analytic approach to moral philosophy which was different from the idealist tendency to treat ethics as a subordinate theme dependent on a metaphysical world-view. Yet we can also see how in the subsequent phase of ethical discussion philosophers have at length been led to doubt whether ethics can profitably be confined in a watertight compartment as a study of the language of morals.[2]

4. To turn now to realism in the United States of America. In

[1] See, for example, *Ethics Since 1900* by M. Warnock (London, 1960).
[2] Professor Stuart Hampshire's *Thought and Action* (London, 1959) is an example of this tendency.

March 1901 William Pepperell Montague (1873–1953) published in *The Philosophical Review* an article entitled 'Professor Royce's Refutation of Realism'. And in October of the same year Ralph Barton Perry (1876–1957) published in *The Monist* a paper on 'Professor Royce's Refutation of Realism and Pluralism'. Both articles, therefore, were answers to Royce's attack on realism as destructive of the possibility of knowledge. And in 1910 the two writers, together with E. B. Holt (1873–1946), W. T. Marvin (1872–1944), W. B. Pitkin (1878–1953), and E. G. Spaulding (1873–1940), published in the *Journal of Philosophy* 'The Program and First Platform of Six Realists'.[1] This was followed by the publication in 1912 of a volume of essays by these authors under the title, *The New Realism: Co-operative Studies in Philosophy*.

As was stated in the 1910 programme and as the sub-title of *The New Realism* indicates, this group of philosophers aimed at making philosophy a genuine co-operative pursuit, at least among those thinkers who were prepared to accept the basic tenets of realism. They insisted on a scrupulous care of language as the instrument of all philosophy, on analysis considered as 'the careful, systematic and exhaustive examination of any topic of discourse',[2] on separating vague complex problems into definite questions which should be dealt with separately, and on a close association with the special sciences. By this approach to philosophy the new realist hoped, therefore, to overcome the subjectivism, looseness of thought and language, and disregard of science which in their opinion had tended to bring philosophy into disrepute. In other words, a reform of philosophy in general was to go hand in hand with the development of a realist line of thought.

The new realists were at any rate agreed on the truth of a basic tenet, namely that, as Pitkin expressed it, 'things known are not products of the knowing relation nor essentially dependent for their existence or behaviour upon that relation'.[3] This tenet corresponds with our natural spontaneous belief, and it is demanded by the sciences. Hence the burden of proof rests fairly and squarely on the shoulders of those who deny it. But the disproofs offered by the idealists are fallacious. For instance, they slide from a truism, that it is only when objects are known that we

---

[1] This programme was reprinted as an Appendix in *The New Realism*.

[2] *The New Realism*, p. 24. As far as care for language and breaking up vague and complex problems into manageable and quite definite questions were concerned, the new realists' idea of proper philosophical procedure was similar to that of G. E. Moore in England.

[3] *Ibid.*, p. 477.

know that they exist, or from the tautology 'no object without a subject', to a substantial but unproven conclusion, namely that we know that objects exist only as objects, that is, only when they are known, as terms of the knowing relation.

This obviously implies that knowledge is an external relation. As Spaulding puts it, knowledge is 'eliminable',[1] in the sense that a thing can exist when it is not known and that, when not known, it can be precisely what it is when it is known, with the obvious difference that it is then not the term of the external relation of knowing. There must thus be at least one kind of external relation. And we can say in general that the new realists accepted the theory of relations as external to their terms. This view obviously favoured pluralism rather than monism in metaphysics. And it also pointed to the impossibility of deducing the world-system *a priori*.

The ordinary man's spontaneous reaction to the basic tenet of realism would undoubtedly be one of unqualified acceptance. For he is obviously accustomed to think of physical objects as existing quite independently of the knowing relation and as being entirely unaffected by this relation in their natures or characteristics. But reflection shows us that some account has to be taken of illusions, hallucinations and such like phenomena. Are they to be described as objects of knowledge? If so, can they reasonably be said to be real independently of the subject? And what of apparently converging railway-lines, sticks which appear bent when half immersed in water, and so on? Can we say that such percepts exist independently of perception? Must we not at any rate modify realism in such a way as to be able to assert that some objects of consciousness exist independently while others do not?

Holt's way of dealing with the matter is to make a distinction between being and reality. Realism does not commit us to holding that all perceived things are real. 'While all perceived things are things, *not* all perceived things are *real* things.'[2] It does not follow, however, that 'unreal' objects of perception or of thought are to be described as 'subjective' in character. On the contrary, the unreal has being and 'subsists of its own right in the all-inclusive universe of being'.[3] In fine, 'the universe is not all real; but the universe all is'.[4]

---

[1] *The New Realism*, p. 478.　　　　[2] *Ibid.*, p. 358.
[3] *Ibid.*, p. 366. The unreal object must be distinguished from the unthinkable, such as a round square.
[4] *Ibid.*, p. 360.

Obviously, some explanation of this use of terms is required. And in the first place what does Holt mean by reality? The answer, 'as to what reality is, I take no great interest',[1] is not very promising. But Holt goes on to say that, if challenged, he would 'hazard the guess that perhaps reality is some very comprehensive system of terms in relation. . . . This would make reality closely related to what logic knows as "existence" '.[2] This suggests that an hallucinatory object, for example, is unreal in the sense that it cannot be fitted, without contradiction, into the most universal system of related terms. But Holt remarks that 'I shall not call an hallucinatory object necessarily "unreal" '.[3] The point on which he insists, however, is that unreality does not exclude objectivity. If, for instance, I assume certain geometrical premisses at will and deduce a consistent system, the system is 'objective', even if it is described as 'unreal'. And to say that the unreal is objective, not subjective, is what Holt means by saying that it has being.

As for converging railway lines, sticks which appear bent in water and so on, Holt maintains that a physical object has innumerable projective properties, with which there correspond different specific responses in the nervous systems of different percipient organisms. Hence if we abstract from the particular purpose or purposes which lead us to select one appearance as a thing's 'real' appearance, we can say that all its appearances are on the same footing. They are all objective, and they subsist as projective properties. We are thus offered the picture of 'a general universe of being in which all things physical, mental, and logical, propositions and terms, existent and non-existent, false and true, good and evil, real and unreal *subsist*'.[4]

As Montague was afterwards to point out when discussing the differences between himself and some of his colleagues in the neo-realist group, there are considerable objections to putting all these things on the same footing. In the first place, the relations between objects of perception can be asymmetrical. For instance, on the assumption that the stick partly immersed in water is straight, we can easily explain why it appears bent. But if we assume that it is bent, we cannot explain why it appears straight in the circumstances in which it does appear to be straight. And this difficulty is certainly not overcome by saying that the stick is bent when it is partly immersed in water, while it is straight

[1] *Ibid.*, p. 366.   [2] *Ibid.*,
[3] *Ibid.*, p. 367.   [4] *Ibid.*, p. 372.

when it is out of the water. Again, some objects can produce effects only indirectly by means of the subject which conceives them, while other objects can also produce effects directly. For example, a dragon, as object of thought, might conceivably stimulate a man to make a voyage of exploration; but it could not produce the effects which can be produced by a lion. And we need to be able to make clear distinctions between the ontological statuses of these different classes of objects.

The new realists also concerned themselves with discussing the nature of consciousness. Holt and Perry, partly under the influence of William James, accepted the doctrine of neutral monism, according to which there is no ultimate substantial difference between mind and matter. And they tried to eliminate consciousness as a peculiar entity by explaining awareness of an object as a specific response by an organism. Montague interpreted this as meaning that the response consists of a motion of particles. And he asked how this theory, which he described as behaviourism, could possibly explain, for example, our awareness of past events. He himself identified the specific response which constitutes consciousness with 'the relation of self-transcending implication, which the brain-states sustain to their extra-organic causes'.[1] But it is not at all clear how brain-states can exercise any such self-transcending function. Nor does it help very much to be told that the possibility of the cortical states transcending themselves and providing awareness of objects is 'a matter for psychology rather than epistemology'.[2]

However, it is at any rate clear that the new realists were intent on maintaining that, as Montague put it, 'cognition is a peculiar type of relation which may subsist between a living being and any entity . . . [that it] belongs to the same world as that of its objects . . . [and that] there is nothing transcendental or supernatural about it'.[3] They also rejected all forms of representationalism. In perception and knowledge the subject is related directly to the object, not indirectly by means of an image or some sort of mental copy which constitutes the immediate term of the relation.

5. This rejection by the neo-realists of all representationalism seemed to some other philosophers to be naïve and uncritical. It was this rejection which led to physical and hallucinatory objects

---

[1] *The New Realism*, p. 482. [2] *Ways of Knowing* (1925), p. 396.
[3] *The New Realism*, p. 475.

being placed on the same footing. And it made it impossible to explain, for instance, our perception of a distant star when the star has ceased to exist. Thus there soon arose a movement of critical realism, formed by philosophers who agreed with the neo-realists in rejecting idealism but who found themselves unable to accept their thoroughgoing rejection of representationalism.

Like neo-realism, critical realism found expression in a joint-volume, *Essays in Critical Realism: A Co-operative Study of the Problems of Knowledge*, which appeared in 1920. The contributors were D. Drake (1898–1933), A. O. Lovejoy (1873–1962), J. B. Pratt (1875–1944), A. K. Rogers (1868–1936), G. Santayana (1863–1952), R. W. Sellars (b. 1880), and C. A. Strong (1862–1940).

The strength of critical realism lay in attack. For example, in *The Revolt against Dualism* (1930), Lovejoy argued that while neo-realists originally appealed to common sense in their rejection of representationalism, they then proceeded to give an account of objects which was incompatible with the common sense point of view. For to maintain with Holt that all the appearances of a thing are on the same footing as its objective projective properties is to commit oneself to saying that railway lines are both parallel and convergent, and that the surface of, say, a penny is both circular and elliptical.

In expounding their own doctrine, however, the critical realists encountered considerable difficulties. We can say that they were agreed in maintaining that what we directly perceive is some character-complex or immediate datum which functions as a sign of or guide to an independently existing thing. But they were not in full agreement about the nature of the immediate datum. Some were prepared to speak about such data as mental states.[1] And in this case they would presumably be in the mind. Others, such as Santayana, believed that the immediate data of consciousness are essences, and ruled out any question as to their whereabouts on the ground that they exist only as exemplified. In any case, if representationalism is once admitted, it seems to follow that the existence of physical objects is inferred. And there then arises the problem of justifying this inference. What reason have I for supposing that what I actually perceive represents something

---

[1] In an essay on the development of American realism Montague attributes to the critical realists in general the doctrine that we know directly only 'mental states or ideas'. Cf. *Twentieth Century Philosophy* (1943). edited by D. D. Runes, p. 441.

other than itself? Further, if we never perceive physical objects directly, how can we discriminate between the representative values of different sense-data?

The critical realists tried to answer the first question by maintaining that from the very start and by their very nature the immediate data of perception point to physical objects beyond themselves. But they differed in their accounts of this external reference. Santayana, for instance, appealed to animal faith, to the force of instinctive belief in the external reference of our percepts, a belief which we share with the animals, while Sellars relied on psychology to explain how our awareness of externality develops and grows in definiteness.

As for the question, how can we discriminate between the representative values of sense-data if we never perceive physical objects directly? one may be tempted to answer, 'In the way that we actually do discriminate, namely by verification'. And this may be an excellent answer from the practical point of view. After all, travellers in the desert, interpreting a mirage as a prediction that they will find water ahead of them, find by bitter experience that the prediction is not verified. At the same time a theoretical difficulty still remains for the representationalist to solve. For on his premisses the process of verification terminates in sensory experience or the having of sense-data and is not a magic wand which, when waved, gives us direct access to what lies beyond sense-data. True, if what we are seeking is the sensory experience of a slaking of thirst, having this experience is all that is required from the practical point of view. But from the point of view of the theory of knowledge the representationalist seems to remain immersed in the world of 'representation'.

The fact of the matter is, of course, that on the level of common sense and practical life we can get along perfectly well. And in ordinary language we have developed distinctions which are quite sufficient to cope for all practical purposes with sticks partially immersed in water, converging railway lines, pink rats, and so on. But once we start to reflect on the epistemological problems to which such phenomena appear to give rise, there is the temptation to embrace some overall solution, either by saying that all the objects of awareness are objective and on the same footing or by saying that they are all subjective mental states or sense-data which are somehow neither subjective nor objective. In the first case we have neo-realism, in the second critical realism, provided, of course, that the immediate data are regarded as representative of or in some way related to independent physical objects. Both positions can be regarded as attempts to reform ordinary language. And though this enterprise cannot be ruled out *a priori*, the fact that both positions give rise to serious difficulties may well prompt us, with the late Professor J. L. Austin, to take another look at ordinary language.

The word 'realism' can have different shades of meaning. In this chapter it has as its basic meaning the view that knowledge is not a construction of the object, that knowing is a relation of compresence between a subject and an object, which makes no difference to the object. We have seen, however, that in the realist movement problems arose about the immediate objects of perception and knowledge. At the same time we do not wish to give the quite erroneous impression that the American philosophers who belonged to the two groups which have been mentioned were exclusively concerned with the problems to which attention has been drawn in this and the preceding sections. Among the neo-realists Perry, for example, became well known as a moral philosopher,[1] and also devoted himself to political and social themes. Among the critical realists Santayana developed a general philosophy,[2] while Strong and Drake expounded a panpsychistic ontology, taking introspection as a key to the nature of reality.[3] Sellars defended a naturalistic philosophy,[4] based on the idea of emergent evolution with irreducible levels and comprising a theory of perception as an interpretative operation. Lovejoy exercised a considerable influence by his studies in the history of ideas.[5]

6. A realist theory of knowledge, in the sense already described, obviously does not exclude the construction of a metaphysical system or world-view. All that is excluded is a metaphysics based on the theory that knowledge is a construction of the object or on

---

[1] He published his *General Theory of Value* in 1926.

[2] Santayana's *Realms of Being* comprises four volumes: *The Realm of Essence* (1927), *The Realm of Matter* (1930), *The Realm of Truth* (1938), and *The Realm of Spirit* (1940).

[3] According to Strong, introspection is the one case in which we are directly aware of 'stuff' as distinct from structure. But neither Strong nor Drake meant to imply that stones, for instance, are conscious. Their panpsychism was linked with the idea of emergent evolution. Even those things which we call 'material' possess a potential energy which at a certain level of evolution manifests itself in consciousness.

[4] As in *The Philosophy of Physical Realism* (1932).

[5] Lovejoy published, for instance, *The Great Chain of Being* in 1936 and *Essays in the History of Ideas* in 1948.

the theory that creative thought or experience is the basic, primary reality. And in point of fact there have been a considerable number of world-views in modern philosophy, which presupposed a realist theory of knowledge. To mention them all is, however, out of the question. And I propose to confine myself to making some remarks about the world-view of Samuel Alexander.

Samuel Alexander (1859–1938) was born in Sydney, Australia, but went to Oxford in 1877, where he came under the influence of Green and Bradley. This influence, however, was supplanted by that of the idea of evolution, as well as by an interest in empirical psychology, which was scarcely a characteristic of Oxford at the time.[1] Later on Alexander received stimulus from the realism of Moore and Russell and came to approach, though he did not altogether accept, the position of American neo-realism. But he regarded the theory of knowledge as preparatory to metaphysical synthesis. And it may well be true that his impulse to metaphysical construction, though not the actual content of his system, was due in some measure to the early influence of idealism on his mind.

In 1882 Alexander was elected a Fellow of Lincoln College, Oxford. And the influence of evolutionary thought can be seen in the book which he published in 1889, *Moral Order and Progress: An Analysis of Ethical Conceptions*. As the title of the book indicates, Alexander considered ethics to be concerned with the analysis of moral concepts, such as good and evil, right and wrong. But he also regarded it as a normative science. In his interpretation of the moral life and of moral concepts he carried on the line of thought represented by Herbert Spencer and Sir Leslie Stephen. Thus in his view the struggle for survival in the biological sphere takes the form in the ethical sphere of a struggle between rival moral ideals. And the law of natural selection, as applying in the moral field, means that that set of moral ideals tends to prevail which most conduces to the production of a state of equilibrium or harmony between the various elements and forces in the individual, between the individual and society, and between man and his environment. There is thus an ultimate and overall ideal of harmony which in Alexander's view includes within itself the ideals upheld by other ethical systems, such as happiness and self-realization. At the same time the conditions of life, physical and

[1] Bradley was interested in psychology. But it is notorious that for many years psychology was frowned on at Oxford and regarded as not qualifying for recognition as a science.

social, are constantly changing, with the result that the concrete meaning of equilibrium or harmony assumes fresh forms. Hence, even though there is in a real sense an ultimate end of moral progress, it cannot be actually attained in a fixed and unalterable shape, and ethics cannot be expressed in the form of a set of static principles which are incapable of modification or change.

To turn to Alexander's realism.[1] His basic idea of knowledge is that it is simply a relation of compresence or togetherness between some object and a conscious being. The object, in the sense of the thing known, is what it is whether it is known or not. Further, Alexander rejects all forms of representationalism. We can, of course, direct our attention explicitly to our mental acts or states. But they do not serve as copies or signs of external things which are known only indirectly. Rather do we 'enjoy' our mental acts while knowing directly objects which are other than the acts by which we know them. Nor are sense-data intermediate objects between consciousness and physical things, they are perspectives of things. Even a so-called illusion is a perspective of the real world, though it is referred by the mind to a context to which it does not belong.[2] Further, in knowing the past by memory we really do know the past. That is to say, pastness is a direct object of experience.

In 1893 Alexander was appointed professor of philosophy in the University of Manchester. In the years 1916–18 he delivered the Gifford Lectures at Glasgow, and the published version appeared in 1920 under the title *Space, Time and Deity*. In this work we are told that metaphysics is concerned with the world as a whole, thus carrying comprehensiveness to its furthest limits. In Aristotelian language we can say that it is the science of being and its essential attributes, investigating 'the ultimate nature of existence if it has any, and those pervasive characters of things, or categories'.[3] But though metaphysics has a wider subject-matter than any special science, its method is empirical, in the sense that, like the sciences, it uses 'hypotheses by which to bring its data into verifiable connection'.[4] At the same time the pervasive and essential attributes of things can be described as non-empirical or

---

[1] The best known of Alexander's articles illustrating his realist theory of knowledge is 'The Basis of Realism', which appeared in the *Proceedings of the British Academy* for 1914.

[2] In other words, the mind does not create the materials of an illusion but derives them from sensible experience. But it can be said to constitute the illusion *as* an illusion by an erroneous judgment in regard to context.

[3] *Space, Time and Deity*, I, p. 2.   [4] *Ibid.*, I, p. 4.

a priori provided that we understand that the distinction between the empirical and the non-empirical lies within the experienced and is not equivalent to a distinction between experience and what transcends all experience. Bearing this in mind, we can define metaphysics as 'the experiential or empirical study of the non-empirical or *a priori*, and of such questions as arise out of the relation of the empirical to the *a priori*'.[1]

According to Alexander, ultimate reality, the basic matrix of all things, is space-time. Precisely how he arrived at this notion, it is difficult to say. He mentions, for example, the idea of a world in space and time formulated by H. Minkowski in 1908. And he refers to Lorentz and Einstein. Further, he speaks with approval of Bergson's concept of real time, though with disapproval of the French philosopher's subordination of space to time. In any case Alexander's notion of space-time as the ultimate reality is obviously opposed to Bradley's relegation of space and time to the sphere of appearance and to McTaggart's theory of the unreality of time. Alexander is concerned with constructing a naturalistic metaphysics or world-view; and he begins with what is for him both the ultimate and, when considered purely in itself, the primitive phase of the evolutionary process.

The naïve way of conceiving space and time is as receptacles or containers. And a natural corrective to this crude image is to depict them as relations between individual entities, relations respectively of co-existence and succession. But this view clearly implies that individual entities are logically prior to space and time, whereas the hypothesis embraced by Alexander is that space and time constitute 'the stuff or matrix (or matrices) out of which things or events are made, the medium in which they are precipitated and crystallized'.[2] If we consider either space or time by itself, its elements or parts are indistinguishable. But 'each point of space is determined and distinguished by an instant in time, and each instant of time by its position in space'.[3] In other words, space and time together constitute one reality, 'an infinite continuum of pure events or point-instants'.[4] And empirical things are groupings or complexes of such events.

Alexander proceeds to discuss the pervasive categories or fundamental properties of space-time, such as identity, diversity and existence, universal and particular, relation, causality and so

---

[1] *Space, Time and Deity*, I, p. 4. [2] *Ibid.*, I, p. 38.
[3] *Ibid.*, I, p. 60. [4] *Ibid.*, I, p. 66.

on. The stage is thus set for an examination of the emergence of qualities and of levels of empirical reality, from matter up to conscious mental activity. We cannot discuss all these themes here. But it is worth drawing attention to Alexander's doctrine of 'tertiary qualities'.

The tertiary qualities are values, such as truth and goodness. They are called 'tertiary' to distinguish them from the primary and secondary qualities of traditional philosophy. But as applied to values the term 'qualities' should really be placed in inverted commas, to indicate that 'these values are not qualities of reality in the same sense as colour, or form, or life'.[1] To speak of them as objective qualities of reality can be misleading. For instance, reality is not, properly speaking, either true or false: it is simply reality. Truth and falsity are properly predicated of propositions as believed, that is, in relation to the mind which believes them, not of things, nor even of propositions when considered simply as mental facts. Similarly, a thing is good, according to Alexander, only in relation to a purpose, as when we speak of a good tool. Again, though a red rose is red whether anyone perceives it or not, it is beautiful only in relation to the mind which appreciates its 'coherence'. But it by no means follows that we are entitled to speak of the tertiary qualities or values as purely subjective or as unreal. They emerge as real features of the universe, though only in relation to minds or conscious subjects. They are, in fine, 'subject-object determinations',[2] which 'imply the amalgamation of the object with the human appreciation of it'.[3]

The relation between subject and object is not, however, invariable. In the case of truth, for example, appreciation by the subject is determined by the object. For in knowledge reality is discovered, not made. But in the case of goodness the quality of being good is determined primarily by the subject, that is, by purpose, by the will. There is, however, a common factor which must be noted, namely that the appreciation of values in general arises in a social context, out of the community of minds. For instance, it is in relation to the judgment of others that I become aware that a proposition is false; and in my judgments about truth or falsity I represent what we can call the collective mind. 'It is social intercourse, therefore, which makes us aware that there is a reality compounded of ourselves and the object, and that in

---

[1] *Ibid.*, II, p. 237.
[3] *Ibid.*

[2] *Ibid.*, II, p. 238.

that relation the object has a character which it would not have except for that relation.'[1]

This doctrine of the emergence of tertiary qualities enables Alexander to insist that evolution is not indifferent to values. 'Darwinism is sometimes thought to be indifferent to value. It is in fact the history of how values come into existence in the world of life.'[2] We thus have the general picture of a process of evolution in which different levels of finite being emerge, each level possessing its own characteristic empirical quality. 'The highest of these empirical qualities known to us is mind or consciousness.'[3] And at this level the tertiary qualities or values emerge as real features of the universe, though this reality involves a relation to the subject, the human mind.

Now, Alexander's work is entitled *Space, Time and Deity*. Hence the question arises, how does Deity fit into this scheme or world-view? The philosopher's answer is that 'Deity is the next higher empirical quality to the highest we know'.[4] We obviously cannot say what this quality is. But we know that it is not any quality with which we are already acquainted. For that it should be any such quality is ruled out by definition.

Does it follow from this that God exists only in the future, so to speak, being identifiable with the next level of finite being to emerge in the process of evolution? To this question Alexander gives a negative answer. As an actually existent being, God is the universe, the whole space-time continuum. 'God is the whole world as possessing the quality of deity. . . . As an actual existent, God is the infinite world with its nisus towards deity, or, to adapt a phrase of Leibniz, as big or in travail with deity.'[5]

Alexander was of Jewish origin and it is not unreasonable to see in his view of God a dynamic version of Spinoza's pantheism, adapted to the theory of evolution. But there is an obvious difficulty in maintaining both that God is the whole world as possessing the quality of Deity and that this quality is a future emergent. Alexander is aware of this, of course. And he concludes that 'God as an actual existent is always becoming deity but never attains it. He is the ideal God in embryo.'[6] As for religion, it can be described as 'the sentiment in us that we are drawn towards Him [God], and caught in the movement of the world to a higher level of existence'.[7]

[1] *Space, Time and Deity*, II, p. 240.   [2] *Ibid.*, II, p. 309.   [3] *Ibid.*, II, p. 345.
[4] *Ibid.*   [5] *Ibid.*, II, p. 353.   [6] *Ibid.*, II, p. 365.
[7] *Ibid.*, II, p. 429.

Given his premisses, Alexander's position is understandable. On the one hand, if Deity is the quality of a future level of being, and if God were identifiable with the actual bearer of this quality, he would be finite. On the other hand, the religious consciousness, Alexander assumes, demands a God who is not only existent but also infinite. Hence God must be identified with the infinite universe as striving after the quality of Deity. But to say this is really to do no more than to apply a label, 'God', to the evolving universe, the space-time continuum. To be sure, there is some similarity between Alexander's view and that of Hegel. At the same time Hegel's Absolute is defined as Spirit, whereas Alexander's is defined as Space-Time. And this renders the label 'God' even more inappropriate. What is appropriate is the description of religion as a 'sentiment'. For in a naturalistic philosophy this is precisely what religion becomes, namely some kind of cosmic emotion.

7. Owing to the development and spread of a current of thought which has been accompanied by a marked distrust of all comprehensive world-views, little attention has been paid to Alexander's philosophy.[1] In any case, in the field of speculative philosophy his star has been completely eclipsed by that of Alfred North Whitehead (1861–1947), the greatest English metaphysical philosopher since Bradley. True, it can hardly be claimed that the influence of Whitehead as a speculative philosopher on recent British philosophy has been extensive or profound. Given the prevailing climate of philosophical thought, one would hardly expect it to have been. Whitehead's influence has in fact been greater in America, where he worked from 1924 until his death, than in his native land. In the last few years, however, interest in his thought has shown itself in a considerable number of books and articles published in Great Britain.[2] And his name has become increasingly known in Europe. In other words, Whitehead is recognized as a major thinker, whereas Alexander tends to be forgotten.

From one point of view, Whitehead's philosophy certainly qualifies for inclusion in this chapter. True, he himself drew attention to the affinity between the results of his philosophizing and absolute idealism. Thus in his preface to *Process and Reality* he notes that 'though throughout the main body of the work I am

[1] In Mr. G. J. Warnock's excellent little book, *English Philosophy Since 1900*, Alexander is passed over in silence.
[2] The increase not only in tolerance of but also in sympathy with 'descriptive metaphysics' has, of course, contributed to this revival of interest in Whitehead.

in sharp disagreement with Bradley, the final outcome is after all not so greatly different'.[1] At the same time Whitehead, who came from mathematics to the philosophy of science and Nature, and thence to metaphysics, intended to return to a pre-idealist attitude and point of departure. That is to say, just as some of the pre-Kantian philosophers had philosophized in close association with the science of their time, Whitehead considered that the new physics demanded a fresh effort in speculative philosophy. He did not start from the subject-object relation or from the idea of creative thought, but rather from reflection on the world as presented in modern science. His categories are not simply imposed by the *a priori* constitution of the human mind; they belong to reality, as pervasive features of it, in much the same sense as Aristotle's categories belonged to reality. Again, Whitehead gives a naturalistic interpretation of consciousness, in the sense that it is depicted as a developed, emergent form of the relation of 'prehension' which is found between all actual entities. Hence when he notes the affinity between the results of his speculative philosophy and some features of absolute idealism he also suggests that his type of thought may be 'a transformation of some main doctrines of Absolute Idealism on to a realistic basis'.[2]

But though Whitehead's philosophy, as standing on what he calls a realistic basis, certainly qualifies for consideration in this chapter, it is far too complicated to summarize in a few paragraphs. And after some consideration the present writer has decided not to make the attempt. It is, however, worth noting that Whitehead was convinced of the inevitability of speculative or metaphysical philosophy. That is to say, unless a philosopher deliberately breaks off at a certain point the process of understanding the world and of generalization, he is inevitably led to 'the endeavour to frame a coherent, logical, necessary system of general ideas in terms of which every element of our experience can be interpreted'.[3] Moreover, it is not simply a question of synthesizing the sciences. For the analysis of any particular fact and the determination of the status of any entity require in the long run a view of the general principles and categories which the fact embodies and of the entity's status in the whole universe. Linguistically speaking, every proposition stating a particular fact requires for its complete analysis an exhibition of the general character of the universe as exemplified in this fact. Ontologically

---

[1] *Process and Reality*, p. vii (1959 edition).   [2] *Ibid.*, p. viii.   [3] *Ibid.*, p. 4.

speaking, 'every definite entity requires a systematic universe to supply its requisite status'.[1] Wherever we start, therefore, we are led to metaphysics, provided that we do not break off the process of understanding on the way.

This point of view assumes, of course, that the universe is an organic system. And it is Whitehead's sustained attempt to show that the universe is in fact a unified dynamic process, a plurality-in-unity which is to be interpreted as a creative advance into novelty, that constitutes his philosophical system. As already noted, the total result of his speculation bears some resemblance to absolute idealism. But the world as presented by Whitehead is certainly not the dialectical working-out of an absolute Idea. The total universe, comprising both God and the world, is said to be caught 'in the grip of the ultimate metaphysical ground, the creative advance into novelty'.[2] It is 'creativity',[3] not thought, which is for him the ultimate factor.

---

[1] *Ibid*, p. 17.   [2] *Ibid.*, p. 529.

[3] 'Creativity', as described by Whitehead, is not an actual entity, like God, but 'the universal of universals' (*Process and Reality*, p. 31).

CHAPTER XVIII

G. E. MOORE AND ANALYSIS

Life and writings—Common sense realism—Some remarks on Moore's ethical ideas—Moore on analysis—The sense-datum theory as an illustration of Moore's practice of analysis.

1. In the last chapter we had occasion to consider briefly some Oxford realists. But when one thinks of the collapse of idealism in England and of the rise of a new dominating current of thought, one's mind naturally turns to the analytic movement which had its origins at Cambridge and which in the course of time established itself firmly at Oxford and in other universities. It is true that in its later phase it has become commonly known as 'Oxford philosophy'; but this does not alter the fact that the three great pioneers of and stimulative influences in the movement, Moore, Russell and Wittgenstein, were all Cambridge men.

George Edward Moore (1873–1958) went up to Cambridge in 1892, where he began by studying classics. He has remarked that he does not think that the world or the sciences would ever have suggested to him philosophical problems. In other words, left to himself he tended to take the world as he found it and as it was presented by the sciences. He appears to have been entirely free from Bradley's dissatisfaction with all our ordinary ways of conceiving the world, and he did not hanker after some superior way of viewing it. Still less was he tortured by the problems which beset Kierkegaard, Jaspers, Camus and such-like thinkers. At the same time Moore became interested in the queer things which philosophers have said about the world and the sciences; for example, that time is unreal or that scientific knowledge is not really knowledge. And he was diverted from classics to philosophy, partly under the influence of his younger contemporary, Bertrand Russell.

In 1898 Moore was awarded a Prize-Fellowship at Trinity College, Cambridge. And in 1903 he published *Principia Ethica*. After an absence from Cambridge he was appointed Lecturer in Moral Science in 1911; and in the following year he published his little work, *Ethics*, in the Home University Library Series. In 1921 he succeeded G. F. Stout as editor of *Mind*; and in 1922 he published *Philosophical Studies*, consisting for the most part of reprinted articles. In 1925 Moore was elected to the Chair of Philosophy at Cambridge on the retirement of James Ward. In 1951 he was awarded the *Order of Merit*; and in 1953 he published *Some Main Problems of Philosophy*. *Philosophical Papers*, a collection of essays prepared for publication by Moore himself, appeared posthumously in 1959, while his *Commonplace Book, 1919–53*, a selection from his notes and jottings, was published in 1962.

2. According to Bertrand Russell, it was Moore who led the rebellion against idealism. And Moore's early realism can be illustrated by reference to an article on the nature of judgment, which he published in *Mind* during the year 1899.

In this article Moore takes as his text Bradley's statement that truth and falsity depend on the relation between ideas and reality, and he refers with approval to Bradley's explanation that the term 'ideas' does not signify mental states but rather universal meanings.[1] Moore then proceeds to substitute 'concept' for 'idea' and 'proposition' for 'judgment', and to maintain that what is asserted in a proposition is a specific relation between concepts. In his view this holds good also of existential judgments. For 'existence is itself a concept'.[2] But Moore rejects the theory that a proposition is true or false in virtue of its correspondence or lack of correspondence with a reality or state of affairs other than itself. On the contrary, the truth of a proposition is an identifiable property of the proposition itself, belonging to it in virtue of the relation obtaining, within the proposition, between the concepts which compose it. 'What kind of relation makes a proposition true, what false, cannot be further defined, but must be immediately recognized.'[3] It is not, however, a relation between the proposition and something outside it.

Now, as Moore says that concepts are 'the only objects of knowledge',[4] and as propositions assert relations between concepts and are true or false simply in virtue of the relation asserted, it looks at first sight as though he were expounding a theory which is the reverse of anything which could reasonably be described as realism. That is to say, it looks as though Moore were creating an unbridgeable gulf between the world of propositions, which is the sphere of truth and falsity, and the world of non-propositional reality or fact.

[1] In other words, Moore approves of Bradley's protest against the psychologizing of logic.
[2] *Mind*, Vol. 8 (1899), p. 180.   [3] *Ibid.*   [4] *Ibid.*, p. 182.

We have to understand, however, that for Moore concepts are not abstractions, mental constructs formed on the basis of the material provided by sense-data, but rather objective realities, as with Meinong. Further, we are invited 'to regard the world as formed of concepts'.[1] That is to say, an existent thing is a complex of concepts, of universals such as whiteness for example, 'standing in a unique relation to the concept of existence'.[2] To say this is not to reduce the world of existing things to mental states. On the contrary, it is to eliminate the opposition between concepts and things. And to say that concepts are the objects of knowledge is to say that we know reality directly. When, therefore, Moore says of concepts that they must *be* something before they can enter into a relation with a cognitive subject and that 'it is indifferent to their nature whether anybody thinks them or not',[3] we can see what he means. He is saying that knowledge makes no difference to the object. It doubtless has its causes and effects; but 'these are to be found only in the subject'.[4] Construction of the object is certainly not one of the effects of knowing.

If a proposition consists of concepts standing in a specific relation to one another, and if concepts are identical with the realities conceived, it obviously follows that a true proposition must be identical with the reality which it is commonly considered as representing and with which it is commonly said to correspond. And in an article on truth,[5] Moore did not hesitate to maintain that the proposition 'I exist' does not differ from the reality 'my existence'.

As Moore was well aware at the time of writing, this theory sounds extremely odd. But what is more serious than its oddity is the difficulty in seeing how it does not eliminate the distinction between true and false propositions. Suppose, for example, that I believe that the earth is flat. If what I believe is a proposition, it seems to follow from the account of propositions explained above, that the earth being flat is a reality. Moore, therefore, came to throw overboard the idea that what we believe is propositions. In fact he came to jettison the idea of propositions at all, at any rate in the sense in which he had formerly postulated them. At the same time he clung to a realist view of knowledge as a unique unanalyzable relation between a cognitive subject and an object, a relation which makes no difference to the nature of the object.

---

[1] *Mind*, Vol. 8, p. 182.   [2] *Ibid.*, p. 183.   [3] *Ibid.*, p. 179.   [4] *Ibid.*
[5] In Baldwin's *Dictionary of Philosophy and Psychology.*

As for the truth or falsity of beliefs, he came to admit that this must depend in some sense on correspondence or the lack of it, though he felt unable to give any clear account of the nature of this correspondence.

Now, if being the term of the unique and indefinable relation in which knowledge consists makes no difference to the nature of the object, there must be at any rate one external relation. And in point of fact Moore, having ascribed to the idealists the view that no relation is purely external, in the sense that there is no relation which does not affect the natures or essences of the terms, proceeds to reject it. Thus in an article on the concept of the relative[1] he distinguishes between the terms 'relative' and 'related' and asserts that the former term, when predicated of a thing, implies that the relation or relations referred to are essential to the subject of which the term is predicated. But this implies that the relation of something which is a whole to something else is identical with or a part of the whole. And this notion, Moore maintains, is self-contradictory. In other words, a thing is what it is, and it is not definable in terms of its relations to anything else. Hence a thing's nature cannot be constituted by the nature of the system to which it belongs; and idealist monism is thus deprived of one of its main foundations.

Moore's best-known criticism of idealism is, of course, his article entitled *The Refutation of Idealism.*[2] In it he maintains that if modern idealism makes any general assertion at all about the universe, it is that the universe is spiritual. But it is not at all clear what this statement means. And it is thus very difficult to discuss the question whether the universe is or is not spiritual. When we examine the matter, however, we find that there is a large number of different propositions which the idealist has to prove if he is to establish the truth of his general conclusion. And we can inquire into the weight of his arguments. Obviously, the statement that the universe is spiritual in character might still be true even if all the arguments advanced by idealists to prove its truth were fallacious. At the same time to show that the arguments were fallacious would be at any rate to show that the general conclusion was entirely unproved.

According to Moore, every argument used to prove that reality is spiritual has as one of its premises the proposition *esse est*

---

[1] Article 'Relative' in Baldwin's *Dictionary of Philosophy and Psychology.*
[2] *Mind*, Vol. 12 (1903), reprinted in *Philosophical Studies.*

percipi, to be is to be perceived. And one's natural reaction to this contention is to comment that belief in the truth of *esse est percipi* is characteristic of Berkeley's idealism, and that it should not be attributed to Hegel, for instance, or to Bradley. But Moore understands *percipi* as including 'that other type of mental fact, which is called "thought" ',[1] and as meaning, in general, to be experienced. And on this interpretation of *percipi* Bradley could be counted as subscribing to the thesis *esse est percipi*, inasmuch as everything is for him a constituent element in one all-comprehensive absolute experience.

As Moore understands *esse est percipi* in such a broad sense, it is not surprising that he finds the thesis ambiguous and capable of being interpreted in several ways. However, let us take it that acceptance of the thesis commits one to holding, among other things, that the object of a sensation cannot be distinguished from the sensation itself, or that, insofar as a distinction is made, it is the result of illegitimate abstraction from an organic unity. Moore undertakes to show that this view is false.

In the first place we are all aware, for example, that the sensation of blue differs from that of green. Yet if they are both sensations, they must have something in common. And Moore calls this common element 'consciousness', while the differentiating elements in the two sensations he calls their respective 'objects'. Thus 'blue is one object of sensation and green is another, and consciousness, which both sensations have in common, is different from either'.[2] On the one hand, as consciousness can co-exist with other objects of sensation besides blue, we obviously cannot legitimately claim that blue is the same thing as consciousness alone. On the other hand, we cannot legitimately claim that blue is the same thing as blue together with consciousness. For if we could, the statement that blue exists would have the same meaning as the statement that blue co-exists with consciousness. And this cannot be the case. For if, as has already been admitted, consciousness and blue are distinct elements in the sensation of blue, it makes sense to ask whether blue can exist without consciousness. And it would not make sense if the statement that blue exists and the statement that blue co-exists with consciousness had exactly the same meaning.

It may be objected that by using the term 'object' instead of 'content' this line of argument simply begs the question. In point

[1] *Philosophical Studies*, p. 7.   [2] *Ibid.*, p. 17.

of fact blue is the content, rather than the object, of the sensation of blue. And any distinction which we may make between the elements of content and consciousness or awareness is the result of an operation of abstraction performed on an organic unity.

For Moore, however, an appeal to the concept of organic unity is tantamount to an attempt to have things both ways. That is to say, a distinction is allowed and prohibited at the same time. In any case Moore is not prepared to admit that 'content' is a more appropriate term than 'object'. It is legitimate to speak of blue as part of the content of a blue flower. But a sensation of blue is not itself blue: it is awareness or consciousness of blue as an object. And 'this relation is just that which we mean in every case by "knowing" '.[1] To know or be aware of blue is not to have in the mind a representative image of which blue is the content or part of the content; it is to be directly aware of the object 'blue'.

According to Moore, therefore, the awareness which is included in sensation is the same unique relation which basically constitutes every kind of knowledge. And the problem of getting out of the subjective sphere or circle of our sensations, images and ideas is a pseudo-problem. For 'merely to have a sensation is already to *be* outside that circle. It is to know something which is as truly and really *not* a part of *my* experience, as anything which I can ever know.'[2]

It can be added, with reference to the idealist thesis that reality is spiritual, that according to Moore we possess precisely the same evidence for saying that there are material things as we possess for saying that we have sensations. Hence to doubt the existence of material things entails doubting the existence of our sensations, and of experience in general. To say this is not to say, or even to suggest, that nothing is spiritual. It is to say that if the statement that reality is spiritual entails denying the existence of material things, we have no possible reason for making the statement. For 'the only *reasonable* alternative to the admission that matter exists *as well as* spirit, is absolute scepticism—that, as likely as not, *nothing* exists at all'.[3] And this is not a position which we can consistently propose and maintain.

In his discussion of sensation and perception, a discussion to which we shall have to return presently, Moore can be said to be concerned with phenomenological analysis. But it is obvious that his general attitude is founded on a common sense realism. And

[1] *Ibid.*, p. 25.   [2] *Ibid.*, p. 27.   [3] *Ibid.*, p. 30.

this element in his thought comes out clearly in the famous essay entitled *A Defence of Common Sense*,[1] where he maintains that there are a number of propositions, the truth of which is known with certainty. Thus I know that there is at present a living human body which is my body. I know also that there are other living bodies besides my own. I know too that the earth has existed for many years. Further, I know that there are other people, each of whom knows that there is a living body which is his own body, that there are other living bodies besides his own, and that the earth has existed for many years. Again, I know not only that these people are aware of the truth of these propositions but also that each of them knows that there are other people who are aware of the same truths. Such propositions belong to the common sense view of the world. And it follows, according to Moore, that they are true. There may indeed be differences of opinion about whether a given proposition belongs or not to the common sense view of the world. But if it does, it is true. And if it is known to belong, it is known to be true. And it is known to be true because of the reasons which we actually have for stating that it is true, not for any supposedly better reasons which philosophers may claim to be able to provide. It is no more the philosopher's business to prove the truth of propositions which we already know to be true than it is his business to disprove them.

Moore's defence of common sense has been referred to here simply as an illustration of one aspect of his realism. We shall have to return to the subject in connection with his conception of analysis. Meanwhile we can profitably take a glance at some of his ethical ideas, which, apart from their intrinsic interest, seem to illustrate the fact that his realism is not a 'naturalistic' realism.

3. Some moral philosophers, Moore remarks, have considered adequate the description of ethics as being concerned with what is good and what is bad in human conduct. In point of fact this description is too narrow. For other things besides human conduct can be good, and ethics can be described as 'the general inquiry into what is good'.[2] In any case, before we ask the question 'what is good?', meaning 'what things and which kinds of conduct possess the property of being good?', it seems logically proper to ask and answer the question, 'what is good?', meaning 'how is

---

[1] *Contemporary British Philosophy*, Second Series, edited by J. H. Muirhead (1925) and reprinted in *Philosophical Papers* (1959).

[2] *Principia Ethica*, p. 2, s.2 (1959 reprint). In reference to this work the letter 's' signifies the section.

good to be defined?', 'what is goodness in itself?' For unless we know the answer to this question, it may be argued, how can we discriminate between good and bad conduct and say what things possess the property of goodness?

Moore insists that when he raises the question, 'how is good to be defined?', he is not looking for a purely verbal definition, the sort of definition which consists simply in substituting other words for the word to be defined. Nor is he concerned with establishing or with justifying the common usage of the word 'good'. 'My business is solely with that object or idea, which I hold, rightly or wrongly, that the word is generally used to stand for. What I want to discover is the nature of that object or idea.'[1] In other words, Moore is concerned with phenomenological rather than with linguistic analysis.

Having raised the question, Moore proceeds to assert that it cannot be answered, not because good is some mysterious, occult and unrecognizable quality but because the idea of good is a simple notion, like that of yellow. Definitions which describe the real nature of an object are only possible when the object is complex. When the object is simple, no such definition is possible. Hence good is indefinable. This does not entail the conclusion that the things which are good are indefinable. All that is being maintained is that the notion of good as such is a simple notion and hence 'incapable of any definition, in the most important sense of that word'.[2]

From this doctrine of good as an indefinable property or quality there follow some important conclusions. Suppose, for example, that someone says that pleasure is the good. Pleasure may be one of the things which possess the property of being good; but if, as is probably the case, the speaker imagines that he is giving a definition of good, what he says cannot possibly be true. If good is an indefinable property, we cannot substitute for it some other property, such as pleasurable. For even if we admitted, for the sake of argument, that all those things which possess the property of being good also possess the property of being pleasurable, pleasure would still not be, and could not be, the same as good. And anyone who imagines that it is or could be the same, is guilty of the 'naturalistic fallacy'.[3]

Now, the fallacy in question is basically 'the failure to distinguish clearly that unique and indefinable quality which we mean

---

[1] *Ibid.*, p. 6, s.6.   [2] *Ibid.*, p. 9, s.10.   [3] *Ibid.*, p. 10, s.10.

by good'.[1] Anyone who identifies goodness with some other quality or thing, whether it be pleasure or self-perception or virtue or love, saying that this is what 'good' *means*, is guilty of this fallacy. These things may perfectly well possess the quality of goodness in the sense, for example, that what is pleasurable also possesses the quality of being good. But it no more follows that to be pleasurable is the same thing as to be good than it would follow, on the supposition that all primroses are yellow, that to be a primrose and to be yellow are the same thing.

But, it may well be asked, why should this fallacy be described as 'naturalistic'? The only real reason for so describing it would obviously be the belief that goodness is a 'non-natural' quality. Given this belief, it would follow that those who identify goodness with a 'natural' quality are guilty of a naturalistic fallacy. But though in *Principia Ethica* Moore does indeed maintain that goodness is a non-natural quality, he greatly complicates matters by distinguishing between two groups of philosophers who are both said to be guilty of the naturalistic fallacy. The first group consists of those who uphold some form of naturalistic ethics by defining good in terms of 'some one property of things, which exists in time'.[2] Hedonism, which identifies pleasure and goodness, would be an example. The second group consists of those who base ethics on metaphysics and define good in metaphysical terms, in terms of or by reference to a supersensible reality which transcends Nature and does not exist in time. According to Moore, Spinoza is an example, when he tells us that we become perfect in proportion as we are united with Absolute Substance by what he calls the intellectual love of God. Another example is provided by those who say that our final end, the supreme good, is the realization of our 'true' selves, the 'true' self not being anything which exists here and now in Nature. What, then, is meant by saying that good is a 'non-natural' quality, if at the same time those who define good in terms of or with reference to a 'non-natural' reality or quality or experience are said to be guilty of the naturalistic fallacy?

The answer which immediately suggests itself is that there is no incompatibility between asserting that good is an indefinable non-natural quality and denying that it can be defined in terms of some other non-natural quality. Indeed, the assertion entails the denial. But this consideration by itself does not tell us in what

[1] *Principia Ethica*, p. 59, s.36.   [2] *Ibid.*, p. 41, s.27.

sense good is a non-natural quality. In *Principia Ethica* Moore makes it clear that he has not the slightest intention of denying that good can be a property of natural objects. 'And yet I have said that "good" itself is not a natural property.'[1] What, then, is meant by saying that good can be, and indeed is, a non-natural property of at least some natural objects?

The answer provided in *Principia Ethica* is extremely odd. A natural property, or at any rate most natural properties, can exist by themselves in time, whereas good cannot. 'Can we imagine "good" as existing *by itself* in time, and not merely as a property of some natural object?'[2] No, we certainly cannot imagine this. But neither can we imagine a natural quality such as being brave existing *by itself* in time. And when Professor C. D. Broad, for example, pointed this out, Moore said that he completely agreed. It is not surprising, therefore, to find him eventually admitting roundly that 'in *Principia* I did not give any tenable explanation of what I meant by saying that "good" was not a natural property'.[3]

In his essay on the conception of intrinsic value in *Philosophical Studies* Moore gave another account of the distinction between natural and non-natural properties. He later admitted that this account was really two accounts; but he maintained that one of them might possibly be true. If one ascribes to a thing a natural intrinsic quality, one is always describing it to some extent. But if one ascribes to a thing a non-natural intrinsic quality, one is not describing the thing at all.

Obviously, if good is a non-natural intrinsic quality, and if to ascribe this quality to an object is not to describe the object in any way at all, the temptation immediately arises to conclude that the term 'good' expresses an evaluative attitude, so to speak, and that to call a thing good is to express this attitude and at the same time a desire that others should share this attitude. But if this conclusion is drawn, the view that goodness is an intrinsic quality of things has to be abandoned. And Moore was not prepared to abandon it. He believed that we can recognize what things possess the quality of being good, though we cannot define the quality. And when he wrote *Principia Ethica*, he was convinced that it is one of the main tasks of moral philosophy to determine values in this sense, namely to determine what things possess the

---

[1] *Ibid.*, p. 41, s.26. [2] *Ibid.*, p. 41, s.26.
[3] In 'A Reply to my Critics' contained in *The Philosophy of G. E. Moore*, edited by P. A. Schilpp, p. 582 (New York, 1952, 2nd edition).

quality of goodness and what things possess it in a higher degree than others.[1]

Obligation was defined by Moore in terms of the production of good. 'Our "duty", therefore, can be defined as that action which will cause more good to exist in the Universe than any possible alternative.'[2] Indeed, in *Principia Ethica* Moore went so far as to say that it is demonstrably certain that the assertion that one is morally bound to perform an action is identical with the assertion that this action will produce the greatest possible amount of good in the Universe. When, however, he came to write *Ethics*, he was no longer prepared to claim that the two statements were identical. And later on he recognized the necessity of distinguishing clearly between the statement that that action is morally obligatory which will produce the greatest amount of good as an effect *subsequent* to the action and the statement that that action is morally obligatory which, by reason of its being performed, by reason of its intrinsic nature, makes the Universe intrinsically better than it would be if some other action were performed. In any case the point to notice is that Moore does not regard his theory of good as an indefinable non-natural property as being in any way incompatible with a teleological view of ethics, which interprets obligation in terms of the production of good, that is, in terms of the production of things or experiences possessing the intrinsic quality of goodness. Nor in fact does there appear to be any incompatibility.

From this theory of obligation it does not follow, however, that in any set of circumstances whatsoever we are morally obliged to perform a certain action. For there might be two or more possible actions which, as far as we can see, would be equally productive of good. We can then describe these actions as right or morally permissible, but not as morally obligatory, even though we were obliged to perform either the one or the other.

Moore certainly assumed and implied that if a man passes a specifically moral judgment or an action, his statement, considered precisely as a moral judgment, is capable of being true or false. Take, for example, the assertion that it was right of Brutus to stab Julius Caesar. If this assertion is intended in a specifically

---

[1] In *Principia Ethica* Moore laid most stress on the values of personal affection and aesthetic enjoyment, that is, the appreciation of the beautiful in art and Nature. And this attitude exercised a considerable influence at the time on what was known as the Bloomsbury Circle.

[2] *Ibid.*, p. 148, s.89.

ethical sense, it is reducible neither to the statement that the speaker has a subjective attitude of approval towards Brutus's action nor to the statement that as a matter of historical fact Brutus stabbed Caesar. And in its irreducible moral character it is either true or false. Hence the dispute between the man who says that Brutus's action was right and the man who says that it was wrong is a dispute about the truth or falsity of a moral proposition.

When, however, he was confronted with the so-called emotive theory of ethics, Moore began to feel doubt about the truth of the position which he had hitherto adopted. As can be seen from his 'A Reply to My Critics', he conceded that Professor C. L. Stevenson might be right in maintaining that the man who says that Brutus's action was right, when the word 'right' is being used in a specifically ethical sense, is not saying anything of which truth or falsity can be predicated, except perhaps that Brutus actually did stab Caesar, a statement which is clearly historical and not ethical. Further, Moore conceded that if one man says that Brutus's action was right while another says that it was wrong, 'I feel some inclination to think that their disagreement *is* merely a disagreement in attitude, like that between the man who says "Let's play poker" and the other who says, "No; let's listen to a record": and I do not know that I am not *as much* inclined to think this as to think that they are making incompatible assertions'.[1] At the same time Moore confessed that he was also inclined to think that his old view was true; and he maintained that in any case Stevenson had not shown that it was false. 'Right', 'wrong', 'ought', may have merely emotive meaning. And in this case the same must be said of 'good' too. 'I am *inclined* to think that this is so, but I am also inclined to think that it is not so; and I do not know which way I am inclined most strongly.'[2]

These hesitations can reasonably be described as typical of Moore. He was, as has often been remarked, a great questioner. He raised a problem, tried to define it precisely and offered a solution. But when he was faced with criticism, he never brushed it aside. When he thought that it was based on misunderstanding of what he had said, he tried to explain his meaning more clearly. When, however, the criticism was substantial and not simply the fruit of misunderstanding, it was his habit to give serious

[1] *The Philosophy of G. E. Moore*, edited by P. A. Schilpp, pp. 546–7.
[2] *Ibid.*, p. 554.

consideration to the critic's remarks and to give due weight to his point of view. Moore never assumed that what he had said must be true and what the other fellow said must be false. And he did not hesitate to give a candid expression to his reflections and perplexities. We have to remember, therefore, that he is thinking aloud, so to speak, and that his hesitations are not necessarily to be taken as a definite retraction of his former views. He is engaged in weighing a new point of view, suggested to him by a critic, and in trying to estimate the amount of truth in it. Further, as we have seen, he is extremely frank about his subjective impressions, letting his readers know, without any attempt at concealment, that he is inclined to accept the new point of view, while at the same time he is inclined to stick to his own former view. Moore never felt that he was irretrievably committed to his own past, that is, to what he had said in the past. And when he became convinced that he had been wrong, he said so plainly.

In regard, however, to the question whether truth and falsity can legitimately be predicated of moral judgments, we are not entitled to say that Moore became *convinced* that his former view had been wrong. In any case the ethical theses which are for ever associated with his name are those of the indefinability of good, considered as a non-natural intrinsic quality, and of the need for avoiding any form of the so-called naturalistic fallacy. Moore's ethical position, especially as developed in *Principia Ethica*, can be said to be realist but not naturalistic; realist in the sense that good is regarded as an objective and recognizable intrinsic quality, not naturalistic in the sense that this quality is described as non-natural. But Moore never succeeded in explaining satisfactorily what was meant by saying, for example, that good is a non-natural quality of natural objects. And it is understandable that the emotive theory of ethics eventually came to the fore in philosophical discussion. After all, this theory can itself claim to be free from the 'naturalistic fallacy' and can use this claim as a weapon for dealing blows at rival theories. At the same time the theory is immune from the accusation of committing what Moore called the naturalistic fallacy only because 'good' is removed altogether from the sphere of objective intrinsic qualities.[1]

[1] It is not, of course, my intention to suggest that Moore's ethics must pass into the emotive theory. What I suggest is simply that it is understandable if to some minds the emotive theory appears more intelligible and tenable. But this theory in its original form was very soon seen to constitute a gross over-simplification of complex issues, And subsequent ethical discussion became much more sophisticated and also, in a real sense, more ecumenical.

4. Mention has already been made of the fact that as an under-graduate at Cambridge Moore was struck by some of the odd things which philosophers have said about the world. McTaggart's denial of the reality of time was a case in point. What, Moore wondered, could McTaggart possibly mean by this? Was he using the term 'unreal' in some peculiar sense which would deprive the statement that time is unreal of its paradoxical character? Or was he seriously suggesting that it is untrue to say that we have our lunch after we have had our breakfast? If so, the statement that time is unreal would be exciting but at the same time preposterous: it could not possibly be true. In any case, how can we profitably discuss the question whether time is real or unreal unless we first know precisely what is being asked? Similarly, according to Bradley reality is spiritual. But it is not at all clear what it means to say that reality is spiritual. Perhaps several different proposi-tions are involved. And before we start discussing whether reality is spiritual or not, we must not only clarify the question but make sure that it is not really several separate questions. For if it is, these questions will have to be treated in turn.

It is important to understand that Moore had no intention whatsoever of suggesting that all philosophical problems are pseudo-problems. He was suggesting that the reason why philo-sophical problems are often so difficult to answer is sometimes that it is not clear in the first place precisely what is being asked. Again, when, as so often happens, disputants find themselves at cross-purposes, the reason may sometimes be that the question under discussion is not really one question but several. Such suggestions have nothing at all to do with any general dogma about the meaninglessness of philosophical problems. They represent an appeal for clarity and accuracy from the start, an appeal prompted by enlightened common sense. They express, of course, the predominantly analytic turn of Moore's mind; but they do not make him a positivist, which he certainly was not.

When, however, we think of Moore's idea of philosophical analysis, we generally think of it in connection with his contention that there are common sense propositions which we all know to be true. If we know them to be true, it is absurd for the philosopher to try to show that they are not true. For he too knows that they are true. Nor is it the business of the philosopher, according to Moore, to attempt to prove, for example, that there are material things outside the mind. For there is no good reason to suppose that the philosopher can provide better reasons than those which we already have for saying that there are material things external to the mind. What, however, the philosopher can do is to analyze propositions, the truth or the falsity of which is established by other than specifically philosophical argument. The philosopher can, of course, try to make explicit the reasons which we already have for accepting some common sense propositions. But this does not turn the reasons into specifically philosophical reasons, in the sense that they have been added, as it were, by the philosopher to our stock of reasons.[1]

The question arises, therefore, what is meant by analyzing a proposition? It obviously cannot signify simply 'giving the meaning'. For if I know that a proposition is true, I must know what it means. Normally at any rate we would not be prepared to say that a man knew, or could know, that a proposition was true, if at the same time he had to admit that he did not know what the proposition meant.[2] And from this we can infer that analysis, as envisaged by Moore, does not consist simply in putting what has been said into other words. For instance, if an Italian asks me what it means to say 'John is the brother of James' and I reply that it means 'Giovanni è il fratello di Giacomo', I have explained to the Italian what the English sentence means, but I can hardly be said to have analyzed a proposition. I have not analyzed anything.

Analysis means for Moore conceptual analysis. He admitted later that he had sometimes spoken as though to give the analysis of a proposition was to give its 'meaning'. But he insisted that what he really had in mind was the analysis of concepts. The use of the word 'means' implies that analysis is concerned with verbal

---

[1] In a well-known essay on 'Moore and Ordinary Language' (*The Philosophy of G. E. Moore*, edited by P. A. Schilpp, Chapter 13), Professor N. Malcolm maintained that Moore's way of proving the denials of common sense propositions to be false was to appeal to ordinary language. Moore himself (*ibid.*, pp. 668–9) admitted that he considered the sort of argument referred to by Malcolm as a good argument, and that he himself had said that this sort of argument amounted to a disproof of the proposition 'there are no material things'. He added, however, that in the case of such a proposition as 'we do not know for certain that there are material things', something more is required if the proposition is to be proved to be false. For in point of fact many more philosophers have held that we do not *know* that there are material things than have held that there are actually no material things.

[2] I say 'normally at any rate', because if a man was convinced that all statements made by a certain authority were necessarily true, he might wish to claim that he knew that any such statement was true, even if he was not at all sure of what it meant.

expression, with defining words, whereas it is really concerned with defining concepts. The *analyzandum*, that which is to be analyzed, is a concept, and the *analyzans*, the analysis, must also be a concept. The expression used for the *analyzans* must be different from the expression used for the *analyzandum*, and it must be different in that it explicitly means or expresses a concept or concepts not explicitly mentioned by the expression used for the *analyzandum*. For instance, to give an example employed by Moore himself, '*x* is a male sibling' would be an analysis of '*x* is a brother'. It is not a question of merely substituting one verbal expression for another in the sense in which 'fratello' can be substituted for 'brother'. 'Male sibling' is indeed a different verbal expression from 'brother', but at the same time it explicitly mentions a concept which is not explicitly mentioned in '*x* is a brother'.

And yet, of course, as Moore admits, if the analysis is correct, the concepts in the *analyzandum* and the *analyzans*, in the proposition to be analyzed and in its analysis, must be in some sense the same. But in what sense? If they are the same in the sense that no distinction can be made between them except in terms of verbal expression, analysis seems to be concerned simply with the substitution of one verbal expression for another. But Moore has said that this is not the case. He is therefore faced with the task of explaining in what sense the concepts in *analyzandum* and *analyzans* must be the same if the analysis is to be correct, and in what sense they must be distinct if analysis is to be more than the mere substitution of an equivalent verbal expression for a given verbal expression. But Moore does not feel able to give a really clear explanation.

In a general way it is, of course, easy enough to give a cash-value to the idea of philosophical analysis. True, if we are told that '*x* is a male sibling' is an analysis of '*x* is a brother', we may be inclined to wonder what possible philosophical relevance analysis of this kind can possess. But consider the non-philosopher who knows perfectly well how to use causal expressions in concrete contexts. If someone tells him that the banging of the door was caused by a sudden gust of wind through the open window, he knows perfectly well what is meant. He can distinguish between cases of *post hoc* and cases of *propter hoc*, and he can recognize particular causal relations. In a sense, therefore, he is well aware what causality means. But if the non-philosopher were asked to give an abstract analysis of the concept of causality, he would find himself at a loss. Like Socrates's young friends in a similar situation, he would probably mention instances of the causal relation and be unable to do anything more. Yet philosophers from Plato and Aristotle onwards have tried to give abstract analyses of concepts such as causality. And we can call this sort of thing philosophical analysis.

Though, however, this idea of philosophical analysis seems at first sight to be plain sailing, it can be and has been challenged. Thus those who sympathize with the attitude expressed in certain remarks in Wittgenstein's *Philosophical Investigations* would maintain that if one is asked what causality is, the proper answer is precisely to mention examples of the causal relation. It is a mistake to look for one single and profounder 'meaning' of the term. Either we already know what causality is (how the word is used) or we do not. And if we do not, we can be informed by having examples of the causal relation pointed out to us. Similarly, it is a mistake to suppose that because we describe a variety of things as beautiful, there must necessarily be one single 'real' meaning, one genuine analysis of a unitary concept, which the philosopher can, as it were, dig out. We can, of course, say that we are looking for a definition. But one can be found in the dictionary. And if this is not what we are looking for, then what we really need is to be reminded of the ways in which the word in question is actually used in human language. We shall then know what is 'means'. And this is the only 'analysis' which is really required.

It is not the intention of the present writer to defend this more 'linguistic' idea of analysis. His sympathies lie rather with the older idea of philosophical analysis, provided, of course, that we avoid the fallacy of 'one word, one meaning'. At the same time the notion of conceptual analysis is not at all so clear as it may seem to be at first sight. Difficulties arise which require to be considered and, if possible, met. But we cannot find any adequate answers to such difficulties in Moore's account of analysis.

This is not, however, surprising. For the fact of the matter is that Moore devoted himself for the most part to the *practice* of philosophical analysis. That is to say, he concerned himself with the analysis of particular propositions rather than with analyzing the concept of analysis. And when he was challenged to give an abstract account of his method and its aims, he felt able to remove some misunderstandings but unable to answer all questions to his own satisfaction. With his characteristic honesty, he did not hesitate to say so openly.

Obviously, therefore, to obtain some concrete idea of what Moore understood by analysis we have to look primarily at his actual practice. But before we turn to a line of analysis which occupied a great deal of his attention, there are two points which must be emphasized. In the first place Moore never said, and never intended to say, that philosophy and analysis are the same thing, and that the philosopher can do nothing more than analyze propositions or concepts. And when this view was attributed to him, he explicitly rejected it. The bent of his mind was indeed predominantly analytic; but he never laid down any dogma about the limits of philosophy. Other people may have done so, but not Moore. In the second place he never suggested that all concepts are analyzable. We have already seen, for example, that according to him the concept of good is simple and unanalyzable. And the same can be said of the concept of knowing.

5. In his well-known paper *Proof of an External World*, which he read to the British Academy in 1939,[1] Moore maintained that it is a good argument for, and indeed sufficient proof of, the existence of physical objects external to the mind if we can indicate one or more such objects. And he proceeded to claim that he could prove that two hands exist by the simple expedient of holding up his two hands, making a gesture with the right hand while saying 'here is one hand' and then making a gesture with the left hand while saying 'and here is the other'.

This may sound extremely naïve. But, as someone has said, Moore always had the courage to appear naïve. The trouble is, however, that while we may all come to believe that there is an external world by becoming aware of external objects, the only person who can possibly need a proof of the existence of an external world is the person who professes to doubt it. And if he professes to doubt, his doubt covers the existence of any extra-mental physical object. Hence he is not likely to be impressed when Moore, or anyone else, exhibits two hands. He will simply say that he doubts whether what he sees, when he is shown two hands, are really external physical objects.

And yet, of course, Moore's position is not really as naïve as it appears to be at first sight. For the determined sceptic is not going to be convinced by any proof. And what Moore is saying to

[1] *Proceedings of the British Academy*, Vol. 25, 1939.

the sceptic is more or less this: 'The only evidence which I can offer you is the evidence which we already have. And this is sufficient evidence. But you are looking for evidence or proof which we have not got, and which in my opinion we can never have. For I see no reason to believe that the philosopher can offer better evidence than the evidence we have. What you are really demanding is something which can never be provided, namely proof that the existence of an external world is a necessary truth. But it is not a necessary truth. Hence it is futile to look for the sort of evidence or proof which you insist on demanding.' This is clearly a reasonable point of view.

Now, as we have already indicated, while thinking that it is not the philosopher's job to try to prove by some special means of his own the truth of such a proposition as 'there are material things' or 'there are extra-mental physical objects', Moore believes that analysis of such propositions does form part of the philosopher's job. For while the truth of a proposition may be certain, its correct analysis may not be at all certain. But the correct analysis of such general propositions such as those just mentioned 'depends on the question how propositions of another and simpler type are to be analyzed'.[1] And an example of a simpler proposition would be 'I am perceiving a human hand'.

This proposition, however, is itself a deduction from two simpler propositions which can be expressed as 'I am perceiving *this*' and '*this* is a human hand'. But what is '*this*'? In Moore's opinion it is a sense-datum. That is to say, what I directly apprehend when I perceive a human hand is a sense-datum. And a sense-datum, even if we assume it to be somehow part of a human hand, cannot be identified with the hand. For the hand is in any case much more than what I actually see at a given moment. Hence a correct analysis of 'I perceive a human hand' involves one in specifying the nature of a sense-datum and its relation to the relevant physical object.

In a paper entitled *The Nature and Reality of Objects of Perception* which he read to the Aristotelian Society in 1905 Moore maintained that if we look at a red book and a blue book standing side by side on a shelf, what we really see are red and blue patches of colour of certain sizes and shapes, 'having to one another the spatial relation which we express by saying they are side by side'.[2] Such objects of direct perception he called 'sense-contents'. In the

---

[1] *Philosophical Papers*, p. 53.   [2] *Philosophical Studies*, p. 68.

lectures which he gave in the winter of 1910–11[1] Moore used the term 'sense-data'. True, in a paper entitled *The Status of Sense-Data*, which he read to the Aristotelian Society during the session 1913–14, Moore admitted that the term 'sense-datum' is ambiguous. For it suggests that the objects to which this term is applied can exist only when they are given, a view to which Moore did not wish to commit himself. Hence he proposed as 'more convenient'[2] the use of the term 'sensible'. But to all intents and purposes 'sense-data' is Moore's name for the immediate objects of direct perception. And in *A Defence of Common Sense* we find him saying that 'there is no doubt at all that there are sense-data, in the sense in which I am now using the term,'[3] that is, in a sense which makes it true to say that what we directly perceive when we look at a hand or at an envelope is a sense-datum but which leaves open the question whether this sense-datum is or is not part of the physical object which in ordinary language we are said to be seeing.

Now, Moore was careful to distinguish between sensations and sense-data. When, for example, I see a colour, the *seeing* the colour is the sensation and *what* is seen, the object, is the sense-datum. It therefore makes sense, at any rate at first sight, to ask whether sense-data can exist when they are unperceived. It would hardly make sense to ask whether a 'seeing' can exist when no sentient subject is seeing. But it does make sense to ask whether a colour exists when it is not perceived. If, of course, sense-data were described as existing 'in the mind', it would hardly make sense to ask whether they can exist unperceived. But Moore was unwilling to describe sense-data in this way, namely as being 'in the mind'.

But if sense-data are not 'in the mind', *where* are they? Provided that sense-data exist, and do not exist in the mind, the question arises whether or not they exist when they are not objects of perception. Do they then exist in a public physical space? One difficulty in saying this is the following. When two men look at a white envelope, we commonly say that they are seeing the same object. But according to the sense-datum theory there must be two sense-data. Further, the shape and spatial relations of one man's sense-datum do not seem to be precisely the same as those of the other man's sense-datum. If, therefore, we take it that the

---

[1] These lectures form the text of *Some Main Problems of Philosophy*, which will be referred to in notes as *Main Problems*.

[2] *Philosophical Studies*, p. 171.

[3] *Philosophical Papers*, p. 54.

shape and size and spatial relations of a physical object existing in public space are the same for all, must we not say that the one man's sense-datum exists in one private space and the other man's sense-datum in another private space?

Further, what is the relation between a sense-datum and the relevant physical object? For example, if I look at a coin from such an angle of vision that its surface appears to me as elliptical, is my sense-datum a part of the coin as a physical object, the surface of which we take to be roughly circular? Ordinary language suggests that it is. For I should normally be said to be seeing the coin. But if I look at the coin at another moment from a different position, or if another man looks at the same coin at the same moment as I do, there are different sense-data. And they differ not merely numerically but also qualitatively or in content. Are all these sense-data parts of the physical object? If they are, this suggests that the surface of a coin can be both elliptical and circular at the same time. If they are not, how are we to describe the relations between the sense-data and the physical object? Indeed, how do we know that there is a physical object for the sense-data to be related to?

These are the sort of problems with which Moore grappled on and off throughout his life. But he did not succeed in solving them to his own satisfaction. For example, we have already seen that in his attack on idealism Moore denied the truth of 'to be is to be perceived'; and his natural inclination was to claim that sense-data can exist even when they are unperceived. But though this point of view may appear reasonable when it is a question of a visual sense-datum such as a colour, it by no means appears reasonable if a toothache, for instance, is admitted into the category of sense-data, nor perhaps if sweet and bitter are taken as examples of sense-data rather than colour, size and shape. And in 'A Reply to My Critics' we find Moore saying that while he had once certainly suggested that sense-data such as blue and bitter could exist unperceived, 'I am inclined to think that it is as impossible that anything which has the sensible quality "blue", and more generally, *anything whatever which is directly appre-hended*, any *sense-datum*, that is, should exist unperceived, as it is that a headache should exist unfelt'.[1]

In this case, of course, as Moore notes, it follows that no sense-datum can possibly be identical with or part of the surface of a

[1] *The Philosophy of G. E. Moore*, edited by P. A. Schilpp, p. 658.

physical object. And to say this is to say that no physical surface can be directly perceived. The question, therefore, of how we know that there are physical objects distinct from sense-data becomes acute. Needless to say, Moore is well aware of the fact. But he is certainly not prepared to jettison his conviction that we do know the truth of the propositions which he regards as propositions of common sense. He is not prepared to throw overboard what, in *A Defence of Common Sense*, he called 'the Common Sense view of the world'.[1] And in a lecture entitled *Four Forms of Scepticism*, which Moore delivered on various occasions in the United States during the period 1940–4, we find a characteristic denial of Russell's contention that 'I do not know for certain that this is a pencil or that you are conscious'.[2] I call the denial 'characteristic' for this reason. Moore remarks that Russell's contention seems to rest on four distinct assumptions; that one does not know these things (that this is a pencil or that you are conscious) immediately; that they do not follow logically from anything which one does know immediately; that, in this case, one's knowledge of or belief in the propositions in question must be based on an analogical or inductive argument; and that no such argument can yield certain knowledge. Moore then proceeds to say that he agrees that the first three assumptions are true. At the same time 'of no one even of these three do I feel *as* certain as that I do know for certain that this is a pencil. Nay more: I do not think it is *rational* to be as certain of any one of these four propositions, as of the proposition that I do know that this is a pencil.'[3]

It is, of course, open to anyone to say that in his opinion the sense-datum theory as expounded by Moore leads logically to scepticism or at any rate to agnosticism in regard to the physical world as distinct from sense-data. But it is certainly not correct to speak of Moore as a sceptic. He was no such thing. He started, as we have seen, with the assumption that we know with certainty that there are external physical objects or material things; but he was doubtful of the correct analysis of such a proposition. And though his analysis may have led him into a position which was difficult to reconcile with his initial conviction, he did not abandon this conviction.

It has not been possible here to follow Moore through all his struggles with the theory of sense-data and its implications. The fulfilment of such a task would require a whole book. The theme

[1] *Philosophical Papers*, p. 45.   [2] *Ibid.*, p. 226.   [3] *Ibid.*

has been discussed in brief primarily in order to illustrate Moore's practice of analysis. But what sort of analysis is it? In a sense, of course, it is concerned with language. For Moore is out to analyze propositions, such as 'I see a human hand' or 'I see a penny'. But to describe his analysis as being concerned 'simply with words', as though it were a case of choosing between two sets of linguistic conventions, would be grossly misleading. Part at any rate of what he does can best be described, I think, as phenomenological analysis. For example, he raises the question, what exactly is it that happens when, as would ordinarily be said, we see a material object? He then explains that he is in no way concerned with the physical processes 'which occur in the eye and the optic nerves and the brain'.[1] What he is concerned with is 'the mental occurrence—the act of consciousness—which occurs (as is supposed) as a consequence of or accompaniment—of these bodily processes'.[2] Sense-data are introduced as objects of this act of consciousness. Or, rather, they are 'discovered', as Moore believes, as its immediate objects. And the process by which they are discovered is phenomenological analysis. But sense-data are not, of course, confined to visual sense-data. Hence we can say that Moore is concerned with the phenomenological analysis of sense-perception in general.

It is not my intention to suggest that this is all that Moore is concerned with, even within the restricted context of the sense-datum theory. For if we assume that sense-data can properly be said to exist, the question of their relation to physical objects can be described as an ontological question. Further, Moore concerns himself with epistemological questions; how do we know this or that? But part at any rate of his activity can better be described as phenomenological analysis than as linguistic analysis. And though the stock of the sense-datum theory has slumped greatly in recent years,[3] the judgment of Dr. Rudolf Metz was not entirely unreasonable, that in comparison with Moore's meticulous phenomenological analysis of perception 'all earlier studies of the problem seem to be coarse and rudimentary'.[4]

[1] *Main Problems*, p. 29. [2] *Ibid.*
[3] We have only to think, for example, of the late J. L. Austin's attack on the theory.
[4] *A Hundred Years of British Philosophy*, p. 547 (London, 1938).

CHAPTER XIX

BERTRAND RUSSELL (1)

Introductory remarks—Life and writings up to the publication of Principia Mathematica; *Russell's idealist phase and his reaction against it, the theory of types, the theory of descriptions, the reduction of mathematics to logic—Ockham's razor and reductive analysis as applied to physical objects and to minds— Logical atomism and the influence of Wittgenstein—Neutral monism—The problem of solipsism.*

1. WE have already had occasion to remark that of all present-day British philosophers Bertrand Russell is by far the best known to the world at large. This is partly due to the fact that he has published a very considerable number of books and essays on moral, social and political topics which are salted with amusing and provocative remarks and are written at a level which can be understood by a public that is scarcely capable of appreciating his more technical contributions to philosophical thought. And it is largely this class of publications which has made of Russell a prophet of liberal humanism, a hero of those who regard themselves as rationalists, free from the shackles of religious and metaphysical dogma and yet at the same time devoted to the cause of human freedom, as against totalitarianism, and of social and political progress according to rational principles. We can also mention, as a contributing cause to Russell's fame, his active self-commitment at various periods of his life to a particular side, sometimes an unpopular side, in issues of general concern and importance. He has always had the courage of his convictions. And the combination of aristocrat, philosopher, Voltairean essayist and ardent campaigner has naturally made an impact on the imagination of the public.

It scarcely needs to be said that the fame of a philosopher during his lifetime is not an infallible indication of the value of his thought, especially if his general reputation is largely due to his more ephemeral writings. In any case the varied character of Russell's writing creates a special difficulty in estimating his status as a philosopher. On the one hand he is justly renowned for his work in the field of mathematical logic. But he himself regards this subject as belonging to mathematics rather than to philosophy. On the other hand it is not fair to Russell to estimate his status as a thinker in terms of his popular writings on concrete moral issues or on social and political topics. For though in view of the traditional and common view of the word 'philosophy' he recognizes that he has to resign himself to having his moral writings labelled as philosophical works, he has said that the only ethical topic which he regards as belonging properly to philosophy is the analysis of the ethical proposition as such. Concrete judgments of value should, strictly speaking, be excluded from philosophy. And if such judgments express, as Russell believes that they do, basic emotive attitudes, he is doubtless entitled to express his own emotive attitudes with a vehemence which would be out of place in discussing problems which, in principle at least, can be solved by logical argument.

If we exclude from philosophy mathematical logic on the one hand and concrete moral, valuational and political judgments on the other, we are left with what can perhaps be called Russell's general philosophy, consisting, for example, of discussions of epistemological and metaphysical questions. This general philosophy has passed through a series of phases and mutations, and it represents a strange mixture of acute analysis and of blindness to important relevant factors. But it is unified by his analytic method or methods. And the changes are hardly so great as to justify a literal interpretation of Professor C. D. Broad's humorous remark that, 'as we all know, Mr. Russell produces a different system of philosophy every few years.'[1] In any case Russell's general philosophy represents an interesting development of British empiricism in the light of later ways of thought, to which he himself made an important contribution.

In the following pages we shall be concerned mainly, though not exclusively, with Russell's idea and practice of analysis. But a thorough treatment, even of this limited theme, will not be possible. Nor indeed could it legitimately be expected in a general history of western philosophy.

2. (i) Bertrand Arthur William Russell was born in 1872. His parents, Lord and Lady Amberley, died when he was a small child,[2] and he was brought up in the house of his grandfather,

---

[1] In *Contemporary British Philosophy*, First Series, edited by J. H. Muirhead, p.79.
[2] In 1937 Russell published, together with Patricia Russell, *The Amberley Papers* in two volumes, containing the letters and diaries of his parents.

Lord John Russell, afterwards Earl Russell.[1] At the age of eighteen he went up to Cambridge, where he at first concentrated on mathematics. But in his fourth year at the university he turned to philosophy, and McTaggart and Stout taught him to regard British empiricism as crude and to look instead to the Hegelian tradition. Indeed, Russell tells us of the admiration which he felt for Bradley. And from 1894, the year in which he went down from Cambridge, until 1898 he continued to think that metaphysics was capable of proving beliefs about the universe which 'religious' feeling led him to think important.[2]

For a short while in 1894 Russell acted as an honorary attaché at the British Embassy in Paris. In 1895 he devoted himself to the study of economics and German social democracy at Berlin. The outcome was the publication of *German Social Democracy* in 1896. Most of his early essays were indeed on mathematical and logical topics, but it is worth noting that his first book was concerned with social theory.

Russell tells us that at this period he was influenced by both Kant and Hegel but sided with the latter when the two were in conflict.[3] He has described as 'unadulterated Hegel'[4] a paper on the relations of number and quantity which he published in *Mind* in 1896. And of *An Essay on the Foundations of Geometry* (1897), an elaboration of his Fellowship dissertation for Trinity College, Cambridge, he has said that the theory of geometry which he presented was 'mainly Kantian',[5] though it was afterwards swept away by Einstein's theory of relativity.

In the course of the year 1898 Russell reacted strongly against idealism. For one thing, a reading of Hegel's *Logic* convinced him that what the author had to say on the subject of mathematics was nonsense. For another thing, while lecturing on Leibniz at Cambridge in place of McTaggart, who was abroad, he came to the conclusion that the arguments advanced by Bradley against the reality of relations were fallacious. But Russell has laid most emphasis on the influence of his friend G. E. Moore. Together with Moore he adhered to the belief that, whatever Bradley or

[1] Bertrand Russell succeeded to the earldom in 1931.
[2] Russell abandoned belief in God at the age of eighteen. But he continued to believe for some years that metaphysics could provide a theoretical justification of emotive attitudes of awe and reverence towards the universe.
[3] Whether Russell ever had a profound knowledge of Hegel's general system is, of course, another question.
[4] *My Philosophical Development*, p. 40.
[5] *Ibid.*

McTaggart might say to the contrary, all that common sense takes to be real is real. Indeed, in the period in question Russell carried realism considerably further than he was later to do. It was not simply a question of embracing pluralism and the theory of external relations, nor even of believing in the reality of secondary qualities. Russell also believed that points of space and instants of time are existent entities, and that there is a timeless world of Platonic ideas or essences, including numbers. He thus had, as he has put it, a very full or luxuriant universe.

The lectures on Leibniz, to which reference has been made above, resulted in the publication in 1900 of Russell's notable work *A Critical Exposition of the Philosophy of Leibniz*. In it he maintained that Leibniz's metaphysics was in part a reflection of his logical studies and in part a popular or exoteric doctrine expounded with a view to edification and at variance with the philosopher's real convictions.[1] From then on Russell remained convinced that the substance-attribute metaphysics is a reflection of the subject-predicate mode of expression.

(ii) Considerable importance is attached by Russell to his becoming acquainted at an international congress at Paris in 1900 with the work of Giuseppe Peano (1858–1932), the Italian mathematician. For many years, in fact since he began to study geometry, Russell had been perplexed by the problem of the foundations of mathematics. At this time he did not know the work of Frege, who had already attempted to reduce arithmetic to logic. But the writings of Peano provided him with the stimulus for tackling his problem afresh. And the immediate result of his reflections was *The Principles of Mathematics*, which appeared in 1903.

But there were weeds in the mathematical garden. Russell finished the first draft of *The Principles of Mathematics* at the end of 1900, and early in 1901 he came upon what seemed to him to be an antinomy or paradox in the logic of classes. As he defined number in terms of the logic of classes, a cardinal number being 'the class of all classes similar to the given class',[2] the antinomy evidently affected mathematics. And Russell had either to solve it or to admit an insoluble antinomy within the mathematical field.

The antinomy can be illustrated in this way. The class of pigs is

---

[1] For some brief comments on Russell's view of Leibniz see Vol. IV of this *History*, pp. 270–2.

[2] *The Principles of Mathematics*, p. 115 (2nd edition, 1937). Two classes are said to be 'similar' when they 'have the same number' (*ibid.*, p. 113).

evidently not itself a pig. That is to say, it is not a member of itself. But consider the notion of the class of all classes which are not members of themselves. Let us call this class X and ask whether X is a member of itself or not. On the one hand, it seems that it cannot be a member of itself. For if we assume that it is, it follows logically that X has the defining property of its members. And this defining property is that any class of which it is a property is not a member of itself. Hence X cannot be a member of itself. On the other hand, it seems that X must be a member of itself. For if we begin by assuming that it is not a member of itself, it follows logically that it is not a member of those classes which are not members of themselves. And to say this is to say that X is a member of itself. Hence whether we begin by assuming that X is a member of itself or that it is not a member of itself, we seem in either case to be involved in self-contradiction.

Russell communicated this antinomy or paradox to Frege, who replied that arithmetic was tottering. But after some struggles Russell hit upon what seemed to him to be a solution. This was the doctrine or theory of types, a preliminary version of which was presented in *Appendix B* in *The Principles of Mathematics*. Every propositional function, Russell maintained, 'has in addition to its range of truth, a range of significance.'[1] For example, in the propositional function 'X is mortal', we can obviously substitute for the variable X a range of values such that the resultant propositions are true. Thus 'Socrates is mortal' is true. But there are also values which, if substituted for X, would make the resultant propositions neither true nor false but meaningless. For instance, 'the class of men is mortal' is meaningless. For the class of men is not a thing or object of which either mortality or immortality can be meaningfully predicated. From 'if X is a man, X is mortal' we can infer 'if Socrates is a man, Socrates is mortal'; but we cannot infer that the class of men is mortal. For the class of men neither is nor could be a man. In other words, the class of men cannot be a member of itself: in fact it is really nonsense to speak of its either being or not being a member of itself. For the very idea of a class being a member of itself is nonsensical. To take an example given by Russell,[2] a club is a class of individuals. And it can be a member of a class of another type, such as an association of clubs, which would be a class of classes. But neither the class nor the class of classes could possibly be a member of itself.

[1] *Ibid.*, p. 523.   [2] *Ibid.*, p. 524.

And if the distinctions between types are observed, the antinomy or paradox in the logic of classes does not arise.

To deal with further difficulties Russell produced a 'branching' or ramified theory of types. But we cannot discuss it here. Instead we can draw attention to the following point. Having made it clear that a class of things is not itself a thing, Russell goes on in *Principia Mathematica* to what he has called 'the abolition of classes'.[1] That is to say, he interprets classes as 'merely symbolic or linguistic conveniences"[2] as incomplete symbols. And it is not surprising to find him later on adopting a sympathetic attitude towards a linguistic interpretation of the theory of types and saying, for example, that 'difference of type means difference of syntactical function'.[3] Having once implied that differences between types are differences between types of entities, Russell came to recognize that the differences lie between different types of symbols, which 'acquire their type-status through the syntactical rules to which they are subject'.[4] In any case it is safe to say that one of the general effects of Russell's theory of types was to encourage belief in the relevance to philosophy of 'linguistic analysis'.

The theory of types has, of course, a variety of possible applications. Thus in his introduction to Ludwig Wittgenstein's *Tractatus Logico-Philosophicus* Russell, writing in 1922, suggested that Wittgenstein's difficulty about not being able to say anything within a given language about the structure of this language could be met by the idea of a hierarchy of languages. Thus even if one were unable to say anything within language *A* about its structure, one might be able to do so within language *B*, when they belong to different types, *A* being a first-order language, so to speak, and *B* a second-order language. If Wittgenstein were to reply that his theory of the inexpressible in language applies to the totality of languages,[5] the retort could be made that there is not, and cannot

---

[1] *The Principles of Mathematics*, p. x (Introduction to 2nd edition).

[2] *Principia Mathematica*, I, p. 72.

[3] *The Philosophy of Bertrand Russell*, edited by P. A. Schilpp, p. 692. As Russell notes in the introduction to the second edition of *The Principles of Mathematics*, he had been convinced by F. P. Ramsey's *The Foundations of Mathematics* (1931), that there are two classes of paradoxes. Some are purely logical or mathematical and can be cleared up by the simple (original) theory of types. Others are linguistic or semantic, such as the paradox arising out of the statement 'I am lying'. These can be cleared up by linguistic considerations. [4]*Ibid.*

[5] It seems to the present writer that in the *Tractatus* Wittgenstein so defines the essence of the proposition that it follows logically that any proposition *about* propositions is a pseudo-proposition, devoid of 'sense' (*Sinn*). In this case to avoid the conclusion one has to reject the definition.

be, such a thing as a totality of languages.[1] The hierarchy is without limit.

What Russell has to say in developing the theory of types also has its application in metaphysics. For example, if we once accept the definition of the world as the class of all finite entities, we are debarred from speaking of it as being itself a contingent entity or being, even if we regard contingency as belonging necessarily to every finite being. For to speak in this way would be to make a class a member of itself. It does not follow, however, that the world must be described as a 'necessary entity'. For if the world is to be defined as the class of entities, it cannot itself be an entity, whether contingent or necessary.

(iii) It has already been mentioned, by way of anticipation, that in *Principia Mathematica* Russell maintains that the symbols for classes are incomplete symbols. 'Their *uses* are defined, but they themselves are not assumed to mean anything at all.'[2] That is to say, the symbols for classes undoubtedly possess a definable use or function in sentences, but, taken by themselves, they do not denote entities. Rather are they ways of referring to other entities. In this respect the symbols for classes are 'like those of descriptions'.[3] And something must now be said about Russell's theory of descriptions, which he developed between the writing of *The Principles of Mathematics* and the publication of *Principia Mathematica*.[4]

Let us consider the sentence 'the golden mountain is very high'. The phrase 'the golden mountain' functions as the grammatical subject of the sentence. And it may appear that as we can say something about the golden mountain, namely that it is very high, the phrase must denote an entity of some sort. True, it does not denote any existing entity. For though it is not logically impossible for there to be a golden mountain, we have no evidence that there is one. Yet even if we say 'the golden mountain does not exist', we seem to be saying something intelligible *about* it, namely that it does not exist. And in this case it appears to follow that 'the golden mountain' must denote an entity, not indeed an actually existing entity, but none the less a reality of some sort.

---

[1] That is, there can no more be a totality of languages than there can be a class of all classes. The latter notion was for Russell self-contradictory. A class of *all* classes would be additional to *all* classes. It would also be a member of itself which is ruled out by the theory of types.

[2] *Principia Mathematica*, I, p. 71.   [3] *Ibid.*

[4] The theory found a preliminary expression in Russell's article *On Denoting* in *Mind* for 1905.

This line of reasoning can be applied, of course, to the grammatical subjects in sentences such as 'the king of France is bald' (uttered or written when there is no king of France) or 'Sherlock Holmes wore a deerstalker's cap'. We thus get the sort of over-populated, or at any rate very well populated, universe in which Russell originally believed in the first flush of his realist reaction against the way in which idealists such as Bradley and McTaggart described as unreal several factors in the universe which common sense spontaneously regards as real. It is understandable, therefore, that Russell devoted himself to the study of Meinong, who also accepted a luxuriant universe in which room was found for entities which do not actually exist but which are none the less realities in some sense. At the same time it was precisely his study of Meinong which raised serious doubts in Russell's mind about the validity of the principle that phrases such as 'the golden mountain', which can function as grammatical subjects in sentences, denote entities of some sort. Indeed, when taken by themselves, have such phrases as 'the golden mountain', 'the king of France' and so on any 'meaning'? It was one of the functions of the theory of descriptions to show that they have not.

According to this theory such phrases are not 'names', denoting entities, but 'descriptions'. In his *Introduction to Mathematical Philosophy* (1919) Russell distinguishes between two sorts of descriptions, indefinite and definite.[1] Phrases such as 'the golden mountain' and 'the king of France' are definite descriptions; and we can confine our attention here to this class. The theory of descriptions purports to show that they are incomplete symbols, and though they can function as grammatical subjects in sentences, these sentences can be restated according to their logical form in such a way that it becomes clear that the phrases in question are not the real logical subjects in the sentences in which they occur as grammatical subjects. When this has become clear, the temptation to think that they must denote entities should vanish. For it is then understood that, taken by themselves, the phrases in question have no denoting function. The phrase 'the golden mountain', for example, does not denote anything at all.

Let us take the sentence 'the golden mountain does not exist'. If this is translated as 'the propositional function "X is golden and a mountain" is false for all values of X', the meaning of the

---

[1] 'An indefinite description is a phrase of the form "a so-and-so" and a definite description is a phrase of the form "the so-and-so" (in the singular)', *Introduction to Mathematical Philosophy*, p. 167.

original sentence is revealed in such a way that the phrase 'the golden mountain' disappears and, with it, the temptation to postulate a subsisting non-actual entity. For we are no longer involved in the awkward situation which arises in view of the fact that the statement 'the golden mountain does not exist' can prompt the question *what* does not exist?', implying that the golden mountain must have some sort of reality if we can say of it significantly that it does not exist.

This is all very well, it may be said, but it is extremely odd to claim, in regard to descriptions in general, that they have no meaning when they are taken by themselves. It seems indeed to be true that 'the golden mountain' does not mean anything, provided that by meaning one understands denoting an entity. But what about a phrase such as 'the author of *Waverley*'? According to Russell, it is a description, not a proper name. But is it not evident that it means Scott?

If 'the author of *Waverley*' meant Scott, Russell replies, 'Scott is the author of *Waverley*' would be a tautology, declaring that Scott is Scott. But it is evidently not a tautology. If, however, 'the author of *Waverley*' meant anything else but Scott, 'Scott is the author of *Waverley*' would be false, which it is not. The only thing to say is, therefore, 'the author of *Waverley*' means nothing. That is to say, taken in isolation it does not denote anyone. And the statement 'Scott is the author of *Waverley*' can be restated in such a way that the phrase 'the author of *Waverley*' is eliminated. For example, 'for all values of X, "X wrote *Waverley*" is equivalent to "X is Scott" '.[1]

It seems indeed that we can very well say 'the author of *Waverley* is Scotch', and that in this case we are predicating an attribute, namely being Scotch, of an entity, namely the author of *Waverley*. Russell, however, maintained that 'the author of *Waverley* is Scotch' implies and is defined by three distinct propositions; 'at least one person wrote *Waverley*', 'at most one person wrote *Waverley*', and 'whosoever wrote *Waverley* was Scotch'.[2] And this can be stated formally as 'there is a term c such that "X wrote *Waverley*" is equivalent, for all values of X, to "X is c", and "c is Scotch" '.

Needless to say, Russell has no doubt that the author of *Waverley* was Scotch, in the sense that Sir Walter Scott wrote

[1] *My Philosophical Development*, p. 84.
[2] *Introduction to Mathematical Philosophy*, p. 177.

Waverley and was a Scotsman. The point is, however, that if the descriptive term 'the author of *Waverley*' is not a proper name and does not denote anyone, the same can be said of such a descriptive term as 'the king of France'. 'The author of *Waverley* was Scotch' can be restated in such a way that the translation is a true proposition but does not contain the descriptive phrase 'the author of *Waverley*', and 'the king of France is bald' can be restated in such a way that the translation does not contain the descriptive phrase 'the king of France' but is a false, though significant proposition. It is thus in no way necessary to postulate any non-actual entity denoted by 'the king of France'.

It is understandable that Russell's theory of descriptions has been subjected to criticism. For example, G. E. Moore has objected[1] that if in 1700 an Englishman had made the statement 'the king of France is wise', it would certainly have been correct to say that 'the king of France' denoted an entity, namely Louis XIV. In this case, therefore, 'the king of France' would not have been an incomplete symbol. But in other circumstances it might be. There can be sentences in which 'the king of France' does not denote anyone; but, equally, there can be sentences in which it does denote someone.

It seems to the present writer that in his criticism of Russell's theory of descriptions Moore is appealing to ordinary linguistic usage. This is, of course, the strength of his criticism. Russell himself, however, is concerned not so much with mapping-out ordinary language as with constructing a theory which will deprive of its linguistic basis the notion that it is necessary to postulate non-existent but real entities such as 'the golden mountain', 'the king of France' (when there is no king of France), and so on. It is perfectly legitimate criticism, it seems to me, to object that the theory involves an interpretation of such phrases which is too narrow to square with actual linguistic usage.[2] But in the present context it is more important to draw attention to Russell's aim, to what he thinks that he is accomplishing by means of his theory.

It would obviously be a great mistake to suppose that Russell imagines that translation of 'the golden mountain is very high' into a sentence in which the descriptive phrase 'the golden

---

[1] *The Philosophy of Bertrand Russell*, edited by P. A. Schilpp, ch. 5.
[2] Some analytic philosophers might wish to say that Russell was trying to 'reform' language, to create an ideal language. But he did not intend, of course, to prohibit people from saying what they are accustomed to say.

mountain' does not occur proves that there is no golden mountain. Whether there is or is not a golden mountain in the world is an empirical question; and Russell is perfectly well aware of the fact. Indeed, if the translation to which reference has just been made proved that there is in fact no golden mountain, then the fact that 'the author of *The Principles of Mathematics* is English' can be restated in such a way that the descriptive phrase 'the author of *The Principles of Mathematics*' disappears would prove that there is no Bertrand Russell.

It would also be a mistake to suppose that according to Russell the ordinary man, the non-philosopher, is misled into thinking that there must be some sort of non-existing but real object corresponding to the phrase 'the golden mountain' because we can say 'the golden mountain does not exist'. Russell is not attributing any mistakes of this kind to the ordinary man. His point is that for philosophers, who reflect on the implications or apparent implications of linguistic expressions, descriptive phrases such as 'the golden mountain' may occasion, and in Russell's opinion have occasioned, the temptation to postulate entities with a queer status between actual existence and non-entity. And the function of the theory of descriptions is to remove this temptation by showing that descriptive phrases are incomplete symbols which, according to Russell, mean nothing, that is, do not denote any entity. The paradoxical aspect of the theory of descriptions is that, because of its generality, it applies equally both to phrases such as 'the golden mountain' or 'the king of France' and to phrases such as 'the author of *The Principles of Mathematics*', not to speak of the other class of phrases such as 'the round square'. But its function is to contribute to clearing away the fictitious entities with which certain philosophers, not the man in the street, have over-populated the universe. It thus serves the purpose of Ockham's razor and can be brought under the general heading of reductive analysis, a theme to which we shall have to return.

A final point. We have noted that when a phrase such as 'the golden mountain' or 'the author of *Waverley*' occurs as the grammatical subject of a sentence, Russell maintains that it is not the logical subject. The same line of reasoning can, of course, be applied to grammatical objects. In 'I saw nobody on the road' the grammatical object is 'nobody'. But 'nobody' is not a special kind of 'somebody'. And the sentence can be restated in such a way (for example, 'it is not the case that I saw any person on the road') that the word 'nobody' disappears. In general, therefore, Russell's contention is that the grammatical form of a sentence is by no means the same as its logical form, and that philosophers can be seriously misled if they do not understand this fact. But though Russell may have generalized this idea, it is historically inaccurate to suggest that he was the first man to make this discovery.[1] For example, in the twelfth century St. Anselm pointed out that to say that God created the world out of nothing is not to say that the world was created out of nothing as some kind of pre-existing material. It is to say that God did not create the world out of anything, that is, out of any pre-existing material.

(iv) The three volumes of *Principia Mathematica*, which were the fruit of the joint work of Russell and A. N. Whitehead, appeared in 1910–13. The point which aroused most interest was the attempt to show that pure mathematics is reducible to logic, in the sense that it can be shown to follow from purely logical premisses and employs only concepts which are capable of being defined in logical terms.[2] In practice, of course, we cannot simply take a complicated mathematical formula at random and express it without more ado in purely logical terms. But in principle the whole of pure mathematics is ultimately derivable from logical premisses, mathematics being, as Russell has put it, the manhood of logic.

As Russell believed that in *Principia Mathematica* he had demonstrated the truth of his thesis, he also believed that he had provided a decisive refutation of Kantian theories of mathematics. For example, if geometry is derivable from purely logical premisses, to postulate an *a priori* intuition of space is entirely superfluous.

Russell and Whitehead had, needless to say, their predecessors. George Boole (1815–64)[3] had attempted to 'algebraicize' logic and had developed a calculus of classes. But he regarded logic as subordinate to mathematics, whereas William Stanley Jevons (1835–82)[4] was convinced that logic is the fundamental science. John Venn

---

[1] This is understood nowadays. But in the past statements have sometimes been made which said or implied that Russell was the discoverer of this distinction between grammatical and logical form.

[2] Russell has expressed his disappointment that comparatively little attention was paid to the mathematical techniques developed in the course of the work.

[3] Author of *The Mathematical Analysis of Logic* (1847), and *An Investigation of the Laws of Thought* (1854).

[4] Author of *Pure Logic* (1864) and other logical studies. Whereas Boole was a professor of mathematics, Jevons occupied a chair of political economy and did not possess Boole's 'mathematicizing' turn of mind, though he invented a calculating machine to carry out the processes of inference.

(1834–1923),[1] however, while attempting to remedy the defects in Boole's system and to overcome the contemporary chaos in symbolic notation, looked on logic and mathematics as separate branches of symbolic language, neither being subordinate to the other. In America C. S. Peirce modified and developed the logical algebra of Boole and showed how it could accommodate a revised version of the logic of relations formulated by Augustus De Morgan (1806–71).

In Germany Friedrich Wilhelm Schröder (1841–1902) gave a classical formulation to Boole's logical algebra as modified by Peirce. More important, Gottlob Frege (1848–1925) attempted to derive arithmetic from logic in his works *Die Grundlagen der Arithmetik* (1884) and *Grundgesetze der Arithmetik* (1893–1903). As has been mentioned, Russell was not at first aware that he had rediscovered for himself ideas which had already been proposed by Frege. But when he became aware of Frege's work, he drew attention to it,[2] though it was not until a considerably later period that the German mathematician's studies obtained general recognition in England.

In Italy Peano and his collaborators tried to show, in their *Formulaires de mathématiques* (1895–1908), that arithmetic and algebra can be derived from certain logical ideas, such as those of a class and of membership of a class, three primitive mathematical concepts and six primitive propositions. As we have seen, Russell became acquainted with Peano's work in 1900. And he and Whitehead made use of Peano's logical symbolism or notation in the construction of *Principia Mathematica*, which carried further the work of both Peano and Frege.

The present writer is not competent to pass any judgment on the contents of *Principia Mathematica*. It must suffice to say that though the thesis of the reducibility of mathematics to logic has by no means won the consent of all mathematicians,[3] nobody would question the historic importance of the work in the development of mathematical logic. Indeed, it stands out above all other English contributions to the subject.[4] In any case, though Russell

[1] Author of *The Logic of Chance* (1866), *Symbolic Logic* (1881), and *The Principles of Empirical or Inductive Logic* (1889).

[2] *Appendix A* in *The Principles of Mathematics* is devoted to 'the logical and arithmetical doctrines of Frege'.

[3] It was rejected both by the 'Formalists', such as David Hilbert (1862–1943) and by the 'Intuitionists' who followed Luitzen Brouwer (b. 1881).

[4] It is a notorious fact that since the publication of *Principia Mathematica* comparatively little attention has been paid in England to symbolic logic. This is not to say that no good work has subsequently been done in England on logical theory. But, generally speaking, the attention of philosophers has been concentrated rather on 'ordinary language'. It is Polish and American logicians who have been most prominent in the field of symbolic logic.

himself may understandably regret that more attention was not paid to the mathematical techniques evolved in the work, the present writer's principal aim in drawing attention here to *Principia Mathematica* is to illustrate the background to Russell's conception of reductive analysis. For example, to say that mathematics is reducible to logic obviously does not mean that there is no such thing as mathematics. Nor is it tantamount to a denial that there are any differences between logic and mathematics as they actually exist or have actually been developed. Rather does it mean that pure mathematics can in principle be derived from certain fundamental logical concepts and certain primitive indemonstrable propositions, and that, in principle, mathematical propositions could be translated into logical propositions with equivalent truth-values.

Before we pass on to Russell's general idea of reductive analysis, it is worth noting that the reducibility of mathematics to logic does not mean that mathematics is based on laws of thought in the psychological sense of laws governing human thinking. In the earlier years of this century Russell believed that mathematics carries us beyond what is human 'into the region of absolute necessity, to which not only the actual world, but every possible world, must conform'.[1] In this ideal world mathematics forms an eternal edifice of truth; and in the contemplation of its serene beauty man can find refuge from a world full of evil and suffering. Gradually, however, though reluctantly, Russell came to accept Wittgenstein's view that pure mathematics consists of 'tautologies'. This change of mind he has described as 'a gradual retreat from Pythagoras'.[2] One effect of the First World War on Russell's mind was to turn it away from the idea of an eternal realm of abstract truth, where one can take refuge in the contemplation of timeless and non-human beauty, to concentration on the actual concrete world. And this meant, in part at least, a turning away from purely logical studies to the theory of knowledge and to the parts of psychology and linguistics which seemed to be relevant to epistemology.

3. We have seen Russell getting rid of superfluous entities such as 'the golden mountain'. And in the course of writing *Principia Mathematica* he found that the definition of cardinal numbers as

---

[1] From *The Study of Mathematics*, written in 1902 and first published in the *New Quarterly* in 1907. See *Philosophical Essays*, p. 82, and *Mysticism and Logic*, p. 69.

[2] *My Philosophical Development*, p. 208.

classes of classes, together with the interpretation of class-symbols as incomplete symbols, rendered it unnecessary to regard cardinal numbers as entities of any kind. But there remained, for example, points, instants and particles as factors in the physical world. And these figured in *The Problems of Philosophy* (1912), which can be said to represent Russell's incursion into the general philosophical field, as distinct from the more restricted sphere of logical and mathematical theory. Whitehead, however, woke him from his 'dogmatic slumbers' by inventing a way of constructing points, instants and particles as sets of events, or as logical constructions out of sets of events.[1]

The technique of reductive analysis as illustrated in the case of points, instants and particles was regarded by Russell as an application of the method already employed in *Principia Mathematica*. In this work the task was to find for mathematics a minimum vocabulary in which no symbol would be definable in terms of the others. And the result of the inquiry was the conclusion that the minimum vocabulary for mathematics is the same as that for logic. In this sense mathematics was found to be reducible to logic. If a similar technique, Russell came to think, is applied to the language used to describe the physical world, it will be found that points, instants and particles do not appear in the minimum vocabulary.

Now, talk about finding a minimum vocabulary tends to suggest that the operation in question is purely linguistic, in the sense of being concerned only with words. But in the context of propositions about the physical world finding a minimum vocabulary means for Russell discovering by analysis the uneliminable entities in terms of which inferred entities can be defined. If, for example, we find that the inferred non-empirical entity, or putative entity, X can be defined in terms of a series of empirical entities a, b, c, and d, X is said to be a logical construction out of a, b, c, and d. This reductive analysis as applied to X has indeed a linguistic aspect. For it means that a proposition in which X is mentioned can be translated into a set of propositions in which there is no mention of X but only of a, b, c, and d, the relation between the original proposition and the translation being such that if the former is true (or false) the latter is true (or false) and *vice versa*. But the reductive analysis has at the same time an

---

[1] See *My Philosophical Development*, p. 103 and *The Principles of Mathematics*, p. xi (in the Introduction to the second edition).

ontological aspect. True, if X can be interpreted as a logical construction out of a, b, c, and d, we are not necessarily committed to denying the existence of X as a non-empirical entity distinct from or over and above a, b, c, and d. But it is unnecessary to postulate the existence of such an entity. Hence the principle of parsimony (or economy) or Ockham's razor forbids us to *assert* the existence of X as an inferred non-empirical entity. And the principle itself can be stated in this form: 'whenever possible logical constructions are to be substituted for inferred entities'.[1]

This quotation is taken from a paper on the relation of sense-data to physics, which Russell wrote at the beginning of 1914. In this paper he maintains that physical objects can be defined as functions of sense-data, a sense-datum being a particular object, such as a particular patch of colour, of which a subject is directly aware. Sense-data, therefore, are not to be confused with sensations, that is, with the acts of awareness of which they are the object.[2] Nor are they mental entities, in the sense of being purely within the mind. We must thus admit, to speak paradoxically, sense-data which are not actual data, not objects of actual awareness on the part of a subject. But the paradox can be avoided by calling these unsensed sense-data *sensibilia*, potential sense-data. And the physical objects of common sense and of science are to be interpreted as functions of sense-data and *sensibilia* or, to put the matter in another way, as the classes of their appearances.

There is, however, a major difficulty in admitting *sensibilia* as being on the same level, so to speak, as actual sense-data. For Russell's programme demands that the physical objects of common sense and of science should be interpreted, if possible, as logical constructions out of purely empirical, non-inferred entities. But *sensibilia* are inferred entities. The only relevant non-inferred entities are *actual* sense-data. Hence it is not surprising to find Russell saying, in his paper on the relation of sense-data to physics, that 'a complete application of the method which substitutes constructions for inferences would exhibit matter wholly in terms of sense-data, and even, we may add, of the sense-data of a single person, since the sense-data of others cannot be known without some element of inference'.[3] But he goes on to add that the carrying out of this programme is extremely difficult, and that

---

[1] *Mysticism and Logic*, p. 155.
[2] It will be noted that Russell and Moore are at one on this matter.
[3] *Mysticism and Logic*, p. 157.

he proposes to allow himself two kinds of inferred entities, the sense-data of other people and *sensibilia*.

In *Our Knowledge of the External World* (1914) Russell depicts the physical objects of common sense and science as logical constructions out of actual sense-data, *sensibilia* or possible sense-data being defined with reference to them. At any rate 'I think it may be laid down quite generally that, *in so far* as physics or common sense is verifiable, it must be capable of interpretation in terms of actual sense-data alone'.[1] However, in a lecture on the ultimate constituents of matter which he delivered early in 1915, Russell remarks that while the particles of mathematical physics are logical constructions, useful symbolic fictions, 'the actual data in sensation, the immediate objects of sight or touch or hearing, are extra-mental, purely physical, and among the ultimate constituents of matter'.[2] Similarly, 'sense-data are merely those among the ultimate constituents of the physical world, of which we happen to be immediately aware'.[3] Whether the statement that sense-data are 'among' the ultimate constituents of the physical world is equivalent to the admission of *sensibilia* as members of this class, or whether it means simply that sense-data are the only ultimate constituents of which we are directly aware, is not quite clear. In any case, if the world of common sense and of science is to be regarded as a logical construction, or hierarchy of logical constructions, out of the actual sense-data of a single person, it is difficult to see how solipsism can be successfully avoided. However, it was not long before Russell abandoned the doctrine of sense-data as here presented. And his ideas on solipsism will be considered later.

So far we have been concerned only with analysis of the physical objects of common sense and science. But what of the subject or mind which is aware of objects? When Russell rejected monism and embraced pluralism, he made a sharp distinction between the act of awareness and its object. Originally indeed, as he himself tells us, he accepted the view of Brentano that in sensation there are three distinct elements, 'act, content and object'.[4] He then came to think that the distinction between content and object is superfluous; but he continued to believe in the relational character of sensation, that is to say, that in sensation a subject is aware of an object. And this belief found

[1] *Our Knowledge of the External World*, pp. 88–9.
[2] *Mysticism and Logic*, p. 128.   [3] *Ibid.*, p. 143.
[4] *My Philosophical Development*, p. 134.

expression in, for example, *The Problems of Philosophy* (1912). In this work Russell admitted, even if tentatively, that the subject can be known by acquaintance. It does not follow, of course, that he accepted the idea of a permanent mental substance. But he held at any rate that we are acquainted with what one might perhaps call the momentary self, the self precisely as apprehending an object in a given act of awareness. In other words, it was a question of the phenomenological analysis of consciousness rather than of metaphysical theory.

When, however, we turn to an essay on the nature of acquaintance, which Russell wrote in 1914, we find him expressing his agreement with Hume that the subject is not acquainted with itself. He does indeed define acquaintance as 'a dual relation between a subject and an object which need not have any community of nature'.[1] But the term 'subject', instead of denoting an entity with which we can be acquainted, becomes a description. In other words, the self or mind becomes a logical construction; and in his 1915 address on the ultimate constituents of matter Russell suggests that 'we might regard the mind as an assemblage of particulars, namely, what would be called "states of mind", which belong together in virtue of some specific common quality. The common quality of all states of mind would be the quality designated by the word "mental".'[2] This suggestion is indeed advanced only in the context of a discussion of the theory, rejected by Russell, that sense-data are 'in the mind'. But it is clear that the subject, considered as a single entity, has become a class of particulars. At the same time these particulars possess a quality which marks them off as mental. In other words, an element of dualism is still retained by Russell. He has not yet adopted the neutral monism, of which something will be said presently.

Needless to say, the theory of logical constructions is not intended to imply that we ought to give up talking about minds on the one hand and the physical objects of common sense and science on the other. To say, for example, that sentences in which a table is mentioned can in principle be translated into sentences in which only sense-data are referred to and the word 'table' does not occur is not equivalent to a denial of the utility of talking about tables. Indeed, within the context of ordinary language and its purposes it is perfectly true to say that there are tables, though

---

[1] *Logic and Knowledge*, p. 127.   [2] *Mysticism and Logic*, pp. 131–2.

from the point of view of the analytic philosopher a table is a logical construction out of sense-data. The language of atomic physics, for instance, does not render ordinary language illegitimate. For the purposes of ordinary life we are perfectly entitled to go on talking about trees and stones; we do not have to talk about atoms instead. And if philosophical analysis leads us to regard the entities of physical science, such as atoms, as logical constructions, this does not render illegitimate the language of physical science. The different levels of language can co-exist and are employed for different purposes, within different contexts. They should not, of course, be confused; but the one level does not exclude the other levels.

It is thus easy to understand the contention that the issue between the sense-datum theory and the common sense view of the world is a purely linguistic matter; that is, that it is simply a question of choosing between two alternative languages. But, as has already been indicated, this contention does not adequately represent Russell's point of view. Obviously, analysis as he practises it takes different forms.[1] Sometimes it is predominantly a logical analysis which has ontological implications only in the sense that it removes the ground for postulating superfluous entities. But in its application to the physical objects of common sense and science it professes to reveal the ultimate constituents of such objects. In other words it professes to increase our understanding not only of language but also of extra-linguistic reality. To be sure, Russell has at times expressed a very sceptical view about the knowledge which is actually attainable in philosophy. But his aim at any rate has been that of attaining impersonal truth. And the primary method of doing so is for him analysis. His point of view is thus opposed to that of Bradley, who thought that analysis, the breaking-up of a whole into its constituent elements, distorts reality and leads us away from the truth which is, as Hegel said, the whole. Later on, especially when treating of the relation of philosophy to the empirical sciences, Russell is ready to emphasize the role of synthesis, of bold and wide philosophical hypotheses about the universe. But at the period of which we have been writing the emphasis is placed on analysis.

[1] So far as the present writer is aware, Russell has never given a systematic account of the methods of analysis practised by himself, comparing them with one another and noting both their common and their differentiating features. On this subject the reader can profitably consult *The Unity of Russell's Philosophy* by Morris Weitz in *The Philosophy of Bertrand Russell*, edited by P. A. Schilpp.

And it would be extremely misleading to describe analysis, as practised by Russell, as being purely 'linguistic'.

This point can also be illustrated in the following way. In *The Problems of Philosophy* Russell accepted universals as ultimate conceptual constituents of reality, universals being said 'to *subsist* or *have being*, where "being" is opposed to "existence" as being timeless'.[1] And though he has progressively depopulated the world of universals, he has never entirely rejected his former view. For he has continued to believe not only that a minimum vocabulary for the description of the world requires some universal term or terms but also that this fact shows something about the world itself, even if he has ended by being uncertain about precisely what it shows.

4. In *My Philosophical Development*,[2] Russell tells us that from August 1914 until the end of 1917 he was wholly occupied with matters arising out of his opposition to the war. These matters presumably cover *Principles of Social Reconstruction* and *Justice in War-Time*, both of which appeared in 1916, in addition to a number of articles and addresses relating to the war. However, during the period 1914–19 Russell published an important series of philosophical articles in *The Monist*.[3] In 1918 he published *Mysticism and Logic and Other Essays* and *Roads to Freedom: Socialism, Anarchism and Syndicalism*. His *Introduction to Mathematical Philosophy*, to which reference has already been made, was written in 1918, during his six months imprisonment,[4] and was published in 1919.

Shortly before the First World War Wittgenstein gave Russell some notes on various logical points. And these, together with the conversations which the two men had had during Wittgenstein's first sojourn at Cambridge, 1912–13, affected Russell's thought during the years when he was cut off from contact with his friend and former pupil.[5] In fact he prefaced his 1918 lectures on the philosophy of logical atomism with the remark that they were largely concerned with ideas which he had learned from Wittgenstein.

As for the term 'atomism' in 'logical atomism' Russell says that

---

[1] *The Problems of Philosophy*, p. 156. [2] P. 128.

[3] The lectures on logical atomism which Russell delivered in 1918 and which were published in *The Monist*, 1918–19, have been reprinted in *Logic and Knowledge*, edited by R. Marsh (London, 1956).

[4] This was the result of a second prosecution, arising, like the first, out of Russell's outspoken opposition to the First World War.

[5] Wittgenstein, then still an Austrian citizen, joined the Austrian army and was subsequently a prisoner-of-war of the Italians.

he wishes to arrive at the ultimate constituent elements of reality in a manner analogous to that in which in *Principia Mathematica* he worked back from 'result' to the uneliminable logical 'premisses'. But he is looking, of course, for logical and not physical atoms. Hence the use of the term 'logical'. 'The point is that the atom I wish to arrive at is the atom of logical analysis, not the atom of physical analysis.'[1] The atom of physical analysis (or, more accurately, whatever physical science at a given time takes to be ultimate physical constituents of matter) is itself subject to logical analysis. But though in his final lecture on logical atomism Russell makes what he calls an excursus into metaphysics and introduces the idea of logical constructions or, as he puts it, logical fictions, he is mainly concerned with discussing propositions and facts.

We can, of course, understand the meaning of a proposition without knowing whether it is true or false. But a proposition which asserts or denies a fact is either true or false; and it is its relation to a fact which makes it true or false.[2] As we have seen, the grammatical form of a sentence may be different from its logical form. But in a logically perfect language 'the words in a proposition would correspond one by one with the components of the corresponding fact, with the exception of such words as "or", "not", "if', "then", which have a different function'.[3] In such a language therefore there would be an identity of structure between the fact asserted or denied and its symbolic representation, the proposition. Hence if there are atomic facts, there can be atomic propositions.

The simplest imaginable kind of fact, according to Russell, is that which consists in the possession of a quality by a particular, the quality being called a 'monadic relation'. This kind of fact is an atomic fact, though not the only kind. For it is not required, in order that a fact should be atomic, that it should comprise only one term and a monadic relation. There can be a hierarchy of atomic facts; facts which comprise two particulars and a (dyadic) relation, facts which comprise three particulars and a (triadic) relation, and so on. It must be understood, however, that 'particulars',

---

[1] *Logic and Knowledge*, p. 179.
[2] Russell notes that it was Wittgenstein who first drew his attention to the truth that propositions are not names for facts. For to every proposition there 'correspond' at least two propositions, one true, the other false. The false proposition 'corresponds with' the fact in the sense that it is its relation to the fact which makes it false.
[3] *Logic and Knowledge*, p. 197.

defined by Russell as the terms of relations in atomic facts, are to be understood in the sense of what would be for him genuine particulars, such as actual sense-data, not in the sense of logical constructions. 'This is white' would thus be an atomic proposition, provided that 'this' functions as a proper name denoting a sense-datum. So would 'these are white', provided again that 'these' denotes genuine particulars.

Now, an atomic proposition contains a single verb or verbal phrase. But by the use of words such as 'and', 'or' and 'if', we can construct complex or molecular propositions.[1] It would appear to follow, therefore, that there are molecular facts. But Russell shows hesitation on this point. Let us suppose, for example, that 'either today is Sunday or I made a mistake in coming here' is a molecular proposition. Does it make any sense to speak of a disjunctive fact? However, though Russell expresses some doubt about molecular facts, he admits 'general facts'. For instance, if we could enumerate all the atomic facts in the world, the proposition 'these are all the atomic facts there are' would express a general fact. Russell is also prepared to admit negative facts, even if with some hesitation. He suggests, for example, that 'Socrates is not alive' expresses an objective negative fact, an objective feature of the world.

We cannot refer to all the topics mentioned by Russell in his lectures on logical atomism. But there are two points to which attention can profitably be drawn. The first is the doctrine that every genuine particular is completely self-subsistent, in the sense that it is logically independent of every other particular. 'There is no reason why you should not have a universe consisting of one particular and nothing else.'[2] True, it is an empirical fact that there is a multitude of particulars. But it is not logically necessary that this should be the case. Hence it would not be possible, given knowledge of one particular, to deduce from it the whole system of the universe.

The second point is Russell's analysis of existence-propositions. I know, for example, that there are men in Canton; but I cannot mention any individual who lives there. Hence, Russell argues, the proposition 'there are men in Canton' cannot be about actual individuals. 'Existence is essentially a property of a propositional

---

[1] When the truth or falsity of a molecular proposition depends simply on the truth or falsity of its constituent propositions it is said to be a truth-function of these constituents.

[2] *Logic and Knowledge*, p. 202.

function.'[1] If we say 'there are men' or 'men exist', this means that there is at least one value of X for which it is true to say 'X is a man'. At the same time Russell recognizes 'existence-facts', such as that corresponding to 'there are men', as distinct from atomic facts.

It has already been mentioned that according to Russell's own explicit declaration his 1918 lectures on logical atomism were partly concerned with explaining theories suggested to him by Wittgenstein. But at that time, of course, he was acquainted with Wittgenstein's ideas only in a preliminary or immature form. Shortly after the armistice, however, Russell received from Wittgenstein the typescript of the *Tractatus Logico-Philosophicus*. And though he found himself in agreement with some of the ideas expressed in it, there were others which he was unable to accept. For example, at that time Russell accepted Wittgenstein's picture-theory of the proposition,[2] his view that atomic propositions are all logically independent of one another, and his doctrine that the propositions of logic and pure mathematics are 'tautologies' which, in themselves,[3] neither say anything about the actual existing world nor reveal to us another world of subsistent entities and timeless truths. But Russell did not accept, for instance, Wittgenstein's contention that the form which a true proposition has in common with the corresponding fact cannot be 'said' but can only be 'shown'. For Russell, as we have already noted, believed in a hierarchy of languages. Even if in language *a* nothing can be said *about* this language, there is nothing to prevent us employing language *b* to talk about *a*. Again, Wittgenstein's denial that anything can be said about the world as a whole, for example about 'all the things that there are in the world,' was more than Russell could stomach.[4]

Every student of recent British philosophy is aware that Russell has shown a marked lack of sympathy with Wittgenstein's later ideas, as expressed above all in *Philosophical Investigations*. But he admired the *Tractatus*; and in spite of the important points on which he disagreed with its author, his own logical atomism was, as we have seen, influenced by Wittgenstein's ideas. It does not follow, however, that the approaches of the two men

[1] *Ibid.*, p. 232.
[2] Later on Russell came to doubt this theory and to believe that, even if it is true in some sense, Wittgenstein exaggerated its importance.
[3] Needless to say, neither Wittgenstein nor Russell questioned the fact that logic and mathematics can be applied.
[4] Russell discusses the impact of Wittgenstein on his thought in ch. X of *My Philosophical Development*.

were precisely the same. Wittgenstein thought of himself as writing simply as a logician. He thought that logical analysis demanded elementary propositions, atomic facts and the simple objects which enter into atomic facts and are named in elementary propositions.[1] But he did not think that it was his business as a logician to give any examples of simple objects, atomic facts or elementary propositions. Nor did he give any. Russell, however, while approaching analysis by way of mathematical logic rather than from the point of view of classical empiricism, very soon became interested in discovering the actual ultimate constituents of the world. And, as we have seen, he did not hesitate to give examples of atomic facts. 'This is white' would be an example, when 'this' denotes an actual sense-datum. Similarly, while in the *Tractatus* Wittgenstein described psychology as a natural science and so as having nothing to do with philosophy, Russell, in his lectures on logical atomism, applied reductive analysis not only to the physical objects of common sense and science but also to the human person. 'A person is a certain series of experiences',[2] the members of the series having a certain relation R between them, so that a person can be defined as the class of all those experiences which are serially related by R.

It is true that while he had previously regarded the goal of analysis as a knowledge of simple particulars, Russell later came to think that while many things can be known to be complex, nothing can be *known* to be simple.[3] But the reason why he came to think this was because in science what was formerly thought to be simple has often turned out to be complex. And the conclusion which he drew was simply that the logical analyst should refrain from any dogmatic assertion that he has arrived at a knowledge of what is simple. In other words, though Russell undoubtedly approached logical atomism with a background of mathematical logic, his attitude was much more empirical than that of Wittgenstein as manifested in the *Tractatus*. And in the application of reductive analysis to physical objects and minds he

[1] In the opinion of the present writer the theory of the world which is found at the beginning of the *Tractatus* has nothing to do with inductive metaphysics. For Wittgenstein, the world exists for us only in so far as it is describable, in so far as we can speak meaningfully about states of affairs in the world. And the theory of atomic facts and simple objects is really an answer to the question, what *must* the world (any world) be like as a necessary condition for meaningful descriptive language? The approach, in other words, is *a priori*. The theory of the world is not an induction from observation of simple objects and atomic facts.

[2] *Logic and Knowledge*, p. 277.

[3] Cf. *My Philosophical Development*, pp. 165–6.

carried on the tradition of British empiricism, a tradition which hardly figured in Wittgenstein's mental furniture.

5. After the First World War Russell found his mind turning to the theory of knowledge and relevant topics, mathematical logic remaining more or less a past interest. This is not to say that his interest in social and political subjects abated. In 1920 he visited Russia, though his impressions were unfavourable, as is clear from *The Practice and Theory of Bolshevism* (1920). A succeeding visit to China bore fruit in *The Problems of China* (1922). Meanwhile he had published in 1921 *The Analysis of Mind*,[1] one of his best known books in the field of philosophy as he understands the term.

When Russell embraced pluralism in 1898, he accepted a dualist position. And, as we have seen, this position was maintained for some time, even if in an attenuated form. Russell was indeed acquainted with William James's theory of neutral monism, according to which the mental and physical are composed of the same material, so to speak, and differ only in arrangement and context.[2] But in his 1914 essay on the nature of acquaintance he first quoted passages from Mach and James and then expressed his disagreement with neutral monism as being incapable of explaining the phenomenon of acquaintance, which involves a relation between subject and object.

In the 1918 lectures on logical atomism, however, the sharpness of Russell's rejection of neutral monism is greatly diminished. In fact he states roundly that 'I feel more and more inclined to think that it may be true'.[3] He is indeed conscious of difficulties in accepting a view which does not distinguish between a particular and experiencing it. At the same time he is no longer sure that the difficulties are insuperable. And it is clear that while he has not yet embraced neutral monism, he would like to be able to do so.

It is thus no matter for surprise if in *The Analysis of Mind* we find Russell announcing his conversion to neutral monism,[4]

[1] This was followed by *The Analysis of Matter* in 1927, the same year in which *An Outline of Philosophy* appeared. Needless to say, the intervening period between 1921 and 1927 was punctuated not only by articles but also by books, such as *The Prospects of Industrial Civilization* (1923), *The ABC of Atoms* (1923), *The ABC of Relativity* (1925), and *On Education* (1926).

[2] As Russell notes, this was much the same view as that held by Ernst Mach. See Vol. VII of this *History*, p. 359.

[3] *Logic and Knowledge*, p. 279.

[4] It should hardly be necessary to point out that neutral monism is not the opposite of pluralism. It is 'monistic' in the sense that it admits no ultimate specific difference between the natures of mental and physical particulars or events. In themselves these particulars are neither specifically mental nor specifically physical or material. Hence the term 'neutral'.

which is conceived as providing a harmonization of two conflicting tendencies in contemporary thought. On the one hand many psychologists emphasize more and more the dependence of mental on physical phenomena; and one can see a definite tendency, especially among the behaviourists, to a form of methodological materialism. Obviously psychologists of this kind really consider physics, which has made a much greater advance than psychology, as the basic science. On the other hand there is a tendency among the physicists, particularly with Einstein and other exponents of the theory of relativity, to regard the matter of old-fashioned materialism as a logical fiction, a construction out of events. These two apparently conflicting tendencies can be harmonized in neutral monism, that is, by recognizing that 'physics and psychology are not distinguished by their material'.[1] Both mind and matter are logical constructions out of particulars which are neither mental nor material but neutral.

Obviously, Russell has now to abandon his former sharp distinction between the sense-datum and awareness of it. He mentions Brentano's theory of the intentionality of consciousness,[2] the theory that all consciousness is consciousness 'of' (an object), and Meinong's distinction between act, content and object. And he then remarks that 'the *act* seems unnecessary and fictitious. . . . Empirically, I cannot discover anything corresponding to the supposed act; and theoretically I cannot see that it is indispensable.'[3] Russell also tries to get rid of the distinction between content and object, when the content is supposed to be something in the external physical world. In fine, 'my own belief is that James was right in rejecting consciousness as an entity'.[4] Russell admits, of course, that he formerly maintained that a sense-datum, a patch of colour for example, is something physical, not psychical or mental. But he now holds that 'the patch of colour may be both physical and psychical',[5] and that 'the patch of colour and our sensation in seeing it are identical'.[6]

How, then, are the spheres of physics and psychology to be distinguished? One way of doing so is by distinguishing between different methods of correlating particulars. On the one hand we can correlate or group together all those particulars which common sense would regard as the appearances of a physical thing in

[1] *The Analysis of Mind*, p. 307.
[2] For some brief remarks about Brentano see Vol. VII of this *History*, pp. 430–1.
[3] *The Analysis of Mind*, pp. 17–18.
[4] *Ibid.*, p. 25.   [5] *Ibid.*, p. 143.   [6] *Ibid.*

different places. This leads to the construction of physical objects as sets of such appearances. On the other hand we can correlate or group together all events in a given place, that is, events which common sense would regard as the appearances of different objects as viewed from a given place. This gives us a perspective. And it is correlation according to perspectives which is relevant to psychology. When the place concerned is the human brain, the perspective 'consists of all the perceptions of a certain man at a given time'.[1]

Now, we have spoken of Russell's 'conversion' to neutral monism. It must be added, however, that this conversion was not complete. For example, while accepting the idea that sensation can be described in terms of a neutral material which in itself is neither mental nor material, he adds that in his opinion 'images belong only to the mental world, while those occurrences (if any) which do not form part of any "experience" belong only to the physical world'.[2] Russell does indeed say that he would be 'glad to be convinced that images can be reduced to sensations of a peculiar kind';[3] but this does not alter the fact that in *The Analysis of Mind* he maintains, even if hesitantly, that images are purely mental. Again, when discussing differentiation between physics and psychology in terms of causal laws, Russell is prepared to admit that 'it is by no means certain that the peculiar causal laws which govern mental events are not really physiological';[4] but at the same time he expresses his belief that images are subject to peculiar psychological laws, which he calls 'mnemic' and that the unperceived entities of physics cannot be brought under psychological causal laws. Further, though, as we have seen, Russell expresses agreement with James in rejecting consciousness as an entity, he clearly feels some hesitation on the point, as well he might. Thus he remarks that whatever the term 'consciousness' may mean, consciousness is 'a complex and far from universal characteristic of mental phenomena'.[5] It thus cannot be used to distinguish the psychical from the physical. And we ought to try to exhibit its derivative character. But to say this is not quite the same thing as to deny the existence of consciousness.

In 1924 Russell published a well-known essay on logical atomism, his contribution to the First Series of *Contemporary British Philosophy*, edited by J. H. Muirhead. The ultimate constituents

---

[1] *Ibid.*, p. 105.   [2] *Ibid.*, p. 25.   [3] *Ibid.*, p. 156.
[4] *Ibid.*, p. 139.   [5] *Ibid.*, p. 308.

of the world are there said to be 'events',[1] each of which stands to a certain number of other events in a relation of compresence. The mind is defined as 'a track of sets of compresent events in a region of space-time where there is matter peculiarly liable to form habits'.[2] As this refers especially to the brain, the definition is more or less the same as the provisional definition offered in 1927 in *An Outline of Philosophy*.[3] But though both minds and physical objects are interpreted as logical constructions out of events, the former are constructed out of sensations and images, while the latter are constructions out of sensations and unperceived events.[4] And we have seen that Russell finds difficulty in regarding images as being anything else but purely mental, and unperceived events as anything else but purely physical.

Reviewing the course of his reflections in *My Philosophical Development* (1959) Russell remarks that 'in *The Analysis of Mind* (1921), I explicitly abandoned "sense-data"'.[5] That is to say, he abandoned the relational theory of sensation, according to which sensation is a cognitive act, sense-data being physical objects of psychical awareness. This meant that there was not the same need as before to regard physical and psychical occurrences as fundamentally different; and to this extent he was able to embrace neutral monism. He adds, however, that when dualism has been got rid of at one point, it is very difficult not to re-introduce it at another, and that it is necessary to re-interpret and re-define such terms as 'awareness', 'acquaintance' and 'experience'. An effort in this direction was made in *An Inquiry into Meaning and Truth* (1940);[6] but Russell does not pretend to have solved all his problems. It is thus not quite accurate to say that Russell embraced neutral monism only to reject it. It is rather that he has found himself unable in practice to carry through the requisite programme of re-interpretation, without, however, being prepared to assert that it could not be carried through.

6. Now, if the physical objects of common sense and science are first interpreted as logical constructions out of sense-data, and if sense-data, considered as extra-mental objects of awareness, are

---

[1] In *An Outline of Philosophy* an event is said to be 'something occupying a small finite amount of space-time' (p. 287), and each minimal event is said to be a 'logically self-subsistent entity' (p. 293).

[1] *Contemporary British Philosophy*, First Series, p. 382.

[3] P. 300.

[4] On unperceived events see *The Analysis of Matter*, pp. 215–16.

[5] *My Philosophical Development*, p. 135.

[6] In this work 'acquaintance' is replaced by 'noticing'. Cf. pp. 49 f.

then eliminated, it seems to follow that we have no direct knowledge or awareness of any external object. For example, when the
occurrence takes place which would ordinarily be called seeing the
sun, the direct object of my awareness seems to be an event or
events, sensations, which are in some sense 'in me'.[1] And the
same must be said about my awareness of other persons. We are
then faced with the difficulty that the direct objects of experience
or awareness are not the physical objects of common sense and of
science, while at the same time it is only what we directly experience that gives us any real reason for believing that there are such
objects.

Of the possible ways of dealing with this problem 'the simplest
is that of solipsism',[2] which Russell is prepared to admit as a
logically possible position. For example, after saying that in his
opinion the universe in itself is without unity and continuity he
remarks, 'indeed there is little but prejudice and habit to be said
for the view that there is a world at all'.[3] Similarly, though as a
matter of fact my experience leads me to believe in the existence
of other minds, 'as a matter of pure logic, it would be possible for
me to have these experiences even if other minds did not exist'.[4]
One can, of course, appeal to causal inference. But even at best
such inference cannot provide demonstrative certainty and thus
cannot show that solipsism is utterly untenable.

Though, however, solipsism may be logically possible, it is
hardly credible. If it is taken as involving the dogmatic assertion
that 'I alone exist', nobody really believes it. If it is taken to mean
simply that there is no valid reason either for asserting or denying
anything except one's own experiences, consistency demands that
one should doubt whether one has had a past and whether one
will have a future. For we have no better reason for believing that
we have had experiences in the past than we have for believing in
external objects. Both beliefs depend on inference. And if we
doubt the second, we should also doubt the first. But 'no solipsist
has ever gone as far as this'.[5] In other words, no solipsist is ever
consistent.

The alternative to what Russell calls 'solipsism of the moment',[6]
the hypothesis that the whole of my knowledge is limited to what
I am now noticing at this moment, is the hypothesis that there are

[1] Cf. *The Analysis of Matter*, p. 197, and *The Scientific Outlook* (1931), pp. 74–5.
[2] *My Philosophical Development*, p. 104.   [3] *The Scientific Outlook*, p. 98.
[4] *My Philosophical Development*, p. 195.   [5] *Ibid.*
[6] *Human Knowledge, Its Scope and Limits* (1948), p. 197.

principles of non-deductive inference which justify our belief in the existence of the external world and of other people. When these two alternatives are clearly presented, nobody, Russell argues, would honestly and sincerely choose solipsism. He is doubtless right. But in this case an examination of the relevant principles of inference becomes a matter of importance.[1]

[1] Obviously, the problem of solipsism presupposes the epistemological theses which give rise to it. And one's natural comment is that these theses might well be re-examined. But this is not the path which Russell chooses.

CHAPTER XX

BERTRAND RUSSELL (2)

The postulates of non-demonstrative inference and the limits of empiricism—Language; the complexity of language and the idea of a hierarchy of languages, meaning and significance, truth and falsity—Language as a guide to the structure of the world.

1. RUSSELL has drawn attention to three books in particular as representing the outcome of his reflections in the years after the First World War on the theory of knowledge and relevant subjects.[1] These are *The Analysis of Mind* (1921), *An Inquiry into Meaning and Truth* (1940), and *Human Knowledge: Its Scope and Limits* (1948). In this section, where we shall be considering Russell's ideas about non-demonstrative inference, we shall be referring mainly to the last-named book.[2]

If we assume with Russell that the physical objects of common sense and of science are logical constructions out of events and that each event is a logically self-sufficient entity, it follows that from one event or group of events we cannot infer with certainty the occurrence of any other event or group of events. Demonstrative inference belongs to logic and pure mathematics, not to the empirical sciences. Indeed, on the face of it it appears that we have no real ground for making any inferences at all in science. At the same time we are all convinced that valid inferences, leading to conclusions which possess varying degrees of probability, can be made both on the level of common sense and in science. To be sure, not all inferences are valid. Many scientific hypotheses have had to be discarded. But this does not alter the fact that no sane man doubts that by and large science has increased and is increasing human knowledge. On this assumption, therefore, the question arises, how can scientific inference be theoretically justified?

Some philosophers would say, and the plain man would probably be inclined to agree with them, that scientific inference stands in need of no other justification than a pragmatic one, namely its success. Scientists can and do make successful predictions.

[1] Cf. *My Philosophical Development*, p. 128.
[2] It will be referred to simply as *Human Knowledge*.

Science works. And the philosopher who looks for a further justification is looking for what cannot be had and is in any case not required.

In Russell's opinion this attitude is equivalent to blocking inquiry from the outset. He is, needless to say, as well aware as anyone else that by and large science delivers the goods. But he is also acutely aware of the fact that purely empiricist premises lead to the conclusion that the factual success of scientific inference is simply fortuitous. Yet nobody really believes that this is the case. Hence we must look for some justification of scientific inference other than its factual success. To attempt to block inquiry at the outset is unworthy of a genuine philosopher. And if inquiry leads us to the conclusion that pure empiricism is an inadequate theory of knowledge, we just have to accept the fact and not shut our eyes to it.

Russell regards his task as that of finding 'the minimum principles required to justify scientific inference'.[1] Such principles or premises[2] must state something about the world. For inference from the observed to the unobserved or from one group of events to another can be justified only 'if the world has certain characteristics which are not logically necessary'.[3] It is not a question of logically necessary principles which are known to possess absolute validity independently of all experience. For scientific inference is non-demonstrative inference. Rather is it a question of reflecting on actual scientific inference and discovering the minimum number of principles, premises or postulates which are required to justify them.

The matter has, however, to be expressed more precisely. There is obviously no question of justifying all inferences and generalizations. For, as we know by experience, some generalizations are false. What we are looking for is the minimum number of principles which will confer an antecedent finite probability on certain inferences and generalizations and not on others. In other words, we have to examine what are universally regarded as genuine instances of scientific inference and generalization and discover the principles which are required in order to justify these types of inference and generalization by conferring on them an antecedent finite probability that is not conferred on the types which

---

[1] *Human Knowledge*, p. 11.
[2] Russell calls them 'postulates'. The reason for this will be discussed presently.
[3] *Human Knowledge*, p. 10.

experience has taught us to reject as inherently fallacious and unscientific.[1]

To cut a long story short, Russell finds five principles or premisses of scientific inference. But he lays no particular emphasis upon the number five. He considers indeed that the principles which he enunciates are sufficient; but he allows for the possibility that the number might be reduced. Further, he does not insist on his actual formulation of the principles.[2] Greater precision might well be possible. It is to be noted, however, that all the principles state probabilities only, not certainties, and that they are conceived as conferring a finite antecedent probability on certain types of inductive inference.

The first principle, described by Russell as the postulate of quasi-permanence, states that, given any event A, it frequently happens that an event very similar to A occurs in a neighbouring place at a neighbouring time. This postulate enables us to operate, for instance, with the common sense concepts of person and thing without introducing the metaphysical notion of substance. For the 'very similar' event can be regarded as part of the history of the series of events which constitutes the person or thing.

The second principle, the postulate of separable causal lines, states that it is often possible to form a series of events such that from one or two members of the series we can infer something about the other members. This principle or postulate is clearly essential for scientific inference. For it is only on the basis of the idea of causal lines that we can infer distant from near events.

The third principle, the postulate of spatio-temporal continuity, which presupposes the second principle and refers to causal lines, denies action at a distance and states that when there is a causal connection between non-contiguous events, there will be found to be intermediate links in the chain.

The fourth principle, 'the structural postulate', states that when a number of structurally similar complex events occur around a centre from which they are not too widely separated, it is generally the case that all are members of causal lines which have their origin in an event of similar structure at the centre. Suppose, for

---

[1] Russell thus presupposes that what is generally regarded as scientific knowledge really is knowledge. If we start with undiluted scepticism, we shall get nowhere. After all, the problem of justifying scientific inference only arises because we are convinced that there is such a thing but at the same time see no adequate basis for it in pure empiricism.

[2] For Russell's actual formulation of the five principles the reader is referred to *Human Knowledge*, pp. 506 ff.

example, that a number of persons are situated in different parts of a public square where an orator is holding forth or a radio is blaring, and that they have similar auditory experiences. This postulate confers antecedent probability on the inference that their similar experiences are causally related to the sounds made by the orator or radio.[1]

The fifth principle, the postulate of analogy, states that if, when two classes of events, A and B, are observed, there is reason to believe that A causes B, then if, in a given case, A occurs but we cannot observe whether B occurs or not, it is probable that it does occur. Similarly, if the occurrence of B is observed while the occurrence of A cannot be observed, it is probable that A has occurred. According to Russell, an important function of this postulate is to justify belief in other minds.

This doctrine of the principles of non-demonstrative inference is partly intended to solve a problem raised by J. M. Keynes (1883–1946) in his *Treatise on Probability* (1921).[2] But the point to which we wish to draw attention here is the unprovability of the principles. They are not offered as eternal truths which can be intuited *a priori*. Nor are they supposed to be deducible from such truths. At the same time they cannot be proved nor even rendered probable by empirical arguments. For they are the very principles on which the validity of such arguments rests. If we tried to justify them by appealing to scientific inference, we should be involved in a vicious circle. Hence the principles must necessarily be described as 'postulates' of scientific inference.

In view of the fact that these postulates cannot be proved, nor even rendered probable, by empirical argument, Russell explicitly admits the failure of empiricism, in the sense that it is inadequate as a theory of knowledge and is unable to justify the presuppositions on which all inferred empirical knowledge depends for its validity. It has therefore sometimes been said that he approaches a Kantian position. But the similarity is limited to a common recognition of the limitations of pure empiricism. Russell is very far from developing a theory of the *a priori* on the lines of Kant's first *Critique*. Instead he proceeds to give a biological-psychological account of the origins of the postulates of non-demonstrative

---

[1] Obviously, the ordinary man would comment: 'I don't need any postulate to know this'. But it must be remembered that for Russell it is *logically* possible that the similarity of experiences should be causally independent, and that in pure empiricism there is nothing which makes it objectively more probable that the similar experiences have a common causal origin than that they do not.

[2] Cf. *My Philosophical Development*, pp. 200 f.

inference. If, for example, an animal has a habit of such a kind
that in the presence of an instance of A it behaves in a manner in
which, before acquiring the habit, it behaved in the presence of an
instance of B, it can be said to have 'inferred' and to 'believe' that
every instance of A is usually followed by an instance of B. This
is, of course, an anthropomorphic way of speaking. The animal
does not consciously make inferences. None the less there is such
a thing as animal inference. It is a feature of the process of adaptation to environment, and there is continuity between it and
inference in man. That is to say, our 'knowledge' of the principles
or postulates of non-demonstrative inference 'exists at first solely
in the form of a propensity to inferences of the kind that they
justify'.[1] Man, unlike the animal, is capable of reflecting on
examples of these inferences, of making the postulates explicit
and of using logical technique to improve their foundations. But
the relatively *a priori* character[2] of the principles is explicable
in terms of a propensity to make inferences in accordance with
them, a propensity which is continuous with that manifested in
animal inference.

Now, we have seen that Russell set out to discover a theoretical
justification of scientific inference. But though he justifies
scientific inference in terms of certain postulates, the postulates
themselves are then explained through a biological-psychological
account of their origin. And this account, which goes back
ultimately to the process of adaptation to environment, appears
to be quite compatible with the theory of what Nietzsche called
biologically useful fictions. In other words, it is arguable that
Russell does not in fact fulfil his programme of providing a
theoretical justification of non-demonstrative inference, not at
least if to justify this inference theoretically means to supply
premisses which warrant the assertion that it is theoretically
valid.

It may appear, therefore, that in the long run we are thrown back
on a pragmatic justification, on an appeal to the fact that the
postulates work, that 'their verifiable consequences are such as
experience will confirm'.[3] Indeed, Russell explicitly says that the

---

[1] *Human Knowledge*, p. 526

[2] The postulates are *a priori* in the sense of being logically antecedent to the
inferences made in accordance with them; but they exist first of all in the form
of an empirical propensity and are recognized as postulates only through an
examination of examples of non-demonstrative inferences. They are not absolutely
a priori eternal truths.

[3] *Human Knowledge*, p. 527.

postulates 'are justified by the fact that they are implied in inferences which we all accept as valid, and that, although they cannot be proved in any formal sense, the whole system of science and everyday knowledge, out of which they have been distilled, is, within limits, self-confirmatory'.[1] The fact that the postulates or principles lead to results which are in conformity with experience 'does not logically suffice to make the principles even probable'.[2] At the same time the whole system of science, of probable knowledge, which rests on the postulates, is self-confirmatory, self-justifying in a pragmatic sense. Hence Russell can say that while he does not accept the idealist coherence theory of truth, there is, in an important sense, a valid coherence theory of probability.[3]

In this case we may be inclined to ask why Russell does not accept from the start the position of those who claim that scientific inference is sufficiently justified by its results, by the fact that it leads to verifiable predictions. But Russell would presumably answer that to content oneself with this position from the start is equivalent to suppressing a real problem, to shutting one's eyes to it. Consideration of the problem leads to a recognition of the indemonstrable postulates of scientific inference, and thus to a recognition of the limitations and inadequacy of pure empiricism as a theory of knowledge. Recognition of these facts is a real intellectual gain; and it cannot be obtained if the attempt to discover a theoretical justification of non-demonstrative inference is prohibited from the outset.

The comment might be made, of course, that though this attitude is reasonable enough when considered within the framework of Russell's general empiricist analysis of the world, the fact remains that while explicitly recognizing the limitations of pure empiricism as a theory of knowledge he does not really go beyond it. His biological explanation of the origin of a propensity to make inferences in accordance with certain implicit postulates or expectations can be seen as a continuation and development of Hume's doctrine of natural beliefs. But to go beyond empiricism, in the sense of substituting for it a genuinely non-empiricist theory of knowledge, would obviously have demanded a much more radical revision of his opinions than Russell was prepared either to undertake or to recognize as justified.

2. We have noted Russell's statement that after the First World

---

[1] *My Philosophical Development*, p. 204.   [2] *Human Knowledge*, p. 526.
[3] Cf. *My Philosophical Development*, p. 204.

War his thoughts turned to the theory of knowledge and to the relevant parts of psychology and linguistics. It is appropriate, therefore, to say something about the last-mentioned theme, Russell's theory of language. Reference has already been made, however, to the theory of the relation between language and fact as expounded in the 1918 lectures on logical atomism. And we can confine ourselves here mainly to Russell's ideas as set out in *An Inquiry into Meaning and Truth* and as repeated or modified in *Human Knowledge*.[1]

(i) Philosophers, Russell remarks, have been chiefly interested in language as a means of making statements and conveying information. But 'what is the purpose of language to a sergeant-major?'[2] The purpose of commands is obviously to influence the behaviour of others rather than to state facts or convey information. Besides, the sergeant-major's language is also sometimes directed to expressing emotive attitudes. Language, in other words, has a variety of functions.

Though, however, Russell recognizes the complex and flexible character of language, he himself is chiefly interested, like the philosophers to whom he vaguely refers, in descriptive language. This is indeed only to be expected. For Russell regards philosophy as an attempt to understand the world. And his attention is thus naturally centred on language as an instrument in fulfilling this task.[3] This is indeed one reason for his marked lack of sympathy with any tendency to treat language as though it were an autonomous, self-sufficient entity, which can be profitably studied by the philosopher without reference to its relation to non-linguistic fact.[4]

Reference has already been made to Russell's idea of a hierarchy of languages, an idea which is connected with the theory of types. In *An Inquiry into Meaning and Truth* he assumes this idea and maintains that though the hierarchy extends indefinitely upwards, it cannot extend indefinitely downwards. In other words, there

[1] Some discussion of language can also be found in *The Analysis of Mind* and *The Outline of Philosophy*.

[2] *Human Knowledge*, p. 71.

[3] Russell refuses to commit himself to the general statement that there can be no thought without language. But in his opinion complicated, elaborate thought at any rate requires language.

[4] Russell's well-known reference to the type of linguistic analysis which 'is, at best, a slight help to lexicographers, and, at worst, an idle tea-table amusement' (*My Philosophical Development*, p. 217), is obviously polemical and constitutes an exaggeration if considered as a description of 'Oxford philosophy' as a whole; but at the same time it illustrates, by way of contrast, the direction of his own interest, namely in language as an instrument in understanding the world.

must be a basic or lowest-type language. And Russell proceeds to discuss one possible form of such a language, though he does not claim that it is the only possible form.

The basic or primary language suggested by Russell is an object-language, consisting, that is to say, of object-words. A word of this type can be defined in two ways. Logically, it is a word which has meaning in isolation. Hence the class of object-words would not include terms such as 'or'. Psychologically, an object-word is one the use of which can be learned without its being necessary to have previously learned the uses or meanings of other words. That is to say, it is a word the meaning of which can be learned by ostensive definition, as when one says to a child 'pig', while pointing to an example of this kind of animal.

It does not follow, however, that an object-language of this kind would be confined to nouns. For it would admit verbs such as 'run' and 'hit' and adjectives such as 'red' and 'hard'. And, according to Russell, 'theoretically, given sufficient capacity, we could express in the object-language every non-linguistic occurrence',[1] though this would admittedly involve translating complicated sentences into a kind of 'pidgin'.

Now, meaningful statements expressed in this primary language would *be* either true or false. But we should not be able to *say*, within the limits of the primary language, that any statement expressed in it was true or false. For these logical terms would not be available. It would be necessary to use a second-order language for this purpose. Actual language, of course, includes both object-words and logical words. But the artificial isolation of a possible object-language serves to illustrate the idea of a hierarchy of languages and shows how we can cope with any difficulty arising out of the contention that nothing can be said within a given language *about* this language.[2]

(ii) Truth and falsity obviously presuppose meaning. We could not properly say of a meaningless statement that it was either true or false. For there would be nothing to which these terms could apply. But it does not follow that every meaningful utterance is either true or false. 'Right turn!' and 'Are you feeling better?' are meaningful utterances, but we would not say of either that it is true or false. The range of meaning is thus wider than the

[1] *An Inquiry into Meaning and Truth*, p. 77. This work will be referred to henceforth as *Inquiry*.
[2] Reference has already been made to the special case of Wittgenstein's contention in the *Tractatus*.

range of logical truth and falsity.[1] And in the *Inquiry* Russell tells us that indicative sentences 'alone are true or false',[2] though subsequently we are told that 'truth and falsehood, in so far as they are public, are attributes of sentences, either in the indicative or in the subjective or conditional'.[3]

Hitherto we have attributed 'meaning' both to object-words and to sentences. But Russell tends, though without uniform consistency, to restrict the term 'meaning' to object-words and to speak of sentences as having 'significance'. And we can say that 'although meanings must be derived from experience, significance need not'.[4] That is to say, we can understand the significance of a sentence which refers to something which we have never experienced, provided that we know the meanings of the words and that the sentence observes the rules of syntax.

Meaning, when attributed to object-words, signifies reference. And it is said to be fundamental. For it is through the meanings of object-words, learned by experience, that 'language is connected with non-linguistic occurrences in the way that makes it capable of expressing empirical truth or falsehood'.[5] But whereas we might expect a purely logical definition of meaning in this sense, Russell introduces psychological considerations based on what he believes to be the way in which a child, for example, comes to acquire the habit of using certain words correctly. Thus we are told that a word is said to mean an object 'if the sensible presence of the object causes the utterance of the word, and the hearing of the word has effects analogous, in certain respects, to the sensible presence of the object'.[6]

This methodological, though not dogmatic, behaviourism can be found also in, for instance, Russell's account of imperatives. An uttered imperative 'expresses' something in the speaker, a desire coupled with an idea of the intended effect, while it 'means' the external effect intended and commanded. And the heard imperative is understood 'when it causes a certain kind of bodily movement, or an impulse towards such a movement'.[7]

Imperative sentences, however, though significant, are not said to be true or false. So let us consider indicative sentences, which are said to indicate fact. Russell also calls them assertions, maintaining that 'an assertion has two sides, subjective and

---

[1] This follows in any case from Russell's view of object-words as meaningful in isolation. 'Hard' by itself, for example, is neither true nor false.

[2] *Inquiry*, p. 30.   [3] *Human Knowledge*, p. 127.   [4] *Inquiry*, p. 193.
[5] *Ibid.*, p. 29.   [6] *Human Knowledge*, p. 85.   [7] *Ibid.*, p. 86.

objective'.[1] Subjectively, an assertion expresses a state of the person who makes the assertion, a state which can be called a belief.[2] Objectively, the assertion is related to something which makes it true or false. An assertion is false if it intends to indicate a fact but fails to do so, true if it succeeds. But true and false assertions are equally meaningful. Hence the significance of an assertion cannot be equated with actual indication of a fact, but lies rather in what the assertion expresses, namely a certain belief or, more accurately, the object of this belief, what is believed. And a heard assertion is said to be significant, from a psychological point of view, if it can cause belief, disbelief or doubt in the hearer.

Russell's insistence on studying language in the context of human life is doubtless largely responsible for his introducing a number of perhaps somewhat confusing psychological considerations. But the main issue can be simplified in this way. The significance of a sentence is that which is common to a sentence in one language and its translation into another language. For example, 'I am hungry' and 'J'ai faim' have a common element which constitutes the significance of the sentence. This common element is the 'proposition'. We cannot ask, therefore, if a proposition is significant. For it *is* the significance. But in the case of indicative sentences at any rate we can properly ask whether the proposition is true or false. Significance is thus independent of truth.

Now, we have noted Russell's insistence that, given certain conditions, we can understand the significance of an assertion which refers to something which we have not personally experienced. It can now be added that he does not wish to tie down the significance of assertions or statements even to the experienceable. And this naturally leads him to adopt a critical attitude towards the logical positivist criterion of meaning. True, in some respects he regards logical positivism with a benevolent eye, chiefly perhaps because of its interpretation of logic and pure mathematics and its serious concern with empirical science. But though he agrees with the positivists in rejecting the idea of 'ineffable knowledge',[3] he has consistently refused to accept the criterion of

[1] *Inquiry*, p. 171.
[2] Russell uses the term 'belief' in such a wide sense that even animals can be said to have beliefs. Cf. *Inquiry*, p. 171 and *Human Knowledge*, p. 329. But we are here concerned with language, and so with human beings.
[3] 'Ineffable knowledge' is not identical with knowledge of what goes beyond our experience.

meaning, according to which the meaning of a factual proposition is identical with the mode of its verification.

In general, Russell argues, the logical positivist criterion of meaning implies two things. First, what cannot be verified or falsified is meaningless. Secondly, two propositions verified by the same occurrences have the same meaning or significance. 'I reject both.'[1] In regard to the first point, the propositions which are most nearly certain, namely judgments of perception, cannot be verified, 'since it is they that constitute the verification of all other empirical propositions that can be in any degree known. If Schlick were right, we should be committed to an endless regress.'[2] In regard to the second point, the hypothesis that the stars exist continuously and the hypothesis that they exist only when I see them are identical in their testable consequences. But they do not have the same significance. Of course, the principle of verifiability can be modified and interpreted as claiming that a factual state-ment is meaningful if we can imagine sensible experiences which would verify it, if it were true. But Russell comments that in his opinion this is a sufficient but not a necessary criterion of significance.[3]

(iii) In 1906–9 Russell wrote four essays dealing with the subject of truth, especially in relation to pragmatism, which were reprinted in *Philosophical Essays*. At a later date he took up the subject again, the results of this second phase of reflection being embodied in the *Inquiry*. The topic is also treated in *Human Knowledge*. And in *My Philosophical Development* Russell devotes the fifteenth chapter to a review of the course of his investigations.

A certain looseness in the use of terminology is characteristic of Russell. Thus in different places we are told that truth and falsity are predicated of indicative sentences, of sentences in the indica-tive or in the subjunctive or conditional, of assertions, of proposi-tions and of beliefs. But it does not follow, of course, that all these ways of speaking are mutually incompatible. The significance of a sentence is a proposition; but propositions, according to Russell, express states of belief. Hence we can say that 'it is in fact primarily beliefs that are true or false; sentences only become so through the fact that they can express beliefs'.[4] In any case the main lines of Russell's theory of truth are clear enough.

In the first place Russell rejects the idealist interpretation of

<hr/>

[1] *Human Knowledge*, p. 465.
[2] *Inquiry*, p. 308.
[3] Cf. *Inquiry*, pp. 175 and 309.
[4] *Human Knowledge*, p. 129.

truth as coherence. In an early article he argued that if every particular true judgment, when isolated from the total system of truth, is only partially true, and if what would normally be called false judgments are partially true and have their place in the complete system of truth, it follows that the statement 'Bishop Stubbs was hanged for murder' is not completely false but forms part of the whole truth.[1] But this is incredible. And, in general, the coherence theory simply blurs the distinction between truth and falsehood.

In the second place Russell rejects the pragmatist theory of truth. When he paraphrased William James's statement that the true is only the expedient in our way of thinking as 'a truth is anything which it pays to believe', he was accused of gross misinterpretation. Russell retorted, however, that James's explanation of the real meaning of the statement was even sillier than what he, Russell, had taken the statement to mean. Russell did indeed owe a number of important ideas to James; but he had no sympathy with the American philosopher's account of truth.

In the third place Russell protests against any confusion between truth and knowledge. Obviously, if I can properly be said to know that something is the case, the statement which expresses my knowledge is true. But it by no means follows that a true proposition must be known to be true. Indeed, Russell is prepared to admit the possibility of propositions which are true, though we cannot know them to be true. And if it is objected that this admission is tantamount to an abandonment of pure empiricism, he replies that 'pure empiricism is believed by no one'.[2]

We are left, therefore, with the correspondence theory of truth, according to which 'when a sentence or belief is "true", it is so in virtue of some relation to one or more facts'.[3] These facts are called by Russell 'verifiers'. To know what an assertion or statements means, I must, of course, have some idea of the state of affairs which would make it true. But I need not know that it is true. For the relation between statement and verifier or verifiers is an objective one, independent of my knowledge of it. Indeed, in Russell's opinion I need not be able to mention any particular instance of a verifier in order to know that a statement is meaningful and that it is thus either true or false. And this thesis enables him to maintain that a statement such as 'there are facts which I

---

[1] Cf. *Philosophical Essays*, p. 156.   [2] *Inquiry*, p. 305.
[3] *My Philosophical Development*, p. 189. Cf. *Human Knowledge*, pp. 164–5.

cannot imagine' is meaningful and either true or false. In Russell's view at any rate I could not mention any particular instance of a fact which cannot be imagined. At the same time I can conceive 'general circumstances'[1] which would verify the belief that there are facts which I cannot imagine. And this is sufficient to render the statement intelligible and capable of being true or false. Whether it *is* true or false, however, depends on a relation which is independent of my knowledge of it. In popular language the statement either corresponds or does not correspond with the facts. And the relation which actually obtains is unaffected by my knowing or not knowing it.

The theory of truth as correspondence with fact does not apply, of course, to the analytic propositions of logic and pure mathematics. For in their case truth 'follows from the form of the sentence'.[2] But in its application to empirical statements or assertions the theory can be said to represent a common sense position. The ordinary man would certainly argue that an empirical factual statement is made true or false by its relation to a fact or facts.[3] Difficulty arises only when we try to give a precise and adequate account of the idea of correspondence in this context. What precisely is meant by it? Russell is conscious of this difficulty. But he tells us that 'every belief which is not merely an impulse to action is in the nature of a picture, combined with a yes-feeling or a no-feeling; in the case of a yes-feeling it is "true" if there is a fact having to the picture the kind of similarity that a prototype has to an image; in the case of a no-feeling it is "true" if there is no such fact. A belief which is not true is called "false". This is a definition of "truth" and "falsehood".'[4]

In the opinion of the present writer the introduction of terms such as 'yes-feeling' and 'no-feeling' into a definition of truth is hardly felicitous. This point apart, however, it is clear that correspondence is conceived by Russell according to the analogy of pictorial representation. But though we may perhaps speak of true and false pictures, that which is strictly speaking true or

---

[1] *Human Knowledge*, p. 169. Some further specification of these 'general circumstances' seems to be required.

[2] *Ibid.*, p. 128.

[3] It is not necessary that the facts should be extra-linguistic. For we can, of course, make statements about *words*, which are made true or false by their relation to linguistic facts. Obviously, this would not apply, for example, to stipulative definitions. But these would in any case be excluded by Russell's custom of predicating truth or falsity of *beliefs*. For a mere declaration that one intends to use a given word in a certain sense cannot be described as a belief.

[4] *Human Knowledge*, p. 170.

false is not the picture but the statement that it does or does not correspond with an object or set of objects. So presumably the relation of correspondence which makes a statement true must be, as in Wittgenstein's *Tractatus*, a structural correspondence between the proposition and the fact or facts which count as its verifier or verifiers. Russell notes, however, that the relation is by no means always simple or of one invariable type.

3. It scarcely needs saying that no amount of inspection of a belief, as Russell puts it, or of an empirical statement will tell us whether it is true or false. To ascertain this we have to consider the factual evidence. But Russell has claimed that in some other sense or senses we can infer something about the world from the properties of language. Moreover, this is not a claim which he has put forward only once or in passing. For example, in *The Principles of Mathematics* he remarked that though grammatical distinctions cannot legitimately be assumed without more ado to indicate genuine philosophical distinctions, 'the study of grammar, in my opinion, is capable of throwing far more light on philosophical questions than is commonly supposed by philosophers'.[1] Again, even in *An Outline of Philosophy*, where he went as far as he could in a behaviourist interpretation of language, he suggested that 'quite important metaphysical conclusions, of a more or less sceptical kind',[2] can be derived from reflection on the relation between language and things. At a later date, in the *Inquiry*, he explicitly associated himself with those philosophers who 'infer properties of the world from properties of language'[3] and asserted his belief that 'partly by means of the study of syntax, we can arrive at considerable knowledge concerning the structure of the world'.[4] Moreover, in *My Philosophical Development* he quotes the paragraph in which this last assertion occurs with the endorsement 'I have nothing to add to what I said there'.[5]

Russell obviously does not mean that we can infer, without more ado, properties of the world from grammatical forms as they exist in ordinary language. If we could do this, we could infer the substance-accident metaphysics from the subject-predicate form of sentence, whereas we have seen that Russell eliminates the concept of substance by reductive analysis.[6] Nor does Russell mean that from the fact that a term can be eliminated, in the sense that sentences in which this term occurs can be translated into

[1] P. 42.   [2] P. 275.   [3] P. 341.   [4] P. 347.   [5] P. 173.
[6] According to Russell, if Aristotle had thought and written in Chinese instead of in Greek, he would have evolved a somewhat different philosophy.

sentences of equivalent truth-value in which the term does not occur, we can infer that no entity exists corresponding to the term in question. As has already been noted, the fact that the term 'the golden mountain' can be eliminated does not prove that there is no golden mountain. It may show that we need not postulate such a mountain. But our grounds for thinking that there actually is no such mountain are empirical, not linguistic, grounds. Similarly, if 'similarity' can be eliminated, this does not by itself prove that there is no entity corresponding to 'similarity'. It may show that we cannot legitimately infer such an entity from language; but to show that language does not provide any adequate ground for inferring a subsistent entity 'similarity' is not the same thing as to prove that there is in fact no such entity. When referring to sentences in which the word 'similarity' cannot be replaced by 'similar' or some such word, Russell remarks that 'these latter need not be admitted'.[1] And it seems obvious that he has already decided, and rightly decided, but on grounds which were not purely linguistic, that it would be absurd to postulate an entity named 'similarity'. For this reason he says that if there are sentences in which 'similarity' cannot be replaced by 'similar', sentences of this class 'need not be admitted'.

The question can thus be formulated in this way. Can we infer properties of the world from the indispensable properties of a logically purified and reformed language? And the answer to this question seems to depend very largely on the sense which is given to the term 'infer' in this context. If it is suggested that a logically purified language can serve as an ultimate premiss from which we can deduce properties of the world, the validity of this idea appears to me questionable. For one thing it would have to be shown that no ontological decisions, made on grounds which could not reasonably be described as purely linguistic, had influenced the construction of the logically purified language. In other words, it would have to be shown that assessment of the indispensable features of language had not been influenced and guided by empirically-based convictions about features of extra-linguistic reality.

If, however, the claim that we can infer properties of the world from properties of language simply means that if we find that it is necessary to speak of things in certain ways, there is at least a strong presumption that there is some reason in things themselves

[1] *Inquiry*, p. 347.

for this necessity, the claim seems to be reasonable. Language has developed through the centuries in response to man's experience and needs. And if we find, for example, that we cannot get along without being able to say of two or more things that they are similar or alike, it is probable that some things are indeed of such a kind that they can be appropriately described as similar or alike, and that the world does not consist simply of entirely heterogeneous and unrelated particulars. But in the long run the question whether there actually are things which can appropriately be described in this way, is a question which has to be decided empirically.

It might perhaps be objected that we cannot talk of 'things' at all without implying similarity. For if there are things, they are necessarily similar in being things or beings. This is doubtless true. And in this sense we can infer from language that similarity is a feature of the world. But this does not alter the fact that it is ultimately through experience, and not from language, that we know that there are things. Reflection on language can doubtless serve to sharpen our awareness of features of extra-linguistic reality and to make us notice what we possibly had not noticed before. But that language can serve as an ultimate premiss for inferring properties of the world seems to be highly questionable.

CHAPTER XXI

BERTRAND RUSSELL (3)

*Introductory remarks—Russell's earlier moral philosophy and
the influence of Moore—Instinct, mind and spirit—The relation
of the judgment of value to desire—Social science and power—
Russell's attitude towards religion—The nature of philosophy
as conceived by Russell—Some brief critical comments.*

1. WE have been concerned so far with the more abstract aspects
of Russell's philosophy. But we noted that his first book was on
German Social Democracy (1896). And concomitantly with or in
the intervals between his publications on mathematics, logic, the
theory of knowledge, the philosophy of science and so on he has
produced a spate of books and articles on ethical, social and
political topics. At the 1948 International Philosophical Congress
at Amsterdam a Communist professor from Prague took it upon
himself to refer to Russell as an example of an ivory-tower
philosopher. But whatever one's estimate may be of Russell's
ideas in this or that field of inquiry and reflection, this particular
judgment was patently absurd. For Russell has not only written
on matters of practical concern but also actively campaigned in
favour of his ideas. His imprisonment towards the close of the
First World War has already been mentioned. During the Second
World War he found himself in sympathy with the struggle against
the Nazis, and after the war, when the Communists were staging
take-overs in a number of countries, he vehemently criticized some
of the more unpleasant aspects of Communist policy and conduct.
In other words, his utterances were for once in tune with the official
attitude in his own country. And in 1949 he received the Order of
Merit from King George VI.[1] In more recent years he has not only
campaigned for the introduction of a system of world-government
but also sponsored the movement for nuclear disarmament. In fact
he carried his sponsorship to the extent of taking a personal part
in the movement of civil disobedience. And as he refused to pay the
imposed fine, this activity earned him a week or so in gaol.[2] Thus

[1] I do not mean to imply, of course, that this high honour was not a tribute to
Russell's eminence as a philosopher.
[2] The short period was passed in the prison infirmary, it is only fair to add, not
in the usual conditions of prison life.

even at a very advanced age Russell has continued to battle on behalf of the welfare of humanity, as he sees it. And the charge of 'ivory-tower philosopher' is obviously singularly inappropriate.

In the following section, however, we shall be concerned with the more theoretical aspects of Russell's ethical and political thought. To the general public he is, of course, best known for his writing on concrete issues. But it would be out of place in a history of philosophy to discuss Russell's opinions about, say, sex[1] or nuclear disarmament, especially as he himself does not regard discussion of such concrete issues as pertaining to philosophy in a strict sense.

2. The first chapter in *Philosophical Essays* (1910) is entitled 'The Elements of Ethics' and represents a conflation of an article on determinism and morals which appeared in the *Hibbert Journal* in 1908 and of two articles on ethics which appeared in 1910 in the February and May issues of the *New Quarterly*. At this period Russell maintained that ethics aims at discovering true propositions about virtuous and vicious conduct, and that it is a science. If we ask why we ought to perform certain actions, we eventually arrive at basic propositions which cannot themselves be proved. But this is not a feature peculiar to ethics, and it does not weaken its claim to be a science.

Now, if we ask for reasons why we ought to perform certain actions and not to perform others, the answer generally refers to consequences. And if we assume that an action is right because it produces good consequences or leads to the attainment of a good, it is clear that some things at any rate must be good in themselves. Not all things can be good. If they were, we could not distinguish between right and wrong actions. And some things may be considered good as means to something else. But we cannot do without the concept of things which are intrinsically good, possessing the property of goodness 'quite independently of our opinion on the subject, or of our wishes or other people's'.[2] True, people often have different opinions about what is good. And it may be difficult to decide between these opinions. But it does not follow from this that there is nothing which *is* good. Indeed, '*good* and *bad* are

[1] We may remark in passing that in 1940 Russell's appointment to the College of the City of New York was cancelled because of his views on marriage and sexual conduct. True, he was given a chair at the Barnes Foundation, Philadelphia, but this appointment lasted only until 1943. The New York episode led to a good deal of acrid controversy, on which the present writer does not feel called upon to pass any comment.

[2] *Philosophical Essays*, p. 10.

qualities which belong to objects independently of our opinions, just as much as *round* and *square* do'.[1]

Though goodness is an objective property of certain things, it is indefinable. It cannot therefore be identified with, say, the pleasant. That which gives pleasure may be good. But, if it is, this is because it possesses, over and above pleasantness, the indefinable quality of goodness. 'Good' no more means 'pleasant' than it means 'existent'.

Now if we assume that goodness is an intrinsic, indefinable property of certain things, it can be perceived only immediately. And the judgment in which this perception is expressed will be insusceptible of proof. The question arises, therefore, whether differences between such judgments do not weaken or even entirely undermine the thesis that there can be knowledge of what is good. Russell obviously does not deny that there have been and are different judgments about what things are good and bad. At the same time such differences, in his opinion, are neither so great nor so widespread as to compel us to relinquish the idea of moral knowledge. In fact, genuine differences between the judgments of different people in regard to intrinsic goodness and badness 'are, I believe, very rare indeed'.[2] Where they exist, the only remedy is to take a closer look.

In Russell's view genuine differences of opinion arise not so much in regard to intrinsic goodness and badness as in regard to the rightness and wrongness of actions. For an action is objectively right 'when, of all that are possible, it is the one which will probably have the best results'.[3] And it is obvious that people may come to different conclusions about means, even when they are in agreement about ends. In these circumstances the moral agent will act in accordance with the judgment at which he arrives after the amount of reflection which is appropriate in the given case.

The thesis that goodness is an intrinsic, indefinable property of certain things, together with the subordination of the concepts of right and obligation to the concept of the good, obviously show the influence of Russell's friend, G. E. Moore. And this influence persists, to some extent at least, in *Principles of Social Reconstruction* (1916). Russell is here mainly concerned with social and political themes; and he tells us that he did not write the book in his capacity as a philosopher. But when he says that 'I consider

[1] *Ibid.*, p. 11.   [2] *Ibid.*, p. 53.   [3] *Ibid.*, p. 30.

the best life that which is most built on creative impulses'[1] and explains that what he means by creative impulses are those which aim at bringing into existence good or valuable things such as knowledge, art and goodwill, his point of view is certainly in harmony with that of Moore.

3. At the same time, though there is certainly no explicit recantation in *Principles of Social Reconstruction* of the views which Russell took over from Moore, we can perhaps see in certain aspects of what he says the manifestation of a tendency to make good and bad relative to desire. In any case there is a marked tendency to interpret morality in the light of anthropology, of a certain doctrine about human nature. I do not mean to imply that this is necessarily a bad thing. I mean rather that Russell is moving away from a purely Moorean point of view in ethics.

'All human activity', Russell agrees, 'springs from two sources: impulse and desire.'[2] As he goes on to say that the suppression of impulse by purposes, desires and will means the suppression of vitality, one's natural tendency is to think that he is talking about conscious desire. But the desire which lies at the basis of human activity is presumably in the first instance unconscious desire. And in *The Analysis of Mind* Russell insists, under the influence of psycho-analytic theory, that 'all primitive desire is unconscious'.[3]

The expression of natural impulse is in itself a good thing because men possess 'a central principle of growth, an instinctive urgency leading them in a certain direction, as trees seek the light'.[4] But this approval of natural impulse, which sometimes puts us in mind of Rousseau, stands in need of qualification. If we follow natural impulse alone, we remain in bondage to it, and we cannot control our environment in a constructive manner. It is mind, impersonal objective thought, which exercises a critical function in regard to impulse and instinct and enables us to decide what impulses need to be suppressed or diverted because they conflict with other impulses or because the environment makes it impossible or undesirable to satisfy them. It is also mind which enables us to control our environment to a certain extent in a constructive manner. So while he insists on the principles of 'vitality', Russell does not give a blanket approval to impulse.

We have seen that Russell attributes human activities to two sources, impulse and desire. Later on he attributes it to 'instinct,

---

[1] *Principles of Social Reconstruction*, p. 5.
[2] *Ibid.*, p. 12.   [3] P. 76.
[4] *Principles of Social Reconstruction*, p. 24.

mind and spirit'.[1] Instinct is the source of vitality, while mind exercises a critical function in regard to instinct. Spirit is the principle of impersonal feelings and enables us to transcend the search for purely personal satisfaction by feeling the same interest in other people's joys and sorrows as in our own, by caring about the happiness of the human race as a whole and by serving ends which are in some sense supra-human, such as truth or beauty or, in the case of religious people, God.

Perhaps we can adopt the suggestion of Professor J. Buchler[2] that for Russell impulse and desire are the basic modes of initial stimulus, while instinct, mind and spirit are the categories under which human activities as we know them can be classified. In any case Russell obviously has in mind a progressive integration of desires and impulses under the control of mind, both in the individual and in society. At the same time he insists on the function of spirit, considered as the capacity for impersonal feeling. For 'if life is to be fully human it must serve some end which seems, in some sense, outside human life'.[3]

4. Even if in *Principles of Social Reconstruction* Russell retained, though with some misgiving, the Moorean idea that we can have intuitive knowledge of intrinsic goodness and badness, he did not retain the idea very long. For example, after having remarked in a popular essay, *What I Believe* (1925), that the good life is one inspired by love and guided by knowledge, he explains that he is not referring to ethical knowledge. For 'I do not think there is, strictly speaking, such a thing as ethical knowledge'.[4] Ethics is distinguished from science by desire rather than by any special form of knowledge. 'Certain ends are desired, and right conduct is what conduces to them.'[5] Similarly, in *An Outline of Philosophy* (1927) Russell explicitly says that he has abandoned Moore's theory of goodness as an indefinable intrinsic quality, and he refers to the influence on his mind in this respect of Santayana's *Winds of Doctrine* (1926). He now holds that good and bad are 'derivative from desire'.[6] Language is, of course, a social phenomenon, and, generally speaking, we learn to apply the word 'good' to the things desired by the social group to which we belong. But 'primarily, we call something "good" when we desire it, and "bad" when we have an aversion from it'.[7]

[1] *Ibid.*, p. 205.
[2] In *The Philosophy of Bertrand Russell*, edited by P. A. Schilpp, p. 524.
[3] *Principles of Social Reconstruction*, p. 245.   [4] P. 37.   [5] P. 40.
[6] *An Outline of Philosophy*, p. 238.   [7] *Ibid.*, p. 242.

To say nothing more than this, however, would be to give an over-simplified account of Russell's ethical position. In the first place the utilitarian element in his earlier ethical ideas, an element common to him and to Moore, has remained unchanged. That is to say, he has continued to regard as right those actions which produce good consequences and as wrong those actions which produce bad consequences. And in this restricted field knowledge is possible. For example, if two men agree that a certain end X is desirable and so good, they can perfectly well argue about which possible action or series of actions is most likely to attain this end. And in principle they can come to an agreed conclusion representing probable knowledge.[1] But though the context would be ethical, the knowledge attained would not be in any way specifically different from knowledge of the appropriate means for attaining a certain end in a non-ethical context. In other words it would not be a case of a peculiar kind of knowledge called 'ethical' or 'moral'.

When we turn, however, from an examination of the appropriate means for attaining a certain end to value-judgments about ends themselves, the situation is different. We have seen that Russell once maintained that differences of opinion about values are not so great as to make it unreasonable to hold that we can and do have immediate knowledge of intrinsic goodness and badness, ethical intuition in other words. But he abandoned this view and came to the conclusion that a difference of opinion about values is basically 'one of tastes, not one as to any objective truth'.[2] If, for instance, a man tells me that cruelty is a good thing,[3] I can, of course, agree with him in the sense of pointing out the practical consequences of such a judgment. But if he still stands by his judgment, even when he realizes what it 'means', I can give him no theoretical proof that cruelty is wrong. Any 'argument' that I may employ is really a persuasive device designed to change the man's desires. And if it is unsuccessful there is no more to be said. Obviously, if someone professes to deduce a certain value-judgment from other value-judgments and one thinks that the alleged deduction is logically erroneous, one can point this out. And if a man meant by 'X is good' no more than

---

[1] It would not be certain or demonstrative knowledge. But neither is scientific knowledge certain knowledge.

[2] *Religion and Science* (1935), p. 238.

[3] The statement 'I think that cruelty is good' or 'I approve of cruelty' would be an ordinary empirical statement, relating to a psychological fact. 'Cruelty is good', however, is a value-judgment.

that X has certain empirical consequences, we could argue about whether X does or does not tend in practice to produce these effects. For this would be a purely empirical matter. But the man would not be likely to say, even in this case, 'X is good' unless he approved of the consequences; and his approval would express a desire or taste. In the long run, therefore, we ultimately reach a point where theoretical proof and disproof no longer have a role to play.

The matter can be clarified in this way. Russell may have sometimes expressed himself in such a way as to imply that in his opinion judgments of value are a matter of purely personal taste, without involving other people in any way. But this is certainly not his considered opinion. In his view judgments of value are really in the optative mood. To say 'X is good' is to say 'would that everyone desired X', and to say 'y is bad' is to say 'would that everyone felt an aversion from y'.[1] And if this analysis is accepted, it is obvious that 'cruelty is bad', when taken as meaning 'would that everyone had an aversion from cruelty', is no more describable as true or false than 'would that everyone appreciated good claret'. Hence there can be no question of proving that the judgment 'cruelty is bad' is true or false.

Obviously, Russell is perfectly aware that there is a sense in which it is true to say that it does not matter much if a man appreciates good wine or not, whereas it may matter very much whether people approve of cruelty or not. But he would regard these practical considerations as irrelevant to the purely philosophical question of the correct analysis of the value-judgment. If I say 'cruelty is bad', I shall obviously do anything which lies in my power to see that education, for example, is not so conducted as to encourage the belief that cruelty is admirable. But if I accept Russell's analysis of the value-judgment, I must admit that my own evaluation of cruelty is not theoretically provable.

Now, Russell has sometimes been criticized for giving vehement expression to his own moral convictions, as though this were inconsistent with his analysis of the value-judgment. But he can make, and has made, the obvious retort that as in his opinion judgments of value express desires, and as he himself has strong desires, there is no inconsistency in giving them vehement expression. And this reply seems to be quite valid, as far as it goes.

[1] In his *Replies to Criticism* Russell says: 'I do not think that an ethical judgment *merely* expresses a desire; I agree with Kant that it must have an element of universality'. *The Philosophy of Bertrand Russell*, edited by P. A. Schilpp, p. 722.

At the same time, when we remember that he is prepared to condemn certain lines of conduct, such as the treatment of the
unfortunate prisoners at Ausschwitz, even if it could be shown
that such conduct would ultimately benefit the human race and
increase the general happiness, it is very difficult to avoid the
impression that he really does think after all that some things
are intrinsically bad, whether other people think they are bad
or not.

Indeed, Russell himself seems to have a suspicion that this is
the case. For after having remarked that he sees no logical
inconsistency between his ethical theory and the expression of
strong moral preferences, he adds that he is still not quite satisfied.
His own theory of ethics does not satisfy him, but then other
people's theories he finds even less satisfactory.[1] Hence we can
perhaps say that while Russell would like to be able to return to
the idea of intrinsic goodness and badness, he is at the same time
convinced that a truly empirical and scientific philosophy can
neither discover Moore's indefinable property of goodness nor
admit self-evident moral principles.

One possible line of objection against Russell's analysis of the
value-judgment is that it does not at all represent what ordinary
people think that they are saying when they make such judgments.
But Russell has never been the man to worry much about what
the non-philosopher thinks. Nor has he ever been a devotee of
'ordinary language'. It is understandable, however, if some
younger moral philosophers[2] have tried to give an account of the
judgment of values, which pays more attention to ordinary
language and its implications and yet refrains from re-introducing
Moore's indefinable non-natural property.

5. There is at least one part of ethics which Russell regards as
belonging to philosophy in a strict sense, namely the analysis of
the judgment of value, the doctrine that to exhibit the logical
form of such judgments one has to express them in the optative
rather than in the indicative mood. But social and political theory
is regarded by Russell as lying wholly outside the sphere of
philosophy in the proper sense. Hence, though it might be considered odd to say nothing at all about them, no apology is needed
for treating them in a very brief and sketchy manner.

In a famous essay which he wrote in 1902 Russell spoke of 'the

---

[1] Cf. *The Philosophy of Bertrand Russell*, edited by P. A. Schilpp, p. 724.
[2] I am thinking, for example, of Mr. R. M. Hare of Oxford.

tyranny of non-human power',[1] Nature's triumphant indifference to human ideals and values, and he also condemned the worship of naked power, of force, and the creed of militarism. He envisaged man turning his back on unthinking power and creating his own realm of ideal values, even if this realm is doomed in the end to utter extinction. It may therefore be somewhat surprising at first sight to find Russell saying in 1938 that those economists are mistaken who think that self-interest is the fundamental motive in social life, and that the basic concept in social science is that of power.[2] For if the word 'power' were interpreted in the same sense in which Russell condemned power in 1902, it would seem to follow that in 1938 he has either radically altered his opinions or is urging men to turn their backs on social and political life, something which is very far from being his intention.

In point of fact, however, Russell has never altered his dislike of 'naked power' and his condemnation of the love of power for its own sake. When he says that power is the basic concept in social science and that the laws of social dynamics cannot be stated except in terms of it, he is using the term to mean 'the production of intended effects'.[3] And when he says that though the desire of commodities and material comfort certainly operates in human life, the love of power is more fundamental, he means by 'love of power' 'the desire to be able to produce intended effects upon the outer world, whether human or non-human'.[4] Whether the love of power in this sense is a good or a bad thing depends on the nature of the effects which a man or group desires to produce.

The matter can be put in this way. In *Power* Russell assumes that energy is the basic concept in physics. He then looks for a basic concept in social science and finds it in power. And as power, like energy, is constantly passing from one form to another, he assigns to social science the task of discovering the laws of the transformation of power. But though Russell rejects the economic theory of history as unrealistic, that is, as minimizing the role of the fundamental motive-force in social life, he does not attempt to classify all human activities in terms of power. For example, it is possible to pursue knowledge for the sake of power, that is, of control; and this impulse has become increasingly conspicuous in modern science. But it is also possible to pursue knowledge in a

---

[1] *Mysticism and Logic*, p. 49 (also *Philosophical Essays*, p. 62).

[2] Cf. *Power: A New Social Analysis* (1938), p. 10. This work will be referred to simply as *Power*.

[3] *Power*, p. 35.   [4] *Ibid.*, p. 274

contemplative spirit, for love of the object itself. Indeed, 'the lover, the poet and the mystic find a fuller satisfaction than the seeker after power can ever know, since they can rest in the object of their love'.[1]

If power is defined as the production of intended effects and love of power as the desire to produce such effects, it obviously follows that power is not an end in itself but a means to the attainment of ends other than itself. And in Russell's opinion 'the ultimate aim of those who have power (and we all have some) should be to promote social co-operation, not in one group as against another, but in the whole human race'.[2] Democracy is upheld as a safeguard against the arbitrary exercise of power.[3] And the ideal of social co-operation in the whole human race is represented as leading to the concept of a world-government possessing the authority and power to prevent the outbreak of hostility between nations.[4] Science has helped to unify the world on the technological plane. But politics has lagged behind science; and we have not yet achieved an effective world-organization capable of utilizing the benefits conferred by science and at the same time of preventing the evils which science has made possible.

It does not follow, of course, that social organization is for Russell the one worthwhile aim of life. In fact it is itself a means rather than an end, a means to the promotion of the good life. Man has acquisitive and predatory impulses; and it is an essential function of the State to control the expression of these impulses in individuals and groups, just as it would be the function of a world-government to control their expression as manifested by States. But man also has his creative impulses, 'impulses to put something into the world which is not taken away from anybody else'.[5] And it is the function of government and law to facilitate the expression of such impulses rather than to control them. Applied to world-government, this idea implies that different nations should remain free to develop their own cultures and ways of life.

[1] The Scientific Outlook (1931), p. 275.   [2] Power, p. 283.
[3] Russell can be called a socialist, but he has emphasized the dangers of socialism when divorced from effective democracy.
[4] If in recent years Russell has paid more attention to campaigning for nuclear disarmament than for a world-government, this is doubtless because the prospect of achieving effective world-government by agreement seems to be somewhat remote, whereas a suicidal world-war could break out at any time.
[5] Authority and the Individual (1949), p. 105. In this work Russell discusses the problem of combining social cohesion with individual liberty in the light of concrete possibilities.

Russell's analysis of social dynamics in terms of the idea of power is doubtless open to criticism on the ground of oversimplification. But the point to notice is that he has consistently subordinated fact to value, in the sense that he has always insisted on the primacy of ethical ends and on the need for organizing human society with a view to facilitating the harmonious development of the human personality. It scarcely needs to be added that Russell does not claim that his judgments about the ethical ends of social and political organization and about what constitutes a good life are exempt from his own analysis of the judgment of value. He would admit that they express personal desires, personal recommendations. And it is for this very reason, of course, that he does not regard them as pertaining to philosophy in a strict sense.

6. Except for noting that Russell abandoned belief in God at an early age, we have not yet said anything about his attitude to religion. To look for a profound philosophy of religion in his writings would be to look in vain. But as he has often referred to the subject, it seems appropriate to give a general indication of his views.

Though, like J. S. Mill before him, Russell evidently thinks that the evil and suffering in the world constitute an unanswerable objection to belief in a God who is described both as infinitely good and as omnipotent, he would not claim that the non-existence of a divine being transcending the world can be proved. Technically speaking, therefore, he is an agnostic. At the same time he does not believe that there is any real evidence for the existence of a God. And it is indeed clear from the whole character of his philosophy that the traditional arguments for God's existence are excluded. On a phenomenalistic analysis of causality no causal inference to a meta-phenomenal being can be valid. And if 'order, unity and continuity are human inventions just as truly as are catalogues and encyclopaedias',[1] we cannot get very far with an argument based on order and finality in the world. As for the arguments adduced by some modern scientists, there is, for example, nothing in evolution to warrant the hypothesis that it manifests a divine purpose. And even if a case can be made out for the thesis that the world had a beginning in time, we are not entitled to infer that it was created. For it might have begun spontaneously. It may seem odd that it should have done so;

[1] *The Scientific Outlook*, p. 101.

'but there is no law of nature to the effect that things which seem odd to us must not happen'.[1]

Though, however, Russell does not think that there is any evidence for the existence of God, he has made it clear that belief in God, taken by itself, would no more arouse his hostility than belief in elves or fairies. It would simply be an example of a comforting but unsupported belief in a hypothetical entity, which does not necessarily make a man a worse citizen than he would otherwise be. Russell's attacks are directed primarily against the Christian religious bodies, which in his view have generally done more harm than good, and against theology only in so far as it has been invoked in support of persecution and religious wars and as a warrant for preventing the taking of means to certain ends which he considers desirable.

At the same time, though Russell often writes in a Voltairean manner, he is not simply a spiritual descendant of *les philosophes*. He attaches value to what we may call religious emotion and a religious attitude of serious concern about life. And in so far as he can be said to have a religion, it is the life of the 'spirit' as sketched in *Principles of Social Reconstruction*. True, this book appeared in 1916, but at a much later date he has remarked that the expression of his own personal religion which seems to him 'least unsatisfactory is the one in *Social Reconstruction*'.[2]

Russell's polemics against Christianity do not concern us here. It is sufficient to point out that though on occasion he pays tribute to, for example, the ideal of love and to the Christian idea of the value of the individual, attack is more prominent than commendation. And while Russell undoubtedly draws attention to some familiar black patches in Christian history, he tends to exaggerate and, sometimes, to sacrifice accuracy to wit and sarcasm. More relevant here, however, is the consideration that he has never tried systematically to dissociate what he regards as valuable in religion from theological belief. If he had, he might possibly have had second thoughts about his position, though it is probably too much to expect that he would ask himself seriously whether God is not in some sense an implicit presupposition of some of the problems which he himself has raised.

7. It is not possible to sum up Russell's view of the nature of philosophy in a concise statement. For he speaks in different ways

---

[1] *The Scientific Outlook*, p. 122.
[2] *The Philosophy of Bertrand Russell*, edited by P. A. Schilpp, p. 726.

at different times.[1] And he has never been a man for gathering together all the threads and showing in detail how they fit together, how they form an intelligible pattern. He has been too intent with getting on with the next matter in hand. At the same time it is not, I think, very difficult to understand how he came to express rather different views about the nature and scope of philosophy. Nor is it very difficult to discover persistent elements in his concept of philosophy.

As far as its basic motive is concerned, philosophy has always been for Russell a pursuit of knowledge, of objective truth. And he has expressed his conviction that one of the main tasks of philosophy is to understand and interpret the world, even to discover, as far as this is possible, the ultimate nature of reality. True, Russell believes that in practice philosophers have often set out to prove preconceived beliefs; and he has referred to Bradley's famous saying that metaphysics is the finding of bad reasons for what one believes by instinct. He is also convinced that in practice some philosophers have employed thought and argument to establish comforting beliefs which have seemed to them to possess pragmatic value. Further, when comparing the aims and ambitions of philosophy with the actual results achieved, he has sometimes spoken as though science were the only means of attaining anything which could properly be called knowledge. But all this does not alter the fact that in regard to what ought to be the attitude, motive and aims of the philosopher Russell has maintained what can reasonably be described as a traditional view. This is apparent in his earlier writings; and it is also apparent in his later attack on 'linguistic' philosophy, that is, on philosophy as concerned exclusively with mapping out so-called ordinary language, on the ground that the philosophers who represent this tendency have abandoned the important task of interpreting the world.[2]

As we have noted, however, the method on which Russell lays the chief emphasis is analysis. In general philosophy this means that the philosopher starts with a body of common knowledge or what is assumed to be knowledge. This constitutes his data. He then reduces this complex body of knowledge, expressed in

---

[1] Russell is, of course, as free as anybody else to change his mind. But, this fact apart, we have to remember, in regard to utterances which, abstractly considered, are scarcely compatible, that in a given context and for polemical reasons he sometimes exaggerates one particular aspect of a subject.

[2] Cf. *My Philosophical Development*, p. 230.

propositions which are somewhat vague and often logically inter-dependent, to a number of propositions which he tries to make as simple and precise as possible. These are then arranged in deductive chains, depending logically on certain initial propositions which serve as premisses. 'The discovery of these premisses belongs to philosophy; but the work of deducing the body of common knowledge from them belongs to mathematics, if "mathematics" is interpreted in a somewhat liberal sense.'[1] In other words, philosophy proceeds by logical analysis from the complex and relatively concrete to what is simpler and more abstract. It thus differs from the special sciences, which proceed from the simpler to the more complex, and also from purely deductive mathematics.

The philosopher may find, however, that some of the logically implied premisses of a common body of assumed knowledge are themselves open to doubt. And the degree of probability of any consequence will depend on the degree of probability of the premiss which is most open to doubt. Thus logical analysis does not simply serve the purpose of discovering implied initial propositions or premisses. It also serves the purpose of helping us to estimate the degree of probability attaching to what commonly passes for knowledge, the consequences of the premisses.

Now, there can be little doubt that the method of analysis was suggested to Russell by his work in mathematical logic. And it is thus understandable that he has spoken of logic as the essence of philosophy and has declared that every philosophical problem, when properly analyzed, is found to be either not really a philosophical problem at all or else a logical problem, in the sense of being a problem of logical analysis.[2] This analysis is inspired by the principle of economy or Ockham's razor and leads to logical atomism.

We have noted, however, how Russell was converted to Wittgenstein's theory of the propositions of formal logic and pure mathematics as systems of 'tautologies'. And if we look at the matter from this point of view, it is perfectly understandable that he has emphasized the difference between logic and philosophy. For example, 'logic, I maintain, is not part of philosophy'.[3] But to say that formal logic, as a system of tautologies, falls outside philosophy is not, of course, incompatible with an insistence on

---

[1] *Our Knowledge of the External World*, p. 214.　　[2] Cf. *Ibid.*, p. 42.
[3] *Human Knowledge*, p. 5.

the importance in philosophy of logical analysis, the reductive analysis which has been characteristic of Russell's thought. True, in proportion as his early work in mathematical logic has receded into the distance, Russell has become less and less inclined to speak of logic as the essence of philosophy. And the more he has come to emphasize the tentative character of philosophical hypotheses, so much the wider has he made the gap between philosophy and logic in the strict sense. Thus there is no question of maintaining that there has been no change in Russell's attitude. After all, having once said that logic is the essence of philosophy, he has declared at a later date that logic is not part of philosophy at all. At the same time we have to remember that when Russell made the first of these statements he meant, in part at any rate, that the method of philosophy is or ought to be the method of logical analysis. And he has never abandoned belief in the value of this method.

Though, however, Russell has retained his belief in the value of the reductive analysis which is a characteristic feature of his thought and has defended this sort of analysis against recent criticism, it is undeniable that his general conception of philosophy underwent a considerable change. We have seen that there was a time when he sharply distinguished between philosophical method on the one hand and scientific method on the other. Later on, however, we find him saying that the philosopher should learn from science 'principles and methods and general conceptions'.[1] In other words, Russell's reflections on the relation between philosophy and science, reflections which were posterior to his work in mathematical logic and to the first conception and employment of reductive analysis, had a considerable influence on his general idea of philosophy. Thus whereas at the time when he was saying that logic is the essence of philosophy, he tended to give the impression that if philosophical problems were properly analyzed and reduced to precise manageable questions they could be solved one by one, he later came to emphasize the need for bold and sweeping provisional hypotheses in philosophy. At the same time he has shown a marked tendency on occasion to question the philosopher's ability to find any real solutions to his problems. Perhaps the following remarks on Russell's ideas about the relation between philosophy and the empirical sciences may serve to make his different utterances more intelligible.

[1] *An Outline of Philosophy*, p. 2.

Philosophy, according to Russell, presupposes science, in the sense that it should be built upon a foundation of empirical knowledge.[1] It must therefore in some sense go beyond science. It is obvious that the philosopher is not in a better position than the scientist to solve problems which are recognized as pertaining to science. He must therefore have his own problems to solve, his own work to do. But what is this work?

Russell has said that the most important part of philosophy consists in criticism and clarification of notions which are apt to be regarded as ultimate and to be accepted in an uncritical manner.[2] This programme presumably covers the critical examination and 'justification' of scientific inference to which reference was made in the previous chapter. But it also includes criticism and clarification of supposedly basic concepts such as those of minds and physical objects. And the fulfilment of this task leads with Russell, as we have seen, to the interpretation of minds and physical objects as logical constructions out of events. But we have also seen that Russell does not consider reductive analysis in this context to be simply a linguistic affair, that is, simply a matter of finding an alternative language to that of minds and physical objects. In a real sense analysis is conceived as aiming at a knowledge of the ultimate constituents of the universe. And the entities of physical science, atoms, electrons and so on, are themselves interpreted as logical constructions. Philosophical analysis, therefore, does not go beyond science in the sense of trying to clarify confused concepts which science takes for granted. On the scientific level the concept of the atom is not confused. Or, if it is, it is hardly the philosopher's business to clarify it. Philosophy goes beyond science in the sense that it advances an ontological or metaphysical hypothesis.

It is in no way surprising, therefore, that Russell should have asserted that one of the jobs of philosophy is to suggest bold hypotheses about the universe. But a question at once arises. Are these hypotheses to be regarded exclusively as hypotheses which science is not yet in a position to confirm or refute, though it could in principle do so? Or is the philosopher entitled to propose hypotheses which are in principle unverifiable by science? In other

---

[1] Cf. for example, *My Philosophical Development*, p. 230, where Russell is criticizing linguistic philosophy, which he regards as trying to effect a divorce of philosophy from science.

[2] *Contemporary British Philosophy*, First Series, p. 379, and *Logic and Knowledge*, p. 341.

words, has philosophy or has it not problems about the universe which are peculiarly its own?

Russell does indeed speak of the problems of philosophy as problems which 'do not, at least at present, belong to any of the special sciences',[1] and which science is thus not yet in a position to solve. Moreover, if the hypotheses of science are provisional, the hypotheses which philosophy advances as solutions to its problems are much more provisional and tentative. In fact, 'science is what you more or less know and philosophy is what you do not know'.[2] True, Russell has admitted that this particular statement was a jocular remark; but he considers that it is a justifiable joke provided that we add that 'philosophical speculation as to what we do not yet know has shown itself a valuable preliminary to exact scientific knowledge'.[3] If philosophical hypotheses are verified, they then become part of science and cease to be philosophical.

This point of view represents what we may call the positivist side of Russell. I do not mean to suggest that he has ever been a 'logical positivist'. For, as we have seen, he has always rejected the logical positivist criterion of meaning. When he says that unverified philosophical hypotheses do not constitute knowledge, he is not saying that they are meaningless. At the same time the statement that 'all *definite* knowledge—so I should contend—belongs to science'[4] can be described as positivist, if we mean by positivism the doctrine that it is only science which provides positive knowledge about the world. It is, however, worth remarking that when Russell makes statements of this nature, he seems to forget that on his theory of the unprovable postulates of scientific inference it is difficult to see how science can be asserted with confidence to provide definite knowledge, though, admittedly, we all believe that it is capable of doing so.

This positivist attitude, however, represents only one aspect of Russell's conception of the problems of philosophy. For he has also depicted the philosopher as considering problems which are not in principle capable of receiving scientific solutions. True, he seems generally to be referring to philosophy in the popular or in the historical sense. But he certainly remarks that 'almost all the questions of most interest to speculative minds are such as science cannot answer'.[5] Further, it is in the business of philosophy to study such questions, for example the problem of the end or ends

---

[1] *An Outline of Philosophy*, p. 1.　　[2] *Logic and Knowledge*, p. 281.
[3] *Unpopular Essays* (1950), p. 39.
[4] *History of Western Philosophy* (1945), p. 10.　　　　[5] *Ibid.*

of life, even if it cannot answer them. Obviously, such problems would be essentially philosophical problems. And even if Russell is sceptical about philosophy's capacity to answer them, he certainly does not regard them as meaningless. On the contrary, 'it is one of the functions of philosophy to keep alive interest in such questions'.[1]

There are indeed some perplexing juxtapositions of conflicting statements in Russell's writings. For example, in the very paragraph in which he says that 'philosophy should make us know the ends of life'[2] he also states that 'philosophy cannot itself determine the ends of life'.[3] Again, having said, as already mentioned, that philosophy should keep alive an interest in such problems as whether the universe has a purpose, and that 'some kind of philosophy is a necessity to all but the more thoughtless',[4] he proceeds to say that 'philosophy is a stage in intellectual development, and is not compatible with mental maturity'.[5]

It is, of course, possible that such apparent inconsistencies can be made to disappear by suitable distinctions in meaning and context. But it is unnecessary to embark here upon detailed exegesis of this sort. It is more to the point to suggest that in Russell's view of philosophy there are two main attitudes. On the one hand he feels strongly that through its impersonal pursuit of truth and its indifference to preconceived beliefs and to what one would like to be true science provides a model for theoretical thinking, and that metaphysical philosophy has a bad record in this respect. He is convinced too that though scientific hypotheses are always provisional and subject to possible revision, science gives us the nearest approach to definite knowledge about the world which we are capable of attaining. Hence such statements as 'whatever can be known, can be known by means of science'.[6] From this point of view the ideal situation would be that philosophy should give way altogether to science. And if in practice it cannot, as there will always be problems which science is not yet in a position to solve, philosophy should become as 'scientific' as possible. That is to say, the philosopher should resist the temptation to use philosophy to prove preconceived or comforting beliefs or to serve as a way of salvation.[7] And concrete judgments of

---

[1] *Unpopular Essays*, p. 41. [2] *An Outline of Philosophy*, p. 312.
[3] *Ibid.* [4] *Unpopular Essays*, p. 41.
[5] *Ibid.*, p. 77. [6] *History of Western Philosophy*, p. 863.
[7] 'In itself philosophy sets out neither to solve our troubles nor to save our souls', *Wisdom of the West* (1959), p. 6.

value, as well as reflections depending on such judgments, should be excluded from 'scientific' philosophy.

On the other hand not only is Russell well aware that 'philosophy' in the popular and historical senses of the term covers a great deal more than would be admitted by the concept of 'scientific' philosophy, but he also feels that there are significant and important questions which science cannot answer but awareness of which broadens our mental horizons. He refuses to rule out such questions as meaningless. And even if he thinks that 'what science cannot discover, mankind cannot know',[1] he is also convinced that if such problems were to be forgotten 'human life would be impoverished',[2] if only because they show the limitations of scientific knowledge. In other words, a certain sympathy with positivism in a general sense is balanced by a feeling that the world has enigmatic aspects, and that to refuse to recognize them is the expression either of an unwarranted dogmatism or of a narrow-minded philistinism.

The matter can be expressed in this way. On his own confession one of the sources of Russell's original interest in philosophy was the desire to discover whether philosophy could provide any defence for some sort of religious belief.[3] He also looked to philosophy to provide him with certain knowledge. On both counts he was disappointed. He came to the conclusion that philosophy could not provide him either with a rational foundation for religious belief or with certainty in any field. There was, of course, mathematics; but mathematics is not philosophy. Russell thus came to the conclusion that science, however provisional its hypotheses may be and to whatever extent scientific inference may rest on unprovable postulates, is the only source of what can reasonably be called definite knowledge. Hence philosophy in a strict sense cannot be much more than philosophy of science and general theory of knowledge, together with an examination of problems which science is not yet in a position to solve but the raising and discussion of which can have a positive stimulative value for science by supplying the required element of anticipatory vision. At the same time Russell has always been passionately interested in the welfare of humanity, as he sees it. Hence he has never hesitated to go beyond the limits of 'scientific' philosophy and to treat of those subjects which involve explicit judgments of

---

[1] *Religion and Science*, p. 243.   [2] *Unpopular Essays*, p. 41.
[3] Cf. *My Philosophical Development*, p. 11.

value and which are certainly covered by 'philosophy' in the popular sense of the term. A good many at any rate of the apparent inconsistencies in his thought are explicable in terms of these considerations. Some of the rest may be partly due to his reluctance to go back over his writings and to exclude differences in the use of the same term or, alternatively, to explain on each occasion in what precise sense he is using the term. It is also perhaps a relevant point that while Russell has recommended the piecemeal tackling of philosophical problems by logical analysis, he has always shown himself appreciative of the grandeur and attraction of sweeping hypotheses and theories.

8. In 1950 Russell received the Nobel Prize for Literature. And there is no doubt but that he is an elegant and, if one prescinds from a certain looseness in the use of terminology, clear writer. Obviously, his early work in mathematical logic is not for the general public. But apart from this, he has brought philosophical reflection to a wide circle of readers who would be unlikely to embark on Kant's first *Critique* or Hegel's *Phenomenology of Spirit*. In literary style he thus stands in the tradition of Locke and Hume and J. S. Mill, though his more popular writings remind one more of the French philosophers of the Enlightenment. In fact with the general public Russell has become the patron of rationalism and non-religious humanism.

Among philosophers nobody questions, of course, Russell's influence on modern British philosophy and similar currents of thought elsewhere. There has doubtless been a tendency in some countries, notably Germany, to dismiss him as an 'empiricist' who did some good work in mathematics in his early days. But he has discussed philosophical problems of interest and importance, such as the foundations of scientific inference and the nature of the judgment of value. And though some of the devotees of the cult of ordinary language may have criticized Russell's reductive analysis, in the opinion of the present writer such criticism is quite inadequate if it is framed entirely in linguistic terms. For example, if reductive analysis is taken to imply that in principle 'Russia invaded Finland' could be translated into a number of sentences in which the term 'Russia' would not occur but individuals only would be mentioned,[1] the relation between the original sentence and the translation being such that if the former is true (or false)

---

[1] The individuals who ordered the invasion, who planned it, who contributed in any way by fighting, making munitions, acting as doctors, and so on.

the latter is true (or false) and *vice versa*, the ontological implication is that the State is not in any way an entity over and above its members. And it seems a quite inadequate criticism if it is simply pointed out that we cannot get along in ordinary language without using such terms as 'Russia'. It is true enough. But then we want to know what is the ontological implication of this point of view. Are we to say that the State *is* something over and above its members? If not, how is the concept of the State to be clarified? In terms of individuals related in certain ways? In what ways? It may be said that these questions can be answered by looking at the ways in which terms such as 'State' are actually used. But it seems obvious that in the process of looking we shall find ourselves referring to extra-linguistic factors. Similarly, it is not sufficient to criticize the statement, say, that the world is the class of things on the ground that we cannot get along without being able to refer to 'the world'. This is true. But then we can quite sensibly ask, 'Do you mean that the world cannot properly be regarded as the class of things? If so, how do you conceive it? Your way may be better; but we want to know what it is.'

These remarks are, however, not intended as a general apologia for Russell's use of reductive analysis. For it may very well be that on examining a particular case of such analysis we find that an essential feature is left out. And in the present writer's opinion this is verified, for example, in the case of Russell's analysis of the self. There was a time, as we have seen, when he thought that the phenomenology of consciousness or awareness implies that the I-subject is uneliminable. Later on, however, he depicted the self as a logical construction out of events, thus developing the phenomenalism of Hume. But it seems to me perfectly clear that when sentences beginning with the pronoun 'I' have been trans-lated into sentences in which only 'events' are mentioned and the word 'I' does not appear, an essential feature of the original sentence has simply been omitted, with the result that the translation is inadequate. In a sense Wittgenstein saw this clearly when he spoke in the *Tractatus* about the metaphysical subject. True, he remarked that if I wrote a book about what I found in the world, I could not mention the metaphysical subject. But it could not be mentioned simply because it is subject and not object, not one of the objects which 'I' find in the world. Empirical psychology, therefore, can carry on without the concept of the metaphysical or transcendental ego or I-subject. But for the phenomenology of consciousness it is uneliminable, as Wittgenstein appears to have seen. Russell, however, attempted to eliminate it by eliminating consciousness. And the present writer does not consider his attempt to have been a success. This is not, of course, an argument against reductive analysis as such. What is genuinely superfluous should doubtless be dealt with by Ockham's razor. But it by no means follows that all that Russell thought superfluous *is* superfluous. The attempt, however, to eliminate the uneliminable may have a pragmatic value, in the sense that it can serve to show what cannot be eliminated by analysis.

This may perhaps sound as though the present writer looks on reductive analysis as *the* philosophical method but disagrees with some of Russell's applications of it. This would, however, be an erroneous impression. I think that reductive analysis has its uses. I do not see how exception can be taken to it as *a* possible method. But I certainly do not think that it is the only philosophical method. For one thing, we become aware of the I-subject, the transcendental ego, by the method of transcendental reflection, not by reductive analysis. True, I have suggested that the failure of reductive analysis to eliminate the I-subject may serve to draw attention to the subject. But in actual fact the failure serves this purpose only if it stimulates a transition to phenomenology, to transcendental reflection. The failure as such simply leaves us perplexed, as it did David Hume. For another thing, if reductive analysis is assumed to be *the* philosophical method, this seems to presuppose a metaphysics, an 'atomic' metaphysics opposed to the 'monistic' metaphysics of absolute idealism. And if one's choice of method presupposes a metaphysics, it is no good claiming that this metaphysics is the only 'scientific' one, unless it is uniformly successful in accounting for experience whereas other methods are not.

To turn to another point. We have seen that Russell set out to obtain certainty. And he has said that 'philosophy arises from an unusually obstinate attempt to arrive at real knowledge'.[1] This presupposes that reality, the universe, is intelligible.[2] But a few years later we are told that 'order, unity and continuity are human inventions'.[3] In other words, the intelligibility of the universe is imposed by man, by the human mind. And this enables Russell to

[1] *An Outline of Philosophy*, p. 1.
[2] It is worth noting that inquiry also presupposes a value-judgment, about the value of truth as a goal for the human mind.
[3] *The Scientific Outlook*, p. 101.

dispose, for example, of the claim of Sir James Jeans, the astronomer, that the world should be conceived as the expressed thought of a divine mathematician. For the fact that the world can be interpreted in terms of mathematical physics is to be attributed to the skill of the physicist in imposing a network. It may be said, of course, that even if the original attempt to understand the world presupposes its intelligibility, this presupposition is simply an hypothesis, and that Russell afterwards comes to the conclusion that the hypothesis is not verified. But the refutation of the hypothesis is the result of an examination of the world, an analysis which itself presupposes the intelligibility of what is examined and analyzed. And in any case, if order, unity and continuity are human inventions, what becomes of the claim that science provides definite knowledge? It seems that what is provided is knowledge simply of the human mind and of its operations. And the very same thing might be said, of course, of the results of Russell's reductive analysis. But in any case can we really believe that science does not provide us with any objective knowledge of the extra-mental world? Nobody would deny that science 'works', that it has pragmatic value. In this case, however, the question immediately arises whether the world must not have certain intelligible characteristics for science to possess this pragmatic value. And if the intelligibility of reality is once admitted, the door is again opened to metaphysical questions which Russell is inclined to dismiss in a cavalier manner.

To conclude. Russell's total literary achievements, ranging from abstract mathematical logic to fiction,[1] is extremely impressive. In the history of mathematical logic his place is obviously assured. In general philosophy his development of empiricism with the aid of logical analysis, together with his recognition of the limitations of empiricism as a theory of knowledge, constitutes an important phase in modern British philosophical thought. As for his popular writings in the fields of ethics, politics and social theory, these obviously cannot be put on the same level as, say, *Human Knowledge*, much less *Principia Mathematica*. Yet they reveal, of course, a personality of interest, a humanist who has said, for example, that his intellect leads him to the conclusion that there is nothing in the universe which is higher than man, though his emotions violently rebel. He admits that he has always desired to

---

[1] Russell published a book of short stories, *Satan in the Suburbs*, in 1953 and *Nightmares of Eminent Persons* in 1954.

find in philosophy some justification for the 'impersonal emotions'. And even if he has failed to find it, 'those who attempt to make a religion of humanism, which recognizes nothing greater than man, do not satisfy my emotions'.[1] Russell may be the great patron of non-religious humanism in Great Britain in the present century; but he has his reservations, at least on the emotive level.

It is thus difficult to classify Russell in an unambiguous manner, for example as an 'empiricist' or as a 'scientific humanist'. But why should we wish to do so? After all, he is Bertrand Russell, a distinct individual and not simply a member of a class. And if in his old age he has become, as it were, a national institution, this is due not simply to his philosophical writing but also to his complex and forceful personality, aristocrat, philosopher, democrat and campaigner for causes in one. It is indeed natural that those of us who hold firm beliefs which are very different from his and which he has attacked, should deplore certain aspects of his influence. But this should not blind one to the fact that Russell is one of the most remarkable Englishmen of the century.

[1] *The Philosophy of Bertrand Russell*, edited by P. A. Schilpp, p. 19.

EPILOGUE

WE have seen that though Bertrand Russell has often expressed very sceptical views about the philosopher's ability to provide us with definite knowledge about the world and though he has certainly little sympathy with any philosopher who claims that his particular system represents final and definitive truth, he has always looked on philosophy as motivated by the desire to understand the world and man's relation to it. Even if in practice philosophy can provide only 'a way of looking at the results of empirical inquiry, a frame-work, as it were, to gather the findings of science into some sort of order',[1] this idea, as put forward by Russell, presupposes that science has given us new ways of seeing the world, new concepts which the philosopher has to take as a point of departure. The scope of his achievement may be limited, but it is the world with which he is ultimately concerned.

In an important sense G. E. Moore was much closer to being a revolutionary. He did not indeed lay down any restrictive dogmas about the nature and scope of philosophy. But, as we have seen, he devoted himself in practice exclusively to analysis as he understood it. And the effect of his example was to encourage the belief that philosophy is primarily concerned with analysis of meaning, that is, with language. True, Russell developed logical analysis and was often concerned with language; but he was concerned with much else besides. Both men, of course, directed attention, in their different ways, to analysis. But it was Moore rather than Russell who seems to us, on looking back, to be the herald, by force of example rather than by explicit theory, of the view that the primary task of the philosopher is the analysis of ordinary language.

For an explicit dogmatic statement about the nature and scope of philosophy we have, however, to turn to Ludwig Wittgenstein. We have noted that it was Wittgenstein who converted Russell to the view that the propositions of logic and pure mathematics are 'tautologies'. In the *Tractatus Logico-Philosophicus*[2] Wittgenstein

[1] *Wisdom of the West*, p. 311.
[2] The original version of this work appeared in 1921 in Ostwald's *Annalen der Philosophie*. The work was published for the first time as a book, with facing German and English texts, in 1922 (reprint with a few corrections, 1923). An edition with a new translation by D. F. Pears and B. P. McGuiness was published in 1961.

explained that what he meant by a tautology was a proposition which is true for all possible states of affairs and which therefore has as its opposite a contradiction, which is true for no possible state of affairs. A tautology, therefore, gives us no information about the world, in the sense of saying that things are one way when they could be another way. A 'proposition', however, as distinct from a tautology, is a picture or representation of a possible fact or state of affairs in the world. A proposition in this sense is either true or false; but we cannot know by inspecting its meaning (*Sinn*) whether it is true or false. To know this we have to compare it, as it were, with reality, with the empirical facts.[1] On the one hand therefore we have the tautologies of logic and pure mathematics which are necessarily true but give us no factual information about the world, while on the other hand there are propositions, empirical statements, which say something about how things are in the world but which are never necessarily true.

Now, propositions, in Wittgenstein's technical use of the term in the *Tractatus*, are identified by him with the propositions of the natural sciences.[2] This identification seems to be unduly restrictive. For there is no good reason, on Wittgenstein's premisses that is to say, why an ordinary empirical statement, which would not normally be called a scientific statement, should be excluded from the class of propositions. But Wittgenstein would presumably admit this, in spite of the identification of the totality of propositions with the totality of the natural sciences. In any case the important point is that propositions are not philosophical. A scientific statement is not a philosophical proposition. Nor, of course, is a statement such as 'the dog is under the table'. Nor are tautologies philosophical propositions. Mathematics is no more philosophy than is natural science. It follows therefore that there is no room in Wittgenstein's scheme for philosophical propositions. In fact there are no such things.[3] And if there are no such things, it

---

[1] A complex proposition is for Wittgenstein a truth-function of elementary propositions. For example, proposition X, let us suppose, is true if propositions a, b and c are true. In such a case it is not necessary to verify X directly in order to know whether it is true or false. But at some point there must be verification, a confrontation of a proposition or of propositions with empirical facts.

[2] *Tractatus*, 4.11. Empirical psychology is included among the natural sciences.

[3] If one were to say to Wittgenstein that 'the continuum has no actual parts' is a philosophical proposition, he would doubtless reply that it is in fact a tautology or a definition, giving the meaning, or part of it, of the word 'continuum'. If, however, it were understood as asserting that there are in the world actual examples of a continuum, it would be an ordinary empirical statement.

obviously cannot be the business of philosophy to enunciate them.[1]

What, then, is the function of philosophy? It is said to consist in the clarification of propositions.[2] And the propositions to be clarified are obviously not philosophical ones. Indeed, if we take literally Wittgenstein's identification of propositions with those of the natural sciences, it follows logically that the business of philosophy is to clarify scientific propositions. But it is by no means immediately clear how and in what sense the philosopher can do this. Further, though the logical positivists of the Vienna Circle certainly attributed to philosophy a modest positive function as a kind of handmaid of science,[3] from what Wittgenstein says elsewhere in the *Tractatus*[4] he appears to be thinking primarily of a sort of linguistic therapeutic, designed to clear up logical confusion. For example, as Russell pointed out, in ordinary or colloquial language the grammatical form of a sentence often disguises the logical form. Hence there can arise for the philosopher the temptation to make 'metaphysical' statements (for instance, that 'the golden mountain' must have some peculiar kind of ontological status half-way between actual existence and nonentity) which are the result of not understanding the logic of our language. The philosopher who sees this can clear up the confusion in his colleague's mind by restating the misleading sentence so as to exhibit its logical form, on the lines of Russell's theory of descriptions. Again, if someone tries to say something 'metaphysical', it can be pointed out to him that he has failed to give any definite meaning (*Bedeutung*, reference) to one or more terms. An example actually given by Wittgenstein, who is extremely sparing of examples in the *Tractatus*, is 'Socrates is identical'. For the word 'identical' has no meaning when used in *this* way as an adjective. But what Wittgenstein has to say would doubtless apply, under certain conditions, to a question such as 'what is the cause of the world?' For if we assume that causality signifies a relation *between* phenomena, it makes no sense to ask for the

---

[1] The *Tractatus* is, of course, a philosophical work and contains 'philosophical propositions'. But with admirable consistency Wittgenstein does not hesitate to embrace the paradoxical conclusion that the propositions which enable one to understand his theory are themselves nonsensical (*unsinnig*, 6.54).

[2] *Tractatus*, 4.112.

[3] For example, the logical positivists of the Vienna Circle envisaged the philosopher as concerned with the language of science and as trying to construct a common language which would serve to unify the particular sciences, such as physics and psychology.

[4] Cf. 4.002–4.0031, 5.473, 5.4733 and 6.53.

cause of *all* phenomena. Further, on Wittgenstein's premisses, we cannot talk about the world as a totality.[1]

Wittgenstein's *Tractatus* was one of the writings which exercised an influence on the Vienna Circle, the group of logical positivists who more or less recognized as their leader Moritz Schlick (1882–1936), professor of philosophy in the University of Vienna.[2] And there are certainly points of agreement between the doctrine of the *Tractatus* and logical positivism. Both are agreed, for example, about the logical status of the propositions of logic and pure mathematics and about the fact that no empirical statement is necessarily true.[3] Further, both the *Tractatus* and logical positivism exclude metaphysical propositions, that is, if considered as providing, or as capable or providing, information about the world, which is either true or false. But while in the *Tractatus* this exclusion follows from Wittgenstein's definition of the proposition and his identification of the totality of propositions with the totality of scientific propositions, in logical positivism it follows from a certain criterion of meaning, namely that the meaning of a 'proposition' or factually informative statement is identical with the mode of its verification, verification being understood in terms of possible sense-experiences. And it is at any rate disputable whether this criterion of meaning is necessarily implied by what Wittgenstein has to say in the *Tractatus*. To be sure, if a proposition asserts or denies a possible state of affairs, we cannot be said to know what it means unless we have sufficient knowledge of the state of affairs which would make it true to be able to distinguish between this state of affairs and the state of affairs which would make it false. In this sense we must know what would verify the proposition. But it by no means necessarily follows that the meaning of the proposition or factually informative statement is identical with the mode of its verification, if 'mode of verification' signifies what we or anyone else could *do* to verify the statement.

In any case, even if those are right who think that the logical

[1] Such talk is obviously excluded if every proposition is a picture or representation of a possible state of affairs *in* the world. True, Wittgenstein himself speaks about the world as a whole. But he is perfectly ready to admit that to do so is to attempt to say what cannot be said.

[2] The Vienna Circle was not a group of 'disciples' of Schlick but rather a group of like-minded persons, some of them philosophers, others scientists or mathematicians, who agreed on a common general programme.

[3] These two points, if taken alone, do not constitute logical positivism. Taken alone, they would admit, for example, the possibility of an inductive metaphysics which proposed its theories as provisional hypotheses.

positivist criterion of meaning is implicitly contained in the *Tractatus*, there seems to be a considerable difference of atmosphere between this work and the typical attitude of the logical positivists in the heyday of their early enthusiasm. The positivists admitted indeed that metaphysical statements could possess an emotive-evocative significance;[1] but some of them at least made it clear that in their opinion metaphysics was a pack of nonsense in the popular, and not simply in a technical, sense. If, however, we consider what Wittgenstein has to say about the metaphysical subject,[2] we can discern a certain seriousness and profundity of thought. To attempt to say something about the metaphysical subject, the I-subject as a pole of consciousness, is inevitably to reduce it to the status of an object. All statements about the metaphysical subject are thus attempts to say what cannot be said. At the same time in a real sense the metaphysical subject shows itself as the limit of 'my world', as the correlative of the object. Strictly speaking, not even this can be said. None the less attempts to do so can facilitate our in some sense 'seeing' what cannot be *said*. But the 'mysticism' which makes an occasional appearance in the *Tractatus* was not congenial to the logical positivists.

To all intents and purposes logical positivism was introduced into England by the publication in 1936 of *Language, Truth and Logic*[3] by A. J. Ayer (b. 1910). This book, with its drastic and lively attack on metaphysics and theology, enjoyed a *succès de scandale*; and it remains as probably the clearest exposition of dogmatic logical positivism. But though logical positivism, as mediated by this work, certainly attracted a great deal of attention, it can hardly be said to have won a notable degree of acceptance among professional philosophers in Great Britain.[4] For the matter of that, Professor Ayer himself has considerably modified his views, as can be seen from his later writings.[5] And it

[1] A statement is said to possess emotive-evocative significance if it expresses an emotive attitude and is designed, not so much by conscious intention as by its nature, to evoke a similar emotive attitude in others.

[2] Cf. *Tractatus*, 5.62–5.641. Cf. also *Notebooks, 1914–1916* (Oxford, 1961), pp. 79–80, where a certain influence by Schopenhauer is evident.

[3] Second edition, 1946.

[4] We can note in passing that Professor R. B. Braithwaite of Cambridge has made a much-discussed attempt to reconcile his logical positivism with his adherence to Christianity. See, for example, his lecture, *An Empiricist's View of the Nature of Religious Belief*, Cambridge, 1955.

[5] These include *The Foundations of Empirical Knowledge* (1940), *Thinking and Meaning* (1947), *Philosophical Essays* (1954), *The Concept of a Person and Other Essays* (1963).

is now generally recognized that logical positivism constituted an interlude in the development of modern British philosophy.[1]

Meanwhile Wittgenstein was engaged in changing his views.[2] In the *Tractatus* he had tried to exhibit the 'essence' of the proposition. And the effect of his definition had been to place descriptive language in a privileged position. For it was only descriptive statements which were recognized as possessing meaning (*Sinn*). He came, however, to see more clearly the complexity of language, the fact that there are many kinds of propositions, descriptive statements forming only one class. In other words, Wittgenstein came to have a clearer view of actual language as a complex vital phenomenon, as something which in the context of human life has many functions or uses. And this understanding was accompanied by a radical change in Wittgenstein's conception of meaning. Meaning became use or function and was no longer dentical with 'picturing'.

If we apply these ideas to logical positivism, the result is the dethronement of the language of science from the position of a uniquely privileged language. For logical positivism meant in effect the selection of the language of science as the model language. Its criterion of meaning, as applied to synthetic propositions in general, was the result of an extension or extrapolation of a certain analysis of the scientific statement, namely as a prediction of certain possible sensible experiences. And, apart from the question whether or not this analysis of the scientific statement is tenable, the dethronement of scientific language as the model language involved the abandonment of the logical positivist criterion of meaning, if considered as a general criterion. Hence, whatever one may think of the precise relation between the *Tractatus* and logical positivism, Wittgenstein's later ideas about language were certainly incompatible with dogmatic logical positivism.

At the same time Wittgenstein had no intention of resuscitating the idea of the philosopher which was excluded by the *Tractatus*, the idea, that is to say, of the philosopher as capable of extending our factual knowledge of the world by pure thought or philosophical reflection. The difference between the concept of the

[1] This is not always recognized by continental philosophers, some of whom still seem to be under the impression that practically all British philosophers are logical positivists.

[2] These are represented by posthumously published writings. *The Blue and Brown Books* (Oxford, 1958), contains notes dictated to pupils in the period 1933-5. *Philosophical Investigations* (Oxford, 1953) represents Wittgenstein's later ideas.

function of philosophy offered in the *Tractatus* and that offered in *Philosophical Investigations* is not one between a revolutionary concept and a traditional concept. Wittgenstein sees himself as having attempted in the *Tractatus* to reform language, to interfere with its actual use, by, for example, equating the proposition with the descriptive statement, and indeed, if we take literally his identification of the totality of propositions with the totality of the natural sciences, with the scientific statement. In *Philosophical Investigations*, however, we are told that 'philosophy may in no way interfere with the actual use of language; it can in the end only describe it'.[1] Negatively, philosophy uncovers examples of nonsense resulting from our not understanding the limits of language;[2] positively, it has the function of describing the actual use of language.

The sort of thing that Wittgenstein has in mind can be explained with the aid of his own analogy of games.[3] Suppose that someone asks me what a game is. And suppose that I reply in this way: 'Well, tennis, football, cricket, chess, bridge, golf, racquets, baseball are all games. And then there are others too, playing at Red Indians, for example, or hide-and-seek.' The other man might retort impatiently: 'I am perfectly well aware of all this. But I did not ask you what activities are customarily called "games": I asked you what a game is, that is to say, I wanted to know the definition of a game, what is the essence of "game". You are as bad as Socrates' young friends who, when asked what beauty is, started mentioning beautiful things or people.' To this I might reply: 'Oh, I see. You imagine that because we use one word "game", it must signify one meaning, one single essence. But this is a mistake. There are only games. There are indeed resemblances, of various sorts. Some games are played with a ball, for example. But chess is not. And even in the case of games which are played with a ball the balls are of different kinds. Consider football, cricket, golf, tennis. True games have some sort of rules, explicit or implicit. But the rules differ with different games. And in any case a definition of "game" in terms of rules would hardly be adequate. There are rules of conduct in criminal courts, but the processes of law are not generally recognized as games. In other words, the only proper answer to your original question is to remind you how the word "game" is used in actual language. You

---

[1] I, s. 124.   [2] I, s. 119.
[3] Cf. *Philosophical Investigations*, I, ss. 66–9, 75.

may not be satisfied. But in this case you are evidently still labouring under the mistaken idea that there must be a single meaning, a single essence, corresponding to each common word. If you insist that we must find such a meaning or essence, you are really insisting on a reform of or interference with language.'

In using this sort of analogy Wittgenstein is clearly thinking primarily of his own attempt in the *Tractatus* to give the essence of the proposition, whereas in point of fact there are many kinds of propositions, many kinds of sentences, descriptive statements, commands, prayers, and so on.[1] But his point of view possesses a wider field of application. Suppose, for example, that a philosopher identifies the 'I' or self with the pure subject or, alternatively, with the body in the sense in which we commonly use the term 'body'. Has he given the essence of 'I', of the self or ego? Wittgenstein might point out that neither interpretation of the pronoun 'I' is compatible with the actual use of language. For example, the identification of the 'I' with the metaphysical subject is not compatible with such a sentence as 'I go for a walk'. Nor is the identification of the 'I' with the body in the ordinary sense compatible with such a sentence as 'I consider Tolstoy a greater writer than Ethel M. Dell'.

This way of disposing of exaggerated philosophical theories, interpreted as attempts to 'reform' language, is described by Wittgenstein as bringing words 'back from their metaphysical to their everyday usage'.[2] And it obviously presupposes that actual language is all right as it is. Consequently, it is all the more necessary to understand that Wittgenstein is not excluding, for example, the technical language which has been developed in order to express man's growing scientific knowledge and new scientific concepts and hypotheses. What he is opposed to is the belief that the philosopher is capable of digging out, as it were, or revealing hidden meanings, hidden essences. And the only reform of language which he allows the philosopher is the restatement which may be required in order to clear up those confusions and misunderstandings which give rise to what Wittgenstein considers to be bogus philosophical problems and theories. Reform of this kind, however, is simply designed to bring out the real logic of actual language. Philosophy can thus be said to aim at the elimination of difficulties, perplexities, problems, which arise from our not understanding the actual use of language. In spite,

---

[1] Cf. *Philosophical Investigations*, I, s. 23.　　　　[2] *Ibid.*, I, s. 116.

therefore, of the change in Wittgenstein's view of language, his general idea of philosophy as a kind of linguistic therapeutic remains the same in broad outline.

Though, however, Wittgenstein himself did not hesitate to dogmatize about the nature and function of philosophy, those philosophers who either have been influenced by his post-*Tractatus* line of reflection or have thought much the same thoughts for themselves, have, generally speaking, refrained from dogmatic pronouncements of this sort. For example, in his 1931 paper on 'Systematically Misleading Expressions'[1] Professor Gilbert Ryle of Oxford (b. 1900), while announcing that he had come to the conclusion that the business of philosophy was at least, and might be no more than, the detection in linguistic idioms of recurrent misconstructions and absurd theories, added that his conversion to this view was reluctant and that he would like to be able to think that philosophy had a more sublime task. In any case if one looks at the writings of those British philosophers who sympathize with Wittgenstein's later ideas, one can see that they have devoted themselves to the implementation of the positive programme of 'describing' the actual use of language rather than simply to the rather negative task of eliminating puzzles or difficulties.

The implementation of the positive programme can take various forms. That is to say, the emphasis can be differently placed. It is possible, for example, to concentrate on exhibiting the peculiar characteristics of different types of language in the sense in which the language of science, the language of morals, the language of the religious consciousness and aesthetic language constitute different types; and one can compare one type of language with another. When the logical positivists turned scientific language into a model language, they tended to lump together a number of other different kinds of propositions as possessing only emotive-evocative significance. The dethronement, however, of scientific language from the position of the model language, except, of course, for specific purposes, naturally encouraged a more careful examination of other types of language, taken separately. And a great deal of work has been done on the language of morals.[2] Again, there has been an appreciable amount

---

[1] Originally published in the *Proceedings of the Aristotelian Society*, this paper was reprinted in *Logic and Language*, Vol. I (Oxford, 1951), edited by A. G. N. Flew.

[2] Cf., for example, *The Language of Morals* (Oxford, 1952) and *Freedom and Reason* (Oxford, 1963), by R. M. Hare.

of discussion of the language of religion. If, for instance, we wish to determine the range of meaning of the term 'God', it is not of much use to say that it is 'meaningless' because it is not a scientific term. We have to examine its uses and functions in the language which, as Wittgenstein puts it, is 'its native home'.[1] Further, one can compare the use of images and analogies in religious language with their use in, say, the language of poetry. It is indeed probably true to say that in the discussion of religious language in recent British philosophy the factor which has attracted the most public attention has been the contention of some philosophers that this or that religious statement really says nothing because it excludes nothing.[2] But it must be remembered that the discussion as a whole brought once more into prominence the subject of analogical language, a theme which was treated by a number of medieval thinkers but which, with some exceptions, was little treated by later philosophers.[3]

It is also possible to concentrate not so much on different general types of language in the sense mentioned above as on the different kinds of sentences in ordinary colloquial language and on the distinctions made in or implied by such language. This kind of mapping-out of ordinary language was characteristic of the late Professor J. L. Austin (1911-60) of Oxford, who distinguished himself by his meticulous care in differentiating between types of 'speech-acts'[4] and showed by actual analysis how inadequate was the logical positivist classification of propositions, and how much more complex and subtle ordinary language is than one might think.

Not unnaturally a good deal of criticism has been levelled against this concentration on ordinary language. For at first sight it looks as though philosophy were being reduced to a trivial occupation or a practically useless game played for its own sake by a number of university professors and lecturers. But though the practitioners of the analysis of ordinary language, notably Austin, have deliberately chosen examples of sentences which make those

---

[1] *Philosophical Investigations*, i, s. 116.

[2] See, for instance, the discussion on 'Theology and Falsification' which was reprinted in *New Essays in Philosophical Theology*, edited by A. G. N. Flew and A. MacIntyre (London, 1955).

[3] Berkeley has something to say on the matter. Kant refers to symbolic language in a theological context. And Hegel, of course, discusses the 'pictorial' language of religion in its relation to aesthetics on the one hand and philosophy on the other.

[4] See, for example, Austin's posthumously published *Philosophical Papers* (Oxford, 1961) and *How to do Things with Words* (Oxford, 1962).

who are accustomed to talk about Being raise their eyebrows, in the opinion of the present writer such analysis is by no means useless. For example, in the development of language in response to experience human beings have expressed in a concrete way a multitude of distinctions between varying degrees of responsibility. And the activity of reflecting on and mapping out these distinctions can be of considerable use. On the one hand it serves the purpose of drawing our attention to factors which have to be taken into account in any adequate discussion of moral responsibility. On the other hand it sets us on our guard when confronted with philosophical theories which ride roughshod, in one direction or another, over the distinctions which human experience has found it necessary to express. It may indeed be objected that ordinary language is not an infallible criterion by which to judge philosophical theories. But Austin did not say that it was. He may have tended to act as though he thought this. But in word at least he disclaimed any such dogmatism, simply observing that in a conflict between theory and ordinary language the latter was more likely to be right than the former, and that in any case philosophers, when constructing their theories, neglected ordinary language at their peril.[1] In any case, even if we consider that the importance of ordinary language has been exaggerated, it does not necessarily follow that we have to consider examination of such language useless or irrelevant to philosophy.

The point can be made clearer perhaps by reference to Professor G. Ryle's celebrated book, *The Concept of Mind* (London, 1949). From one point of view it is a dissolution of the theory of 'the ghost in the machine', the dualistic theory attributed to Descartes, by means of an examination of what we are accustomed to say about man and his mental activities in ordinary language. But from another point of view it might be considered as an attempt to exhibit the concept of mind, and indeed of the nature of man, which finds concrete expression in the sentences of ordinary language. And such an attempt is undoubtedly useful and relevant to philosophy.[2] Obviously, if one works backwards, as it were, from a philosophical theory to a view implicit in ordinary language, one is returning to a point antecedent to the raising of

[1] In *Sense and Sensibilia* (Oxford, 1962), a posthumous work representing courses of lectures, Austin tries to dispose of a particular philosophical theory, namely the sense-datum theory.
[2] Whether Professor Ryle's attempt is successful or unsuccessful and how far it embodies the author's own theories, are not questions which need detain us here.

philosophical problems. And the only valid reason for stopping there would be the belief that any real problems which then arise are not philosophical in character but psychological or physiological or both, belonging, that is to say, to science and not to philosophy. At the same time it is useful to remind oneself and obtain a clear view of what we ordinarily say about man. For ordinary language certainly favours a view of man as a unity; and in so far as this view can be considered as expressing man's experience of himself, it has to be taken into account.

And yet, of course, it is a great mistake to oppose ordinary language to theory, as though the former were entirely free of the latter. Apart from the fact that theories and beliefs of one kind or another leave their deposits, as it were, in ordinary language, our language is not in any case a simple photograph of bare facts. It expresses interpretation. Hence it cannot be used as a touchstone of truth. And philosophy cannot be simply uncritical of so-called ordinary language. Nor can it be critical without indulging in theory.

Needless to say, this is not a discovery of the present writer. It is a matter of common recognition.[1] Hence it is only to be expected that in recent years the concept of philosophy should have tended to broaden, even within the analytic movement itself. One expression of this process, in certain circles at least, has been the displacement of the dogmatic restriction of the nature and scope of philosophy, which was characteristic of Wittgenstein, by an attitude of tolerance which is willing to give a hearing even to the avowed metaphysician, provided, of course, that he is prepared to explain why he says what he does. But it is not simply a matter of toleration, of the growth of a more 'ecumenical' spirit. There have also been signs of a developing conviction that analysis is not enough. For example, in *Thought and Action*,[2] Professor Stuart Hampshire observed that the language of ethics cannot be adequately treated unless it is examined in the light of the function of such language in human life. Hence the need for a philosophical anthropology.

The concentration on ordinary language, however, which is in harmony with the ideas expounded by Wittgenstein in *Philosophical Investigations*, represents only one tendency, even if a prominent one, in the analytic movement as a whole. For it has

[1] See, for instance, Professor A. J. Ayer's inaugural lecture at Oxford, which forms the first chapter in his book, *The Concept of a Person*.
[2] London, 1959.

long been recognized that a great deal of what was popularly called 'linguistic analysis' would be far better described as 'conceptual analysis'. And the idea of conceptual analysis can open up wide vistas. For instance, in his well-known book *Individuals: An Essay in Descriptive Metaphysics*[1] Mr. P. F. Strawson of Oxford spoke of descriptive metaphysics as exploring and describing the actual structure of our thought about the world, that is, as describing the most general features of our conceptual structure, whereas revisionary metaphysics is concerned with changing our conceptual structure, with making us see the world in a new light. Revisionary metaphysics was not condemned, but descriptive metaphysics, in the sense explained, was said to need no further justification than that of inquiry in general.

In so far as generalization in this matter is legitimate, it seems safe to say that the following remarks represent an attitude towards metaphysics which is not uncommonly adopted by contemporary British philosophers. To describe metaphysics as meaningless, as the logical positivists did, is to pass over the obvious fact that the great metaphysical systems of the past often expressed visions of the world which can be stimulating and, in their several ways, illuminating. Further, in the context of logical positivism to say that metaphysical propositions are meaningless is really to say that they are different from scientific propositions.[2] This is true enough; but it contributes little to an understanding of metaphysics as an historical phenomenon. To obtain this understanding we have to examine actual metaphysical systems with a view to sorting out the various types of metaphysics and the different kinds of arguments employed.[3] For it is a mistake to suppose that they all conform to one invariable pattern. Again, we cannot legitimately take it for granted that metaphysics is simply an attempt to answer questions which arise out of 'the bewitchment of our intelligence by means of language'.[4] This is a matter for detailed examination. Moreover, it is clear that the

[1] London, 1959.

[2] That is to say, this is the essential factual content of the description. A judgment of value may also, of course, be included or implied.

[3] *The Nature of Metaphysics* (edited by D. F. Pears, London, 1957) represents a series of broadcast talks by different philosophers, including Professor Ryle. The general attitude to metaphysics is critical but comparatively sympathetic. A considerably more extensive examination of metaphysics is undertaken by Professor W. H. Walsh of Edinburgh University in *Metaphysics* (London, 1963).

[4] *Philosophical Investigations*, I, s. 109. The fact that some writers have appealed to psycho-analysis as perhaps capable of explaining the recurrence of a particular type of metaphysics, such as monism, shows at any rate that they consider metaphysics to have roots which go deeper than linguistic or logical confusion.

impulse to develop a unified interpretation of the world in terms of a set of concepts and categories is not something intrinsically improper or blameworthy. True, since the time of Kant we cannot accept the idea that the philosopher is capable of deducing the existence of any entity in an *a priori* manner. Further, before attempting to construct large-scale syntheses it would be wiser to do more spade-work by tackling precise questions separately. At the same time philosophical problems tend to interlock; and in any case it would be absurd to attempt to ban metaphysical synthesis. The construction of a world-view or *Weltanschauung* is indeed a somewhat different activity from that of trying to answer particular questions to which, in principle, quite definite answers can be given. But while the demand that philosophers who are interested in pursuing the second sort of activity should devote themselves to synthesis instead is unjustified, a wholesale condemnation of metaphysical synthesis is also unreasonable.

As far as it goes, this growth of a more tolerant attitude towards forms of philosophy other than the microscopic analysis which has been a conspicuous feature of recent British thought is something to be welcomed. Taken by itself, however, it leaves a good many questions unanswered. Suppose, for the sake of argument, that we accept the restriction of philosophy to the clarification of propositions which are not philosophical propositions, the restriction which is made in the *Tractatus*. The presupposition is clear enough, namely that philosophy is not a discipline with a special subject-matter of its own, alongside the particular sciences.[1] The philosopher cannot enunciate philosophical propositions which increase our knowledge of the world. If, however, we drop the dogmatic restriction of the nature and scope of philosophy and show ourselves prepared to regard metaphysics, at least in some recognizable form, as a legitimate philosophical activity, we can reasonably be expected to explain what change in the concept of philosophy is implied by this concession. It is really not sufficient to say that we do not undertake to reform language, and that the word 'philosophy', as actually used, certainly covers metaphysics, whereas it no longer covers physics or biology. For the following question can always be asked: 'When you say that you have no wish to prohibit metaphysics, do you mean simply that if some people feel the urge to develop theories which are akin to poetic and imaginative visions

[1] This is explicitly stated in the *Tractatus*, 4.111.

of reality, and which cannot legitimately lay claim to represent or increase knowledge, you have no desire to interfere with them? Or are you seriously prepared to admit the possibility that metaphysics is capable in some sense of increasing our knowledge? If so, in what sense? And what do you think that metaphysical knowledge is or could be about or of?'

The analytic philosophers might, of course, reply that it is simply a question of their being prepared to give the metaphysician a hearing instead of barring the way in advance to all dialogue and mutual understanding. It is the metaphysician's business to explain what he is about. When he has done so, his own account of his activities can be examined.

Though, however, this line of reply is reasonable up to a point, it seems to neglect two facts. First, if we repudiate a dogmatic restrictive definition of philosophy, this repudiation has implications. And it is not unreasonable if we are invited to make them explicit. Secondly, as the analytic philosophers like to point out, they do not constitute a completely 'homogeneous' school. On the contrary, several rather different tendencies are discernible; and it is obvious enough from an examination of their writings that a number of philosophers who would popularly be classed as 'analysts' are doing something very different from what could accurately be described as 'linguistic analysis'. It is all very well for them to say that they are doing 'philosophy'. No doubt they are. But what is philosophy in this wide sense? What precisely is its nature, function and scope? It is in regard to their British colleagues' view on such general issues that the continental philosopher of a different tradition is apt to find himself hopelessly at sea.

The conclusion to be drawn is perhaps that the so-called revolution in philosophy has lost any clearly defined shape, and that no clear concept of the nature of philosophy has yet taken the place of the various restrictive definitions proposed by the logical positivists, by the *Tractatus* and then again by *Philosophical Investigations*. This obviously does not prevent British philosophers from doing valuable work on particular themes. But it means that the external observer may well be left wondering what particular game is being played, and why. What is the relevance of philosophy to life? And why is it thought necessary to have chairs of philosophy in universities? Such questions may be naïve, but they require an answer.

APPENDIX A

JOHN HENRY NEWMAN

Introductory remarks—Newman's approach to the problem of religious belief in his university sermons—The approach in The Grammar of Assent—*Conscience and God—The convergence of probabilities and the illative sense—Final remarks.*

1. To say that we are concerned here with John Henry Newman (1801–90) simply as a philosopher is perhaps somewhat misleading. For it might be understood as suggesting that in addition to his many other interests and activities Newman devoted himself to philosophical problems for their own sake, for their intrinsic interest as theoretical puzzles. And this would be far from the truth. Newman's approach to the philosophical topics which he discussed was that of a Christian apologist. That is to say, he wrote from the point of view of a Christian believer who asks himself to what extent, and in what way, his faith can be shown to be reasonable. Newman made no pretence of temporarily discarding his faith, as it were, in order to give the impression of starting all over again from scratch. He tried, of course, to understand other people's points of view. But his discussion of religious belief was conducted, as it might be expressed, within the area of faith. That is to say, it was a question of faith seeking understanding of itself rather than of an unbelieving mind wondering whether there was any rational justification for making an act of faith. At the same time the attempt to show that Christian belief is in fact reasonable led Newman to develop philosophical ideas. To put the matter in another way, his attempt to exhibit the insufficiency of contemporary rationalism and to convey a sense of the Christian vision of human existence led him to delineate lines of thought which, while certainly not intended to present the content of Christian belief as a set of conclusions logically deduced from self-evident principles, were meant to show to those who had eyes to see that religious faith was not the expression of an irrational attitude or a purely arbitrary assumption. And even if it involves a certain mutilation of his thought as a whole, we can pick out for brief consideration here some of the lines of thought which can reasonably be described as philosophical.

Now there have been apologists who concerned themselves not so much with the reasons people actually have for believing as with developing arguments which, in their opinion, should convince the minds of any unbelievers capable of understanding the terms used, though the ordinary believer may never have thought of these arguments at all and might even be incapable of understanding and appreciating them if they were presented to him. Newman, however, is more concerned with showing the reasonableness of faith as it actually exists in the great mass of believers, most of whom know nothing of abstract philosophical arguments. And he tries to make explicit what seems to him to be the chief ground which he himself and other people have for a living belief in God.[1] In other words, he tries to outline a phenomenological analysis of the spontaneous movement of the mind culminating in assent to the existence of God as a present reality. At the same time he obviously does not intend to write simply as a psychologist who may describe various reasons why people believe in God, even if some or all these reasons appear to him unable to justify assent to God's existence. On the contrary, Newman argues that the main empirical ground on which belief rests is a sufficient ground.

An analogy may clarify the point. We all have a practical belief in the objective existence of external objects independently of their being perceived by us. And there is clearly a difference between making explicit the grounds which people actually have for this belief and trying, as some philosophers have done, to justify the belief by excogitating philosophical arguments which are thought to provide better and sounder grounds for belief than those which people actually have, even if they are not reflectively aware of them. Indeed, it is arguable that the philosopher is not in a position to provide better grounds for the belief in question than those on which our belief actually, if implicitly, rests. Analogously, Newman is very conscious of the difference between showing that religious belief, as it actually exists, is reasonable and showing that it would be reasonable if people had other grounds for believing than those which they in fact have.

There is a further point which is worth noticing. When Newman talks about belief in God, he is thinking of what we might call a living belief, a belief which involves an element of personal commitment to a personal being apprehended as a present reality and which tends to influence conduct, not about a mere notional assent to an abstract proposition. Hence when he is reflecting on grounds for belief in God, he tends to neglect impersonal metaphysical arguments addressed simply to the intellect and to concentrate on the movement of the mind which, in his opinion, brings a man up against God as a present reality, as manifested in the voice of conscience. His line of thought is therefore addressed to the man who has a lively sense of moral obligation. Similarly, when dealing with the evidences for the truth of Christianity he is speaking primarily to the genuine and open-minded

---

[1] Newman does not, of course, exclude the role of grace. But he prescinds from it when he is trying to show that a sufficient ground for belief in God is available to all.

inquirer, particularly to the man who already believes in God, and who has, as Newman puts it, a presentiment of the possibility of revelation. In both cases he presupposes certain subjective conditions, including moral conditions, in his reader. He does not profess to provide demonstrations modelled on those of mathematics.

Given this approach, it is not surprising that the name of Newman has often been linked with that of Pascal. Both men were concerned with Christian apologetics, and both fixed their attention on effective belief and on the way in which people actually think and reason in concrete issues rather than on a mathematical model of demonstration. The 'spirit of geometry' was alien to both minds. And both emphasized the moral conditions for appreciating the force of arguments in favour of Christianity. If therefore someone excludes Pascal from the class of philosophers on the ground that he was a special pleader, he is likely to treat Newman in the same way. Conversely, if someone recognizes Pascal as a philosopher, he is likely to accord a similar recognition to Newman.[1]

Newman's philosophical background was, however, very different from that of Pascal. For it was constituted to a large extent by British philosophy. As a student Newman acquired some knowledge of Aristotle. And though nobody would call him an Aristotelian, the Greek philosopher certainly exercised some influence on his mind. As for Platonism, which in certain respects he found congenial, Newman's knowledge of it seems to have been obtained mainly from certain early Christian writers and the Fathers. Of British philosophers he certainly studied Francis Bacon, and he knew something of Hume, whom he considered acute but dangerous; but in the *Apologia* he states that he never studied Berkeley. For Locke, however, he felt a profound respect. He tells us explicitly that he felt this respect 'both for the character and the ability of Locke, for his manly simplicity of mind and his outspoken candour';[2] and he adds that 'there is so much in his remarks upon reasoning and proof in which I fully concur, that I feel no pleasure in considering him in the light of an opponent to views which I myself have ever cherished as true'.[3] Besides Locke we must mention Bishop Butler,[4] who exercised an obvious and admitted influence on Newman's mind.

Later on Newman studied the writings of Dean Mansel (1820–71),

[1] It is as well to remember that the constructors of original metaphysical systems have often employed argument to commend views of reality already present to their minds, at least in outline. Yet this fact does not by itself show that a given argument is devoid of force. Analogously, the fact that Newman writes as a Christian believer does not necessarily entail the conclusion that his philosophical reflections are valueless.

[2] *An Essay in Aid of a Grammar of Assent* (3rd edition, 1870), p. 155. This work will be referred to as *GA*.

[3] *Ibid.*

[4] For Bishop Joseph Butler (1692–1752), see Vol. V of this *History*, pp. 165–70 and 184–91.

of some of the Scottish philosophers and the *Logic* of J. S. Mill. Further, in spite of a disclaimer on his part, it can be shown that he had some acquaintance with Coleridge. Of German thought, however, Newman appears to have known little, particularly at first-hand. If therefore we leave the early study of Aristotle out of account, we can say that his philosophical ideas were formed in the climate of British empiricism and of the influence of Butler. Newman's varied interests and activities left him indeed little time and energy for serious philosophical reading, even if he had had the inclination to read widely in this field. But in any case what he did read was simply a stimulus for forming his own ideas. He was never what would be called a disciple of any philosopher.

As for Scholastic philosophy, Newman knew little about it. In later years he at any rate possessed some writings by pioneers in the revival of Scholasticism. And when Leo XIII published his Encyclical *Aeterni Patris* in 1870, urging the study of St. Thomas, Newman composed, even if he did not send, an appreciative letter to the Pope. But it is fairly evident from the letter that what he had in mind was a revival of intellectual life in the Church, in continuity with the thought of the Fathers and Doctors, rather than of Thomism in particular. And in any case the old-fashioned textbook Thomism would hardly have been congenial to Newman's mind. It is true that since his death a number of Scholastic philosophers have adopted or adapted lines of thought suggested by his writings and have used them to supplement traditional arguments. But it scarcely needs saying that this fact provides no adequate reason for making out that Newman was 'really' a Scholastic. His approach was quite different, though he was quite willing to admit that other approaches might have their uses.

2. In a university sermon which he preached at Oxford in 1839 Newman insists that faith 'is certainly an exercise of Reason'[1]. For the exercise of reason lies 'in asserting one thing, because of some other thing.'[2] It can be seen in the extension of our knowledge beyond the immediate objects of sense-perception and of introspection;[3] and it can be seen also in religious belief or faith, inasmuch as this is 'an acceptance of things as real, which the senses do not convey, upon certain previous grounds'.[4] In other words, as Newman does not postulate any faculty of intuiting God (or indeed any external immaterial being), he must admit that in some sense at least the existence of God is inferred.

Reasoning, however, is not necessarily correct: there can be faulty reasoning. And Newman is well aware that for the rationalist any

---

[1] *Oxford University Sermons (Fifteen sermons preached before the University of Oxford)* (3rd edition, 1872), p. 207. This work will be referred to as *OUS*. Newman obviously means that faith presupposes an exercise of reason.

[2] *Ibid.*

[3] We can see here a reflection of the empiricist point of view.

[4] *OUS*, p. 207.

process of reasoning or inference presupposed by religious faith is invalid. According to the popular or common idea of reason and its exercise we should exclude the influence of all prejudices, preconceptions and temperamental differences and proceed simply according to 'certain scientific rules and fixed standards for weighing testimony and examining facts'[1], admitting only such conclusions 'as can produce their reasons'.[2] It is evident, however, that most believers are unable to produce reasons for their belief. And even when they are, it by no means follows that they began to believe for this reason or that they will cease believing if the reasons are challenged or placed in doubt. Further, 'faith is a principle of action, and action does not allow time for minute and finished investigations'.[3] Faith does not demand unquestionable demonstration; and it is influenced by antecedent probabilities and presumptions. True, this is frequently verified in the case of non-religious belief. For example, we frequently believe what we read in the newspapers, without any examination of the evidence. But though this behaviour is undoubtedly necessary for life, the fact remains that what appears probable or credible to one man may appear in quite a different light to someone else. 'It is scarcely necessary to point out how much our inclinations have to do with our belief.'[4] It is thus easy to understand the rationalist depreciation of faith as the expression of wishful thinking.

In a real sense, of course, unbelief or scepticism is in the same boat as faith. For unbelief 'really goes upon presumptions and prejudices as much as Faith does, only presumptions of an opposite nature. . . . It considers a religious system so improbable, that it will not listen to the evidence of it; or, if it listens, it employs itself in doing what a believer could do, if he chose, quite as well . . .; viz., in showing that the evidence might be more complete and unexceptionable than it is.'[5] Sceptics do not really decide according to the evidence; for they make up their minds first and then admit or reject evidence according to their initial assumption. Hume provides a signal example of this when he suggests that the impossibility of miracles is sufficient refutation of the testimony of witnesses. 'That is, the antecedent improbability is a sufficient refutation of the evidence.'[6]

Newman seems to be quite justified in suggesting that unbelievers often proceed according to assumptions, and that they are as open as anyone else to the influence of inclination and temperament. But though this is a polemical point of some value, it obviously does not show that faith, considered as what Newman calls an exercise of reason, measures up to the standard demanded by the rationalist, if this standard is understood as that of strict logical demonstration from self-evident principles. Newman, however, has no intention of pretending

[1] *OUS*, p. 229.   [2] *Ibid.*, p. 230.   [3] *Ibid.*, p. 188.
[4] *Ibid.*, p. 189.   [5] *Ibid.*, p. 230.   [6] *Ibid.*, p. 231.

that it does. He argues instead that the rationalist conception of reasoning is far too narrow and does not square with the way in which people actually, and legitimately, think and reason in concrete issues. It must be remembered that his contention is that faith is reasonable, not that its content is logically deducible according to the model of mathematical demonstration.

It is no valid argument against the reasonableness of religious faith to say that it assumes what are judged to be antecedent probabilities. For we all find ourselves under the necessity of making assumptions, if we are to live at all. We cannot live simply by what is logically demonstrable. For example, we cannot demonstrate that our senses are trustworthy, and that there is an objective external world with which they put us in contact. Nor can we demonstrate the validity of memory. Yet in spite of our being sometimes deceived, to express the matter in a popular way, we assume and cannot help assuming that our senses are fundamentally trustworthy, and that there is an objective external world. Indeed, nobody but the sceptic questions scientific inference as such, though the scientist does not prove the existence of a public physical world but assumes it. Again, we do not allow our mistakes and slips to destroy all belief in the validity of memory. Further, unless we try to adopt a position of complete scepticism, a position which we cannot maintain in practice, we necessarily assume the possibility of valid reasoning. We cannot demonstrate it *a priori*; for any attempt at demonstration presupposes what we are trying to demonstrate. In fine, 'whether we consider processes of Faith or other exercise of Reason, men advance forward on grounds which they do not, or cannot produce, or if they could, yet could not prove to be true, on latent or antecedent grounds which they take for granted'[1].

We can note in passing that in Newman's readiness to say that the existence of a public external world is an unprovable assumption we can perhaps discern an echo of his impression at an early age, an impression recorded in the first chapter of the *Apologia*, that there were only two luminously self-evident beings, himself and his Creator. But we are also reminded of Hume's contention that though we cannot prove the existence of bodies apart from our perceptions, Nature has placed us under the necessity of believing in it. A philosopher can indulge in sceptical reflections in his study; but in ordinary life he, like the rest of mankind, has a natural belief in the continued objective existence of bodies even when they are not perceived. Reason cannot demonstrate the truth of this belief. But the belief is none the less reasonable. The unreasonable man would be the one who tried to live as a sceptic and not to act on any assumption which could not be proved.

It is indeed obviously true that men cannot help believing in the

[1] *Ibid.*, pp. 212–13.

existence of an external, public world,[1] and that it would be un-reasonable to attempt to act on any other assumption. If we refused to act on anything but logically demonstrated conclusions, we could not live at all. As Locke aptly remarked, if we refused to eat until it had been demonstrated that the food would nourish us, we should not eat at all. But it can be objected that belief in God is not a natural belief comparable to that in the existence of an external world. We cannot help believing in practice that bodies exist independently of our perception; but there does not seem to be any such practical necessity to believe in God.

Newman's line of argument is that there is something, namely conscience, which belongs to human nature as much as do the powers of perceiving and of reasoning, and which predisposes to belief in God, in the sense that it carries with it a 'presentiment' of the divine existence. A belief in God which is based on conscience is thus not grounded simply on the temperamental idiosyncrasy of certain individuals, but rather on a factor in human nature as such or at least on a factor in every human nature which is not morally stunted or maimed. The voice of conscience does not indeed carry with it any proof of its own credentials. In this sense it is an 'assumption'. But it manifests the presence of a transcendent God; and assent to the existence of the God so manifested is reasonable.

Before, however, we consider Newman's argument from conscience to the existence of God a little more closely, we can turn our attention to his approach to the problem of religious belief as outlined in his much later work, *The Grammar of Assent*, which was published in 1870.[2]

3. Assent, as Newman uses the term, is given to a proposition and is expressed by assertion. But I cannot properly be said to assent to a proposition unless I understand its meaning. This understanding is called by Newman apprehension. Hence we can say that assent pre-supposes apprehension.

There are, however, two types of apprehension, corresponding to two types of propositions. 'The terms of a proposition do or do not stand for things. If they do, then they are singular terms, for all things that are, are units. But if they do not stand for things they must stand for notions, and are common terms. Singular nouns come from experience,

---

[1] The present writer has no intention of committing himself to the view that we cannot properly be said to know that there is an external world. Of course, if we so define knowledge that only the propositions of logic and mathematics can be said to be known to be true, it follows that we do not know that things exist when we are not perceiving them. But as the word 'know' is used in ordinary language, we can perfectly well be said to know it.

[2] It would be misleading to describe *The Grammar of Assent* as a philosophical work, for in the long run it is concerned with 'the arguments adducible for Christianity' (*GA*, p. 484). But these arguments are placed in a general logical and epistemological context.

common from abstraction. The apprehension of the former I call real, and of the latter notional.'[1]

Exception might be taken to some of the expressions and statements in this quotation. But the general thesis seems to be reasonably clear. Apprehension or understanding of a term which stands for a thing or person is called real, while apprehension of an abstract idea or universal concept is called notional. If we apply this distinction to propositions, apprehension of, for example, a proposition in geometry would be notional, while the apprehension of the statement 'William is the father of James' would be real.

It follows from this that we must also distinguish between two types of assent. Assent given to a proposition apprehended as notional, as concerned with abstract ideas or universal terms, is notional assent, while that which is given to propositions apprehended as real, as concerned directly with things or persons, is real assent.

Now Newman takes it that things and persons, whether objects of actual experience or presented imaginatively in memory, strike the mind much more forcibly and vividly than do abstract notions. Real apprehension therefore is 'stronger than notional, because things, which are its objects, are confessedly more impressive and effective than notions, which are the object of notional [apprehension]. Experiences and their images strike and occupy the mind, as abstractions and their combinations do not.'[2] Similarly, although, according to Newman, all assent is alike in being unconditional,[3] acts of assent 'are elicited more heartily and forcibly, when they are made upon real apprehension which has things for its objects, than when they are made in favour of notions and with a notional apprehension'.[4] Further, real assent, though it does not necessarily affect conduct, tends to do so in a way in which purely notional assent does not.[5]

Real assent is also called belief by Newman. And it is obvious that the belief in God with which he is primarily concerned as a Christian apologist is a real assent to God as a present reality, and an assent which influences life or conduct, not simply a notional assent to a proposition about the idea of God. True, if assent is given to propositions, real assent will in this case be given to the proposition 'God exists' or 'there is a God'. But it will be given to the proposition apprehended as real, the term 'God' being understood as signifying a present reality, a present personal being. And from this it follows that Newman is not, and cannot be, primarily interested in a formal demonstrative inference to God's existence. For in his view, which recalls that of Hume, demonstration exhibits the logical relations between notions or ideas. That is to say, it derives conclusions from

---

[1] *GA*, pp. 20–1. [2] *Ibid.*, p. 35.
[3] So-called doubtful assent is for Newman unconditional assent to the statement that the truth of a given proposition is doubtful.
[4] *GA*, p. 17. [5] Cf. *ibid.*, p. 87.

premisses, the terms of which stand for abstract or general ideas. Thus the assent given to the conclusion is notional and lacks that element of personal commitment which Newman associates with real assent to the existence of God.

As has already been mentioned, however, Newman does not postulate in man any power of intuiting God directly. Hence some sort of inference is required, some movement of the mind from what is given in experience to what transcends immediate experience or perception. At the same time it must not be the type of inference which leads to notional rather than to real assent. Thus the following questions arise: 'Can I attain to any more vivid assent to the Being of a God, than that which is given merely to notions of the intellect? . . . Can I believe as if I saw? Since such a high assent requires a present experience or memory of the fact, at first sight it would seem as if the answer must be in the negative; for how can I assent as if I saw, unless I have seen? But no one in this life can see God. Yet I conceive a real assent is possible, and I proceed to show how.'[1] Newman's attempt to show how this real assent is possible will be considered in the next section.

4. We have seen that according to Newman even our non-religious beliefs rest on at any rate latent assumptions.[2] Something is taken for granted, whether explicitly or implicitly. There is some point of departure which is taken as given, without proof. In the case of belief in God this point of departure, the given basis of the movement of the mind, is conscience. Conscience is as much a factor in human nature, in the complex of mental acts, 'as the action of memory, of reasoning, of imagination, or as the sense of the beautiful'.[3] And it is 'the essential principle and sanction of Religion in the mind'.[4]

Conscience, however, can be considered under two aspects which, though not separate in fact, are none the less distinguishable. In the first place we can consider it as a rule of right conduct, as judging about the rightness or wrongness of particular actions. And it is an empirical fact that different people have made different ethical judgments. Some societies, for example, have approved conduct which other societies have condemned. In the second place we can consider conscience simply as the voice of authority, that is, as imposing obligation. And the sense of obligation is essentially the same in all who possess a conscience. Even if A thinks that he ought to act in one way while B

---

[1] *GA*, p. 99.

[2] As for formal demonstrative inference, this, Newman insists, is conditional. That is to say, the truth of the conclusion is asserted on the condition of the premisses being true. And though Newman himself does not deny that there are self-evident principles, he points out that what seems self-evident to one man does not necessarily seem self-evident to another. In any case the possibility of valid reasoning is assumed. If we try to prove everything and to make no assumptions whatsoever, we shall never get anywhere.

[3] *GA*, p. 102.   [4] *Ibid.*, p. 18.

thinks that he ought to act in another way, the consciousness of obligation, considered in itself, is similar in both men.

Considered under this second aspect, as the voice of internal authority,
conscience 'vaguely reaches forward to something beyond self, and
dimly discerns a sanction higher than self for its decisions, as evidenced
in that keen sense of obligation and responsibility which informs
them'.[1] The inward law of conscience does not indeed carry with it any
proof of its own validity, but it 'commands attention to it on its own
authority'.[2] The more this inward law is respected and followed, the
clearer become its dictates, and at the same time the clearer becomes
the presentiment or vague awareness of a transcendent God, 'a supreme
Power, claiming our habitual obedience'.[3]

A lively sense of obligation thus carries the mind forward to the
thought of something beyond the human self. Further, conscience
possesses an emotive aspect, on which Newman lays considerable
emphasis. Conscience produces 'reverence and awe, hope and fear,
especially fear, a feeling which is foreign for the most part, not only to
Taste, but even to the Moral Sense, except in consequence of accidental
associations'.[4] And Newman argues that there is an intimate connection
between affections and emotions on the one hand and persons on the
other. 'Inanimate things cannot stir our affections; these are correlative
with persons.'[5] Hence 'the phenomena of Conscience, as a dictate, avail
to impress the imagination with the picture of a Supreme Governor, a
Judge, holy, just, powerful, all-seeing, retributive'.[6] In other words,
conscience can produce that 'imaginative' awareness of God which is
required for the vivid assent to which reference has already been made.

What Newman says on this matter was doubtless verified in his own
case. When he spoke of the mind of a child who recognizes obligation
and who has been preserved from influences destructive of his 'religious
instincts'[7] as reaching forward 'with a strong presentiment of the
thought of a Moral Governor, sovereign over him, mindful and just',[8]
we may well discern a generalization from his own experience. Further,
if we consider what he has to say as a descriptive account of the basis
of real assent to God, it is doubtless verified in many other cases. For
it is certainly arguable that with many believers respect for the dictates
of conscience is a powerful influence in keeping alive the consciousness
of God as a present reality. True, it is possible to neglect and disobey
the dictates of conscience and still believe in God. But it is also probably
true that if one habitually turns a deaf ear to the voice of conscience,
so that it becomes dim or obscured, belief in God, if retained, tends to

---

[1] *Ibid.*, p. 104. [2] *OUS*, p. 19. [3] *Ibid.*
[4] *GA*, pp. 104–5. By Taste Newman means the aesthetic sense, considered as
the sense of the beautiful, while by Moral Sense he means in this context a sense
of the fittingness or deformity of actions, involving moral approval or disapproval.
[5] *Ibid.*, p. 106. [6] *Ibid.*, p. 107. [7] *Ibid.*, p. 109.
[8] *Ibid.*

degenerate into what Newman would call a purely notional assent. In other words, from the phenomenological point of view Newman's account of the relation between conscience and belief in or real assent to God has an indubitable value. There are indeed other factors which have to be considered in a phenomenological analysis of belief in God. But Newman certainly illustrates one aspect of the matter.

At the same time Newman is not concerned simply with describing the way in which, in his opinion, people come to believe in God, as though the belief were or could be on the same level as a belief, say, in the existence of elves and fairies. He wishes to show that belief in God is reasonable, and in some sense or other he intends to indicate the outlines of a 'proof' of God's existence. For instance, he says explicitly that the argument from conscience is 'my own chosen proof of that fundamental doctrine [God's existence] for thirty years past'.[1] And elsewhere he remarks that while he does not intend to prove 'here' the existence of a God, 'yet I have found it impossible to avoid saying where I look for the proof of it'.[2]

But what sort of a proof is it? In a sermon preached in 1830 Newman says that 'Conscience implies a relation between the soul and a something exterior, and that, moreover, superior to itself; a relation to an excellence which it does not possess, and to a tribunal over which it has no power'.[3] In spite, however, of the use of the word 'imply', he can hardly mean that the idea of conscience implies the idea of God in such a way that to assert the existence of conscience and deny the existence of God constitutes a logical contradiction. Moreover, elsewhere Newman uses phrases which suggest a causal inference. For instance, he says of conscience that 'from the nature of the case, its very existence carries on our minds to a Being exterior to ourselves; for else whence did it come?'[4] And we have already noted his remark, when speaking of the emotive aspect of conscience, that 'inanimate things cannot stir our affections; these are correlative with persons'.[5] But Newman is, of course, aware that by no means all philosophers would agree that we can legitimately infer the existence of God from the sense of obligation. And if he skates lightly over views different from his own, it is fairly evident that he is really concerned not so much with a causal inference to an explanatory hypothesis, analogous to causal inference in science, as with inviting his hearers or readers to enter into themselves and to reflect on the question whether they are not in some sense aware of God as manifested in the voice of conscience.

In other words, Newman seems to be primarily concerned with

---

[1] From the 'Proof of Theism', a paper published for the first time in Dr. A. J. Boekraad's *The Argument from Conscience to the Existence of God according to J. H. Newman* (Louvain, 1961), p. 121.
[2] *GA*, p. 101.　　　　　　　　　　[3] *OUS*, p. 18.
[4] *Sermons Preached on Various Occasions* (2nd edition, 1858), p. 86.
[5] *GA*, p. 106.

personal insight into the 'significance' or 'implications' of the awareness of obligation in a sense of these terms which it is difficult to define. And his line of thought appears to bear more resemblance to the phenomenological analyses performed in our own day by Gabriel Marcel than to metaphysical arguments of the traditional type. Newman admits indeed that a generalized inductive argument is possible. Just as from sense-impressions 'we go on to draw the general conclusion that there is a vast external world',[1] so by induction from particular instances of awareness of an inner imperative, an awareness which opens the mind to the thought of God, we can conclude to 'the Ubiquitous Presence of One Supreme Master'.[2] But assent to the conclusion of a generalized inductive argument will be, for Newman, a notional assent. Hence an argument of this kind appears to fall into the same class as arguments from Nature to God, of which he says in one place that while he has no intention of questioning their beauty and cogency, he certainly does question 'whether in matter of fact they make or keep men Christians'.[3] For such an argument to be 'effective', yielding real assent, we have to 'apply our general knowledge to a particular instance of that knowledge'.[4] That is to say, for assent to the conclusion of a generalized moral argument to become a living belief and the basis of religion, I have to enter within myself and hear the voice of God manifesting itself in the voice of conscience.[5] It is the personal appropriation of the truth which counts for Newman, not a mere intellectual assent to an abstract proposition.

In other words, Newman really wants to make us 'see' something for ourselves in the context of our personal experience rather than to argue that one proposition follows logically from another. After all, he says himself that he does not intend to deal 'with controversialists'.[6] In a real sense he wishes to make us see what we are. Without conscience a man is not really a man. And unless conscience leads us to belief in God by bringing us, so to speak, up against God as a present reality manifested in the sense of obligation, it remains stunted. Human nature expands, as it were, in faith. It is from the start open to God. And in Newman's view this potential openness is realized, basically, through personal insight into the 'phenomenon' of conscience. It is thus probably a mistake to interpret his argument from conscience to God as a public proof of the existence of God. True, the phenomenological analysis is public in the sense that it is a written explicitation of what Newman regards as the spontaneous movement of the unspoiled mind. But the public analysis cannot possibly do what Newman wishes it to do, to

---

[1] *Ibid.*, pp. 60–1. [2] *Ibid.*, p. 61.
[3] *Sermons Preached on Various Occasions*, p. 98. [4] *GA*, p. 61.
[5] It should be noted that Newman did not hold that the moral law depends on the arbitrary *fiat* of God. He maintained that in recognizing our obligation to obey the moral law we implicitly recognize God as Father and Judge.
[6] *GA*, p. 420.

facilitate real assent, unless it is interiorized, applied, as he puts it, to the particular instance.

5. We cannot examine here Newman's discussion of the evidences for the truth of Christianity. But there is a logical point connected with the discussion which is worth mentioning.

Formal demonstrative inference can, of course, be employed within theology, to exhibit the implications of statements. But when we are considering the evidences for Christianity in the first place, we are largely concerned, Newman takes it, with historical matters, with matters of fact. And at once a difficulty arises. On the one hand in reasoning about matters of fact rather than about the relations between abstract ideas our conclusions enjoy some degree of probability, perhaps a very high degree, but still only probability. On the other hand all assent, Newman insists, is unconditional. How then can we be justified in giving unconditional assent, such as is demanded of the Christian, to a proposition which is only probably true?

To answer this objection Newman makes use of ideas found in Pascal, Locke and Butler and argues that an accumulation of independent probabilities, converging towards a common conclusion, can render this conclusion certain. In his own words, where there is a 'cumulation of probabilities, independent of each other, arising out of the nature and circumstances of the case which is under review; probabilities too fine to avail separately, too subtle and circuitous to be convertible into syllogisms, too numerous and various for such conversion, even were they convertible',[1] but which all, taken together, converge on a certain conclusion, this conclusion can be certain.

It can doubtless be admitted that we do in fact often take a convergence of probabilities as sufficient proof of the truth of a proposition. But it can still be objected against Newman that no definite rule can be given for determining when the truth of a certain conclusion is the only possible rational explanation of a given convergence. Hence though we may be perfectly justified in assuming the truth of the conclusion for all practical purposes, an unconditional or unqualified assent is unjustified. For any hypothesis remains revisible in principle. It is all very well for Newman to say that in the case of religious inquiry we are 'bound in conscience to seek truth and to look for certainty by modes of proof, which, when reduced to the shape of formal propositions, fail to satisfy the severe requisitions of science'.[2] The fact remains that if unconditional assent to a proposition is taken to exclude the possibility of the proposition turning out to be false, it cannot legitimately be given to a conclusion drawn from a convergence unless we are able to show that at some point probability is transferred into certainty.

Obviously, Newman can hardly mean by unconditional assent one which excludes all possibility of the relevant proposition turning out to

[1] *GA*, p. 281.　　　　　[2] *Ibid.*, p. 407.

be false. For if all assent is unconditional, it must include assent to propositions which we very well know might turn out to be false. In its most general form the statement that all assent is unconditional can hardly mean more than that assent is assent. However, in the case of adherence to Christianity Newman clearly has in mind an absolute self-commitment, an unqualified assent in the fullest sense. And though he would doubtless admit that there is no infallible abstract rule for determining when a convergence of possibilities is such that the conclusion is certain, he argues that man possesses a 'faculty' of the mind, analogous to the Aristotelian *phronesis*, which is susceptible of different degrees of development and which is in principle capable of discerning the point at which the convergence of probabilities amounts to conclusive proof. This is the illative sense. 'In no class of concrete reasonings, whether in experimental science, historical research, or theology, is there any ultimate test of truth and error in our inferences besides the trustworthiness of the Illative Sense that gives them its sanction.'[1] We either 'see' or we do not see that a given inference is valid. Similarly, we either see or we do not see that the only rational explanation of a given accumulation of converging independent probabilities is the truth of the conclusion on which they converge. By the nature of the case there can be no further criterion of judgment than the mind's estimate of the evidence in a particular case.

It may seem that Newman places the emphasis on subjective or psychological states. He says, for example, that 'certitude is a mental state: certainty is a quality of propositions. Those propositions I call certain, which are such that I am certain of them.'[2] And this may give the impression that in his opinion any proposition is certainly true if it causes the feeling of being certain in a human being. But he goes on to say that in concrete questions certitude is not a 'passive impression made upon the mind from without . . . but . . . an active recognition of propositions as true. . . .'[3] And as 'everyone who reasons is his own centre',[4] there can be no further criterion of evidence or of the validity of inference in concrete matters of fact than seeing that the evidence is sufficient or that the inference is valid. Newman has no intention of denying the objectivity of truth. He means rather that if we think that a man's reasoning in questions of fact is faulty, we can only ask him to look again at the evidence and at his process of reasoning. If it is objected that there can be a 'logic of words',[5] the sort of deduction which can be performed by a machine, Newman does not deny this. But he insists that a distinction must be made between the logic of words and reasoning about matters of fact. The former leads to purely notional assent; and this does not interest him when he is writing as a

---

[1] *Ibid.*, p. 352. The illative sense is 'the power of judging about truth and error in concrete matters' (*ibid.*, p. 346).
[2] *Ibid.*, p. 337.   [3] *Ibid.*   [4] *Ibid.*, p. 338.   [5] *Ibid.*

Christian apologist who wishes to justify real assent. He does not set out to argue that reasoning about Christian evidences can be reduced to the logic of words, to formal demonstrative inference. What he wishes to show is rather that in all concrete issues of fact we have to employ inference which is not so reducible, and that the believer's assent to the conclusion of reasoning about the evidences for Christianity cannot therefore be justifiably described as a mere leap or as the result of wishful thinking because it does not conform to a pattern of demonstration which certainly has its uses but which is inappropriate outside a certain limited field.

6. We have already had occasion to refer to a certain affinity between Newman's reflections on conscience and Gabriel Marcel's phenomenological analyses. But the intellectual antecedents and formations of the two men were, needless to say, very different; and whereas Newman was out to prove something, to show that Christian belief is reasonable, the apologetic motive is much less obvious with Marcel. Indeed, Marcel's philosophical reflections helped to bring him to Christianity, whereas Newman's philosophical reflections presuppose the Christian faith, in the sense that it is a case of faith reflecting on itself. At the same time there are certain limited affinities.

Similarly, in spite of the great differences between the two men Newman's preoccupation with the personal appropriation of truth as a basis for life and with personal self-commitment may put us in mind of Kierkegaard,[1] whose span of life (1813–55) fell entirely within that of Newman. This is not to suggest, of course, that Newman knew anything at all about the Danish thinker, or even of his existence. But though Newman certainly did not go so far as Kierkegaard in describing truth as subjectivity, there is none the less a certain degree of spiritual affinity between the two men.

As for Newman's insistence on the moral conditions for the fruitful pursuit of truth in religious inquiry, this has become a commonplace of the newer apologetics, as has indeed Newman's approach from within the soul rather than from external Nature. In other words, there is at any rate some affinity between Newman's approach to apologetics and that associated in modern times with the name of Maurice Blondel (1861–1949).

The point of these remarks is this. If we take Newman simply as he stands, there are a good many questions which modern British logicians and philosophers would wish to ask, and objections which they would feel inclined to make. But it seems safe to say that Newman is not now regarded, except possibly by a few devotees, as a philosopher whose thought one either accepts or rejects, as the case may be. By saying that he is not 'now' regarded I do not mean to imply that he was ever looked on in this light. I mean rather that the growth of interest in his

[1] For Kierkegaard see ch. 17 of Vol. VII of this *History*.

philosophical thought and in his style of apologetics has coincided with the spread of movements in philosophy and in apologetics which, on our looking back, are seen to have certain affinities with elements in Newman's reflections. Hence those who take an interest in his philosophical reflections tend to look on them as a source of stimulus and inspiration rather than as a rigid, systematic doctrine, which, of course, Newman himself never intended them to be. And in this case detailed criticism of particular points necessarily seems pedantic and appears, to those who value Newman's general approach, as more or less irrelevant.

APPENDIX B

A SHORT BIBLIOGRAPHY

General Works

For the sake of brevity titles of general histories of philosophy mentioned in the first section of the Bibliography in Volume VII of this *History* have not been repeated here. Nor have I attempted to supply bibliographies for all the philosophers mentioned in the text of the present volume. In the case of a considerable number of philosophers works are mentioned in the text or in footnotes, which have not been listed here.

Adams, G. P. and Montague, W. P. (editors). *Contemporary American Philosophy*. 2 vols. New York, 1930. (Personal Statements.)

Anderson, P. R. and Fisch, M. H. *Philosophy in America*. New York, 1939.

Blau, J. L. *Men and Movements in American Philosophy*. New York, 1939.

Bochenski, I. M. *Contemporary European Philosophy*, translated by D. Nicholl and K. Aschenbrenner. London and Berkeley, 1956.

Brinton, Crane. *English Political Thought in the Nineteenth Century*. Cambridge (Mass.), 1949.

Deledalle, G. *Histoire de la philosophie américaine de la guerre de sécession à la seconde guerre mondiale*. Paris, 1955.

Lamanna, A. P. *La filosofia del novecento*. Florence, 1964.

Merz, J. T. *History of European Thought in the Nineteenth Century*. 4 vols. London, 1896–1914.

Metz, R. *A Hundred Years of British Philosophy*, translated by J. W. Harvey, T. E. Jessop and H. Sturt. London, 1938. (An account of British philosophy from about the middle of the nineteenth century onwards.)

Muelder, W. E. and Sears, L. *The Development of American Philosophy*. Boston, 1940.

Muirhead, J. H. (editor). *Contemporary British Philosophy: Personal Statements*. 2 vols. London, 1924–5. (The first volume includes statements by, for example, Bosanquet, McTaggart, Bertrand Russell and Schiller, the second by James Ward and G. E. Moore.)

Passmore, J. *A Hundred Years of Philosophy*. London, 1957. (A useful account of philosophy, mainly but not exclusively British, from J. S. Mill, with a concluding chapter on existentialism.)

Riley, I. W. *American Thought from Puritanism to Pragmatism and Beyond*. New York, 1923 (2nd edition).

Schneider, H. W. *A History of American Philosophy*. New York, 1946,
Seth (Pringle-Pattison), A. *English Philosophers and Schools of Philo-
sophy*. London, 1912. (From Francis Bacon to F. H. Bradley.)
Warnock, G. J. *English Philosophy Since 1900*. London, 1958. (A clear
and succinct account of the development of the modern analytic
movement.)
Warnock, M. *Ethics Since 1900*. London, 1960.
Werkmeister, W. H. *A History of Philosophical Ideas in America*. New
York, 1949.

Part I: Chapters I–V

1. *General Works Relating to the Utilitarian Movement.*

Albee, E. *A History of English Utilitarianism*. London, 1902.
Davidson, W. L. *Political Thought in England: Bentham to J. S. Mill*.
London, 1950.
Guyau, J. M. *La morale anglaise contemporaine*. Paris, 1904 (5th ed.).
Halévy, E. *The Growth of Philosophic Radicalism*, translated by M.
Morris, with a preface by A. D. Lindsay. London, 1928.
Laski, H. J. *The Rise of European Liberalism*. London, 1936.
Leslie, S. W. *Political Thought in England. The Utilitarians from
Bentham to Mill*. London and New York, 1947.
Mondolfo, R. *Saggi per la storia della morale utilitaria*. 2 vols. Verona
and Padua, 1903–4.
Plamentaz, J. *The English Utilitarians*. Oxford, 1949.
Stephen, L. *The English Utilitarians*. 3 vols. London, 1900. (The
volumes are devoted respectively to Bentham, James Mill and
J. S. Mill.)

2. *Bentham*
Texts

The Works of Jeremy Bentham, edited by John Bowring. 11 vols.
Edinburgh, 1838–43.
Benthamiana, Select Extracts from the Works of Jeremy Bentham,
edited by J. H. Burton. Edinburgh, 1843.
Oeuvres de Jérémie Bentham, translated by E. Dumont. 3 vols.
Brussels, 1829–30.
Colección de obras del célebre Jeremias Bentham, compiled by E.
Dumont with commentaries by B. Anduaga y Espinosa. 14 vols.
Madrid, 1841–3.
An Introduction to the Principles of Morals and Legislation, edited by
L. Lafleur. New York, 1948. (The 1876 Oxford edition is a
reprint of the 1823 edition.)
Theory of Legislation, translated from the French of E. Dumont by
R. Hildreth. London, 1896.

Bentham's Theory of Legislation, edited by C. K. Ogden. London, 1950.

A Fragment on Government, edited by F. C. Montague. London, 1891.

Bentham's Theory of Fictions, edited by C. K. Ogden. London, 1932.

Bentham's Handbook of Political Fallacies, edited by H. A. Larrabee. Baltimore, 1952.

Deontology, or the Science of Morality, edited by J. Bowring. 2 vols. London, 1834.

The Limits of Jurisprudence Defined, edited by C. W. Everett. New York, 1945.

Jeremy Bentham's Economic Writings, Critical Edition based on his Printed Works and Unprinted Manuscripts, edited by W. Stark. 3 vols. London, 1952–4. (Each volume contains an introductory essay. The second appendix, contained in the third volume, is a systematic survey of the surviving Bentham manuscripts.)

Catalogue of the Manuscripts of Jeremy Bentham in the Library of University College, London, edited by A. T. Milne. London, 1937.

Studies

Atkinson, C. M. *Jeremy Bentham, His Life and Work*. London, 1905.

Baumgardt, D. *Bentham and the Ethics of Today*. Princeton (U.S.A.) and London, 1952.

Busch, J. *Die moralische und soziale Ethik Benthams*. Neisse, 1938.

Everett, C. W. *The Education of Jeremy Bentham*. New York, 1931.

Jones, W. T. *Masters of Political Thought: From Machiavelli to Bentham*. London, 1947.

Keeton, G. W. and Schwarzenberger, G. (editors). *Jeremy Bentham and the Law*. London, 1948.

Laski, H. J. *Political Thought in England: Locke to Bentham*. London, 1950.

Mack, M. P. *Jeremy Bentham: An Odyssey of Ideas, 1748–1792*. London, 1962.

Mill, J. S. *Mill on Bentham and Coleridge*, edited by F. R. Leavis. London, 1950.

Quintodamo, N. *La morale utilitaristica del Bentham e sua evoluzione nel diritto penale*. Naples, 1936.

Stephen, L. *The English Utilitarians: Vol. I, Jeremy Bentham*. London, 1900.

3. James Mill

Texts

History of India. 3 vols. London, 1817. (4th edition, 9 vols., 1848; 5th edition, with continuation by M. H. Wilson, 10 vols., 1858.)

Elements of Political Economy. London, 1821 (3rd and revised edition, 1826).

Analysis of the Phenomena of the Human Mind, edited by J. S. Mill, with notes by A. Bain, A. Findlater and G. Grote. 2 vols. London, 1869.
A Fragment on Mackintosh. London, 1835.

Studies

Bain, A. *James Mill, A Biography*. London 1882.
Bower, G. S. *Hartley and James Mill*. London, 1881.
Hamburger, J. *James Mill and the Art of Revolution*. Yale, 1964.
Ressler, A. *Die Beiden Mill*. Cologne, 1929.
Stephen, L. *The English Utilitarians: Vol. II, James Mill*. London, 1900.

4. *J. S. Mill*
Texts

Collected Works of John Stuart Mill, general editor F. E. L. Priestley. Toronto and London. Vols. XII–XIII, *The Earlier Letters, 1812–1848*, edited by F. E. Mineka, 1963; vols. II–III, *The Principles of Political Economy*, with an introduction by V. W. Bladen, edited by J. M. Robson, 1965.
Autobiography, edited by H. J. Laski. London, 1952. (Among other editions there is the one edited by J. J. Cross, New York, 1924.)
The Early Draft of J. S. Mill's Autobiography, edited by J. Stillinger. Urbana (Ill.), 1961.
Mill's Utilitarianism reprinted with a Study of the English Utilitarians, by J. Plamentaz. Oxford, 1949.
On Liberty, Considerations on Representative Government, edited with an introduction by R. B. McCallum. Oxford, 1946.
Considerations on Representative Government, edited with an introduction by C. V. Shields. New York, 1958.
A System of Logic. London, 1949 (reprint).
Examination of Sir William Hamilton's Philosophy. London, 1865.
John Stuart Mill's Philosophy of Scientific Method, edited by E. Nagel. New York, 1950. (Selections, with introductory material, from the *Logic* and the *Examination*.)
Dissertations and Discussions. 5 vols. Boston (U.S.A.), 1865–75.
Mill on Bentham and Coleridge, edited by F. R. Leavis. London, 1950.
Auguste Comte and Positivism. London, 1865.
Inaugural Address at St. Andrews. London, 1867.
Three Essays on Religion. London, 1874. (*Theism*, edited by R. Taylor. New York, 1957.)
John Stuart Mill and Harriet Taylor: Their Friendship and Subsequent Marriage, edited by F. A. Hayek. Chicago, 1951. (Contains the Mill–Taylor correspondence.)

Lettres inédites de John Stuart Mill à Auguste Comte, publiées avec les résponses de Comte, edited by L. Lévy-Bruhl. Paris, 1899.

Bibliography of the Published Works of John Stuart Mill, edited by N. MacMinn, J. R. Hinds and J. M. McCrimmon. London, 1945.

Studies

Anschutz, R. P. *The Philosophy of J. S. Mill*. Oxford, 1953. (Illustrates very well the different tendencies in Mill's thought.)

Bain, A. *John Stuart Mill: A Criticism with Personal Recollections*. London, 1882.

Borchard, R. *John Stuart Mill, the Man*. London, 1957.

Britton, K. *John Stuart Mill*. Penguin Books, 1953.

Casellato, S. *Giovanni St. Mill e l'utilitarismo inglese*. Padua, 1951.

Castell, A. *Mill's Logic of the Moral Sciences: A Study of the Impact of Newtonism on Early Nineteenth-Century Social Thought*. Chicago, 1936.

Courtney, W. L. *The Metaphysics of John Stuart Mill*. London, 1879.

Cowling, M. *Mill and Liberalism*. Cambridge, 1963.

Douglas, C. *J. S. Mill: A Study of His Philosophy*. London, 1895.
Ethics of John Stuart Mill. Edinburgh, 1897.

Grude-Oettli, N. *John Stuart Mill zwischen Liberalismus und Sozialismus*. Zürich, 1936.

Hippler, F. *Staat und Gesellschaft bei Mill, Marx, Lagarde*. Berlin, 1934.

Jackson, R. *An Examination of the Deductive Logic of John Stuart Mill*. London, 1941.

Kantzer, E. M. *La religion de John Stuart Mill*. Caen, 1914.

Kennedy, G. *The Psychological Empiricism of John Stuart Mill*. Amsterdam, 1928.

Kubitz, O. A. *The Development of John Stuart Mill's System of Logic*. Urbana (Ill.), 1932.

McCosh, J. *An Examination of Mr. J. S. Mill's Philosophy*. New York, 1890 (2nd edition).

Mueller, I. W. *John Stuart Mill and French Thought*. Urbana (Ill.), 1956.

Packe, M. St. John. *The Life of John Stuart Mill*. New York, 1954.

Pradines, M. *Les postulats métaphysiques de l'utilitarisme de Stuart Mill et Spencer*. Paris, 1909.

Ray, J. *La méthode de l'économie politique d'après John Stuart Mill*. Paris, 1914.

Roerig, F. *Die Wandlungen in der geistigen Grundhaltung John Stuart Mills*. Cologne, 1930.

Russell, Bertrand. *John Stuart Mill*. London, 1956. (Bristol Academy Lecture.)

Saenger, S. *John Stuart Mill, Sein Leben und Lebenswerk*. Stuttgart, 1901.

Schauchet, P. *Individualistische und sozialistische Gedanken im Leben John Stuart Mills*. Giessen, 1926.

Stephen, L. *The English Utilitarians:* vol. III, *John Stuart Mill*. London, 1900.

Towney, G. A. *John Stuart Mill's Theory of Inductive Logic*. Cincinnati, 1909.

Watson, J. *Comte, Mill and Spencer*. Glasgow, 1895.

Zuccante, G. *La morale utilitaristica dello Stuart Mill*. Milan, 1899. *Giovanni S. Mill e l'utilitarismo*. Florence, 1922.

5. *Herbert Spencer*
Texts

A System of Synthetic Philosophy. 10 vols. London, 1862–93. (For some detailed information about the various editions of the books comprising the *System* see pp. 240–1.)

Epitome of the Synthetic Philosophy, by F. H. Collins. London, 1889 (5th edition, 1901).

Essays, Scientific, Political and Speculative. 3 vols. London, 1891. (Two volumes of *Essays, Scientific, Political and Speculative* appeared at London in 1857 and 1863 respectively and one volume of *Essays, Moral, Political and Aesthetic* at New York in 1865.)

Education, Intellectual, Moral, Physical. London, 1861.

The Man versus The State. London, 1884.

The Nature and Reality of Religion. London, 1885.

Various Fragments. London, 1897.

Facts and Comments. London, 1902.

Autobiography. 2 vols. New York, 1904.

Studies

Allievo, G. *La psicologia di Herbert Spencer*. Turin, 1914 (2nd edition).

Ardigò, R. *L'Inconoscibile di Spencer e il noumeno di Kant*. Padua, 1901.

Asirvatham, E. *Spencer's Theory of Social Justice*. New York, 1936.

Carus, P. *Kant and Spencer*. Chicago, 1889.

Diaconide, E. *Étude critique sur la sociologie de Herbert Spencer*. Paris, 1938.

Duncan, D. *The Life and Letters of Herbert Spencer*. London, 1912.

Elliott, H. *Herbert Spencer*. London, 1917.

Ensor, R. C. *Some Reflections on Spencer's Doctrine that Progress is Differentiation*. Oxford, 1947.

Fiske, J. *Outlines of Cosmic Philosophy.* 2 vols. London, 1874. (These lectures are critical as well as expository of Spencer's thought.)

Gaupp, O. *Herbert Spencer.* Stuttgart, 1897.

Guthmann, J. *Entwicklung und Selbstentfaltung bei Spencer.* Ochsenfurt, 1931.

Häberlin, P. *Herbert Spencers Grundlagen der Philosophie.* Leipzig, 1908.

Hudson, W. H. *Introduction to the Philosophy of Herbert Spencer.* London, 1909.

Jarger, M. *Herbert Spencers Prinzipien der Ethik.* Hamburg, 1922.

Macpherson, H. *Herbert Spencer, The Man and His Work.* London, 1900.

Parisot, E. *Herbert Spencer.* Paris, 1911.

Parker-Bowne, B. *Kant and Spencer.* New York, 1922.

Ramlow, L. *A. Riehl und Spencer.* Berlin, 1933.

Royce, J. *Herbert Spencer: An Estimate and Review with a chapter of Personal Reminiscences by J. Collier.* New York, 1904.

Rumney, J. *Herbert Spencer's Sociology: A Study in the History of Social Theory.* London, 1934.

Sergi, G. *La sociologia di Herbert Spencer.* Rome, 1903.

Sidgwick, H. *Lectures on the Ethics of T. H. Green, Mr. Herbert Spencer, and J. Martineau.* London, 1902.

Solari, G. *L'opera filosofica di Herbert Spencer.* Bergamo, 1904.

Stadler, A. *Herbert Spencers Ethik.* Leipzig, 1913.

Thompson, J. A. *Herbert Spencer.* London, 1906.

Tillett, A. W. *Spencer's Synthetic Philosophy: What It is All About. An Introduction to Justice, 'The Most Important Part'.* London, 1914.

Part II: Chapters VI–X

1. *General Works Relating to British Idealism*

Abbagnano, N. *L'idealismo inglese e americano.* Naples, 1926.

Cunningham, G. W. *The Idealistic Argument in Recent British and American Philosophy.* New York, 1933.

Dockhorn, K. *Die Staatsphilosophie des englischen Idealismus, ihre Lehre und Wirkung.* Pöppinghaus, 1937.

Haldar, H. *Neo-Hegelianism.* London, 1927.

Milne, A. J. M. *The Social Philosophy of English Idealism.* London, 1962.

Muirhead, J. M. *The Platonic Tradition in Anglo-Saxon Philosophy.* London, 1931.

Pucelle, J. *L'idéalisme en Angleterre de Coleridge à Bradley.* Neuchatel and Paris, 1955. (Can be highly recommended.)

2. *Coleridge*
Texts

Works, edited by W. G. T. Shedd. 7 vols. New York, 1884.

The Friend. 3 vols. London, 1812. (2 vols, 1837).

Biographia Literaria. London, 1817. (Everyman Library, 1906 and reprints.)

Aids to Reflection. 2 vols. London, 1824–5 (with addition of the *Essay on Faith*, 1890).

On the Constitution of Church and State, edited by H. N. Coleridge. London, 1839.

Confessions of an Inquiring Spirit, edited by H. N. Coleridge. London, 1840.

Treatise on Method. London, 1849 (3rd edition).

Essays on His Own Times. 3 vols. London, 1850.

Anima Poetae, edited by E. H. Coleridge. London, 1895.

Letters, edited by E. H. Coleridge. London, 1895.

Unpublished Letters. London, 1932.

The Political Thought of Coleridge, selected by R. J. White. London, 1938.

The Philosophical Lectures of S. T. Coleridge, Hitherto Unpublished, edited by K. Coburn. London, 1949.

The Notebooks of S. T. Coleridge, edited by K. Coburn. 2 vols. London, 1957–62.

Studies

Blunden, E. and Griggs, E. L. (editors). *Coleridge Studies*. London, 1934.

Campbell J. D. *Life of S. T. Coleridge*. London, 1894.

Chambers, E. K. *S. T. Coleridge: A Biographical Study*. Oxford, 1938.

Chinol, E. *Il pensiero di S. T. Coleridge*. Venice, 1953.

Coburn, K. *Inquiring Spirit. A New Presentation of Coleridge* (from published and unpublished writings). London, 1931.

Ferrando, G. *Coleridge*. Florence, 1925.

Green, J. H. *Spiritual Philosophy, Founded on the Teaching of the late S. T. Coleridge*. 2 vols. London, 1865.

Hanson, L. *Life of S. T. Coleridge Early Years*. London, 1938.

Kagey, R. *Coleridge: Studies in the History of Ideas*. New York, 1935.

Lowes, J. L. *The Road to Xanadu: A Study in Ways of the Imagination*. London, 1927 (revised edition 1930).

Muirhead, J. H. *Coleridge as Philosopher*. London, 1930.

Richards, I. A. *Coleridge on Imagination*. London, 1934.

Snyder, A. D. *Coleridge on Logic and Learning*. New Haven, 1929.

Wellek, R. *Immanuel Kant in England*. Princeton, 1931. (Only partly on Coleridge.)

Winkelmann, E. *Coleridge und die kantische Philosophie.* Leipzig, 1933.

Wunsche, W. *Die Staatsauffassung S. T. Coleridge's.* Leipzig, 1934.

3. *Carlyle*
Texts

Works, edited by H. D. Traill. 31 vols. London, 1897–1901.
Sartor Resartus. London, 1841, and subsequent editions.
On Heroes, Hero-Worship and the Heroic in History. London, 1841.
Correspondence of Carlyle and R. W. Emerson. 2 vols. London, 1883.
Letters of Carlyle to J. S. Mill, J. Sterling and R. Browning, edited by
   A. Carlyle. London, 1923.

Studies

Baumgarten, O. *Carlyle und Goethe.* Tübingen, 1906.
Fermi, L. *Carlyle.* Messina, 1939.
Garnett, R. *Life of Carlyle.* London, 1887.
Harrold, C. F. *Carlyle and German Thought, 1819–34.* New Haven,
   1934.
Hensel, P. *Thomas Carlyle.* Stuttgart, 1901.
Lammond, D. *Carlyle.* London, 1934.
Lea, F. *Carlyle, Prophet of Today.* London, 1944.
Lehman, B. H. *Carlyle's Theory of the Hero.* Duke, 1939.
Neff, E. *Carlyle and Mill: Mystic and Utilitarian.* New York, 1924.
   Carlyle. New York, 1932.
Seillière, E. *L'actualité de Carlyle.* Paris, 1929.
Storrs, M. *The Relation of Carlyle to Kant and Fichte.* Bryn Mawr,
   1929.
Taylor, A. C. *Carlyle et la pensée latine.* Paris, 1937.
Wilson, D. A. *Carlyle.* 6 vols. London, 1923–34.

4. *T. H. Green*
Texts

Works, edited by R. L. Nettleship, 3 vols. London, 1885–8. (Contains
   Green's *Introductions to Hume's Treatise,* lectures on Kant, on
   Logic and on *The Principles of Political Obligation,* together with
   a memoir of the philosopher by Nettleship.)
Introductions to Hume's Treatise in vols. 1 and 2 of the *Philosophical
   Works of David Hume* edited by T. H. Green and T. M. Grose.
   London, 1874.
Prolegomena to Ethics, edited by A. C. Bradley. London, 1883.
Principles of Political Obligation. London, 1895.

Studies

Günther, O. *Das Verhältnis der Ethik Greens zu der Kants.* Leipzig,
   1915.

Fairbrother, W. H. *The Philosophy of T. H. Green*. London, 1896.

Fusai, M. *Il pensiero morale di T. H. Green*. Florence, 1943.

Lamont, W. D. *Introduction to Green's Moral Philosophy*. New York, 1934.

Muirhead, J. H. *The Service of the State: Four lectures on the Political Teaching of Green*. London, 1908.

Pucelle, J. *La nature et l'esprit dans la philosophie de T. H. Green. I, Métaphysique–Morale*. Louvain, 1961. (A thorough and sympathetic study.)

5. E. Caird
Texts

A Critical Account of the Philosophy of Kant. Glasgow, 1877. (Revised edition in 2 vols. with the title *The Critical Philosophy of Kant*, Glasgow, 1889.)

Hegel. Edinburgh, 1883.

The Social Philosophy and Religion of Comte. Glasgow, 1885.

Essays on Literature and Philosophy. 2 vols. Glasgow, 1892.

The Evolution of Religion. 2 vols. Glasgow, 1893.

The Evolution of Theology in the Greek Philosophers, 2 vols. Glasgow, 1904.

Studies

Jones, H. and Muirhead, J. H. *The Life and Philosophy of Edward Caird*. London, 1921.

6. Bradley
Texts

The Presuppositions of Critical History. London, 1874.

Ethical Studies. London, 1876 (2nd edition, 1927).

Mr. Sidgwick's Hedonism. London, 1877.

The Principles of Logic. London, 1883 (2nd edition with Terminal Essays in 2 vols, 1922.)

Appearance and Reality. London, 1893 (2nd edition with Appendix, 1897).

Essays on Truth and Reality. London, 1914.

Aphorisms. Oxford, 1930.

Collected Essays. 2 vols. Oxford, 1935. (This work includes *The Presuppositions of Critical History*.)

Studies

Antonelli, M. A. *La metafisica di F. H. Bradley*. Milan, 1952.

Campbell, C. A. *Scepticism and Construction. Bradley's Sceptical Principle as the Basis of Constructive Philosophy*. London, 1931.

Chappuis, A. *Der theoretische Weg Bradleys*. Paris, 1934.

Church, R. W. *Bradley's Dialectic*. London, 1942.

De Marneffe, J. *La preuve de l'Absolu chez Bradley. Analyse et critique de la méthode*. Paris, 1961.

Kagey, R. *The Growth of Bradley's Logic*. London, 1931.

Keeling, S. V. *La nature de l'expérience chez Kant et chez Bradley*. Montpellier, 1925.

Lomba, R. M. *Bradley and Bergson*. Lucknow, 1937.

Lofthouse, W. F. *F. H. Bradley*. London, 1949.

Mack, R. D. *The Appeal to Immediate Experience. Philosophic Method in Bradley, Whitehead and Dewey*. New York, 1945.

Ross, G. R. *Scepticism and Dogma: A Study in the Philosophy of F. H. Bradley*. New York, 1940.

Schüring, H.-J. *Studie zur Philosophie von F. H. Bradley*. Meisenheim am Glan, 1963.

Segerstedt, T. T. *Value and Reality in Bradley's Philosophy*. Lund, 1934.

Taylor, A. E. *F. H. Bradley*. London, 1924. (British Academy lecture.)

Wollheim, R. *F. H. Bradley*. Penguin Books, 1959.

In *Mind* for 1925 there are articles on Bradley by G. D. Hicks, J. H. Muirhead, G. F. Stout, F. C. S. Schiller, A. E. Taylor and J. Ward.

7. *Bosanquet*
Texts

Knowledge and Reality. London, 1885.

Logic, or the Morphology of Knowledge. 2 vols. London, 1888.

Essays and Addresses. London, 1889.

A History of Aesthetic. London, 1892.

The Civilization of Christendom and Other Studies. London, 1893.

Aspects of the Social Problem. London, 1895.

The Essentials of Logic. London, 1895.

Companion to Plato's Republic. London, 1895.

Rousseau's Social Contract. London, 1895.

Psychology of the Moral Self. London, 1897.

The Philosophical Theory of the State. London, 1899.

The Principle of Individuality and Value. London, 1912.

The Value and Destiny of the Individual. London, 1913.

The Distinction between Mind and Its Objects. London, 1913.

Three Lectures on Aesthetics. London, 1915.

Social and International Ideals. London, 1917.

Some Suggestions in Ethics. London, 1918.

Implication and Linear Inference. London, 1920.

What Religion Is. London, 1920.

The Meeting of Extremes in Contemporary Philosophy. London, 1921.

Three Chapters on the Nature of Mind. London, 1923.
Science and Philosophy and Other Essays, edited by J. H. Muirhead
and R. C. Bosanquet. London, 1927.

Studies

Bosanquet, H. *Bernard Bosanquet.* London, 1924.
Houang, F. *La néo-hégelianisme en Angleterre: la philosophie de
Bernard Bosanquet.* Paris, 1954.
           *De l'humanisme à l'absolutisme. L'évolution de la pensée
religieuse du néo-hégelien anglais Bernard Bosanquet.*
Paris, 1954.
Muirhead, J. H. (editor). *Bosanquet and His Friends: Letters Illus-
trating Sources and Development of His Philosophical Opinions.*
London, 1935.
Pfannenstil, B. *Bernard Bosanquet's Philosophy of the State.* Lund,
1936.

8. McTaggart
Texts

Studies in the Hegelian Dialectic. Cambridge, 1896 (2nd edition 1922).
Studies in the Hegelian Cosmology. Cambridge, 1901 (2nd edition,
1918).
Some Dogmas of Religion. London, 1906, (2nd edition, with bio-
graphical introduction by C. D. Broad, 1930).
A Commentary on Hegel's Logic. Cambridge, 1910 (new edition, 1931).
The Nature of Existence. 2 vols. Cambridge, 1921–7. (The second vol.
is edited by C. D. Broad.)
Philosophical Studies, edited, with an introduction by S. V. Keeling,
London, 1934. (Mainly a collection of published articles, includ-
ing that on the unreality of time.)

Studies

Broad, C. D. *Examination of McTaggart's Philosophy.* 2 vols. Cambridge, 1933–8.
Dickinson, G. Lowes. *McTaggart, a Memoir.* Cambridge, 1931.

Part III: Chapters XI–XIII

1. *General Works Relating to Idealism in America*
Abbagnano, N. *L'idealismo inglese e americano.* Naples, 1926.
Adams, G. P. *Idealism and the Modern Age.* New Haven, 1919.
Barrett, C. and Others. *Contemporary Idealism in America.* New
York, 1932.

Cunningham, G. W. *The Idealistic Argument in Recent British and American Philosophy*. New York, 1933.

Frothingham, O. B. *Transcendentalism in New England*. New York, 1876.

Jones, A. L. *Early American Philosophers*. New York, 1898.

Miller, P. *The New England Mind: The Seventeenth Century*. New York, 1939.

Parrington, V. L. *Main Currents of American Thought*. New York, 1927.

Riley, I. W. *American Philosophy: The Early Schools*. New York, 1907.

Rogers, A. K. *English and American Philosophy Since 1800*. New York, 1922.

Royce, J. *Lectures on Modern Idealism*. New Haven, 1919.

Schneider, H. W. *The Puritan Mind*. New York, 1930.

    A History of American Philosophy. New York, 1946.

Stovall, F. *American Idealism*. Oklahoma, 1943.

2. *Emerson*

Texts

The Complete Works of Ralph Waldo Emerson, edited by E. W. Emerson. 12 vols. Boston, 1903–4. (Fireside edition, Boston, 1909.)

Works, 5 vols. London, 1882–3.

    6 vols., edited by J. Morley, London, 1883–4.

The Journals of Ralph Waldo Emerson, edited by E. W. Emerson and W. F. Forbes. 10 vols. Boston, 1909–14.

The Letters of Ralph Waldo Emerson, edited by R. L. Rusk. New York, 1939.

Studies

Alcot, A. B. *R. W. Emerson, Philosopher and Seer*. Boston, 1882.

Bishop, J. *Emerson on the Soul*. Cambridge (Mass.), and London, 1965.

Cabot, J. E. *A Memoir of R. W. Emerson*. 2 vols. London, 1887.

Cameron, K. W. *Emerson the Essayist: An Outline of His Philosophical Development through 1836*. 2 vols. Raleigh (N.C.), 1945.

Carpenter, F. I. *Emerson and Asia*. Cambridge (Mass.), 1930.

    Emerson Handbook. New York, 1953.

Christy, A. *The Orient in American Transcendentalism*. New York, 1932.

Firkins, O. W. *R. W. Emerson*. Boston, 1915.

Garnett, R. *Life of Emerson*. London, 1888.

Gray, H. D. *Emerson: A Statement of New England Transcendentalism as Expressed in the Philosophy of Its Chief Exponent*. Palo Alto (Calif.), 1917.

Hopkins, V. C. *Spires of Form: A Study of Emerson's Aesthetic Theory*. Cambridge (Mass.), 1951.

James, W. *Memories and Studies*. New York, 1911. (Includes an address on Emerson.)

Masters, E. L. *The Living Thoughts of Emerson*. London, 1948.

Matthiessen, F. O. *American Renaissance: Art and Expression in the Age of Emerson and Whitman*. London and New York, 1941.

Michaud, R. *Autour d'Emerson*. Paris, 1924.
        La vie inspirée d'Emerson. Paris, 1930.

Mohrdieck, M. *Demokratie bei Emerson*. Berlin, 1943.

Paul, S. *Emerson's Angle of Vision*. Cambridge (Mass.), 1952.

Perry, B. *Emerson Today*. New York, 1931.

Reaver, J. R. *Emerson as Myth-Maker*. Gainesville (Flor.), 1954.

Rusk, R. L. *The Life of Ralph Waldo Emerson*. New York, 1949.

Sahmann, P. *Emersons Geisteswelt*. Stuttgart, 1927.

Sanborn, F. B. (editor). *The Genius and Character of Emerson*. Boston, 1885.

Simon, J. *R. W. Emerson in Deutschland*. Berlin, 1937.

Whicher, S. B. *Freedom and Fate: An Inner Life of Ralph Waldo Emerson*. Philadelphia, 1953.

3. *Royce*
Texts

The Religious Aspect of Philosophy. Boston, 1885.

California: A Study of American Character. Boston, 1886.

The Spirit of Modern Philosophy. Boston, 1892.

The Conception of God: A Philosophical Discussion concerning the Nature of the Divine Idea as a Demonstrable Reality. New York, 1897. (This work, by several authors, includes Royce's intervention at a philosophical discussion in 1895.)

Studies of Good and Evil. New York, 1898.

The World and the Individual. 2 vols. New York, 1900-1.

The Conception of Immortality. Boston, 1900.

The Philosophy of Loyalty. New York, 1908.

Race Questions, Provincialisms and Other American Problems. New York and London, 1908.

William James and Other Essays on the Philosophy of Life. New York, 1911.

The Sources of Religious Insight. Edinburgh, 1912.

The Problem of Christianity. 2 vols. New York, 1913.

War and Insurance. New York, 1914.

Lectures on Modern Idealism. New Haven, 1919. (Edition by J. E. Smith, New York and London, 1964.)

Royce's Logical Essays, edited by D. S. Robinson. Dubuque (Iowa), 1951.

Josiah Royce's Seminar 1913–14, as recorded in the notebooks of
H. Costello, edited by G. Smith. New Brunswick, 1963.

Studies

Albeggiani, F. *Il sistema filosofico di Josiah Royce*. Palermo, 1930.

Amoroso, M. L. *La filosofia morale di Josiah Royce*. Naples, 1929.

Aronson, M. J. *La philosophie morale de Josiah Royce*. Paris, 1927.

Cotton, J. H. *Royce on the Human Self*. Cambridge (Mass.), 1954.

Creighton, J. E. (editor). *Papers in Honor of Josiah Royce on His
Sixtieth Birthday*. New York, 1916.

De Nier, M. *Royce*. Brescia, 1950.

Dykhuizen, G. *The Conception of God in the Philosophy of Josiah
Royce*. Chicago, 1936.

Fuss, P. *The Moral Philosophy of Josiah Royce*. Cambridge (Mass.),
1965.

Galgano, M. *Il pensiero filosofico di Josiah Royce*. Rome, 1921.

Humbach, K. T. *Einzelperson und Gemeinschaft nach Josiah Royce*.
Heidelberg, 1962.

Loewenberg, J. *Royce's Synoptic Vision*. Baltimore, 1955.

Marcel, G. *La métaphysique de Royce*. Paris, 1945.

Olgiati, F. *Un pensatore americano: Josiah Royce*. Milan, 1917.

Smith, J. E. *Royce's Social Infinite*. New York, 1950.

Part IV: Chapters XIV–XVI

1. *General Works Relating to Pragmatism*

Baumgarten, E. *Der Pragmatismus: R. W. Emerson, W. James, J.
Dewey*. Frankfurt, 1938.

Bawden, H. H. *Pragmatism*. New York, 1909.

Berthelot, R. *Un romantisme utilitaire*. 3 vols. Paris, 1911–13.

Childs, J. L. *American Pragmatism and Education: An Interpretation
and Analysis*. New York, 1956.

Chiocchetti, E. *Il pragmatismo*. Milan, 1926.

Hook, S. *The Metaphysics of Pragmatism*. Chicago, 1927.

Kennedy, G. (editor). *Pragmatism and American Culture*. Boston,
1950.

Lamanna, E. P. *Il pragmatismo anglo-americano*. Florence, 1952.

Leroux, E. *Le pragmatisme américain et anglais*. Paris, 1922.

Mead, G. H. *The Philosophy of the Present*. Chicago, 1932.

Moore, A. W. *Pragmatism and Its Critics*. Chicago, 1910.

Moore, E. C. *American Pragmatism: Peirce, James and Dewey*. New
York, 1961.

Morris, C. W. *Six Theories of Mind*. Chicago, 1932.

Murray, D. L. *Pragmatism*. London, 1912.

Perry, R. B. *Present Philosophical Tendencies.* New York, 1912.

Pratt, J. B. *What is Pragmatism?* New York, 1909.

Simon, P. *Der Pragmatismus in der modernen französischen Philosophie.* Paderborn, 1920.

Spirito, U. *Il pragmatismo nella filosofia contemporanea.* Florence, 1921.

Stebbing, L. S. *Pragmatism and French Voluntarism.* Cambridge, 1914.

Sturt, H. (editor). *Personal Idealism.* London, 1902.

Van Wessep, H. B. *Seven Sages: The Story of American Philosophy.* New York, 1960. (Includes Chapters on James, Dewey and Peirce.)

Wahl, J. A. *Les philosophies pluralistes d'Angleterre et d'Amérique.* Paris, 1920.

Wiener, P. P. *Evolution and the Founders of Pragmatism.* Cambridge (Mass.), 1949.

2. Peirce

Texts

Collected Papers of Charles Sanders Peirce. 8 vols. Cambridge, Mass. Volumes I–VI, edited by C. Hartshorne and P. Weiss and first published 1931–5, have been re-issued in 1960 as three volumes. Volumes VII–VIII, edited by A. W. Burke, were published in 1958.

There are also some books of selections, such as:

Chance, Love and Logic, edited by M. R. Cohen, with a supplementary essay by J. Dewey, New York, 1923.

The Philosophy of Peirce. Selected Writings, edited by J. Buchler. London, 1940 (reprint, New York, 1955).

Essays in the Philosophy of Science, edited by V. Tomas. New York, 1957.

Values in a Universe of Chance, edited by P. P. Wiener. Stanford and London, 1958.

Studies

Boler, J. F. *Charles Peirce and Scholastic Realism. A Study of Peirce's Relation to John Duns Scotus.* Seattle, 1963.

Buchler, J. *Charles Peirce's Empiricism.* London, 1939.

Carpenter, F. I. *American Literature and the Dream.* New York, 1955. (Includes a chapter on Peirce.)

Feibleman, J. K. *An Introduction to Peirce's Philosophy Interpreted as a System.* New York, 1946; London, 1960.

Freeman, E. *The Categories of Charles Peirce.* La Salle (Ill.), 1934.

Gallie, W. B. *Peirce and Pragmatism.* Penguin Books, 1952.

Goudge, T. A. *The Thought of C. S. Peirce.* Toronto and London, 1950.

Guccione Monroy, A. *Peirce e il pragmatismo americano.* Palermo, 1959.

Kempski, J. V. *C. A. Peirce und der Pragmatismus.* Stuttgart and Cologne, 1952.

Mullin, A. A. *Philosophical Comments on the Philosophies of C. S. Peirce and L. Wittgenstein.* Urbana (Ill.), 1961.

Murphey, M. G. *The Development of Peirce's Philosophy.* Cambridge (Mass.), 1961.

Thompson, M. *The Pragmatic Philosophy of C. S. Peirce.* Chicago and London, 1953.

Wennerberg, H. *The Pragmatism of C. S. Peirce.* Lund, 1963.

Wiener, P. P. and Young F. H. (editors). *Studies in the Philosophy of Charles Sanders Peirce.* Cambridge (Mass.), 1952.

3. *James*
Texts

The Principles of Psychology. New York, 1890.

The Will to Believe and Other Essays. New York and London, 1897 (reprint New York, 1956).

The Varieties of Religious Experience. New York and London, 1902.

Pragmatism. New York and London, 1907.

The Meaning of Truth. New York and London, 1909.

A Pluralistic Universe. New York and London, 1909.

Some Problems of Philosophy. New York and London, 1911.

Memories and Studies. New York and London, 1911.

Essays in Radical Empiricism. New York and London, 1912.

Collected Essays and Reviews. New York and London, 1920.

The Letters of William James, edited by H. James. 2 vols. Boston, 1926.

Annotated Bibliography of the Writings of William James, edited by R. B. Perry. New York, 1920.

Studies

Bixler, J. S. *Religion in the Philosophy of William James.* Boston, 1926.

Blau, T. *William James: sa théorie de la connaissance et de la verité.* Paris, 1933.

Boutroux, E. *William James.* Paris, 1911. (English translation by A. and B. Henderson, London, 1912.)

Bovet, P. *William James psychologue: l'intérêt de son oeuvre pour les éducateurs.* Saint Blaise, 1911.

Busch, K. A. *William James als Religionsphilosoph.* Göttingen, 1911.

Carpio, A. P. *Origen y desarrollo de la filosofia norteamericana. William James y el pragmatismo.* Buenos Aires, 1951.

Castiglioni, G. *William James.* Brescia, 1946.

Compton, C. H. (compiler). *William James: Philosopher and Man.* New York, 1957. (Quotations and References in 652 books.)

Cugini, U. *L'empirismo radicale di W. James.* Naples, 1925.

Kallen, H. M. *William James and Henri Bergson.* Chicago, 1914.

Knight, M. *William James.* Penguin Books, 1950.

Knox, H. V. *The Philosophy of William James.* London, 1914.

Le Breton, M. *La personnalité de William James.* Paris, 1929.

Maire, G. *William James et le pragmatisme religieux.* Paris, 1934.

Menard, A. *Analyse et critique des 'Principes de la Psychologie' de William James.* Paris, 1911.

Morris, L. *William James.* New York, 1950.

Nassauer, K. *Die Rechtsphilosophie von William James.* Bremen, 1943.

Perry, R. B. *The Thought and Character of William James.* 2 vols. Boston, 1935. (This is the standard biography.)
  The Thought and Character of William James. Briefer Version. New York, 1954.
  In the Spirit of William James. New Haven, 1938.

Reverdin, H. *La notion d'expérience d'après William James.* Geneva, 1913.

Roback, A. A. *William James, His Marginalia, Personality and Contribution.* Cambridge (Mass.), 1942.

Royce, J. *William James and Other Essays on the Philosophy of Life.* New York, 1911.

Sabin, E. E. *William James and Pragmatism.* Lancaster (Pa.), 1916.

Schmidt, H. *Der Begriff der Erfahrungskontinuität bei William James und seine Bedeutung für den amerikanischen Pragmatismus.* Heidelberg, 1959.

Switalski, W. *Der Wahrheitsbegriff des Pragmatismus nach William James.* Braunsberg, 1910.

Turner, J. E. *Examination of William James' Philosophy.* New York, 1919.

There are several collections of essays by various authors such as:
Essays Philosophical and Psychological in Honor of William James. New York, 1908.
In Commemoration of William James, 1842–1942. New York, 1942.
William James, the Man and the Thinker. Madison (Wis.), 1942.

4. *Schiller*
Texts

Riddles of the Sphinx. First published anonymously (by 'a Troglodyte') at London in 1891, then with the author's name at New York in 1894.
New edition, with sub-title *A Study in the Philosophy of Humanism.* London, 1910.

Axioms as Postulates, in *Personal Idealism*, edited by H. Sturt, London, 1902.

Humanism, Philosophical Essays. London, 1903 (2nd edition, 1912).

Studies in Humanism. London, 1907 (2nd edition, 1912).

Plato or Protagoras? London, 1908.

Formal Logic: A Scientific and Social Problem. London, 1912 (2nd edition, 1931).

Problems of Belief. London, 1924.

Why Humanism?, in *Contemporary British Philosophy*, First Series, edited by J. H. Muirhead. London, 1924.

Tantalus, or The Future of Man. London, 1924.

Eugenics and Politics. London, 1926.

Pragmatism, in *Encyclopædia Britannica*, 14th edition, 1929.

Logic for Use: An Introduction to the Voluntarist Theory of Knowledge. London, 1929.

Social Decay and Eugenical Reform. London, 1932.

Must Philosophers Disagree? and Other Essays in Popular Philosophy. London, 1934.

Studies

Abel, R. *The Pragmatic Humanism of F. C. S. Schiller*. New York and London, 1955.

Marett, R. *Ferdinand Canning Scott Schiller*. London, 1938. (British Academy lecture.)

White, S. S. *A Comparison of the Philosophies of F. C. S. Schiller and John Dewey*. Chicago, 1940.

5. Dewey
Texts

Psychology. New York, 1887 (3rd revised edition, 1891).

Leibniz's New Essays Concerning the Human Understanding. A Critical Exposition. Chicago, 1888.

The Ethics of Democracy. Ann Arbor, 1888.

Applied Psychology. Boston, 1889.

Outlines of a Critical Theory of Ethics. Ann Arbor, 1891.

The Study of Ethics: A Syllabus. Ann Arbor, 1894.

The Psychology of Number and Its Applications to Methods of Teaching Arithmetic (with J. A. McLellan). New York, 1895.

The Significance of the Problem of Knowledge. Chicago, 1897.

My Pedagogic Creed. New York, 1897.

Psychology and Philosophic Method. Berkeley, 1899.

The School of Society. Chicago, 1900 (revised edition, 1915).

The Child and the Curriculum. Chicago, 1902.

The Educational Situation. Chicago, 1902.

Studies in Logical Theory (with Others). Chicago, 1903.

Logical Conditions of a Scientific Treatment of Morality. Chicago, 1903.

Ethics (with J. H. Tufts). New York, 1908.

How We Think. New York, 1910.

The Influence of Darwin on Philosophy and Other Essays in Contemporary Thought. New York, 1910.

Educational Essays, edited by J. J. Findlay. London, 1910.

Interest and Effort in Education. Boston, 1913.

German Philosophy and Politics. New York, 1915 (revised edition, 1942).

Schools of Tomorrow (with E. Dewey). New York, 1915.

Democracy and Education. New York, 1916.

Essays in Experimental Logic. Chicago, 1916.

Reconstruction in Philosophy. New York, 1920 (enlarged edition, 1948).

Letters from China and Japan (with A. C. Dewey, edited by E. Dewey. New York, 1920).

Human Nature and Conduct: An Introduction to Social Psychology. New York, 1922.

Experience and Nature. Chicago, 1925 (revised edition, 1929).

The Public and Its Problems. New York, 1927 (2nd edition, 1946).

Characters and Events. Popular Essays in Social and Political Philosophy, edited by J. Ratner. 2 vols. New York, 1929.

Impressions of Soviet Russia and the Revolutionary World, Mexico, China, Turkey. New York, 1929.

The Quest for Certainty. New York, 1929.

Individualism, Old and New (reprinted articles), New York, 1930.

Philosophy and Civilization. New York, 1931.

Art as Experience. New York, 1934.

A Common Faith. New Haven, 1934.

Education and The Social Order. New York, 1934.

Liberalism and Social Action. New York, 1935.

The Teacher and Society (with Others). New York, 1937.

Experience and Education. New York, 1938.

Logic: The Theory of Inquiry. New York, 1938.

Intelligence in the Modern World: John Dewey's Philosophy, edited by J. Ratner. New York, 1939. (Mostly selections from published writings.)

Theory of Valuation. Chicago, 1939.

Freedom and Culture. New York, 1939.

Education Today, edited by J. Ratner. New York, 1940.

Knowing and the Known (with A. F. Bentley). Boston, 1949.

There are several books of selections and compilations based on Dewey's writings, such as:

Intelligence in the Modern World: John Dewey's Philosophy, edited by J. Ratner. New York, 1939.

Dictionary of Education, edited by R. B. Winn. New York, 1959.
Dewey on Education, selected with an introduction and notes by M. S. Dworkin. New York, 1959.
For fuller bibliographies see:
A Bibliography of John Dewey, 1882–1939, by M. H. Thomas and H. W. Schneider, with an introduction by H. W. Schneider. New York, 1939.
The Philosophy of John Dewey, edited by P. A. Schilpp. New York, 1951 (2nd edition).

Studies

Baker, M. *Foundation of John Dewey's Educational Theory*. New York, 1955.

Baumgarten, E. *Der Pragmatismus: R. W. Emerson, W. James, J. Dewey*. Frankfurt, 1938.

Bausola, A. *L'etica di John Dewey*. Milan, 1960.

Brancatisano, F. *La posizione di John Dewey nella filosofia moderna*. Turin, 1953.

Buswell, J. O. *The Philosophies of F. R. Tennant and J. Dewey*. New York, 1950.

Child, A. *Making and Knowing in Hobbes, Vico and Dewey*. Berkeley, 1953.

Corallo, G. *La pedagogia di Giovanni Dewey*. Turin, 1950.

Crosser, P. K. *The Nihilism of John Dewey*. New York, 1955.

Edman, I. *John Dewey, His Contribution to the American Tradition*. Indianopolis (Ind.), 1955.

Feldman, W. T. *The Philosophy of John Dewey. A Critical Analysis*. Baltimore, 1934.

Fleckenstein, N. J. *A Critique of John Dewey's Theory of the Nature and the Knowledge of Reality in the Light of the Principles of Thomism*. Washington, 1954.

Geiger, G. R. *John Dewey in Perspective*. London and New York, 1938.

Gillio-Tos, M. T. *Il pensiero di John Dewey*. Naples, 1938.

Grana, G. *John Dewey e la metodologia americana*. Rome, 1955.

Gutzke, M. G. *John Dewey's Thought and Its Implications for Christian Education*. New York, 1956.

Handlin, O. *John Dewey's Challenge to Education: Historical Perspectives on the Cultural Context*. New York, 1959.

Hook, S. *John Dewey: An Intellectual Portrait*. New York, 1939.

Leander, F. *The Philosophy of John Dewey. A Critical Study*. Göteborg, 1939.

Levitt, M. *Freud and Dewey on the Nature of Man*. New York, 1960.

Mack, R. D. *The Appeal to Immediate Experience. Philosophic Method in Bradley, Whitehead and Dewey*. New York, 1945.

Mataix, A. (S.J.), *La norma moral en John Dewey*. Madrid, 1964.

Nathanson, J. *John Dewey*. New York, 1951.
Roth, R. J., (S.J.). *John Dewey and Self-Realization*. Englewood Cliffs (N.J.), 1963.
Thayer, H. S. *The Logic of Pragmatism: An Examination of John Dewey's Logic*. New York and London, 1952.
White, M. G. *The Origin of Dewey's Instrumentalism*. New York, 1943.
White, S. S. *A Comparison of the Philosophies of F. C. S. Schiller and John Dewey*. Chicago, 1940.

Symposia on Dewey:

John Dewey, The Man and His Philosophy, edited by S. S. White. Cambridge (Mass.), 1930. (Discourses in honour of Dewey's seventieth birthday.)
The Philosopher of the Common Man, edited by S. S. White. New York, 1940. (Essays in celebration of Dewey's eightieth birthday.)
The Philosophy of John Dewey, edited by P. A. Schilpp. New York, 1951 (2nd edition).
John Dewey: Philosopher of Science and Freedom, edited by S. Hook. New York, 1950.
John Dewey and the Experimental Spirit in Philosophy, edited by C. W. Hendel. New York, 1959.
John Dewey: Master Educator, edited by W. W. Brickman and S. Lehrer. New York, 1959.
Dialogue on John Dewey, edited by C. Lamont. New York, 1959.
John Dewey: His Thought and Influence, edited by J. Blewett. New York, 1960.

Part V: Chapters XVII–XXI[1]

1. *Some general works describing or illustrating recent philosophy, especially in Great Britain.*

Adams, G. P. and Montague, W. P. (editors). *Contemporary American Philosophy*. 2 vols. New York, 1930.
Ayer, A. J. and Others. *The Revolution in Philosophy*. London, 1956. (Broadcast Talks.)
Black, M. *Language and Philosophy*. Ithaca and London, 1949.
       Problems of Analysis: Philosophical Essays. Ithaca and London, 1954.
Blanshard, B. *Reason and Analysis*. London and New York, 1962. (A critical discussion of linguistic philosophy.)
Boman, L. *Criticism and Construction in the Philosophy of the American New Realism*. Stockholm, 1955.

[1] No bibliography has been supplied for Wittgenstein, as his philosophical ideas have been mentioned only in general discussion or incidentally.

Charlesworth, M. *Philosophy and Linguistic Analysis*. Pittsburgh and Louvain, 1959. (Critical as well as historical.)

Drake, D. and Others. *Essays in Critical Realism*. New York and London, 1921.

Flew, A. G. N. (editor). *Logic and Language* (first series). Oxford, 1951.
    Logic and Language (second series). Oxford, 1955.
    Essays in Conceptual Analysis. Oxford, 1953.
    New Essays in Philosophical Theology. London, 1955.

Gellner, E. *Words and Things*. London, 1959. (A very critical treatment of linguistic philosophy in England.)

Ginestier, P. *La pensée anglo-saxonne depuis 1900*. Paris, 1956.

Holt, E. B. and Others. *The New Realism*. New York, 1912.

Kremer, R. P. *Le néo-realisme américain*. Louvain, 1920.
    La théorie de la connaissance chez les néo-realistes anglais. Louvain, 1928.

Lewis, H. D. (editor). *Contemporary British Philosophy* (third series). London, 1956.

Linsky, L. (editor). *Semantics and the Philosophy of Language*. Urbana (Ill.), 1952.

Mace, C. A. (editor). *British Philosophy in the Mid-Century*. London, 1957.

MacIntyre, A. (editor). *Metaphysical Beliefs*. London, 1957.

Muirhead, J. H. *Rule and End in Morals*. London, 1932. (Discusses the ethical issues treated by Prichard, Carritt, Ross, Joseph, and others.)

Pears, D. F. (editor). *The Nature of Metaphysics*. London, 1957. (Broadcast Talks.)

Sellars, R. W. and Others. *Essays in Critical Realism*. New York and London, 1920.

Urmson, J. O. *Philosophical Analysis. Its Development between the Two World Wars*. Oxford, 1956.

Warnock, G. J. *English Philosophy Since 1900*. (A clear account of the development of the analytic movement.)

Warnock, M. *Ethics Since 1900*. London, 1960. (Mainly on the development of English ethical theory from Bradley. But discusses the ideas of the American philosopher C. L. Stevenson and contains a chapter on Sartre.)

2. *G. E. Moore*
Texts

Principia Ethica. Cambridge, 1903 (2nd edition, 1922; new edition, 1960).

Ethics. London, 1912 (and reprints).

Philosophical Studies. London, 1922 (new edition, 1960). (This work includes 'The Refutation of Idealism' from *Mind*, 1903.)

Some Main Problems of Philosophy. London, 1953. (This volume includes some hitherto unpublished lectures delivered in the winter of 1910–11.)

Philosophical Papers. London, 1959. (This volume includes 'A Defence of Common Sense' from *Contemporary British Philosophy*, Second Series, 1925.)

Commonplace Book, 1919–1953, edited by C. Lewy. London, 1962.

Studies

Braithwaite, R. B. *George Edward Moore, 1873–1958*. London, 1963. (British Academy lecture.)

Schilpp, P. A. (editor). *The Philosophy of G. E. Moore*. New York, 1952.

White, A. R. *G. E. Moore: A Critical Exposition*. Oxford, 1958.

3. *Russell*

Texts

German Social Democracy. London and New York, 1896.

An Essay on the Foundations of Geometry. Cambridge, 1897.

A Critical Exposition of the Philosophy of Leibniz. Cambridge, 1900.

The Principles of Mathematics. Cambridge, 1903.

Principia Mathematica (with A. N. Whitehead). 3 vols. Cambridge, 1910–13 (2nd edition, 1927–35).

Philosophical Essays (reprinted articles). London and New York, 1910.

The Problems of Philosophy. London and New York, 1912.

Our Knowledge of the External World as a Field for Scientific Method in Philosophy. London and Chicago, 1914 (revised edition, 1929).

The Philosophy of Bergson (controversy with Professor H. W. Carr). London, Glasgow and Cambridge, 1914.

Scientific Method in Philosophy. Oxford, 1914.

War, the Offspring of Fear (pamphlet). London, 1915.

Principles of Social Reconstruction. London, 1916 (2nd edition, 1920).

Policy of the Entente, 1904–1914: A Reply to Professor Gilbert Murray (booklet). Manchester and London, 1916.

Justice in War-Time. London and Chicago, 1916 (2nd edition, 1924).

Political Ideals. New York, 1917.

Mysticism and Logic and Other Essays (reprinted essays). London and New York, 1918.

Roads to Freedom: Socialism, Anarchism and Syndicalism. London, 1918.

Introduction to Mathematical Philosophy. London and New York, 1919.

The Practice and Theory of Bolshevism. London and New York, 1920 (2nd edition, 1949).

The Analysis of Mind. London, 1921, New York, 1924.

The Problem of China. London and New York, 1922.

Free Thought and Official Propaganda (lecture). London and New York, 1922.

The Prospects of Industrial Civilization (with D. Russell). London and New York, 1923.

The ABC of Atoms. London and New York, 1923.

Icarus, or the Future of Science (booklet). London and New York, 1924.

How To Be Free and Happy (lecture). New York, 1924.

The ABC of Relativity. London and New York, 1925 (revised edition, 1958).

On Education, Especially in Early Childhood. London and New York, 1926. (In America with the title *Education and the Good Life*.)

The Analysis of Matter. London and New York, 1927 (reprint, 1954).

An Outline of Philosophy. London and New York, 1927. (In America with the title *Philosophy*.)

Selected Papers of Bertrand Russell (selected and introduced by Russell). New York, 1927.

Sceptical Essays (largely reprints). London and New York, 1928.

Marriage and Morals. London and New York, 1929.

The Conquest of Happiness. London and New York, 1930.

The Scientific Outlook. New York, 1931.

Education and the Social Order. London and New York, 1932. (In America with the title *Education and the Modern World*.)

Freedom and Organization, 1814–1914. London and New York, 1934. (In America with the title *Freedom versus Organization*.)

In Praise of Idleness and Other Essays. New York, 1935.

Religion and Science. London and New York, 1935.

Which Way to Peace? London, 1936.

The Amberley Papers (with P. Russell.) 2 vols. London and New York, 1937.

Power: A New Social Analysis. London and New York, 1938.

An Inquiry into Meaning and Truth. London and New York, 1940.

Let the People Think (essays). London, 1941.

A History of Western Philosophy: Its Connection with Political and Social Circumstances from the Earliest Times to the Present Day. London and New York, 1945 (2nd edition, 1961).

Human Knowledge: Its Scope and Limits. London and New York, 1948.

Authority and the Individual. London and New York, 1949.

Unpopular Essays (largely reprints). London and New York, 1950.

The Impact of Science on Society (lectures). New York, 1951.

New Hopes for a Changing World. London, 1951.

Human Society in Ethics and Politics. London and New York, 1954.

Logic and Knowledge: Essays, 1901–1950, edited by R. C. Marsh. London and New York, 1956. (This volume includes Russell's 1918 lectures on the philosophy of logical atomism, also the article on logical atomism written for *Contemporary British Philosophy*, First Series, 1924.)

Why I am not a Christian, and Other Essays. London and New York, 1957.

My Philosophical Development. London and New York, 1959.

Wisdom of the West. London, 1959.

Has Man a Future? Penguin Books, 1961.

Fact and Fiction. London, 1961.

Studies

Clark, C. H. D. *Christianity and Bertrand Russell.* London, 1958.

Dorward, A. *Bertrand Russell.* London, 1951. (A booklet written for the British Council and the National Book League.)

Feibleman, J. K. *Inside the Great Mirror. A Critical Examination of the Philosophy of Russell, Wittgenstein and their Followers.* The Hague, 1958.

Fritz, C. A. *Bertrand Russell's Construction of the External World.* New York and London, 1952.

Götlind, E. *Bertrand Russell's Theories of Causation.* Upsala, 1952.

Jourdain, P. E. B. *The Philosophy of Mr. Bertrand Russell* (satire). London and Chicago, 1918.

Leggett, H. W. *Bertrand Russell* (pictorial biography). London, 1949.

Lovejoy, A. O. *The Revolt Against Dualism.* Chicago, 1930. (Chapters 6–7 treat of Russell's theory of mind.)

McCarthy, D. G. *Bertrand Russell's Informal Freedom.* Louvain, 1960 (doctorate dissertation).

Riveroso, E. *Il pensiero di Bertrand Russell.* Naples, 1958.

Santayana, G. *Winds of Doctrine.* London, 1913. (Includes a study of Russell's philosophy.)

Schilpp, P. A. (editor). *The Philosophy of Bertrand Russell.* New York, 1946 (2nd edition).

Urmson, J. O. *Philosophical Analysis. Its Development between the Two World Wars.* Oxford, 1956. (Includes a critical discussion of Russell's reductive analysis. Russell's reply, together with replies to criticisms by G. J. Warnock and P. F. Strawson, is reprinted in chapter 18 of *My Philosophical Development*.)

Wood, A. *Bertrand Russell, The Passionate Sceptic* (biographical). London, 1957.

        Russell's Philosophy: A Study of Its Development (an unfinished essay printed at the end of Russell's *My Philosophical Development*).

Wood, M. G. *Why Mr. Bertrand Russell is not a Christian*. London, 1928.

There are, of course, many articles on particular points or aspects of Russell's thought in *Mind, Analysis, The Proceedings of the Aristotelian Society, The Philosophical Review,* and other periodicals. But they cannot possibly be listed here.

INDEX

(The principal references are in heavy type. Asterisked numbers refer to bibliographical information.)